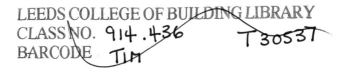

Paris

timeout.com/paris

Published by Time Out Guides Ltd, a wholly owned subsidiary of Time Out Group Ltd.
Time Out and the Time Out logo are trademarks of Time Out Group Ltd.

© Time Out Group Ltd 2005
Previous editions 1989, 1990, 1992, 1995, 1997, 1998, 1999, 2000, 2001, 2002, 2003, 2004.

10 9 8 7 6 5 4 3 2 1

This edition first published in Great Britain in 2005 by Ebury
Ebury is a division of The Random House Group Ltd,
20 Vauxhall Bridge Road, London SW1V 2SA

Random House Australia Pty Limited, 20 Alfred Street, Milsons Point, Sydney, New South Wales 2061, Australia
Random House New Zealand Limited, 18 Poland Road, Glenfield, Auckland 10, New Zealand
Random House South Africa (Pty) Limited, Endulini, 5A Jubilee Road, Parktown 2193, South Africa

Random House UK Limited Reg. No. 954009

Distributed in USA by Publishers Group West
1700 Fourth Street, Berkeley, California 94710

Distributed in Canada by Penguin Canada Ltd
10 Alcorn Avenue, Toronto, Ontario, Canada M4V 3B2

For further distribution details, see www.timeout.com

ISBN 1-904978-30-4

A CIP catalogue record for this book is available from the British Library

Colour reprographics by Icon, Crowne House, 56-58 Southwark Street, London SE1 1UN

Printed and bound in Germany by Appl
Papers used by Ebury Press are natural, recyclable products made from wood grown in sustainable forests

Time Out Guides Limited
Universal House
251 Tottenham Court Road
London W1T 7AB
Tel + 44 (0)20 7813 3000
Fax + 44 (0)20 7813 6001
Email guides@timeout.com
www.timeout.com

Editorial
Editor Peterjon Cresswell
Consultant Natasha Edwards
Deputy Editor Simon Cropper
Listings Editors David Smith, Oliver Brock
Proofreader John Pym
Indexer Jackie Brind

Editorial/Managing Director Peter Fiennes
Series Editor Ruth Jarvis
Deputy Series Editor Lesley McCave
Business Manager Gareth Garner
Guides Co-ordinator Holly Pick
Accountant Sarah Bostock

Design
Art Director Mandy Martin
Deputy Art Director Scott Moore
Senior Designer Tracey Ridgewell
Designers Oliver Knight, Tessa Kar
Junior Designer Chrissy Mouncey
Digital Imaging Dan Conway
Ad Make-up Charlotte Blythe, Philippe Thareaut

Picture Desk
Picture Editor Jael Marschner
Deputy Picture Editor Tracey Kerrigan
Picture Researchers Ivy Lahon, Monica Roche, Simon Cropper, Peterjon Cresswell

Advertising
Sales Director Mark Phillips
International Sales Manager Ross Canadé
International Sales Executive James Tuson
Sales & Administration Manager Paris Philippe Thareaut
Advertising Executives Paris Ellen Green, Keri Stone

Marketing
Marketing Director Mandy Martinez
US Publicity & Marketing Associate Rosella Albanese

Production
Production Director Mark Lamond
Production Controller Samantha Furniss

Time Out Group
Managing Director Paris Karen Albrecht

Chairman Tony Elliott
Managing Director Mike Hardwick
Group Financial Director Richard Waterlow
Group Commercial Director Lesley Gill
Group General Manager Nichola Coulthard
Group Circulation Director Jim Heinemann
Group Art Director John Oakey
Online Managing Director David Pepper
Group Production Director Steve Proctor
Group IT Director Simon Chappell

Contributors
Introduction Simon Cropper. **History** Simon Cropper, Peterjon Cresswell (*Revolution rock* Natalie Whittle). **Paris Today** Richard Woodruff, Alex Duvel-Smith. **Delanoë's Dream** Alex Duvel-Smith. **Haute Couture or High Street?** Tina Isaac. **Architecture** Natasha Edwards. **Where to Stay** Heather Stimmler-Hall (*Unknown pleasures* Toby Rose). **Sightseeing** Natasha Edwards, Simon Cropper (*Tours* Oliver Brock; *Hidden Paris* Alison Culliford; *Paris against the clock, Tiptoe through the tombstones* Natalie Whittle; *On the waterfront* Dora Whitaker). **The Louvre** Alison Culliford, Natasha Edwards (*The cult of the Code* Heather Stimmler-Hall). **Museums** Alison Culliford, Natasha Edwards. **Restaurants** Rosa Jackson, Alec Lobrano. **Cafés & Bars** Kate Spenley, Peterjon Cresswell, David Smith, Anna Brooke. **Shops & Services** Kate van den Boogert (*Market forces*, food & drink Rosa Jackson; *That old black magic* Lucia Scazzocchio). **Festivals & Events** Kate van den Boogert (*No Plage like home* Alison Culliford; *Ol' four eyes is back* Simon Cropper). **Cabaret, Circus & Comedy** Anna Brooke. **Children** Sally Parr. **Dance** Marie-Laure Ferreyra. **Film** Simon Cropper. **Galleries** Natasha Edwards. **Gay & Lesbian** Toby Rose. **Music: Classical & Opera** Stephen Mudge. **Music: Popular Music** David Smith. **Nightlife** Lucia Scazzocchio. **Sport & Fitness** Heather Stimmler-Hall, Richard Woodruff, Peterjon Cresswell (*A day at the races* Alison Culliford; *Friday night fever* Dora Whitaker). **Theatre** Catherine Bredeson. **Trips Out of Town** Heather Stimmler-Hall, Anna Brooke, Dora Whitaker (*Rock back in time* Natasha Edwards, Anna Brooke; *Faites vos jeux* Natalie Whittle). **Directory** Simon Cropper, Richard Woodruff, Oliver Brock.

Maps JS Graphics (john@jsgraphics.co.uk).

Photography by Karl Blackwell, except: pages 10, 20 MEPL; pages 15, 16, 19 AKG; pages 25, 27, 33 Corbis; pages 32, 84, 87, 148, 277, 291 Adam Eastland; page 37 Patrice Stable; pages 72, 105 Oliver Knight; pages 79, 80, 81, 278, 304 Jonathan Perugia; page 175 Jean-Marie Périer; page 283 Gallimard; pages 293, 294, 295, 296 Agathe Poupeney/CND; page 301 Gaumont-Franco Film-Aubert/Photofest; page 314 Thierry Ardouin/Cité de la musique; page 317 L.Willaert; page 341 Cosimo Mirco Magliocca; page 346 J B Leroux; pages 352, 358 Images of France.
The following images were provided by the featured establishments/artists: 37, 38, 48, 52, 64, 68, 163, 187, 214, 228, 285, 323, 342, 343, 356, 361, 357.

Contents

Introduction

Why? An introduction? After all, we're talking about the city that – of all the capitals in all the world – most roundly and most richly deserves the 'Needs No Introduction' label. (If you feel even a faint twinge of disbelief while reading that statement, think of all the famous quotations, lines from songs and popular sayings that name, say, London – and then of all the same that name Paris. We guarantee Paris will get the higher score.) So, again, why this preamble?

First, because we're proud to announce that there's far more to Paris than any song lyric might suggest. And secondly, we've never been in thrall to its easy clichés – peddled, it has to be said, by Parisians as much as anyone. You all know the tune: city of light, city of love, springtime when it drizzles, *oh bla bla*. To hear some people talk about Paname (bet you didn't know *that* nickname), you'd think the place had frozen solid in 1905.

And therein lies the danger. Paris is so well known, so often filmed, photographed, fêted, painted, hymned, written up, visited, dreamed of – that it's often taken for granted. Hence the real purpose of this introduction, a recommendation we can't make strongly enough: look again, and look harder. Even if this is your first visit, you already have a detailed mental picture of the place; try, if at all possible, to forget it. And stop thinking of Paris as a tourist destination. No one who flits round the main monuments (Mona Lisa, tick! Sacré-Coeur, tick! Eiffel Tower, tick!) without taking the time to stand still, to look at the bits between all those *sights* or follow their nose without reference to a map, can hope to see what makes this city unique.

Unique, and constantly on the move. Paris is not wedded to the past – far from it. This is a city that loves technology (ride its new tramway or driverless trains on Métro line 14 for a taste of the future), that dares to be bold (in the construction zones of the 13th district and on the site of an earlier, disastrous bit of boldness at Les Halles), a city that dares to have Olympic ambitions. The clichés don't even come close.

If Thomas Jefferson was right when he said that France is everyone's second country, then Paris is everyone's second city. You could spend the best part of a lifetime trying to understand it, so just love it for what it is: always different, always the same.

ABOUT TIME OUT CITY GUIDES

Time Out Paris is one of an expanding series of travel guides produced by the people behind London and New York's successful listings magazines. Our guides are all written and updated by resident experts who have striven to provide you with all the most up-to-date information you'll need to explore the city, whether you're a local or first-time visitor.

THE LOWDOWN ON THE LISTINGS

Above all, we've tried to make this book as useful as possible. Websites, telephone numbers, transport information, opening times, admission prices and credit card details are all included in our listings. And, as far as possible, we've given details of facilities, services and events, all checked and correct at the time we went to press. However, owners and managers can change their arrangements at any time. Before you go out of your way, we'd strongly advise you to call and check opening times, dates of exhibitions and other particulars. While every effort has been made to ensure the accuracy of the information contained in this guide, the publishers cannot accept responsibility for any errors it may contain.

PRICES AND PAYMENT

Prices are given in euros, and have been verified with each venue or business. We have noted whether shops, hotels, restaurants and other establishments accept credit cards or not but have only listed the major cards – American

Express (AmEx), Diners Club (DC), MasterCard (MC) and Visa (V). Many businesses will also accept other cards. Please note that the Visa card is referred to locally as the Carte Bleue.

The prices we've supplied should be treated as guidelines, not gospel. Fluctuating exchange rates and inflation can cause charges, in shops and restaurants particularly, to change rapidly. If prices vary wildly from those we've quoted, ask whether there's a good reason. If not, go elsewhere. Then please write and let us know. We aim to give the best and most up-to-date advice, so we always want to know if you've been badly treated or overcharged.

THE LIE OF THE LAND

To make the book (and the city) easier to navigate, we have divided Paris into areas. They are: The Islands; Right Bank (The Louvre, Palais-Royal and Les Halles; Opéra & Grands Boulevards; the Champs-Elysées & western Paris; Montmartre & Pigalle; Beaubourg & the Marais; Bastille & eastern Paris; North-east Paris) and Left Bank (The Latin Quarter & the 13th; St-Germain-des-Prés & Odéon; Montparnasse & beyond; The 7th & the 15th). These are our breakdowns, and are not the official *arrondissements* you will see signposted around town – although every address listed here gives its district number.

TELEPHONE NUMBERS

The country code for France is 33. All Paris telephone numbers begin with 01. If dialling Paris from abroad, drop the initial 0. If calling within France, dial all ten digits. A handful of numbers listed begin with 08 – these can be free, at low rate or high rate. For details, check www.agence.francetelecom.com. For more information on telephones and codes, *see p385.*

ESSENTIAL INFORMATION

For all the practical information you might need for visiting the city, including visa and customs information, advice on disabled facilities and access, emergency telephone numbers, a list of useful websites and the lowdown on the local transport network – turn to the Directory at the back of this guide. It starts on p365.

MAPS

We've included a series of fully indexed colour street maps to the city at the back of this guide – they start on p402 – and, where possible, we've printed a grid reference for each address given in the guide. There's a district overview map on p400 and a Métro map on p414.

LET US KNOW WHAT YOU THINK

We hope you enjoy *Time Out Paris*, and we'd like to know what you think of it. We welcome tips for places that you consider we should include in future editions and take notice of your criticism of our choices. You can email us on guides@timeout.com.

Advertisers

We would like to stress that no establishment has been included in this guide because it has advertised in any of our publications and no payment of any kind has influenced any review. The opinions given in this book are those of Time Out writers and entirely independent.

There is an online version of this book, along with guides to over 45 other international cities, at **www.timeout.com**.

In Context

Vercingetorix
lays his arms
before Caesar.
See p11.

History

Besieged, invaded and occupied, and in revolt almost once in every century, Paris has always been a dangerous place to live – but never dull.

THE FIRST VISITORS

The earliest settlers seem to have arrived in Paris around 120,000 years ago. One of them lost a flint spear-tip on the hill we now call Montmartre, and the still dangerous-looking weapon is to be seen today in the Stone Age collection at the **Musée des Antiquités Nationales** (*see p171*). There was a Stone Age weapons factory under present-day Châtelet, and the redevelopment of Bercy in the 1990s managed to unearth ten Neolithic canoes, five of which are now high and dry in the **Musée Carnavalet** (*see p176*). The fluctuating level of the river, however, probably forced people to dwell on one of the area's many hills.

By 250BC, a Celtish tribe known as the Parisii had put the place on the map, and given the modern capital its name. The Parisii were river traders, wealthy enough to mint gold coins. The **Musée de la Monnaie** (*see p177*)

has a good collection of their small change. Their most important *oppidum*, a primitive fortified town, was located on an island in the Seine, which is generally thought to have been the present Ile de la Cité.

ROMAN PARIS

Superb strategic location and the capacity to generate hard cash were guaranteed to attract the attention of the Romans. Julius Caesar arrived in southern Gaul as proconsul in 58BC and soon used the pretext of dealing with invading barbarians to stick his Roman nose into the affairs of northern Gaul. The Gauls didn't appreciate the attention, and in 54BC the Eburones from the Meuse valley rebelled against the Romans. Other tribes joined in: in 51BC the Parisii rose up with the rest of Gaul.

Caesar had his hands full dealing with the great Gaul marauder Vercingetorix, so he sent his general Labienus with four legions and part of the cavalry to secure the passage of the Seine at Lutetia, as they called Paris. The Gauls were massacred, although a contingent of Parisii escaped to be defeated later with Vercingetorix at the battle of Alesia. Then the surrender of Vercingetorix in 52BC left the Paris region and the rest of Gaul in Roman hands.

Roman Lutetia was a prosperous town of around 8,000 inhabitants. Apart from centrally-heated villas and a temple to Jupiter on the main island (remains of both are visible in the **Crypte Archéologique**, *see p85*), there were the sumptuous baths (now the **Musée National du Moyen Age**, *see p173*), and the 15,000-seater **Arènes de Lutèce** (*see p130*).

CHRISTIANITY

Christianity arrived in around 250 in the shape of Denis of Athens, who went on to become first bishop of Paris. Legend has it that when he was decapitated by Valerian on Mons Martis, the mount of the martyrs (today better known as Montmartre), Denis picked up his head and walked with it to what is now St-Denis, to be buried there. The event is depicted in Henri Bellechose's glorious 'Retable de Saint-Denis', to be found in the **Louvre** (*see pp152-160*).

Gaul was still a tempting prize. Waves of barbarian invaders – Alamans, Francs and others – began crossing the Rhine from 275 onwards. They sacked more than 60 cities in Gaul, including Lutetia, where the population was decimated and the buildings on the Montagne Ste-Geneviève were pillaged and burned. The bedraggled survivors used the rubble to build a rampart around the Ile de la Cité and to fortify the forum, although few citizens remained in the shadow of its walls.

It was at this time that the city was renamed Paris. Protected by the Seine and the new fortifications, its main role now was as a rear base for the Roman armies defending Gaul, and it was here in 360 that Julian was proclaimed emperor by his troops. In the same year, the first Catholic council of Paris was held, condemning the Arian branch of Christianity as heresy. The city's inhabitants, however, had concerns more pressing than theology.

Around 450, with the arrival of the Huns in the region, the people of Paris prepared once again to flee. They were dissuaded by a feisty woman named Geneviève, who was famed in the Christian community for her piety. Seeing the walls of the city defended against him, no less a pillager than Attila the Hun turned back and was defeated soon afterwards.

CLOVIS

In 464, Paris managed to resist another siege, this time by the Francs under Childeric. However by 486, after a further blockade lasting ten years, Geneviève had no option but to surrender the city to Childeric's successor, Clovis, who went on to conquer most of Gaul and founded the Merovingian dynasty. He chose Paris as capital of his new kingdom, and it stayed that way until the 7th century, in spite of various conflicts among his successors.

Under the influence of his wife, Clotilde, Clovis converted to Christianity. He founded

Revolution rock 1358

Next time you find yourself on Métro line 4, spare a thought for the first French revolution. The station one stop north of Les Halles has been named to commemorate failed rabble-rouser, Etienne Marcel. A hero to some, but certainly no Spartacus: Marcel came from an established bourgeois family in Paris, and he fought largely for bourgeois rights, too.

In the 1350s, France had shrugged off the Black Plague, but was still lumbered with the hideously expensive Hundred Years War against the English. To fund the conflict, King Jean II tried to introduce new tax laws – unsuccessfully. When Jean was captured by the English at Poitiers in 1356, his problems passed to his 18-year-old son, Charles.

The Etats Généraux, consultant body to the throne, was summoned to the royal palace on the Ile de la Cité to discuss the country's woes. The teenage king was beseiged with angry demands for reform, particularly from Etienne Marcel, then provost of the local merchants. Marcel seized control of Paris and began a bitter power struggle with the crown; in 1357, fearing widespread revolt, Charles fled to Compiègne. But as he ran, he had Paris blockaded.

Marcel now needed help. He called on the peasants, who were also raging against taxes, but they were quickly crushed. He then called on Charles 'The Bad' of Navarre, ally to the English, but his arrival in Paris just made many of Marcel's supporters nervous. On 31 July 1358, Marcel was murdered and the revolution was over.

Just to make sure, however, the returning Charles built a new stronghold to protect Paris: the Bastille.

and was buried in the basilica of the Saints Apôtres, later re-dedicated to Saint Geneviève when the saviour and future patron saint of Paris was interred there in 512. All that remains of the basilica today is a single pillar in the grounds of the modern Lycée Henri IV; but there's a shrine dedicated to Saint Geneviève and some relics in the fine Gothic church of **St-Etienne-du-Mont** (*see p129*) next door.

Geneviève and Clovis had set a trend. The Ile de la Cité was still the heart of the city, but, under the Merovingians, the Left Bank was the up-and-coming area for fashion-conscious Christians, with 11 churches built here in the period (against only four on the Right Bank and one on the Ile de la Cité). Not everyone was sold on the joys of city living, though. From 614 onwards, the Merovingian kings preferred the *banlieue* at Clichy, or wandered the kingdom trying to keep rebellious nobles in check. By the time one of the rebels, Pippin 'the Short', decided to do away with the last Merovingian in 751, Paris was starting to look passé.

Pippin's son, Charlemagne, built his capital at Aix-la-Chapelle, while his successors, known as the Carolingian dynasty, moved from palace to palace, consuming the local production.

> ## 'The Norsemen sacked the city, and Charles II had to cough up 7,000 pounds of silver to get them to leave.'

Paris, meanwhile, was doing quite nicely for itself as a centre for Christian learning, and the city had grown to house a population of 20,000 by the beginning of the ninth century. This was the high point in the popularity and political power of the great abbeys like St-Germain-des-Prés, where transcription of the Latin classics was helping to preserve much of Europe's Roman cultural heritage. Power in the Paris region was exercised by the Counts of Paris.

THE VIKINGS

In 845 the Vikings appeared before the walls. Unopposed, the Norsemen sacked the city, and King Charles II, 'the Bald', had to cough up 7,000 pounds of silver to get them to leave. Recognising a soft touch when they saw one, the Vikings returned to sack the city repeatedly between 856 and 869, burning churches with heathen abandon. Better late than never, Charles organised the defence of the city. Fortified bridges were built – the Grand Pont over the northern and the Petit Pont over the southern branch of the Seine, blocking the passage of the Viking ships further upstream.

In 885, Gozlin, bishop of Paris, had just finished repairing the Roman walls when the Vikings showed up once again; this time they found the city defended against them. After a siege lasting a year, King Charles III 'the Fat' arrived at the head of an army but, deciding that discretion is indeed the better part of valour, handed over 700 pounds of silver and politely invited the Norsemen to pillage some other part of his kingdom. The Count of Paris, Eudes, having performed valiantly in the siege of 885-886, was offered the royal crown when Charles was deposed in 888. Although the Carolingians recovered the throne after his death in 898, Eudes' great-nephew, Hugues Capet, was elected king of France in 987, adding what remained of the Carolingian dominions to his territories around Paris.

PARIS FINDS ITS FEET

Under the Capetian dynasty, although Paris was now at the heart of the royal domains, the city did not yet dominate the kingdom. Robert 'the Pious', king from 996 to 1031, stayed more often in Paris than his father, restoring the royal palace on the Ile de la Cité, while Henri I (1031-1060) issued more of his charters in Paris than in Orléans. In 1112, the abbey of **St-Denis** (*see p149*) replaced St-Benoît-sur-Loire as principal monastery, so confirming the pre-eminence of Paris over Orléans.

Paris itself still consisted of little more than the Ile de la Cité and small settlements under the protection of the abbeys on each bank. On the Left Bank, royal largesse helped to rebuild the abbeys of St-Germain-des-Prés, St-Marcel, and Ste-Geneviève, although it took more than 150 years for the destruction wrought there by the Vikings to be fully repaired. The Right Bank, where mooring was easier, prospered from river commerce, and three boroughs grew up around the abbeys of St-Germain-l'Auxerrois, St-Martin-des-Champs and St-Gervais. Bishop Sully of Paris began building the cathedral of Notre-Dame in 1163.

The growing complexity of government during the 12th century, and the departure of kings on crusade, meant that the administration tended to stay in the Palais de la Cité and the royal treasure in the fortress of the Temple (built by the newly founded order of the Templars). The wisdom of this approach was confirmed by the disaster of Fréteval in 1194, where King Philippe-Auguste was defeated by Richard the Lionheart, losing much of his treasure and his archives in the process.

This minor hiccup aside, the reign of Philippe-Auguste (1180-1223) was a turning point in the history of Paris. Before, the city was a confused patchwork of royal, ecclesiastical and feudal authorities, exercising various powers, rights and privileges. Keen to raise revenues, Philippe favoured the growth of the guilds, especially the butchers, drapers, furriers, haberdashers and merchants: so began the rise of the bourgeoisie.

He also ordered the building of the first permanent market buildings at Les Halles, and a new city wall, first on the Right Bank to protect the commercial heart of Paris, and later on the Left Bank. At the western end, Philippe built a castle, the Louvre, to defend the road from the ever-menacing Normandy, whose duke was also King of England.

A GOLDEN AGE

Paris was now the principal residence of the king and the uncontested capital of France. No longer threatened by foreign invasion, the city found itself overrun by a new and altogether deadlier menace that exists to this day: lawyers. And barristers, bailiffs, prosecutors, sergeants, accountants, judges, clerks and all the bureaucratic trappings of royal government.

> **'Masters and students of the Sorbonne were already gaining a reputation for rowdiness.'**

To accommodate the rapidly growing royal administration, the Palace of the Cité, site and symbol of power for the previous thousand years, was remodelled and enlarged. Work was begun by Louis IX (later Saint Louis) in the 1240s, and later continued under Philippe IV ('le Bel'). This architectural complex, of which the **Ste-Chapelle** and the **Conciergerie** (for both, see p85) can still be seen today, was inaugurated with great pomp at Pentecost 1313. Philippe invited Edward II of England and his Queen, Isabelle of France. The English were impressed: they soon came back for a long stay.

The palace was quickly filled with functionaries, so the king spent as much of his time as he could outside Paris at the royal castles of **Fontainebleau** (see p351) and, especially, **Vincennes** (see p149). The needs of the plenipotentiaries left behind to run the kingdom were met by a rapidly growing city population, piled into rather less chic buildings.

Paris was also reinforcing its identity as a major religious centre: as well as the local clergy and dozens of religious orders, the city was home to the masters and students of the university of the **Sorbonne** (established in 1253, see p129), who were already gaining a reputation for rowdiness. An influx of scholars

from all over Europe gave the city a cultural and intellectual cachet it was never to lose.

By 1328, Paris housed around 200,000 inhabitants, making it the most populous city in Europe. However, that year was to be the last of the golden age: the line of Capetian kings spluttered to an inglorious halt as Charles IV died heirless. The English claimed the throne for the young Edward III, son of Philippe IV's daughter. Refusing to recognise his descent through the female line, the late king's cousin, Philippe de Valois, claimed the crown as Philippe VI. So began the Hundred Years' War, – which in fact lasted for 116 years.

TROUBLES AND STRIFE

To make matters worse, the Black Death (bubonic plague) ravaged Europe from the 1340s. Those not zapped by the plague had to contend with food shortages, ever-increasing taxes, riots, repression, currency devaluations and marauding mercenaries. Meanwhile, in Paris, the honeymoon period for the king and the bourgeoisie was coming to an end. Rich and populous, Paris was expected to bear the brunt of the war burden; and as defeat followed defeat (notably the disaster at Crécy in August 1346) the bourgeoisie and people of the city were increasingly exasperated by the futility of the sacrifices they were making. It was around this time, in 1358, to be precise, that a chap called Etienne Marcel briefly seized control of Paris (see p11 **1358**).

By 1420, following the French defeat at Agincourt, Paris was in English hands; in 1431, Henry VI of England was crowned King of France in Notre-Dame. He didn't last. Five years later, Henry and his army had been driven back to Calais by the Valois king, Charles VII. Charles owed his grasp on power to Jeanne d'Arc, who led the victorious French in the battle of Orléans, only to be betrayed by her compatriots who decided she was getting too big for her boots. She was captured and sold to the English, who had her burnt as a witch.

By 1436, Paris was once again the capital of France. But the nation had been nearly bled dry by war, and was still divided politically, with powerful regional rulers continuing to threaten the monarchy. The ambitions of the Austrian Hapsburg dynasty represented a serious external worry. In a general atmosphere of instability, disputes over trade, religion and taxation were all simmering dangerously.

RENAISSANCE AND REFORMATION

In the closing decades of the 15th century, the restored Valois monarchs sought to reassert their position. A wave of building projects was the public sign of this effort, giving us such

Revolution rock 1789

Louis XVI, the 40th king of France, had poor control of his country's swelling problems. French intervention in the Seven Years War and the American War of Independence had left the country practically bankrupt, and subsequent attempts to introduce new taxes met with strong opposition from the bourgeoisie. Thrown into Louis' woes was a year of bad weather in 1788. First, a terrible hailstorm, which ruined the Paris harvest. Then a hard winter, which froze the rivers that brought food into the city. Bread prices soared, as did discontent. Springtime in 1789 brought riots on the rue du Faubourg-St- Antoine, where factory workers' wages had been cut. The parlements, or high courts, urged Louis to call a meeting of the *états généraux* – the representative body for the First Estate (the clergy), the Second Estate (the nobility) and the Third Estate (the bourgeoisie and commoners).

On 5 May 1789, the king reluctantly faced the états at Versailles. The Third Estate, which had as many members as the other two combined, demanded that the three merge into a single assembly, with one vote per member. Louis refused. On 20 June, the Third Estate reconvened on the playing courts at the Jeu de Paumes at Versailles and swore to establish a national constitution. The embattled Louis eventually conceded and allowed the états to form the Assemblée Nationale. But behind the scenes, the king was gathering troops to disband the assembly; on 12 July he publicly, and foolishly, dismissed the commoner's ally, finance minister Jacques Necker, prompting a violent counter-coup. On 13 July, Camille Desmoulins, a young unemployed lawyer, empassioned an angry crowd gathered in the Palais-Royal garden to take action. The next day, the crowd pillaged Les Invalides for arms, marched on the Bastille prison, and proceeded to tear it down. Only seven prisoners were imprisoned there, but the symbolic victory was immense (and enduring, as the annual *quatorze juillet* celebrations show, see p281). An emasculated Louis came to Paris on 17 July to acknowledge the crowds at Hôtel de Ville.

The establishment of the constitution forged ahead, and sparked furious debate. Tax breaks for the nobility and clergy were abolished, the country was divided into local governments and Roman Catholic Church property was seized. Two Parisian convents hosted two newly formed political clubs. On the Left Bank, at a 13th-century Franciscan convent (some parts of which are still standing, 15 rue de l'Ecole de Médicine), the Cordeliers club charged its members, mostly the poor *sans-culottes* (so-called because they couldn't afford breaches), a few cents to hear monarchy-bashing speeches by its leading lights. These included the figures of Desmoulins and Marat. On the Right Bank, the more radical Jacobins, who included Mirabeau, Danton and Robespierre, took up residency in a Dominican convent on rue St-Honoré, later destroyed by Napoleon. Before the monks were expelled, they hired the convent's library for 200 francs a year, holding forth beneath a fresco of Saint Thomas Aquinas.

One of Louis' original problems, the price of bread, had not budged. In October, a mob of starving women marched the 12 miles to Versailles and demanded that the king come to Paris. He promised to send the women grain, an offer they rejected by decapitating some of his guards. Louis wisely transferred to the Tuileries. In the months that followed the Jacobins roused powerful Republican feeling. Fearing greater danger at home and hoping to gain support abroad, the king and his family attempted to flee Paris on 20 June 1791. With Louis disguised as a valet, they got as far as Varennes, where a commoner recognised Louis' face from his portrait on a coin. Louis, Marie-Antoinette and family were brought back to Paris in disgrace, crowds throwing things at their coach, and poking their heads through the window and spitting.

On 14 September, Louis accepted the new constitution, and the revolution appeared to be over. But other monarchies were plotting to reinstate the King. In 1792, Austrian and Prussian troops invaded France, gaining rapidly on Paris with easy battles against a weak French army. The Republicans, rightly, suspected Louis of conspiring with the enemy, and scrabbled together their own army to capture him, ringing out the cannons on Pont Neuf to enrol the public. On the morning of 10 August, the Tuileries palace rang with gunfire. Swiss guards enlisted to defend the king put up a staunch fight, but were hacked to death along with all the

The Storming of the Bastille in 1789.

palace staff. Two bloody days later, the royal family was incarcerated in the Temple prison by the radical Commune de Paris, headed by Danton, Marat and Robespierre.

Next, massacre. Rampant suspicions about possible traitors led the revolutionaries to the gates of the city's prisons. They invaded, and murdered 2,000 so-called traitors, including the princess of Lamballe, whose head was stuck on a spike and paraded to the royal family through a window at the Temple. The monarchy was abolished on 22 September; the king was executed on 21 January. A trial, Robespierre claimed, was out of the question, since it would put 'the Revoultion itself in the dock'. The guillotine, a symbol of the revolution's brutality (in fact invented by Dr Guillotin as a humane method of execution) stood at the place de la Révolution and took thousands of heads, including that of Louis' widow, Marie-Antoinette, almost a year later. She awaited her fate in a wallpapered prison cell at the **Conciergerie** (*see p85*).

There was precious little dignity to this particular period of the Revolution. Within the Revolutionary Convention, which had replaced the Assemblée Nationale, the Jacobins had expelled the monarchist Girondins (a young Girondist, Charlotte Corday, retaliated by stabbing Marat to death at his home) and were gathering dictatorial momentum. Headed by 'l'incorruptible' Robespierre, the Jacobins in September 1793 vowed to wage terror against all rebels, Girondins and dissidents. In the Great Terror of 1794, the guillotine was transferred to place du Trône Renversé ('Overturned Throne', now place de la Nation), and sliced through 1,300 necks in six weeks. Bodies were dumped in the Picpus garden (now **Cimetière de Picpus**, *see p109*). The tumbrils, or two-wheeled carts which carried the dead, were painted green to disguise their bloody load.

Almost everybody wanted the Terror to end. The French army had successfully beaten off foreign forces, and the incessant killing began to look unecessary. Robespierre and his cohorts attempted some democratic reform, but most people wanted them gone. On 28 July 1794, he was executed and the reign of terror collapsed. The biggest and bloodiest revolution was over.

masterpieces as St-Etienne-du-Mont, **St-Eustache** (*see p100*) and private homes like the Hôtel de Cluny (which now houses the Musée National du Moyen-Age) and the **Hôtel de Sens** (*see p106*), which today houses the **Bibliothèque de Forney** (*see p167*). The Renaissance in France climaxed under François I. As well as being involved in the construction of magnificent châteaux at Fontainebleau, **Blois** and **Chambord** (for both, *see p362*), François was responsible for transforming the Louvre from a fortress into a royal palace. He held open house for such luminaries as Leonardo Da Vinci and Benvenuto Cellini. He also established the Collège de France to encourage humanist learning outside the control of the clergy-dominated universities.

Despite burning heretics by the dozen, François was unable to stop the spread of Protestantism, launched in Germany by Martin Luther in 1517. Resolutely Catholic, Paris was the scene of some horrific violence against Huguenots, as supporters of the new faith were called. The picture was complicated by the political conflict opposing the Huguenot Prince de Condé and the Catholic Duc de Guise.

By the 1560s, the situation had degenerated into open warfare. Catherine de Médicis, the scheming Italian widow of Henri II, was the real force in court politics. It was she who connived to murder prominent Protestants gathered in Paris for the marriage of the king's sister on St Bartholomew's Day (23 August 1572). Catherine's main aim was to dispose of her powerful rival, Gaspard de Coligny, but the situation got out of hand, and as many as 3,000 people were butchered. Henri III attempted to reconcile the religious factions and eradicate the powerful families directing the conflict, but the people of Paris turned against him and he was forced to flee. His assassination in 1589 brought the Valois line to an end.

THE BOURBONS
The throne of France being up for grabs, Henri of Navarre declared himself King Henri IV, launching the Bourbon dynasty. Paris was not impressed. The city closed its gates against the Huguenot king and the inhabitants endured a four-year siege by supporters of the new ruler. Henri broke the impasse by converting to Catholicism (and later quipped, *'Paris vaut bien une messe'* – Paris is well worth a Mass).

Louis XIV. See p17.

> ### 'François Ravaillac fatally stabbed the king while he was stuck in traffic.'

Henri set about rebuilding his ravaged capital. He completed the **Pont Neuf** (*see p80*), the first bridge to span the whole of the Seine. He commissioned place Dauphine and the city's first enclosed residential square – the place Royale – now **place des Vosges** (*see p105*). The square was the merry scene of jousting competitions and countless duels.

Henri also tried to reconcile his Catholic and Protestant subjects, issuing the Edict of Nantes in 1598, effectively giving each religion equal status. The Catholics hated the deal, and the Huguenots were suspicious. Henri was the victim of at least 23 attempted assassinations by fanatics of both persuasions. Finally, in 1610, a Catholic by the name of François Ravaillac fatally stabbed the king while he was stuck in traffic on rue de la Ferronnerie.

TWO CARDINALS
Since Henry's son, Louis XIII, was only eight at the time of his father's death, the widow, Marie de Médicis, took up the reins of power. We can

Revolution rock 1830

The fuss kicked up by the Napoleonic years appeared to be settling down. Bourbon blood once again took control of the country, with Louis XVI's exiled brother installed on the throne in 1814 as Louis XVIII. Old Catholic regimes die hard, and the new King's Charter of Liberties was not a wholly sincere expression of how he meant to rule. Liberal intellectual activity flourished nevertheless, with figures such as the caricaturist Daumier poking satirical fun at the bourgeoisie.

In 1824, Louis XVIII's youngest brother, Charles X, took the crown. Like his predecessor, he yearned for the ways of the *ancien régime*. But in the 1830 elections, the liberals won a hefty majority in the Chamber of Deputies, the legislative body. Charles'

unpopular minister Prince Polignac, a returned emigré, promptly dissolved the Chamber, announced a date for new elections and curtailed the number of voters.

Polishing off this collection of bad decisions was a decree abolishing the freedom of the press. The day after its issue, 26 July, 5,000 print workers and journalists filled the streets and three newspapers went to press. When police tried to confiscate copies, they sparked a three-day riot, *Les Trois Glorieuses*, with members of the disbanded National Guard manning the barricades. On 30 July he dismissed Polignac, but it was too late. He had little choice but to abdicate, and fled to England. As French revolutions go, it was a neat, brief affair.

thank her for the **Palais du Luxembourg** (*see p136*) and the 24 paintings she commissioned from Rubens, now part of the Louvre collection.

Louis took up his royal duties in 1617, but Cardinal Richelieu, chief minister from 1624, was the man who ran France. Something of a schemer, he outwitted the king's mother, his wife, Anne of Austria, and a host of princes and place-seekers. Richelieu helped to strengthen the power of the monarch, and he did much to limit the independence of the aristocracy. The cardinal was also a great architectural patron. He commissioned Jacques Lemercier to build what is now the **Palais-Royal** (*see p88*), and ordered the rebuilding of the Sorbonne.

The Counter-Reformation was at its height, and lavish churches such as the Baroque **Val-de-Grâce** (*see p130*) were an important reassertion of Catholic supremacy. The 16th century was 'Le Grand Siècle', a time of patronage of art and artists, even if censorship forced the brilliant mathematician and philosopher, René Descartes, into exile.

The first national newspaper, *La Gazette*, hit the streets in 1631; Richelieu used it as a propaganda tool. The cardinal founded the **Académie Française** (*see p134*), a sort of literary think-tank which is still working, slowly, on the dictionary of the French language which Richelieu commissioned from them in 1634. Richelieu died in 1642; Louis XIII followed suit a few months later. The new king, Louis XIV, was five years old. Anne of Austria became regent, with the Italian Cardinal Mazarin, a Richelieu protégé, as chief minister. Rumour has it that Anne and Mazarian may

have been married. Mazarin's townhouse is now home to the **Bibliothèque Nationale de France – Richelieu** (*see p167*).

Endless wars against Austria and Spain had depleted the royal coffers, and left the nation drained by exorbitant taxation. In 1648, the royal family was chased out of Paris by a popular uprising, 'la fronde', named after the catapults used by some of the rioters. Parisians soon tired of the anarchy that followed. When Mazarin's army retook the city in 1653, the boy-king was warmly welcomed. Mazarin died in 1661 and Louis XIV, now 24 years old, decided he would rule France without the assistance of any chief minister.

SHINE ON, SUN KING

The 'Roi Soleil', or Sun King, was an absolute monarch. 'L'état, c'est moi,' (I am the State) was his vision of power. To prove his grandeur, the king embarked on wars against England, Holland and Austria. He also refurbished and extended the Louvre, commissioned **place Vendôme** (*see p90*) and **place des Victoires** (*see p93*), constructed the Observatory and laid out the grands boulevards along the lines of the old city walls. The triumphal arches at **Porte St-Denis** and **Porte St-Martin** (*see p97*) date from this time, too. His major project was the palace at **Versailles** (*see p354*), a massive complex which drew on the age's finest architectural, artistic and landscape-design talents. Louis moved his court there in 1682.

Louis XIV owed much of his brilliant success to the work of Jean-Baptiste Colbert, nominally in charge of state finances, but eventually taking control of all the important levers of the state machine. Colbert was the force behind the Sun King's redevelopment of Paris. The **Hôtel des Invalides** (*see p138*) was built to accommodate the crippled survivors of Louis' wars, the **Salpêtrière** (*see p145*) to shelter fallen women. In 1702, Paris was divided into 20 '*quartiers*' (not until the Revolution was it re-mapped into '*arrondissements*'). **Le Procope** (*see p133*), the city's first café, opened in 1686. Although its original proprietor, Francesco Procopio dei Coltelli, would no longer recognise it since a 1989 facelift, the place is still in business. Colbert died in 1683, and Louis' luck on the battlefield ran out. Hopelessly embroiled in the War of the Spanish Succession, the country was devastated by famine in 1692.

The Sun King died in 1715, leaving no direct heir. His five-year-old great-grandson, Louis XV, was named king, with Philippe d'Orléans as regent. The court moved back to Paris. Installed in the Palais-Royal, the regent set about enjoying his few years of power, hosting lavish dinners which regularly degenerated into orgies. The state, meanwhile, remained chronically in debt.

THE ENLIGHTENMENT

Some of the city's more sober residents were making Paris the intellectual capital of Europe. Enlightenment thinkers such as Diderot, Montesquieu, Voltaire and Rousseau were all active during the reign of Louis XV. Literacy rates were increasing – 50 per cent of French men could read, 25 per cent of women – and the publishing industry was booming.

The king's mistress, Madame de Pompadour, encouraged him to finance the building of the **Ecole Militaire** (*see p139*) and the laying out of place Louis XV, known to us as **place de la Concorde** (*see p89*). The massive church of **St-Sulpice** (*see p136*) was completed in 1776. Many of the great houses in the area bounded by rue de Lille, rue de Varenne and rue de Grenelle date from the first half of the 18th century. The private homes of aristocrats and wealthy bourgeois, these would become the venues for numerous salons, the informal discussion sessions often devoted to topics raised by Enlightenment questioning.

The Enlightenment spirit of rational humanism finally took the venom out of the Catholic-Protestant power struggle, and the increase in public debate helped to change views about the nature of the State and the place and authority of the monarchy. As Jacques Necker, Louis XVI's finance minister on the eve of the Revolution, put it, popular opinion was 'an invisible power that, without treasury, guard or army, gives its laws to the city, the court and even the palaces of kings.'

Thanks to the Enlightenment, and an ever-growing burden of taxation on the poorest strata of society to prop up the wealthiest, that power was about to overturn the status quo for good (*see p14* **1789**).

NAPOLEON

Amid the post-Revolutionary chaos, and after the fall of Robespierre, power was divided between a two-housed Assembly and a Directory of five men. The French public reacted badly to hearing of England's unsuccessful attempts to promote more popular rebellion; when a royalist rising in Paris needed to be put down, a young officer from Corsica was the man to do it: Napoleon Bonaparte. Napoleon quickly became the Directory's right-hand man. When they needed someone to lead an Italian campaign against Austria, Napoleon was the man. Victory saw France – and Napoleon – glorified. After a further, aborted, campaign to Egypt in 1799, Napoleon returned home to put down another royalist plot, made himself the chief of the newly governing three-man Consul – and by 1804 he was emperor.

After failing to squeeze out the English by setting up the Continental System to block trade across the Channel, Napoleon waged wars of massive scope against Britain, Russia and Austria. On his way to the disaster of Moscow, Napoleon gave France the lycée educational system, the Napoleonic Code of civil law, the Legion of Honour, the Banque de France, the **Pont des Arts** (*see p81*), the **Arc de Triomphe** (*see p110*), the **Madeleine** church (he re-established Catholicism as the State religion; *see p95*), the **Bourse** (*see p93*), and the **rue de Rivoli**. He was also responsible for the centralised bureaucracy which still manages to drive Frenchmen mad.

As France became invaded by Russian troops who had chased Napoleon's once mighty army all the way from Moscow and Leipzig, Paris came under threat. Montmartre, then named Montnapoléon had a telegraph machine at its summit, one that had given so many of the emperor's orders and transmitted news of so many victories. The hill fell to Russian troops. Napoleon gave the order to blow up the city's main powder stores, and thus Paris itself. The officer refused. Paris accommodated carousing Russian, Prussian and English soldiers while Napoleon was sent to exile in Elba.

A hundred days later, he was back, leading an army against the Wellington and Blücher's troops in the mid-summer mud of Waterloo, near Brussels. A further defeat saw the end of him. Paris survived further foreign occupation. The diminutive Corsican died on the south Atlantic prison island of St Helena in 1821.

Revolution rock 1848

The 'citizen king'. The 'bourgeois monarch'. Such were the catchlines that stuck to Louis-Philippe. Famed for his habit of always carrying an umbrella, he was hardly a thrusting Napoleonic figure, and nor was his rule particularly adventurous – or popular. To the bourgeoisie, Louis looked kindly – more landowners, businessmen and lawyers were given the vote – but the poor were given a decidedly cold shoulder. As France's industrial revolution pitched up a few gears in the 1830s, latticing the country with roads, canals and railways, pestilence and poverty seeped into growing urban slums. The back-breaking hours worked in the factories would not be curbed by legislation: 'Whatever the lot of the workers is, it is not the manufacturer's responsibility to improve it,' said one trade minister. In Left Bank cafés, a new bohemian tribe of students derided the materialistic government. Workers' pamphlets and newspapers, such as *La Ruche Populaire*, gave voice to the starving, crippled poor. A majority of ill-feeling was stacking up against the King.

23 February 1848: along the boulevards, lit by gas lamps, hundreds of Parisians – men, women and students – moved towards a public banquet at La Madeleine. The king's minister, François Guizot, had forbidden direct campaigning by opposition parties in the forthcoming election; as a way around this, the parties held banquets instead of meetings. One diarist of the time noted that some of the crowd had stuffed swords and daggers underneath their shirts, but the demonstration was largely peaceful – until the troops on the boulevard des Capucines opened fire. The gunshots ignited a riot.

As barricades were springing up all over the city, a trembling Louis-Philippe abdicated and a liberal provisional government declared a republic. The virtual epidemic of poverty and unemployment was stemmed by creating national ateliers, or workshops, but such 'radical' reforms made the Right extremely nervous. A conservative government took power in May 1848, and shut down the ateliers. A month later, the poor were back in the streets. Some 50,000 toook part in these 'June Days' protests, but they were quite comprehensively crushed by the troops of General Cavaignac. In the final analysis, about 1,500 Parisians died and some 5,000 were deported.

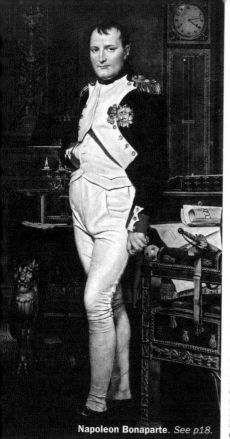

Napoleon Bonaparte. *See p18.*

ANOTHER ROUND OF BOURBONS

Having sampled revolution and military dictatorship, the French were now ready to give monarchy a second chance. The Bourbons got back in business, briefly, in 1815 in the person of Louis XVIII, Louis XVI's elderly brother. Several efforts were made to adapt the monarchy to the new political realities, but the forces unleashed during the Revolution, and the divisions which had opened in French society as a result, were not to be ignored. When another brother of Louis XVI, Charles X, became king in 1824, he decided that enough royal energy had been wasted trying to reconcile the nation's myriad factions. It was time for a spot of old-fashioned absolutism. The people were happy to respond with old-fashioned rebellion (*see p17* **1830**).

Another leftover from the *ancien régime* was now winched onto the throne – Louis-Philippe, Duc d'Orléans, who had some Bourbon blood in his veins. A father of eight who never went out without his umbrella, he was eminently acceptable to the newly powerful bourgeoisie. But the poor who had risked their lives in two attempts to change French society were unimpressed by the new king's promise to embrace a moderate and liberal version of the Revolutionary heritage.

THE NINETEENTH CENTURY

Philosopher Walter Benjamin declared Paris 'the capital of the nineteenth century', and he had a point. For sure, it was smaller than London, but in intellectual and cultural spheres it reigned supreme. On the demographic front, its population doubled to one million between 1800 and 1850. Most of the new arrivals were rural labourers who came to work on the ever-expanding city's building sites. The middle classes were doing well, thanks to the late arrival of the industrial revolution in France, and the solid administrative structures inherited from Napoleon. The poor were as badly off as ever, only there were more of them. When troops fired on a crowd of the unemployed on boulevard des Capucines on 23 February 1848, they triggered another revolution (*see p19* **1848**).

As the pamphleteer Alphonse Karr said of the revolution's aftermath, 'plus ça change, plus c'est la meme chose' (the more things change, the more they stay the same). In December 1848, Louis Bonaparte – nephew of Napoleon – was elected president. By 1852, he had moved into the Tuileries Palace and declared himself Emperor Napoleon III. Hugo called him Little Napoleon, but the diminutive Bonaparte held on to power for 22 years – significantly longer than his 'bigger' diminutive forebear.

THE SECOND EMPIRE

The emperor appointed a lawyer as *préfet* to mastermind the reconstruction of Paris. In less than two decades, prefect Georges-Eugène Haussmann had created the most magnificent city in Europe. His goals included better access to railway stations, better water supplies, an extended sewer system and a long list of new hospitals, barracks, theatres and mairies. It was a colossal, revolutionary project, and it transformed the capital. Haussmann created a network of wide, arrow-straight avenues that were better ventilated and more hygienic than the narrow streets they replaced – particularly in the old quarters on the islands and just off the Seine, whose rapid improvement would see the largest slum clearance ever accomplished in Europe. Now, with their unobstacled vistas, these streets were far more aesthetic. Their dimensions also had political advantages: the streets would be harder to barricade, and troops would be able to reach the scene of any future insurrection faster and in greater numbers. (Boulevard de Sébastopol, in particular, was conceived as a military fast track to the centre.)

So synonymous is Haussmann with the recasting of the city, and with a certain architectural style, that he's sometimes believed to have designed the buildings himself. He was indeed a formidable administrator, but no civil engineer: architectural detail he left to others. Shrewdly, he refused to employ the official architects of the day and hired instead more modest practitioners – people like Gabriel Davioud – who were much easier to command. The tree-lined streets radiating out from **place Charles de Gaulle** (see p111) are the classic expression of Haussmann's vision, while the rich mix of styles in Charles Garnier's **Opéra** (see p95) is often seen as typical of Second Empire self-indulgence.

Not everyone was happy. Haussmann's works destroyed thousands of buildings, including beautiful Middle Ages monuments; on the whole of Ile de la Cité only Notre-Dame survived. Entire residential areas were wiped off the map, and only the owners of buildings themselves were compensated; tenants were merely booted out and left to fend for themselves. Writers and artists lamented the loss of the more quirky Paris they used to know, and criticised the unfriendly grandeur of the new city. But there was no going back.

The emperor's meddling foreign policy would be his downfall. After the relatively successful Crimean War of the mid 1850s, he tried in vain to impose the Catholic Maximilian as ruler of Mexico. Maximilian's execution was the subject of Edouard Manet's famous painting. Manet would be the precursor of the burgeoning

Revolution rock 1871

When the emperor's away, the revolutionaries come out to play. In 1870 the over-reaching foreign policies of Louis-Napoleon (otherwise known as Napoleon III) had led France into an unwise war with the German states. Outmuscled by the viciously efficient Prussian army, Louis was forced to surrender at Sedan, and was dispatched to a prison cell in Germany, where he remained.

The war continued, and back in Paris, a provisional government hastily took power. Elections gave conservative monarchists the majority, though the Paris vote was firmly Republican. Former prime minister Adolphe Thiers assumed executive power. Meanwhile, Prussian forces prowled at the city gates and the beseiged city starved, picking rats from the gutter for food. Léon Gambetta, a young politician, escaped in style (by hot air balloon) but failed to raise an army in the south. In January 1871 the provisional government signed a bitter armistice that relinquished Alsace Lorraine and agreed to pay a five-million franc indemnity. German troops would stay on French soil until the bill was paid.

But with occupying army camps stationed around it, Paris considered the treaty a dishonour. Thiers ordered his soldiers to enter the city and strip it of its cannons, but the insurgents cut them short. The new government scuttled off to the haven of Versailles, while on 26 March Paris elected its own municipal body, the Commune, so called in memory of the spirit of 1792. The 92 members of the Commune hailed from the left and working classes; their agenda was liberal (schools would be secularised, debts suspended) but war-like (Germany must be defeated). Paris itself was given a little makeover: the column jutting Napoleonic glory into place Vendôme was pulled down, and statues of the great emperor were smashed up all over town.

Thiers would not stand by and watch. (The Germans, however, kept their ringside seats throughout.) Artillery fire picked at the communards' sandbag barricades on the edges of Paris. The suburbs fell by 11 April. In the sixth week of fighting, troops broke in through the Porte de St-Cloud and covered the springtime city in blood. The ill-equipped *Communards* faced a massacre: 25,000 were killed in days. In revenge, hostages were taken and shot, including the Archbishop of Paris (later honoured with the Sacré-Coeur). The infamous *pétroleuses*, women wielding petrol bombs, burnt off their anger, torching the Tuileries and the Hôtel de Ville. On the last day of *la semaine sanglante*, 28 May, 147 communards were trapped and shot in Père Lachaise cemetery, against the 'Mur des Fédérés', which remains an icon of the Commune struggle. The dead were buried in the streets; the prisons were crammed with some 40,000 arrested Communards. Thousands of others were deported.

Today, the tragic story of the Paris Commune is memorably documented in the collection of the **Musée d'Art et d'Histoire de St-Denis** (see p149).

Impressionist movement, which would include Monet, Renoir, Degas and Cézanne. Napoleon's next misadventure, the Franco-Prussian war of 1870, divided the figureheads of this artistic movement. They either fought or fled. Monet's stay in London marked him, discovering the light techniques used by Turner. After the war, Manet, Monet and Renoir would move to bucolic, riverside locations, to experiment with the contrasting use of colours and light. Artists flocked to Paris to emulate them. Impressionism begat Fauvism and Matisse, Cubism and Picasso. Paris was the mecca of the art world.

At home, the city's rapid industrialisation saw the rise of Socialism and Communism amid the disgruntled working class. Napoleon III gave limited rights to Trades Unions. Abroad, though, the now constitutional monarch was a disaster. A sick man, dominated by his wife Eugénie, he allowed himself to be drawn into a war with Prussia. France was soon defeated. At Sedan, in September 1870, 100,000 French troops were forced to surrender to Bismarck's Prussians; Napoleon III himself was captured. He never returned. In the humiliating deal which put a temporary end to hostilities, France lost the industrial heartlands of Alsace and Lorraine to Germany. The Prussians marched on Paris and lay seige to the city. Brave Paris held out, starving, for four brave months. By following spring, it had organised itself into a Commune. (*See p21* **1871**.)

General de Gaulle. *See p23.*

THE THIRD REPUBLIC

Out of the ruins of the Second Empire rose the Third Republic, a hastily flung together compromise given little chance of survival even by those who supported it. In fact, its makeshift constitution was to survive until 1940, thus becoming the most enduring – so far – in modern French history.

Thanks mainly to the huge economic boost provided by colonial expansion in Africa and Indo-China, the horrors of the Commune were soon forgotten in the self-indulgent materialism of the turn of the century. The **Eiffel Tower** (*see p140*) was built as the centrepiece of the 1889 Universal Exhibition. In 1891 the first line of the Métro opened, linking Porte Maillot and Vincennes in 25 minutes. For the World Exhibition of 1900, the **Grand Palais** (*see p168*) and **Petit Palais**, the **Pont Alexandre III** (*see p81*) and the Gare d'Orsay (now **Musée d'Orsay**, *see p164*) were built to affirm France's position as a dominant world power. The first cinema had opened (1895), and clubs like the **Moulin Rouge** (*see p117*) were buzzing. The lurid life of Montmartre, depicted by Toulouse-Lautrec – and its cheap rents – would attract the city's artistic community.

AN AFFAIR TO REMEMBER

In 1894, a Jewish army officer, Captain Alfred Dreyfus, had been dismissed in disgrace from the army and deported to Devil's Island, convicted of selling state secrets to the Prussians. The affair rocked the French establishment to its self-satisfied roots. Emile Zola famously championed the Jewish officer's cause in *J'Accuse!*, an open letter to President, as did statesmen such as Georges Clemenceau and Jean Jaurès. The Catholic right wing sided with the army, and lost heavily when Dreyfus was proven innocent.

THE GREAT WAR

As France, England and Germany outdid each other to industrialise and carve up the atlas, in 1904 France and England came to a political understanding: the Entente Cordiale. Once this included Russia, the Triple Entente, this was slowly stacking up against the Triple Alliance of Germany, Italy and Austro-Hungary. Nationalist tensions rose as European empires crumbled. On 3 August 1914 Germany declared war on France.

Although the Germans never made it to Paris in World War I, France became a battleground. German troops were stopped 20km short of Paris by French victory in the Battle of the Marne, although the artillery was audible. The city, and French society, suffered terribly in the war, despite ultimate victory.

The nations gathered at Versailles to make the peace and established new Europe states. A League of Nations was formed. Amid the post-war idealism, artists had responded to the horrors and absurdity of conflict with Surrealism. It was a movement founded in Paris by André Breton, a doctor who had treated troops in the trenches, and who had embraced Freud's theories of the unconscious. In 1924 it had a manifesto, a year later its first exhibition. Again, artists (and photographers) – Dali, Man Ray – flocked to Paris. By now Montmartre was too dear, and Montparnasse became the hub of artistic life. The interwar years were a whirl of activity in artistic and political circles. Paris became the avant-garde capital of the world, recorded by Hemingway, F Scott Fitzgerald and Gertrude Stein who had made the city their home and source of inspiration.

'The Vichy government was so eager to please the Germans, it organised anti-Semitic measures without prompting.'

Meanwhile, the Depression unleashed a wave of political violence, Fascists fighting Socialists and Communists for control. The election in 1936 of Léon Blum's Front Populaire saw the introduction of such social benefits as paid holidays for workers. At the same time, many writers were leaving Paris to Spain to cover – and indeed, to take part in – the Civil War. Across the German border, the contentious territories of Alsace-Lorraine – and the burden of the World War I peace agreements signed in Paris – became one of many bugbears held by the new Chancellor, Hitler. As war broke out, France had believed that its Maginot line would hold strong against the German threat. The Nazis simply bypassed it through Belgium.

THE SECOND WORLD WAR

Paris was in German hands within weeks of the start of hostilities. The city fell without a fight. A pro-German government in was set up in Vichy, a spa resort with enough hotels to accommodate the number of administrators. It was headed by the ageing World War I hero Marshall Pétain, popularly known as 'the victor of Verdun', while a young army officer, Charles de Gaulle, went to London to organise the Free French opposition. For those happy to get along with the German army, the period of the Occupation presented few hardships and, indeed, some good business opportunities. Food was rationed and tobacco and coffee went out of

circulation, but the black market thrived. In other ways, life went on much as before: each month during the winter of 1939-40, 800,000 Parisians still managed to go to the cinema.

For those who chose to resist, however, there were the Gestapo torture chambers at avenue Foch or rue Lauriston. The Germans further discouraged uncooperative behaviour with occasional executions: one victim, whose name now adorns a Métro station on line 5, was Jacques Bonsergent, an engineering student who was caught fly-posting and subsequently shot because he refused to reveal the names of his luckier (they got away) friends.

Paris was also a bad place in which to be Jewish. The Vichy government was so eager to please the Germans, it organised antisemitic measures without prompting from the occupier. As of the spring of 1941, the French authorities deported Jews to the death camps, frequently via the internment camp at Drancy. Prime minister Pierre Laval claimed it was a necessary concession to his Third Reich masters. (Laval would later flee to Spain, be refused political asylum by Franco and be handed to the Americans. After a failed attempt at poisoning himself, he was shot in 1945.) In July 1942, 12,000 Jewish French citizens were rounded up in the Vélodrome d'Hiver, a sports complex on quai de Grenelle, and then dispatched to Auschwitz. (In July 1994, a memorial to the victims was finally erected near the site of the long-demolished sports arena.)

THE LIBERATION

Paris survived the war practically unscathed, ultimately due to the bravery of one of its captors. On 23 August 1944, as the Allied armies of liberation approached the city, Hitler ordered his commander, Dietrich Von Choltitz, to detonate the explosives which had been set all over town in anticipation of a retreat. Von Choltitz refused. On 25 August 1944, French troops, tactfully placed at the head of the US forces, entered the city, and General de Gaulle led the parade down the Champs-Elysées.

Writers and artists swept back into Paris to celebrate and seek out old haunts. Hemingway held court at the Hotels Ritz and Scribe with the great journalists of the day, clinking glasses with veterans of the Spanish Civil War such as photographer Robert Capa and George Orwell. Picasso's studio was besieged by well-wishers.

However, the Liberation was not the end of France's troubles. De Gaulle was the hero of the hour, but relations between the interim government he commanded and the Resistance – largely Communist – were still tricky. Orders issued to *maquis* leaders in the provinces were often ignored. The Communists wanted a revolution, and De Gaulle suspected them of hatching plans to seize Paris prior to August 1944. Meanwhile, De Gaulle knew he had to commit every available French soldier to the march on Germany, or risk being sidelined by the other allies after the war. With no military forces to spare for domestic law and order, he had to leave homeland security to the very people – the 'patriotic militias' – who were most likely to be at least sympathetic to the Communist cause; or, even more dubiously, gendarmes who had previously worked with the occupying power.

When it came to rebuilding the country, the uncomfortable compromises multiplied – even to the point of injustice. Companies that had worked with the Germans were the best equipped, and thus the most useful; and while a handful of collaborating industrialists, including the motor vehicle baron Louis Renault, were imprisoned, many got off scot free. In any case, recovery was slow to come. There were shortages of everything. Food was as hard to come by as it had been during the war; indeed, many complained they had been better off under the Germans. Medical supplies were inadequate, as were more basic necessities. Even in the ministries, paper was so scarce that for a while, correspondence had to be sent out on Vichy letterhead, with the sender crossing out 'Etat Français' at the top and writing 'République Française' instead. It was an embarrassing state of affairs.

THE IMMEDIATE POST WAR

On Tuesday, 8 May 1945, De Gaulle made a broadcast to the nation to announce Germany's surrender. Paris went wild. Cars hooted their horns, church bells rang, sirens wailed, artillery boomed and low-flying aircraft zoomed overhead. Crowds packed out the Champs-Elysées and the city's fountains were switched back on. It was a hell of a party.

> **'A vote was passed maintaining de Gaulle in his position as head of state – but he remained an antagonistic leader.'**

The euphoria didn't last. There were strikes. And more strikes. Liberation had proved to be a restoration, not the revolution the Communists, now the most powerful political force in the land, had hoped for. The Communist Party was, in at least one respect, as pragmatic as everyone else: it did its utmost to turn parliamentary democracy to its advantage, to wit, getting as

many of the top jobs as it could. (It even lobbied to get members into the Académie Française.) The pragmatism stopped, however, at its tendency to see fascists and fifth columnists in every shadow; the French Communist leader, Maurice Thorez, would travel around town only in an armoured limousine with bodyguards in tow, for fear of assassination attempts.

A general election was held on 21 October 1945. The Communists secured 159 seats, the Socialists got 146, and the Catholic Mouvement Républicain Populaire got 152. At the Assemblée Nationale's first session a fortnight later, a unanimous vote was passed maintaining de Gaulle in his position as head of state – but he remained an antagonistic leader. His reluctance to take a firm grip of the disastrous economic situation alienated many intellectuals and industrialists who had previously been loyal to him, and his characteristic aloofness only made the misgivings of the general populace worse. He, on the other hand, was disgusted by all the political chicanery – what he called its *pourriture*, or rot. On 20 January 1946, he abruptly resigned.

France, meanwhile, looked to swift industrial modernisation under an ambitious plan put forward by internationalist politician Jean Monnet. While the economy and daily life remained grim, brash new fashion designer Christian Dior put together a stunning collection of strikingly simple clothes: the New Look. (*See pp37-39* **Haute couture or high street?**) Such extravagance horrified many locals, but the fashion industry boomed. Meanwhile, the divisions in Paris between its fashionable and its run-down working class areas became more pronounced. The northern and eastern edges – areas only revived in the late 20th century by a taste for retro, industrial decor and cheap rent – were forgotten about.

DE GAULLE IN THE DESERT

Félix Gouin, the new Socialist premier, quickly nationalised the bigger banks and the coal industry. But the right wing was growing, and there was even a rise of royalist hopes. A referendum was held in May 1946 to determine the crucial tenet of the Fourth Republic's constitution: should the Assemblée Nationale have absolute or restricted power? The results were a narrow victory for those who, like de Gaulle, had insisted the Assemblée's power should be qualified. De Gaulle's prestige increased, but it was to be another 12 years, and a whole new constitution – the Fifth Republic – before he got his hands back on the levers of power. He spent much of his *'passage du désert'* writing his memoirs.

In Context

THE ALGERIAN WAR AND MAY 1968

The post-war years were marked by the rapid disintegration of France's overseas interests – and her rapprochement with Germany to create what would become the European Community.

When revolt broke out in Algeria in 1956, almost 500,000 troops were sent in to protect national interests. A protest by Algerians in Paris on 17 October 1961 led to the deaths of hundreds of people at the hands of the city's police. The extent of the violence was officially concealed for decades, as was the use of torture against Algerians by French troops. Algeria became independent in 1962.

Meanwhile, the slow, painful discoveries of collaboration in World War II, often overlooked in the rush to put the country back on its feet, were being faced. The younger generation began to question the motives of the older one.

De Gaulle's Fifth Republic was felt by many to be grimly authoritarian. There are certainly those who believe that he designed it to be an elected monarchy, which is interesting when you consider that it's the constitution still in use today. In the spring of 1968, students unhappy with overcrowded university conditions took to the streets of Paris at the same time as striking Renault workers. The protest turned violent

(*see p26* **1968**). The real significance of May 1968 is still debated, but de Gaulle certainly took it seriously, fleeing to Germany on 29 May as the street violence reached its peak. He came back, of course, and went on to win the elections that June – but his career was over.

MITTERRAND

Following the largely anonymous presidencies of Georges Pompidou and Valéry Giscard d'Estaing, the Socialist François Mitterrand took up the task in 1981. The verdict on Mitterrand is still not in: the early part of his presidency saw him introducing some radical political and economic reforms, but the necessities of pragmatism and compromise led to their reversal, and he left the Socialist party in some disarray. At any rate, Mitterrand made a big difference to Paris and visitors to the city can thank him for his *Grands Projets* without worrying about suggestions that they might represent a most unrepublican form of self-aggrandisement. Mitterrand was responsible for IM Pei's Louvre **pyramid** (*see p153*), the **Grande Arche de la Défense** (*see p149*), the **Opéra Bastille** (*see p318*), and the more recent **Bibliothèque Nationale de France – François Mitterrand** (*see p167*).

American troops march down the Champs-Elysées at the **Liberation of Paris**. *See p23*.

Revolution rock 1968

The *soixante-huitards* sprang the greatest public revolt in French living memory. For that, and for the Left, at least, the revolutionaries of 1968 are revered as heroes. At the time, they were students – post-war baby boomers who had grown up in a France ill at ease with its post-war identity. They were then crammed into universities that had been somewhat cheaply expanded to accommodate them. Talk of politics grew across the campuses, turning against the government's stranglehold on the media and President de Gaulle's poor grasp of the economy. Ministers did indeed at the time have a sinister habit of leaning on the leading newspaper editors, and television was dubbed to be 'the government in your dining room'. Inflation was high, and the gap between the working classes and the bourgeoisie was becoming a chasm.

But still, de Gaulle echoed many when he said the events of May 1968 were simply 'incompréhensible'. The touchpaper was lit at overcrowded Nanterre university, on the outskirts of Paris, where students had been protesting against the war in Vietnam and the tatty state of the campus.

On May 2, exhausted by the protests, the authorities closed the university down and threatened to expel some of the students. The next day, a sit-in was held in sympathy at the Sorbonne. Police were called to intervene, but made things worse, charging into the crowd with truncheons, tear gas and a comprehensive lack of judgement. The city's streets were soon flooded with thousands of incensed student demonstrators, now officially on strike. The trades unions followed, as did the lycées. By mid May, nine million people were on strike, and not just in Paris: factories all over the country were occupied by workers, including the Renault plant in Rouen and Sud Aviation near Nantes.

On 24 May de Gaulle intervened – naturally via the nation's television sets. His speech warned of civil war, and pleaded for support. It didn't go down too well: riots broke, with students storming the Bourse, only to be thwarted by more police tear gas. Barricades sprung up all over the Latin Quarter, which had become something of a battleground, with the Odéon theatre and the amphitheatre of the Sorbonne packed every night with activists and students.

Five days later, prime minister Pompidou sent tanks to the edges of Paris, but the crisis did not quite come to such extremes. Pompidou conceded pay rises of between seven and ten per cent and an increase in the minimum wage; the country went back to work. A general election was called prematurely for 23 June, by which time the Right had gathered enough red-fearing momentum to gain a safe majority.

The revolt of 1968 was over, and the city slowly tried to get back to a more normal state of affairs, starting by scrubbing off the colourful, anti-Gaullist graffiti that by then was scrawled all over Paris.

CHIRAC, BUSH AND IRAQ

France may still boast the world's fourth-largest economy, the nuclear deterrent and a permanent seat on the UN Security Council, but her influence on the world stage had been waning for years until President Chirac, flushed from re-election and well aware he was onto a PR winner, stood up in early 2003 to oppose the US-led invasion of Iraq. France's official disapproval of George Bush culminated in the threat to use its Security Council veto against any resolution authorising the use of force without UN say-so, a move inspired by Chirac's hunger for an international role, his fear of the consequences among France's five million Muslims of an attack on Iraq, traditional Gallic anti-Americanism, or a genuine belief that this particular war at this particular time in this particular place was wrong.

Whatever the reason, it did Chirac no harm at all. His personal approval ratings soared at home, at one stage breaking the 80 per cent barrier, and abroad he became the darling of the Islamic world, Africa, Asia and large swathes of continental Europe. He also acquired a most-hated-man status in America rivalled only by Osama Bin Laden and Saddam Hussein, but that was a small price to pay.

Chirac's domestic popularity didn't last. His prime minister, Jean-Pierre Raffarin, and the centre-right government began attacking some of France's more prized national institutions with a programme of long-overdue reforms, starting with the state pension system. The blindingly obvious fact that a steadily greying population plus fewer people in work equals serious pension shortfall did not prevent some of the largest nationwide protests France has

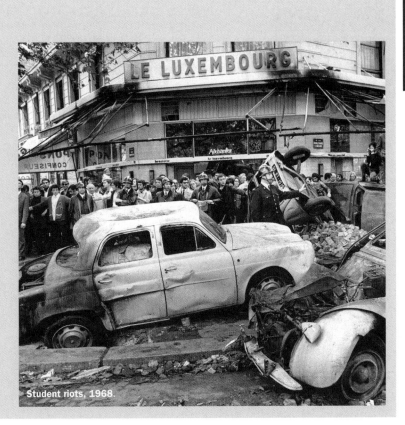

Student riots, 1968.

seen since 1995, with striking Métro, hospital workers, postmen, teachers and binmen bringing the city to a virtual standstill.

Planned restrictions on the uniquely Gallic, exceptionally generous (and heavily indebted) system of unemployment benefit for out-of-work performing arts professionals like actors, musicians and backstage staff led to a further round of protests, as well as the cancellation of France's equivalents of Edinburgh and Glyndebourne, the Avignon and Aix summer cultural festivals.

Then came the official mismanagement and aloofness that characterised, for all of France, the murderous two-week heatwave of August 2003, during which as many as 14,000 elderly people died, Government ministers put their heads in the sands, and Chirac did not deign to open his mouth, still less cut short holiday in

Canada. The popularity of president and prime minister plummeted to all-time lows, from which they have barely recovered.

Today, the great white hope of the right wing is a young chap by the name of Nicolas Sarkozy, at just 50 a refreshingly youthful and dynamic (and, crucially, media-savvy) whose sights are set unabashedly on the presidential chair. After a near-faultlessly popular stint as minister of the interior, he was shunted by Chirac to the lower-wattage job of finance minister, but is widely tipped as a hot ticket for the next presidential election in 2007.

The left has the Mayor of Paris, Bertrand Delanoë. His popular vision of a traffic-free city (*see pp33-35* **Delanoë's Dream**) is slowly transforming the capital. Should he also earn Paris the right to host the Olympic Games of 2012, presidency may be just reward.

Key events

EARLY HISTORY

250BC Lutetia founded on the Ile de la Cité by a Celtic tribe, the Parisii.
52BC Paris conquered by the Romans.
260AD St Denis executed on Mount Mercury.
360 Julian, Governor of Lutetia, is proclaimed Roman Emperor by his troops.
451 Attila the Hun nearly attacks Paris.
496 Frankish king Clovis baptised at Reims.
508 Clovis makes Paris his capital.
543 Enormous Benedictine Monastery of St-Germain-des-Prés founded.
635 King Dagobert establishes international Fair of St-Denis.
800 Charlemagne becomes first Holy Roman Emperor. Moves his capital from Paris to Aix-la-Chapelle (Aachen).
845-880 Paris sacked by the Vikings.
987 Hugues Capet, Count of Paris becomes king of France.

THE CITY TAKES SHAPE

1136 Abbot Suger begins the construction of the Basilica of St-Denis.
1163 Building of Notre-Dame begins.
1181 Philippe-Auguste establishes a new market at Les Halles.
1190-1202 Philippe-Auguste constructs a protective city wall.
1215 University of Paris is recognised by Rome with the Papal Charter.
1246-48 Louis IX (later St-Louis) constructs Sainte-Chapelle.
1253 Sorbonne founded.
1340 Hundred Years War with England begins – lasting 116 years.
1357 Revolt by Etienne Marcel.
1364 Charles V moves royal court to the Louvre and builds Bastille and Vincennes fortresses.
1420-36 Paris under English rule.
1422 Henry V of England dies at the Château de Vincennes.
1463 First printing press in Paris.

THE WARS OF RELIGION AND AFTER

1528 François I, the Renaissance King, begins rebuilding the Louvre.
1572 23 August: the brutal massacre of Protestants on St Bartholemew's Day.
1589 Henri III assassinated.
1593 Henri IV converts to Catholicism, ending Wars of Religion.
1605 The construction of place des Vosges and Pont Neuf.

1610 Henri IV assassinated.
1635 Académie Française founded.
1643 Cardinal Mazarin becomes regent.
1648-53 Paris under continual threat by the *Fronde* rebellion.
1661 Louis XIV begins personal rule – and the transformation of Versailles; the fall of Fouquet.
1667 Paris given its first street lighting.
1671 Building of Les Invalides.
1672 Creation of the Grands Boulevards on line of Charles V's city wall. Portes St-Denis and St-Martin built.
1680 Comédie-Française founded.
1682 Louis XIV transfers court to Versailles.

ROYALTY TO REPUBLICANISM

1700 Beginning of the 15-year War of the Spanish Succession.
1715 Death of Louis XIV; Philippe d'Orléans becomes regent.
1753 Place Louis XV (later place de la Concorde) begun.
1785 Fermiers Généraux Tax Wall built.
1789 The first meeting of Etats-Généraux since 1614.
1789 14 July: Paris mob takes the Bastille. Oct: Louis XVI forced by protesters to leave Versailles for Paris.
1791 21 June: Louis XVI attempts to escape Paris – unsuccessfully.
1792 September Massacres. 22 Sept: Republic declared. Royal statues removed.
1793 Execution of Louis XVI and Marie-Antoinette. Louvre museum opens to the public.
1794 The Terror – 1,300 heads fall in six weeks. July: Jacobins overthrown; Directoire takes over. A young officer from Corsica, Napoleon Bonaparte, is their right-hand man.
1799 Napoleon returns from Egypt to stage a military coup – becomes First Consul.
1804 Napoleon crowns himself emperor at a grand ceremony at Notre-Dame.
1806 Napoleon commissions the building of the Arc de Triomphe.
1814 Napoleon defeated; Russian army occupies Paris; Louis XVIII grants the Charter of Liberties.
1815 Napoleon regains power (the 'Hundred Days'), before defeat at Waterloo. Bourbon monarchy restored, with Louis XVIII.
1830 July: Charles X overthrown; Louis-Philippe of Orléans becomes king.
1836 Completion of Arc de Triomphe.

1838 Daguerre creates first daguerreotype photos. Paris gradually becomes a global mecca for visual arts.
1848 Louis-Philippe overthrown, replaced by Second Republic. Most men get the vote. Louis-Napoleon Bonaparte elected President.

CULTURAL EVOLUTION
1852 Louis-Napoleon declares himself Emperor Napoleon III: Second Empire. Bon Marché, first department store, opens.
1853 Haussmann made Préfet de Paris.
1862 Construction of Palais Garnier begins. Hugo's *Les Misérables* published.
1866 *Le Figaro* daily newspaper founded.
1870 Prussian victory at Sedan; siege of Paris. Napoleon III abdicates.
1871 Commune takes over Paris; May: *la semaine sanglante*.
1874 First Impressionist exhibition in Nadar's atelier on bd des Capucines.
1875 Bizet's *Carmen* at Opéra Comique.
1889 Paris Exhibition on the centenary of Revolution: Eiffel Tower built. Moulin Rouge opens. Montmartre becomes the artistic hub.
1894-1900 Dreyfus case polarises opinion.
1895 Dec: world's first public film screening by the Lumière brothers at the Jockey Club, now the Hôtel Scribe.
1900 Paris' *Exposition Universelle*: Grand Palais, Petit Palais, Pont Alexandre III built. First Métro line opened.

THE WORLD WAR YEARS
1914 As World War I begins, Germans beaten back from Paris at the Marne.
1918 11 Nov: Armistice signed in the forest of Compiègne.
1919 Peace conference held at Versailles.
1927 La Coupole opens in Montparnasse. Paris again the cultural and literary mecca as writers and artists flock here in the inter-war years. Surrealism flourishes.
1934 Fascist demonstrations.
1936-37 France elects Popular Front under Léon Blum; first paid workers' holidays.
1940 Germans occupy Paris. 18 May: De Gaulle's call to arms from London. Life in occupied Paris goes on.
1941-42 Mass deportations of Paris Jews.
1944 Aug: Paris liberated.
1946 Fourth Republic established. Women given the vote.
1947 Christian Dior launches the New Look. Marshall Plan gives post-war aid to France.

1949 Simone de Beauvoir's *The Second Sex* published.
1955-56 Revolt begins in Algeria; demonstrations on the streets in Paris.
1957 Opening of CNIT in new La Défense business district.
1958 De Gaulle President: Fifth Republic.

EUROPEAN UNION AND NEW WORLD ORDER
1958 France founder member of what would become the European Economic Community – today's European Union.
1962 Algerian War ends.
1968 May: student riots and workers' strikes in Paris and across France.
1969 De Gaulle resigns, Pompidou becomes President.
1973 Boulevard Périphérique inaugurated.
1977 Centre Pompidou opens. Jacques Chirac wins first mayoral elections.
1981 François Mitterrand elected President; abolition of the death penalty.
1989 Bicentenary of the Revolution: Louvre Pyramid and Opéra Bastille completed.
1995 Jacques Chirac elected President.
1997 General election: Socialist government elected under Lionel Jospin.
2001 Socialist Bertrand Delanoë elected Mayor of Paris. He begins the gradual transformation of Paris by introducing a series of crowd-pleasing civic projects. *Le Monde* declares 'We Are All Americans' after the destruction of the World Trade Center.
2002 The success of National Front leader Jean-Marie Le Pen in the first round of the presidential elections paves the way for Jacques Chirac's landslide re-election. Jean-Pierre Raffarin becomes Prime Minister as France becomes governed by the centre-right.
2003 Jacques Chirac threatens to veto any US-led attempt to construct a UN resolution authorising military action against Iraq. Parliament approves legislation to devolve wide-ranging powers to France's regions and departments, perhaps signalling a move away from highly centralised government. Jean-Pierre Raffarin's government's proposals to reform the state retirement pension and unemployment benefit allowance causes widespread strikes. An estimated 15,000 French people die in the August heat wave. Compensation awarded to orphaned victims of the Nazi occupation of 1940-44.

Paris Today

Paris is gripped by a new urban dynamism. While rents rise, so do hopes that the city will host the 2012 Olympics.

According to a major poll conducted last year, Parisians would like to see their city with fewer cars, better public transport and less pollution. Aware that their city's reputation and character rely greatly on its past, they would also like to see the city's historical buildings better protected. Happily for Mayor Bertrand Delanoë, who instigated the poll, these results neatly reflect his own plans and policies for Paris. Since coming to power in 2001, the charismatic Socialist mayor has made most of the right moves, and his growing popularity recently confirmed by his debut in the bi-annual survey of the nation's 50 favourite French personalities. (The list was again topped by Zinédine Zidane, who risks losing his place after his retirement from international football.)

Traffic and public transport have been a priority, with the creation of multiple bus lanes (sometimes physically divided from the road by potted bamboo) and cycle lanes making a real difference to daily life in the city. Construction has begun on a new tramway around the edge of town. Due to open in 2006, the initial section of the line (around Les Maréchaux in the south) will be bordered by 36,000m² of lawns and over a thousand trees. Projects envisage the creation of more green space, and the extension of several existing Métro lines to link up with a tram network due to be built in the suburbs.

Fun is also high on the agenda, as Delanoë's flagship Paris-Plage (*see p280* **No Plage like home**) event testifies. How else to construe the transformation of the Seine-side quays into a sand-filled beach complete with showers, palm trees and ice-cream outlets? While the summer-time event may have raised some initial concerns about the frivolous spending of tax-payers' money, it has since achieved a genuine popularity, and will celebrate its fourth year in 2005. The other 'fun' innovation is the all-night **Nuit Blanche** (*see p282*), which sees various artistic installations, concerts and swimming sessions organised throughout the city during a weekend night in early autumn. This event, too, has become a crowd-puller, and no doubt helped contribute to the mayor's public appeal (*see also pp33-35* **Delanoë's Dream**).

There is one issue where Delanoë meets with local disapproval: his insistence on resurrecting the long-taboo debate about putting up skyscrapers. Tower blocks, he argues, are the only way to resolve the city's housing shortage. While the outcome of this particular battle remains uncertain, current urban development projects are proving highly successful. Delanoë's plans to re-engineer the Les Halles gardens and subterranean shopping centre, widely recognised as an architectural disaster, have unsurprisingly been given the thumbs up, while the major regeneration of the previously abandoned site east of the Gare d'Austerlitz in the 13th goes from strength to strength. Visual artists from the suburbs have been moving in, making it one of the most exciting exercises in urban renewal anywhere in Europe. The first group put itself on the map when it moved into a squat dubbed **Les Frigos** ('The Fridges'; www.les-frigos.com) because it was a disused cold-store by the railway sidings of Austerlitz. At the same time, the **Bibliothèque Nationale François Mitterrand** (*see p167*) was being built, and other artists took up residence in rue Louise-Weiss and surrounding streets. By the time Delanoë was elected, he saw no option but to integrate them in his vision for the city. Meanwhile, new buildings are springing up around the Bibliothèque in the form of social housing, plush apartments and international company headquarters, while four universities will take up residence by 2006. Last year, links were further improved with the extension of the driverless line 14 Métro to Gare St-Lazare, and the line is being lengthened in the other direction, towards Olympiades in the 13th. (*See p146* **The lucky 13th**.)

> ## 'Between 2000 and 2003, property prices rose by an average of one per cent per month. In the first half of 2004, they went up by a staggering 13.1 per cent.'

While provisions have been made to build more social housing, those who do not qualify are faced with the ever-spiralling cost of property in Paris. Between 2000 and 2003, property prices rose by an average of one per cent per month. In the first half of 2004, residential prices went up by a staggering 13.1 per cent. Consequently, trendy young professionals (or *bobos*) have taken their search for affordable flats to more genuinely working-class quartiers like the Goutte d'Or and Ste-Marthe in the north, simultaneously inflicting the capital's highest inflation on these areas (18.2 per cent in the 10th alone). One effect of these increasing property prices and rents is the emergence of *la colocation*, or flat-sharing. (*See p381* **Vive la colocation!**) While still a relatively uncommon practice compared with most Anglophone countries, the phenomenon has given rise to a change in living culture.

Construction elsewhere is of a cultural kind, with the inauguration or regeneration of a number of museums. Most eagerly awaited

(in 2006) is the Musée du Quai Branly, with a prime site by the Eiffel Tower. In the south-west, the long-forgotten Renault factory on Ile Séguir in the middle of the Seine is to be bulldozed to make way for a museum designed by Tadao Ando which will house the extensive modern art collection of businessman François Pinault. During 2005, the new Musée du Cinéma is set to open at an existing Frank Gehry-designed building at Bercy, while the Palais de Chaillot at Trocadéro should receive some much-needed reinvigoration with the opening of the Cité de l'Architecture et du Patrimoine.

Paris, though, is not just about culture. As a popular gastronomic trend demonstrates, it's OK to have fun, too. *Le fooding* is a term still bandied about, even if few seem sure of its meaning. Combining 'food' with 'feeling', it was coined as a backlash against traditional ways of evaluating food. Instead of focusing on the quality of the food, *fooding* also looks at atmosphere, decor, music and service. The phenomenon has spawned a *Fooding Guide*, published by trendy *Nova* magazine, and an annual Fooding Week, during which awards are given to the year's best fooding restaurants. Free fooding events over the summer serve food, wine and music to those who know the day's password (available on www.lefooding.com).

Fun aside, Delanoë has just one man to rival his popularity in political circles: current Minister of Finance, Nicolas Sarkozy. Widely viewed as the man most likely to take over from Chirac as president, the ambitious 50-year-old remains well-supported despite announcing some controversial privatisation projects. A hefty public deficit that breaches EU limits has forced Sarkozy to press on with the partial sell-off of aero engine firm SNECMA, France Telecom, and energy utilities Electricité de France and Gaz de France. Passing the bill for the last two sparked a series of strikes that saw energy supplies cut to the Eiffel Tower and the homes of several leading politicians.

Despite this, Sarkozy's energy and charisma have won him an image as saviour of the ruling centre-right UMP party, especially after its embarrassing defeats at the 2004 local and European elections. Chirac quite rightly sees his Finance Minister as a threat, particularly since losing loyal right-hand man Alain Juppé. Party chairman Juppé was last year convicted of illegal funding in a scandal that implicated Chirac himself, although the president managed to escape relatively unscathed. Meanwhile, Prime Minister Jean-Pierre Raffarin continues to hone a reputation for ineptness, following his poor handling of the 2003 heatwave that claimed thousands of lives and his failure to pass a bill aimed at raising money for the aged.

More Seine-side revelry.

compared with the previous year. Japanese and Middle Eastern tourists have also started coming back. Although the tourist industry is still not as buoyant as it was back in 2002, the crisis is relative; France still leads the world in terms of tourist arrivals (75 million) in 2003, the year of the Iraq war, forest fires and strikes by performance artists.

The French themselves are starting to take holidays outside their own country. France remains the holiday destination of choice for the French, but the first half of 2004 saw a 21 per cent increase in non-business stays abroad compared with the same period in 2003. One explanation is the arrival of budget airlines in France. While the dominance of Air France (which has merged with KLM to become Europe's biggest airline) seems to have killed off any domestic budget airlines, foreign airlines have begun to set up routes to and from Paris. Low-cost travel abroad is now provided by the likes of Ryanair, easyJet and bmibaby.

'The bid has created a buzz around town... If Paris wins, the Olympics will transform the city.'

The arrival of new air routes bodes well for international tourism, and it also serves a more distant goal of the capital: that of winning the 2012 Olympic Games. Indeed, accessibility and transport is one of the areas where Paris scores highly relative to its rival candidate cities (London, New York, Madrid and Moscow). The International Olympic Committee (IOC) has also expressed satisfaction with the city's security measures, its accommodation potential, and the proposed financial and architectural plans. On top of this, Paris boasts the successful experiences of hosting the 1998 World Cup and the 2003 World Athletics Championships. It also has many of the necessary sporting arenas – notably the **Stade de France** (*see p333*), **Longchamp hippodrome** (*see p335*), and the **Roland Garros** tennis complex (*see p333*). The bid has already created a buzz around town, uniting not just the city's population (three-quarters of Parisians want the Games), but its politicians, with Delanoë presiding on the bid committee and Chirac offering his full backing. The IOC gives its decision in July 2005. If Paris wins, the Olympics will transform the city. Although, by 2012, Delanoë hopes to have already created a greener, more liveable Paris – and if his high-reaching ambitions are realised, it's around that date he'll be standing for President of the Republic.

Uproar also greeted the government's move to ban students from wearing 'conspicuous' religious apparel – notably headscarves – in schools. The new law was passed in September 2004, despite Iraqi militants threatening to kill journalist hostages Georges Malbrunot and Christian Chesnot if the ruling were not reversed.

The hostage affair was perhaps particularly shocking to the French as they had been at pains to keep a distance from the Iraq situation. Indeed, the big 'no' to the war (which famously saw French fries re-baptised 'Freedom fries' in certain transatlantic eateries) not only sullied international relations, but contributed to a drop in tourism of nine per cent in 2003. Differences with Britain, however, were laid aside as the two nations celebrated 100 years of the Entente Cordiale, the diplomatic agreement signed to ally two ancient adversaries.

Transatlantic relations, meanwhile, were probably not aided by the Cannes Film Festival jury (admittedly presided over by American Quentin Tarantino) bestowing the Palme d'Or on Michael Moore's anti-Bush documentary *Fahrenheit 9/11*. It's a commonly held view that Franco-American relations will not improve greatly until the States gets a new president – in 2008. Nonetheless, American tourists have begun to return to France, with figures for overnight stays up by 15.6 per cent in July 2004

Delanoë's Dream

The current mayor has plans that go well beyond Seine-side beaches and city-wide cycle lanes.

The summer of 2004 marked the halfway mark in Bertrand Delanoë's first term as mayor of Paris. It rained. And rained. One after the other, screenings in the open-air cinema season were cancelled. As gale-force winds whipped France, the blue deckchairs and sunshades of Paris-Plage were folded away. The open-air dance on place de la Bastille to mark the 60th anniversary of the Liberation of Paris was a soggy affair. All these Delanoë-inspired crowd-pleasers were a wash-out. Parisians sat inside their cafés and grumbled about being robbed of summer. Everyone knew they could not really blame the mayor for the weather, but it did begin to feel like life under the 54-year-old socialist was only fine when the sun shone.

The challenge to this former businessman in the run-up to the 2007 mayoral elections is to prove that there is more to him than fun and dance. Paris has become a feel-good capital since 2001 when he became the first socialist to run the Hôtel de Ville and the first openly gay mayor of a major French city. Under Delanoë, it is permitted to sit and walk on the grass in municipal parks. **Paris-Plage** (*see p280* **No Plage like home**) and the annual **Nuit Blanche** all-night arts festival (*see p282*) offer a hint of subsidised hedonism that breaks with the pomp of his right-wing predecessors. Bus drivers wear badges proclaiming: 'I will try to speak English', and Métro trains have been decorated with a smiley-face logo suggesting we should all 'get together for a more caring transport system'.

Whether Delanoë is delivering the goods is another matter. His supporters say give him time. His detractors claim his plans are far too ambitious, unless he intends to plunge the capital into debt.

Apart from a homophobic stabbing that put him out of action for three months after the first Nuit Blanche in October 2002, the road so far has been easy for Delanoë. As the tarnished reputation of his predecessor, Jean Tibéri, became darkened by allegations of fraud, the tweed-suited socialist promised Parisians that his would be a lean, clean regime, with no tax increases, a democratic housing programme, more crèches and complete accounting transparency. After former prime minister and City Hall financial boss Alain Juppé was found guilty of syphoning off Parisian money to boost the right-wing's fighting fund, the socialists secured a landslide victory in the 2004 regional elections. This gave Delanoë an army of political allies in and around the capital – his dreams may yet turn into reality.

'Delanoë dreams of a city without cars. Work has begun on a tramline due to circle Paris and replace the PC bus that follows the route of the *périphérique*.'

The dreams include transforming the sprawling Les Halles shopping centre and transport hub from a urine-stinking rabbit warren in which 800,000 commuters battle every day to keep their cool. Four plans are on the table, ranging from a moderately costly revamp of the existing plasticky architecture to the construction of 20 colourful towers of flats, artists' studios, boutiques, with access to public transport. At Les Halles and beyond, Delanoë needs to redynamise the city centre from which businesses are fleeing because office space has become too pricy. His solution is to build skyscrapers – a controversial move, which he has so far partially won and which will require scrapping a 30-year-old ban on practically all buildings over eight storeys.

Delanoë dreams of a city without cars. Work has already begun – between pont de Garigliano in the 15th arrondissement and porte d'Ivry in the 13th – on a tramline that is ultimately due to circle Paris and replace the PC bus that follows the route of the roaring *périphérique*. He would like Parisians to cycle more – at weekends several busy routes, such as the quayside of Canal St-Martin, are closed to traffic. At five locations, including Les Halles and place de la République, bicycles are offered for rent at a nominal charge. At the same time, more bus and cycle lanes are being introduced and major thoroughfares – such as boulevard Magenta in the 10th – are being narrowed by the creation of islands of greenery.

Green or grey, Paris is lucky because it has enough going for it that when its bohemians pair up and have children, they do not all move to the suburbs. A zero-interest mortgage

programme helps keep younger and lower-paid residents in the city centre. They also expect child care to be available. In 2001, Delanoë promised 4,500 new crèche places in six years. So far he has produced 1,500.

Under Tibéri and, before him, Jacques Chirac, social housing had become so limited and its allocation so corrupt that most Parisians assumed you needed to know someone in authority to qualify for a low-cost council flat. After his election, Delanoë quickly sent the signal that he wanted to ease the process and take action to move disadvantaged families into high-income neighbourhoods. Since 2001, more than 7,000 new flats have been built, including some in the stuffy 8th and 16th districts.

There is a new emphasis on student life with a plan to build halls of residence offering a further 3,000 beds by 2007. Student numbers are set to increase in the capital, anyway, as the Paris VII faculty expands in 2005 into the 13th district in the shadow of the four glass towers of the Bibliothèque François Mitterrand. In fact, the entire Left Bank area east of the Gare d'Austerlitz – where the present mayor first gained a parliamentary seat at the age of 31 – is emerging as a kind of Delanoë laboratory of modern inner-city living. Centred around the enormous library built by the late president – a mentor to Delanoë – the area is to combine offices, 5,000 new homes (half of them municipal) and all facets of student life, set in plenty of greenery. *See p146* **The lucky 13th**.

Delanoë won the 2001 elections thanks to his Green allies and they have been put in charge of the environment and the parks. Parisians retain a deep-seated mental block against gestures such as poop-scooping or sorting their rubbish into dustbins for bottles (white lids), for packaging (yellow lids) and the rest (green lids). Yet the mayor believes his two million citizens will, eventually, learn through '*concertation civile*', the catch-all phrase which has led to greater spending on newsletters and magazines and a new stress on neighbourhood associations. A new Citizens' Council now represents non-Europeans who cannot vote in municipal elections.

Tunisia-born with a British grandmother, Delanoë has a fixation for grass-roots consultation, and is seen to do so. (He even travels to work by Métro.) Some critics might call it pseudo-democracy, served up by a consummate politician (and former national spokesman of the Socialist Party) to camouflage an authoritarian and image-conscious nature. His plans to redevelop Les Halles only became known to Parisians by accident when one of the architects he had consulted mentioned them to the press. To parry accusations that the mayor was trying to sneak through a grand project unilaterally, the Hôtel de Ville in no time at all sent out 200,000 questionnaires. These – unsurprisingly – showed that Parisians wanted Les Halles to be modernised.

The image thing is a niggle. Speak to the men sipping *panachés* beneath the rainbow flags of the Marais district and they will tell you they elected Delanoë to be '*notre dame de Paris*'. Delanoë used to be pretty well-known in the 4th and in the bars of Montmartre. Dressed in leather jeans, he was a follower of iconic disco singer Dalida and a stalwart at the Palace nightspot. Somehow that tweed suit seems a little ill-fitting.

'For the 60th anniversary of the Liberation of Paris, the Hôtel de Ville paid for a thousand Parisians to be taught to do the jitterbug.'

The Hôtel de Ville itself has changed radically under Delanoë. The opulent 600m² mayoral apartments have been turned emblematically into a crèche and, to signal restraint, wine of only one colour is served throughout the courses in the dining room. The cheese course has been scrapped altogether. Delanoë's office is all natural oak because one of his first moves was to get out the paint stripper and remove a lot of gold and brown paint. The only hedonistic excess Delanoë seems to allow himself is an annual feast for the eye of tanned beach volley players who are given a sandpit beneath his office windows during Paris-Plage.

The potted palms and deckchairs will again be brought out in July 2005, even though many Parisians are bored with the concept and say it has become merchandised beyond good taste. Nuit Blanche, which lasts 24 hours and includes museums staying open all night and colourful lighting displays on public buildings, is more flexible and may have the scope to reinvent itself for several years. Both concepts share the goal of getting Parisians back on to the streets and mixing – an idea used to great effect, whatever the weather, at the one-off event on 26 August 2004 to mark the 60th anniversary of the Liberation of Paris. The Hôtel de Ville paid for a thousand Parisians to be taught to do the jitterbug. Before the street party, they were invited to sew 1940s costumes for themselves at workshops supervised by pensioners with memories of World War II.

Delanoë needs to keep his administration dynamic-looking but, as the years go by, he will also need to show evidence of progress in the

Bertie's beach: **Paris-Plage**.

shape of jobs created by businesses returning from the suburbs, a liveable Les Halles area, and cleaner air. Disabled people are no fans of the mayor's piecemeal policies as far as they are concerned. Environmentalists have strong reservations over his approach to reducing traffic by making drivers feel the heavy charge of congestion – increased traffic jams – rather than by introducing a fee, London-style.

If the political speculators are to be believed, there is far more at stake for Delanoë than the 2007 municipal elections. His autobiography, *La Vie, Passionnément*, published in September 2004, is a first move, they claim, in a tactical game that will lead him to the presidency of France in 2012 – the year he hopes Paris will host the Olympic Games.

Such a victorious combination of image and timing would outclass even Jacques Chirac's carefully calculated ascent from the Hôtel de Ville in 1977 to the Elysée-Palace in 1995. But Paris-Plage might have to weather a few more rainy summers before then.

Dior.

Gaultier.

Haute couture or high street?

Paris' waning fashion houses aim to balance traditional haute couture with high-street chic.

Whither haute couture? Living on borrowed time, thanks to an ageing clientele, this wonderfully archaic craft and bastion of French culture is trying every which way to adapt itself to a fast-moving, off-the-peg world. Prior to a restricted three-day couture week (no Versace, no Ungaro, no five-day extravaganza) in Paris in July 2004, the industry's ruling body debated the notion of bringing in other high-end goods to shore up subsequent galas. Once the pinnacle of decades of delicate handicraft, this feast of high fashion would feature the few remaining couture houses and, as part of a 'luxury week' under consideration by the Fédération Française de la Couture, shoes, boots, perfumes, jewellery and… chocolates. Has it really come to this?

France and fashion: the two are inextricably linked. The country's textile traditions have made it a fashion epicentre since the 16th century, when François I decided to circumvent expensive imports by making Lyon the hub of silk production. It was a move that brought great prosperity: the Rhône-Alps region is France's second-largest economy, with textile production ranking second only to high technology, and it boasts one of the world's most important textile museums.

Louis XIV promoted the local industry by sending fashion dolls to courts across Europe. The sartorial caprices of the court of Versailles, thanks to such figures as Madame de Pompadour (mistress of Louis XV) and Marie-Antoinette (whose milliner Rose Bertin was nicknamed 'the minister of fashion'), inspired legions of followers and made Paris a fashion bellwether. The reputation stuck right through the 1789 Revolution, the two Empires, and up until the modern era. And when Adolf Hitler wanted to move haute couture to Germany, key designer Madame Grès refused. Hitler gave in.

The nation and the city of Paris consider fashion part of their heritage. The cultural attachment to fashion and the expression of personal flair are a vital part of the French social fabric. For anyone looking to make it in the fashion world – as a designer, stylist,

Karl Lagerfeld *en personne...*

... and **John Galliano** *lui-même.*

photographer, model or journalist – Paris remains the gateway and a rite of passage.

If Paris continues to hold centre stage, and if the 'Made in France' label remains the ultimate imprimatur of luxury, it's thanks to haute couture, a uniquely French institution founded by an Englishman, Charles Frederick Worth. A dressmaker who set up shop on the rue de la Paix in the mid 19th century, Worth rose to become the fashion arbiter of the day. By 1865, his architectural silhouettes and lavish embellishments had caught the eye of Empress Eugénie; the courts of Austria, Russia, Italy and Spain, as well as a wealthy American clientele, soon bought in. A flamboyant dresser himself, Worth was the first to put labels in his clothes and show them on live models – thus becoming the first designer to steer style rather than simply execute customers' specifications. In 1868 he created fashion's governing body, la Chambre Syndicale, and established the intricate set of rules and regulations to which qualifying *maisons* must comply. Among these criteria, modified only slightly over the years, are the presentation of collections in Paris twice a year, featuring a minimum of 35 designs for day and evening.

'The handiwork is as breathtaking as the price, even if there are only 1,500 clients in the world who can pay for a gown that costs five figures.'

In addition, a house must employ at least 15 *petites-mains* ('little hands') to ensure the artisanal integrity of the atelier. Today, for example, it may take three people 500 hours to create elaborate embroidery for a gown, such as those in the Sissi-inspired collection by John Galliano for Christian Dior for autumn-winter collection of 2004/5. The handiwork is as breathtaking as the price tag, and if in the end there are no more than an estimated 1,500 clients in the world who can pay for a gown that costs well into five figures – and even if the expense of mounting a runway show can easily run into the millions – there is no calculating the inspiration that haute couture inspires. It is a priceless shop window and creative laboratory for French know-how, and its influence radiates from catwalk and red carpet to the glossies and right on down to the high street. Look no further than Karl Lagerfeld at Chanel to see where all those trendy frayed tweeds of recent seasons came from.

CHANEL, DIOR AND SAINT LAURENT

By the early 20th century, Worth had been succeeded by his disciple Paul Poiret, who championed the applied arts and encouraged clients to drop cumbersome corsetry in favour of Orientalist, columnar designs and even harem pants. He was also the first, in 1911, to create a designer perfume and cosmetics line, which he named after his daughter Rosine. But it was Gabrielle Chanel who, by the 1920s, was dominating the fashion scene with a look that was both revolutionary and comfortable, made up of borrowings from men's wardrobes such as tweed and jersey. In 1921 she introduced Chanel No.5, becoming the first to demonstrate how perfume can be key and foundation to a fashion house's success. The classic 'little black dress' followed in 1926. Other great names included Madeleine Vionnet (innovator of the bias cut), Patou (sportswear), Lanvin, Rochas and Schiaparelli (witty Surrealist-inspired designs; she was also the first to use zips).

In the immediate post-war era, Christian Dior's New Look had re-established French fashion as the standard-bearer that it remains to this day. Haute couture hit its zenith in the 1950s, with over a hundred houses led by such names as Cristóbal Balenciaga, Jacques Fath, Pierre Balmain, Hubert de Givenchy, Pierre Cardin (who later topped fashion's rich list through licensing) and Dior, who, after his death in 1957, was succeeded by a rising star named Yves Saint Laurent. By the 1960s, Saint Laurent opened his own *maison* to much acclaim. Though his contributions to fashion from the Mondrian dress to the dinner jacket are too numerous to list, it was he who in 1966 rocked the fashion world by establishing his Rive Gauche label – thus becoming the first designer to offer couture, prêt-à-porter and accessories under one roof. The rest of the fashion world followed suit. Other notable names that emerged at that time were future-fixated Paco Rabanne, miniskirt inventor André Courrèges, Emanuel Ungaro and Jean-Louis Scherrer. By the label-conscious 1980s, fashion designers had attained rock-star status.

It was Jean-Paul Gaultier, a disciple of Saint Laurent, whose entry into the fashion world with irreverent, whimsical designs – such as Madonna's cone-shaped corset and a perfume packaged in a tin can – made him the enfant terrible of French fashion. Gaultier entered the couture arena in 1997; his witty and undeniably Parisian collections have today earned him the role of couture's saviour and heir apparent.

The future of couture has been the subject of furious debate in recent seasons. In the decade after Christian Dior restored France to fashion predominance with the New Look, the number of couture houses was halved to 50. When Yves Saint Laurent closed his 40-year career with a glorious finale in January 2002, a dozen houses were left. Today, there are a handful of majors: Chanel, Dior, Gaultier, Scherrer, Lacroix and Givenchy, plus a smattering of invited guests, such as the eternal Valentino and Ralph Rucci (the first American to present couture in Paris since Mainbocher in the 1930s). The hundreds of speciality ateliers that supplied couture houses with the embroidery, feathers, fur and other lavish trimmings have dwindled. Faced with the impending demise of these métiers, Chanel moved to preserve the heritage of couture arts by acquiring the fabled ateliers of Lesage (embroidery), Lemarié (feathers and flowers), Desrues (costume finery), Massaro (haute shoemaking) and Michel (millinery).

> **'In 2003, haute couture generated revenues of €520 million, only five per cent of France's global fashion turnover, and half the revenues of a decade ago.'**

Other fabled couture houses have risen from obscurity in recent years to attain critical acclaim and reinvent a couture spirit through ready-to-wear, thanks to the talent of designers such as Alber Elbaz at Lanvin, Nicolas Ghesquière at Balenciaga or Olivier Theyskens at Rochas. The house of Grès, steeped in couture history, closed its doors for good in 2004, and the future of others, such as Balmain, remains uncertain.

The argument can be made that given decreasing numbers, a dwindling clientele, the lightning speed at which the high street can replicate catwalk looks – and the fact that few French designers are rising through the ranks – together mean that haute couture is riding on the coat-tails of history. In 2003, it generated revenues of €520 million, only five per cent of France's global fashion turnover, and half the revenues of a decade ago.

But haute couture is the stuff of dreams. It continues to draw the crowds and with fewer big houses to overshadow them, new talents keep the creative laboratory churning and vie for the attentions of buyers and press. Call it luxury prêt-à-porter, 'ready couture' or 'semi-couture' – as Gaultier himself dubbed his in-store concept, expected in 2005 – for those with a taste for the dream, even if that means taking home just one handbag or a perfume, there will always be room for luxury. And for that, we will always have Paris.

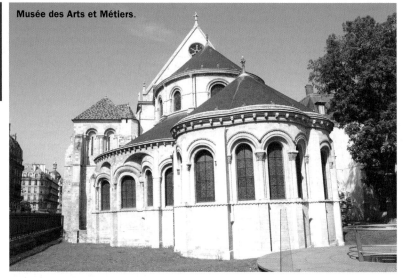

Musée des Arts et Métiers.

Architecture

History writ large in golden Paris stone.

The story of Paris architecture parallels the growth of the city, spreading outwards over the centuries in concentric rings as the population grew and the city burst out of its walls. It can be read from its historic hub to its 19th- and 20th-century rim. It is a tale of materials and techniques – the long use of golden Paris stone has given the city an apparent uniformity that belies the variety of styles.

ROMANESQUE AND GOTHIC

Medieval Paris centred on the Ile de la Cité, the Latin Quarter and around Châtelet and Les Halles. Although the main public buildings of Roman Paris were on the Left Bank, the Roman wall had only ever encircled the Ile de la Cité. During the Viking invasions, the population took refuge on the island. It was not until the medieval wall of Philippe-Auguste in 1190 that ramparts came to protect what is now part of the 5th and 6th districts, from rue Dauphine to rue du Cardinal-Lemoine on the Left Bank and the Louvre to St-Paul on the Right Bank. In the 1350s, Charles V began a new wall, stretching as far east as his new fortress at the Bastille.

The main medieval thoroughfares, rue St-Martin, rue St-Jacques and rue Mouffetard, followed those of Roman Paris. Paris had powerful Romanesque abbeys outside the city walls, but remains of this style are few. The tower of **St-Germain-des-Prés** (*see p134*) built circa 1000, topped by a later spire, still has its rounded arches, and some decorated capitals survive in the nave, while the church of the **Prieuré St-Martin-des-Champs** (then an important Cluniac monastery now a dramatic exhibition space in the **Musée des Arts et Métiers**; *see p180*) has ornate capitals and a complex ring of early 12th-century chapels.

It was in the **Basilique St-Denis** (*see p149*) that the Gothic trademarks of pointed arches, ogival vaulting and flying buttresses were first combined, to develop a style that is particularly associated with Paris and northern Europe. Vaulting allowed buildings to span large spaces and let light in, hence an aesthetic of brightness and verticality. A spate of building followed with cathedrals at **Chartres** (*see p349*), as well as **Notre-Dame** (*see p84*) in Paris. This incorporated all the features of the style: twin-towered west front, soaring nave, intricate rose windows and buttressed east end. Gothic style was a combination of architectural structure and decoration, not just in the fancy finials and gargoyles, but in its elaborate vaults, developed at Chartres where the sculpted statues formed part of the doorway structure itself.

Ribbed vaulting became more refined and columns more slender, in the Rayonnant or High Gothic style. Mason and architect Pierre de Montreuil continued work on St-Denis, and his masterpiece, the 13th century **Sainte-Chapelle** (*see p85*), took Gothic to its height, reducing stonework on the upper level to a minimum around the stained glass.

The later Flamboyant Gothic style saw a wealth of decoration, in the **Eglise St-Séverin** (*see p125*), with its twisting spiral column and the pinnacles and gargoyles of the early 16th-century Tour St-Jacques. In the 1190s, Philippe-Auguste began the **Louvre** (*see pp152-159*), part of whose keep can still be seen within the museum complex, but the royal family continued to live in the Palais de la Cité, where early 14th-century vaulted halls can be seen in **La Conciergerie** (*see p85*). The oldest domestic buildings constructed in wood have rarely survived – only ecclesiastical buildings were generally put up in more prestigious stone – and the building of half-timbered ones was banned because of the frequent fires. Much of the tight medieval ground plan survives, especially in the Latin Quarter – from the tower of Notre-Dame you can see just how tightly packed the streets still are. Buildings have been put up over ancient medieval cellars or updated with new façades to keep up with the times. The Hôtel de Sens and Hôtel de Cluny (now the **Bibliothèque Forney** and the **Musée National du Moyen-Age**; *see p167 and p173*) are examples of surviving domestic architecture. Cluny set the pattern for the later *hôtels particuliers*, though is distinctly Gothic in its windows, doorways and chapel.

THE RENAISSANCE

The Italian Renaissance, with its revival of classical motifs and the antique principles of construction and rediscovery of the dome under Brunelleschi, Michelangelo et al, came late to Paris, and was largely due to François I. He installed Leonardo Da Vinci at **Amboise** (*see p362*), and also called in Primaticcio and Rosso at **Fontainebleau** (*see p352*), where the fireplaces epitomise the virtuoso distortion of 16th-century Mannerism. **Eglise St-Eustache** (*see p100*) with classical façade and columns, but a floor-plan based on Notre-Dame, and pretty **Eglise St-Etienne-du-Mont** (*see p129*) show that, even at its most developed,

Renaissance style remained largely superficial. The **Hôtel Lamoignon** (*see p103*) in the Marais, begun in the 1580s, with its giant order pilasters and Greek key motifs, and the **Hôtel Carnavalet** (*see p176*), with its sculpted façades, are the best examples of Renaissance mansions. Patrons looked to the antique world, but required new levels of domestic comfort.

THE ANCIEN REGIME – BAROQUE

Henri IV built **Pont Neuf** (*see p80*) and place Dauphine on the Ile de la Cité and **place des Vosges** (*see p105*) in the Marais. The latter were both symmetrical, built in red brick with stone facing, steeply pitched slate roofs, and vaulted ground-floor arcades.

The 17th century was a high point in French power; the monarchy desired buildings to reflect its grandeur, and both church and state looked to Rome to provide models: baroque. The Palais du Luxembourg combined classic French château with elements of the Pitti Palace in Marie de Médicis' native Florence. Its architect Salomon de Brosse added the new classical west front to the **Eglise St-Gervais St-Protais** (*see p106*) in 1621, the first in Paris to use the three-tier classical order (Doric, Ionic, Corinthian). With classical façades and domed structures, Counter-Reformation churches – the **Eglise St-Paul St-Louis** (*see p106*), **Eglise du Dôme** (*see p138*) at Les Invalides, and the **Eglise du Val-de-Grâce** (*see p130*), designed by Mansart and Lemercier – followed the Gesù in Rome as the Catholic church reasserted its influence after the Wars of Religion.

But even at colossal **Versailles** (*see p354*), with glittering Hall of Mirrors, French baroque never reached the excesses of Italy or Austria, as local architects kept a restrained classicism and followed Cartesian principles of harmony and balance. François Mansart in particular was a master of graceful proportions, as seen in the monastic buildings of the Val de Grâce, though he was notoriously slow, and few of his projects were ever quite finished as planned.

Nouveaux riches and royal officials flocked to build themselves fine mansions in the newly drained Marais and the Ile St-Louis. Those in the Marais follow a symmetrical U-shaped plan, with the main façade behind a majestic, walled entrance courtyard and gardens behind, as at the **Hôtel de Sully** (*see p170* **Capturing defining moments**), Hôtel Salé (**Musée National Picasso**; *see p166*) or Hôtel St-Aignan (**Musée d'Art et d'Histoire du Judaïsme**; *see p176*). Baroque heralded new ideas of urbanism. The vistas and promenades of Le Nôtre's gardens at Versailles and **the Tuileries** (*see p91*) are also seen in the long esplanade of **Les Invalides** (*see p138*). Under

Place Vendôme.

Colbert, Louis XIV's chief minister, the creation of stage sets to magnify the Sun King's power proceeded apace. The Louvre grew as Claude Perrault created the west façade with its long colonnade, while Hardouin-Mansart's **place des Victoires** (*see p94*) and **place Vendôme** (*see p92*) were designed to show off equestrian statues of the king. Royal victories meant that Paris was no longer at risk of invasion. Charles V's city wall was demolished and replaced by the Grands Boulevards, soon lined by aristocratic residences. **Portes St-Martin** and **St-Denis** (for both, *see p97*) were put up at strategic points to celebrate the victories in evocation of imperial Rome.

ROCOCO & NEO-CLASSICISM

In the early 18th century, the creation of new boulevards (boulevards de l'Hôpital, du Montparnasse and des Invalides) on the Left Bank saw the Faubourg St-Germain, an area previously outside the city, overtaking the Marais as the chic new *quartier*. Spacious aristocratic demeures were put up, many of which survive, such as the Hôtel Bouchardon (**Musée Maillol**; *see 166*) on rue de Grenelle, with its elaborate fountain at the entrance, and the Hôtel Matignon on rue de Varenne. Under Louis XV, the severe lines of the previous century were softened by rounded corners and decorative detailing, as satyr masks over doorways, at the Hôtel Chenizot (51 rue St-Louis-en-l'Ile) and Hôtel d'Albret (31 rue des Francs-Bourgeois). The main developments came in interior decoration, as frivolous rococo style reached a peak in the Hôtel de Soubise, decorated by Boucher, Restout and Van Loo.

From the 1750s, geometry was back as Rome inspired Jacques-Ange Gabriel's neo-classical **place de la Concorde** (*see p92*) as well as Soufflot's **Panthéon** (*see p129*). Classicism was also used for the **Théâtre de l'Odéon** (*see p344*). In the Mur des Fermiers-Généraux, a new wall was put up for the collection of duties.

Utopian architect Ledoux's toll gates played with geometrical forms: circular at **Parc Monceau** (*see p113*) and La Rotonde de La Villette; rectangular pairs at **place Denfert-Rochereau** (*see p144*) and place de la Nation.

NINETEENTH-CENTURY REVIVALS

The Revolution largely confined itself to pulling buildings down. Royal statues bit the dust, and churches became 'temples of reason' or grain stores. Napoleon brought Paris back to a proper sense of its grand self. Land confiscated from aristocracy and church was built up. A stern classicism was preferred for the **Arc de Triomphe** (*see p112*), Greek temples inspired **the Madeleine** (*see p95*) and **the Bourse** (*see p94*). A few rare examples of Napoleonic decoration survive at Malmaison and in the **Petit Hôtel Bourrienne** (*see p98*) in the 10th.

By the 1840s, classical style was under challenge from a Gothic revival led by Eugène Viollet-le-Duc, helped by the Romantic movement's enthusiasm for the Middle Ages and the success of Victor Hugo's *Notre-Dame de Paris*. Viollet-le-Duc defended the return to Gothic as a form of rationalism, in which Gothic architecture was the style best adapted to the needs of society: the most efficient way of building a stone church because it maximised height and luminosity. Though controversial, his restorations of the Sainte-Chapelle, Notre-Dame, St-Denis (as well as Carcassonne and Vézélay) did save them from ruin. He admitted that his 'restorations' were not a return to the actual buildings as they had been constructed haphazardly over decades, but to 'a complete state that perhaps never existed at a given moment'. He removed or added elements as necessary, according to architectural principles.

Eclecticism ruled, however. Neo-Renaissance was chosen for the **Eglise de la Trinité** (*see p96*), the **Hôtel de la Païva** (*see p118*) on place St-Georges, the reconstruction of the **Hôtel de Ville** (*see p103*) and also for some of the grandiose new district town halls and banks in the late 19th century. Byzantium and the Romanesque also made a comeback from the 1870s, notably in **Sacré-Coeur** (*see p116*).

> ## 'Haussmann masterminded the transformation of the rapidly growing capital into the most modern city of the day.'

The greatest change to the face of Paris came from Baron Haussmann. Appointed Napoleon III's Préfet de la Seine in 1853, Haussmann was not an architect but an administrator. Aided by architects and engineers including Baltard, Hittorff, Alphand and Belgrand, Haussmann masterminded the transformation of the rapidly growing capital into the most modern city of the day. Broad streets and boulevards were cut through the old city, answering communication and health problems, but also ensuring that the city could be more easily governed – and keeping up Colbert's idea of perspectives and vistas, as the broad boulevards often led to a focal point, whether a train station, an opera or the Arc de Triomphe. Haussmann constructed asylums, prisons, schools, churches, hospitals, and the water and sewage systems. He gave Paris its new cast-iron market pavilions at **Les Halles** (*see p99*) and landscaped the **Bois de Boulogne** (*see p114*) and **Bois de Vincennes** (*see p109*), the **Parc des Buttes-Chaumont** (*see p123*) and **Parc Montsouris** (*see p145*) with waterfalls, lakes and grottos. The city acquired the Haussmannian apartment block lining the new boulevards of St-Michel and Sébastopol, as Paris and its new districts expanded. The model lasted until well into the 20th century. (*See p45* **Haussmann's house**.)

Charles Garnier's sumptuous **Palais Garnier** (*see p95*) of 1862-75 epitomised Second Empire style. In fact it was every style: barely a centimetre is left unadorned in this glorious confection of coloured marble, carved stone, gilding, crystal chandeliers, allegorical paintings and sheer excess.

Breakthroughs in engineering made the use of iron frames increasingly popular. Henri Labrouste's reading room at the **Bibliothèque Ste-Geneviève** (1844-50; *see p127*), Hittorff's **Gare du Nord** (1861-65; *see p98*), the Grande Galerie de l'Evolution (**Muséum d'Histoire Naturelle**; *see p180*) and **Musée d'Orsay** (*see p139*) are but shells around an iron frame. In the 1850s, Haussmann persuaded Baltard to build new Les Halles market pavilions not in stone but using a visible iron structure. It was

such a success that the style was soon copied in numerous local markets of which a few, such as the Marché St-Quentin, remain. The most daring iron structure of them all was of course the **Eiffel Tower** (*see p140*), built in 1889 for the Exposition Universelle, and at the time the tallest structure in the world.

ART NOUVEAU AND MODERNISM

The 20th century began with an outburst of extravagance for the 1900 Exposition Universelle and another excuse to put up prestigious showcases with the **Grand Palais** and the **Petit Palais** (for both, *see p112*). Laloux's Gare d'Orsay (now Musée d'Orsay) and the **Train Bleu** brasserie (*see p207*) were ornate examples of the heavy beaux arts floral style and eclectic classical motifs of the period, but with the Brasserie Julien (16 rue du Fbg St-Denis, 10th, 01.47.70.12.06) and Maxim's (3 rue Royale, 8th, 01.42.65.27.94) came in the new, naturalistic art nouveau style. Art nouveau looked to nature and fluid forms for inspiration and using brick, ceramic tiles and wrought iron as new expressions – in Paris it was seen at its most extravagant in Guimard's flamboyant Métro entrances and **Castel Béranger** (*see p114*). Henri Sauvage's tiled studio building in the 16th district and apartment complex on rue

Palais Garnier.

Vavin are fascinating examples of proto-Modernism, cleverly using stepped back terraces to let daylight pierce large blocks.

'The mass housing of Le Corbusier's Villes Radieuses became so influential and so debased across Europe after 1945.'

The period after World War I saw the rise of Auguste Perret and Le Corbusier. Perret stayed within a classical aesthetic, but his use of reinforced concrete gave new liberty to floor plans and façades, cleverly using a golden-coloured concrete that blended with Paris stone. Le Corbusier tried out his ideas (pilotis, strip windows, built-in furniture) in luxury houses, such as Villas La Roche and Jeanneret. His Pavillon Suisse at the **Cité Universitaire** (*see p144*) and the Armée du Salut hostel in the 13th can be seen as an intermediary between these villas and the mass housing of his Villes Radieuses, which became so influential and so debased across Europe after 1945. Robert Mallet-Stevens is unrivalled for his elegance, most clearly on rue Mallet-Stevens, though the most radical modern building, Pierre Chereau's 1931 glass block and steel Maison de Verre in the 7th, is not visible from the street. Avant-garde architects built houses for wealthy

patrons in the developing 14th and 16th, and Boulogne-Billancourt, but Modern Movement influence spread to public housing, schools and suburban town halls in the socially conscious 1930s. Art deco love of chrome, steel and glass found its way into La Coupole brasserie and **Le Grand Rex** cinema (*see p97 and p298*). Clean Modernist lines were also adapted in a new classical revival in the massive **Palais de Chaillot** (*see p112*) and **Palais de Tokyo** (*see p169*) built for the Exposition Universelle of 1937, marked by pared-back colonnades and sculptors such as Bouchard and Bourdelle.

POSTWAR AND HIGH-TECH
The aerodynamic aesthetic of the 1950s saw the **UNESCO building** (*see p140*) and the first beginnings of La Défense with the **CNIT building** (*see p151*). The shanty towns that had emerged to house immigrant workers cried out for a solution. In the 1960s and '70s tower blocks sprouted in the suburbs. Redevelopment inside Paris was limited, but regulations allowed taller buildings, noticeably the **Tour Montparnasse** (*see p144*) and in the 13th. These laws subsequently changed so that a second Tour Montparnasse could never appear. Massive housing blocks were put up along rue de Flandres in the 19th, while France's biggest university faculty was put up at Jussieu.

Opened in 1977, Piano and Rogers' high-tech **Centre Pompidou** (*see p103*) was the first of the prestige projects that have become a

Opéra Bastille. *See p45*.

Haussmann's house

In Georges Perec's *La Vie Mode d'Emploi* (Life: A User's Manual), a multi-generational, multi-storey story takes place over a Haussmannian apartment building from the cellars with its boiler and gurgling pipes, via the two apartments on each floor up to the *chambres de bonne* (maid's rooms) in the mansard roof. In this jigsaw puzzle of different lives, the apartment building becomes a microcosm of French society.

The Haussmannian apartment model is perhaps the archetype of the Préfet's 19th-century transformation of Paris. Though of course derived from earlier rental building precursors, new regulations of 1859 controlled details such as the pitch of the roof and ratio of building height to street width. It conveyed a sort of uniformity on the city but also proved brilliantly habitable, and adaptable to different budgets (a similar format could be used for prosperous five-bedroom flats and humble two- bedroom ones, for large reception rooms or small), to varying degrees of decoration and to the

different architectural styles that followed. This continued well into the 20th century as a similar floor plan was adopted by belle époque and art deco apartment blocks. A typical pattern developed. There were two flats on each floor on either side of a central staircase (18th-century rented buildings generally had one flat on each floor), full-length wrought-iron balconies along the second floor and the fifth floor, which was stepped back to allow additional daylight into the building, small balconies on other floors, and mansard windows in the sixth-floor roof. A second set of flats was often reached through a courtyard. The hierarchy of front and back staircases, the prime flats with grand balconies and the humble *chambres de bonne*, ensure a degree of social mix even in the grandest districts. This is perhaps even more true today, as *chambres de bonne* have become the domaine of students and the single, and – as with Paris' earlier ancient tenements – continue to ensure a density of population in the city centre.

trademark of modern Paris, a radical sculptural insertion inside a historic quarter. Its steel-and-glass structure with exposed services (heating, air-conditioning, escalators, lifts) left totally adaptable spaces inside; walls could be moved around for galleries and performance spaces.

Mitterrand's *Grands Projets* dominated the 1980s and early '90s as the president sought to leave his stamp on Paris with IM Pei's **Louvre Pyramid** (*see p153*), Jean Nouvel's **Institut du Monde Arabe** (*see p130*), Sprecklesen's **Grande Arche de La Défense** (*see p151*), as well as Ott's radically controversial **Opéra Bastille** (*see p318*), Perrault's **Bibliothèque Nationale** (*see p167*) and, in Bercy, Chemetov's new finance ministry. Urban renewal during the 1990s transformed previously industrial areas to return the balance of Paris eastwards around La Villette, Bercy and in the 13th (*see p146* **The lucky 13th**) – witness Wilmotte's **MK2 Bibliothèque** arthouse multiplex cinema (*see p298*). Postmodern Paris with new decorative symbolism saw Philippe Starck's late-lamented Café Costes, Christian de Portzamparc's Café Beaubourg at 43 rue St-Merri, and Ricardo Bofill's place de Catalogne; Frédéric Borel's housing in the 20th district created radical, irregular spaces with slanting planes.

One of the architects who has most marked late 20th century Paris has been Jean Nouvel. Using sleek materials in which transparency is the buzzword, he offers a masterful play of light, with the dappled shadowy effects and curved façade echoing the bend in the Seine of the Institut du Monde Arabe. His **Fondation Cartier** (*see p168*) building creates a series of false glass façades between the street before reaching the real building.

Although the age of *Grands Projets* has gone, Chirac's **Musée du Quai Branly** (Jean Nouvel again; *see p161*) is currently under construction by the Seine. In collaboration with garden designer Gilles Clément, it looks as if it will be a sort of new ecological take on high-tech, with a long sweep of etched glass and wooden shades inserted within a screen of vegetation and trees.

Paris has gained two footbridges: passerelle de Solférino by Mimram and the future passerelle de Bercy by Feichtinger. Building continues in the ZAC Rive Gauche around the Bibliothèque Nationale, bringing in architects under Christian de Portzamparc. After hard-fought battles, the tear-it-all down ethos has been rejected – some of the area's industrial spaces will be integrated with schemes such as the Grands Moulins de Paris, to be rehabilitated as a university building by Rudi Ricciotti.

Where to Stay

Where to Stay

75,000 hotel rooms to choose from. *Beaux rêves!*

Hôtel Meurice. *See p51.*

For some, a hotel is simply a base at which to sleep and scrub up before stepping out again to explore the city. For others, it's a feature of the holiday worth savouring in its own right. Whatever your take, there's a Paris hotel that fits the bill. We've selected the best of the bunch in every category, starting with marble-clad palaces fit for a Sun King, and moving down the price slope to the cramped-yet-cosy hotels with exposed wooden beams and vaulted, bare-stone breakfast rooms, via sleek boutique hotels with their flat-screen TVs and daring colour schemes. And, of course, we've got a pick of budget addresses where there's no need to stay any longer than it takes to get some shut-eye and a shower.

CLASSIFICATION AND FACILITIES

Hotels are graded according to an official star rating system designed to sort palace from pit stop – but we haven't followed it in this guide. Said star ratings usually reflect room size and

mere presence of a lift (rather than decor, staff or atmosphere), and we don't think the system is of much practical value when making your choice. Instead, we've divided the hotels into four categories, according to these prices for one night in a double room with shower/bath facilities: Deluxe €300+; Expensive €200-€300; Moderate €100-€200; Budget up to €100.

Deluxe hotels usually offer air-conditioning, double-glazed windows, bar and restaurant (except in the smaller boutique hotels), and can arrange babysitting and airport shuttle service; in-room services often include modem connection and room service, plus other extras depending on the hotel. Expensive hotels offer similar amenities and services. The moderate hotels should have in-room phone, modem connection and breakfast service; at the budget hotels you can normally be assured of a TV and in-room phone. We provide a list of the key services below the description of each hotel. For **gay hotels**, *see p313.*

NEED TO KNOW

Note that all hotels in France charge an additional room tax (*taxe de séjour*) of around €1 per person, sometimes included in the posted rate. Hotels are often booked solid during the major trade fairs (January, May, September), and it's hard to find a quality pillow on which to lay your head during fashion weeks (January and early July for haute couture, March and October for prêt-à-porter). However, at quieter times, including July and August, hotels often offer reasonable special deals at short notice; phone ahead or check their websites to find out. Same-day reservations can be made in person, for a small fee, at the **Office de Tourisme de Paris** (*see chapter* **Directory**).

Several websites offer discount booking: **www.parishotels.com** guarantees the lowest prices online, which can be up to 70 per cent off the rack rate; and **www.ratestogo.com** offers big discounts on four-star hotels for last-minute reservations (up to two weeks in advance).

The Islands

Expensive

Hôtel du Jeu de Paume

54 rue St-Louis-en-l'Île, 4th (01.43.26.14.18/fax 01.40.46.02.76/www.jeudepaumehotel.com). M° Pont Marie. **Rates** €160-€225 single; €240-€285 double; €480 suite; €15 breakfast. **Credit** AmEx, DC, MC, V. **Map** p408 K7.

An oh-so-discreet courtyard entrance, the original 17th-century beams, private garden and a unique timbered breakfast room that was once a real tennis court, built under Louis XIII: this is a charming hotel. It's now filled with a nicely slung-together array of modern and classical art. A dramatic glass lift and catwalks lead to the rooms, simple and tasteful with Pierre Frey fabric walls.

Hotel services *Bar. Gym. Disabled access. Internet (web TV). Room service.*

Moderate

Hôtel des Deux-Îles

59 rue St-Louis-en-l'Île, 4th (01.43.26.13.35/fax 01.43.29.60.25/www.deuxiles-paris-hotel.com). M° Pont Marie. **Rates** €140 single; €158 double; €10 breakfast. **Credit** AmEx, MC, V. **Map** p408 K7.

This peaceful 17th-century townhouse offers 17 soundproofed, air-conditioned rooms done out in faintly colonial style. Attractive features include a tiny courtyard off the lobby, and a vaulted stone breakfast room with fireplace (which helps it feel less like a cellar than many such breakfast rooms). Staff are friendly and helpful; the very pleasant Hôtel Lutèce, nearby at No.65 (01.43.26.23.52), is run by the same management.

Hotel services *Concierge. Internet. TV.*

Budget

Hospitel Hôtel Dieu

1 pl du Parvis-Notre-Dame, 4th (01.44.32.01.00/fax 01.44.32.01.16/www.hotel-hospitel.com). M° Cité or Hôtel de Ville. **Rates** €88.50 single; €99.50 double; €7.60 breakfast. **Credit** MC, V. **Map** p408 J7.

Hospitel has 14 spotless rooms with colourful contemporary decor and a limited view of the spires of Notre-Dame. It's used by families of the Hôtel Dieu hospital's in-patients and staff; they usually take up about half the hotel's capacity. A medical smell is present but not strong, bathrooms are quite large, and you couldn't ask for a better sightseeing base.

Hotel services *Bar. Disabled access. Internet. No-smoking room(s). Room service.*

The Louvre, Palais-Royal & Les Halles

Deluxe

Hôtel Costes

239 rue St-Honoré, 1st (01.42.44.50.00/fax 01.42.44.50.01/www.hotelcostes.com). M° Tuileries. **Rates** €350 single; €500-€600 double; €700-€1,400 suite; €30 breakfast. **Credit** AmEx, DC, MC, V. **Map** p403 G5.

If attitude is more important than service, this temple of stylish notoriety is for you. And don't even

The best **Hotel spas**

Four Seasons George V

Five-star pampering in indulgent luxury. *See p57.*

Le Grand InterContinental

New spa specialising in seawater treatments. *See p53.*

Hôtel Costes K

Cool spa in ultra-hip surroundings. *See p51.*

Hôtel Meurice

Vinotherapy at the vast Espace Bien-Etre. *See p51.*

Hôtel Royal Monceau

Eight relaxing massages, aromatherapy and hydrotherapy among the one- to ten-day courses. *See p59.*

Hôtel Westminster

Top-floor fitness centre with beautifully tiled steam room. *See p57.*

think of whipping out your autograph book, no matter how many A-listers you find at the low-lit bar (*see p222* **Hot hotel haunts**). The Costes boasts one of the best pools in Paris, a sybaritic Eastern-inspired affair with an underwater CD system. The same management also run the sleek Hôtel Costes K in the 16th (*see below*) – smashing spa and all.
Hotel services *Bar. Concierge. Gym. Parking (€30). Pool (indoor). Restaurant. Room service. Spa. TV.*
Other locations: *Hôtel Costes K, 81 av Kléber, 16th (01.44.05.75.75).*

Hôtel de Crillon
10 pl de la Concorde, 8th (01.44.71.15.00/fax 01.44.71.15.02/www.crillon.com). M° Concorde. **Rates** €585 single; €665-€865 double; €1,130-€14,300 suite; €30-€45 breakfast. **Credit** AmEx, DC, MC, V. **Map** p403 F4.

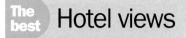

Hotel views

Le Degrés de Notre-Dame
Cathedral gawping from rooms 47 and 501. See p65.

Hôtel Brighton
Cut-price vistas of the Tuileries gardens and beyond. See p52.

Hôtel la Demeure
Lovely views from the wrap-around balustrades of the corner rooms. See p67.

Hôtel Edouard VII
Garnier's opera house in full view from facing balconies. See p55.

Hôtel Louvre Ste-Anne
Book early for top-floor balcony views of Sacré-Coeur. See p52.

Hôtel Meurice
Perfect 360º panorama from the Belle Epoque Suite. See p51.

Hôtel du Panthéon
Soufflot's neo-classical masterpiece observed from many rooms. See p67.

Terrass Hôtel
Gaze at the Eiffel Tower from the bath of room No.704. See p61.

Timhotel Montmartre
Stunning vistas of Montmartre from the fourth or fifth floors. See p61.

Le Walt
Sixth-floor sights of Eiffel's iron. See p73.

The height of neo-classic European magnificence, the Crillon lives up to its palace reputation with a decor heavy in marble, mirrors and gold leaf. The Michelin-starred Les Ambassadeurs (*see p199*) has a hot new chef, and the Winter Garden tearoom has a gorgeous terrace and live harp music. You can even learn how to recreate those trendy flower arrangements seen throughout the hotel at regular classes given by the city's top floral designers.
Hotel services *Bar. Business centre. Concierge. Disabled access. Gym. Internet. No-smoking room(s). Parking (free). Restaurants (2). Room service. TV.*

Hôtel Meurice
228 rue de Rivoli, 1st (01.44.58.10.10/fax 01.44.58.10.15/www.meuricehotel.com). M° Tuileries. **Rates** €500-€600 single; €650-€720 double; €1,050-€10,000 suites; €32-€45 breakfast. **Credit** AmEx, DC, MC, V. **Map** p403 G5.
Having spruced up its opulent Louis XVI decor and intricate mosaic tiled floors in a lengthy facelift, Le Meurice is rejuvenated. All of its 195 rooms are done out in distinct historical styles; among the 35 suites, the Belle Epoque offers 360-degree views of Paris. If you tire of the baggy-trousered lounge DJ in the Winter Garden (replacing the classic pianist), run to the huge spa with its *vinothérapie* treatments – or, to get grape products directly into your bloodstream, head to the intimate Bar Fontainebleau.
Hotel services *Bar. Business centre. Concierge. Disabled access. Gym. Internet. No-smoking room(s). Restaurants (2). Room service. Spa. TV.*

Hôtel Ritz
15 pl Vendôme, 1st (01.43.16.30.30/fax 01.43.16.31.78/www.ritzparis.com). M° Concorde or Opéra. **Rates** €610-€770 single or double; €880-€8,500 suite; €34-€43 breakfast. **Credit** AmEx, DC, MC, V. **Map** p403 G4.
This grande dame of Paris hotels has proffered hospitality to Coco Chanel, the Duke of Windsor, Proust and Dodi and Di; today's guests have the choice of 142 bedrooms and 45 suites, from the romantic 'Frédéric Chopin' to the glitzy 'Impérial'. There are plenty of corners in which to strike poses or quench a thirst, from Hemingway's elegant cigar bar and the plush Victorian Champagne bar to the poolside bar inspired by Ancient Greece. *See also p222* **Hot hotel haunts**.
Hotel services *Bars (3). Business centre. Gym. Internet. Parking (€44). Pool (indoor). Restaurant. Room service. Spa. TV.*

Hôtel Sofitel le Faubourg
15 rue Boissy-d'Anglas, 8th (01.44.94.14.00/fax 01.44.94.14.28/www.sofitel.com). M° Concorde. **Rates** €365 single; €435-€495 double; €575-€995 suites; €2,000-€2,500 apartment; €28 breakfast. **Credit** AmEx, DC, MC, V. **Map** p403 G4.
The old offices of *Marie Claire* are unsurprisingly close to the major couture boutiques; the rooms have Louis XVI armchairs, large balconies, Roger & Gallet smellies in the bathrooms, and walk-in wardrobes. For shopping widowers, there's a small

gym and a hammam. And it's quiet: since the 2001 terrorist attacks, the street has been closed to traffic (the American Embassy is on the corner). **Hotel services** *Bar. Business centre. Concierge. Disabled access. Gym. Internet. No-smoking room(s). Parking (€26). Restaurant. Room service. Spa. TV.*

Moderate

Hôtel Brighton
218 rue de Rivoli, 1st (01.47.03.61.61/fax 01.42. 60.41.78/www.esprit-de-france.com). M° Tuileries. **Rates** €119-€160 single or double; €169-€260 triple; €238 suite; €8 breakfast. **Credit** AmEx, DC, MC, V. **Map** p403 G5.

With several rooms overlooking the stunning Tuileries gardens, this hotel is excellent value. The Brighton, all faux-marble and mosaic decor, was opened at the start of the 20th century as the Entente Cordiale began. All of the rooms are reasonably priced and spacious, but those with prime views should be booked as early as possible.
Hotel services *Concierge. Disabled access. Room service (morning). TV.*

Hôtel Louvre Ste-Anne
32 rue Ste-Anne, 1st (01.40.20.02.35/fax 01.40.15. 91.13/www.louvre-ste-anne.fr). M° Pyramides. **Rates** €99-€122 single; €111-€184 double; €10 breakfast. **Credit** AmEx, MC, V. **Map** p403 H5.

Treat yourself to a five-star pamper

If you ever land a once-in-a-lifetime stay at the **Four Seasons George V** (pictured; *see also* p57), here's a tip: arrive a couple of hours before check-in time. If your room isn't ready, ignore the intimidating expanse of Italian marble in the lobby, and take up the invite to go down to the spa. Change into a fuzzy robe, and prepare for one of the city's most indulgent cocoons. Like a little slice of Marie-Antoinette's Versailles, the spa steers clear of the clinically chlorinated and commonplace contemporary atmosphere of most hotel spas and instead goes right in for decadent pampering. Welcome to heaven.

At the desk, where guests are greeted by name, is the lounge and juice bar. A large bay window overlooks the 6m by 9m pool and hot tub, surrounded by trompe-l'oeil murals of Versailles' gardens and a ceiling of perfectly peaceful blue sky with puffy white clouds.

Within, a 750m^2 (8,065sq ft) spa is decorated in luxurious Louis XVI style with delicate furnishings in creamy colours and pale marble columns. Real Toiles de Jouy fabrics cover the walls. The lights are all softly dimmed under lampshades, and the spa's signature scent wafts through the air.

And then there are the treatment rooms! The menu is mouth-watering: a two-hour Forget Jet Lag package, traditional Japanese shiatsu with green tea service, a Margarita Body Scrub, a Punta Mita massage with tequila (be on your best behaviour if you want a sip), and the ultimate six-hour Vision of Beauty package that includes a facial, full massage, complete body wax, hair cut, manicure and pedicure, lunch, and make-up by a beautician. The hands-down best of the 11 is the VIP room, with two massage tables and a private jacuzzi, sauna, steam room and shower. Perfect for a late afternoon rendezvous *à deux*. The spa uses the typically French Carita and Decléor products, and Bobbi Brown cosmetics. There's also a barber, personal fitness trainer, and special packages for men. Even the changing rooms are indulgent, with sauna, steam room, a private dressing room and individual safety deposit boxes in each locker.

Intended for the sole pleasure of hotel guests, visitors can book treatments on weekdays, but the pool and fitness facilities are off-limits. It's still worth every euro.

The height of European magnificence at the **Hôtel de Crillon**. *See p51.*

The friendly staff at this centrally located hotel do a lot to make guests feel at home. The 20 fine air-conditioned rooms are done with a Provençal peach and ivy theme; for extra space and balcony views of Sacré-Coeur, book one of the top-floor rooms – more expensive, but worth the outlay.
Hotel services *Concierge. Disabled access. Internet (wireless). Room service. TV.*

Hôtel Mansart

5 rue des Capucines, 1st (01.42.61.50.28/fax 01.49.27.97.44/www.esprit-de-france.com). M° Opéra. **Rates** €110-€300 double; €17 extra bed; €10 breakfast. **Credit** AmEx, DC, MC, V. **Map** p403 G4.
Stay near the ritzy place Vendôme without the sky-high prices: this welcoming, spacious hotel has real style, with a light, roomy lobby decorated in geometric murals inspired by formal gardens. The 57 bedrooms in assorted colour schemes boast pleasant fabrics, period furniture and paintings, and the lovely Vendôme duplex has an excellent view of the square (ideal for planning a jewel heist).
Hotel services *Bar. Concierge. Internet. No-smoking room(s). TV.*

Hôtel des Tuileries

10 rue St-Hyacinthe, 1st (01.42.61.04.17/fax 01.49.27.91.56/www.hotel-des-tuileries.com). M° Tuileries. **Rates** €135-€200 single; €150-€270 double; €215-€270 triple; €13 breakfast. **Credit** AmEx, DC, MC, V. **Map** p403 G5.
The fashion pack adores this 18th-century hotel, a property of Marie-Antoinette's lady-in-waiting now located in prime shopping territory. The current style is a kind of comfy *Ab Fab*, with ethnic rugs and the odd splattering of animal print and bright art, combined with traditional antique furniture, exposed beams and a listed staircase.
Hotel services *Bar. Concierge. Internet. No-smoking room(s). Room service (24hr). TV.*

Le Relais Saint-Honoré

308 rue St-Honoré, 1st (01.42.96.06.06/fax 01.42.96.17.50). M° Tuileries. **Rates** €190 double; €280-€320 suite; €12 breakfast. **Credit** AmEx, DC, MC, V. **Map** p403 G5.
This entirely renovated 17th-century hotel offers 13 rooms and two suites with elegant, traditional decor. The attention to detail is immaculate, and the welcome delightfully warm.
Hotel services *Business centre. Concierge. Internet. Room service. TV.*

Budget

Hôtel du Cygne

3 rue du Cygne, 1st (01.42.60.14.16/fax 01.42.21.37.02/www.hotelducygne.fr). M° Etienne Marcel or Châtelet/RER Châtelet Les Halles. **Rates** €72-€110 single; €99-€121 double; €7 breakfast. **Credit** AmEx, MC, V. **Map** p404 J5.
This traditional hotel in a 17th-century building offers 20 compact, cosy and simple rooms with thoughtful, distinctive touches such as homemade furnishings and antiques. It's set on a pedestrian street in the bustling Les Halles district, so light sleepers might prefer one of the rooms that look over the courtyard; No.35 is the most spacious.
Hotel services *Bar. TV.*

Opéra & Grands Boulevards

Deluxe

Le Grand InterContinental

2 rue Scribe, 2nd (01.40.07.32.32/fax 01.42.66.12.51/www.paris-le-grand.intercontinental. com). M° Opéra. **Rates** €610-€680 double; €710-€3,000 suite; €31 breakfast. **Credit** AmEx, MC, V. **Map** p403 G4.

This 1862 landmark hotel is the chain's European flagship – but, given its sheer size, perhaps 'mother ship' would be more appropriate. An enormous palace that occupies the entire block (three wings, almost 500 rooms) next to the Garnier opera house, the Grand certainly lives up to its name. Following an 18-month, multi-million-euro refit, it reopened in 2003 sporting the latest technological conveniences, splendid innards revamped by illustrious decorator Pierre-Yves Rochon (who also did up the George V), and a new spa specialising in seawater treatments. *Hotel services Bar. Business centre. Concierge. Disabled access. Gym. Internet. No-smoking room(s). Parking (€30). Restaurants (2). Room service. Spa. TV.*

Hôtel Concorde St-Lazare

108 rue St-Lazare, 8th (01.40.08.44.44/fax 01.40.08.44.69/www.concordestlazare-paris.com). M° St-Lazare. **Rates** €360-€450 double; €685-€1,580 suite; €24 breakfast. **Credit** AmEx, DC, MC, V. **Map** p403 G3.
Here guests are cocooned in soundproofed luxury, a welcome respite from the bustling crowds of the nearby Grands Magasins department stores and St-Lazare railway station. The hotel's 19th-century Eiffel-inspired lobby is a historic landmark, and the high ceilings, marble pillars, and sculptures look much as they have for over a century. Rooms are spacious, with double entrance doors and exclusive Annick Goutal toiletries; the belle-époque brasserie Café Terminus and sexy Golden Black Bar were styled by the fashion designer Sonia Rykiel. Guests have access to a fitness centre a short distance away. *Hotel services Bar. Business centre. Concierge. Internet (wireless). No-smoking room(s). Restaurant. Room service. TV.*

Hôtel Edouard VII.

Expensive

Hôtel Ambassador

16 bd Haussmann, 9th (01.44.83.40.40/fax 01.42.46.19.84/www.hotelambassador-paris.com). M° Richelieu Drouot. **Rates** €360-€450 double; €545-€990 suite; €60 extra bed; €10-€22 breakfast. **Credit** AmEx, DC, MC, V. **Map** p403 H4.
If you're looking for vintage style but can't stomach another gilded hotel à la Louis XIV, check into this historic, Haussmann-era hotel, completely redecorated in 2002 in slate, taupe and pale turquoise hues for a sexy, masculine feel. The low-lit Lindbergh Bar is named after the pilot who stopped in for a drink and a cigar after his record-breaking transatlantic flight in 1927. Ideally situated for shopping at the Grands Magasins or clubbing around the Grands Boulevards. Its summer rates are excellent value. *Hotel services Bar. Business centre. Concierge. Gym. No-smoking room(s). Restaurant. Room service. TV.*

Hôtel Edouard VII

39 av de l'Opéra, 2nd (01.42.61.56.90)/fax 01.42.61.47.73/www.edouard7hotel.com). M° Opéra. **Rates** €236-€271 single; €309-€465 double; €509-€680 suite; €22 breakfast. **Credit** AmEx, DC, MC, V. **Map** 403 G4.

Owned by the same family for five generations, this refined hotel includes artful touches such as Murano glass lights, smooth wooden features and contemporary sculptures in the entrance hall. The stylish bar and restaurant Angl'Opéra (with resident star chef Gilles Choukroun) are decked out in dark mahogany and comfortable stripes, and some of the individually decorated bedrooms offer wonderful balcony views of the Garnier opera house.
Hotel services Bar. Business centre. Concierge. Disabled access. Internet. No-smoking room(s). Restaurants. Room service. TV.

Hôtel Westminster

13 rue de la Paix, 2nd (01.42.61.57.46/fax 01.42. 60.30.66/www.warwickwestminsteropera.com). M° Opéra. **Rates** €420 single or double; €700-950 suite; breakfast €23-€28. **Credit** AmEx, DC, MC, V. **Map** p403 G4.
This luxury hotel near place Vendôme has more than a touch of British warmth about it, no doubt owing to the influence of its favourite 19th-century guest, the Duke of Westminster (after whom the hotel was named; the current Duke reportedly still stays here). The hotel fitness centre has a top-floor location, with a beautiful tiled steam room and views over the city, while the cosy bar features deep leather chairs, fireplace and live jazz at weekends.
Hotel services Bar. Business centre. Concierge. Gym. No-smoking room(s). Parking (€21). Restaurant. Room service. Spa. TV.

Park Hyatt Paris-Vendôme

5 rue de la Paix, 2nd (01.58.71.12.34/fax 01.58.71.12.35/www.paris.hyatt.com). M° Opéra. **Rates** €410-€580 single or double; €600-€4,000 suite; €32 breakfast. **Credit** AmEx, DC, MC, V. **Map** p403 G4.
Opened in 2002, this hotel is a luxurious mix of dark mahogany, pale limestone, matte gold and neutral fabrics under high ceilings – set off by liberal use of rough bronze sculptures serving as light sconces and doorknobs. Rooms have the latest Bang & Olufsen TVs and spa-like bathrooms with huge dressing areas, artful shower-bath areas and under-floor heating. There's a circular gourmet restaurant, Le Park, where guests can watch chefs prepare food in the open kitchen, and a Med-style courtyard for lunch and dinner in summer.
Hotel services Bar. Business centre. Concierge. Disabled access. Gym. Internet. No-smoking room(s). Parking. Restaurants (2). Room service. Spa. TV.

Moderate

Résidence Hôtel des Trois Poussins

15 rue Clauzel, 9th (01.53.32.81.81/fax 01.53.32.81.82/www.les3poussins.com). M° St-Georges. **Rates** €130 single; €145 double; €163 triple; €215 quad; €145-€230 studios with kitchenette; €10 breakfast. **Credit** AmEx, DC, MC, V. **Map** p403 H2.
Just off the beaten track in a pleasant *quartier*, and within walking distance (uphill) of Montmartre, the Résidence offers the rare opportunity to stay in Paris

in a self-catering studio. Decor is traditional, with a preference for yellow. Don't forget to mention *Time Out Paris* upon reservation for a 15% discount.
Hotel services Concierge. Diabled access. Internet. No-smoking room(s). Parking (€23). TV.

Budget

Hôtel Langlois

63 rue St-Lazare, 9th (01.48.74.78.24/fax 01.49. 95.04.43/www.hotel-langlois.com). M° Trinité or Notre-Dame de-Lorette. **Rates** €84-€94 single; €94-€104 double; €140 suite; €8.60 breakfast. **Credit** AmEx, DC, MC, V. **Map** p403 G3.
Built as a bank in 1870, this great-value belle-époque building was converted into the Hôtel des Croisés in 1896. Its 27 spacious bedrooms are all individually decorated in art nouveau style; look out for the delightful hidden bathrooms in some of the larger ones. In 2001, after featuring in the Jonathan Demme film *Charade*, the establishment changed its name to Langlois in honour of the celebrated founder of the Cinémathèque Française.
Hotel services Concierge. Internet. Room service. TV.

Hôtel Madeleine Opéra

12 rue Greffuhle, 8th (01.47.42.26.26/fax 01.47. 42.89.76/www.hotel-madeleine-opera.com). M° Madeleine. **Rates** €78-€85 single or double; €99 triple; €6 breakfast. **Credit** AmEx, DC, MC, V. **Map** p404 J4.
This bargain hotel in the heart of the city's theatre and Grands Magasins shopping district is just the other side of the Eglise Madeleine. Its sunny lobby sits behind a 200-year-old façade that was once a shopfront. The 24 rooms are maybe a touch basic but still nice enough, and breakfast is brought to your room every morning.
Hotel services Concierge. Internet. Room service (morning). TV.

Champs-Elysées & western Paris

Deluxe

Four Seasons George V

31 av George-V, 8th (01.49.52.70.00/fax 01.49. 52.70.10/www.fourseasons.com). M° George V. **Rates** €650-€860 single; €650-€890 double; €1,250-€9,000 suite; €34-€45 breakfast. **Credit** AmEx, DC, MC, V. **Map** p402 D4.
There's no denying that the George V is serious about luxury: chandeliers, marble and tapestries; almost over-attentive staff; glorious flower arrangements; divine bathrooms; and ludicrously comfortable beds surrounded by the largest guestrooms in Paris. The sybaritic spa includes whirlpools, saunas and an impressive menu of services, including treatments for the unabashedly Metrosexual clientele. *See p52* **Treat yourself to a five-star pamper.**

Hotel services *Bar. Business centre. Concierge. Disabled access. Gym. Internet. No-smoking room(s). Pool (indoor). Restaurant. Room service. Spa. TV.*

Hôtel le A

4 rue d'Artois, 8th (01.42.56.99.99/fax 01.42.56. 99.90/www.paris-hotel-a.com). M° St-Philippe du-Roule or Franklin D. Roosevelt. Rates €240-€576 double; €439 suite; €21 breakfast. Credit AmEx, DC, MC, V. Map p403 E4.

The black and white decor of this designer boutique hotel provides a fine backdrop for the models, artists and media types hanging out in the lounge bar area; the only splashes of colour come from the graffiti-like artworks by conceptual artist Fabrice Hybert. The 26 rooms all have granite bathrooms and continue the neutral tones, and the starched white slipcovers on all furniture, changed after each guest, make the smallish space seem larger than first appears. The dimmer switches are a nice touch – as are the lift lights that change colour at each floor.
Hotel services *Bar. Concierge. Disabled access. Internet (wireless). No-smoking room(s). Room service. TV.*

Hôtel Plaza Athénée

25 av Montaigne, 8th (01.53.67.66.67/fax 01.53. 67.66.76/www.plaza-athenee-paris.com). M° Alma Marceau. Rates €555 single; €695-€750 double; €910-€6,500 suite; €35-€46 breakfast. Credit AmEx, DC, MC, V. Map p402 D5.

Follow in the Manolo'd footsteps of *Sex in the City*'s Carrie Bradshaw by admiring the Eiffel Tower from your balcony at this historic hotel, before stepping out for some power shopping at Chanel, Vuitton, Dior and the other avenue Montaigne boutiques. Material girls and boys will like the high-tech room amenities, including remote controlled air-con, internet and video game access on TV with infra-red keyboard, and mini hi-fi. The ever-stylish bar, full of rock stars and hot shots, has a modern decor matched by a good cocktail list (*see p222* **Hot hotel haunts**) and staff who know what service is about.
Hotel services *Bar. Concierge. Disabled access. Gym. Internet. No-smoking room(s). Parking (€25). Restaurants (2; 3 in summer). Room service. TV.*

Hôtel Royal Monceau

37 av Hoche, 8th (01.42.99.88.00/fax 01.42.99.89.90/ www.royalmonceau.com). M° Charles de Gaulle Etoile. Rates €495-€695 double; €750-€2,450 suite; €27-€40 breakfast. Credit AmEx, DC, MC, V. Map p402 H5.

As if the acres of marble and tapestries, a romantic, Michelin-starred garden restaurant, and posh health spa with pool weren't luxurious enough, the historic Royal Monceau will up the ante with a complete renovation in 2005, turning 203 rooms and 45 suites into 180 spacious *chambres* and 52 suites redecorated by Costes' darling Jacques Garcia. One to watch.
Hotel services *Bar. Business centre. Concierge. Disabled access. Gym. Internet (wireless). Parking (€30). Pool (indoor). Restaurants (2). Room service. Spa. TV.*

Hôtel de Vigny

9-11 rue Balzac, 8th (01.42.99.80.80/fax 01.42. 99.80.40/www.hoteldevigny.com). M° George V. Rates €395 single; €450-€540 double; €725 suite; €21-€28 breakfast. Credit AmEx, MC, V. Map p403 H5.

The capital's only Relais & Château hotel has the feel of a private, plush, townhouse. Although it's just off the Champs-Elysées, the Vigny is a discreet hotel that pulls in a discerning, low-key clientele; its 21 rooms have marble bathrooms and individual decor in tasteful striped or floral fabrics. Enjoy dinner in the art deco Baretto restaurant, or a cup of tea in front of the library fireplace.
Hotel services *Bar. Concierge. Internet. No-smoking room(s). Parking (€23). Restaurant. Room service. TV.*

Pershing Hall

49 rue Pierre-Charron, 8th (01.58.36.58.00/fax 01.58.36.58.01/www.pershinghall.com). M° George V. Rates €390-€500 double; €720-€1,000 suite; €27 breakfast. Credit AmEx, DC, MC, V. Map p402 D4.

The refreshing mix of 19th-century grandeur and contemporary comfort make the Pershing Hall feel quite large, but this luxury hotel is really a cleverly disguised boutique hotel with just 26 rooms. Chic locals frequent the stylish bar and restaurant terrace set off by a dramatic vertical garden. Designed by Andrée Putman, the neat white-on-white bedrooms emphasise natural materials, with stained grey oak floors, and particularly fine mosaic-tiled bathrooms with geometric styling and copious towels.
Hotel services *Bar. Business centre. Concierge. Disabled access. Gym. Internet. No-smoking room(s). Parking (€8). Restaurant. Room service. TV.*

Expensive

Hôtel Pergolèse

3 rue Pergolèse, 16th (01.53.64.04.04/fax 01.53. 64.04.40/www.hotelpergolese.com). M° Charles de Gaulle Etoile. Rates €175-€375 single; €195-€420 double; €13-€20 breakfast. Credit AmEx, DC, MC, V. Map p402 B3.

The Pergolèse was one of the first designer boutique hotels in town, but still looks contemporary a decade or more after being decorated by Rena Dumas-Hermès with Philippe Starck furniture and Hilton McConnico rugs. Rooms are done out in pastel tones with blonde wood furniture, and come with Bang & Olufsen TVs and cool white-tiled bathrooms.
Hotel services *Bar. Concierge. Internet (wireless). No-smoking room(s). Room service. TV.*

Hôtel Square

3 rue de Boulainvilliers, 16th (01.44.14.91.90/fax 01.44.14.91.99/www.hotelsquare.com). M° Passy/ RER Kennedy Radio France. Rates €255-€400 single or double; €500 suite; €14-€20 breakfast. Credit AmEx, DC, MC, V. Map p406 A7.

Located in the upmarket 16th hard by the Maison de la Radio, this courageously modern hotel has a

dramatic yet welcoming interior, and attentive service that comes from having to look after only 22 rooms. These are decorated in amber, brick or slate colours, with exotic woods, quality fabrics and bathrooms seemingly cut from one huge chunk of Carrara marble. Check the exhibitions in the atrium gallery or mingle with the media types at the hip Zebra Square restaurant and DJ lounge bar (which has a branch in Monaco).

Hotel services *Bar. Business centre. Concierge. Disabled access. Internet. Parking (€20). Restaurant. Room service. TV.*

Moderate

Hôtel Elysées Ceramic

34 av de Wagram, 8th (01.42.27.20.30/fax 01.46. 22.95.83/www.elysees-ceramic.com). M° Charles de Gaulle Etoile. **Rates** €175 single; €200 double; €230 triple; €10 breakfast. **Credit** AmEx, DC, MC, V. **Map** p402 C3.

A comfortable hotel between the Arc de Triomphe and the Eiffel Tower, this has a listed art nouveau ceramic façade as old as its foundation in 1904; the theme continues inside, with a ceramic cornice around the reception. The 57 rooms are clean and modern, with stencilled patterns; there's a roomy, cactus-filled breakfast room in the basement.

Hotel services *Concierge. Disabled access. Internet (wireless). No-smoking room(s). Room service (until 4pm). TV.*

Hôtel Regent's Garden

6 rue Pierre-Demours, 17th (01.45.74.07.30/fax 01.40.55.01.42/www.hotel-paris-garden.com). M° Charles de Gaulle Etoile or Ternes. **Rates** €127-€276 single; €139-€276 double; €12 breakfast. **Credit** AmEx, DC, MC, V. **Map** p402 C3.

This elegant hotel – built for Napoleon III's physician – features appropriately Second Empire high ceilings and plush upholstery, and a lounge looking over a lovely walled garden; there are 39 large bedrooms, some with gilt mirrors and fireplaces. An oasis of calm ten minutes from the Champs-Elysées.

Hotel services *Concierge. Internet (wireless). No-smoking room(s). Parking (€12). TV.*

Budget

Hôtel Keppler

12 rue Keppler, 16th (01.47.20.65.05/fax 01.47. 23.02.29/www.hotelkeppler.com). M° Kléber or George V. **Rates** €90-€100 single; €100-€115 double; €120-€135 triple; €6 breakfast. **Credit** AmEx, MC, V. **Map** p402 C4.

It's quite a surprise to find value this good so close to the upmarket shopping and entertainment district of the Champs-Elysées. The Keppler is a pleasing budget hotel with the high ceilings and spacious rooms typical of the area, decorated in simple, old-fashioned style.

Hotel services *Bar. Concierge. Internet. Room service. TV.*

Hôtel Ambassador. See p55.

Montmartre & Pigalle

Expensive

Terrass Hôtel

12-14 rue Joseph-de-Maistre, 18th (01.46.06.72.85/ fax 01.42.52.29.11/www.terrass-hotel.com). M° Place de Clichy. **Rates** €206-€250 single; €244-€290 double; €326 suite; breakfast included. **Credit** AmEx, DC, MC, V. **Map** p403 G1.
There's nothing particularly spectacular about this classic hotel, but for those willing to pay top euro for the best views in town, Terrass fits the bill. Ask for room 704 and you can lie in the bath and look out at the Eiffel Tower (and people on the Eiffel Tower could possibly see you in the bath).
Hotel services *Bar. Concierge. Disabled access. Internet. No-smoking room(s). Restaurant. Room service. TV.*

Moderate

Hôtel Roma Sacré-Coeur

101 rue Caulaincourt, 18th (01.42.62.02.02/fax 01.42.54.34.92/www.hotelroma.fr). M° Lamarck Caulaincourt. **Rates** €75-€115 single; €80-€125 double; €7 breakfast. **Credit** AmEx, DC, MC, V. **Map** p403 H1.
This hotel is located on the trendier, north side of Montmartre, far from the postcard shops and coach parties, but still within walking distance (uphill) of

Sacré-Coeur. From the tiny lobby, a whimsical, Astroturf-covered staircase leads to the 57 rooms, simply decorated in pastels; the priciest enjoy views of the basilica. Air-conditioned rooms are available on floors five to seven, for an extra €10 per day.
Hotel services *Concierge. Room service (morning only). TV.*

Timhotel Montmartre

11 rue Ravignan, 18th (01.42.55.74.79/fax 01.42. 55.71.01/www.timhotel.fr). M° Abbesses. **Rates** €115-€130 single; €115-€200 double; €150-€180 triple; €10 breakfast. **Credit** AmEx, DC, MC, V. **Map** p403 H1.
The location on picturesque place Emile-Goudeau makes this one of the most popular hotels in the Timhotel chain. It has 60 nice rooms, comfortable without being plush; try to bag one of on the fourth or fifth floor for stunning views over Montmartre.
Hotel services *Concierge. Disabled access. Internet. No-smoking room(s). TV.*

Budget

Blanche Hôtel

69 rue Blanche, 9th (01.48.74.16.94/fax 01.49. 95.95.98). M° Blanche. **Rates** €26-€57 single; €31-€89 double; €50-€95 triple; €61-€100 quad; €6 breakfast. **Credit** AmEx, MC, V. **Map** p403 G2.
If you're prepared to forgo frills and don't mind the rather racy aspect of the neighbourhood, this is a

good-value bet. The interior is less than palatial and features less-than-luxurious 1970s furniture, but the rooms are of good size and there's a bar in the lobby. **Hotel services** *Bar. Concierge. TV.*

Hôtel Ermitage

24 rue Lamarck, 18th (01.42.64.79.22/fax 01.42. 64.10.33). M° Lamarck Caulaincourt. **Rates** €76 single; €86 double; €113 triple; €133 quad; breakfast included. **No credit cards. Map** p403 H1.
This 12-room hotel stands on the calm, non-touristy north side of Montmartre, only five minutes from Sacré-Coeur and within 20 minutes (by Métro) of the Champs-Elysées. Rooms are large and endearingly over-decorated; some higher ones have fine views. **Hotel services** *Internet. No-smoking room(s). Parking (€15). Room service.*

Royal Fromentin

11 rue Fromentin, 9th (01.48.74.85.93/fax 01.42. 81.02.33/www.hotelroyalfromentin.com). M° Pigalle. **Rates** €69-€130 single; €79-€155 double; €114-€193 triple; €134-€231 quad; breakfast included. **Credit** AmEx, DC, MC, V. **Map** p403 H2.
Wood panelling, art deco windows and a vintage glass lift betray the hotel's origins as a 1930s cabaret hall; its theatrical atmosphere has attracted such rock stars as Blondie and Nirvana. The 47 rooms, many with views of Sacré-Coeur, have been recently renovated in traditional French style with richly coloured fabrics.
Hotel services *Bar. Concierge. Internet.*

Beaubourg & the Marais

Deluxe

Murano Urban Resort

13 bd du Temple, 3rd (01.42.71.20.00/fax 01.42.71. 21.01/www.muranoresort.com). M° Filles du Calvaire. **Rates** €350 single; €450-€650 double; €650-€2,000 suite; €22-€28 breakfast. **Credit** AmEx, DC, MC, V. **Map** p404 L5.
Supercool and luxurious hotel in the heart of the Marais; *see p64* **Unknown pleasures.**
Hotel services *Bar. Disabled access. Gym. Internet. No-smoking room(s). Parking. Pool. Restaurant. Room service. Spa. TV.*

Pavillon de la Reine

28 pl des Vosges, 3rd (01.40.29.19.19/fax 01.40. 29.19.20/www.pavillon-de-la-reine.com). M° Bastille or St-Paul. **Rates** €350-€510 double; €480-€780 suite; €20-€25 breakfast. **Credit** AmEx, DC, MC, V. **Map** p408 L6.
The owner of this cosy hotel, set back from place des Vosges, makes guests feel they're being welcomed into her own home. The warmly coloured fabrics and exposed wooden beams ooze traditional Paris style, with smatterings of modernity – reflected in some of the newer duplex suites, which are decked out in taffeta and plush purple velvets.
Hotel services *Bar. Concierge. Internet. No-smoking room(s). Parking. Room service. TV.*

Expensive

Hôtel Bourg Tibourg

19 rue du Bourg-Tibourg, 4th (01.42.78.47.39/fax 01.40.29.07.00/www.hotelbourgtibourg.com). M° Hôtel de Ville. **Rates** €150 single; €200-€250 double; €350 suite; €12 breakfast. **Credit** AmEx, MC, V. **Map** p408 K6.
Same owners, same interior decorator – but don't expect this jewel box of a boutique hotel to look like a miniature Hôtel Costes. Aside from the enviable location in the heart of the Marais district and the fashion-pack fans, this tiny hotel is all about Jacques Garcia's neo-Gothic-cum-Byzantine decor. Exotic, scented candles, mosaic-tiled bathrooms, luxurious fabrics in rich colours and the cool contrast of crisp white linens create the perfect escape from the outside world. There's no restaurant or bar for striking a pose – that's done in the neighbourhood bars.
Hotel services *Concierge. Disabled access. Room service. TV.*

Moderate

Hôtel Axial Beaubourg

11 rue du Temple, 4th (01.42.72.72.22/fax 01.42. 72.03.53/www.axialbeaubourg.com). M° Hôtel de Ville. **Rates** €110-€125 single; €155-€200 double; €11 breakfast. **Credit** AmEx, DC, MC, V. **Map** p408 K6.
This stylish boutique hotel decorated with white marble floors, mud coloured walls, crushed velvet sofas and exposed beams is just a few yards from the Centre Pompidou. Rooms are not large, but exude refinement and comfort. Great value.
Hotel services *Concierge. Disabled access. Internet. Room service. TV.*

Hôtel de la Bretonnerie

22 rue Ste-Croix-de-la-Bretonnerie, 4th (01.48.87. 77.63/fax 01.42.77.26.78/www.bretonnerie.com). M° Hôtel de Ville. **Rates** €110-€145 double; €180 suite; €9.50 breakfast. **Credit** AmEx, MC, V. **Map** p408 K6.
With their wrought ironwork, exposed stone and wooden beams, the labyrinth of corridors and passages in this 17th-century *hôtel particulier* are full of historic atmosphere. Tapestries, rich colours and the odd four-poster bed give a sense of individuality to the 29 suites and bedrooms. No air-conditioning, but each room has a fan.
Hotel services *Room service. TV.*

Hôtel St-Louis Marais

1 rue Charles V, 4th (01.48.87.87.04/fax 01.48. 87.33.26/www.saintlouismarais.com). M° Sully Morland or Bastille. **Rates** €59-€91 single; €107-€125 double; €7.50 breakfast. **Credit** MC, V. **Map** p408 L7.
Built as part of a 17th-century Célestin convent, this peaceful hotel between the Ile St-Louis and place des Vosges was completely refurbished in 2003. Rooms are compact and cosy, with characteristic wooden

beams and traditional decor; book one of the more expensive rooms if you're claustrophobic.
Hotel services *Concierge. Internet. No-smoking room(s). Parking (€12).*

Hôtel St-Merry
78 rue de la Verrerie, 4th (01.42.78.14.15/fax 01.40.29.06.82). M° Hôtel de Ville. **Rates** €160-€230 double; €205-€275 triple; €335 suite; €11 breakfast. **Credit** MC, V. **Map** p408 K6.
The Gothic-style decor of this former presbytery attached to the historic Eglise St-Merry is almost perfect for a Dracula set, with wooden beams, stone walls and plenty of iron. Behind the door of room No.9 a flying buttress straddles the bed – perfect for escaping honeymooners. On the down side, the historic building has no lift and only the suite has a telly. The Hôtel Saintonge Marais (16 rue de Saintonge, 01.42.77.91.13) is run by the same people.
Hotel services *Concierge. No-smoking room(s). Room service. TV.*

Budget

Grand Hôtel Jeanne d'Arc
3 rue de Jarente, 4th (01.48.87.62.11/fax 01.48.87.37.31). M° St-Paul. **Rates** €57 single; €80 double; €112 triple; €140 quad; €6 breakfast. **Credit** AmEx, MC, V. **Map** p408 L6.

Unknown pleasures

Paris' latest and most stylish boutique lodging certainly lives up to its billing. The **Murano Urban Resort** (*see p63*) even has private swimming pools to prove it. Opened in the summer of 2004, the first fashion hotel in the Marais is aiming to compete with the Hôtel Costes, which seems to have abandoned plans to open a sister establishment nearby, giving the new kid on the block a clear run at the arty set.

Design, glass and gadgets are immediately brought to the fore. Behind an eye-catching white multi-storey façade, designed to demarcate it from the commerce along unremarkable boulevard du Temple, automatic doors made of Murano glass swish open. Liveried staff nod as guests pass into a central low-level atrium, where, along one side, dancing flames flicker in a knee-high alcove. From this vantage point you can admire the low-lit multicoloured bar and its 19-hour-a-day louche lounge ambience.

In the baroque-meets-contemporary dining room, an upended set of irregular white organ pipes reaches down from the ceiling; the upholstery is raging purple with raspberry-coloured cushions. Lunch and evening meals consist of reassuring classic fare at reassuring prices, although Sunday brunch is not yet on the menu.

A bright, fabric-lined lift leads to the 43 rooms and nine suites. Bedrooms follow the signature loud colours and low light of Murano glass, and are the real interface with high technology. Fingerprint access on the door complements the truly Murano touch, echoing the namesake Venetian glass: the colour light cordinator. Yup, you can change your room colour from purple haze to Big Bird yellow at the press of a button. Spacious bathrooms of black slate provide a suitably sombre accompaniment.

Step outside – especially after the spa opens, planned for late 2004 – and the Murano Urban surpasses itself. As well as the warm-water pool, hammam and massages promised by the spa (although you can have the masseur come to your room), and a common swimming pool already in place, two private pools await guests paying top dollar. Urban chic so contemporary it hurts combined with your own en-suite swimming pool – can anyone top that?

This hotel's strong point is its location on a quiet road round the corner from pretty place du Marché-Ste-Catherine in the Marais. Recent refurbishment has made the reception area striking, and the huge mirror on the wall adds real wow value (plus, of course, the illusion of extra space). Rooms are colourful (you like orange, right?) and, for this price range, are well sized, comfortable and clean.
Hotel services *Concierge. Disabled access. Internet. Room service (morning). TV.*

Hôtel de Roubaix

6 rue Greneta, 3rd (01.42.72.89.91/fax 01.42.72. 58.79/www.hotel-de-roubaix.com). M° Réaumur Sébastopol or Arts et Métiers. **Rates** €54-€60 single; €66 double; €74-€84 triple; €80-€90 quad; breakfast included. **Credit** MC, V. **Map** p404 K5.
You're two blocks from the Centre Pompidou, the Marais, and the trendy shops of rue Etienne Marcel. You've got an immaculately clean bathroom, TV, telephone, and a lift to take you to your room. So why are the rates so low? Could be the granny-friendly decor or the squishy mattresses; but since the hotel's 53 rooms are invariably booked solid, it seems no one's too discouraged.
Hotel services *Concierge. TV.*

Hôtel du Septième Art

20 rue St-Paul, 4th (01.44.54.85.00/fax 01.42.77. 69.10). M° St-Paul. **Rates** €59-€75 single; €75-€130 double; €7 breakfast. **Credit** AmEx, DC, MC, V. **Map** p408 L6.
Cinema aficionados will adore this black-and-white hotel, styled in homage to the 'seventh art': vintage posters and signed photos of stars compete for every inch of wall space. Nothing else is lavishly Hollywood, but there is a fitness room in the cellar if you want to work off those Paris pastries.
Hotel services *Bar. Gym. Internet. TV.*

Bastille & eastern Paris

Moderate

Hôtel Beaumarchais

3 rue Oberkampf, 11th (01.53.36.86.86/fax 01.43. 38.32.86/www.hotelbeaumarchais.com). M° Filles du Calvaire or Oberkampf. **Rates** €75-€90 single; €110-€150 double; €10 breakfast. **Credit** AmEx, MC, V. **Map** p404 L5.
This contemporary hotel in the edgy, happening Oberkampf area is within walking distance of the Marais and Bastille districts. Its 31 rooms are all brightly decorated (colourful walls, mosaics in the bathrooms, wavy headboards and Milan glass bedside lamps); breakfast is served on the tiny garden patio or in your room.
Hotel services *Concierge. Internet. Room service. TV.*

Libertel Terminus Est

5 rue du 8-mai 1945, 10th (01.55.26.05.05/fax 01.55.26.05.00/www.libertel-hotels.com). M° Gare de l'Est. **Rates** €137-€231 single; €147-€289 double;

€195-€490 suite; €14 breakfast. **Credit** AmEx, DC, MC, V. **Map** p404 K3.
Conveniently located right across from the Gare de l'Est, this great railway hotel combines modern interior design with elements that evoke the age of steam: leather luggage handles on wardrobes, retro bathroom fittings and a library in the lobby. The 200 rooms and public areas have WiFi capacity.
Hotel services *Bar. Concierge. Disabled access. Gym. Internet (wireless). No-smoking room(s). Room service. TV.*

Le Pavillon Bastille

65 rue de Lyon, 12th (01.43.43.65.65/fax 01.43. 43.96.52/www.pavillon-bastille.com). M° Bastille. **Rates** €130 double; €213 suite; €12 breakfast. **Credit** AmEx, DC, MC, V. **Map** p409 M7.
The best thing about this hotel is its location between the Bastille opera house and Gare de Lyon. The 25 rooms follow a strict, contemporary yellow and blue code, and are clean and fresh (though too small for cat-swinging). If you're feeling classy, try out the €24 Forfait VIP, for a bathrobe, bowl of fruit, slippers and more flexible checking out times.
Hotel services *Bar. Business centre. Concierge. Internet. No-smoking room(s). Room service. TV.*

Budget

Hôtel Moderne du Temple

3 rue d'Aix, 10th (01.42.08.09.04/www.hotel modernedutemple.com). M° Goncourt or République. **Rates** €26-€40 single; €34-€44 double; €4 breakfast. **Credit** MC, V. **Map** p404 L4.
Just off the bazaar-like rue du Faubourg-du-Temple, this budget hotel is basic but pleasant and comfy. Many of the rooms have big mirrors, and all have satellite TV; the least expensive rooms have shared facilities in the hall. Don't miss the diminutive, quaint patio or the small, top floor lounge kitted out with cane furniture.
Hotel services *TV.*

The Latin Quarter & the 13th

Moderate

Les Degrés de Notre-Dame

10 rue des Grands-Degrés, 5th (01.55.42.88.88/ fax 01.40.46.95.34/www.lesdegreshotel.com). M° St-Michel. **Rates** €70 single; €100-€160 double; €100 studio; breakfast included. **Credit** MC,V. **Map** p408 J7.
On a tiny street across the river from Notre-Dame, this vintage hotel is a gem. Its ten rooms are full of character, with such features as original paintings, antique furniture and exposed wooden beams (Nos.47 and 501 have views of the cathedral). They also have an adorable restaurant, a few streets away, two studio apartments where you can live just as Parisians do.
Hotel services *Bar. Concierge. Internet. Room service. Restaurant. TV.*

Hôtel la Demeure

*51 bd St-Marcel, 13th (01.43.37.81.25/fax 01.45.
87.05.03/www.hotel-paris-lademeure.com). M° Les
Gobelins.* **Rates** €119 single or double; €141 twin;
€198 suite; €12 breakfast. **Credit** AmEx, DC, MC, V.
Map p408 K10.

This comfortable, modern hotel on the edge of the
Latin Quarter is run by a friendly father and son. It
has 43 air-conditioned rooms with internet access,
plus suites with sliding doors to separate sleeping
and living space. The wrap-around balustrades of
the corner rooms offer lovely views of the city, and
bathrooms feature either luxurious tubs or elaborate
shower heads with elaborate massage possibilities.
Hotel services *Bar. Concierge. Internet. Parking
(€17). Room service. TV.*

Hôtel des Grandes Ecoles

*75 rue du Cardinal-Lemoine, 5th (01.43.26.79.23/
fax 01.43.25.28.15/www.hotel-grandes-ecoles.com).
M° Cardinal Lemoine.* **Rates** €105-€130 single or
double; €20 extra bed; €8 breakfast. **Credit** MC, V.
Map p408 K8.

A breath of fresh air in the heart of the Latin Quarter,
this country-style hotel has 51 old-fashioned rooms
set around a leafy garden where breakfast is served
in summer. The largest of the three buildings houses the reception area and an old-fashioned breakfast
room with gilt mirror and piano.
Hotel services *Concierge. Disabled access. Internet.
Parking (€30). Room service.*

Hôtel du Panthéon

*19 pl du Panthéon, 5th (01.43.54.32.95/fax
01.43.26.64.65/www.hoteldupantheon.com). RER
Luxembourg/M° Cardinal Lemoine.* **Rates** €168-
€233 single or double; €198-€244 triple; €10
breakfast. **Credit** AmEx, DC, MC, V. **Map** p408 J8.

The 34 rooms of this elegant hotel are beautifully
decorated in classic French Toile de Jouy fabrics,
antique furniture and painted woodwork. Some
enjoy impressive views of the Panthéon; others
squint out on to a hardly-less-romantic courtyard,
complete with chestnut tree. The Hôtel des Grands
Hommes (01.46.34.19.60) next door is run by the
same management.
Hotel services *Bar. Concierge. Internet (wireless).
TV.*

Hôtel Résidence Henri IV

*50 rue des Bernardins, 5th (01.44.41.31.81/
01.46.33.93.22/www.residencehenri4.com). M°
Maubert Mutualité.* **Rates** €133-€155 single or
double; €130-€260 apartments; €9 breakfast. **Credit**
AmEx, DC, MC, V. **Map** p408 K7.

With a mere nine rooms and five apartments, all
guests at this belle époque-style hotel can be assured
of the staff's full attention. It's well-situated on a
quiet cul-de-sac next to leafy square Paul-Langevin,
a few minutes' walk from Notre-Dame. The apartment rooms come with a handy mini-kitchen,
although you may be reduced to eating on the beds
in the smaller apartments.
Hotel services *Concierge. Internet (wireless). TV.*

Select Hôtel

*1 pl de la Sorbonne, 5th (01.46.34.14.80/fax 01.46.
34.51.79/www.selecthotel.fr). M° Cluny La Sorbonne.*
Rates €139-€175 double; €179-€189 triple; €212
duplex; breakfast included. **Credit** AmEx, DC, MC,
V. **Map** p408 J7.

Set at the foot of the Sorbonne, this 68-room hotel is
an appealing blend of modern art deco features and
traditional Parisian exposed stone walls and wood-
en beams. A patio, atrium Winter Garden and 1920s
bar offer plenty of places to lounge around while
planning your day.
Hotel services *Bar. Concierge. Internet. Room
service (limited). TV.*

Budget

Familia Hôtel

*11 rue des Ecoles, 5th (01.43.54.55.27/fax 01.43.
29.61.77/www.hotel-paris-familia.com). M° Maubert
Mutualité or Jussieu.* **Rates** €76 single; €93-€123
double; €128-€149 triple; €169 quad; breakfast
included. **Credit** AmEx, DC, MC, V. **Map** p408 J7.

Located on a bustling Latin Quarter street, this old
fashion-styled hotel offers a warm and enthusiastic
welcome from owner Eric Gaucheron, balconies
hung with tumbling plants and walls hung with
French tapestry replicas. The 30 rooms have such
personalised touches as sepia murals, cherry wood
furniture and stone wall cladding. The Gaucherons
also own the Minerve (01.43.26.26.04), just next door,
which offers the same fantastic package. Both places
are in demand; book well in advance.
Hotel services *. Concierge. Disabled access.
Internet (wireless). Parking (€20). TV.*

Hôtel Esmeralda

*4 rue St-Julien-le-Pauvre, 5th (01.43.54.19.20/fax
01.40.51.00.68). M° St-Michel or Maubert Mutualité.*
Rates €35 single; €65-€95 double; €110 triple;
€120 quad; €7 breakfast. **Credit** AmEx, MC, V.
Map p408 J7.

An off-beat piece of historic Paris, the Esmeralda
has 19 floral rooms with antique furnishings and
aged wallpaper, as well as the uneven floors and
wonky staircase you'd expect in a building dating
back to 1640. The larger rooms overlooking Notre-
Dame are popular with honeymooners. Book ahead.
Hotel services *Concierge. Internet.*

Hôtel de la Sorbonne

*6 rue Victor-Cousin, 5th (01.43.54.58.08/fax 01.40.
51.05.18/www.hotelsorbonne.com). M° Cluny La
Sorbonne/RER Luxembourg.* **Rates** €100-€120
single or double; €8 breakfast. **Credit** AmEx, MC, V.
Map p408 J8.

This cosy hotel between the Luxembourg Gardens
and the Panthéon features wooden floors, beams and
a fire in the salon. The 37 rooms are pale green or
lavender, with cheerful geranium-filled window
boxes. Bathrooms are tiny but new; choose one with
a shower rather than one with a gnome-sized tub.
Hotel services *Concierge. Internet (wireless). No-
smoking room(s). TV.*

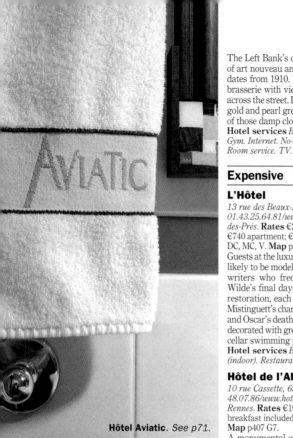

Hôtel Aviatic. *See p71.*

The Left Bank's only palace hotel is a masterpiece of art nouveau and early art deco architecture that dates from 1910. It has a plush jazz bar and lively brasserie with views of the chic Bon Marché store across the street. Its 250 rooms, revamped in purple, gold and pearl grey, maintain a 1930s feel – slip out of those damp clothes and into a dry Martini.
Hotel services *Bar. Business centre. Concierge. Gym. Internet. No-smoking room(s). Restaurants (2). Room service. TV.*

Expensive

L'Hôtel

13 rue des Beaux-Arts, 6th (01.44.41.99.00/fax 01.43.25.64.81/www.l-hotel.com). M° St-Germain-des-Prés. **Rates** €255-€640 double; €640 suite; €740 apartment; €17 breakfast. **Credit** AmEx, DC, MC, V. **Map** p407 H6.
Guests at the luxuriously decorated L'Hôtel are more likely to be models and film stars than the starving writers who frequented the place during Oscar Wilde's final days. Under Jacques Garcia's careful restoration, each room has its own special theme; Mistinguett's chambre retains its art deco mirror bed and Oscar's deathbed room has, appropriately, been decorated with green peacock murals. Don't miss the cellar swimming pool and fumoir.
Hotel services *Bar. Concierge. Internet. Pool (indoor). Restaurant. Room service. TV.*

Hôtel de l'Abbaye

10 rue Cassette, 6th (01.45.44.38.11/fax 01.45.48.07.86/www.hotel-abbaye.com). M° St-Sulpice or Rennes. **Rates** €195-€313 double; €363-€449 suite; breakfast included. **Credit** AmEx, MC, V. **Map** p407 G7.
A monumental entrance leads the way through a courtyard into this tranquil hotel, originally part of a convent. Wood panelling, well-stuffed sofas and an open fireplace in the drawing room make for a relaxed atmosphere, but, best of all, there's a surprisingly large garden where breakfast is served in the warmer months. The 42 rooms are tasteful and luxurious, and the suites have rooftop terraces.
Hotel services *Bar. Concierge. Internet. Room service. TV.*

La Villa

29 rue Jacob, 6th (01.43.26.60.00/fax 01.46.34.63.63/www.villa-saintgermain.com). M° St-Germain-des-Prés. **Rates** double €220-€345; suite €375-€445; extra bed €40; breakfast €15. **Credit** AmEx, DC, MC, V. **Map** p407 H6.
Refreshingly modern and stylish, charismatic and likeable, La Villa has cool faux crocodile skin on the bedheads and crinkly taffeta on the taupe-coloured walls. Wonderfully, your room number is projected on to the floor outside your door if drunken homecomings are becoming a challenge. Look out for great offers on last-minute bookings.
Hotel services *Bar. Concierge. Disabled access. Internet. Room service. TV.*

St-Germain-des-Prés & Odéon

Deluxe

Esprit Saint-Germain

22 rue St-Sulpice, 6th (01.53.10.55.55/fax 01.53.10.55.56/www.espritsaintgermain.com). M° Mabillon. **Rates** €235-€285 single; €265-€380 double; €380-€675 suite; €16 breakfast. **Credit** AmEx, DC, MC, V. **Map** p407 H7.
Opened in August 2004, this stylish boutique hotel is all about texture. Its 31 rooms feature long velvet curtains and wall hangings, leather headboards and green or grey slate bathrooms. On the top floor is a small room with a sauna, steam room and exercise machine. No restaurant, but a bar in the lounge.
Hotel services *Bar. Concierge. Disabled access. Gym. No-smoking room(s). Room service. Spa. TV.*

Hôtel Lutetia

45 bd Raspail, 6th (01.49.54.46.46/fax 01.49.54.46.00/www.lutetia-paris.com). M° Sèvres-Babylone. **Rates** €400-€550 double; €750-€2,500 suite; €22 breakfast. **Credit** AmEx, DC, MC, V. **Map** p407 G7.

Moderate

Le Clos Médicis

56 rue Monsieur-le-Prince, 6th (01.43.29.10.80/fax 01.43.54.26.90/www.closmedicis.com). M° Odéon/ RER Luxembourg. **Rates** €125-€215 single; €175-€215 double; €260 triple; €12 breakfast. **Credit** AmEx, DC, MC, V. **Map** p408 H7.

Designed more like a stylish, private townhouse than a hotel, Le Clos Médicis is located by the beautiful Luxembourg gardens: perfect if you fancy starting every morning with a stroll among the trees. The hotel's decor is refreshingly modern and eminently chic, with rooms done out with taffeta curtains, chenille bedcoverings and bathrooms featuring antique floor tiles. The cosy lounge has a working fireplace for those chilly winter nights.

Hotel services *Bar. Concierge. Disabled access. Internet. No-smoking room(s). Room service. TV.*

Grand Hôtel de l'Univers

6 rue Grégoire-de-Tours, 6th (01.43.29.37.00/fax 01.40.51.06.45/www.hotel-paris-univers.com). M° Odéon. **Rates** €130-€170 single; €150-€215 double; breakfast included. **Credit** AmEx, DC, MC, V. **Map** p407 H7.

Making the most of its 15th-century origins, this hotel features exposed wooden beams, high ceilings, antique furnishings and toile-covered walls. Manuel Canovas fabrics lend a posh touch, but there are also practical features such as a laptop for rent. The same helpful team runs the Hôtel St-Germain-des-Prés close by (36 rue Bonaparte, 6th, 01.43.26.00.19, www.hotel-paris-saint-germain), with a medieval-themed room and the sweetest attic in Paris.

Hotel services *Bar. Concierge. Internet. No-smoking room(s). TV.*

Hôtel des Marronniers

21 rue Jacob, 6th (01.43.25.30.60/fax 01.40.46. 83.56/www.paris-hotel-marronniers.com). M° St-Germain-des-Prés. **Rates** €110 single; €153-€168 double; €208 triple; €230 quad; €10-€12 breakfast. **Credit** MC, V. **Map** p407 H6.

Hidden smack in the centre of the lively St-Germain district through a leafy courtyard, this hotel offers welcome peace and quiet. Afternoon tea is served in the lovely conservatory overlooking a garden at the back where you'll find the chestnut trees that give the hotel its name. The 37 rooms are mostly reasonably sized, with pretty canopies and fabrics.

Hotel services *Internet. TV.*

Budget beds

In addition to the great budget deals listed in this chapter, we've chosen the following hotels for their superb value and quirky style. Every one of the addresses below can supply a good night's sleep for under €85.

Hôtel Chopin

46 passage Jouffroy or 10 bd Montmartre, 9th (01.47.70.58.10/fax 01.42.47.00.70). M° Grands Boulevards. **Rates** €64-€72 single; €72-€84 double; €7 breakfast. **Credit** AmEx, MC, V. **Map** p404 J4.

Set in a historic, glass-covered arcade, the Chopin's original 1846 façade adds to the old-fashioned appeal. The 30 quiet and functional rooms have salmon-coloured walls and green carpet.

Hôtel Eldorado

18 rue des Dames, 17th (01.45.22.35.21/ fax 01.43.87.25.97/www.eldoradohotel.fr). M° Place de Clichy. **Rates** €25-€45 single; €50-€70 double; €50-€80 triple; €6 breakfast. **Credit** MC, V. **Map** p403 F2.

An eccentric hotel decorated with funky flea-market finds. The Eldorado's winning features include a wine bar, one of the best garden patios in town and a loyal fashionista following.

Hôtel de Lille

8 rue du Pélican, 1st (01.42.33.33.42). M° Palais Royal Musée du Louvre. **Rates** €38-€46 single; €46-€60 double; no breakfast. **No credit cards. Map** p404 H5.

Tiny hotel with 14 clean, spacious rooms in belle-époque style.

Hôtel de Nesle

7 rue de Nesle, 6th (01.43.54.62.41). M° Odéon. **Rates** €50-€60 single; €60-€100 double; no breakfast. **Credit** MC, V. **Map** p408 H6.

Minimal hotel services and only nine of the 20 rooms are en-suite; but all have colourful murals and many overlook a charming garden courtyard.

Hôtel Résidence Gobelins

9 rue des Gobelins, 13th (01.47.07.26.90/ fax 01.43.31.44.05/www.hotelgobelins. com). M° Les Gobelins. **Rates** €55 single; €73-€75 double; €89 triple; €99 quad; breakfast €7. **Credit** AmEx, MC, V. **Map** p408 K10.

A tiny lift leads to the colourful rooms equipped with satellite TV, telephone and fan. The bright breakfast room overlooks a private garden courtyard. Friendly service.

Hôtel des Saints-Pères

*65 rue des Sts-Pères, 6th. (01.45.44.50.00/fax
01.45.44.90.83). M° St-Germain-des-Prés.* **Rates**
€105 single; €135-€190 double; €260 suite; €290
apartment; €12 breakfast. **Credit** AmEx, MC, V.
Map p407 G7.
Built in 1658 by one of Louis XIV's architects, this
discreet hotel now occupies an enviable place among
St-Germain-des-Prés' hottest designer boutiques. It
boasts a charming garden and a sophisticated if
small bar. The most coveted room is No.100, with
its fine 17th-century ceiling by painters from the
Versailles School; it also has an open bathroom, so
you can gaze at scenes from the myth of Leda and
the Swan while you scrub.
Hotel services *Bar. Concierge. Internet.
Room service. TV.*

Budget

Hôtel Delambre

*35 rue Delambre, 14th (01.43.20.66.31/fax 01.45.
38.91.76/www.hoteldelambre.com). M° Edgar Quinet
or Vavin.* **Rates** €85-€95 single or double; €145
suite; €8 breakfast. **Credit** AmEx, MC, V.
Map p407 G9.
Occupying a slot in a small street between
Montparnasse and St-Germain, this hotel was home
to Surrealist André Breton in the 1920s. Today it's
modern and friendly, with cast-iron touches in the
30 rooms and newly installed air-conditioning. The
mini suite in the attic is particularly pleasing, if not
really suitable for the more generously framed.
Hotel services *Concierge. Disabled access.
Internet. TV.*

Hôtel du Globe

*15 rue des Quatre-Vents, 6th (01.43.26.35.50/fax
01.46.33.62.69). M° Odéon.* **Rates** €85.80 single;
€105.80-€120.80 double; €8 breakfast. **Credit** MC,
V. **Map** p408 H7.
The Globe has retained much of its 17th-century
character, and very pleasant it is, too. Gothic
wrought-iron doors lead into florid corridors, and an
unexplained suit of armour supervises guests from
a post in the tiny inner hall. Rooms with baths are a bit
bigger than those with showers. Take care on the
small, winding staircase.
Hotel services *Disabled access. Internet. TV.*

Regents Hôtel

*44 rue Madame, 6th (01.45.48.02.81/fax 01.45.
44.85.73). M° St-Sulpice.* **Rates** €75-€80 single; €85-
€100 double; €110 triple; €125 quad; €7 breakfast.
Credit AmEx, MC, V. **Map** p407 G7.
In Paris as much as elsewhere, it's rare to find a budget option with style, but this discreet hotel in a quiet
street in St-Germain is a nice surprise, its courtyard
garden used for breakfast in summer. Reception
rooms are a sunny Provençal blue and yellow, bedrooms are comfortable with new bathrooms, and
some have small balconies.
Hotel services *Concierge. Disabled access. TV.*

Montparnasse

Moderate

Hôtel Aviatic

*105 rue de Vaugirard, 6th (01.53.63.25.50/fax
01.53.63.25.50/www.aviatic.fr). M° Montparnasse
Bienvenüe or St-Placide.* **Rates** €132-€210 double; €12
breakfast. **Credit** AmEx, DC, MC, V. **Map** p407 H7.
This historic hotel has tons of character, from the
Empire-style lounge and garden atrium to the bistro-
style breakfast room. The polished floor in the lobby
(watch your feet) and the hints of marble and brass
lend an impressive touch of glamour. The pricier
'*supérieure*' rooms are worth it for the space and
such extras as bathrobes and a modem connection.
Hotel services *Concierge. Internet. No-smoking
room(s). Parking (€22). TV.*

Budget

Hôtel Istria-Montparnasse

*29 rue Campagne-Première, 14th (01.43.20.91.82/
fax 01.43.22.48.45). M° Raspail.* **Rates** €96 double;
€110 twin; €10 breakfast. **Credit** AmEx, DC, MC, V.
Map p407 G9.
Behind this unassuming façade is the place where
the artistic royalty of Montparnasse's heyday – Man
Ray, Marcel Duchamp, Louis Aragon – once lived.
The Istria has been modernised since then, but it still
has lots of charm with 26 simply furnished rooms,
a cosy cellar breakfast room and comfortable living
area. Film fans take note: the tiled artists' studios
next door featured in Godard's *A Bout de Souffle.*
Hotel services *Concierge. No-smoking. TV.*

The 7th & the 15th

Deluxe

Hôtel Duc de Saint-Simon

*14 rue de Saint-Simon, 7th (01.44.39.20.20/fax
01.45.48.68.25/www.hotelducdesaintsimon.com).
M° Rue du Bac.* **Rates** €220-€280 double; €350-
€375 suite; €15 breakfast. **Credit** AmEx, MC, V.
Map p407 F6.
A lovely courtyard leads the way into this popular
hotel situated on the edge of St-Germain-des-Prés.
The 34 romantically decorated bedrooms include
four with terraces above a closed-off leafy garden.
A perfect pitch for lovers, though if you can do with-
out a four-poster bed, there are cheaper and more
spacious rooms than the Honeymoon Suite.
Hotel services *Bar. Parking (€30). Room service.
TV (on request).*

Le Montalembert

*3 rue de Montalembert, 7th (01.45.49.68.68/fax
01.45.49.69.49/www.montalembert.com). M° Rue du
Bac or Solférino.* **Rates** €340-€430 double; €560-
€780 suite; €20-€28 breakfast. **Credit** AmEx, DC,
MC, V. **Map** p407 G6.

Grace Leo-Andrieu's impeccable boutique hotel opened in 1989 remains a benchmark of quality and service. It has everything *mode* maniacs (who flock here for Fashion Week) could want: bathrooms stuffed with Contemporel toiletries, a set of digital scales and 360° mirrors to check the silhouette. Decorated in pale lilac, cinnamon and olive tones, the entire hotel is WiFi-compatible, and the clattery two-person staircase lifts are a nice nod to old fashionability in a hotel that is otherwise *tout moderne*. **Hotel services** *Bar. Concierge. Internet (wireless). No-smoking room(s). Restaurant. Room service. TV.*

Expensive

Le Walt

37 av de La Motte-Picquet, 7th (01.45.51.55.83/fax 01.47.05.77.59/www.inwoodhotel.com). M° Ecole Militaire. **Rates** €250-€300 single; €270-€320 double; €12 breakfast. **Credit** AmEx, DC, MC, V. **Map** p406 D7.

Feel like a star walking down the spotlit red carpet to your room at this well-appointed boutique hotel. Each of the 25 rooms are decorated in warm milk-chocolate tones, with wooden floors, modern walnut furniture and a giant painting above the bed. Many on the sixth floor have views of the Eiffel Tower. The hotel restaurant, decorated in burgundy velour and caramel with purple gossamer curtains, spills out into the chic little courtyard on warmer days. **Hotel services** *Bar. Concierge. Disabled access. Internet. No-smoking room(s). Restaurant. Room service. TV.*

Moderate

Hôtel de La Bourdonnais

111 av de La Bourdonnais 7th (01.47.05.45.42/ fax 01.45.55.75.54/www.hotellabourdonnais.com). M° Ecole Militaire. **Rates** €125 single; €145 double or twin; €165 triple; €185 quad; €205 suite; €10 breakfast. **Credit** AmEx, MC, V. **Map** p406 D6.

The family-owned La Bourdonnais feels more like a traditional French bourgeois townhouse than a hotel, with 60 bedrooms decorated in rich colours, antiques and Persian rugs. The main lobby opens on to a jungle-like winter garden and patio, where guests take breakfast, or an intimate lounge ideal for reading the papers over coffee, or checking e-mail at the internet station. **Hotel services** *Concierge. Disabled access. Internet. Parking (€15). TV.*

Hôtel Lenox

9 rue de l'Université, 7th (01.42.96.10.95/fax 01.42.61.52.83/www.lenoxsaintgermain.com). M° St-Germain-des-Prés. **Rates** €125-€204 double; €260-€275 duplex; €290-€305 triple; €10-€12.50 breakfast. **Credit** AmEx, DC, MC, V. **Map** p407 G6.

The location may be the seventh, but this venerable literary and artistic haunt is unmistakeably part of the St-Germain district. The art deco styled Lenox Club Bar, open to the public, features comfortable

Mealtime at chic hostel **MIJE**. *See p73.*

leather club chairs and jazz instruments on the walls. Bedrooms, reached by an astonishing glass lift, have more traditional decor and city views. **Hotel services** *Bar. Internet. Room service. TV.*

Budget

Grand Hôtel Lévêque

29 rue Cler, 7th (01.47.05.49.15/fax 01.45.50.49.36/ www.hotel-leveque.com). M° Ecole Militaire. **Rates** €57 single; €87-€93 double; €122 triple; €8 breakfast. **Credit** AmEx, MC, V. **Map** p406 D6.

Recently renovated with new air-conditioning, the Lévêque is great value for its location on the market street of chic rue Cler. A charming tiled entrance leads to 50 well-equipped rooms, with sparkling bathrooms in all except the basin-only singles. **Hotel services** *Concierge. TV.*

Hôtel Eiffel Rive Gauche

6 rue du Gros-Caillou, 7th (01.45.51.24.56/fax 01.45.51.11.77/www.hotel-eiffel.com). M° Ecole Militaire. **Rates** €79 single; €89-€95 double; €105-€119 triple; €129-€149 quad; €9 breakfast. **Credit** MC, V. **Map** p406 D6.

The Provençal decor and warm welcome make this hotel a cosy retreat. For the quintessential Paris view at a bargain price, ask for one of the upper floors of this well-situated hotel; you can see the Eiffel Tower

from nine of the 30 rooms. They feature Empire-style bedheads and modern bathrooms. There is also a tiny, tiled courtyard with a bridge.
Hotel services *Internet. TV.*

Youth Accommodation

Auberge Internationale des Jeunes
10 rue Trousseau, 11th (01.47.00.62.00/fax 01.47.00.33.16/www.aijparis.com). Mº Ledru-Rollin.
Open 24hrs daily; rooms closed 10am-3pm. **Rates** *Nov-Feb* €13. *Mar-Oct* €14. Breakfast included.
Credit AmEx, MC, V. **Map** p409 N7.
Cleanliness is a high priority at this large (120-bed) hostel close to Bastille and within easy distance of the Marais. Rooms hold two to six people, and the larger ones have their own bathroom. Bookings can be made; at the lowest rates in central Paris, the place fills quickly in summer.
Hostel services *Internet.*

Auberge Jules Ferry
8 bd Jules-Ferry, 11th (01.43.57.55.60/fax 01.43.14.82.09/www.fuaj.fr). Mº République or Goncourt.
Rates €19.50 per person; breakfast & linens included. **Credit** MC, V. **Map** p405 M4.
This friendly IYHF hostel has 100 beds in rooms for two to six. There is no need to – indeed no way to – make advance reservations. No curfew, though rooms are closed between 10am and 2pm.
Hostel services *Internet.*

BVJ Paris/Quartier Latin
44 rue des Bernardins, 5th (01.43.29.34.80/fax 01.53.00.90.91/www.bvjhotel.com). Mº Maubert Mutualité. **Rates** €26 per person dormitory; €35 single; €28 per person double; breakfast included.
No credit cards. **Map** p408 K7.
The BVJ hostel has clean rooms, with 100 beds and homely tartan quilts in bare modern dorms (for up to ten) and singles. There's also a TV lounge and a work room suitable for writing up your journal.
Hostel services *Internet.*
Other locations: *BVJ Paris/Louvre, 20 rue Jean-Jacques-Rousseau, 1st (01.53.00.90.90).*

MIJE
6 rue de Fourcy, 4th (01.42.74.23.45/fax 01.40.27.81.64/www.mije.com). Mº St-Paul. **Rates** dorm €27 per person (18-30s sharing rooms); single €42; double €32 per person; triple €28 per person; membership €2.50; breakfast included. **No credit cards**. **Map** p408 L6, L7, K6.
MIJE runs two 17th-century Marais residences and a former convent (see addresses below) that provide the most attractive hostel sleeps in Paris. Plain, clean rooms have snow-white sheets and sleep up to eight; all have a shower and basin. The Fourcy address has its own restaurant. Don't miss the 1am curfew.
Other locations *11 rue du Fauconnier, 4th; 12 rue des Barres, 4th.*

Bed & Breakfast

Alcove & Agapes
Le Bed & Breakfast à Paris, 8bis rue Coysevox, 18th (01.44.85.06.05/fax 01.44.85.06.14/www.bedand breakfastinparis.com).
This B&B service offers over 100 homes (€50-€125 for a double) with hosts from artists to grannies. The multi-lingual website provides good descriptions and photos for each property.

Good Morning Paris
43 rue Lacépède, 5th (01.47.07.28.29/fax 01.47.07.44.45/www.goodmorningparis.fr).
This company has 100 rooms in the city. Prices range from €46 for one person to €87 for three. They also have apartments for two to four people from €104. Minimum stay is two nights.

Apart-Hotels & Short-Stay Rental

A deposit is usually payable on arrival. Small ads for private short-term lets run in the fortnightly anglophone *FUSAC* (www.fusac.org).

Citadines Apart'hotel
Central reservations 01.41.05.79.79/fax 01.41.05.78.87/www.citadines.com. **Rates** €108 studio; €180 apartment. **Credit** AmEx, DC, MC, V.
The 17 modern Citadines complexes across Paris (around the Louvre, Opéra and St-Germain) tend to attract a mainly business clientele. Room sizes vary from slightly cramped studios to two-bedroom apartments, all with a kitchenette and dining table suitable for those with children. There are discounts available for longer stays.

Eurogroup Hotel Residences
Central reservations 04.79.65.07.65/fax 04.79.65.08.08/www.eurogroup-vacances.com. **Rates** from €104 studio; from €139 apartment for four.
Résidence Champ de Mars *2bis rue Alasseur, 15th (01.53.86.85.00/01.53.86.85.28). Mº La Motte-Picquet Grenelle.*
Villa Montmartre *44 rue de Clignancourt, 18th (01.42.59.97.38/fax 01.42.59.97.39). Mº Château Rouge.*
Comfortable studios and apartments.

Paris Appartements Services
20 rue Bachaumont, 2nd (01.40.28.01.28/fax 01.40.28.92.01/www.paris-apts.com). **Open** 9am-7pm Mon-Fri; 10am-noon Sat. **Rates** €61 studio; from €135 two-room apartment; five-night minimum stay. **Credit** MC, V.
This organisation provides furnished studios and one-bedroom flats in the 1st to 4th districts, with weekly maid service, and a 24-hour helpline manned by bilingual staff. A daily breakfast service and cleaning can also be arranged.

Sightseeing

Features

Introduction

Welcome to the city of light.

Monuments old and new: the **Eiffel Tower** and **Mur de la Paix** (*see p140*).

Paris is a sightseer's dream. It's not only that there's such a long list of things worth seeing – so much history, so many monuments, all those museums, all that *food*; as a bonus, the bag that holds this dizzying number of goodies is one of reassuringly manageable dimensions. You can get a good feel for Paris even on a day trip, something you can't say of many capital cities; and while its famed beauty certainly doesn't extend to every last cranny, there are few streets that are not worth walking along.

Walking: that's the secret. The Métro is a world champion among public transport networks and merits a ride in its own right; the buses are clean, frequent and cheap; and there are plenty of guided tours to show you around. By all means, time permitting, try them all. But your best chance of hearing this city's heartbeat lies in putting one foot in front of the other, above ground, among the people who live and work here; only then will you be able to see the 'museum city' clichés for what they are. Paris is alive, thriving: joyous proof that a city can love the trappings of the modern world without forgetting – or fossilising – its past.

Its 20 districts spiral out, clockwise and in ascending order, from the Louvre. These are the *arrondissements*, the pieces that together make a jigsaw puzzle compared by novelist Julien Green to medical models of the human brain, and each piece has its connotations. 5th: *intello*. 6th: chic. 16th: affluent and stuffy. 18th, 19th, 20th: lively and multicultural. Rightly or wrongly, residents are often assessed, at least on first encounter, by their postcodes – and many will tell you that Paris is not a city but, in fact, a coagulation of distinct villages.

We've divided the **Sightseeing** chapter into four sections: the Seine & Islands; Right Bank; Left Bank; and Beyond the Périphérique. The Right Bank and Left Bank sections are also sub-divided by areas which, roughly, follow district guidelines, starting from the centre and working out. If you want to cut to the chase, follow our recipe for a potted Paris weekend (*see p78* **Paris against the clock**).

▶ For **Museums**, see pp161-184.
▶ For the **Louvre**, see pp152-160.
▶ For **Disneyland Paris**, see p356.
CM refers to the **Carte Musées et Monuments**; see p161.

Guided tours

For boat tours, *see p86.*

Coach tours

Les Cars Rouges

(01.53.95.39.53/www.lescarsrouges.com).
Departs from Trocadéro 9.30am-6.30pm
every 10-20 min daily. **Admission** €22;
€11 4-12s. **Credit** AmEx, DC, MC, V.
Red double-deckers follow a set route around
the major monuments. Hop on or off at any
of nine stops (including Eiffel Tower, Notre-
Dame, Louvre, Opéra). Recorded commentary.

Cityrama

*4 pl des Pyramides, 1st (01.44.55.61.00/
www.grayzlineparis.com). M° Palais Royal
Musée du Louvre.* **Departs** *Winter* 10am,
11.30am, 2pm. *Summer* 10am, 11.30am,
2pm, 3.30pm. **Admission** €15; €7.50 concs.
Credit AmEx, DC, MC, V.
Another double-decker outfit with multi-lingual
recorded commentary.

Paris Vision

*214 rue de Rivoli, 1st (01.42.60.30.01/
www.parisvision.fr). M° Tuileries.* **Departs**
times vary. **Admission** €19-€92; €9.50-€92
4s-11s. **Credit** AmEx, DC, MC, V.
Large air-conditioned coaches take you round
the sights. The commentary is rather basic,
and you should make sure you get a top-
deck seat. Tours last between two hours and
a full day; the longer ones include lunch or a
river cruise. Call or see the website for
minibus tours.

Tours on two wheels

City-bird

08.26.10.01.00/www.city-bird.com.
Admission €70-€90. **Credit** AmEx, DC, MC, V.
For the money-rich and time-poor, a new
sightseeing tool: the motorbike. A friendly,
knowledgeable driver comes to pick you up,
then weaves you through the traffic,
supplying banter and history over an
intercom, while Paris sights whirl around
you as if by accident. A simple 'taxi-scooter'
service is also offered.

Fat Tire Bike Tours

*(01.56.58.10.54/www.fattirebiketoursparis.
com).* Meet *Pilier Sud, Tour Eiffel, Champs de
Mars, 7th. M° Bir-Hakeim.* **Departs** *Nov-Feb* by
appointment. *Mar-May* 11am daily; 7pm Tue,
Thur, Sun. *June-July* 11am, 3pm, 7pm daily.
Aug-15 Oct 11am, 7pm. *16 Oct-Nov* 11am
daily; 7pm Tue, Thur, Sun. **Admission** *Day*
€24; €22 students. *Night* €28; €26 students.
Both €48; €44 students. **No credit cards**.
Day and night tours in English around the
major sights. Wet-weather gear is provided in
the rain. Call or see the website for Segway
tours (€70 per person) and tours of Giverny
and Versailles.

Paris à vélo, c'est sympa!

*28 rue Baudin, 11th (01.48.87.60.01/
www.parisvelosympa.com). M° Richard Lenoir.*
Departs *1 Nov-31 Mar* 10am, 2pm Sat,
Sun. *May-Sept* 6am Sun. *1 Apr-31 Oct* 10am
Mon, Fri; 3pm Wed; 10am, 3pm Sat, Sun.
Admission €32.50; €28 under-26s; €18
under-12s. **Credit** MC, V.
Multilingual guided cycle tours with a variety
of themes, including nocturnal Paris and Paris
at dawn. Reservation required. Call or see the
website for tours outside Paris.

Sightseeing

Paris against the clock

You've got a mere 48 hours – or maybe 36, or perhaps just 24 – to spend in the city of light. As well as the must-do must-see list – the Eiffel Tower, Notre-Dame, Arc de Triomphe, the Louvre, the Musée d'Orsay, the Sacré-Coeur – there are some other delights worth squeezing into a swift *séjour*. Here are a few ideas.

Day one

A delicious croissant is an important Paris rite of passage. Start the day with mouthfuls of crisply buttery flakes and soft, squishy dough – in other words, a croissant, ideally from **Au Levain du Marais** (32 rue de Turenne, 3rd), an easy stroll from the magnificent 17th-century place des Vosges. Sip an espresso at one of several cafés that face the square.

Now for a look at a bit more of the Marais. Traditionally the Jewish quarter, it's abuzz with culture, retail and bars. Many of its beautiful *hôtels particuliers* – old aristocratic mansions – now house important cultural institutions like the **Musée Carnavalet** (*see p176*), **Musée National Picasso** (*see p166*) and **Maison Européene de la Photographie** (*see p170*). Boutique safarists, meanwhile will find joy in the streets leading off the main shopping thoroughfare of rue des Francs-Bourgeois. The area is also an enclave

of contemporary art galleries and, particularly around rue Vieille-du-Temple, a thriving bar scene, both straight and gay.

There are several unsung panoramas in Paris. The **Institut du Monde Arabe** (*see p174*), a behemoth glass building designed by French superstar architect Jean Nouvel, has a fine collection of Middle Eastern art and a rooftop café with fabulous views looking down the Seine. Clambering up to the small temple that marks the summit of the **Parc des Buttes-Chaumont** (*see p123*) shows beautifully landscaped swathes of green below, and miles of city beyond. Save **Sacré-Coeur** (*see p116*) for dusk, when the tourists have largely departed and the night lights have begun to smoulder.

Meander along the stone quays that border the Seine and leaf through old *revues* and tatty paperbacks at the riverside *bouquiniste* stalls (*see p245*), which are folded away into their iconic green boxes at night. From the quays you can either hop on a sightseeing boat, or pause to explore the islands. The **Paris Mémorial de la Déportation** (*see p85*) on the Ile de la Cité is an under-visited tribute to the people deported to concentration camps during World War II. On the Ile St-Louis, the deliciousness of ice cream from

Berthillon (31 rue St-Louis-en-l'Ile, 4th, 01.43.54.31.61) is no secret; if the weather's warm you'll have to queue. We recommend the blackcurrant (*cassis*) flavour.

Evenings start with aperitifs. Join the sociable crowd on the terrace seats at **Le Bar du Marché** (*see p132*) and watch the Left Bank people traffic pass by over a kir, served by one of the eccentric, dungaree-wearing waiters. And now you're almost certainly in the mood for a little nocturnal revelry. Cross the river for the **Rex** nightclub (*see p329*) for an electronica blowout. Post-dancefloor hunger pangs can be satiated at welcoming Les Halles bistro La Poule au Pot (10 rue de Vauvilliers, 1st, 01.42.36.32.96), which thoughtfully stays open until 6am. Near the Champs, La Maison de l'Aubrac (37 rue Marbeuf, 8th, 01.43.59.05.14) is a bonhomie-filled outpost of the Auvergne, grilling *côte du boeuf* to perfection until 7am, every day of the week. Finish your *nuit blanche* in style with a coffee at gorgeous art deco brasserie Le Vaudeville (29 rue Vivienne, 2nd, 01.40.20.04.62), which opens its doors from 7am.

Day two

Cross the Pont des Arts and head south through the narrow Left Bank streets to St Sulpice church, then stroll to the **Jardin du Luxembourg** (*see p130*), pull up two green chairs (this is the accepted protocol – you need the extra one as a footrest) and size up the park life: children sailing toy boats past the ducks on the central pond, tai chi groups doing bizarre stretches and old timers playing unhurried chess. The adjacent museum, the **Musée National du Luxembourg** (*see p168*), hosts world-class art exhibitions – Botticelli, Modigliani and so on.

Amble along the tree-lined **Canal St-Martin** (*see p121* **On the waterfront**), crossing from side to side over its romantic green bridges, to explore the little shops and gently buzzing bars that have made this an up-and-coming area. On Sundays, traffic is outlawed from the quai de Valmy and the bar-lined quai de Jemmapes, replaced by streams of in-line skaters, cyclists and baby buggies. Boutiques such as princessy outfitter **Stella Cadente** (93 quai Valmy, 10th, 01.42.09.27.00) and kitsch merchants **Antoine et Lili** (*see p256*) are both open on Sundays. For coffee and a slice of chocolate cake, try wood-floored,

chandeliered café Le Sporting (3 rue des Récollets, 10th, 01.46.07.02.00); for a swift *demi* that you can drink by the water, go for friendly bar **Le Jemmapes** (*see p233*).

Modern art lovers should visit the superb collection at the **Musée de l'Art Moderne de la Ville de Paris** (*see p162*), which is neighbour to the new contemporary art space, the **Palais de Tokyo** (*see p169*). From here you can walk to the Champs-Elysées and make a nighttime hike up the Arc de Triomphe to see the lit avenue stretching into the city.

As a parting gesture, sink into a comfy Chesterfield and relax with an expertly shaken cocktail at the classy neo-colonial **China Club** (*see p230*). Cigar and cigarette smokers can wallow in the fug of the *fumoir* upstairs.

WEEKEND TIPS

Buy a *carnet* of 10 tickets (€10) if you're staying less than two days; for long weekends it's worth investing in a *coupon hebdomidaire*, or weekly pass, for €14.50. You can use these tickets on the Métro, RER and buses.

The Seine & Islands

Giving insularity a good name.

Even the sprites are knocked sideways by **Pont Alexandre III**. *See p81.*

The Seine

The Seine is at once divide, transport route and tourist attraction. In the first category, the division is as much psychological as physical, between a Left Bank still popularly perceived as chic and intellectual and a Right Bank seen as mercantile. In the second, the Seine is still used to transport building materials; and in the third, as all the boat tours attest (*see p86* **Boat tours**), it's a must-see feature.

It hasn't always been so. For much of the 19th and 20th centuries, the Seine was barely given a second thought by anyone who didn't work on it or roar along its quay roads. Then, in the 1980s, the banks along the stretch now known as quai François-Mitterrand became a popular gay cruising area (*see p309*), and in 1990 UNESCO added 12 kilometres of Paris riverbank to its World Heritage register. The Parc Tino-Rossi was created on the Left Bank, where riverside tango became a regular event. Then the floating venues – **Batofar** (*see p328*) and its ilk – became super-trendy; and in the last ten years, it's been one Seine-side cultural attraction after another. Stretches of riverside roads are closed on Sundays to give free rein to cyclists and rollerskaters. The Port de Javel becomes an open-air dancehall in the summer. And then there's the summer riverside jamboree of Paris-Plage (*see p280* **No Plage like home**).

The bridges

The Seine is crossed by 39 bridges, including three footbridges and two railway ones. From the recently cleaned, honey-coloured arches of ancient Pont Neuf to Pont Charles-de-Gaulle with its smooth lines of aerodynamic magic, the bridges within Paris number 36 and afford some of the most seductive reasons to visit the city – and some of the best views. The date of the very first construction traversing the Seine is shrouded in mystery, but the position of today's Petit Pont was established when the **Parisii Celts** (*see p10*) were making a mint as river traders and toll-bridge operators in the first century BC. The Romans quickly put up a cross-island thoroughfare in the guise of a reinforced Petit Pont and Grand Pont (now called Pont de Notre-Dame), creating a straight route from Orléans to Belgium.

Paris *ponts* have been bombed, bashed to bits by buses, boats and barges, weather-beaten to destruction and even trampled to toppling point in 1634, when Pont St-Louis collapsed under the weight of a religious procession. During the Middle Ages, the handful of bridges linking the islands to its banks were lined with shops and houses, but the flimsy wooden constructs regularly caught fire or got washed away. The Petit Pont sank 11 times before councillors decided to ban building on top of bridges.

Pont Neuf was inaugurated in 1607 and has been standing sturdy, gargoyles a-goggle, ever since. This was the first bridge to be built with no houses to obstruct the view of the river. It had a raised stretch of road at the edge to keep walkers separate from traffic and horse dung (the new-fangled 'pavement' soon caught on); the semi-circular alcoves that now make handy smooching pit-stops were once filled with teeth pullers, peddlers and *bouquinistes* (*see p245*).

The 19th century saw a bridge boom – 21 of them in all in fact, including the city's first suspension, steel and iron bridges. Pont de la Concorde used up what was left of the Bastille after the storming of 1789; romantic Pont des Arts was the first solely pedestrian crossing (built in 1803, rebuilt in the 1980s). The most glitteringly exuberant would have to be the gilded torch-headed Pont Alexandre III to which Tsar Nicholas II laid the first stone. The most pleasingly practical is the Pont de l'Alma, with its Zouave statue. This has long been a popular flood level measure: when his toes get wet the state raises the flood alert and starts to close the quay-side roads; when he's up to his ankles in Seine, it's no longer possible to navigate the river by boat. This offers some indication of how devastating the great 1910 flood must have been, when the plucky Zouave disappeared up to his neck – as did large parts of central Paris.

The 20th century also welcomed some fab additions to the line-up. Pont Charles-de-Gaulle, for example, stretches resplendent like a huge aeroplane's wing, and iron Viaduc d'Austerlitz (1905) is striking yet elegant in the way it cradles Métro line 5. Planned for 2006, the Passerelle de la Bibliothèque Nationale, as the city's 37th bridge, has a lot to live up to. Plans show a low-lying, cabled construction without any ground supports between the banks, and a walkway that stretches 180 metres.

Ile de la Cité

In the 1st and 4th districts.
The Ile de la Cité is where Paris began around 250BC at this convenient bridging point on the Seine when the Parisii, a tribe of Celtic Gauls,

moved here and founded a settlement (*see p10*). Romans, Merovingians and Capetians followed, in what went on to be a centre of political and religious power right into the Middle Ages: royal authority concentrated at one end around the Capetian palace, and the church at the other end around Notre-Dame.

When Victor Hugo wrote *Notre-Dame de Paris* in 1831, the Ile de la Cité was still a bustling quarter of narrow medieval streets and tall houses: 'the head, heart and very marrow of Paris'. Assuming the metaphor was apt, Baron Haussmann performed a marrow transplant when he supervised the expulsion of 25,000 people from the island, razing tenements and some 20 churches, leaving behind large, official buildings – the law courts, **La Conciergerie**, Hôtel-Dieu hospital, the police headquarters and the cathedral. The lines of the old streets are traced into the parvis in front of **Notre-Dame**.

Perhaps the most charming spot is the western tip, where the Pont Neuf spans the Seine. Despite its name, it is in fact the oldest remaining bridge in Paris, begun under the reign of Henri III and Catherine de Médicis in 1578 and taking 30 years in all to complete. With the absence of houses on top, the arches of the Pont Neuf are lined with grimacing faces, supposedly modelled on courtiers of Henri III.

View from **Pont Notre-Dame.**

Down the steps is a leafy triangular garden, square du Vert-Galant, an ideal spot for picnics. You can also take to the water on the **Vedettes du Pont Neuf** moored on the quay (*see p86* **Boat tours**). In the centre of the bridge is an equestrian statue of Henri IV, erected in 1635, melted down to make cannons during the Revolution and replaced in 1818. On the island side of the bridge, triangular place Dauphine, home to restaurants, wine bars and the ramshackle Hôtel Henri IV, was built in 1607, on what was then a sandy bar that flooded every winter. It was commissioned by Henri IV, who named it in honour of his son, the future King Louis XIII. The red brick and stone houses, similar to place des Vosges (though subsequently much altered in the interest of sun terraces), look out on to the quays and square. The third, eastern side was demolished in the 1860s, when the new Préfecture de Police was built, known by its address, quai des Orfèvres, and immortalised on screen by Clouzot's film and Simenon's Maigret novels. It's a tranquil secluded spot, though you may not agree with André Malraux, who, borrowing from Freud no doubt, summed up its appeal – 'the sight of its triangular formation with slightly curved lines, and of the slit which bisects its two wooded spaces. It is, without doubt, the vagina of Paris'.

The towers of the Conciergerie dominate the island's north bank. Along with the Palais de Justice, it was originally part of the Palais de la Cité, residential and administration complex of the Capetian kings. It occupies the site of an earlier Merovingian fortress and, before that, the Roman governor's house. Etienne Marcel's uprising prompted Charles V to move the royal retinue to the Louvre in 1358, and the Conciergerie was assigned a

more sinister role as a prison for those awaiting execution. The interior is worth a visit with its prison cells and vaulted Gothic halls. On the corner of boulevard du Palais, the Tour de l'Horloge, built in 1370, was the first public clock in Paris.

Sainte-Chapelle, Pierre de Montreuil's masterpiece of stained glass and slender Gothic columns, nestles amid the nearby law courts. Surrounding the chapel, the Palais de Justice evolved alongside the Conciergerie. Behind elaborate wrought iron railings, most of the present buildings with their fine neo-classical

Hidden Paris Island of Dr Moreau

Now the most expensive real estate in Paris, the Ile St-Louis was not always so posh. In the mid 19th century the Hôtel Pimodan, now called the Hôtel de Lauzun, housed a dyer's workshop while the flats up above were inhabited by, among others, Baudelaire, Théophile Gautier and Fernand Boissard, who formed the famous Club des haschichins. Encouraged by the psychologist Dr Moreau of Tours, the group of writers and artists experimented with the drug, which they took in the form of jam, in an effort to find 'intellectual electricity' and an 'artificial paradise'. Gautier's novel *Le Club des*

haschichins recounts how one night, driven by an irrepressible desire to commit collective suicide, they headed to the 'suicide bridge' in the Buttes-Chaumont, only to duck out once they got there. Now with its beautiful 17th-century interiors restored, the *hôtel* belongs to the authorities and is used for private functions and occasional theatre and concerts. It opens to the public during the **Journées du Patrimoine** (*see p282*).

Hôtel de Lauzun

17 quai d'Anjou, 4th (01.43.54.27.14).
M° Pont Marie or Sully Morland.

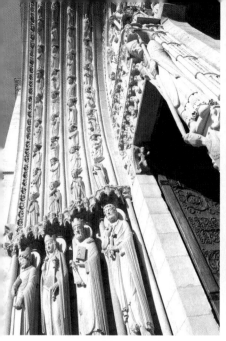

Cathédrale Notre-Dame de Paris. *See p84.*

entrance courtyard dates from the 1780s reconstruction by Desmaisons and Antoine. After passing through security, you can visit the Salle des Pas Perdus, busy with plaintiffs and barristers, and sit in on cases in the civil and criminal courts. The Palais is still the centre of the French legal system, although it has been rumoured that the law courts will one day be moved out to the 13th or 15th districts.

Across boulevard du Palais, behind the Tribunal du Commerce, place Louis-Lépine is occupied by the green pavilions of the Marché aux Fleurs, where horticultural suppliers sell flowers, cacti and exotic trees. On Sundays, they are joined by twittering caged birds and small animals in the Marché aux Oiseaux. The Hôtel-Dieu, east of the market place, was founded in the seventh century. During the Middle Ages your chances of survival here were, at best, slim; today the odds are much improved. The hospital originally stood on the other side of the island facing the Latin Quarter, but after a series of fires in the 18th century was rebuilt here in the 1860s.

Notre-Dame cathedral dominates the eastern half of the island. On the parvis in front of the cathedral, the bronze marker Kilomètre Zéro is the point from which all distances are measured in the city. The **Crypte Archéologique** under the parvis gives a sense of the island's multi-layered past, when it was a tangle of alleys, houses, churches and cabarets. For all the tourists, Notre-Dame is still a place of worship,

with its **Assumption Day procession** (*see p281*), **Christmas Mass** (*see p283*) and Nativity scene on the parvis through December.

Walk through the garden by the cathedral to appreciate its skeleton of flying buttresses. North-east, a medieval feel persists in the few streets untouched by Haussmann, such as rue Chanoinesse, rue de la Colombe and rue des Ursins, though the crenellated medieval remnant on the corner of rue des Ursins and rue des Chantres was redone in the 1950s for the Aga Khan. The capital's oldest love story unfolded in the 12th century at 9 quai aux Fleurs, where Héloïse lived with her uncle Canon Fulbert, who had her lover and tutor, the scholar Abélard, castrated. Héloïse was sent to a nunnery. Behind the cathedral in a small garden at the eastern end of the island is the **Mémorial des Martyrs de la Déportation**, commemorating those sent to concentration camps.

Cathédrale Notre-Dame de Paris

Pl du Parvis-Notre-Dame, 4th (01.53.10.07.02/ Towers 01.53.10.07.02). M° Cité/RER St-Michel. **Open** *7.45am-6.45pm daily. Towers Oct-Mar 10am-4.45pm daily. Apr-Sept 9am-6.45pm daily.* **Admission** *free. Towers €6.10; €4.10 18-25s; free under-18s.* **Credit** MC, V. **Map** p408 J7.
One of the masterpieces of Gothic architecture, Notre-Dame was commissioned in 1160 by Bishop Maurice de Sully who wanted to rival the smart new abbey that had just gone up in St-Denis. It replaced the earlier St-Etienne basilica built in the sixth

A river runs through it, and that river is the **Seine**. *See p80.*

century by Childebert I on the site of a Gallo-Roman temple to Jupiter. It was constructed between 1163 and 1334, and the amount of time and money spent on it reflected the city's growing prestige. Pope Alexander III may have laid the foundation stone, the choir was completed in 1182, the nave in 1208, the west front and twin towers went up between 1225 and 1250. Chapels were added to the nave between 1235 and 1250 and to the apse between 1296 and 1330. The cathedral was plundered during the French Revolution, and then re-dedicated to the cult of Reason. The original statues of the Kings of Judah from the west front were torn down by the mob (who believed them to represent the kings of France) and rediscovered only during the construction of a car park in 1977 (they are now on view in the Musée National du Moyen-Age; *see p173*). By the 19th century, the cathedral was looking pretty shabby.

Victor Hugo, whose *Notre-Dame de Paris* had been a great success, led the campaign for its restoration. Gothic revivalist Viollet-le-Duc restored Notre-Dame to her former glory in the mid 19th century, although work has been going on ever since with the replacement and cleaning of damaged and eroded finials and sculptures. Although Reims (*see p359*) was the coronation church of the French kings, that didn't stop others with monarchical pretensions: in 1430, Henry VI of England was crowned here; Napoleon made himself Emperor here in 1804, while in 1909 it hosted the beatification of Joan of Arc (you'll find a statue of her inside).

Despite its heavy restoration, the west front remains a high point of Gothic art for the balanced proportions of its twin towers and rose window, and the three doorways with their rows of saints and sculpted tympanums: the Last Judgment (centre), Life of the Virgin (left), Life of St Anne (right). Inside,

admire the long nave with its solid foliate capitals and high altar with marble Pietà by Coustou; the choir was rebuilt in the 18th century by Robert le Cotte but it is surrounded by medieval painted stone reliefs depicting the Resurrection (south) and Nativity (north). Religious paintings, known as the Mays, because they were donated by the guilds every 1 May, hang in many of the side chapels. Off to the south of the choir, the Treasury contains ornate bishops' copes, church plate and reliquaries containing the crown of thorns that long sat in Sainte-Chapelle. To truly appreciate the masonry, climb up the towers (only a limited number are allowed at one time). The route begins up the north tower and descends down the south. Between the two towers you get a close-up view of the gallery of chimeras – the fantastic birds and leering hybrid beasts designed by Viollet-le-Duc along the balustrade, including the pensive Stryga who looks down on the capital from the first corner. After a detour to see the Bourdon, the big bell, a tight spiral staircase leads to the top of the south tower from where you can look down on the spire and pretty much every monument in Paris.

La Conciergerie

2 bd du Palais, 1st (01.53.40.60.97). M° Cité or Châtelet. **Open** *Nov-Feb* 9am-4.30pm daily. *Mar-Oct* 9.30am-6pm daily. **Admission** €6.10; €4.10 12-25s, students; free under-12s; €9 with Sainte-Chapelle. **Credit** MC, V. **Map** p408 J6.

Marie-Antoinette was imprisoned here during the Revolution, as were Danton and Robespierre before their execution. The Conciergerie looks every inch the forbidding medieval fortress, yet much of the pseudo-medieval façade was added in the 1850s. The 13th-century Bonbec tower, built during the reign of St-Louis, the 14th-century twin towers César and Argent, and the Tour de l'Horloge, survive from the Capetian palace. The visit takes you through the Salle des Gardes, the medieval kitchens with four huge chimneys, and the Salle des Gens d'Armes, an impressive vaulted Gothic hall built in 1301-1315 for Philippe le Bel. After the royals moved to the Louvre, the fortress became a prison under the watch of the Concierge. The wealthy had private cells with their own furniture, which they paid for; others were crowded together on beds of straw. A list of Revolutionary prisoners, including a hairdresser, shows that far from all victims were nobles. Marie-Antoinette's cell, the Chapelle des Girondins, has her crucifix, some portraits and a guillotine blade.

La Crypte Archéologique

Pl du Parvis-Notre-Dame, 4th (01.55.42.50.10).
M° Cité/RER St-Michel Notre-Dame. **Open** 10am-5.30pm Tue-Sun. **Admission** €3.30; €2.20 over-60s; €1.60 14-26s; free under-14s. **No credit cards.**
Map p408 J7.
Hidden under the parvis in front of the cathedral lies a surprisingly large expanse revealing bits of Roman quaysides, ramparts and hypocausts, medieval cellars, shops and pavements, the foundations of Ste-Geneviève-des-Ardens (the church where Geneviève's remains had been stored during the Norman invasions), an 18th-century foundling hospital and a 19th-century sewer, excavated since the 1960s. It's not always easy to work out exactly which wall, column or staircase is which but you do get a vivid sense of the sheer layers of history piled up on one another over 16 centuries. There are plans to eventually extend the crypt to reveal part of the foundations of the Merovingian cathedral, slightly further west than the present cathedral.

Mémorial des Martyrs de la Déportation

Square de l'Ile de France, 4th. M° Cité/RER St-Michel Notre-Dame (01.46.33.87.56). **Open** *Winter* 10am-noon; 2-5pm Tue-Sun. *Summer* 10am-noon; 2-7pm Tue-Sun. **Admission** free. **Map** p408 J7.
This sober tribute to the 200,000 Jews, Communists, homosexuals and Resistants deported to concentration camps from France during World War II was opened in 1962 on the eastern tip of the island. A blind staircase descends to river level, where simple chambers are lined with tiny lights and the walls are inscribed with poetry. A barred window looks out onto the Seine.

Sainte-Chapelle

4 bd du Palais, 1st (01.53.40.60.80). M° Cité/RER Châtelet Les Halles. **Open** *Nov-Feb* 9am-4.30pm daily. *Mar-Oct* 9.30am-6pm daily. **Admission** €6.10; €4.10 12-25s, students; free under-12s; €9 with Conciergerie. **Credit** *Shop* MC, V. **Map** p408 J6.
Devout King Louis IX (Saint Louis, 1226-70) had a hobby of collecting holy relics (and children; he fathered 11). In the 1240s he bought what was advertised as the Crown of Thorns, and ordered Pierre de Montreuil to design a suitable shrine. The result was

the exquisite Flamboyant Gothic Sainte-Chapelle. With its 15-metre high windows, the upper level, intended for the royal family and the canons, appears to consist almost entirely of stained glass. The windows depict hundreds of scenes from the Old and New Testaments, culminating with the Apocalypse in the rose window, and on sunny days coloured reflections dapple the stone. The lower chapel with its star-painted vaulting was for the use of palace servants.

Ile St-Louis

In the 4th district.
The Ile St-Louis is one of the most exclusive residential addresses in the city. Delightfully unspoiled, it offers fine architecture, narrow streets and pretty views from the tree-lined quays, and still has the air of a tranquil backwater, curiously removed from city life.

For hundreds of years the island was a swampy pasture belonging to Notre-Dame and a retreat for fishermen, swimmers and courting couples; then it was known as the Ile Notre-Dame. In the 14th century Charles V built a fortified canal through the middle, thus creating the Ile aux Vaches ('Island of Cows'). Its real-estate potential wasn't realised until 1614, when speculator Christophe Marie persuaded

Hôtel Chenizot. *See p86.*

Louis XIII to fill in the canal (today's rue Poulletier) and plan streets, bridges and houses. The island was renamed in honour of the king's pious predecessor and the venture proved a huge success, thanks to society architect Louis Le Vau, who from the 1630s on built fashionable new residences on quai d'Anjou, quai de Bourbon and quai de Béthune (including 3 quai d'Anjou for himself), as well as the **Eglise St-Louis-en-l'Ile**. By the 1660s the island was filled and, unlike the Marais, where the smart reception rooms were at the rear of the courtyard, here they were often at the front to allow their residents riverside views.

The rue St-Louis-en-l'Ile, lined with fine historic buildings now containing quirky gift shops and gourmet food stores (many of them open on Sunday), quaint tea rooms, stone-walled bars, restaurants and hotels, runs the length of the island. The grandiose Hôtel Lambert (2 rue St-Louis-en-l'Ile/1 quai d'Anjou) was built by Le Vau in 1641 for Louis XIII's secretary with sumptuous interiors by Le Sueur, Perrier and Le Brun. At No.51, Hôtel Chenizot, look out for the bearded faun adorning the rocaille doorway which is flanked by the stern dragons supporting the balcony; there's more sculpture on the courtyard façade, while a second courtyard hides craft workshops and an art gallery. Across the street, the Hôtel du Jeu de Paume at No.54 was once a real tennis court, while famous deluxe ice-cream maker Berthillon (No.31) still draws a crowd. There are great views of the flying buttresses of

Boat tours

Most boats depart from the quays under the Eiffel Tower, in the 7th and 8th districts, and go on a circuit around the islands, first along the Left Bank and past the Latin Quarter and Notre-Dame, then along the Right Bank, past the Marais and the Louvre.

Bateaux-Mouches

Pont de l'Alma, 8th (01.42.25.96.10/ recorded info 01.40.76.99.99/www.bateaux-mouches.fr). M° Alma-Marceau. **Departs** *Summer* 10.15am, 11am, 11.30am, 12.15pm, 1pm, 1.45pm & every 30min 8-10pm daily. **Admission** €7; €4 4-12s; free under-4s.

If you're after a whirlwind tour of the essential sites and don't mind crowds of schoolchildren and tourists, this, the oldest cruise operation on the Seine, is the one for you. The four languages that are crammed into the canned commentary and the high speed of the boat mean that you get only the basic facts. By the way, the origins of the 'Mouches' part of the name is cloaked in mystery – sadly, there was no founder called Monsieur Mouche.

Bateaux Parisiens

Tour Eiffel, port de la Bourdonnais, 7th (01.44.11.33.55/www.bateauxparisiens. com). RER Pont de l'Alma. **Departs** *Dec-Mar* every hour 10am-10pm daily. *Apr-Nov* every 30min 10am-11pm daily. **Admission** €9.50; €4.50 under-12s.

BP's trimarans are smarter boats than most, and jaunty Parisian music flavours your cruise. Competent staff provide a live commentary in French, and good English and Spanish. Their glass-topped boats should be avoided on hot days as they turn into floating greenhouses.

Batobus Tour Eiffel

Musée d'Orsay, St-Germain-des-Prés (quai Malaquais), Notre Dame, Jardin des Plantes, Hotel-de-Ville, Louvre and Champs-Elysées (Pont Alexandre III). **Departs** *every 15-25min* from 10am-9pm daily. **Admission** *Short-trip ticket* €7.50; €3.50 under-12s. *Day pass* €11; €5 under-12s. *Two-day pass* €13; €7 under-12s. *One-month pass* €22; €12 under-12s. *Season pass* €50; €30 under-12s.

A public transport and sightseeing hybrid (*pictured*), this is a very pleasurable way to cruise through the city, with eight hop-on-hop-off stops between the Eiffel Tower and the Jardin des Plantes. The polite staff, who give tourist information on request, and the presence of some Parisians, confirm this as a classier choice. It can be combined with L'Open Tour, on a two-day ticket that gives you unlimited access to the 50 bus-stops and eight boat-stops.

Paris Canal

01.42.39.15.00/www.pariscanal.com. Boats leave from Port de l'Arsenal, 50 bd de la Bastille, 12th, M° Bastille, and Bassin de la Villette, 13 quai de la Loire, 19th, M° Jaurès. **Departs** *Port de l'Arsenal* 9.45am, 2.30pm daily. *Bassin de la Villette* 9.45pm, 2.45pm daily. **Admission** €14; €11 students; €8 6-12s; free under-6s.

If the Seine palls, take a trip up the city's second waterway, the Canal St-Martin. The

Notre-Dame at the western end from the terraces of the Brasserie de l'Isle St-Louis and the Flore en l'Ile café. A footbridge crosses from here to the Ile de la Cité.

Baudelaire wrote part of *Les Fleurs du Mal* while living at the Hôtel de Lauzun; he and fellow poet Théophile Gautier also organised meetings of their dope-smokers' club here (*see p82* **Island of Dr Moreau**). Earlier, Racine, Molière and La Fontaine resided as guests of La Grande Mademoiselle, cousin of Louis XIV – and mistress of the Comte de Lauzan. The *hôtel*, built 1656-57, stands out for its scaly sea-serpent drainpipes and trompe-l'oeil interiors.

There are further literary associations to be found at 6 quai d'Orléans: the Adam Mickiewicz library-museum (01.43.54.35.61; open 2-6pm

Thur) is dedicated to the Romantic poet, journalist and zealous campaigner for Polish freedom, who had dashed back to Poland for the failed 1831 uprising only to find himself unable to cross the border. He came to Paris to write poems and political pamphlets, all found here.

Eglise St-Louis-en-l'Ile

19bis rue St-Louis-en-l'Ile, 4th (01.46.34.11.60).
M° Pont Marie. **Open** 9am-noon, 3-7pm Tue-Sun.
Map p408 L7.
Inserted discreetly amid the street façades, the island's church was constructed between 1664 and 1765, following plans by Louis Le Vau and later completed by Gabriel Le Duc. The interior follows the classic baroque model with Corinthian columns and a sunburst over the altar, and is also used as a venue for classical music concerts.

tree-lined canal is a pretty and characterful sight, and the 150-minute trip even goes underground for a stretch, where the tunnel walls are enlivened by a coloured light show. Call for cruises between the Musée d'Orsay and La Villette. *See p121* **On the waterfront**.

Vedettes de Paris

Port de Suffren 7th (01.47.05.71.29/ www.vedettesdeparis.com). M° Bir-Hakeim.
Departs *Nov-Feb* every hour from 11am-6pm daily. *Apr-Oct* every 30 min 10am-10pm Mon-Fri; 10am-11pm Sat, Sun. **Admission** €9; €4 under-12s.
Open boats give the most unobstructed views, and the recorded commentary can

be avoided by choosing the children's cruise: the French-only tour guide on board soon tires of the bridge-naming game.

Vedettes de Pont-Neuf

Square du Vert Galant, 1st (01.46.33.98.38/ www.vedettesdupont neuf.com). M° Pont Neuf. **Departs** *Nov-Feb* 10.30am-10pm Mon-Fri, 10.30am-10.30pm Sat, Sun. *Mar-Oct* 10am-10.30pm daily. **Admission** €10; €5 under-12s.
Big boats that give you the option of sitting inside just a foot or two above water level or outside on the top deck – where you may get drenched by pranksters throwing water from bridges as you pass underneath.

The Right Bank

Take off at Concorde, scale Sacré-Coeur, storm Bastille, end at Père-Lachaise.

Sightseeing

The Louvre to Concorde

In the 1st district.

It may no longer be the centre of French power but the Louvre (*see pp152-160* **The Louvre**) still exerts its presence, first of all as a grandiose architectural ensemble, a palace within the city; and, secondly, as a symbol of cultural Paris. When the monarchs moved from the Ile de la Cité in the 14th century, the Louvre became the new base of royal power, and later that of the empire. What had been simply a fortress along Philippe-Auguste's city wall in 1190 was transformed into a residence with all the latest Gothic comforts by Charles V; François I turned it into a sumptuous Renaissance palace. For centuries it was a work in progress – everyone wanted to add his bit, right up to the most monarchical of presidents, François Mitterrand, who added IM Pei's glass pyramid, doubled the exhibition space and added the subterranean Carrousel du Louvre shopping mall, auditorium and food halls. Hundreds of people have always swarmed around the palace, first courtiers and ministers, then artists and, since 1793, when the palace was first turned into a museum, art lovers (although the last bit of the finance ministry only moved out in 1991). Around the palace, other subsidiary palaces grew up: Catherine de Médicis commissioned Philibert Delorme to begin a palace at the Tuileries; Richelieu built the Palais Cardinal, later the Palais-Royal.

On place du Louvre, opposite Claude Perrault's grandiose western façade of the Louvre, is **Eglise St-Germain-l'Auxerrois**, once the French kings' parish church and home to the only original Flamboyant Gothic porch in Paris, built in 1435. Mirroring it to the left of the belfry is the 19th-century neo-Gothic 1st district town hall, with its own fanciful rose window and classical porch, alongside chic bar **Le Fumoir** (*see p219*), with its very own Mona Lisa of Amaretto, orange juice and champagne. You can walk through the Louvre from here, through the ornate Cour Carrée, although the main museum entrance is now the pyramid or from Palais Royal Musée du Louvre Métro.

Across rue de Rivoli from the Louvre, past the **Louvre des Antiquaires** antiques emporium (*see p272*) and nightspot **Le Cab** (*see p331*), stands the understatedly elegant

Arc du Carrousel. *See p89.*

Palais-Royal, once Cardinal Richelieu's private mansion and now the Conseil d'Etat and Ministry of Culture. With its quiet gardens, it's hard to believe that this was once the most debauched corner of the capital and starting point of the French Revolution.

In the 1780s the Palais was a rumbustious centre of Paris life, where aristocrats and the financially challenged inhabitants of the faubourgs rubbed shoulders, and the coffee houses in its arcades attracted radical debate. Here Camille Desmoulins called the city to arms on the eve of Bastille Day (*see p14* **1789**). After the Napoleonic Wars, Wellington and Field Marshal von Blücher lost so much money at the gambling dens that Parisians claimed they had won back their entire dues for war reparations.

Only haute cuisine restaurant **Le Grand Véfour** (founded as Café de Chartres in the 1780s; *see p193*) survives from this era, albeit with decoration from a little later. The **Comédie-Française** theatre ('La Maison de Molière'; *see p342*) stands on the southwest corner. The company, created by Louis XIV in 1680, moved here in 1799. Molière himself is honoured in the fountain on the corner of rue Molière and rue de Richelieu. Brass-fronted Café Nemours on place Colette (who used to buy cigars at old-fashioned A la Civette at 157 rue St-Honoré) is also a thespian favourite, while the Métro station in front by artist Jean-Michel Othoniel puts a kitsch slant on Guimard's classic art nouveau design by decorating the aluminium struts with glass baubles.

Today the arcades of the Palais-Royal are an eccentric world of antique dealers, philatelists and specialists in tin soldiers and musical boxes nestled under the arcades. You'll find the chic vintage clothes specialist **Didier Ludot** (*see p259*) and the elegant parfumery **Salons du Palais-Royal Shiseido** (*see p241*). Passing through the arcades to rue de Montpensier, the neo-rococo Théâtre du Palais-Royal and the centuries-old theatre café L'Entr'acte (47 rue de Montpensier, 1st, 01.42.97.57.76), you'll find narrow, stepped passages that stretch between here and rue de Richelieu. This small area, along with parallel rue Ste-Anne, is the focus of Paris' Japanese community with sushi restaurants and noodle bars.

On the other side of the palace towards Les Halles, off rue Jean-Jacques Rousseau, galerie Véro-Dodat, built by prosperous *charcutiers* during the Restoration, has beautifully preserved neo-classical wooden shopfronts. Browse the bijou selection of antique dolls, the made-to-measure make-up boutiques and luxury leather goods. On the corner of rue St-Honoré and rue Croix-des-Petits-Champs, don't miss the controversial new façade of an annexe of the Ministry of Culture by architect Francis Solers that unites a 19th-century Haussmannian block and a new glass-and-steel extension.

At the western end of the Louvre by rue de Rivoli are the **Musée des Arts Décoratifs**, the **Musée de la Mode et du Costume** and the **Musée de la Publicité** (*see p172*). All are administered independently of the Musée du Louvre, but all were refreshed as part of the Grand Louvre scheme. Across the place du Carrousel from the Louvre pyramid, the Arc du Carrousel, a mini-Arc de Triomphe, was built in polychrome marble for Napoleon in 1806-09. The chariot on the top was originally drawn by the antique horses from San Marco in Venice, handily snapped up by Napoleon but returned in 1815. From the arch the extraordinary

symmetry of the **Jardin des Tuileries**, the **Champs-Elysées** (*see p110*) up to the **Arc de Triomphe** (*see p112*) and on to the **Grande Arche de la Défense** (*see p149*) is evident. Once stretching as far as the Tuileries palace, destroyed in the 1871 Paris Commune (*see p21* **1871**), the Tuileries gardens were laid out in the 17th century by André Le Nôtre and remain a pleasure area with cafés, ice-cream stalls and a summer **funfair** (*see p289*); they also act as an open-air gallery for modern art sculptures. Flanking them overlooking **place de la Concorde** stand the **Musée de l'Orangerie** (due to reopen in 2005) and the **Jeu de Paume**, the latter built for playing real tennis, now a new centre for photographic exhibitions (*see p170* **Capturing defining moments**).

The stretch of rue de Rivoli running beside the Louvre towards Concorde, laid out by Napoleon's architects Percier and Fontaine in 1802-11, is more remarkable for its arcaded façades than its jaded souvenir shops. It runs in a perfect line to place de la Concorde in one direction, and in the other, as rue St-Antoine, to the **Marais** (*see p103*). Old-fashioned hotels remain, along with gentlemen's outfitters, bookshop **WH Smith** (*see p246*) and tearoom Angelina (226 rue de Rivoli, 1st, 01.42.60.82.00). The area evolved into a little England in the 1830s and 1840s as aristocrats, writers and artists flooded across the English Channel after the Napoleonic Wars, staying at the **Hôtel Meurice** (*see p51*), buying their daily English

The best Views

Arc du Carrousel
Look through the Tuileries, the Champs-Elysées up to the Arc de Triomphe, and the Grande Arche de la Défense. *See above.*

Arc de Triomphe
Gander over Paris from 50m up. *See p112.*

Eiffel Tower
Three viewing levels and 1,665 steps for the brave. *See p140.*

Rue de Ménilmontant
See right across to the Centre Pompidou from the eastern outskirts. *See p120.*

Sacré-Coeur
Paris panorama from the dome. *See p116.*

Tour Montparnasse
Ride the lift to the 56th floor. *See p144.*

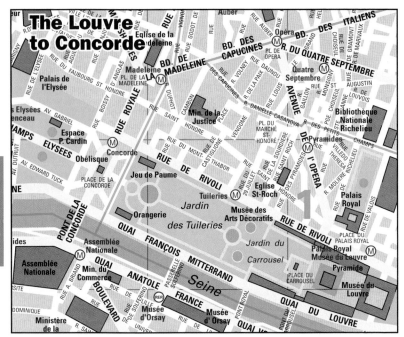

The Louvre to Concorde

newspaper published by bookseller **Galignani** (see p245), and dining at the fancy restaurants of the Palais-Royal.

Place des Pyramides, at the junction of rue de Rivoli and rue des Pyramides, contains a shiny gilt equestrian statue of Joan of Arc. One of four statues of her in the city, it is appropriated every year on May Day by supporters of Jean-Marie Le Pen as a proud symbol of French nationalism. Ancient rue St-Honoré, running parallel to rue de Rivoli, is one of those streets that changes style in different districts – smart shops line up towards place Vendôme, little local cafés and inexpensive bistros towards Les Halles. No.296, the baroque **Church of St-Roch**, is still pitted with bullet holes left by Napoleon's troops when they crushed a royalist revolt in 1795. With its old houses, adjoining rue St-Roch still feels wonderfully authentic; a couple of shops are even built into the side of the church. Further up, at No.263bis, the Chapelle Notre-Dame de l'Assomption (1670-76), now used by the city's Polish community, has a dome so disproportionately large locals dubbed it 'dumb dome' (sot dôme), a pun on 'Sodom'. Much talked-about boutique **Colette** (see p249) has added some oomph to what was once a staid shopping area, recently drawing a swarm of high-concept fashion stores in its wake,

ideally placed for the fashionistas and film stars who touch down at **Hôtel Costes** (see p48) and its chic bar (see p222 **Hot hotel haunts**).

Opposite Colette is rue du Marché St-Honoré, which once led to the covered Marché St-Honoré, since replaced by the shiny offices of the BNP-Paribas bank, in a square lined with trendy restaurants; behind, rue Danielle-Casanova still boasts fine 18th-century houses.

Further west along rue St-Honoré lies wonderful, eight-sided **place Vendôme** and a perspective stretching from rue de Rivoli up to **Opéra** (see p95). At the end of the Tuileries, place de la Concorde, laid out to the glorification of Louis XV, is a masterclass in the use of open space and fabulous when all lit up. The winged Marly horses (copies of the originals now in the Louvre) frame the entrance to the Champs-Elysées. The smart rue Royale, leading to the **Madeleine** (see p94), boasts superior tearoom **Ladurée** (see p223) and the mythic Maxim's restaurant (featured in Lehár's opera *The Merry Widow*; 3 rue Royale, 1st, 01.42.65.27.94), which has a fabulous art nouveau interior. The rue Boissy d'Anglas proffers stylish shops and the perennially popular Le Buddha Bar (No.8, 1st, 01.53.05.90.00); while the ultimate sporting luxuries can be found at **Hermès** (see p254) on rue du Fbg-St-Honoré (a westward extension of rue St-Honoré), as well as designer divas **Yves Saint Laurent** (*see p256*), Gucci (No.2, 1st, 01.42.96.83.27), Guy Laroche (No.28, 1st, 01.40.06.01.70), Chloé (No.54, 1st, 01.44.94.33.00) and others. More tearooms and fine porcelain lurk in the galerie and passage Royale.

Eglise St-Germain-l'Auxerrois
2 pl du Louvre, 1st (01.42.60.13.96). M° Pont Neuf or Louvre Rivoli. **Open** noon-7pm daily. **Map** p408 H6.
The architecture of this former royal church spans several eras: most striking though is the elaborate Flamboyant Gothic porch. Inside, there is the 13th-century Lady Chapel and splendid canopied, carved bench by Le Brun made for the royal family in 1682. The church achieved notoriety on 24 August 1572, when its bell rang to signal the St Bartholomew's Day massacre.

Eglise St-Roch
296 rue St-Honoré, 1st (01.42.44.13.20). M° Pyramides or Tuileries. **Open** 8am-7pm daily. **Map** p403 G5.
Begun in the 1650s in what was then the heart of Paris, this long church was designed chiefly by Jacques Lemercier. Famed, pious parishioners and patrons have left funerary monuments: Le Nôtre, Mignard, Corneille and Diderot are all here, so too busts by Coysevox and Coustou as well as Falconet's statue *Christ on the Mount of Olives* and Anguier's superb *Nativity*. Plus, a baroque pulpit and a cherub-adorned retable behind the rear altar. The bullet holes from a 1795 shoot-out between royalists and conventionists still pit the façade.

Jardin des Tuileries
Rue de Rivoli, 1st. M° Tuileries or Concorde. **Open** 7.30am-7pm daily. **Map** p403 G5.
Stretching between the Louvre and place de la Concorde, the gravelled alleyways of the gardens, named after the tile factories that stood here in the Middle Ages, have been a chic promenade ever since they opened to the public in the 16th century, and the popular entertainment mood persists with the funfair that sets up by the railings in summer. Renowned André Le Nôtre, who began his career as royal gardener here in 1664 before going on to such exalted commissions as Vaux-le-Vicomte and Versailles, created the prototypical French garden with its terraces and central vista running through circular and hexagonal ponds, and down the Grand Axe, along what would become the Champs-Elysées. When the Tuileries palace was burned down by the Paris Commune in 1871, the park was expanded. As part of Mitterrand's Grand Louvre project (*see p154* **Who built the Louvre?**), fragile sculptures such as Coysevox's winged horses were transferred to the Louvre and replaced by copies. and the Maillol sculptures returned to the Jardins du Carrousel. Replanting has restored parts of Le Nôtre's design and renewed damaged trees. A handful of modern sculptures have been added, including bronzes by

Jardin des Tuileries.

Laurens, Moore, Ernst, Giacometti and Dubuffet's *Le Bel Costumé*. There's even a specialist gardeners' bookshop by place de la Concorde.

Palais-Royal

Pl du Palais-Royal, 1st (www.palais-royal.org). M° Palais Royal Musée du Louvre. **Open** *gardens* 7.30am-8.30pm daily. **Map** p404 H5.

Built for Cardinal Richelieu by Jacques Lemercier, the building was originally known as the Palais Cardinal. Richelieu left it to Louis XIII, whose widow, Anne d'Autriche, preferred it to the chilly Louvre and rechristened it when she moved in with her son, the young Louis XIV. In the 1780s, the Duc d'Orléans, Louis XVI's fun-loving brother, enclosed the gardens in a three-storey peristyle and filled it with cafés, theatres, sideshows, shops and flats to raise money to reconstruct the burnt-down opera. In complete contrast to Versailles, the Palais-Royal was a place for people of all social classes to mingle and its arcades came into their own as a social trysting place. Daniel Buren's once-controversial modern installation of black and white striped columns of different heights graces the main courtyard, while the stately buildings house the Conseil d'Etat and the Ministry of Culture.

Place de la Concorde

1st/8th. M° Concorde. **Map** p403 F5.

Place de la Concorde is the city's largest square, with grand perspectives stretching east-west from the Louvre to the Arc de Triomphe, and north-south from the Madeleine to the Assemblée Nationale across the Seine. The royal architect Gabriel designed the square in the 1750s along with the two colonnaded mansions on either side of rue Royale; the west one houses the chic Hôtel de Crillon (*see p51*) and the Automobile Club de France, the other is the Naval Ministry. In 1792, the centre statue of Louis XV was replaced with the revolutionaries'

guillotine for the execution of Louis XVI, Marie-Antoinette and many more (*see p14* **1789**). The square was embellished in the 19th century with sturdy lampposts, the Luxor obelisk, a present from the Viceroy of Egypt, and ornate tiered fountains, which represent river and maritime navigation. The best view is by night, from the terrace by the Jeu de Paume in the Tuileries gardens.

Place Vendôme

1st. M° Tuileries or Opéra. **Map** p403 G4.

Elegant place Vendôme got its name from the *hôtel particulier* built by the Duc de Vendôme previously on this site. Inaugurated in 1699, the eight-sided square was conceived by Hardouin-Mansart to show off an equestrian statue of the Sun King, which was torn down in 1792 and eventually replaced in 1806 by the Colonne de la Grande Armée. Modelled on Trajan's column in Rome and featuring a spiral comic strip illustrating Napoleon's military exploits, it was constructed from 1,250 Russian and Austrian cannons captured at the battle of Austerlitz. During the 1871 Commune this symbol of 'brute force and false glory' was pulled down; the present column is a replica. Hardouin-Mansart himself only designed the façades, with their ground-floor arcade and giant Corinthian pilasters; the buildings behind were put up by nobles and speculators. Today the square is home to sparkling names like Boucheron, Cartier, (for both, *see p262*), Van Cleef & Arpels (*see p263*) and other prestigious jewellers and fashion houses, as well as merchant banks, the Justice Ministry and the Hôtel Ritz (*see p51*), from where Di and Dodi set off on their last journey. At No.12, you can now visit the Grand Salon where Chopin died in 1849, staying at the Comtesse Potocka's; its fabulous allegorical decoration dates from 1777 and has been restored as part of the new museum set above the boutique of venerable jeweller's Chaumet (01.44.77.26.26).

Hidden Paris Going underground

No need to pray with crossed legs at the Madeleine – its celestial glories are almost matched by the subterranean ones at the city's most aesthetic public convenience.

Built in 1905 by Etablissements Porcher, whose bathroom showroom is also nearby, a mosaic staircase descends into the art nouveau lavs, decorated with stained glass, plant-motif tiles, mahogany and brass. The gents and ladies are amalgamated, so men who pay €0.30 rather than €0.41 for a cubicle lack a little privacy behind their stalls.

Each spotless cubicle includes an early 20th-century sink, oval mirror and brass coat hook, making it perfect for changing into your evening dress or putting on a disguise.

In daily charge of the toilets for the last two decades, the characterful Dame-Pipi now wishes to remain anonymous after a Rio-based magazine ran a feature on her and she was deluged by Brazilian fans. She is in fact from Togo, and has filled the glass cases with postcards sent by wellwishers.

This anonymous but popular public servant maintains a jungle of thriving tropical plants, and offers a shoe-shine service on the throne-like mahogany chair for €1.65. Our lady of Madeleine only serves clients from 10am to 6pm, every day. She allows herself to close the doors for an hour at midday – even toilet attendants must be entitled to the daily ritual of a lunch hour.

Place Vendôme. *See p92.*

The Bourse

In the 1st and 2nd districts.
Paris' traditional business district is squeezed
between the elegant calm of the Palais-Royal
and shopping hub, the **Grands Boulevards**
(*see p94*). Along rue du Quatre-Septembre and
around, **La Bourse**, the Stock Exchange, is
where bankers and stockbrokers work in
grandiose buildings whose vast scale seems
intended to dwarf mere mortals. The Banque de
France, France's central bank, has occupied the
17th-century Hôtel de Toulouse since 1811, its
long gallery still hung with old masters.
Nearby, fashion and finance meet at chic **place
des Victoires**, designed by Hardouin-Mansart,
forming an intimate circle of buildings today
dedicated to fashion. West of the square, poke
your nose in shop-lined galerie Vivienne – the
smartest of all the city's covered passages –
adjoining galerie Colbert and temporary
exhibitions at the **Bibliothèque Nationale
Richelieu**. Linger at luxury food and wine
merchant **Legrand** (*see p270*) on the corner of
Vivienne and rue de la Banque, or take a detour
along the passage des Petits-Pères to see the
17th- to 18th-century Eglise Notre-Dame-des-
Victoires, the remains of an Augustine convent,
with a cycle of paintings around the choir by
Carle van Loo.

Rue de la Banque now leads to the Bourse,
behind a commanding neo-classical colonnade.
Generally, the area has a relaxed feel, positively
sleepy on weekends, but animated pockets exist

at places like Le Vaudeville (29 rue Vivienne,
2nd, 01.40.20.04.62) and Gallopin (40 rue Notre-
Dame-des-Victoires, 2nd, 01.42.36.45.38),
brasseries where stockbrokers and journalists
converge for lunch and post-work drinks.
Rue des Colonnes is a quiet street lined with
graceful porticos and acanthus motifs dating
from the 1790s, while its design nemesis, the
1970s concrete and glass HQ of Agence France-
Presse, the country's biggest news agency, lies
just across busy rue du Quatre-Septembre.
Although most newspapers have left, *Le Figaro*
remains in rue du Louvre. Up on the corner of
rue Montmartre and rue du Croissant towards
the Grands Boulevards, take a look at the Café
du Croissant, where Jean Jaurès, socialist
politician and founder of *L'Humanité*
newspaper, was assassinated in 1914.

Bibliothèque Nationale Richelieu

*58 rue de Richelieu, 2nd (01.53.79.53.79/www.
bnf.fr). M° Bourse.* **Open** *Galeries Mansart/Mazarine
exhibitions only* 10am-7pm Tue-Sat; noon-7pm Sun.
Cabinet des Médailles 1-5.45pm Mon-Fri; 1-4.45pm
Sat; noon-6pm Sun. **Admission** *Galerie* €5; €4
under-26s. *Cabinet des Médailles* free. **Credit** MC, V.
Map p404 H4.
The genesis of the French National Library dates
from the 1660s, when Louis XIV moved manuscripts
that could not be housed in the Louvre over to this
lavish Louis XIII townhouse – formerly the private
residence of Cardinal Mazarin. The library was first
opened to the public in 1692, and by 1724 it had
received so many new acquisitions the adjoining
Hôtel de Nevers was added. Some of the original

Palais Garnier.

painted decoration by Romanelli and Grimaldi can still be seen in Galeries Mansart and Mazarine, now used for exhibitions of manuscripts and prints. Antique coins (originally known as *médailles*) and curious royal memorabilia collected by kings from Philippe-Auguste onwards are in the Musée du Cabinet des Médailles (*see p176*). Transformed in the 1860s by the innovative circular vaulted reading room designed by Henri Labrouste, the library is now curiously empty as most books have since been relocated to the Bibliothèque Nationale François Mitterrand (*see p167*), although a number of medieval manuscripts, maps, engravings, musical scores and performing arts material remain here.

La Bourse

Palais Brongniart, pl de la Bourse, 2nd (01.49.27. 55.55/www.bourse-de-paris.fr). M° Bourse. Guided tours call a week in advance. **Admission** €8.50; €5.50 concs. **No credit cards. Map** p404 H4.
After a century at the Louvre, the Palais-Royal and rue Vivienne, the Stock Exchange was transferred in 1826 to this building, a dignified testament to First Empire classicism designed under Napoleon by Alexandre Brongniart. It was enlarged in 1906 to create a cruciform interior, where brokers buzzed around a central enclosure, the *corbeille* ('basket' or 'trading floor'). Computers have rendered the design obsolete, but the daily dash remains frenetic.

Place des Victoires

1st, 2nd. M° Bourse. **Map** p404 H5.
This circular square, the first of its kind, was designed by Hardouin-Mansart in 1685 to show off a statue of Louis XIV which marked victories against Holland. The original went in the Revolution (although the massive slaves from its base are found in the Louvre) and was replaced in 1822 with an equestrian statue by Bosio. Today its sweeping façades house fashion boutiques Kenzo and Victoire.

Opéra & Grands Boulevards

Mainly in the 2nd, 8th, 9th and 10th districts.

Opéra and Madeleine

Charles Garnier's wedding-cake **Palais Garnier** (of Phantom of the Opera legend) is all gilt and grandeur, as an opera house should be. Garnier was also responsible for the ritzy Café de la Paix (12 bd des Capucines, 9th, 01.40.07. 36.36) and **Le Grand Hôtel Intercontinental** (*see p53*) overlooking place de l'Opéra. In the Jockey Club (now the Hôtel Scribe, the centre for Allied war correspondents after the Liberation) behind, the Lumière brothers held the world's first public cinema screening in 1895. Old England, just opposite on the boulevard des Capucines (No.12, 9th, 01.47.42.81.99) with its wooden counters, Jacobean-style ceilings and old-style goods and service, could have served as their costume consultants. The **Olympia** concert hall (*see p321*), the legendary venue of Piaf, The Beatles and anyone in *chanson*, was knocked down, but rose again nearby. Over the road at No.35, pioneering portrait photographer Nadar opened a studio in the 1860s, frequented by writers and artists including Dumas père, Offenbach and Doré. In 1874 it hosted the first Impressionists' exhibition. Pedestrianised rue Edouard-VII, laid out in 1911, leads to the

along with those of almost 3,000 victims of the Revolution, including Camille Desmoulins, Danton, Malesherbes and Lavoisier, were found in 1814 on the exact spot where the altar stands. The year after, the bodies of Louis XVI and Marie-Antoinette were transferred to the Basilique St-Denis (*see p149*); they are now represented by marble statues of Louis XVI supported on an angle and Marie-Antoinette on her knees at the feet of Religion. In January the chapel draws ardent (if currently unfulfilled) royalists for an annual memorial service.

Eglise St-Augustin

46 bd Malesherbes, 8th (01.45.22.23.12). M° St-Augustin. **Open** *Sept-June* 10am-6pm Mon-Fri; 10am-7.30pm Sat, Sun. *July, Aug* 10am-12.45pm, 3.30-6pm Tue-Fri; 10am-noon, 4-7.30pm Sat; 10am-noon, 4.30-6pm Sun. **Map** p403 F3.

St-Augustin, designed in 1860-71 by Victor Baltard, architect of the Les Halles pavilions, is not what it seems. The domed, neo-Renaissance stone exterior is merely a shell, inside is an iron vault structure; even the decorative angels are cast in metal. Bouguereau paintings hang in the transept.

Eglise de la Madeleine

Pl de la Madeleine, 8th (01.44.51.69.00). M° Madeleine. **Open** 9am-7pm Mon-Fri. **Map** p403 G4.

The building of a church on this site began in 1764 and in 1806, Napoleon sent instructions from Poland for Barthélémy Vignon to design a 'Temple of Glory' dedicated to his Grand Army. After the Emperor's fall, construction slowed and the building, by now a church again, was finally consecrated in 1845. The exterior is ringed by huge fluted Corinthian columns, with a double row of columns at the front and a frieze of the Last Judgement just above the portico. Inside are three-and-a-half giant domes, a striking organ and pseudo-Grecian side altars in a sea of multicoloured marble. The painting by Ziegler in the chancel depicts the history of Christianity, the ever-modest Napoleon prominent in the foreground. It's now a favourite venue for society weddings.

Palais Garnier

Pl de l'Opéra, 9th (box office 08.92.89.90.90/www.operadeparis.fr). M° Opéra. **Open** 10am-5pm daily. **Admission** €6; €3 concs. *Guided tours in English* (01.40.01.22.63) 1pm and 2pm Tue-Sun €10; €5-€9 concs. **Credit** AmEx, DC, MC, V. **Map** p403 G4.

Brimming with gilt and red velvet, the Opera House designed by Charles Garnier is a monument to Second Empire high society. The opera company had been founded by Louis XIV in 1669, moving home after fires and assassination attempts. In 1860 a competition for a grander – and safer – new opera house was launched. It was won by then unknown 35-year-old Charles Garnier, who described opera as 'a temple with art for divinity' and designed his new building with auditorium as sanctuary and foyer as nave. Held up by money, fire, the Franco-Prussian war and the Paris Commune, the building was only inaugurated in 1875. The comfortably upholstered

octagonal square of the same name with an equestrian statue of the monarch by Landowski and through an arch, another square contains the belle-époque **Théâtre de l'Athénée-Louis Jouvet** (*see p344*).

The Madeleine, a monument to Napoleon, guards the end of the boulevard. At the head of rue Royale, its classical portico mirrors the Assemblée Nationale on the other side of place de la Concorde over the river, while the interior is a riot of marble and altars. Worth a browse are extravagant delicatessens **Fauchon**, **Maison de la Truffe** (for both, *see p269*) and other luxury foodstores, plus haute-cuisine restaurant **Lucas Carton** (*see p199*), with an art nouveau interior by Majorelle.

Landmark department stores **Printemps** and the **Galeries Lafayette** (for both, *see p240*), which opened just behind the Palais Garnier in the late 19th century, also deserve investigation. Behind the latter stands the Lycée Caumartin, designed as a convent in the 1780s by La Bourse architect Brongniart to become one of the most prestigious lycées under Napoleon. West along Haussmann's boulevard is the small square containing the sober **Chapelle Expiatoire** dedicated to Louis XVI and Marie-Antoinette.

Chapelle Expiatoire

29 rue Pasquier, 8th (01.42.65.35.80). M° St-Augustin. **Open** 1-5pm Thur-Sat. **Admission** €2.50; free under-18s. **Map** p403 F3.

The chapel was commissioned by Louis XVIII in memory of his executed predecessors, his brother Louis XVI and Marie-Antoinette. Their remains, auditorium seats more than 2,000 people and the exterior is just as opulent, with sculptures of music and dance on the façade, Apollo topping the copper dome and nymphs bearing torches. Carpeaux's sculpture *La Danse* shocked Parisians with its frank sensuality; in 1869 someone threw a bottle of ink over its thunderous marble thighs. The original is safe in the Musée d'Orsay (*see p164*), where there is now also a massive maquette of the building. The Garnier hosts productions of both opera and ballet (*see p294 and p318*). The Grand Foyer, its mirrors and parquet, coloured marble, moulded stucco, sculptures and allegorical paintings by Baudry, have all recently been magnificently restored. This was a place of social exchange where during the interval the public of all origins could mix and observe. You can also visit the Grand Staircase, the auditorium with its false ceiling painted by Chagall in 1964, and red satin and velvet boxes (some of which have almost no view), as well as the library and museum – once the emperor's private salons where he could arrive directly by carriage by the ramp at the rear of the building.

Quartier de l'Europe

With its streets named after European cities, the district stretching from Gare St-Lazare towards place de Clichy was the Impressionists' quarter. In those days it epitomised modernity, when the station – the city's first – opened here in 1837 serving the line Paris to St-Germain-en-Laye, later displaced and rebuilt in the 1880s. Today the long shabby commuter station has had a revamp as a glass dome disgorges travellers from the Métro interchange. The next door **Hôtel Concorde St-Lazare** (*see p53*) was the city's first great station hotel, with a grandiose hallway constructed by Eiffel in 1889 for visitors to the Exposition Universelle at the same time as he was building the Eiffel Tower. Monet, who lived nearby in rue d'Edimbourg, depicted the new steam age in the 1870s in *La Gare St-Lazare* and *Pont de l'Europe*; Pissarro and Caillebotte painted views of the new boulevards, while Manet had a studio on rue de St-Petersbourg. Today, rue de Budapest remains a thriving red-light district, while rue de Rome, dubbed the '*rue des luthiers*', has long been home to stringed-instrument makers. Just east of St-Lazare, peruse the imposing **Eglise de la Trinité** and art nouveau brasserie Mollard (115 rue St-Lazare, 8th, 01.43.87.50.22).

Eglise de la Trinité

Pl Estienne d'Orves, 9th (01.48.74.12.77). Mº Trinité. **Open** 7.15am-8pm daily. **Map** p403 G3. Dominated by the tiered belltower, this neo-Renaissance church was built 1861-67 by Théodore Ballu. Composer Olivier Messiaen (1908-92) was organist here for over 30 years.

Eglise de la Madeleine. *See p95.*

The Grands Boulevards

Contrary to popular belief, the string of Grands Boulevards between Madeleine and République (des Italiens, Montmartre, Poissonnière, Bonne-Nouvelle, St-Denis, St-Martin) were not built by Haussmann but by Louis XIV in 1670, replacing the fortifications of King Philippe-Auguste's city wall. Their ramparts have left their traces in the strange changes of levels with stairways climbing up to side streets at the eastern end. They became a place of entertainment, crowded with street sellers, hawkers and entertainers. The boulevards burgeoned after the Revolution, as new residences, theatres and covered passages were built on land repossessed from aristocrats and monasteries. They still offer a glimpse of the city's divergent personalities – a stroll from Opéra to République leads from luxury shops to St-Denis prostitutes – and the phrase *théâtre des boulevards* is still used for lowbrow theatre. Between boulevard des Italiens and rue de Richelieu is place Boïeldieu and the **Opéra Comique** (*see p316*), where *Carmen* was premiered in 1875. Alexandre Dumas fils was born at No.1 in 1824.

The 18th-century Hôtel d'Angny, now the Town Hall of the 9th district, was once home to the infamous '*bals des victimes*', where every guest had to have a relative who had lost their head to the guillotine. The **Hôtel Drouot** auction house (*see also p272*) is surrounded by antique shops, coin and stamp dealers and wine bar Les Caves Drouot, where auction-goers and valuers congregate. There are several grand *hôtels particuliers* on rue de la Grange-Batelière, which leads on one side down curious passage Verdeau, occupied by antiques dealers, and on the other back to the boulevards via passage Jouffroy. With its grand barrel-vaulted glass-and-iron roof, this is home to the lovely Hôtel Chopin (10 bd Montmartre, 9th, 01.47.70.58.10), shop windows of doll's houses, walking sticks, art books and film posters, and the colourful entrance of the **Grévin** waxworks (*see p290*).

Across the boulevard, explore passage des Panoramas, the city's oldest remaining covered passageway. When it was opened in 1800, panoramas – vast illuminated circular paintings – of Rome, Jerusalem, Athens, London and other cities were exhibited here drawing large crowds. Today it contains tea room L'Arbre à Cannelle (No.57, 2nd, 01.45.08.55.87), coin and stamp sellers, furniture-makers and old-fashioned printer Stern (No.47), established here since 1840; it leads into a tangle of other little passages and the stage door of the Théâtre des Variétés (7 bd Montmartre, 2nd, 01.42.33.11.41), a pretty neo-classical theatre, where Offenbach premiered *La Belle Hélène*.

Rue du Faubourg-Montmartre is home to celebrated belle-époque *bouillon* Chartier (No.7, 9th, 01.47.70.86.29), which serves up hundreds of meals a day to the budget minded, and at No.8, late lamented nightspot Le Palace (occupied in 2004 by squatters who gave tours of the legendary music hall turned club). The street is also part of a Jewish quarter, less well-known than the Marais, which grew up in the 19th century. There are several kosher bakers, restaurants and France's largest synagogue at 44 rue de la Victoire, an opulent Second Empire affair completed in 1876. Wander down cobbled Cité Bergère, constructed in 1825 as desirable residences; though most are now budget hotels, the pretty iron-and-glass *portes-cochères* remain. On rue Bergère stands the art deco Folies-Bergère (32 rue Richer, 9th, 08.92.68.16.50), now only sporadically used for cabaret revues. South of boulevard Bonne-Nouvelle lies **Sentier** (*see p99*), while to the north rue du Faubourg-Poissonnière offers its mix of rag-trade outlets and grand *hôtels particuliers*.

Back on the boulevard is evidence of a move north of the Marais by trendsetting hubs: gay club **Le Vogue** (*see p308*), lesbian club **Pulp** (*see p313*), DJ Laurent Garnier's fief **Le Rex** (*see p330*) and chic **De la Ville Café** (*see p221*). Palatial art deco cinema **Le Grand Rex** (*see also p298*) completes the quintet. East of here are Louis XIV's twin triumphal arches, the **Porte St-Martin** and **Porte St-Denis**, symbolic gateways erected at the same time as the fortifications were taken down.

Le Grand Rex

1 bd Poissonnière, 2nd (08.92.68.05.96/www.le grandrex.com). M° Bonne Nouvelle. **Tour** Les Etoiles du Rex every 50 mins 10am-7pm Wed-Sun, school hols. **Admission** €7.50; €6.50 under-16s; €12.50/€11.50 tour and film. Credit MC, V. **Map** p404 J4.

Opened in 1932, the huge art deco cinema was designed by Auguste Bluysen with fantasy Hispanic interiors by US designer John Eberson. Go behind the scenes in the crazy 50-minute guided tour which includes a presentation about the construction of the auditorium, a visit to the production room complete with nerve-jolting Sensurround effects.

Hôtel Drouot

9 rue Drouot, 9th (01.48.00.20.20/www.drouot.fr). M° Richelieu Drouot. **Open** 11am-6pm Mon-Sat. *Auctions* 2pm Mon-Sat. **Map** p404 H3.

A spiky 1970s aluminium-and-marble concoction is the unlikely setting for the centre of France's secondary art market, though now rivalled by Sotheby's and Christie's. Inside, escalators whizz you up to several small salerooms, where at any one time, medieval manuscripts, antique furniture, Oriental arts, modern paintings, posters, jewellery and fine wines might be up for sale. Details of upcoming auctions are published in the weekly *Gazette de L'Hôtel Drouot*, sold at newsstands. Prestige sales are at Drouot-Montaigne, the junkier sell-offs at Drouot Nord.

Other locations: *Drouot-Montaigne, 15 av Montaigne, 8th (01.48.00.20.80); Drouot Nord, 64 rue Doudeauville, 18th (01.48.00.20.90).*

Porte St-Denis & Porte St-Martin

Rue St-Denis/bd St-Denis, 2nd/10th; 33 bd St-Martin, 3rd/10th. **Map** p404 K4.

These twin triumphal gates were erected in 1672 and 1674 at important entry points to the city as part of Colbert's strategy to glorify Paris and celebrate Louis XIV's victories on the Rhine. Modelled on the triumphal arches of ancient Rome, the Porte St-Denis is particularly harmonious, based on a perfect square with a single arch, bearing Latin inscriptions and decorated with military trophies and battle scenes. Porte St-Martin bears allegorical reliefs of some of Louis XIV's many campaigns.

Fbg-St-Denis to Gare du Nord

North of Porte St-Denis and Porte St-Martin, around two of Paris' oldest thoroughfares leading out of the city, the Fbg-St-Denis and Fbg-St-Martin, is an area transformed in the 19th century by the railways – and the two stations of Gare du Nord and Gare de l'Est. The grubby rue du Fbg-St-Denis is almost souk-like with its food shops, narrow passages and sinister courtyards, and pimps surveying the prostitutes hanging in doorways. Amid this, brasserie Julien (16 rue du Fbg-St-Denis, 10th, 01.47.70.12.06) boasts one of the finest art

Sightseeing

nouveau interiors in Paris. Garishly lit passage Brady is a surprising piece of India in Paris, full of restaurants, hairdressers and costume shops, while the art deco passage du Prado is more a continuation of the Sentier rag trade. The Fbg-St-Martin, which follows the trace of the Roman road out of the city, is full of children's clothes wholesalers, along with some atmospheric courtyards and the ornate Mairie for the 10th. Rue des Petites-Ecuries ('Little Stables Street') was once known for saddlers but now has shops, cafés and top jazz venue **New Morning** (*see p324*), and is home to large Afro-Caribbean and Turkish communities. On nearby alleyway Cour des Petites-Ecuries, the Brasserie Flo (No.7, 10th, 01.47.70.13.59) has the allure of an Alsatian tavern; rue de Paradis is known for its porcelain and glass outlets, and the Musée du Cristal has become the **Pinacothèque** art space (*see p169*). Rue d'Hauteville contains hints of the area's grander days, at No.58, not visible from the street, hides the **Petit Hôtel Bourrienne**, a small privately owned time capsule. Opposite, the Cité Paradis is an alleyway of early industrial buildings. At the top of the street, **Eglise St-Vincent de Paul** has twin towers and cascading terraced gardens, and is about as close as Paris gets to Rome's Spanish Steps. Behind, on rue de Belzunce, are modern bistro **Chez Michel** (*see p209*) and offshoot Chez Casimir (*see p197* **No such thing as a cheap lunch?**). Down on boulevard Magenta, the covered Marché St-Quentin, built in the 1860s, is one of the city's few remaining cast-iron, covered market halls.

Popular theatres such as the mosaic-filled neo-Renaissance Théâtre Antoine-Simone Berriau (No.14, 10th, 01.42.08.77.71) and the art deco Eldorado (No.4, 10th, 01.42.38.22.22) line up on boulevard de Strasbourg, cut through in the 19th century to create a vista up to the Gare de l'Est. At No.2, another neo-Renaissance creation houses Paris' last fan maker and the **Musée de l'Eventail** (*see p172*); towards the station, Eglise St-Laurent (69 bd de Magenta/119 rue du Fbg-St-Martin, 10th) is one of the city's oldest churches, an eclectic composition with 12th-century tower, Gothic nave, baroque lady chapel, 1930s stained glass and a 19th-century façade. Sandwiched between Gare de l'Est and **Canal St-Martin** (*see p121* **On the waterfront**) are the newly restored **Couvent des Récollets** and Square Villemin park.

Couvent des Récollets

148 rue du Faubourg-St-Martin, 10th. M° Gare de l'Est. **Map** p404 L3.
Founded as a Franciscan monastery in the 17th century when still outside city walls, this barracks, spinning factory and hospice then became a military

hospital between 1860 and 1968. Abandoned to dereliction, the convent was squatted by artists, les Anges des Récollets, at the start of the 1990s. The buildings were renovated and reopened in 2004. One half, the Maison des Architectes, has a café and a programme of architectural debates. The other half is the Centre International d'Accueil et d'Echanges des Récollets: 85 studios and duplexes for foreign 'creators' – artists and researchers (from painters to neurobiologists) – invited to stay here for extended periods. In rehabilitating the building, architect Frédéric Vincendon decided to leave traces of its checkered history, leaving a ghostly presence in 17th-century stonework, 20th-century reinforced concrete columns and squatters' graffiti.

Eglise St-Vincent de Paul

Pl Franz-Liszt, 10th (01.48.78.47.47). M° Gare du Nord. **Open** *Sept-June* 8am-noon, 2-7pm daily. *July, Aug* 8am-noon, 5-7pm Tue-Sun. **Map** p404 K2.
Set at the top of terraced gardens, this church was begun in 1824 by Lepère and completed 1831-44 by Hittorff. The twin towers, pedimented Greek temple portico and sculptures along the parapet of the four evangelists are in classical mode. The interior has a double-storey arcade of columns, murals by Flandrin, and church furniture by Rude.

Gare du Nord

Rue de Dunkerque, 10th (08.91.36.20.20). M° Gare du Nord. **Map** p404 K2.
The grandest of the great 19th-century train stations (and Eurostar terminal since 1994) was designed by Hittorff in 1861-64. A conventional stone façade, with Ionic capitals and statues representing towns served by the station, hides a vast, bravura iron-and-glass vault. Today, the impressively light and airy refurbishment of the suburban section bordering rue du Fbg-St-Denis makes the Eurostar's glass-topped digs look somewhat drab.

Petit Hôtel Bourrienne

58 rue d'Hauteville, 10th (01.47.70.51.14). M° Poissonnière. **Open** *Guided visits* 1-15 July, 1-30 Sept noon-6pm daily. Rest of year by appointment, Sat. **Admission** €6. **No credit cards.** **Map** p404 K3.
A rare example of the Consulaire style, this quite exceptional, small *hôtel particulier* was built by Célestin-Joseph Happé in 1789-98. From 1795-98 it was occupied by Fortunée Hamelin, born (like her friend the Empress Joséphine) in Martinique. She acquired notoriety for parading topless down the Champs-Elysées. A bedroom-boudoir painted with incredibly detailed tropical birds was all that was decorated for her, before the hôtel was taken over by Louis Fauvelet de Bourrienne, the private secretary of Napoleon. He decorated it according to the latest mode, making sure to keep his political options open (the dining room ceiling is painted with motifs favourable to both monarchy and empire). The two small wings overlooking the garden contain an Egyptian-style bathroom – where guests could be entertained – and a winter garden.

Les Halles & Sentier

In the 1st and 2nd districts.

In Zola's novel *Le Ventre de Paris*, Les Halles is an area groaning with food, swarming and seething with the Parisian populace. While Les Halles remains the belly of Paris, a geographic and symbolic centre, place of commerce and entertainment, with its daily discharge of some 800,000 people from its massive RER-Métro interchange it has become a place to avoid.

For centuries, Les Halles was the city's wholesale food market – covered markets were set up here in 1181 by King Philippe-Auguste. In the 1850s, Baltard's spectacular cast-iron and glass pavilions were erected, 'the lace of Vulcan' as Verlaine described them. In 1969 the market was relocated to the southern suburb of Rungis. Baltard's ten pavilions were knocked down, leaving a giant hole – rudely nicknamed 'le trou des Halles'. After a long political dispute it was filled in the early 1980s by the miserably designed **Forum des Halles** underground shopping and transport hub and the unloved (except by the homeless) Jardin des Halles. One market pavilion was saved and reconstructed at Nogent-sur-Marne.

The problem with what to do with a smelly, crime-ridden transport interchange and poorly conceived shopping mall is a political one. Mayor Bertrand Delanoë has asked four architects and planners to come up with proposals to improve Les Halles, to bring people back to the gardens, and a classier clientele to the shops and to combat the sense of insecurity. With only a loose brief and no definite budget – and the desire of locals to be consulted – it's going to be some time before any one scheme is ready to be put into action. *See pp33-35* **Delanoë's Dream**.

East of the Forum in the middle of place Joachim-du-Bellay stands the Renaissance Fontaine des Innocents. The canopied fountain has swirling stone reliefs of water nymphs and titans by Jean Goujon (the ones you see today are copies, the originals are in the Louvre). It was inaugurated for Henri II's arrival in Paris on 16 June 1549 on the traditional royal route along the rue St-Denis. It was moved and reconstructed here when the nearby Cimetière des Innocents, the city's main burial ground, was demolished in 1786 after flesh-eating rats started gnawing into people's living rooms, and the bones were transferred to the catacombs (*see p143* **The great escape**).

Pedestrianised rue des Lombards is a beacon for live jazz, with **Sunset/Sunside**, **Baiser Salé** and **Au Duc des Lombards** (for all, *see p325*). Nearby, King Henri IV was assassinated in 1610 by Catholic fanatic François Ravaillac on ancient rue de la Ferronnerie when the royal carriage was held up in the traffic. The street has now become an extension of the Marais gay circuit, so the only thing Henri would be held up for today is, perhaps, ridicule.

The ancient easternmost stretch of the rue St-Honoré runs into the southern edge of Les Halles. The Fontaine du Trahoir stands at the corner with rue de l'Arbre-Sec. Opposite, the superb Hôtel de Truden (52 rue de l'Arbre-Sec) was built in 1717 for a wealthy wine merchant; in the courtyard, a shop sells vintage magazines and newspapers, while on rue des Prouvaires, the old market-traders' haunt **La Tour de Montlhéry** (*see p192*) still serves up meaty fare all night long. Fashion chains line the commercial stretch of the rue de Rivoli south of Les Halles, as well as the daisy-bedecked façade of long-established, and now establishment, vibrant art squat Chez Robert Electron Libre. Running towards the Seine, ancient little streets such as rue des Lavandiers-Ste-Opportune and narrow rue Jean-Lantier show a human side of Les Halles that has yet to be swept away. Stretching between the rue de Rivoli and the Pont Neuf is **La Samaritaine** department store (*see p240*), metamorphosed from ugly ducking into serious splendid swan after a takeover by luxury conglomerate LVMH. It has a fantastic art nouveau staircase and glazed verrière, and the Toupary restaurant and

Châtelet. See p102.

tearoom at the top also offers great views. Next door, a former part of the store now contains the smart Kenzo flagship, spa and Philippe Starck-designed **Kong** restaurant and bar (*see p193 and p219*), offering more great views. From here the quai de la Mégisserie, thickly lined with horticultural suppliers and pet shops, leads towards **Châtelet** (*see p102*).

Looming over the northern edge of the Jardin des Halles is the massive **Eglise St-Eustache**, with Renaissance motifs inside and chunky flying buttresses without. At the western end of the gardens is the circular, domed **Bourse de Commerce**. In front of it, an astrological column is all that remains from a grand palace belonging to Marie de Médicis that once stood on this spot. Nearby, the delightfully dusty **E Dehillerin** (*see p274*) continues to supply colossal saucepans, knives and specialist implements to restaurants and regular clients.

The empire of **Agnès b** (*see p256*) stretches along most of rue du Jour, with streetwise outlets such as **Kiliwatch** (*see p259*) and **Diesel** (*see p257*) on rue Tiquetonne and rue Etienne-Marcel, getting progressively more upmarket towards the place des Victoires. The restored **Tour Jean Sans Peur** is a strange relic of the fortified medieval townhouse of Jean Sans Peur, Duc de Bourgogne.

If you're in the mood for food, head to buzzy, pedestrianised rue Montorgueil, lined with grocers, delicatessens and pavement cafés. Historic façades remain from when this was an area where the belle monde and the working class mingled: Pâtisserie Stohrer (No.51, 2nd, 01.42.33.38.20), founded in 1730 and credited with the invention of the sugary Puits d'Amour; Le Rocher de Cancale (No.78, 01.42.33.50.29) and back towards Les Halles, the golden snail sign hanging out in front of L'Escargot Montorgueil (No.38, 1st, 01.42.36.83.51). Glass-roofed passage du Grand-Cerf has been restored and is home to several design consultancies.

Stretching north of here, bordered by boulevard du Bonne-Nouvelle to the north and boulevard Sébastopol to the east, lies Sentier, the historic garment district, while cocky rue St-Denis has long relied on strumpets and strip joints. The tackiness is unremitting into its northern continuation of rue du Fbg-St-Denis, which snakes north from the Forum des Halles.

Rue Réaumur houses striking art nouveau buildings with metal structures constructed as industrial premises in the early 1900s. Between rue des Petits-Carreaux and rue St-Denis is the site of the medieval Cour des Miracles – a refuge where, after a day's begging, paupers would 'miraculously' regain use of their eyes or limbs. An abandoned aristocratic estate, it was a sanctuary for the underworld for decades until it was cleared out in 1667.

Sentier's surrounding maze of streets and passages throng with porters shouldering linen bundles, while sweatshops churn out copies of catwalk creations. No surprise that the area attracts hundreds of illegal and semi-legal foreign workers. Streets such as rue du Caire, d'Aboukir and du Nil, reflect the Egyptian craze following Napoleon's Egyptian campaign in 1798-99 – look out for the sphinxes heads and mock hieroglyphics on 2 place du Caire.

Bourse de Commerce

2 rue de Viarmes, 1st (01.55.65.78.41/tour booking 01.55.65.70.18). Mº Louvre Rivoli. **Open** *for tour groups* 9am-6pm Mon-Fri. **Admission** €42/tour group. **No credit cards. Map** p404 J5.
Housing offices of the Paris Chamber of Commerce, this trade centre for coffee and sugar was built as a grain market in 1767. The circular building was then covered by a wooden dome, damaged by fire and replaced by an avant-garde iron structure in 1809.Once covered in copper, now in glass, it is sadly underused; recent proposals have put forward the idea of a hotel, restaurant or museum.

Eglise St-Eustache

Rue du Jour, 1st (01.40.26.47.99/www.st-eustache. org). Mº Les Halles. **Open** 9am-7.30pm daily. **Map** p404 J5.

Baroque **Eglise St-Roch**. *See p91.*

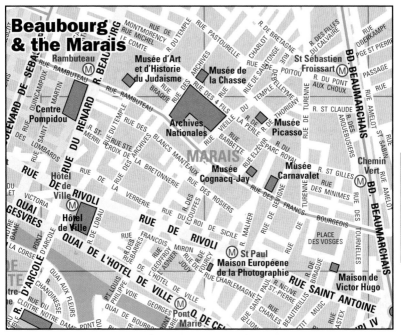

Beaubourg & the Marais

This massive barn-like church, built 1532-1640, has a Gothic structure but Renaissance decoration in its pedimented façade and Corinthian capitals. Among the paintings in the side chapels are a *Descent from the Cross* by Luca Giordano; contemporary pieces by John Armleder were added in 2000. Works by Thomas Couture adorn the 19th-century Lady Chapel. The church has a fine 8,000-pipe organ and gives free recitals at 5.30pm on Sundays.

Forum des Halles

1st. Mº Les Halles/RER Châtelet Les Halles. **Map** p404 J5.
The labyrinthine mall and transport interchange extends three levels underground and includes the Ciné Cité multiplex (www.ugc.fr), the Forum des Images (*see p299*) and a swimming pool (*see p340*), as well as mass-market clothing chains, branches of Darty, Fnac (*see p246*) and Muji, and the Forum des Créateurs, a section given over to young designers. Despite a tiered open central courtyard, an overall sense of cavernous gloom prevails. On Saturdays it is invaded by teenagers pouring in on the RER.

Tour Jean Sans Peur

20 rue Etienne-Marcel, 2nd (01.40.26.20.28/http:// tour.jeansanspeur.free.fr). Mº Etienne Marcel. **Open** *Term-time* 1.30-6pm Wed, Sat, Sun. *School hols* 1.30-6pm Tue-Sun. **Admission** €5; €3 7-18s, students; free under-7s. **Tour** 2pm; €8. **No credit cards.** Map p404 J5.

This Gothic turret (1409-11) is the remnant of the townhouse of Jean Sans Peur, Duc de Bourgogne. He got his nickname (the fearless) from his exploits in Bulgaria – but he was equally responsible for the assassination in 1407 of Louis d'Orléans, his rival and the cousin of Charles VI, which sparked the Hundred Years' War and saw Burgundy allied to the English crown. Jean fled Paris, but returned two years later to add this show-off tower to his mansion – it was also meant to protect him any vengeance on the part of the aggrieved widow of Louis d'Orléans. In 1419 he was assassinated by a partisan of the dauphin, the future Charles VII. Today you can climb the multi-storey tower, with various rooms leading off the stairway. Carved vaulting halfway up depicts naturalistic branches of oak, hawthorn and hops, symbols of Jean Sans Peur and Burgundian power. The huge mansion originally spanned Philippe-Auguste's city wall. The base of a turret is still concealed within.

Beaubourg & the Marais

In the 3rd and 4th districts.
Between boulevard Sébastopol and the Bastille are Beaubourg – site of the **Centre Pompidou** since 1977 – and the Marais, largely built between the 16th and 18th centuries and now jam-packed with boutiques, museums and bars.

Renzo and Rogers' iconic **Centre Pompidou**. *See p103.*

Beaubourg & Hôtel de Ville

Contemporary Parisian architecture began with the Centre Pompidou, designed by Richard Rogers and Renzo Piano, and this international benchmark of inside-out high-tech is as much of an attraction as its contents, which include the **Musée National de l'Art Moderne** (*see p162*). The piazza outside attracts a motley crew of street performers and pavement artists, while on one side the reconstructed **Atelier Brancusi** (*see p164*), the sculptor's studio which he left to the state, was moved here from the 15th district. On the other side of the piazza is rue Quincampoix with its galleries, bars and cobbled passage Molière with its old shopfronts and the Théâtre Molière (01.44.54.53.00). Beside the Centre Pompidou is place Igor Stravinsky and the funky Fontaine Stravinsky, full of splashing, spraying kinetic fountains, including a colourful snake by the late artists Nikki de St-Phalle and Jean Tinguély, and the red-brick **IRCAM** music institute (*see p316*), also designed by Renzo Piano.

The church of St-Merri (78 rue St-Martin, 4th, 01.42.71.40.75), which has a Flamboyant Gothic façade complete with an androgynous demon leering over the doorway, sits on the south side of the square. Inside are a carved wooden organ loft, the joint contender (along with **Eglise St-Séverin**; *see p125*) for the oldest bell in Paris (1331), and 16th-century stained glass.

South of here stands the spiky Gothic **Tour St-Jacques**. Towards the river, on the site of the Grand Châtelet, a fortress put up in the 12th century to defend Pont au Change bridge, place du Châtelet features an Egyptian-themed fountain in the middle framed on each side by twin theatres designed by Davioud as part of Haussmann's urban improvements in the 1860s. They are now two of the city's leading arts venues: the **Théâtre de la Ville** (*see p318 and p344*); and **Théâtre du Châtelet** (*see p295 and p316*), an opera and concert hall.

Beyond Châtelet, the **Hôtel de Ville**, the City Hall and home to the mayor, has been the symbol of municipal power since 1260. The equestrian statue on the embankment in front of the building is of 14th-century merchant leader and rebel, Etienne Marcel. Subsequent revolutionaries made it their base in the 1871 Commune, but the building was set on fire by the Communards themselves and wrecked during savage fighting. (*See p21* **1871**.) It was rebuilt according to the original model, on a bigger scale in fanciful neo-Renaissance style with knights in armour along the roofline and statues of French luminaries from Didot to Corot dotted all over the walls. The square outside was formerly called place de Grève, after the nearby riverside wharf on which goods were unloaded for market. *Grève* has come to be the French word for 'strike', thanks to the numerous demonstrations and protests that gathered here. Protestant heretics were burnt in the square during the 16th-century Wars of Religion, and the dreadful guillotine stood here during the Terror, when Danton, Marat and Robespierre made the Hôtel de Ville their seat of government. Today the square is used for outdoor events such as an ice rink in December for Paris sur glace (*see p282*) and screenings of major sports events. Just across the road stands the popular Bazar de l'Hôtel de Ville department store, or **BHV** (*see p240*).

Centre Pompidou

Rue Beaubourg, 4th (01.44.78.12.33/www.centre pompidou.fr). M° Hôtel de Ville or Rambuteau. **Open** 11am-9pm Mon, Wed-Sun. **Admission** *Museum €7; €5 students; free under-18s. Exhibitions* vary. **Credit** AmEx, DC, MC, V. **Map** p404 K5/K6.
The primary colours, exposed pipes and air ducts make this one of the most well-known sights in Paris. The then unknown Italo-British architectural duo of Renzo Piano and Richard Rogers won the competition with their 'inside-out' boilerhouse approach, which put air-conditioning, pipes, lifts and the escalators on the outside, leaving an adaptable space within. The multi-disciplinary concept of modern art museum (the most important in Europe), library, exhibition and performance spaces and repertory cinema was also revolutionary. When it opened in 1977, its success exceeded all expecta-tions. After a two-year revamp the centre reopened in January 2000 with an enlarged museum, renewed performance spaces, vista-rich Georges restaurant and a mission to get back to the stimulating inter-disciplinary mix of old. Entrance to the forum is free (as is the library which has a separate entrance), but you now have to pay to go up the escalators.

Hôtel de Ville

29 rue de Rivoli, 4th (01.42.76.43.43/www.paris.fr). M° Hôtel de Ville. **Open** 9.30am-7pm Mon-Sat. **Map** p408 K6.
Rebuilt by Ballu after the Commune, the palatial, multi-purpose Hôtel de Ville is both the heart of the city administration and a place to entertain visiting dignitaries. Small exhibitions are held in the Salon d'accueil, the rest of the building accessible only by guided tour (weekly – book in advance) is awash with parquet floors, marble statues, crystal chande-liers and allegorical painted ceilings. Mayor Delanoë himself prefers to live in a dinky, bijou pad in the Marais rather than in the lofty apartment here.

Tour St-Jacques

Square de La-Tour-St-Jacques, 4th. M° Châtelet. **Map** p408 J6.
Loved by the Surrealists, this solitary Flamboyant Gothic belltower with its leering gargoyles is all that remains of the St-Jacques-La-Boucherie church, built for the powerful Butchers' Guild in 1508-22. The statue of Blaise Pascal at the base commemorates his experiments on atmospheric pressure carried out here in the 17th century. A weather station now crowns the 52m tower, not open to the public.

The Marais

The Marais, a bewitching area whose narrow streets are dotted with aristocratic *hôtels particuliers*, art galleries, fashion boutiques and stylish cafés, lies east of Roman rue St-Martin and rue du Renard. While browsing, take the time to look up at the beautiful carved doorways and the early street signs carved into the stone. The Marais, or 'marsh', started life as a piece of swampy ground inhabited by a few monasteries, sheep and market gardens. This was one of the last parts of central Paris to be built up. In the 16th century the elegant Hôtel Carnavalet and Hôtel Lamoignon saw the start of the area's phenomenal rise as an aristocratic residential district; Henri IV began building the **place des Vosges** in 1605. Nobles and royal officials followed, building smart townhouses where famous literary ladies such as Mme de Sévigné and Mlle de Scudéry and influential courtesan Ninon de l'Enclos held court. The area fell from fashion a century later; happily, many of the narrow streets were essentially unchanged as mansions were transformed into industrial workshops, crafts studios, schools and tenements, and even the fire station on rue de Sévigné. Several can be visited as museums, others can be seen only on walking tours or on the **Journées du Patrimoine** (*see p282*). The Marais is a favourite spot for a Sunday stroll, as many of the shops are open, though if you come during the week you have more chance of wandering into some of the elegant courtyards.
Rue des Francs-Bourgeois, crammed with impressive mansions and original boutiques, runs like a backbone right through the Marais, becoming more aristocratic as it leaves the foodshops of rue Rambuteau behind. Two of the most refined early 18th-century residences are Hôtel d'Albret (No.31), a venue for jazz concerts at the **Paris quartier d'été** festival (*see p281*), and the palatial Hôtel de Soubise (No.60), the national archives. Begun in 1704 for the Prince and Princesse de Soubise, interiors by Boucher and Lemoine can be seen as part of the **Musée de l'Histoire de France** (*see p177*), along with the neighbouring Hôtel de Rohan, and a surprising series of rose gardens. On one side of its grandiose, colonnaded Cour d'Honneur, architect Delamair incorporated the turreted, fortified medieval gateway of the Hôtel de Clisson visible on rue des Archives. Facing the Archives Nationaux, the Crédit municipal (No.55), successor of the historic Mont de Piété founded by Louis XVI in 1777, still acts as a sort of municipal pawnshop: people bring in valuables in exchange for cash; items never reclaimed are sold off at auction. Just beyond, by the Centre Culturel Suisse (No.38), an

alleyway with overhanging houses is typical of the little lanes that once ran between the mansions, and still has its central gutter and stone bollards down the side. On the corner of rue Pavée is the austere Renaissance Hôtel Lamoignon, with a magisterial courtyard adorned with giant Corinthian pilasters. Built in 1585 for Diane de France, Henri II's illegitimate daughter, it houses the Bibliothèque Historique de la Ville de Paris (No.24, 4th, 01.44.59.29.40).

Further along the **Musée Carnavalet** (*see p176*), dedicated to the history of Paris, runs across the Hôtel Carnavalet and the later Hôtel le Peletier de St-Fargeau. One of the finest houses in the Marais, the Hôtel Carnavalet set the pattern for many of the *hôtels* to follow with its U-shaped plan behind an entrance courtyard; the reliefs of the four seasons on the façade are possibly by Jean Goujon. It was once home to famous letter-writer Mme de Sévigné.

At its eastern end, rue des Francs-Bourgeois leads into the beautiful brick-and-stone place des Vosges. At one corner is the **Maison de Victor Hugo** (*see p178*), where the writer lived from 1833 to 1848, and across the square is the luxurious Ambroisie restaurant (No.9, 4th, 01.42.78.51.45). An archway in the south-west corner leads to the Hôtel de Sully, now housing the **Patrimoine Photographique** (*see p179 and p170* **Capturing defining moments**). Designed in 1624, it belonged to Henri IV's minister the Duc de Sully. Its two beautifully proportioned courtyards contain reliefs of the four seasons and a rare, surviving orangery.

Several other important museums are also in sumptuous *hôtels*. The Hôtel Salé on rue de Thorigny, built in 1656, was nicknamed ('salty') after its owner, Fontenay, who collected the salt tax. It was beautifully restored and extended in the 1980s to house the **Musée National Picasso** (*see p166*); it has an elegant semi-circular courtyard adorned by sphinxes and a grand baroque stairwell carved with garlands, imperial busts and gambolling cupids. Nearby, the pretty Hôtel Donon, built in 1598 for the royal building inspector, contains the **Musée Cognacq-Jay** (*see p163*) and has remarkable 18th-century panelled interiors (both its own and those brought here from other mansions), while the Hôtel Guénégaud, attributed to François Mansart for its harmonious proportions and sobriety, contains the eclectic collection of the **Musée de la Chasse et de la Nature** hunting museum (*see p176*).

The Marais has also long been a focus for the city's Jewish community. Jews were expelled from France in the Middle Ages, but when they were granted citizenship after the Revolution, the Marais became the natural point of arrival. The community today is centred on rue des Rosiers, rue des Ecouffes and rue Pavée (where there's a synagogue designed by Guimard). Originally made up mainly of Ashkenazi Jews who arrived after the pogroms in Eastern Europe at the end of the 19th century (many were later deported during World War II), the community expanded in the 1950s and '60s with a wave of Sephardic Jewish immigration following French withdrawal from North Africa. As a result, there are now many falafel shops alongside Central European Jewish bakers and delis, such as **Finkelstajn** (*see p268*) and late-opening Jo Goldenberg (7 rue des Rosiers, 4th, 01.48.87.20.16).

The lower ends of rue des Archives and rue Vieille-du-Temple are the centre of café life – including **Petit Fer à Cheval** (*see p229*) and La Chaise au Plafond in the neighbouring rue du Trésor (No.10, 4th, 01.42.76.03.22) – and the hub of the gay scene. Gay bars such as **Open Café** (*see p309*) draw merry crowds for the early-evening happy hour. In their midst at Nos.22-26 rue des Archives, the 15th-century Cloître des Billettes is the only surviving Gothic cloister in Paris.

Workaday rue du Temple, once the road leading to the Templars' church, is full of surprises. Near rue de Rivoli, the **Latina** (*see p301*) specialises in Latin American films and holds tango balls in the room above. At No.41, an archway leads into the former Aigle d'Or coaching inn, now the **Café de la Gare** café-théâtre (*see p286*). Further north, at No.71, the grandiose Hôtel de St-Aignan, built in 1650 for the Conte d'Avaux, contains the **Musée d'Art et d'Histoire du Judaïsme** (*see p176*). A truly majestic courtyard, with giant Corinthian pilasters and carved armorial, the oval galleried staircase and traces of fresco in the café hint at just how splendid this must have been before it was converted into a town hall, workshops and a warren of apartments before being rescued in the 1990s. The top end of rue du Temple and adjoining streets such as rue des Gravilliers are packed with costume jewellery, handbag and rag-trade wholesalers in what is the city's oldest Chinatown. The Quartier du Temple was once a fortified, semi-independent entity under the Knights Templar, until the order grew so powerful it rivalled the monarchy and it was suppressed in 1313 by Philippe le Bel. Their Tour du Temple, a monastery under the Knights Hospitalier de St-Jean, became a prison in the Revolution, where the royal family was held in 1792. The round church and keep have been replaced by Square du Temple and the Carreau du Temple clothes market.

The north-west corner of the Marais hinges on the **Musée des Arts et Métiers** (*see p180*), a science museum with early flying

Hidden Paris Behind closed doors

As people head for one of the many cafés along the Marais' main rue Vielle-du-Temple, few catch sight of the terrifying medusa heads on the heavy doors of No.47. They date from the 1660s, when the Hôtel Amelot de Bisseuil was built – but they are also rather fitting for the skullduggery that went on behind them when it was home of Pierre-Augustin Caron de Beaumarchais a century later. The son of a watchmaker who bought his own title, this playwright, socialite and secret agent would hobnob with thespians at the Comédie-Française while arms dealing for a king who never quite knew whose side he was on. (As an aside, Beaumarchais ran a campaign to encourage breastfeeding.)

It was at this house that Beaumarchais wrote his play *The Marriage of Figaro*, suppressed for its radical ideas, and the source of the libretto of Mozart's opera. He used the address to establish a fake import-export company, Rodrigue Hortalez et Cie, as a cover for shipping arms to American insurgents against the English. Over the door is a portico featuring the initials BA (Amelot de Bisseuil) flanked by goddesses; on the other side, Romulus and Remus. If you get a chance to look in don't miss the sundials in the first courtyard and the wall with theatrical motifs in the second. The hôtel is open during the **Journées du Patrimoine** (*see p282*).

machines displayed in the 12th-century chapel of the former priory of St-Martin-des-Champs, and the adjoining Conservatoire des Arts et Métiers. Across rue St-Martin on square Emile-Chautemps, after a brief, disastrous interlude as a theme park, the Théâtre de la Gaîté Lyrique, which once premiered operettas by Offenbach, is to be renovated as a cultural centre. There are many ancient streets around here, although No.3 rue Volta, long considered to be the oldest house in Paris, is now believed to be merely a bit of retro design, dating from the early 17th-century in disobedience to the laws againt half-timbered structures; a much older house is the Auberge de Nicolas Flamel at No.51 rue de Montmorency built in 1407 by notorious alchemist Nicolas Flamel. He probably never lived here himself but rented out the ground floor workshop (now a restaurant) and lodged the poor for free upstairs.

Despite the Marais' rise to fashion, the less-gentrified streets around the northern stretch of rue Vieille-du-Temple towards place de la République is awash with tiny local bars, designers on the rise and old craft workshops. Some of the city's best contemporary art galleries such as **Yvon Lambert** (*see p305*) hide in elegant *hôtels particuliers*. Amid the foodshops of rue de Bretagne is fashionable couscous stalwart **Chez Omar** (*see p207*) and the renovated Marché des Enfants-Rouges, one of the city's oldest markets founded in 1615, also once a red-uniformed orphanage.

Place des Vosges
4th. M° St-Paul. **Map** p408 L6.
The first planned square in Paris (along with its contemporary place Dauphine) was commissioned in 1605 by Henri IV and inaugurated by his son Louis XIII in 1612. Intimate, with harmonious red-brick-and-stone arcaded façades and steeply pitched slate roofs, it is quite distinct from the pomp of later Bourbon Paris. Laid out on a symmetrical plan with carriageways through the taller Pavillon de la Reine on the north side and Pavillon du Roi on the south, the other lots were sold off as concessions to royal officials and nobles (note that some façades are imi-

Place des Vosges. See p105.

renovated and given a minimalist modern extension as the **Maison Européenne de la Photographie** (*see p179 and p170* **Capturing defining moments**). Down rue de Fourcy towards the river across a medieval formal garden you can see the rear façade of the Hôtel de Sens, a rare medieval mansion built as the Paris residence of the Archbishops of Sens at the end of the 15th century, with a picturesque array of turrets. It houses the **Bibliothèque Forney** (*see p167*), specialising in posters, postcards and exhibitions about graphic design.

Across from the tip of the Ile St-Louis near Pont Sully, are the square Henri-Galli, with a rebuilt fragment of Bastille prison, and the **Pavillon de l'Arsenal** (*see p171*), built by a rich timber merchant to put on art shows, and home to displays about Parisian architecture.

Winding rue François-Miron winds back towards the Hôtel de Ville. At 17 rue Geoffroy l'Asnier, the Mémorial du Martyr Juif Inconnu is currently being extended as the **Mémorial du Shoah**, museum, memorial and study centre devoted to the Holocaust, due to open in January 2005 (*see p178*); note also the Cité des Arts complex of artists' studios, and the ornate lion's head and giant shell motif on the doorway of 17th-century Hôtel de Châlon-Luxembourg at No.26. At 11 and 13 rue François-Miron, two wonky half-timbered houses are probably rare 14th-century structures, though heavily rebuilt in the 1960s. Rue du Pont-Louis-Philippe has arty jewellers, paper shops, and the designer furniture and gifts of **Galerie Sentou** (*see p274*), while stepped rue des Barres is tearoom territory, overlooking the spiky chevet of the Eglise St-Gervais-St-Protais.

tation brick). Originally called place Royale, its name dates from the Napoleonic Wars, when the Vosges was the first region of France to pay its war taxes. Mme de Sévigné, salon hostess and letter-writer, was born at No.1bis in 1626. At that time the garden was the scene of duels and trysts; now it attracts children from the nearby nursery school.

The St-Paul district

In 1559, Henri II was mortally wounded in a jousting tournament on today's rue St-Antoine; he is commemorated by the marble *La Vierge de Douleur* by Pilon in the **Eglise St-Paul-St-Louis**. South of rue St-Antoine is the sedate residential area of St-Paul, though still lined with dignified 17th- and 18th-century façades. The Village St-Paul, a colony of antique sellers, spread over small, linked courtyards between rue St-Paul, rue Charlemagne and quai des Célestins, is a promising source of 1930s and '50s furniture, kitchenware and wine gadgets (open Mon, Thur-Sun). Over on rue des Jardins-St-Paul is the largest surviving section of the fortified wall of Philippe-Auguste. The infamous poisoner Marquise de Brinvilliers lived at Hôtel de Brinvilliers (12 rue Charles-V) in the 1630s. She killed her father and brothers to inherit the family fortune and was only caught after her lover died – of natural causes.

By St-Paul Métro station on the corner of rue François-Miron and rue de Fourcy is another fine mansion, the Hôtel Hénault de Cantorbe,

Eglise St-Gervais-St-Protais

Place St-Gervais, 4th (01.48.87.32.02). M° Hôtel de Ville. **Open** varies. **Map** p408 K6.
Gothic at the rear, classical at the front (the west front is now attributed to Salomon de Brosse, the architect of the Palais de Luxembourg), most of the impressive Flamboyant Gothic interior dates from the 16th century. The nave gives an impression of enormous height with tall columns without capitals that soar up to the vault. There are plenty of fine funerary monuments dotted about, especially the baroque statue of chancellor Le Tellier reclining on a marble sarcophagus. The Couperin family were organists here for generations.

Eglise St-Paul-St-Louis

99 rue St-Antoine, 4th (01.42.72.30.32). M° Bastille or St-Paul. **Open** 9am-8pm Mon-Sat; 9-8.30pm Sun. **Map** p408 L6.
This domed baroque Counter-Reformation church, is modelled, like all Jesuit churches, on the Gesù in Rome. Completed in 1641, it has a single nave, side chapels and a three-storey hierarchical façade with

(replacement) statues of Saints Louis, Anne and Catherine. The provider of confessors to the Kings of France, it was richly endowed until Revolutionary iconoclasts broke into it and stole its treasures, including the hearts of Louis XIII and XIV. In 1802 it again became a church and houses Delacroix's *Christ in the Garden of Olives*.

Fortified wall of Philippe-Auguste

Rue des Jardins-St-Paul, 4th (www.philippe-auguste. com). M° Pont Marie or St-Paul. **Map** p408 L7.
King Philippe-Auguste (1165-1223), the first great Parisian builder since the Romans, enclosed his city within a great wall. The largest surviving section, complete with towers, extends along rue des Jardins-St-Paul. Another chunk is at 3 rue Clovis (5th) and odd remnants of towers are dotted around the Marais, rue du Louvre and St-Germain-des-Prés.

Bastille & eastern Paris

Mainly in the 11th and 12th districts.
Place de la Bastille, traditionally the frontier between central Paris and the more proletarian east, has remained a potent symbol of popular revolt ever since the prison-storming that inaugurated the Revolution. *See p14* **1789**.
While the square is still a favourite gathering point for demonstrations, and setting for the big Bastille Day ball every July (*see p281*), the area has been transformed since the 1980s with the arrival of the **Opéra Bastille** (*see p318*), and trendy cafés, restaurants and bars. The site of the prison itself is now a Société Générale bank while the gap left by the castle ramparts forms the present-day square, dominated by the massive, curved façade of the Opéra. Opened in 1989 on the bicentennial of Bastille Day, it remains controversial, criticised for its poor acoustics and construction – but productions usually sell out. South of the square is the Port de l'Arsenal marina, while north of the square, the canal (*see p121* **On the waterfront**) continues underground, beneath the broad boulevard Richard-Lenoir, site of a long outdoor market on Sunday mornings.

Rue du Faubourg-St-Antoine has been the heart of the furniture makers' district for centuries. Some gaudy furniture showrooms still line the street, but it is increasingly being colonised by clothes shops and bars, including the popular salsa-themed Barrio Latino (Nos. 46-48, 12th, 01.55.78.84.75), and you can't help but feel a twinge of regret for when the last Louis XVI chair or nubian slave candelabra finally disappears. The cobbled rue de Lappe typifies the Bastille's seismic shift, as the last remaining furniture workshops, the 1930s Balajo dance hall (No.9, 11th, 01.47.00.07.87), old Auvergnat bistro La Galoche d'Aurillac (No.41, 11th, 01.47.00.77.15) and grocer Chez

Teil (No.6, 11th, 01.47.00.41.28) hold out against gift shops and theme bars that teem with teens at weekends. Pockets of arty resistance remain on rue de Charonne with the hip Pause Café (No.41, 11th, 01.48.06.80.33) and its busy terrace, old-style bistro **Chez Paul** (*see p211*), art nouveau Bistro du Peintre (116 av Ledru-Rollin, 11th, 01.47.00.34.39) and dealers in colourful '60s furniture. On rue des Taillandiers and rue Keller, the patch is a focus for record shops, streetwear boutiques and, increasingly, young fashion designers.

The main thoroughfares reveal only half the story. Narrow street frontages hide cobbled alleys, lined with craftsmen's workshops or quirky bars and bistros dating from the 18th century. Peruse the cours de l'Ours, du Cheval Blanc, du Bel Air (with hidden garden) and de la Maison Brûlée, the passage du Chantier on Fbg-St-Antoine, the rustic-looking passage de l'Etoile d'Or and the passage de l'Homme with old wooden shop fronts on rue de Charonne. This area was originally outside the city walls on the lands of the Convent of St-Antoine (parts of which survive as the Hôpital St-Antoine). In the Middle Ages skilled furniture makers not belonging to the city's restrictive guilds began a tradition of free-thinking, a development which made this an incendiary area during the 1789 Revolution. *See p109* **Crafty passages**.

Further down rue du Fbg-St-Antoine is place d'Aligre, home to a rowdy North African vegetable market (the cheapest in Paris), a more sedate covered market (*see p267* **Market forces**) and the only fleamarket within the city walls (*see p273* **Hunt the heirloom**), where a handful of *brocanteurs* sell junk and old books and prints for high prices. Marketeers and locals meet on Sunday mornings at the Baron Bouge wine bar (*see p227* **Vintage venues**), where you can take your container to fill up from a cheap barrel wine. The road ends in the major intersection place de la Nation, another grand square. Originally called place du Trône, after a throne that was placed here when Louis XIV and his bride Marie-Thérèse entered the city here in 1660. During the bloody aftermath of the Revolution, the guillotine was moved here and thousands were guillotined between 13 June and 28 July 1799, the bodies carted to nearby **Picpus Cemetery** (*see p109*). The square still has two of Ledoux's toll houses and tall Doric columns from the 1787 Mur des Fermiers-Généraux. Right in the centre stands Jules Dalou's rather grandiose allegorical bronze sculpture, *Le Triomphe de la République*, erected for the centenary of the Revolution in 1889. East of Nation, broad Cours de Vincennes has a busy street market on Wednesday and Saturday mornings and kerb crawlers by night.

Place de la Bastille.

North of place de la Bastille, boulevard
Beaumarchais separates rowdy Bastille from
the elegant Marais, and the polygonal **Cirque
d'Hiver** winter circus (*see p286*), designed by
Hittorff in 1852. East of place Voltaire, on rue de
la Roquette, which heads eastwards towards
Ménilmontant (*see p120*) and the cemetery of
Père-Lachaise (*see p123*), a small park and
playground surrounded by modern housing
marks the site of the prison de la Roquette,
where a plaque remembers the 4,000 Resistance
members imprisoned here in World War II.

Place de la Bastille

4th/11th/12th. Mº Bastille. Map p409 M7.
Nothing remains of the prison which, on 14 July
1789, was stormed by the forces of the plebeian
revolt. Though only seven prisoners remained, the
event provided the rebels with arms and gave the
insurrection momentum. It remains the eternal
symbol of the Revolution, celebrated with a lively
street ball here every 13 July. The prison itself was
quickly torn down, its stones used to build Pont de
la Concorde. Vestiges of the foundations can be seen
in the Métro; there's part of a reconstructed tower at
square Henri-Galli, near Pont de Sully (4th). The
Colonne de Juillet, topped by a gilded *génie* of
Liberty, is a monument to Parisians who fell in the
revolutions of July 1830 and 1848.

Bercy & Daumesnil

The **Viaduc des Arts** is the former Paris-
Vincennes railway viaduct along avenue
Daumesnil, whose glass-fronted arches now
showcase a gentrified a row of craft and design
boutiques and workshops. Atop the viaduct, old
ladies admire the blooms among the bamboo of
the **Promenade Plantée**, which continues
through the Jardin de Reuilly and east to the
Bois de Vincennes. Further along, amid its
comfortable residential blocks, avenue
Daumesnil is fast becoming a Silicon Valley
of computer outlets.

Eglise du St-Esprit is a curious 1920s
concrete copy of Istanbul's Hagia Sofia, while
nearby **Cimetière de Picpus** contains the
graves of many of the Terror's victims, as well
as American War of Independence hero General
La Fayette. Just before the Périphérique, the
fabulous **Palais de la Porte Dorée** (*see
p170*) was built in 1931 for the Exposition
Coloniale with striking, if politically incorrect,
reliefs on the façade and two fabulous art deco
offices designed by Ruhlmann. Originally the
Musée des Colonies, then the Musée des Arts
d'Afrique et d'Océanie (now in storage as the
basis of the future Musée du Quai Branly),
it is currently being used for design exhibitions,
but still has a popular aquarium complete with
crocodiles in the basement (*see p292*).

As recently as the 1980s, wine was still
unloaded off barges at Bercy but now this
stretch of the Seine is firmly part of redeveloped
Paris with the massive Ministère de l'Economie
et du Budget and to the west the peculiar grass-
covered pyramid of the **Palais Omnisports
de Paris-Bercy**, a rock (*see p320*) as well as
sports venue (*see p333*). To the east is the Bercy
Expo exhibition and trade centre. Between the
two lie the modern **Parc de Bercy** and the
former American Center, built in the early 1990s
by Frank Gehry, thus predating his Bilbao
Guggenheim. It is currently being prepared for
its new tenant, the **Cinémathèque Française**
(*see p298*). At the eastern edge of the park, in
contrast to the modern **Ciné Cité** multiplex
(*see p298*), is **Bercy Village** (*see p291* **From
waste ground to playground**). Forty-two
stone wine warehouses have been restored and
opened as shops, wine bars and cafés on either
side of a cobbled street, the Cour St-Emilon; the
result is lively, if somewhat antiseptic. Typical
is **Club Med World** (*see p332*), whose themed
bars and juggling barmen evoke a holiday

resort. Another group has been converted as the Pavillons de Bercy, with the **Musée des Arts Forains** (*see p182*), a collection of fairground rides and Venetian carnival salons.

Bois de Vincennes

12th. M° Porte-Dorée or Château de Vincennes.

This is Paris's biggest park created, like the Bois de Boulogne in the west, when former royal hunting forest was landscaped by Alphand for Baron Haussmann. As well as lawns and woodland, there are cycle paths, four lakes, picnic areas, a Buddhist temple, a racetrack (*see p335* **A day at the races**), restaurants, a baseball field (*see p336*) and a small farm. It also contains the city's main zoo (*see p292*), now largely closed because of lack of maintenance, though the rugged fake mountains look impressive against the skyline, and the Cartoucherie theatre complex (*see p342* **Five go down to the woods**). Boats can be hired out on Lake Daumesnil. The Parc Floral (*see p289*), something between a botanical garden and an amusement park, was laid out in a modern style in 1969, with mock hills, brick turrets, a spiral lake, an iris mound, pine trees and a bonsai garden. A first-rate programme of jazz (*see p324*) and classical concerts takes place on lazy summer weekends by the lake. Dotted around are unusual amusements such as Paris-themed crazy golf, with the water drained from the Seine. Next to the park stands the imposing Château de Vincennes, where England's Henry V died in 1422.

Cimetière de Picpus

35 rue de Picpus, 12th (01.43.44.18.54). M° Nation or Daumesnil or Picpus. **Open** 15 Apr-14 Oct 2-6pm Tue-Sun; 15 Oct-14 Apr 2-4pm Tue-Sun. **Admission** €2.50. **No credit cards. Map** p409 Q8.

Redolent with revolutionary associations, both French and US, this cemetery in a working convent is the resting place for the thousands of victims of the Revolutionary aftermath, guillotined at place du Trône (now place de l'Ile de Réunion) between 14 June and 27 July 1794. At the end of a walled garden is a graveyard of aristocratic French families. In one corner is the tomb of General La Fayette, who fought in the American War of Independence and was married to one of the aristocratic Noailles. Clearly marked are the sites of two communal graves and you can discern the doorway where the carts arrived. It was only thanks to a maid who had seen the carts that the site was rediscovered – plus the cemetery and adjoining convent founded by the descendents of the Noailles family. In the chapel, two tablets on either end of the transept list the names and occupation of the executed: 'domestic', 'farmer' and 'employee' figure alongside 'lawyer', 'abbess' and 'prince and priest'.

Eglise du St-Esprit

186 av Daumesnil, 12th (01.44.75.77.50). M° Daumesnil. **Open** 9.30am-noon, 3-7pm Mon-Fri; 9.30am-noon, 3-6pm Sat. **Map** p409 P9.

Behind a red-brick exterior cladding, this unusual 1920s concrete church follows a square plan around a central dome, lit by a scalloped ring of windows. Architect Paul Tournon was directly inspired by the Hagia Sofia cathedral in Istanbul, though rather than mosaics, the inside is decorated with frescos by Maurice Denis and others.

Parc de Bercy

Rue de Bercy, 12th. M° Bercy or Cour St-Emilion. **Open** from 8am Mon-Fri; from 9am Sat, Sun. Closing times vary. **Map** p409 N9/10.

Hidden Paris Crafty passages

Running east of Bastille, the rue du Fbg-St-Antoine contains the bland commerce of Habitat, Monoprix, showrooms selling life-size ceramic cheetahs – and the vestiges of a dying art. Look down one of the ivy-clad passages running off it and you may glimpse the last *ébénistes* of the Faubourg, who work in tiny ateliers using marquetry, carpentry, varnishing and gilding techniques unchanged for 500 years or more.

The tradition dates back to Louis XI, who gave craftsmen working outside the city limits freedom from the restrictions of the guilds. The result was a rich flowering of French craftsmanship which reached its zenith in the reigns of Louis XIV and XVI – but also the radicalism that led the insurgents of the Faubourg St-Antoine to storm the Bastille and lose so many of their best clients to the

guillotine. The curious names of today's passages recall the old tradesmen's signs: cour de l'Etoile-d'Or, cour de l'Ours, cour de la Maison-Brûlée, passage de la Boule-Blanche and passage de la Main-d'Or.

Rising rents have seen many craftsmen leave, but those who remain congregate in the wonderful ironmonger's at No.151, where Arlette recounts the gossip and chain-smokes amid thousands of brass doorknobs. Down the passage at No.155 Spaniard José Sevilla works with an apprentice restoring carved wood chair legs and frames, while at No.179 Alain Foisy restores Louis XVI furniture and Gérard Brucato is the last hand wood turner in Paris. The workmen don't always welcome chatty visitors, but take a peek nevertheless. When it's all film production offices and loft conversations it will all be too late.

Created in the 1990s, the Bercy park combines the French love of geometry with that of food. There are a large lawn and a grid with square rose, herb and vegetable plots, an orchard and gardens laid out to represent the four seasons.

La Promenade Plantée

Av Daumesnil, 12th. M° Ledru-Rollin or Gare de Lyon. **Map** p409 M8/N8.
The railway tracks atop the Viaduc des Arts have been replaced by a promenade planted with roses, shrubs and rosemary, offering a high-level view into Parisian lives. It continues at ground level through the Jardin de Reuilly and the Jardin Charles Péguy on to the Bois de Vincennes in the east. Rollerbladers are banned, but no one seems to have noticed.

Le Viaduc des Arts

15-121 av Daumesnil, 12th (www.viaduc-des-arts.com). M° Ledru-Rollin or Gare de Lyon. **Map** p409 M8/N8.
Glass-fronted workshops poke out from the arches beneath the Promenade Plantée, providing a showroom for craftspeople, including furniture and fashion designers, picture frame gilders, tapestry restorers, porcelain decorators, and chandelier, violin and flute makers. There's the late-opening Viaduc Café too. Design industry body VIA puts on exhibitions of contemporary work at Nos.29-35.

The Champs-Elysées & western Paris

In the 8th, 16th and 17th districts.
While the 'Elysian Fields' can be a letdown on first, tourist-filled sight, the avenue remains the symbolic gathering place of a nation for sports victories, New Year's Eve and displays of military might on July 14. At night, the head and tail lights of ten lanes of honking traffic form a continuous red and a white ribbon.

Over the past decade, the Champs-Elysées has undergone a renaissance, thanks initially to the facelift – underground car parks and granite paving – instigated by Jacques Chirac. Chi-chi shops and chic hotels have set up in the 'golden triangle' (avenues George-V, Montaigne and the Champs), including **Louis Vuitton** (*see p255*), **Chanel** (*see p254*), **Jean-Paul Gaultier** (*see p254*), **Ladurée** tearoom (*see p223*), **Marriott** (70 av des Champs-Elysées, 8th, 01.53.93.55.00) and **Pershing Hall** (*see p59*) hotels. The **Four Seasons George V** (*see p57*) has enjoyed a revamp, while smart restaurants such as Spoon, Food & Wine (14 rue de Marignan, 8th, 01.40.76.34.44) and Senso (16 rue de la Trémoille, 8th, 01.56.52.14.14), and nightspots like **La Suite** (*see p332*) draw an affluent and screamingly fashionable pack. Crowds line up for the glitzy Lido cabaret (116bis av des Champs-Elysées, 8th, 01.40.76.56.10), the **Queen** nightclub

(*see p332*) and numerous cinemas, or stroll down the avenue to floodlit **place de la Concorde** (*see p92*). Just down from the **Arc de Triomphe**, Locals stock up on late-night wines, magazines and groceries at **Drugstore Publicis** (*see p241*), founded by an ad agency in the 1960s, and recently given a tacky cladding of swirly metal bars by American architect Michele Saee.

This great spine of western Paris started life as an extension to the Tuileries gardens, laid out by Le Nôtre in the 17th century. By the Revolution, the avenue had reached its full stretch, but it was more Sunday stroll territory than thoroughfare. During the Second Empire the Champs-Elysées became a focus of fashionable society, military parades and royal processions. Bismarck was so impressed when he arrived with the conquering Prussian army in 1871 that he had a replica, the Ku'damm, built in Berlin. Here smart residences and hotels sprung up along its upper half, together with streetlights, sideshows, concert halls, theatres and exhibition centres. Hitler's troops made a point of marching down it in 1940; as did their Allied counterparts four years later.

The lower, landscaped reach of the avenue hides behind it two theatres and haute-cuisine restaurants Laurent (41 av Gabriel, 8th,

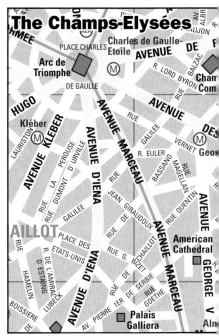

01.42.25.00.39) and Ledoyen (1 av Dutruit, 8th, 01.53.05.10.01), in fancy Napoleon III pavilions. At the Rond-Point des Champs-Elysées, Nos.7 (Artcurial gallery, bookshop and auction house) and 9 hint at the fine mansions that once lined the avenue. From here, it's platinum cards and stick-thin women only as avenue Montaigne rolls out its array of fashion houses: **Christian Dior**, **Chanel** (for both, *see p254*), **Prada** (*see p255*), Jil Sander (No.52, 8th, 01.44.95.06.70), Loewe (No.46, 8th, 01.53.57.92.50), Céline (No.36, 8th, 01.56.89.07.92), Calvin Klein (No.53, 8th, 01.56.88.12.12), Ungaro (No.2, 8th, 01.53.57.00.00) and more. Models and magnates nibble on the terrace at chic eaterie L'Avenue (No.41, 8th, 01.40.70.14.91). You can admire the lavish **Hôtel Plaza Athénée** hotel (*see p59*) and Auguste Perret's innovative 1911-13 **Théâtre des Champs-Elysées** concert hall (*see p318*), a monument to the early 20th-century avant-garde with reliefs by Bourdelle, auditorium painted by Maurice Denis and lights by Lalique. Since 1990 it has been topped by the sleek glass-fronted Maison Blanche restaurant (No.15, 8th, 01.47.23.55.99) with superb views across the river to the Eiffel Tower.

South of the avenue, the glass-domed **Grand Palais** and Petit Palais, both built for the 1900 Exposition Universelle and still used for major art exhibitions, create a magnificent vista across elaborate Pont Alexandre III to Les Invalides. Both are due to emerge from hoardings after major renovations in 2005. At the bridge end of the Petit Palais a bronze statue of Winston Churchill stomps along in an overcoat, while old rival Charles de Gaulle strides at the Champs end of the Grand Palais. The rear wing of the Grand Palais opening on to av Franklin-D.-Roosevelt contains the **Palais de la Découverte** science museum (*see p181*).

To the north of the avenue lie smart shops, antiques dealers and officialdom. On circular place Beauvau wrought-iron gates herald the Ministry of the Interior. The 18th-century Palais de l'Elysée, the official presidential residence, is at No.55-57 rue du Fbg-St-Honoré. Nearby, with gardens extending down to avenue Gabriel are the equally palatial British Embassy and adjoining ambassadorial residence, once the Hôtel Borghèse, where Napoleon's favourite sister Pauline lived from 1803 to 1815.

At the western end of the Champs-Elysées, the Arc de Triomphe towers above place Charles-de-Gaulle, also known as l'Etoile. Initially a project to glorify the victories of Napoleon, the giant triumphal arch was later modified to celebrate the Revolutionary armies. The square with its 12 avenues radiating out

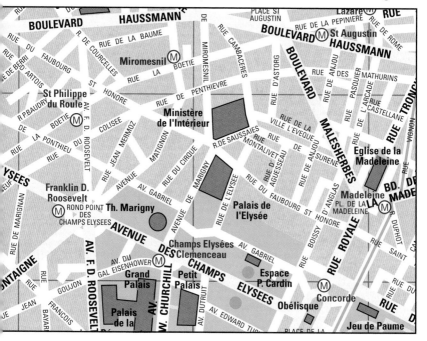

was commissioned later by Haussmann. From the top, gaze upon prize Paris real estate: the swanky mansions along the grassy verges of avenue Foch or the prestige office buildings of avenues Hoche and Wagram.

South of the Arc de Triomphe, avenue Kléber leads to the monumental buildings and terraced gardens of the Trocadéro , with views over the river to the Eiffel Tower. The vast symmetrical 1930s **Palais de Chaillot** dominates the hill and houses four museums plus the **Théâtre National de Chaillot** (see p344). Descending in terraces, Trocadéro's bronze and stone statues showered by powerful fountains form a dramatic ensemble with the backdrop of the Eiffel Tower and Champ de Mars. Across place du Trocadéro is the **Cimetière de Passy**.

To the west of Chaillot on av du Président-Wilson is the **Palais de Tokyo** which houses on one side the **Musée d'Art Moderne de la Ville de Paris** (see p162), and on the other, the wacky **Palais de Tokyo Site de Création Contemporaine** (see p169), which has injected new life into this area. By night the art world mixes with young professionals. Facing the Palais de Tokyo (although entered from av Pierre-1er-de-Serbie) is the **Pavillon Galliera** (see p174 and p175 **Wearing it well**), used for fashion exhibitions, while just up the hill at place d'Iéna are the fabulous Asian and Oriental art collections of the **Musée Guimet** (see p174). Back towards the Champs-Elysées amid the grand 19th-century mansions around place des Etats-Unis, the lavish former townhouse of avant-garde patron Marie-Laure de Noailles has been given a cheeky renovation by Philippe Starck and contains the showroom, museum and Le Cristal Room restaurant of the **Maison Baccarat** (see p171 and p198).

Arc de Triomphe

Pl Charles-de-Gaulle (access via underground passage), 8th (01.55.37.73.77). M° Charles de Gaulle Etoile. **Open** *Oct-Mar* 10am-10.30pm daily. *Apr-Sept* 10am-11pm daily. Closed public hols. **Admission** €7; €4.50 18-25s; free under-18s. **Credit** MC, V. **Map** p402 C3.
Napoleon ordered the arch's construction in 1809 as a monument to the triumph of the republican armies, but almost immediately the empire he'd built began to collapse. The arch, 50m high and 45m wide, was only completed in 1836. Nonetheless it is carved with the names of Napoleon's victories, and decorated with a frieze of battle scenes and sculptures on its flanks, including Rude's celebrated *Le Départ des Volontaires* (or *La Marseillaise*). In 1840, Napoleon's ashes were carried under it on their way to Les Invalides; French troops finally got to march through it victoriously to celebrate the end of World War I; in 1921, France's Unknown Soldier

was buried here. The annual Bastille Day military procession begins here (see p281).

Cimetière de Passy

2 rue du Commandant-Schloesig, 16th (01.47.27. 51.42). M° Trocadéro. **Open** 8am-5.45pm Mon-Fri; 8.30am-5.45pm Sat; 9am-5.45pm Sun. **Map** p402 B5.
Since 1874 this has been considered one of the most elegant places in Paris to be laid to rest. You'll find composers Debussy and Fauré, painters Manet and his sister-in-law Berthe Morisot, writer Giraudoux, and various generals and politicians.

Grand Palais

Av Winston-Churchill, av du Général-Eisenhower, 8th (01.44.97.78.04). M° Champs-Elysées Clemenceau. **Map** p403 E5.
Built for the 1900 Exposition Universelle, the Grand Palais was the work of three different architects, each of whom designed a façade. During World War II it housed Nazi tanks. In 1994 the magnificent glass-roofed central hall was suddenly closed when bits of metal started falling off the roof, although exhibitions continued to be held in the other wings. The bronze horses rearing over the southern corner have recently returned from restoration and the remainder of the building should reopen in 2005.

Palais de Chaillot

Pl du Trocadéro, 16th. M° Trocadéro. **Map** p402 C5.
Looming across the river from the Eiffel Tower, the immense pseudo-classical Palais de Chaillot was constructed by Azéma, Boileau and Carlu for the 1937 international exhibition, with giant sculptures of *Apollo* by Henri Bouchard and *Hercules* by Albert Pommier and inscriptions by Paul Valéry. Ironically, it stands on the foundations of an earlier complex put up for the 1878 World Fair. With two sweeping symmetrical wings astride the central esplanade, it is home to the Cinémathèque cinema (see p299), Musée de la Marine (see p177) and what's left of the Musée de l'Homme in the western wing (see p181; currently staging temporary exhibitions while the ethnology and anthropology sections are in storage awaiting the new museum at Quai Branly). In the east wing are the Théâtre National de Chaillot, and the ex-Musée des Monuments Historiques (see p170), to open in 2005 as the Cité de l'Architecture.

Monceau & Batignolles

Parc Monceau, with its neo-Antique follies and large lily pond, lies at the far end of avenue Hoche (the main entrance is on boulevard de Courcelles, the circular pavilion by Ledoux). Three museums capture the extravagance of the area when it was newly fashionable in the 19th century: the **Musée Jacquemart-André** (see p163), with its fabulous collection of old masters; **Musée Nissim de Camondo** (see p173; 18th-century decorative arts) and **Musée Cernuschi** (see p173; Chinese art). There are some nice exotic touches, too, such as the unlikely red lacquer Galerie Ching Tsai Too (48 rue de Courcelles, 8th), built in 1926 for a dealer in Oriental art near the fancy wrought-iron gates of Parc Monceau, or the onion domes of the Russian Orthodox **Alexander Nevsky Cathedral** on rue Daru. Built in the mid 19th century when a stay in Paris was essential to the education of every Russian aristocrat, it is still at the heart of an émigré little Russia.

Famed for its stand during the 1871 Paris Commune, the Quartier des Batignolles to the north-east towards place de Clichy is more working class, with the lively rue de Lévis street market, tenements lining the deep railway canyon and the attractive square des Batignolles park with the pretty Eglise Ste-Marie de Batignolles overlooking a small semi-circular square. It is fast becoming chic, with a rising restaurant scene. On rue des Dames are the Eldorado hotel (No.18, 17th, 01.45.22.35.21), the **Lush** bar (*see p226*) and trendy bathroom shop SBR (No.29, 17th, 01.43.87.88.00).

Alexander Nevsky Cathedral

12 rue Daru, 17th (01.42.27.37.34). M° Courcelles. **Open** varies. **Map** p402 D3.

The edifice has enough onion domes, icons and incense to make you think you were in Moscow. This Russian Orthodox church was built 1859-61 in the neo-Byzantine Novgorod-style of the 1600s, by the Tsar's architect Kouzmin, who was also respon-sible for the Fine Arts Academy in St Petersburg. Services, on Sunday mornings and Orthodox saints' days, are in Russian.

Cimetière des Batignolles

Rue St-Just, 17th (01.53.06.38.68). M° Porte de Clichy. **Open** *Nov-Mar* 8am-5.30pm Mon-Fri; 8.30am-5.30pm Sat; 9am-5.30pm Sun. *Apr-Oct* 8am-6pm Mon-Fri; 8.30am-6pm Sat; 9am-6pm Sun.

Squeezed inside the Périphérique are the graves of poet Paul Verlaine, Surrealist André Breton, and Léon Bakst, costume designer of the Ballets Russes.

Parc Monceau

Bd de Courcelles, av Hoche, rue Monceau, 8th. M° Monceau. **Open** *Nov-Mar* 7am-8pm daily. *Apr-Oct* 7am-10pm. **Map** p403 E2

Surrounded by grand *hôtels particuliers* and elegant Haussmannian apartments, Monceau is a favourite with well-dressed children and their nannies. It was laid out in the late 18th century for the Duc de Chartres in the then fashionable English style, with an oval lake, spacious lawns and a variety of follies: an Egyptian pyramid, a Corinthian colonnade, Venetian bridge and ancient sarcophagi.

Passy & Auteuil

West of l'Etoile, the massive 16th district is the one that probably suffers the most from prejudices and preconceptions. This is an area

Line up on the **Arc de Triomphe**. *See p112.*

of grandiose apartments and exclusive residences hidden down private roads, yet beyond its bourgeois respectability, it hides some seminal pieces of Modernist architecture (*see pp40-46* **Architecture**) – and some of the city's most important museums.

When **Balzac** lived at No.47 rue Raynouard (*see p178*) in the 1840s, Passy was a country village where a fashionable clientele came to take cures for anaemia at its mineral springs – a name reflected in the rue des Eaux. The village – along with nearby Auteuil – was absorbed into the city with the annexation of 1860. Beyond the Maison de Balzac, at Nos.51-55, is the apartment building and former design offices of avant-garde architect August Perret in his material of predeliction, reinforced concrete. The **Musée du Vin** (*see p183*) is of interest if only for its atmospheric setting in the vaulted cellars of the wine-producing Abbaye de Minimes destroyed in the Revolution. Rue de Passy, once the village high street, and parallel rue de l'Assomption are the focus of local life with fashion shops and traiteurs, revamped department store Franck et Fils (80 rue Passy, 16th, 01.42.15.00.37) and an upmarket covered market. The former Passy station is now La Gare restaurant (19 chaussée de la Muette, 16th, 01.42.15.15.31; see p133 **Bring back the Belt**), ladies who shop watch from the art deco La Rotonde café (12 chaussée de la Muette, 16th, 01.45.24.45.45) or stack up on cakes at Japanese pâtisserie Yamakasi (6 chaussée de la Muette), while a nearby curiosity are three wooden dachas on Villa Beauséjour, built by Russian craftsmen for the 1867 Exposition Universelle and reconstructed here.

West of the Jardin du Ranelagh (originally high-society pleasure gardens, modelled on the endearingly bawdy 18th-century London version) is the Impressionist draw the **Musée Marmottan** (see p163), featuring a fabulous collection of Monet's late water-lily canvases, other Impressionists and Empire furniture.

Next to the Pont de Grenelle stands the circular **Maison de Radio France**, the giant Orwellian home to the state broadcasting bureaucracy. Opened in 1963, it's a constant reminder of the pivotal role that the state still plays in people's lives. You can attend concerts (see p316) or take guided tours around its endless corridors; employees nickname the place 'Alphaville', after the Godard film. From here, in upmarket Auteuil, go up rue Fontaine, the best place to find art nouveau architecture by Hector Guimard. Despite extravagant iron balconies, **Castel Béranger** at No.14 was originally low-rent lodgings; Guimard designed outside and in, right down to the wallpaper and stoves. He also designed the less-ambitious Nos.19, 21 and tiny Café Antoine at No.17. The long neglected Hôtel Mezzara at No.60 has recently been renovated and is sometimes open for exhibitions. Pay literary homage at No.96 where Marcel Proust was born. Guimard lived in the house he built at 122 avenue Mozart.

Nearby around Métro Jasmin is Le Corbusier terrain. The **Fondation Le Corbusier** occupies two of his avant-garde houses in the square du Dr-Blanche. A little further up rue du Dr-Blanche, rue Mallet-Stevens is almost entirely made up of refined houses by Robert Mallet-Stevens, while sculptor Henri Bouchard himself commissoned the studio and house that is now the endearingly dusty Atelier-Musée Bouchard. Much of Auteuil is private territory with exclusive streets of houses off rue Chardon-Lagache, though more villagey bits remain around the Eglise d'Auteuil; the studio of 19th-century sculptor Carpeaux also remains, looking rather lost, at 39 boulevard Exelmans, the top storey added by Guimard.

West of the 16th, across the Périphérique, sprawls the **Bois de Boulogne**, a royal hunting reserve turned park which includes a boating lake and cycle paths. At Porte d'Auteuil are the romantic **Serres d'Auteuil** and the two sports venues of the **Parc des Princes** (see p333), home of flagship football club **Paris St-Germain** (see p334), and **Roland Garros** (see p333), host of the French tennis open.

Bois de Boulogne

16th. M° Porte Dauphine or Les Sablons.
Covering 865 hectares, the Bois was the old Forêt de Rouvray hunting grounds. It was landscaped in the 1860s, when romantic artificial grottos and waterfalls were created around the Lac Inférieur. The Jardin de Bagatelle (route de Sèvres à Neuilly, 16th, 01.40.67.97.00) are famous for their roses, daffodils and water lilies and contain an orangery which rings to the sound of tinkling Chopin in summer. The Jardin d'Acclimatation is a children's amusement park (see p289). The Bois boasts two racecourses (Longchamp and Auteuil; see p335 **A day at the races**), sports clubs and stables, the Musée National des Arts et Traditions Populaires (see p172) and restaurants, including the haute cuisine of Le Pré Catelan (route de Suresnes, 16th, 01.44.14.41.14). There are plans to reduce the traffic and replant some of the scrubby woodland. Boats can be rented on the Lac Inférieur and there's cycle hire nearby. Crowded at weekends with romancing picnickers and dog walkers, at night the Bois is transformed into a parade ground for transsexuals and swingers of every stripe.

Castel Béranger

14 rue La Fontaine, 16th. M° Jasmin. Closed to the general public.
Guimard's masterpiece of 1895-98 epitomises art nouveau in Paris. Here you can see his love of brick and wrought iron, asymmetry and renunciation of harsh angles not found in nature. Along with the whiplash motifs characteristic of art nouveau, there are still many signs of Guimard's earlier taste for fantasy and the medieval: green seahorses climb the façade, and the faces on the balconies are thought to be a self-portrait, inspired by Japanese figures, to ward off evil spirits.

Fondation Le Corbusier

Villa La Roche, 8-10 square du Dr-Blanche, 16th (01.42.88.41.53/www.fondationlecorbusier.asso.fr). M° Jasmin. **Open** 1.30pm-6pm Mon; 10am-12.30pm, 1.30-6pm Tue-Thur; 10am-12.30pm, 1.30-5pm Fri. Closed Aug. **Admission** €2.50; €1.50 13-18s; free under 12s. **No credit cards**.
This house, designed by Le Corbusier in 1923 for a Swiss art collector, shows the visionary architect's ideas in practice with its stilts, strip windows, roof terraces and balconies, built-in furniture and an unsuspected use of colour inside: sludge green, blue and pinky beige. Sculptural cylindrical staircase and split volumes create a variety of geometrical vistas, while inside is decked out with Corb and Perriand's furniture and Corb's own neo-Cubist paintings. The

adjoining Villa Jeanneret, designed by Le Corbusier for his brother, houses the foundation's library.

Le Jardin des Serres d'Auteuil

3 av de la Porte d'Auteuil, 16th (01.40.71.75.23).
M° Porte d'Auteuil. **Open** *Winter* 10am-5pm daily.
Summer 10am-6pm daily. **Admission** €1.
No credit cards.
These romantic glasshouses were opened in 1895 to cultivate plants for Parisian parks and public spaces. Today there are seasonal displays of orchids and begonias. Look out for the steamy tropical pavilion with palms, birds and Japanese ornamental carp.

Montmartre & Pigalle

In the 9th and 18th districts.
Montmartre, the highest point in the whole city, resembles some perched southern hill village, with its tight-packed houses spiralling up round the mound underneath the sugary-white oversized dome of **Sacré-Coeur**. Despite the onslaught of tourists, it is surprisingly easy to leave them all behind and to fall under the spell of the most unabashedly romantic district of Paris. Climb and descend quiet stairways, peer into little alleys, ivy-covered houses and deserted squares, and explore streets like rue des Abbesses, rue des Trois-Frères and rue des Martyrs with their cafés, quirky boutiques and young, arty community.

For centuries, Montmartre was a tranquil, windmill-packed village. When Haussmann sliced through the city centre, working-class families started to move out and peasant migrants poured into an industrialising Paris from across France. Montmartre swelled. The hill was absorbed into the city of Paris in 1860, but remained fiercely independent, and its role in the Paris Commune in 1871, when the Montmartrois fended off the government troops of Adolphe Thiers, is marked by a plaque on rue du Chevalier-de-la-Barre. *See p21* **1871**.

Artists moved into the area from the 1880s. Renoir found subject matter in the cafés and *guinguettes*. Toulouse-Lautrec patronised its bars and immortalised its cabarets in posters; later it was frequented by Picasso and artists of the Ecole de Paris, Utrillo and Modigliani.

The best starting point is the Abbesses Métro, one of only two in Paris (along with Porte Dauphine) to retain its original art-nouveau metal and glass awning designed by Hector Guimard. Across place des Abbesses as you emerge from the station is the art nouveau church of St-Jean-de-Montmartre, a pioneering reinforced concrete structure behind the brick, studded with turquoise mosaics around the door. Along rue des Abbesses and adjoining rue Lepic, which winds its way up the hill, are many excellent food shops, wine merchants,

cafés, including **Le Sancerre** *(see p226)*, and offbeat boutiques. The famous **Studio 28** cinema *(see p301)*, opened in 1928, is where Buñuel's *L'Age d'Or* had a riotous première in 1930. It has its own dinky bar.

In the other direction from Abbesses, at 11 rue Yvonne-Le-Tac, is the Chapelle du Martyr where, according to legend, St Denis picked up his head after his execution by the Romans in the third century (hence the name Montmartre – martyr's mount). Rue Orsel, with a typically Montmartrois cluster of retro design, ethnic and second-hand clothes shops, leads to place Charles-Dullin where cafés overlook the respected Théâtre de l'Atelier (1 place Charles-Dullin, 18th, 01.46.06.49.24). Up the hill, the cafés of rue des Trois-Frères are popular for an evening drink. The street leads into sloping place Emile-Goudeau, whose staircases, wrought-iron streetlights and old houses are particularly evocative. The Bateau Lavoir, a piano factory which stood at No.13, saw the birth of Cubism. Divided into a warren of studios in the 1890s for impoverished artists, it was here that Picasso painted *Les Demoiselles d'Avignon* in 1906-07, when he, Braque and Juan Gris were all residents. The building burned down in 1970 but has since been reconstructed. On rue Lepic, which winds up the hill from rue des Abbesses, are the village's two remaining windmills: the Moulin du Radet, moved here in the 17th century from its hillock in rue des Moulins near the Palais-Royal; and the Moulin de la Galette, site of the celebrated dancehall depicted by Renoir (now in the Musée d'Orsay; *see p164*) and today a restaurant. Vincent Van Gogh and beloved brother Theo lived at No.54 from 1886-88.

On tourist-swamped place du Tertre at the top of the hill, portrait painters compete to sketch you or flog lurid sunset views of Paris; nearby Espace Dali (11 rue Poulbot, 18th, 01.42.64.40.10) offers a slightly more illustrious alternative. Round here, according to legend, the word 'bistro' was born in the early 1800s at the restaurant La Mère Catherine when Russian soldiers shouted '*Bistro!*' ('Quickly!') to be served. Just off the square is the oldest church in the district, St-Pierre-de-Montmartre, whose columns have grown bent with age. Founded by Louis VI in 1133, it is a fine example of early Gothic, and a contrast to its extravagant neighbour, the basilica of Sacré-Coeur.

For all its kitsch and swarms of tourists, though, Sacré-Coeur is well worth the visit for its sheer 19th-century excess. Rather than the main steps, take the staircase down rue Maurice-Utrillo to pause on a café terrace on the small square at the top of rue Muller, or wander down through the adjoining park to the Halle

Pigalle.

St-Pierre. The former covered market is now used for exhibitions of naive art, but the surrounding square and streets, known as the Marché St-Pierre, are packed with fabric shops, laden with rolls of material, and a great source of discounted bin ends.

On the north side of place du Tertre in rue Cortot is the quiet 17th-century manor, which houses the **Musée de Montmartre** (*see p177*), dedicated to the area and its former inhabitants. Dufy, Renoir and Utrillo all had studios in the entrance pavilion. Nearby in rue des Saules is the Montmartre vineyard, planted by local artist Poulbot in 1933 in memory of the ones that once covered the area. The grape picking here each autumn is a ritual celebrated with much pomp. Further down the hill, amid rustic, shuttered houses, is **Au Lapin Agile** cabaret (*see p284*). This old meeting point for local artists got its name from André Gill, who painted the inn sign of a rabbit (lapin A. Gill). Singers still churn out nostalgia here today.

A series of pretty squares leads to rue Caulaincourt, crossing the ravine of the oddly romantic **Cimetière de Montmartre** (enter on avenue Rachel, reached by staircase from rue Caulaincourt or place de Clichy). Winding down the back of the hill, avenue Junot is lined with exclusive residences, such as the avant-garde house built by Adolf Loos for Dadaist poet

Tristan Tzara at No.15, exemplifying his Modernist maxim: 'Ornament is crime'.

Cimetière de Montmartre

20 av Rachel, access by stairs from rue Caulaincourt, 18th (01.53.42.36.30). M° Blanche. **Open** *6 Nov-15 Mar* 8am-5.30 pm Mon-Fri, 8.30am-5.30pm Sat; 9am-5.30pm Sun and hols. *16 Mar-5 Nov* 8am-6pm Mon-Fri; 8.30am-6pm Sat; 9am-6pm Sun and hols. **Map** p405 G1.

You stumble over the famous and infamous here: Truffaut, Nijinsky, Berlioz, Degas, Offenbach, German poet Heine and Surrealist painter Victor Brauner are all buried here. Also La Goulue, the first great cancan star and model for Toulouse-Lautrec, celebrated local beauty Mme Récamier, and the consumptive heroine Alphonsine Plessis, inspiration for Dumas' *La Dame aux Camélias* and Verdi's *La Traviata*. Flowers and messages are still left daily for Egyptian pop diva and gay icon Dalida, who lived on nearby rue d'Orchampt.

Sacré-Coeur

35 rue du Chevalier-de-la-Barre, 18th (01.53.41.89.00). M° Abbesses or Anvers. **Open** *Basilica* 6am-10.30pm daily. *Crypt & dome Winter* 10am-5.30pm daily. *Summer* 9.30am-7pm daily. **Admission** free; *crypt and dome* €5. **Credit** AmEx, DC, MC, V. **Map** p404 J1.

Commissioned as an act of penance after the nation's defeat by the Prussians in 1870, voted by the Assemblée Nationale and financed from public subscription, work began on this enormous mock Romano-Byzantine edifice in 1877. It was finished in 1914 and consecrated in 1919, by which time a jumble of architects had succeeded Paul Abadie, winner of the original competition. The interior is lavishly adorned with gaudy neo-Byzantine mosaics. There's a fantastic view from the dome.

Pigalle

Pigalle has long been the sleaze centre of Paris, but that may be changing. A recent police blitz, instigated in response to increased tourist rip-offs and rough-ups, has shooed away the streetwalkers and many an erotic cabaret, peep show and go-go bar with them. While locals bemoan the sanitising of their atmospherically seedy neighbourhood, the recent relandscaping of boulevards de Clichy and de Rochechouart looks set to continue the clean up.

In the 1890s, Toulouse-Lautrec's posters of Jane Avril at the Divan Japonais, Le Chat Noir, the Moulin Rouge, and of *chansonnier* Aristide Bruant, immortalised the area's cabarets and were a landmark in both art and the art of advertising. At the end of the 19th century, of the 58 houses on rue des Martyrs, 25 were cabarets (a few, such as the drag shows Michou and Madame Arthur, remain today); others were *maisons closes*. But it's still a pretty cool street: Le Divan Japonais is now **Le Divan du Monde** (*see p320*), club and music venue; a hip crowd packs into **La Fourmi** (*see p225*) across the street, and up the hill there's a cluster of atelier-boutiques where designers have set up their sewing machines at the back of the shop. Along the boulevard, behind its bright red windmill, the **Moulin Rouge**, once the image of naughty 1890s Paris, is now a cheesy tourist draw. (*See p285* **Cancan and champers**.) Its befeathered dancers still cancan across the stage but are no substitute for La Goulue and Joseph Pujol – *le pétomane* who could pass wind melodically. In stark contrast is the Cité Véron next door, a cobbled alley with curlicue iron entrance sign, a small theatre and cottagey buildings, among them 6bis where writer and jazz musician Boris Vian lived between 1953 and 1958. The **Elysée Montmartre** belle-époque music hall programmes an eclectic array of music concerts (*see p319*) and cool club nights, but the **Folies Pigalle** nightspot (*see p329*) still retains undeniable Pigalle flavour with its after-parties and drag queens.

La Nouvelle Athènes

Just south of Pigalle and east of the rue Blanche lies this mysterious, often overlooked quarter

dubbed the New Athens when colonised by quantities of artists, writers and composers in the early 19th century. Long-forgotten actresses and demi-mondaines had mansions built here and some of the prettiest can be found in tiny rue de la Tour-des-Dames, which refers to one of the many windmills owned by the once-prosperous Couvent des Abbesses. Wander through the adjoining streets and passageways to glimpse further angles of these miniature palaces, especially on rue St-Lazare (painter Paul Delaroche lived in the Italianate house at No.58) and rue de La Rochefoucauld.

Just off rue Taitbout stands square d'Orléans, a remarkable housing estate built in 1829 by English architect Edward Cresy. This ensemble of flats and artists' studios attracted the glitterati of the day, including George Sand and her lover Chopin. In the house originally built for Dutch painter Ary Scheffer in nearby rue Chaptal, the **Musée de la Vie Romantique** (*see p178*) displays the artist's mementoes.

The **Musée Gustave Moreau** (*see p166*) on rue de La Rochefoucauld, meanwhile, is reason enough for a visit, featuring the artist's cramped apartment and magnificent studio. Fragments of bohemia can still be gleaned in the area, although the Café La Roche, where Moreau would meet Degas for drinks and rows,

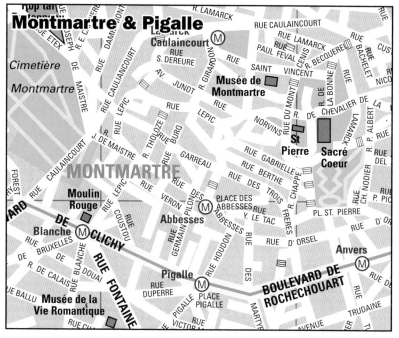

Sacré-Coeur. *See p116.*

has been downsized to La Joconde (57 rue Notre-Dame-de-Lorette, 9th, 01.48.74.10.38). Degas painted most of his memorable ballet scenes round the corner in rue Frochot and Renoir hired his first decent studio at 35 rue St-Georges. A few streets away in Cité Pigalle, a collection of studios, is Van Gogh's last Paris house (No.5), from where he moved to Auvers-sur-Oise. There is a plaque here, but nothing on the building in rue Pigalle where Toulouse-Lautrec drank himself to death in 1903.

The area round the neo-classical Eglise Notre-Dame-de-Lorette, built in the form of a Greek temple, was built up in Louis-Philippe's reign and was famous for its courtesans or *lorettes*, elegant young ladies named after their haunt of rue Notre-Dame-de-Lorette. From 1844 to 1857, Delacroix had his studio at No.58 (by No.56, where Gauguin was born in 1848). The painter later moved to place de Furstenberg in the 6th (now **Musée Delacroix**; *see p165*). Rue St-Lazare still contains some delightfully old-fashioned shops and bistros, including perfumier **Détaille 1905** (*see p243*), and bistro **Chez Jean** (*see p205*). The lower stretch of rue des Martyrs is packed with food shops, while a little further up the hill look out for the prosperous residences of the cité Malesherbes and avenue Trudaine. Place Gustave-Toudouze

contains tearoom Tea Folies (No.6, 9th, 01.42.80.08.44) and the No Stress café (No.2, 9th, 01.48.78.00.27), and glorious circular place St-Georges was home to the true Empress of Napoleon III's Paris: the notorious Madame Païva. She lived in the neo-Renaissance No.28, thought to be outrageous at the time of its construction. 'La Païva' shot herself in the head following the end of her love affair with the millionaire cousin of Chancellor Otto von Bismarck.

La Goutte d'Or

For a less orthodox Paris experience, head for Barbès Rochechouart Métro station and the area north of it. Zola used it as a backdrop for *L'Assommoir*, his novel set among the district's laundries and absinthe cafés. Today heroin has replaced absinthe as the means of escape.

Primarily an African and Arab neighbourhood, La Goutte d'Or can seem like a colourful slice of Africa or a state under perpetual siege due to the frequent police raids. Down rue Doudeauville, you'll find African music shops, while rue Polonceau contains African grocers and Senegalese restaurants. Mayor Delanoë has tried to attract young designers to the area by designating rue des Gardes 'rue de la mode', while square Léon is the focus for **La Goutte** d'Or en Fête in June (*see p281*), which brings together local musicians. Some of them, such as Africando and the Orchestre National de Barbès, have become well known across Paris. There is a lively street market under the Métro tracks (Mon, Wed, Sat morning) along boulevard de la Chapelle, with stalls of exotic vegetables and rolls of African fabrics.

On the northern edge of the city at Porte de Clignancourt is the city's largest flea market, the **Marché aux Puces de St-Ouen** (*see p273* **Hunt the heirloom**).

North-east Paris

In the 10th, 11th, 19th and 20th districts.
Gigantic place de la République stands like a frontier between the old aristocratic Marais and the more proletarian north-east, an area in transition with charming areas abreast grotty, dodgy ones, and modern housing developments beside relics from the old villages of La Villette, Belleville, Ménilmontant and Charonne.

Canal St-Martin to La Villette

Canal St-Martin, built 1805-25, begins at the Seine at Pont Morland – where there's a small marina at Port de l'Arsenal – disappears underground at Bastille, hides under boulevard Richard-Lenoir, then re-emerges after crossing rue du Faubourg-du-Temple, east of place de la République. Faubourg-du-Temple itself, once the country lane that led to Belleville, is scruffy and cosmopolitan, lined with cheap grocers and everything-at-one-euro stores, some surprising hidden courtyards, and some stalwarts of Paris nightlife: **Le Gibus** (*see p329*), lively Brazilian bar-restaurant **Favela Chic** (*see p233*) and vintage dance hall **La Java** (*see p332*), plus the Palais des Glaces (No.37, 10th, 01.42.02.27.17), which puts on seasons of French comics.

The first stretch of the canal lined with shady trees and crossed by iron footbridges and locks has the most appeal. The canal is a favourite spot with local families on Sunday when the quays are traffic-free. Many of the remaining canalside warehouses have been snapped up by artists and designers or turned into loft apartments and the quais and nearby streets have been colonised by trendy bars. You can take a boat up the canal as far as La Villette. *See p121* **On the waterfront.**

East of here, the Hôpital St-Louis (main entrance rue Bichat) was commissioned in 1607 by Henri IV to house plague victims, and was built as a series of isolated pavilions in the brick-and-stone style as **place des Vosges** (*see p105*), far enough from the town to prevent risk of infection. Behind the hospital, the rue de

la Grange-aux-Belles housed the infamous Montfaucon gibbet, put up in 1233, where victims were hanged and left to the elements. Today the street contains music cafés **Chez Adel** (*see p322*) and L'Apostrophe (No.23, 10th, 01.42.08.26.07). East of the hospital, delightful cobbled rue Ste-Marthe and place Ste-Marthe have a provincial air, busy at night with multi-ethnic restaurants and cafés Le Panier (32 pl Ste-Marthe, 10th, 01.42.01.38.18) and the Sainte-Marthe (32 rue Ste-Marthe, 10th, 01.44.84.36.96).

To the north is the Parti Communiste Français, on the place du Colonel-Fabien, a surrealist, curved glass curtain wall raised off the ground on a concrete wing, built in 1968-71 by Brazilian architect Oscar Niemeyer with Paul Chemetov and Jean Deroche. The canal disappears briefly again under place de Stalingrad, one of Paris' dodgiest districts by night. The square was landscaped in 1989 to showcase the Rotonde de La Villette, one of Ledoux's grandiose 1780s toll houses which once marked the boundary of Paris and now houses exhibitions and archaeological finds. Here the canal widens into Bassin de La Villette, and the new developments along the quai de Loire and further quai de la Marne, as well as some of the worst of 1960s and '70s housing in the colossal blocks that stretch along rue de Flandres. At 104 rue d'Aubervilliers the old Pompes Funèbres – former municipal undertaker – is scheduled to be turned into a multimedia art space by 2005.

At the eastern end of the basin is an unusual 1885 hydraulic lifting bridge, Pont de Crimée. Thursday and Sunday mornings add vitality with a canalside market at place de Joinville. East of here, the Canal de l'Ourcq (created in 1813 to provide drinking water, as well as for freight haulage) divides: Canal St-Denis runs north through St-Denis towards the Seine, Canal de l'Ourcq continues through La Villette and suburbs east. Long the city's main abattoir district, still reflected in the Grande Halle de La Villette and by some of the old meaty brasseries along boulevard de La Villette, the neighbourhood has been revitalised since the late 1980s by the post-modern **Parc de La Villette** complex with the **Cité des Sciences et de l'Industrie** (*see p170*) science museum (also incorporating the **Cité des Enfants**; *see p290*), the **Cité de la Musique** concert hall (*see p316 and p324*), and its varied programme of ethnic music, jazz and classical events.

Parc de La Villette

Av Corentin-Cariou, 19th. Mᵒ Porte de La Villette/ av Jean-Jaurès, 19th. Mᵒ Porte de Pantin. (01.40.03. 75.03). **Map** p405 inset.
La Villette's programmes range from avant-garde music to avant-garde circus. Once the city's main

cattle market and abattoir, it was to be replaced by a high-tech slaughterhouse but instead was transformed into the Cité des Sciences et de l'Industrie, a futuristic, interactive science museum. Outside you'll find the shining, spherical La Géode IMAX cinema (*see p298*) and the Argonaute submarine. Dotted with red pavilions or folies, the park itself designed by Swiss architect Bernard Tschumi is a postmodern feast (guided tours 08.03.30.63.06, 3pm Sun in summer). The folies serve as glorious giant climbing frames, as well as a first-aid post, burger bar and children's art centre. Kids shoot down a Chinese dragon slide and an undulating suspended path follows the Canal de l'Ourcq. As well as the big lawns, which are used for an open-air film festival in summer, there are ten themed gardens bearing evocative names such as the Garden of Mirrors, of Mists, of Acrobatics and of Childhood Horrors (all this can be terribly spooky if you lose your way en route to the Cabaret Sauvage circus or nightclub venue; *see p286 and p332*). South of the canal are the Zénith (*see p320*), used for rock concerts, and the Grande Halle de La Villette – remnant of the former cattle market – now used for trade fairs, exhibitions and September's Villette Jazz Festival (*see p282*). It is winged by the Conservatoire de la Musique music school (*see p316*) and the Cité de la Musique, beautifully designed by Christian de Portzamparc, with its concert halls, rehearsal rooms and the Musée de la Musique (*see p179*).

Belleville, Ménilmontant & Charonne

When the city boundaries were expanded in 1860, Ménilmontant, Belleville and Charonne, once villages which kept the capital supplied with wine and fruit and where Parisians would escape at weekends, were all absorbed. They were built up with housing for migrants, first from rural France and later from former French colonies in North Africa and South-east Asia. The main tourist attraction is **Père-Lachaise** cemetery, but the area also encompasses one of the city's most beautiful parks, the romantic **Buttes-Chaumont**. Despite clever attempts to dissipate workers' agitation by splitting the village between the 11th, 19th and 20th administrative districts, Belleville became the centre of opposition to the Second Empire. Cabarets, artisans and workers typified 1890s Belleville; colonised by artists in the 1990s and a centre of counter-culture, now Belleville is becoming a trendy hang-out.

On boulevard de Belleville, Chinese and Vietnamese shops rub up against Muslim and kosher groceries, couscous and falafel eateries, and there's a busy street market on Tuesday and Friday mornings. Legend has it that Edith Piaf was born on the pavement outside 72 rue de Belleville, as commemorated on the plaque: 'On the steps of this house was born on the 19 December 1915, in the greatest poverty, Edith Piaf, whose voice would later move the world'. Aficionados run the nearby appointment-only **Musée Edith Piaf** (*see p178*), a modest two-room museum full of her memorabilia.

North of here, up avenue Simon-Bolivar, is the romantically landscaped Parc des Buttes-Chaumont. This is the most des-res part of north-east Paris with Haussmannian apartments overlooking the park and to the east, near place de Rhin-et-Danube, a small area of tiny, hilly streets lined with small houses and gardens, known as the Quartier Mouzaïa. The art space **Le Plateau** (*see p170*) south of the park attracts contemporary art zealots.

Up on the slopes of the Hauts de Belleville, there are picturesque old stairways and views from rue Piat and rue des Envierges, which lead to the modern but charming Parc de Belleville with its Maison des Vents devoted to birds and kites. Below the park, rue Ramponneau mixes new housing and relics of old Belleville. At No.23 an old smithy has been transformed into La Forge, an artists' squat, many of them members of La Bellevilloise association which is trying to save the area from redevelopment and preserve its original charm.

Mesnil-Montant used to be a few houses on a hill with vines and fruit trees, then came the bistros, bordellos and workers' housing. It became part of Paris in 1860 with Belleville, and has a similar history. Today it's a thriving centre of alternative Paris, as artists and young Parisians have moved in. Boulevard de Ménilmontant divides this trendy café quarter from the cemetery of Père-Lachaise. While side streets still display male-only North African cafés, rue Oberkampf is home to some of the city's most humming bars, many following the success of the pivotal Café Charbon. (*See p231 and p228* **Operation Oberkampf.**)

The area mixes 1960s and '70s monster housing projects with older dwellings, some gentrified, some derelict. Below rue des Pyrénées, which cuts through the 20th district, explore the rustic Cité Leroy or Villa l'Ermitage, cobbled cul-de-sacs of little houses and gardens, and old craft workshops. Rue de l'Ermitage has a curious neo-Gothic house at No.19 – and a bird's eye view from the junction with rue de Ménilmontant, right down the hill to the Centre Pompidou and Tour St-Jacques. Across on rue Boyer, the **Maroquinerie** (*see p321*) puts on an eclectic cultural programme of literary events, political debate and live music, and at 88 rue de Ménilmontant, graffiti-covered art squat La Miroiterie opens house for art shows and the *magasin gratuit*, a free swap shop.

On the waterfront

One of Napoleon's better ideas, the once rundown Canal St-Martin is now one of the city's most desirable place to relax and reside. As an example of the bucolic urban aesthetic, it simply cannot be beat.

For a century, today's waterside tableau of modern art spaces, quirky boutiques and stylish cafés lay unloved and forgotten in the tatty north-east of Paris. St-Martin had been built over two decades in the early 1800s, to link the Canal de l'Ourcq to the Seine. To supervise the project, Napoleon brought in the chief engineer on his 1799 Egyptian campaign, Pierre-Simon Girard, who had spent time studying the Nile. As a working canal, St-Martin had its heyday as the main freight route into Paris some 150 years ago, falling into disuse as stock moved on to the railways. It narrowly escaped a worse fate in the 1960s, when the then President Pompidou tried to level it and turn it into a motorway.

Now this Cinderella of canals, all cobblestones, locks and arched iron footbridges, is the perfect backdrop for a Sunday afternoon's laze. You can take one of two tourist boats (*see p86* **Boat tours**) up to the Parc de La Villette and let the whole intricate system of swing bridges and locks glide by. On land, the first stretch of the canal north from rue du Fbg-du-Temple to the bend at square des Récollets, lined with shady trees, has the most appeal, particularly on Sundays when the embankments are closed off to cars. Locals picnic on the sun-dappled water's edge, browse in arty boutiques such as **Artazart** (*see p245*) and cluster at the busy café terraces of **Le Jemmapes** and **Chez Prune** (for both, *see p233*).

Between the fifth and sixth locks at 101 quai de Jemmapes is the **Hôtel du Nord**, the inspiration for the 1938 Marcel Carné film of the same name. It is now a restaurant and an anglophone stand-up comedy venue (*see p286*). Carné appreciated the atmosphere of the place, and recreated much of it in the studio. Today only the hotel's façade is real, marked with a commemorative plaque. Only the inconspicuous Le Pont Tournant, on the

corner with quai de Jemmapes and quietly overlooking the swing bridge, seems to hark back to canal's past.

The canal disappears briefly again under seedy place de Stalingrad, then widens into Bassin de La Villette, built for Napoleon in 1808, today bordered by new housing developments.The waterway continues into Canal de l'Ourcq, and the major cultural attractions of **Parc de La Villette** (*see p120*).

Clean and convivial, the Canal St-Martin has a new-found community of trendy young professionals and their families. They publish their own magazine, *La Gazette du Canal*, and organise the annual Canal en Fête at the end of June. Stalls of jumble line up down the quays, the organic cake stands do a roaring trade, and rock and jazz bands turn spare bits of kerb into an impromptu stage.

With clean-ups in 1999 and 2002, even the fish have come back. With further renovations planned, the appeal of the Canal St-Martin is so great, property prices rival those of St-Germain-des-Prés.

East of Père-Lachaise on rue de Bagnolet, La Flèche d'Or, a converted station on the Petite Ceinture railway line (*see p133* **Bring back the Belt**), is a bar and music establishment temporarily closed for refurbishment. Nearby Le Gambetta (8 place Gambetta, 20th, 01.46.36.83.02) more than makes up for it with a party crowd and live music. Just beyond, medieval **Eglise St-Germain de Charonne** is at the heart of what is left of the village of Charonne. Sitting at the top of a flight of stairs next to its presbytery, below a hill that was once covered with vines, it is the city's only church, apart from St-Pierre-de-Montmartre, still to have its own graveyard.

Below here, centred on the old village high street of rue St-Blaise, is a prettified backwater of quiet tea rooms and bistros, such as Le Damier (No.29, 20th, 01.43.72.16.95) and Café Noir (No.15, 20th, 01.40.09.75.80), where old shops are now used for art classes. Place des Grès, once the site of the public pillory where justice was meted out to thieves, and nearby renovated houses and little garden squares, form a pristine village fragment before the grim housing estates lower down the street and a massive tower block on rue Vitruve.

Towards Porte de Bagnolet, where rue de Bagnolet and rue des Balkans meet on the edge of a small park, the Pavillon de l'Hermitage is a small aristocratic relic built in 1720s when Françoise-Marie de Bourbon, daughter of Louis XIV, when it was in the grounds of the Château de Bagnolet. A little further south at Porte de

Tiptoe through the tombstones

If any place can claim the accolade of being the 21st district of Paris, it is **Père-Lachaise** (*see p123*). A vast walled city of the dead, the city's main cemetery is embedded into Paris life and memory. Here lie Delacroix, Proust, Bizet – in fact almost anyone dead, talented and French you care to mention. Not even French, actually. Creed and nationality have never prevented entry – you either had to have lived or died in Paris or have an allotted space in a family tomb.

It was opened after the post-Revolution Terror of the 1790s when the city's communal graveyards were piled high with corpses, and disease rife. The state quickly passed a new law to buy land for cemeteries and created a large out-of-town alternative, the Cimetière de l'Est. Later named after the Jesuit Père de La Chaise, Louis XIV's confessor who lived on this estate, it was designed by Alexandre Brongniart to be a public park and cemetery, an abundantly green and pleasant place in which Parisians could ponder and wander.

But Parisians stubbornly wanted to be buried where they had lived, in their native *quartiers*, and snubbed the new project. In a bid to gain popularity, in 1817 the presumed remains of medieval lovers Abélard and Héloïse were moved here, along with those of Molière and La Fontaine. Great ceremonial burials became the norm. In next to no time, thousands of trees were being cut down to make space for new graves: Sarah Bernhardt, Ingres, Balzac, Chopin, Colette and Edith Piaf. When the Little Sparrow passed away in October 1963, 40,000 came to mourn her,

including a detachment of men from the Foreign Legion who had adopted *Non, je ne regrette rien* as their song.

Nearby, a century earlier, the Mur des Fédérés got its name after 147 members of the Paris Commune of 1871 were lined up and shot against it. Further up the hill is a series of Holocaust memorials.

Finding a certain grave can be a pilgrimage without a map. You'll only get an indifferent shrug from the entry guards, so buy a map from the hawkers at the main Père Lachaise Métro entrance or from shops nearby.

Montreuil, cross the Périphérique for the Puces de Montreuil. (*See p273* **Hunt the heirloom**.)

Cimetière du Père-Lachaise

*Bd de Ménilmontant, 20th (01.55.25.82.10). M°
Père-Lachaise.* **Open** *6 Nov-15 Mar* 8am-5.30pm
Mon-Fri; 8.30am-5.30pm Sat; 9am-5.30pm Sun and
hols. *16 Mar-5 Nov* 8am-6pm Mon-Fri; 8.30am-6pm
Sat; 9am-6pm Sun and public hols. **Map** p409 P5.
Thousands of tombs in the city's main cemetery. *See
below* **Tiptoe through the tombstones**.

Eglise St-Germain de Charonne

*Pl St-Blaise, 20th (01.43.71.42.04). M° Porte de
Bagnolet.* **Open** varies.
The old village church of Charonne dates mainly
from the 15th century, though one massive column
and the belltower remain from an earlier structure.

The interior is almost square with triple nave and a
simple organ loft. Two side altars have striking
modern paintings (a crucifixion and a pietà) by Paul
Rambié; a niche contains a wood statue of St Blaise.

Parc des Buttes-Chaumont

*Rue Botzaris, rue Manin, rue de Crimée, 19th.
M° Buttes-Chaumont.* **Open** *Oct-Apr* 7am-8.15pm
daily. *May, mid Aug-end Sept* 7am-9.15pm daily.
June-mid Aug 7am-10.15pm daily. **Map** p409 N2.
With its meandering paths and vertical cliffs, this
lovely park was designed by Adolphe Alphand for
Haussmann in the 1860s. A former gypsum quarry,
tip and public gibbet, waterfalls now cascade out of
a man-made cave, which even has its own fake
stalactites. A bridge (cheerfully named the Pont des
Suicides) crosses the lake to an island crowned by a
mini-temple. Always popular with kids (*see p289*).

The cemetery has as many legends as the
city it serves. Oscar Wilde's headstone
(*pictured*), carved by Epstein, is a winged,
naked, male angel that was considered so
offensive it was neutered by the head keeper,
who used the offending member as a
paperweight. The tomb of romantic poet
Alfred de Musset is used as dead-letter box
by clandestine lovers. And then there's Victor
Noir, a journalist killed in 1870 at the age of
22 by Napoleon's cousin Prince Pierre. He
rests underneath a bronze likeness by Dalou,
whose meticulous chisel freezes the young
hero in his dying pose – including the bullet
tear in Noir's waistcoat, and accentuating his
subject's rigorous youth by giving him a virile
bulge at the groin. Women hoping to conceive
would rub it relentlessly, so much so that it
shone a ruddy bronze, while the rest of his
body slowly became coated in oxidised green.
In the summer of 2004, the authorities put a
respectful end to the ritual by placing an iron
fence around the statue and strategic roses
protecting Noir's modesty.

Rituals are difficult things. The nefarious
stoned ways of Doors fans means the lizard
king has to have his own bodyguard, and to
the annoyance of the authorities, Wilde
devotees have taken to covering his Epstein-
carved headstone of a naked winged angel
with lipsticked kisses. New pilgrimages have
sprung up: the grave of tragic actress Marie
Trintignant, murdered by her lover Bertrand
Cantat, star of rock band Noir Désir, attracts
the most attention. Her burial in 2003 was
the biggest media event here since Edith Piaf
40 years before.

Space and demand dictate that it's not
easy to buy eternal rest. Since 2003, plots
leased for ten, 30 and 50 years have been
added to those that are *temporaires* (about a
century) and *perpetuelles* (until abandoned).
Out of the one million originally buried here,
only 200,000 have managed to enjoy
uninterrupted slumber.

Some 500 graves a year are classified as
'abandoned', either no longer visited and/or
fallen into dangerous disrepair. The need for
maintenance is immense. Walk through the
labyrinthine cobbled alleys and avenues, and
you see the ashen-black layers of pollution,
the decrepit stones and slowly disappearing
epitaphs, the tree roots clamped all over
gravestones. While it adds to the mystery,
such an incredible reliquary cannot be left to
decay. With the bicentennial of the cemetery
in 2004, its preservation policy came under
review, and a more structured way to care for
the site is being considered. On the agenda is
the revival of Brongniart's original '*jardin-
cimetière*' concept, with new plantings and
fewer fellings.

So when should you visit Père-Lachaise?
The quiet early mornings can be magical,
especially in spring, when the white chesnut
blossoms come out in full. A late sunny
September afternoon can have its special
moments too.

For all its two million annual visitors, Père-
Lachaise is too sprawling to ever be crowded.
This is a place for wanderers and, where
everyone seems to have a lot of time on their
hands, *flâneurs* too. Allow at least a morning
or an afternoon.

The Left Bank

It's all academic, really. And literary, of course...

Eiffel Tower. *See p140.*

The Latin Quarter

In the 5th district.

The university quarter since medieval times, the Latin Quarter abounds in fine churches, wonky ancient buildings, studenty bars and learning or learned institutions; despite the rocketing prices of flats, it still has a distinctly intellectual edge. It got its name from the use of Latin as the common language among students who came here from all over Europe in the Middle Ages, but it could just as well refer to the vestiges of Roman Lutetia, of which it was the heart. The first two Roman streets ran where present-day rue St-Jacques (later the pilgrims' route to Compostela) and rue Cujas run today; the forum was probably beneath rue Soufflot. The area has the city's most important Roman remains: the Cluny baths, now part of the **Musée National du Moyen Age**, and the **Arènes de Lutèce** amphitheatre.

Quartier de la Huchette

The boulevard St-Michel, at one time symbolic of student rebellion, is these days a ribbon of fast-food giants, and shoe and clothing shops,

though **Gibert Joseph** and **Gibert Jeune** (for both, *see p245*) continue to furnish books and stationery to students. East of here, the semi-pedestrianised Quartier de la Huchette has retained much of its medieval street plan. Rue de la Huchette and rue de la Harpe have are now best known for their kebabs and pizzas, though if you look past the Turks and tavernas there are 18th-century wrought-iron balconies and carved masks in the latter street. At the tiny **Théâtre de la Huchette** (*see p344*), Ionesco's absurdist drama *La Cantatrice Chauve* ('The Bald Soprano') has been playing continuously since 1957, with some of its original cast. Also of interest are rue du Chat-qui-Pêche, supposedly the city's narrowest street, and rue de la Parcheminerie, named after the parchment sellers and copyists who once lived here. Amid the tourist paraphernalia (and usually fringed by a row of tramps) stands the city's most charming medieval church, the **Eglise St-Séverin**, with leering gargoyles, spiky gabled side chapels and an exuberantly vaulted Flamboyant Gothic interior.

Across ancient rue St-Jacques is the **Eglise St-Julien-le-Pauvre**, built as a resting place for 12th-century pilgrims. Nearby rue Galande has ancient houses, the Trois Mailletz cabaret at No.56 (5th, 01.43.54.00.79), the medieval cellars of the **Caveau des Oubliettes** jazz club (*see p234 and p325*) were used as a prison after the Revolution (*oubliette* is the French word for dungeon, into which prisoners were thrown, then forgotten). At No.42, the **Studio Galande** (*see p301*) arts cinema still draws goths bearing rice and umbrellas for late screenings of *The Rocky Horror Picture Show* every Friday and Saturday. Just outside the church in the square Viviani garden stands what is possibly the city's oldest tree, a false acacia planted in 1602, now half-swamped by an enormous thatch of ivy and propped up by some impressive concrete buttresses. Nearby on rue de la Bucherie, expats in worn tweed jackets sporting leather elbow patches gather at second-hand English bookshop **Shakespeare & Co** (*see p245*), opposite the **bouquinistes** (*see p245*), the book and print sellers whose green boxes line the quays. The little streets between here and the eastern stretch of boulevard St-Germain are among the city's oldest: streets like rue de Bièvre, following the course of the river Bièvre (*see p136* **The lost river**) which flowed into the Seine in the Middle Ages, rue du Maître-Albert and rue des Grands-Degrès, with traces of old shop signs painted on the façades. Remnants of the Collège des Bernardins, built for the Cistercian order, can be seen in rue de Poissy, where the Gothic monks' refectory of the 13th- to 14th-century is being restored after long service as firemen's barracks. Nearby stand Eglise St-Nicolas de Chardonnet (23 rue Bernardins, 5th, 01.44.27.07.90), associated with the most reactionary wing of the Catholic church and still performs Mass in Latin, and the art deco Maison de la Mutualité (24 rue St-Victor, 5th 01.40.46.12.00) whose uses range from trades unions' meetings to the occasional rock concert.

At 47 quai de la Tournelle, the 17th-century Hôtel de Miramion now contains the Musée de l'Assistance Publique (5th, 01.40.27.50.05, www.ap-hop-paris.fr), devoted to the history of Paris hospitals. You'll find food for all budgets along here, from the landmark haute-cuisine restaurant Tour d'Argent (15 quai de la Tournelle, 5th, 01.43.54.23.31), which claims to have been founded as an inn in 1582, to the populist Tintin shrine *café-tabac* Le Rallye (No.11, 5th, 01.43.54.29.65). Place Maubert, today a breezy morning marketplace (Tue, Thur, Sat), witnessed the grim hanging of Protestants during the 16th-century Wars of Religion. Just behind the square, the hideous modern police station is home to a curious array of grisly criminal evidence in the **Musée de la Préfecture de Police** (*see p177*).

On the corner of boulevard St-Germain and boulevard St-Michel stand the striking ruins of the late second-century Thermes de Cluny, the Romans' main baths complex; the adjoining Gothic Hôtel de Cluny provides a suitable setting for the **Musée National du Moyen Age**, the national collection of medieval art. Touching boulevard St-Germain, its garden has been replanted with species found in medieval tapestries, paintings and treatises.

Eglise St-Julien-le-Pauvre

rue St-Julien-le-Pauvre, 5th (01.43.54.52.16). Mº Cluny La Sorbonne. **Open** 9.30am-1pm, 3-6.30pm daily. **Map** p408 J7.
A former sanctuary for pilgrims en route to Compostela, this much-mauled church dates from the late 12th century, on the cusp of Romanesque and Gothic, and has capitals richly decorated with vines, acanthus leaves and winged harpies. Once part of a priory, it became the university church when colleges migrated to the Left Bank and was often the site of riotous university assemblies. Since 1889 it has been used by the Greek Orthodox church.

Eglise St-Séverin

1 rue des Prêtres-St-Séverin, 5th (01.42.34.93.50). Mº Cluny La Sorbonne or St-Michel. **Open** 11am-7.30pm daily. **Map** p408 J7.
Built on the site of the chapel of solitary hermit Séverin, itself on top of a much earlier Merovingian burial ground, this lovely Flamboyant Gothic church was long the parish church of the Left Bank and rebuilt on various occasions to repair damage after ransacking by Normans and to meet the needs of the growing population. The church dates from the 15th century, though the doorway, carved with foliage, was added last century from the demolished Eglise St-Pierre-aux-Boeufs on Ile de la Cité.

The double ambulatory is famed for its forest of 'palm tree' vaulting, which meets at the end in a unique spiral column that inspired a series of paintings by Robert Delaunay. The belltower (a survivor from one of the earlier churches on the site) has the oldest bell in Paris (1412). Around the nave are stained glass windows dating from the 14th and 15th centuries, most of those in the side chapels are by 19th-century Chartres master Emile Hersh, while the choir apse has striking stained glass designed by artist Bazaine in the 1960s. Next door, around the former cemetery, is the only remaining charnel house in Paris, where the bones taken from common burial grounds were placed.

Musée National du Moyen Age – Thermes de Cluny

6 pl Paul-Painlevé, 5th (01.53.73.78.00/www.musee-moyenage.fr). Mº Cluny La Sorbonne. **Open** 9.15am-5.45pm Mon, Wed-Sun. **Admission** €5.50; €4 18s-25s, all Sun; free under-18s, CM. **Credit** *Shop* MC, V. **Map** p408 J7.
The national museum of medieval art is best known for the beautiful, allegorical Lady and the Unicorn

Sightseeing

Rue Mouffetard.

Moules de Bouchot

Moules L'Huitre et demie 11€

Moules marinières 9€

Moules au safran 10€

Moules au Noilly-Prat 10€

tapestry cycle, but also has important collections of medieval sculpture and enamels. The building itself, commonly known as Cluny, is also a rare example of 15th-century secular Gothic architecture, with its foliate Gothic doorways, hexagonal staircase jutting out of the façade and vaulted chapel. It was built in 1485-98 – atop a Gallo-Roman baths complex dating from the second and third centuries – to lodge priests, at the request of Jacques d'Amboise, abbot of the powerful Abbaye de Cluny in Burgundy. With its U-shaped residential building set behind an entrance courtyard, it was a precursor of the Marais *hôtels particuliers* of the 16th and 17th centuries. After serving as a printworks and laundry, the *hôtel* was rented in the 1830s by fervent medievalist Alexandre du Sommerand to house his collection, which laid the foundations of the museum created in 1844. The baths, built in characteristic Roman bands of stone and brick masonry, are the finest Roman remains in Paris. The vaulted frigidarium (cold bath), tepidarium (warm bath), caldarium (hot bath) and part of the hypocaust heating system are all still visible. *See also p173.*

The Sorbonne, Montagne Ste-Geneviève & Mouffetard

The days of horn-rims, pipes and turtle necks are long gone, thanks to an influx of well-heeled residents in the 1980s, who put accommodation here beyond most students' reach. At least the intellectual tradition persists: the Montagne Ste-Geneviève is a concentration of academic institutions, from the Sorbonne to Grandes Ecoles such as the Ecole Normale Supérieure; students throng countless specialist bookstores and the art cinemas of rue Champollion and rue des Ecoles. The district's long association with learning began in about 1100, when a number of scholars, including Pierre Abélard, began to live and teach on the Montagne, independent of the established Canon school of Notre-Dame. This loose association of scholars came to be referred to as a 'university'. The Paris schools attracted disciples from all over Europe, and the 'colleges' – really student residences dotted round the area (some still survive) – multiplied, until the University of Paris was eventually given official recognition with a charter from Pope Innocent III in 1215.

By the 16th century, the university – named the **Sorbonne**, after the most famous of its colleges – had been co-opted by the Catholic Church. A century later, Cardinal Richelieu rebuilt it. Following the Revolution, when the university was forced to close, Napoleon then revived the Sorbonne as the cornerstone of his new, centralised education system. The university participated enthusiastically in the uprisings of the 19th century, and was also a seedbed of the 1968 revolt (*see p26* **1968**). Nowadays it is decidedly less turbulent. The present buildings are mostly 19th century; only the Baroque Chapelle de la Sorbonne survives from Boney's rebuild. By contrast, independent **Collège de France**, also on rue des Ecoles, was founded in 1530 by a group of humanists led by Guillaume Budé under the patronage of François I. Neighbouring Brasserie Balzar (No.49, 5th, 01.43.54.13.67) is a long-standing supplier of fuel for philosophising.

Climb up rue St-Jacques, serpentine rue de la Montagne-Ste-Geneviève or rue des Carmes, with its Baroque chapel (now used by the Syrian church), and rue Valette past the brick-and-stone entrance of the Collège Ste-Barbe, where Ignatius Loyola, Montgolfier and Eiffel studied, to impressive place du Panthéon. Where rue de la Montagne-Ste-Geneviève and rue Descartes meet, cafés and eccentric wine bistros overlook the sculpted 19th-century entrance of the former elite Ecole Polytechnique (since moved to the suburbs and replaced by the research ministry), where there's a small public park, and budget bistro **L'Ecurie** (*see p210*). This old stable burrows down into subterranean layers of medieval cellars.

The huge domed **Panthéon**, inspired by the Pantheon in Rome, was commissioned by Louis XV to honour Geneviève, the city's patron saint, but was converted during the Revolution to a secular temple for France's *grands hommes*. Alexandre Dumas was moved here in October 2002, with much ceremonial hullabaloo. In the surrounding square is one of the city's grand set pieces, also conceived by Panthéon architect Soufflot: the elegant 5th-district town hall, mirrored by the law faculty. On the north side,

the Ste-Geneviève university library (No.10, 5th, 01.44.41.97.97), built by Labrouste with an iron-framed reading room, contains medieval manuscripts. On the other side is the Hôtel des Grands Hommes (No.17, 5th, 01.46.34.19.60, www.hoteldesgrandshommes.com), where Surrealist mandarin André Breton invented 'automatic writing' in the 1920s.

Pascal and Racine, and the remains of Saint Geneviève, are all buried in Eglise St-Etienne-du-Mont (1 rue St-Etienne-du-Mont, 5th, 01.43. 54.11.79), on the north-east corner of the square. Just behind it, within the illustrious and elitist Lycée Henri IV, is the Gothic-Romanesque Tour de Clovis, part of the former Abbaye Ste-Geneviève. Look through the entrance doorway during term time and you'll also catch glimpses of the cloister and other monastic buildings. Further along rue Clovis is a chunk of Philippe-Auguste's 12th-century city wall (other chunks can be spotted at 62 rue du Cardinal-Lemoine and at the rear of buildings on rue Descartes). Exiled monarch James II resided at No.65 in the severe buildings of the former Collège des Ecossais (now a school), founded in 1372 to house Scottish students; King James' brain was preserved here until carried off and lost during the French Revolution. Other well-known ex-residents include Hemingway, who lived at both 79 rue du Cardinal-Lemoine (note the plaque) and 39 rue Descartes in the 1920s; James Joyce completed *Ulysses* while staying at 71 rue du Cardinal-Lemoine; and Rimbaud also lived in rue Descartes. Descartes himself lived on nearby rue Rollin.

This area is still a mix of tourist picturesque and gentle village, where some of the buildings hide surprising courtyards and gardens. Pretty

The best Literary landmarks

Café Flore
The haunt of Sartre and de Beauvoir after the war has now become somewhat touristified and upmarket – but still holds literary and philosophical evenings. *See p132.*

Café Procope
The first café to open in Paris in 1686 was frequented by the likes of Rousseau, Voltaire and Verlaine. Voltaire left his desk behind... *See p133.*

Hôtel du Vieux Paris
The original 'Beat Hotel', now rather more luxurious, is where William Burroughs wrote *The Naked Lunch*. *See p134.*

Rue du Cardinal-Lemoine
Once housed Hemingway at No.79, and James Joyce at No.71, where he completed *Ulysses*. *See p127.*

Rue de Pot-de-Fer
George Orwell lived at No.6, and washed dishes nearby. His experiences are in *Down and Out in Paris and London*. *See p128.*

Shakespeare & Co
The original shop at 12 rue de l'Odéon first published Joyce's *Ulysses*. *See p136.* Its modern counterpart now accommodates budding writers working as staff at 37 rue de la Bûcherie. *See p245.*

place de la Contrescarpe has been a famous rendezvous since the 1530s, when writers Rabelais, Ronsard and Du Bellay frequented the Cabaret de la Pomme de Pin at No.1; it still has lively cafés galore. When George Orwell stayed at 6 rue du Pot-de-Fer in 1928 and 1929, and detailed his experiences as a dishwasher in *Down and Out in Paris and London*, it was a place of astounding poverty; today the street is lined with bargain bars and restaurants, while the restored houses along rue Tournefort bear little relation to the garrets of Balzac's *Le Père Goriot*. Rue Mouffetard, originally the road to Rome and one of the oldest streets in the city, winds southward as a suite of cheap bistros, Greek and Lebanese tavernas, knick-knack shops and tourists; the vibe described by Hemingway – 'that wonderful narrow crowded market street, beloved of bohemians' – has somewhat faded. The busy street market (Tue-Sat, Sun morning) on the lower half seethes on weekends when it spills on to the square and around the cafés in front of the Eglise St-Médard (39 rue Daubenton, 5th, 01.44.08.87.00). There's another busy market, more frequented by locals, at **place Monge** (Wed, Fri, Sun morning; *see p267* **Market forces**).

Heading south beyond rue Soufflot, rue St-Jacques turns pretty. Here you'll find several ancient buildings such as the elegant *hôtel* at No.151, good food shops, vintage bistro Perraudin (No.157, 5th, 01.46.33.15.75), and the Institut Océanographique (No.195, 5th,

01.44.32.10.70, www.oceano.org/io), which has plentiful aquariums much loved by schoolkids. Rue d'Ulm houses the blue chip Ecole Normale Supérieure (No.45, 5th, 01.44.32.30.00), occupied in protest by the unemployed in January 1998; in an echo of 1968, students also joined in.

Turn off up hilly rue des Fossés-St-Jacques to discover place de l'Estrapade; in the 17th century the *estrapade* was a tall wooden tower from which deserters were dropped repeatedly until they died. Nearby in rue des Irlandais, the **Centre Culturel Irlandais** (*see p167*) in the renovated Collège des Irlandais hosts concerts, exhibitions, films, plays and spoken-word events promoting Irish culture.

To the west, rue Soufflot and broad rue Gay-Lussac (a hotspot of May 1968), with their Haussmannian apartment buildings, lead to boulevard St-Michel and the **Jardin du Luxembourg** (*see p130*). Further down rue St-Jacques, in the potters' quarter of Roman Lutetia, is another landmark, the **Eglise du Val-de-Grâce**, the least altered and most ornate of the city's baroque churches. Leading up to it, at 6 rue du Val-de-Grâce, was the home of Alfons Maria Mucha, the Czech art nouveau painter, best known for his posters of actress Sarah Bernhardt.

Collège de France
11 pl Marcelin-Berthelot, 5th (01.44.27.12.11/ www.college-de-france.fr). M° Cluny La Sorbonne. **Map p408 J7.**

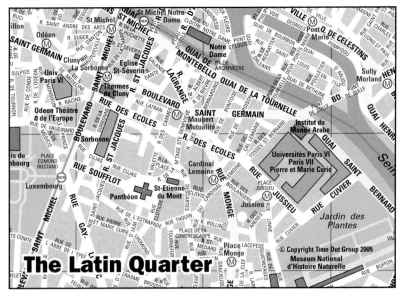

The Latin Quarter

© Copyright Time Out Group 2005

Founded in 1530 with the patronage of François I, the college is both a research institute and a place of learning. The present building dates from the 16th and 17th centuries with a later annexe. All lectures are free and open to the public; some have been given by such eminent names as Claude Lévi-Strauss and Emmanuel Le Roy Ladurie.

Eglise St-Etienne-du-Mont

Pl Ste-Geneviève, 5th (01.43.54.11.79). M° Cardinal Lemoine/RER Luxembourg. **Open** noon-7pm Mon; 8am-7pm Tue-Sun. **Map** p408 J8.

Geneviève, patron saint of Paris, is credited with having miraculously saved the city from the ravages of Attila the Hun in 451, and her shrine has been a popular pilgrimage place ever since. The present church was built in an amalgam of Gothic and Renaissance styles between 1492 and 1626, and once adjoined the abbey church of Ste-Geneviève. The façade mixes Gothic rose windows with rusticated classical columns and reliefs of classically draped figures. The interior is wonderfully tall and light, with soaring columns and a classical balustrade. The stunning Renaissance roodscreen, with its double spiral staircase and ornate stone strapwork, is the only one left in Paris, and was possibly designed by Philibert Delorme. Also worth a look is the ornate canopied wooden pulpit by Germaine Pillon dating from 1651, adorned with figures of the Graces and supported by a muscular Samson sitting on the defeated lion. Saint Geneviève's elaborate neo-Gothic brass-and-glass shrine (shielding the ancient tombstone) is located to the right of the choir, surrounded by assorted reliquaries and countless marble plaques bearing messages of thanks. At the back of the church (reached via the sacristy), the catechism chapel built by Baltard in the 1860s has a cycle of paintings relating the saint's life.

Le Panthéon

Pl du Panthéon, 5th (01.44.32.18.00). M° Cardinal Lemoine/RER Luxembourg. **Open** 10am-5.15pm daily. **Admission** €7; €4.50 18s-25s; free under-18s. **Credit** MC, V. **Map** p408 J8.

Soufflot's neo-classical megastructure with its huge dome was the architectural Grand Projet of its day, commissioned by a grateful Louis XV as an appropriately grandiose way to thank Saint Geneviève for his recovery from illness. By the time it was ready in 1790, the goalposts had moved; during the Revolution, Le Panthéon was re-dedicated as a 'temple of reason' and the resting place of the nation's great men. The austere barrel-vaulted crypt now houses Voltaire, Rousseau, Victor Hugo and Zola, and new heroes are added but rarely: Pierre and Marie Curie's remains were transferred here in 1995, she being the first woman to be interred in her own right. André Malraux, writer, Resistance hero and De Gaulle's culture minister, arrived in 1996; Alexandre Dumas in 2002. Inside are Greek columns and domes, and 19th-century murals of the saint's life by Symbolist painter Puvis de Chavannes, a formative influence on Picasso's blue period.

Eglise St-Séverin. *See p125.*

Up the steep spiral stairs to the colonnade are superb views across the city. The reconstruction of Foucault's pendulum also hangs here. It proved that the earth does indeed spin on its axis, a universal joint letting the direction of the pendulum's swing rotate as the earth revolves.

La Sorbonne

12 rue de la Sorbonne, 5th (01.46.33.08.61/www. sorbonne.fr). M° Cluny La Sorbonne. **Open** Tours by arrangement (01.40.46.22.11). Closed July, Aug. **Map** p408 J7.

Founded in 1253 by Robert de Sorbon, the University of the Sorbonne was at the centre of the Latin Quarter's intellectual activity from the Middle Ages until 1968, when it was occupied by students and stormed by the riot police. The authorities then split the University of Paris into safer outposts, but the Sorbonne still houses the Faculté des Lettres. Rebuilt by Richelieu, reorganised by Napoleon, the present buildings date from the late 1800s, with a labyrinth of classrooms and lecture theatres, as well as an observatory tower. The elegant dome of the 17th-century chapel dominates place de la Sorbonne; Cardinal Richelieu is buried inside. It is only open to the public for exhibitions or concerts.

Eglise St-Médard

141 rue Mouffetard, 5th (01.44.08.87.00). M° Censier Daubenton. **Open** 8am-noon, 2.30-7.30pm daily. **Map** p408 J9.

The original chapel was a dependency of the Abbaye Ste-Geneviève; rebuilding at the end of the 15th century created a much larger, late-Gothic structure with elaborate vaulted ambulatory.

Eglise du Val-de-Grâce

Pl Alphonse-Laveran, 5th (01.40.51.47.28). RER Luxembourg or Port-Royal. **Open** noon-6pm, Tue, Wed, Sat, Sun. **Admission** €5; €2.50 students, 6s-12s; free under-6s. **No credit cards. Map** p408 H9.
Anne of Austria, wife of Louis XIII, vowed to erect 'a magnificent temple' if God blessed her with a son. She got two. The resulting church and surrounding Benedictine monastery – now a military hospital and the Musée du Service de Santé des Armées devoted to military medicine (*see p181*) – were built by François Mansart and Jacques Lemercier. This is the most luxuriously baroque of the city's 17th-century domed churches, its ornate altar decorated with twisted barley-sugar columns. The swirling colours of the dome frescos painted by Pierre Mignard in 1669 (which Molière once eulogised) are meant to prefigure heaven. In stark contrast, the surrounding monastery is the perfect example of Mansart's classical restraint. Make sure to phone ahead to arrange guided visits.

The Jardin des Plantes district

The quiet, easternmost part of the 5th district is home to additional academic institutions, the Paris mosque and another Roman relic. Old-fashioned bistros on rue des Fossés-St-Bernard contrast with the slab-sided 1960s architecture of the massive university campus of Paris VI and VII, the science faculty (known as Jussieu). Built on what had been the site of the important Abbaye St-Victor, it's now the subject of a major asbestos-removal programme. Between the Seine and Jussieu is the strikingly modern, glass-faced **Institut du Monde Arabe**, with a busy programme of concerts and exhibitions, and a restaurant with a great view. The **Jardin Tino Rossi**, along the river, contains the slightly dilapidated **Musée de la Sculpture en Plein Air**, and in summer is a favourite stop for dancing and picnicking.

Stop at the **Arènes de Lutèce**, the Roman amphitheatre, its entrance hidden among the many hotels of rue Monge. The circular arena and its tiers of stone seating were rediscovered in 1869 when the street was being built. Their excavation started in 1883, thanks to the archaeological zeal of Victor Hugo. Nearby you can see the white minaret and green pan-tiled roof of the **Mosquée de Paris**, built in 1922 and official focus for the city's Muslim community, as opposed to the more makeshift or clandestine mosques that have since sprung up elsewhere around the city. Its beautiful Moorish tearoom is a favourite student haunt.

It looks out on to the **Jardin des Plantes**, the city's botanical garden. Established in 1626 as a garden for medicinal plants, it features an 18th-century maze, a winter garden brimming with rare species and the brilliantly renovated Grande Galerie de l'Evolution of the **Museum National d'Histoire Naturelle** (*see p180*). It's also home to **La Ménagerie** zoo (*see p291*), an unlikely by-product of the Revolution, when royal and noble collections of wild animals were impounded. Street names and the lovely animal-themed fountain on the corner of rue Cuvier pay homage to the many naturalists and other scientists who worked here, while up the street from the mosque (5 rue Geoffroy-St-Hilaire), the words 'Chevaux', 'Poneys' and 'Anes' are still visible on the former horse market.

Arènes de Lutèce

Entrances rue Monge, rue de Navarre, rue des Arènes, 5th. M° Cardinal Lemoine or Place Monge. **Open** *Winter* 8am-5.30pm daily. *Summer* 8am-10pm daily. **Map** p408 K8.
The Roman arena, where wild beasts and gladiators fought, could seat 10,000 people. It was still visible during the reign of Philippe-Auguste in the 12th century, then disappeared under rubble. The site was discovered in 1869 and now incorporates a romantically planted garden. These days, it attracts skateboarders, footballers and *boules* players.

Institut du Monde Arabe

1 rue des Fossés-St-Bernard, 5th (01.40.51.38.38/ www.imarabe.org). M° Jussieu. **Open** *Museum* 10am-6pm Tue-Sun. *Library* 1-8pm Tue-Sat. *Café* noon-6pm Tue-Sun. **Admission** *Roof terrace, library* free. *Museum* €3; free under-12s. *Exhibitions* varies. **Credit** MC, V. **Map** p408 K7.
A clever blend of high-tech steel, glass architecture and Arab influences, this wedge-shaped Grand Projet was built in 1980-87 to a design by French architect Jean Nouvel. Endless shuttered windows, inspired by the screens of Moorish palaces, look like and act as camera apertures according to the amount of available light. Inside is a collection of Middle Eastern art, archaeological finds, exhibition spaces, a library and a popular café. The Institute runs a varied agenda of dance and classical Arab music. There's a great view from the roof. *See also p174.*

Jardin des Plantes

Pl Valhubert, rue Buffon or rue Cuvier, 5th. M° Gare d'Austerlitz, Place Monge or Jussieu. **Open** *Main garden* 7.15am-sunset daily. *Alpine garden* Apr-Sept 8-11am, 1.30-5pm daily. *Greenhouses* Apr-Sept 1-5pm Mon, Wed-Fri; 10am-5pm Sat, Sun. *Ménagerie* Apr-Sept 9am-5pm, Mon-Sat; 9am-6.30pm Sun. *Museum: Grande Galerie de l'Evolution* (01.40.79.30.00): 10am-6pm Mon-Wed-Sun; *other galleries* Apr-Sept 10am-5pm Mon, Wed-Fri, 10am-6pm Sat, Sun. **Admission** free. *Greenhouses* €3. *Ménagerie* €6; €3.50 under-18s. *Grande Galerie de l'Evolution* €7; €5 under-18s. **No credit cards. Map** p408 L8.

Literary hotbed of the Latin Quarter – **La Sorbonne**. *See p129*.

Although small and a tad dishevelled, the Paris botanical garden, which contains more than 10,000 species, including tropical greenhouses and rose, winter and Alpine gardens, is worth a visit. Begun by Louis XIII's doctor as the royal medicinal plant garden in 1626, it opened to the public in 1640. It also comprises the Ménagerie, a small zoo, and the Muséum National d'Histoire Naturelle, including the magnificently renovated 1880s Grande Galerie de l'Evolution. Several ancient trees on view include a false acacia planted in 1636 and a cedar planted in 1734, while an 18th-century spiral yew maze climbs up a little hill, A plaque on the former laboratory announces that this is where Henri Becquerel discovered radioactivity in 1896.

Jardin Tino Rossi (Musée de la Sculpture en Plein Air)

Quai St-Bernard, 5th. M° Gare d'Austerlitz. **Open** *from* 8am Mon-Fri; *from* 9am Sat, Sun. Closing times vary. **Admission** free. **Map** p408 K8.

Despite recent replanting, the open-air sculpture museum by the Seine fights a constant battle against graffiti. Still, it is a pleasant enough, if traffic-noisy stroll. Most of the works are second-rate aside from Etienne Martin's bronze *Demeure I* and the Carrara marble *Fenêtre* by Cuban artist Careras.

La Mosquée de Paris

1 pl du Puits-de-l'Ermite, 5th (01.45.35.97.33/ tea room 01.43.31.38.20/Turkish baths 01.43.31. 18.14/www.mosquee-de-paris.com). M° Censier Daubenton. **Open** *Tours* 9am-noon, 2-6pm Mon-Thur, Sat, Sun (closed Muslim hols). *Tea room* 10am-midnight daily. *Restaurant* 7.30pm-10.30pm daily;

baths (women) 10am-9pm Mon, Wed, Sat; 2-9pm Fri; *(men)* 2-9pm Tue; 10am-9pm Sun. **Admission** €2.30; €1.50 7s-25s, over-60s; free under-7s; tea room free; baths €15-€35. **Credit** MC, V. **Map** p408 K9.

The mosque's stunning green-and-white square minaret is the spiritual heart of France's Algerian-dominated Muslim population. Built in 1922-26 in Hispano-Moorish style, with elements inspired by the Alhambra and Fez's Mosque Bou-Inania, the mosque is a series of buildings and courtyards in three sections: religious (grand patio, prayer room and minaret, all for serious worshippers and not inquisitive tourists); scholarly (Islamic school and library); and, entered from rue Geoffroy-St-Hilaire, commercial (domed hammam, Turkish baths, and relaxing Moorish tearoom).

St-Germain-des-Prés & Odéon

The Left Bank once stood for learning – now it has some of the most expensive property in Paris. It is also serious fashion territory, but still a hub for publishers.

The lore of Paris café society and intellectual life was born in St-Germain-des-Prés. Verlaine and Rimbaud drank here; later, Sartre, Camus and de Beauvoir scribbled and squabbled, and musicians congregated around Boris Vian in the post-war jazz boom. Earnest types still pose with weighty tomes, and the literati glitterati still gather on café terraces – to give interviews. With all the local price hikes, the only writers here today are the well-established ones.

Institut de France. *See p134*.

Armani, Louis Vuitton, Dior, Cartier and Céline have all unpacked their bags and the jazz clubs and musicians have crossed the river. In 1997 a band of intellectuals founded 'SOS St-Germain' to halt the tide of commercialism. Fashion designer **Sonia Rykiel** (*see p255*), long in the camp of the *germanopratins* (as residents are called), joined the campaign; **Karl Lagerfeld** (*see p255*) opened his photography gallery on rue de Seine. The upshot is that St-Germain almost rivals **avenue Montaigne** (*see p110*) for designer boutiques.

From the boulevard to the Seine

Hit by shortages of coal during World War II, Sartre shunned his cold flat on rue Bonaparte. 'The principal interest of the Café de Flore,' he noted, 'was that it had a stove, a nearby Métro and no Germans.' Although you can now spend more on a few coffees here than on a week's heating, the **Flore** (172 bd St-Germain, 6th, 01.45.48.55.26) remains an arty favourite and hosts *café-philo* evenings in English. Its rival, **Les Deux Magots** (6 pl St-Germain-des-Prés, 6th, 01.45.48.55.25), facing historic **Eglise St-Germain-des-Prés**, serves a cross-section of tourists. Nearby is celeb fave, Brasserie Lipp (151 bd St-Germain, 6th, 01.45.48.53.91), while art nouveau fans prefer Brasserie Vagenende (142 bd St-Germain, 6th, 01.43.26.68.18); swish late-night bookshop **La Hune** (*see p245*) provides sustenance of a more intellectual kind.

St-Germain-des-Prés grew up around the medieval abbey, the oldest church in Paris and site of an annual fair that drew merchants from across Europe. Traces of its cloister and part of the abbot's palace remain behind the church on rue de l'Abbaye. Constructed in 1586 in red brick with stone facing, the palace prefigured the architecture of **place des Vosges** (*see p105*). Charming place Furstenberg (once the palace stables) is home to upmarket furnishing fabric stores and the house and studio where the elderly Delacroix lived when painting the murals in St-Sulpice; today it is the **Musée National Delacroix** (*see p165*). Wagner, Ingres and Colette lived on rue Jacob; its elegant 17th-century *hôtels particuliers* now contain specialist book, design and antiques shops, pleasant hotels and bohemian throwbacks.

Further east, the rue de Buci hosts a street market and upmarket food shops, and is home to cafés Les Etages (No.5, 6th, 01.46.34.26.26) and Bar du Marché (No.16, 6th, 01.43.26.55.15). Hôtel La Louisiane (60 rue de Seine, 6th, 01.44.32.17.17, www.hotellalouisiane.com) has housed jazz gods Chet Baker and Miles Davis, and Existentialist deities Sartre and de Beauvoir. Rue Bonaparte, where Manet was born at No.5 in 1832, rue de Seine and rue des Beaux-Arts are still packed with small art galleries, mostly specialising in 20th-century abstraction, tribal art and art deco furniture. Here Oscar Wilde complained about the wallpaper and then checked out for good at what was then the Hôtel d'Alsace, now the renovated and fashionably over-the-top **L'Hôtel** (*see p68*). On rue Jacques-Callot, La Palette and Bistro Mazarin are good stopping-off points with enviable terraces; rue Mazarine, with shops of lighting, vintage toys and jewellery, also houses Conran's brasserie **L'Alcazar** (*see p213 and p236*) and hipster club **Wagg** (*see p331*) in a former cabaret. On quai de Conti stands the neo-classical Hôtel des Monnaies, built at the demand of Louis XV by architect Jacques-Denis Antoine, formerly the mint (1777-1973) and now the **Musée de la Monnaie** (*see p177*), a coin museum. Behind the colonnaded façade is a curious combination of elegant salons and industrial premises; commemorative medals are still engraved and struck here today. Next door stands the domed **Institut de France**, cleaned to within an inch of its crisp classical life. Opposite, the iron Pont des Arts footbridge leads to the **Louvre** (*see pp152-160*). Further along, the city's main fine-arts school, the **Ecole Nationale Supérieure des Beaux-Arts**, occupies an old monastery.

Coffee was first drunk in Paris in 1686 at Café Procope (13 rue de l'Ancienne-Comédie, 6th, 01.40.46.79.00). It was used by Voltaire, Rousseau, Benjamin Franklin, revolutionary Danton and later Verlaine. Despite the tourists, look out for Voltaire's desk and a postcard from

Marie-Antoinette. The back opens on to the twee, cobbled passage du Commerce St-André, home to toyshops, jewellers, chintzy tearooms and tapas trove Bistrot La Catalogne (No.4, 6th, 01.55.42.16.19). In the 18th century, Dr Joseph-Ignace Guillotin first tested out his notorious device – designed to make executions more humane – in the cellars of what is now the Pub St-Germain (No.17, 6th, 01.43.25.82.66); the first victim was reputedly a sheep. Jacobin regicide Billaud-Varenne was among those who felt the steel of Guillotin's gadget; his former home (45 rue St-André-des-Arts, 6th) was a location for the first girls' lycée in Paris, the Lycée Fénelon, founded in 1883. Today, rue St-André-des-Arts, which winds toward boulevard St-Michel, is lined with gift shops, crêperies and an arts cinema. Veer off the main drag into such quiet side streets as rue des Grands-Augustins, rue de Savoie and rue Séguier, and you find printers, bookshops and dignified 17th-century *hôtels particuliers*. On the corner of rue and quai des Grands-Augustins, **Lapérouse** restaurant (*see p213*) has a series of private dining rooms, where gentlemen would entertain their demi-monde mistresses; contemporary **Les Bouquinistes** (*see p213*) is easy to peek into. The turreted Hôtel de Fécamp, at 5 rue de Hautefeuille, was the medieval townhouse of

Hidden Paris Bring back the Belt

Wander the outskirts of Paris and you may find fragments of railway that mysteriously vanish into the urban fabric. These are the remnants of the Petite Ceinture, the 'little belt' that once circumnavigated the city a hop from where the Périphérique now roars by. Stretches of the railway can be found running through public parks (**Monsouris** in the 14th, **Georges Brassens** in the 15th and the **Buttes-Chaumont** in the 19th; *see p145, p145 and p123*); in the 20th, a line runs from the station later turned into the now-defunct Flèche d'Or bar. In the west, the old station of Passy La-Muette has become a brasserie incorporating the ticket office and platforms: Restaurant La Gare (19 chaussée de la Muette, 16th, (01.42.15.15.31).

The Ceinture was built between 1852 and 1869, originally to carry freight – but soon someone had the bright idea of turning it into public transport. In 1900 it was the city's pride and joy, carrying 39 million passengers and global tourists visiting the Exposition Universelle. Its life as a passenger line was cut short in 1934, when the steam trains

were replaced by a far less romantic PC bus. The tragic event was recorded in Charles Trenet's popular lament *Ménilmontant*:
'*Quand je revois ma petite gare, où chaque train passait joyeux, j'entends encore dans le tintamarre, des mots bizarres, des mots d'adieux.*' ('When I remember my little station, where every train that passed was happy, I still hear in all the din strange words, words of goodbye.')

For the last few years, a local society has been devoted to the Ceinture's preservation – L'Association pour la Sauvegarde de la Petite Ceinture (www.petiteceinture.org) – and has been lobbying for the return of passenger services on the line. The group has already managed to put the old north-east section back into action for one-off train rides, as well as planting a garden along sidings near the Porte de Clignancourt. If plans go ahead to incorporate a green stretch of the line into the extended T2 tramway from **Parc André Citroen** (*see p140*) as far as **Bibliothèque** (*see p147*), the Petite Ceinture will finally have its dignity restored.

the abbots of Fécamp, begun in 1292. Legend has it, that rue Gît-le-Coeur ('here lies the heart') is so called because one of Henri IV's mistresses lived here. At No.9 is the now rather luxurious Hôtel du Vieux Paris (6th, 01.44.32.15.90), the 'Beat Hotel' where William Burroughs revised *The Naked Lunch*.

Ecole Nationale Supérieure des Beaux-Arts (Ensb-a)

14 rue Bonaparte, 6th (01.47.03.52.15/www. ensba.fr). M° St-Germain des-Prés. **Open** *Courtyard* 9am-5pm Mon-Fri. *Exhibitions* 1-7pm Tue-Sun. **Admission** *Exhibitions* €4; €2.50 students, 12s-18s; free under-12s. **Credit** V. **Map** p407 H6.

The city's most prestigious fine-art school resides in what remains of the 17th-century Couvent des Petits-Augustins, the 18th-century Hôtel de Chimay, some 19th-century additions and some relics of assorted French châteaux moved here after the Revolution (when the buildings briefly served as a museum of French monuments, before becoming the art school in 1816). Exhibitions are often held here – entrance on quai Malaquais.

Eglise St-Germain-des-Prés

3 pl St-Germain-des-Prés, 6th (01.43.25.41.71). M° St-Germain-des-Prés. **Open** 8am-7.45pm Mon-Sat; 9am-8pm Sun. **Map** p407 H7.

The oldest church in Paris. On the advice of Germain (later bishop of Paris), Childebert, son of Clovis, had a basilica and monastery built here around 543; it was originally dedicated to St Vincent and then came to be known as St-Germain-le-Doré because of

its copper roof, and subsequently as St-Germain-des-Prés ('in the fields'). During the Revolution the abbey was burnt and a saltpetre refinery installed; the spire was only added in a clumsy 19th-century restoration. Despite this, most of the present structure is 12th-century, and some ornate carved capitals and the tower remain from the 11th. Illustrious tombs include those of Jean-Casimir, deposed king of Poland, who became abbot of St-Germain in 1669, and Scottish nobleman William Douglas. Under the window in the second chapel is the funeral stone of philosopher-mathematician René Descartes; his ashes have been here since 1819.

Institut de France

23 quai de Conti, 6th (01.44.41.44.41/www.institut-de-france.fr). M° St-Germain-des-Prés. **Open** *Guided tours* Sat, Sun (call ahead for times). **Admission** €3.10. **No credit cards. Map** p408 H6.

The elegant domed building, with two sweeping curved wings, was designed by Louis Le Vau in 1663-84 as a school for provincial children founded by Cardinal Mazarin. In 1805, the five academies of the Institut (Académie Française, Académie des Inscriptions et Belles-Lettres, Académie des Beaux-Arts, Académie des Sciences, Académie des Sciences Morales et Politiques), moved here. Inside is Mazarin's ornate tomb by Hardouin-Mansart, and the Bibliothèque Mazarine (open to over-18s, €15 for a one-year card with ID and two photos). The Académie Française, zealous guardian of the French language, was founded by Cardinal Richelieu in 1635 with the aim of preserving the purity of French from corrupting outside influences (such as English).

Eglise St-Sulpice. *See p136.*

Les Immortels, as the members of the Academy are still modestly known, have never stopped trying to impose archaic rules on a language and population that embrace multicultural input.

St-Sulpice & the Luxembourg

The quarter south of boulevard St-Germain between Odéon and Luxembourg, crammed with historic buildings and interesting shops, epitomises civilised Paris. Just off the boulevard lies the covered market of St-Germain, once the site of the medieval St-Germain fair. It now houses an underground swimming pool, auditorium, food hall and a shopping arcade. There are bars and bistros along rue Guisarde, nicknamed rue de la Soif ('thirst street') thanks to its regular bevy of carousers; it has the late-night Birdland bar (No.8, 6th, 01.43.26.97.59) and a couple of bistros, Mâchon d'Henri (No.8, 6th, 01.43.29.08.70) and Brasserie Fernand (No.13, 6th, 01.43.54.61.47). Rue Princesse and rue des Canettes are a beguiling mix of budget eateries, pizzerias and nocturnal haunts known to a determined few: the Bedford Arms pub (17 rue Princesse, 6th, 01.46.33.43.54) and nightspot Castel (15 rue Princesse, 6th, 01.40.51.52.80).

Pass the fashion boutiques, antiquarian book and print shops and high-class pâtisseries and you come to **Eglise St-Sulpice**, a surprising 18th-century exercise in classical form with two unmatching turrets and a colonnaded façade. The square and fountain in front were designed in the 19th century by Visconti. The square contains Visconti's imposing, lion-flanked Fontaine des Quatre Points Cardinaux (a pun on cardinal points and the statues of Bishops Bossuet, Fénelon, Massilon and Flechier, none of whom was actually a cardinal) and is the centrepiece for today's **Foire St-Germain** (*see p279*), a summer fair for antiques, books and poetry. The Café de la Mairie (8 pl St-Sulpice, 6th, 01.43.26.67.82) is a favourite with intellectuals and students, while amid shops of religious artefacts, the chic boutiques on place and rue St-Sulpice include **Yves Saint Laurent** (*see p256*), Christian Lacroix (2 pl St-Sulpice, 6th, 01.46.33.48.95, www.christian-lacroix.com), **Agnès b** (*see p256*), Vanessa Bruno (25 rue St-Sulpice, 6th, 01.43.54.41.04), Catherine Memmi (11 rue St-Sulpice, 6th, 01.44.07.02.02), popular perfumier Annick Goutal (12 pl St-Sulpice, 6th, 01.46.33.03.15) and milliner Marie Mercié (23 rue St-Sulpice, 6th, 01.43.26.45.83). Prime shopping continues further west: clothes on rue Bonaparte and rue du Four, and accessory and fashion shops on rue du Dragon, rue de Grenelle and rue du Cherche Midi. If you spot a queue in the latter street, it's most likely for the famous bread at **Poilâne** (*see p265*). Across the street at the junction of rue de Sèvres and rue du Cherche Midi, César's spiky bronze Centaur is a tribute by the French sculptor to Picasso.

The early 17th-century chapel of St-Joseph-des-Carmes, once a Carmelite convent, now hidden within the Institut Catholique (21 rue d'Assas, 6th, 01.44.39.52.00, www.icp.fr), was the scene for the killing of 115 priests during the Terror in 1792. To the east lies wide rue de Tournon, lined by such grand 18th-century residences as the elegant Hôtel de Brancas (No.6), with figures of Justice and Prudence over the door. This street opens up to the **Palais du Luxembourg**, which now serves as the Senate, and the adjoining **Jardin du Luxembourg**, the quintessential Paris park.

Towards boulevard St-Germain is the neo-classical **Odéon, Théâtre de l'Europe** (*see p344*), built in 1779, now closed for renovation. Beaumarchais' *Mariage de Figaro* was first performed here in 1784. A house in the square in front was home to Revolutionary hero Camille Desmoulins, who incited the mob to attack the Bastille in 1789. Now it's restaurant La Méditerranée (2 pl de l'Odéon, 6th, 01.43.26.02.30); an arty rendezvous in the 1940s, its menus and plates were designed by Jean Cocteau. Joyce's *Ulysses* was first published in 1922 by Sylvia Beach at the iconic Shakespeare & Co at 12 rue de l'Odéon (no relation to the current Latin Quarter bookshop, whose first owner was given permission to use the name).

Further along the street, at 12 rue de l'Ecole-de-Médecine, is the colonnaded neo-classical Université René Descartes (Paris V) medical school, and the **Musée d'Histoire de la Médecine** (*see p180*). The Club des Cordeliers, set up by Danton in 1790, devised revolutionary plots across the street at the Couvent des Cordeliers (No.15); the 14th-century refectory, all that remains of the monastery founded by St Louis, houses contemporary art exhibitions. Marat, one of the club's leading lights, was stabbed to death in the bathtub at his home in the same street – David subsequently fixing the moment after the crime in his iconic painting *The Death of Marat*. This was the surgeons' district: observe the sculpted doorway of the neighbouring *hôtel* and the domed building at No.5, once the barbers' and surgeons' guild (the two nearly the same thing in early medicine), now university premises. Climb rue André-Dubois to rue Monsieur-le-Prince and budget restaurant Polidor (No.41, 6th, 01.43.26.95.34), in business since 1845, and arts cinema Les 3 Luxembourg (No.67, 6th, 01.46.33.97.77).

Eglise St-Sulpice

Pl St-Sulpice, 6th (01.46.33.21.78). M° St-Sulpice.
Open 8am-7.30pm daily. **Map** p407 H7.
It took 120 years (starting in 1646) and six architects to finish the church of St-Sulpice. The grandiose Italianate façade with its two tier-colonnade was designed by Jean-Baptiste Servandoni, although he died in 1766 before the second tower was finished, leaving one tower a good five metres shorter than the other. Three murals by Delacroix in the first chapel – *Jacob's Fight with the Angel*, *Heliodorus Chased From the Temple* and *St Michael Killing the Dragon* – create a suitably sombre atmosphere.

Jardin and Palais du Luxembourg

Pl Auguste-Comte, pl Edmond-Rostand or rue de Vaugirard, 6th. M° Odéon/RER Luxembourg.
Open *Jardin* dawn-dusk daily. **Map** p407 H8.
The palace was built in the 1620s for Marie de Médicis, widow of Henri IV, by Salomon de Brosse on the site of the former mansion of the Duke of Luxembourg. Its Italianate style, with Mannerist rusticated columns, was intended to remind her of the Pitti Palace in her native Florence. In 1621, she commissioned Rubens to produce for the palace the 24 huge paintings, now in the Louvre, celebrating her life. Reworked by Chalgrin in the 18th century, the palace now houses the French parliamentary upper house, the Sénat (open only by guided visits or on the Journées du Patrimoine, *see p282*).

The mansion next door (Le Petit Luxembourg) is the residence of the Sénat's president. The gardens, though, are the real draw: part formal, with terraces and gravel paths, part 'English garden' of lawns and mature trees, they are the quintessential Paris park. The garden is alive with various sculptures, from the looming Cyclops on the 1624 Fontaine de Médicis to queens of France, a mini Statue of

Hidden Paris The lost river

Of the many scandals lurking under the pavements of Paris, one of the least known is that of the River Bièvre. Before its demise, the Bièvre brought fresh water into the city from its source at Guyancourt, south-west of Versailles; that didn't save it from shameful pollution, nor from being channelled into the sewers in 1850.

It entered Paris near Porte d'Italie, splitting into two at the Butte-aux-Cailles and travelling through the 13th and the 5th, where it flowed into the Seine. The Bièvre's bounty to the city was considerable. It provided drinking water, ice (Glacière Métro station still recalls the ice-collecting that took place here in winter) and limescale-free water for local washerwomen. It turned the mills at the monastery of St-Victor and irrigated the Jardin des Plantes.

But it was used for sluicing down the butcheries, tanneries and dyers of rue Mouffetard. This picturesque street takes its name from the putrid smell (*la mouffe*) of the polluted Bièvre. But the final nail in the coffin

was its abuse by the **Manufacture Nationale des Gobelins** weaving factory (*see p147*) – think of that the next time you splash out on an expensive tapestry.

The lost Bièvre has inspired floods of poetry, odes from Balzac, Ronsard, Hugo and Coppée, and an angry tract by J-K Huysmans who claimed it was a metaphor for feminine poverty exploited by the big city. Every year since 1981, a protest march has taken place through the night in May over the river's original 50-km course. The 'Friends of the Bièvre' often wax lyrical on their website, www.bievre.org.

It's not all been in vain. Plans are afoot to resurrect 1km of the Bièvre from Parc Kellerman to Square René-le-Gall in the 13th, and another 450m by the Jardin des Plantes in the 5th. For the time being, a little stream trickles through the quiet park of René-le-Gall. You'd never know it was the Bièvre (there is certainly no sign to say so), but it symbolises the hope for a cleaner city.

Liberty, wild animals, busts of literary giants Flaubert and Baudelaire, and a monument to Delacroix. There are orchards (300 varieties of apples and pears) and an apiary where you can take beekeeping courses. The Musée du Luxembourg (see p168) hosts prestigious art exhibitions, with lesser art shows in the former Orangerie. Most interesting, though, are the people: an international mix of *flâneurs* and *dragueurs*, chess players and martial arts practitioners; children on ponies, in sandpits, up climbing frames, on roundabouts and playing with the old-fashioned sailing boats on the pond. (See p289.) Then, there are the tennis courts (see p340), *boules* pitches (see p336), a bandstand with concerts on summer afternoons – and acres of park chairs.

The 7th & western Paris

Mainly 7th district, parts of 6th and 15th.
Townhouses spread out westwards from St-Germain into the profoundly establishment 7th district, as the street and café life gives way to tranquil residential blocks and government offices. The 7th easily divides into two halves: the more intimate Faubourg St-Germain to the east, with its historic mansions and fine shops and, west of Les Invalides, windswept wide avenues and the Eiffel Tower.

The Faubourg St-Germain

In the early 18th century, when the Marais went out of fashion, aristocrats built palatial new residences on the Faubourg St-Germain, the district that was growing up around the site of the former city wall. Well-bred Paris continues to reside here today, amid the government ministries and foreign embassies that colour the area with flags and diplomatic number plates. Many fine *hôtels particuliers* survive; glimpse their stone gateways and elegant entrance courtyards on rues de Grenelle, St-Dominique, de l'Université and de Varenne.

Just west of St-Germain, the 'Carré Rive Gauche' or 'Carré des Antiquaires' – the quadrangle of streets enclosed by quai Voltaire, rues des Sts-Pères, du Bac and de l'Université – and is lined with antiques shops. On rue des Sts-Pères, *chocolatier* **Debauve&Gallais** (see p266), with its classic period interior, has been making chocolates since 1800, originally for medicinal purposes. Rue du Pré-aux-Clercs, named after a field where students used to sort out their differences by duelling, is today a favourite with fashion insiders. There are still students to be found on adjoining rue St-Guillaume, home to the prestigious Fondation Nationale des Sciences-Politiques (No.27, 7th, 01.45.49.50.50, www.sciences-po.fr), better known as 'Sciences-Po'.

Rue de Montalembert is home to two of the Left Bank's smartest hotels: the **Hôtel Montalembert** (see p71) and the Hôtel du Pont-Royal, a gastronomone's destination with the addition of the trendy **Atelier de Joël Robuchon** (see p215). By the river, a beaux arts train station houses the unmissable art collections of the **Musée d'Orsay**; the towns once served are still listed on the façade. Outside on the esplanade are 19th-century bronze *animalier* sculptures. Next door is the lovely 1780s Hôtel de Salm, a mansion built for a German prince and now the Musée National de la Légion d'Honneur (2 rue de la Légion d'Honneur, 7th, 01.40.62.84.25), devoted to France's honours system. Across the street, a modern footbridge, the Passerelle Solférino, crosses the Seine to the Tuileries.

Fancy Hôtel Bouchardon now houses the **Musée Maillol** (see p166). At its curved entrance, the Fontaine des Quatre-Saisons by Bouchardon has statues of the seasons surounding allegorical figures of Paris above the rivers Seine and Marne. You'll have to wait for the open-house **Journées du Patrimoine** (see p282) to see the decorative interiors and private gardens of others such as the Hôtel de Villeroy (Ministry of Agriculture; 78 rue de Varenne, 7th), Hôtel Boisgelin (Italian Embassy; 47 rue de Varenne, 7th), Hôtel d'Avaray (Dutch ambassador's residence, 85 rue de Grenelle, 7th), Hôtel d'Estrées (Russian ambassador's residence; 79 rue de Grenelle, 7th), or Hôtel de Monaco (Polish Embassy, 57 rue St-Dominique, 7th). Among the most beautiful is the Hôtel Matignon (57 rue de Varenne, 7th), residence of the Prime Minister. Used by French statesman Talleyrand for lavish receptions, it contains the biggest private garden in Paris. The Cité Varenne at No.51 is a lane of exclusive houses with private gardens.

Then there's rue du Bac, home to the city's oldest and most elegant department store, **Le Bon Marché** ('the good bargain'; see p240), and to unlikely pilgrimage spot the **Chapelle de la Médaille Miraculeuse** On nearby rue de Babylone, handy budget bistro Au Babylone (No.13, 7th, 01.45.48.72.13) has been serving up lunches for decades, but the Théâtre de Babylone where Beckett's *Waiting for Godot* was premiered in 1953 has now long since gone.

At the foot of boulevard St-Germain, facing place de la Concorde across the Seine, is the **Assemblée Nationale**, the lower house of the French parliament. Behind it, elegant place du Palais-Bourbon leads into rue de Bourgogne, a rare commercial thoroughfare amid the official buildings, with some delectable pâtisseries and designer furniture showrooms. Nearby, the mid 19th-century Eglise Ste-Clothilde (12 rue

Martignac, 7th, 01.44.18.62.60), with its skeletal twin spires, is an early example of Gothic Revival. Beside the Assemblée is the Foreign Ministry, often referred to by its address, 'quai d'Orsay'. Beyond it, a long, grassy esplanade leads up to the golden-domed **Invalides**. The vast military hospital complex, with Eglise du Dôme and St-Louis-des-Invalides churches, all built by Louis XIV, epitomises the official grandeur of the Sun King as expression of royal and military power. It now houses the **Musée de l'Armée** (*see p174*), as well as Napoleon's tomb inside the Eglise du Dôme. Stand with your back to the dome to survey cherubim-laden Pont Alexandre III and the **Grand** and **Petit Palais** (*see p112*) over the river, all three put up for the 1900 Exposition Universelle. Just beside Les Invalides is the **Musée Rodin** (*see p166*), housed in the charming 18th-century Hôtel Biron and its romantic gardens. Rodin was invited here in 1908, on the understanding that he would give his work to the state. Many of his great sculptures, including *The Thinker*, *The Burghers of Calais* and the swarming *The Gates of Hell* are displayed in his house and around the gardens. The chapel, at the time of going to press, was undergoing restoration.

Les Invalides.

Assemblée Nationale

33 quai d'Orsay, 7th (01.40.63.60.00/www. assemblee-nat.fr). M° Assemblée Nationale. **Open** 8.40-11.40am, 2-5pm Mon, Fri, Sat. *Guided tours* 10am, 2pm, 3pm Sat. **Admission** free (ID required). **Map** p407 F5.

Like the Sénat, another royal building converted to republicanism, the Assemblée Nationale (also known as the Palais Bourbon) was built in 1722-28 for the Duchesse de Bourbon, daughter of Louis XIV and Madame de Montespan, who also put up the neighbouring Hôtel de Lassay (official residence of the Assembly's president) for her lover the Marquis de Lassay. It was modelled on the Grand Trianon at Versailles, a colonnaded *cour d'honneur* opening on to rue de l'Université and gardens running down to the Seine. Later the Prince de Condé extended the palace, linked the two hôtels and laid out the place du Palais-Bourbon. The Greek temple-style façade by the river (actually the rear of the building) was added only in 1806 to mirror the Madeleine; in front are statues of four great statesmen: L'Hôpital; Sully; Colbert and Aguesseau. The Napoleonic frieze on the pediment was replaced by a monarchist one after the restoration. The present frieze was added in 1838-41, with more conciliatory figures of France, Power and Justice. After the Revolution, the palace became the meeting place for the Conseil des Cinq-Cents, the new legislative body, forerunner of the parliament's lower house which set up here for good in 1827, when the interior was radically altered with the building of the Hémicycle debating chamber. The library is decorated with Delacroix's *History of Civilisation*. Visitors can attend debates.

Chapelle de la Médaille Miraculeuse

Couvent des Soeurs de St-Vincent-de-Paul, 140 rue du Bac, 7th (01.49.54.78.88). M° Sèvres-Babylone. **Open** 7.45am-1pm, 2.30-7pm daily. **Map** p407 F7.

In 1830 saintly Catherine Labouré was said to have been visited by the Virgin, who gave her a medal which performed miracles. Attracting two million pilgrims every year, the kitsch chapel – mosaics, murals and statues, and the embalmed bodies of Catherine and her mother superior – is one of France's most visited sites. Reliefs in the courtyard tell the nun's story; slot machines let you buy a medal of your own.

Les Invalides

Esplanade des Invalides, 7th (01.44.42.54.52/Musée de l'Armée 01.44.42.37.67/www.invalides.org). M° Invalides. **Open** *Oct-Mar* 10am-4.45pm daily. *Apr-Sept* 10am-5.45pm daily. **Admission** *Courtyard* free. *Musée de l'Armée & Eglise du Dôme* €6; €4.50 students under 26; free under-18s, CM. **Credit** MC, V. **Map** p407 E6.

Its imposing gilded dome is misleading: the Hôtel des Invalides was (and in part still is) a hospital. Commissioned by Louis XIV for wounded soldiers, at one time it housed up to 6,000 invalids. Designed by Libéral Bruand and then completed by Jules Hardouin-Mansart, it's a magnificent monument to Louis XIV and Napoleon. The foundations were laid in 1671. Behind lines of topiaried yews and cannons, the main (northern) façade has a relief of Louis XIV (Ludovicus Magnus) and the Sun King's sunburst. Wander through the main courtyard and you'll see

its grandiose two-storey arcades, sundials on three sides and statue of Napoleon glaring out from the end; the dormer windows around the courtyards are sculpted in the form of suits of armour. Now the Invalides houses the impressive Musée de l'Armée, with a staggering display of military paraphernalia, the Musée de l'Ordre de la Libération and the Musée des Plans-Reliefs, the collection of scale models of cities begun by Vauban, and once utilised as an aid to military strategy.

The complex also contains two churches – or, rather, a sort of double church: the Eglise St-Louis was for the soldiers, the Eglise du Dôme for the king, each with its own separate entrance. You'll find an opening behind the altar between the two. The long, barrel-vaulted nave of the church of St-Louisis hung with flags captured from enemy troops. Since 1840 the baroque Eglise du Dôme has been solely dedicated to the worship of Napoleon, whose body was supposedly brought here from St Helena (although this is now in doubt).

On the ground floor, under a dome painted by De la Fosse, Jouvenet and Coypel, are chapels featuring monuments to such generals as Vauban, Foch and Joseph Napoleon – Napoleon's older brother and king of Italy and Spain. Napoleon II (King of Rome) is buried in the crypt with his father the emperor. Two dramatic black figures holding up the entrance to the crypt, the red porphyry tomb, the ring of giant figures and the friezes and texts eulogising the emperor's heroic deeds give the measure of the cult of Napoleon, cherished in France for ruling large swaths of Europe and creating an administrative and educational system that endures today.

Musée d'Orsay

1 rue de la Légion d'Honneur, 7th (01.40.49.48.14/ recorded information 01.45.49.11.11/www.musee-orsay.fr). M° Solférino/RER Musée d'Orsay. **Open** 10am-6pm Tue, Wed, Fri, Sat; 10am-9.30pm Thur, 9am-6pm Sun. **Admission** €7; €5 students, over-60s, Sun; free under-18s; free 1st Sun of mth. **Credit** *Shop* AmEx, MC, V. **Map** p407 G6.

Originally a train station, designed by Victor Laloux to coincide with the 1900 Exposition Universelle. The platforms proved too short for modern trains and, by the 1950s, the station was threatened with demolition. It then became home to a theatre (the Renaud-Barrault), and scenes in Orson Welles' *The Trial* were filmed here. It was saved in the late 1970s when President Giscard d'Estaing decided to turn it into a museum spanning the fertile art period between 1848 and 1914, home to masterpieces by Manet, Monet, Degas, Renoir, Gauguin, Cézanne and Van Gogh among others. (The painter Edouard Détaille had said it looked like a palace of fine art when it was built.) *See also p164.*

West of Les Invalides

South-west of the Invalides is the massive Ecole Militaire (av de la Motte-Picquet, 7th), the military academy built by Louis XV to educate the children of penniless officers. It would later train Napoleon. The severe neo-classical building was designed by Jacques Ange Gabriel. It's still used by the army and closed to the public. From the north-western side of the Ecole Militaire begins the vast Champ de Mars, a market garden converted into a military drilling ground in the 18th century. It was the scene of celebrations after the Revolution and now forms the backdrop to the most celebrated Paris monument of all, the **Eiffel Tower**. At its avenue de la Motte-Picquet end stands the Mur pour la Paix, erected in 2000 to articulate hopes for peace. Opposite its south-eastern edge are the Y-shaped **UNESCO** building, built in 1958, and the Modernist Ministry of Labour. Smart apartments line broad avenues Bosquet and Suffren, though there are also interesting examples of architectural eclecticism: look at the pseudo-Gothic and pseudo-Renaissance houses on avenue de Villars and Lavirotte's fabulous art nouveau doorway at 27 avenue Rapp. For signs of life in this rather stuffy quarter, visit **Saxe-Breteuil** street market on the avenue de Saxe (*see p267* **Market forces**), old-fashioned bistros Thoumieux (79 rue St-Dominique, 7th, 01.47.05.49.75) and Fontaine de Mars (129 rue St-Dominique, 7th, 01.47.05.46.44), set on an arcaded square next to a pretty fountain. The upper reaches of rue Cler have classy food shops.

Les Egouts de Paris

Entrance opposite 93 quai d'Orsay, by Pont de l'Alma, 7th (01.53.68.27.81). M° Alma Marceau/ RER Pont de l'Alma. **Open** 11am-4pm Mon-Wed, Sat, Sun. Closed 3wks Jan. **Admission** €3.80; €3.05 students, over-60s; €2.30 5s-12s; free under-5s, CM. **Map** p402 D5.

For centuries the main source of drinking water in Paris was the Seine, which was also the main sewer. Construction of an underground sewerage system began in 1825 under Napoleon. Today, the Egouts de Paris is a smelly museum; each sewer in the 2,100km system is marked with a replica of the street sign above. The Egouts can be closed after periods of heavy rain.

Eiffel Tower

Champ de Mars, 7th (01.44.11.23.45/recorded information 01.44.11.23.23/www.tour-eiffel.fr). M° Bir-Hakeim/RER Champ de Mars Tour Eiffel. **Open** 1 Sept-13 June 9.30am-11pm daily. 14 June-31 Aug 9am-midnight. **Admission** By lift 1st level €3.70; €2.3 3s-12s. 2nd level €7; €3.90 3s-12s. 3rd level €10.20; €5.50 3s-12s; free under-3s. By stairs (9.30am-6.30pm) 1st & 2nd levels €3.30. **Credit** AmEx, MC, V. **Map** p406 C6.

Maupassant claimed he left Paris because of it, William Morris visited daily to avoid having to see it from afar, and it was meant to be a temporary structure – but today no building better symbolises Paris than the Tour Eiffel. The radical cast-iron tower was built – for the 1889 World Fair and the centenary of the 1789 Revolution – by engineer Gustave Eiffel (whose construction company still exists today). Eiffel made use of new technology that was already popular in iron-framed buildings.

Construction took over two years and used some 18,000 pieces of metal and 2,500,000 rivets. The 300-metre tower stands on four massive concrete piles, and was the tallest building in the world until overtaken by New York's Empire State Building in the 1930s. Vintage double-decker lifts ply their way up and down, or you can walk as far as the second level. There are souvenir shops, an exhibition space, café and even a post office on the first and second levels (the smart Jules Verne restaurant has its own lift in the north tower). At the top (third level), there's Eiffel's cosy salon and a viewing platform with panels pointing out what to see in every direction. Views can reach over 65km on a good day, although the most fascinating perspectives are of the ironwork itself, whether gazing up from underneath or enjoying the changing vision going up in the lift. At night, for ten minutes on the hour, 20,000 flashbulbs provide a beautiful shimmering effect. The tower has some six million visitors a year; to avoid the queues, try coming late at night.
Wheelchair access (1st & 2nd levels only).

UNESCO

7 pl de Fontenoy, 7th (01.45.68.10.00/www.unesco. org). M° Ecole Militaire. **Open** 9.30am-2.30pm Mon-Fri. *Tours* (01.45.68.16.42) 3pm Mon-Fri. **Admission** free. **Map** p407 D7.

The Y-shaped UNESCO headquarters, built in 1958, is home to a swarm of international diplomats. It's worth visiting for the sculptures and paintings by Picasso, Arp, Giacometti, Moore, Calder and Miró, and the Japanese garden, and its contemplation cylinder by minimalist architect Tadao Ando.

Village Suisse

38-78 av de Suffren/54 av de La Motte-Picquet, 15th (01.43.06.44.18). M° La Motte-Picquet Grenelle. **Open** 10.30am-12.30pm; 1.30-7pm Mon, Thur-Sun. **Map** p406 D7.

The mountains and waterfalls created for the Swiss Village at the 1900 Exposition Universelle are long gone, but the village lives on. Rebuilt as blocks of flats, the street level has been colonised by some 150 boutiques offering high-quality, though pricy, antiques and collectibles.

Along the Seine

Downstream from the Eiffel Tower, the high-tech **Maison de la Culture du Japon** stands near Pont Bir-Hakeim on quai Branly. Beyond, the 15th-district Fronts de Seine riverfront, with its tower block developments, was the scene of some of the worst architecture of the 1970s. This would-be brave new world of walkways, suspended gardens, and tower blocks had no obvious means of access, so the Beaugrenelle shopping centre and strange restaurants are hidden underground. Further west things look up: the sophisticated former headquarters of the Canal+ TV channel (2 rue des Cévennes), designed by American architect Richard Meier, is surrounded by fine modern housing; and the **Parc André Citroën**, created in the 1990s on the site of the former Citroën car works (*see p291* **From waste ground to playground**). The park runs down to the Seine quayside, where you'll find the occasional cruise ship and August partygoers.

Parc André Citroën

Rue Balard, rue St-Charles, quai Citroën, 15th. Mᵒ Javel or Balard. **Open** *from* 8am-6pm Mon-Fri; *from* 9am-6pm Sat, Sun, public hols. Closing times vary. **Map** p406 A9.

This park is a fun, postmodern version of a French formal garden by Gilles Clément and Alain Prévost. It comprises glasshouses, computerised fountains, waterfalls, a wilderness and themed gardens with different coloured plants and even sounds. Stepping stones and water jets make it a garden for pleasure as well as philosophy. The tethered Eutelsat helium balloon takes visitors up for marvellous panoramic views over the city.

Maison de la Culture du Japon

101bis quai Branly, 15th (01.44.37.95.00). Mᵒ Bir-Hakeim/RER Champ de Mars Tour Eiffel. **Open** noon-7pm Tue, Wed, Fri, Sat; noon-8pm Thur. **Admission** free. **Map** p406 C6.

Built in 1996 by the Anglo-Japanese architectural partnership of Yamanaka and Armstrong, this opalescent glass cultural centre screens films and puts on exhibitions and theatre. It also has a library, an authentic Japanese tea pavilion on the roof, where you can watch the tea ceremony, and a well-stocked book and gift shop.

Montparnasse & beyond

Mainly 6th and 14th districts, some 13th and 15th.

Artists such as Picasso, Léger and Soutine fled to 'Mount Parnassus' in the early 1900s to escape the rising rents of Montmartre. They were soon joined by Chagall, Zadkine and other escapees from the Russian Revolution, and by Americans, including Man Ray, Henry Miller, Ezra Pound and Gertrude Stein. Between the wars the neighbourhood symbolised modernity. Studio buildings with large north-facing windows were built by avant-garde architects all over this part of Paris, artists, writers and intellectuals drank and debated in the quarter's showy bars and naughty pastimes – such as the tango – flourished.

Today, Montparnasse has lost much of its soul. The high-rise **Tour Montparnasse**, the first skyscraper in central Paris, is the most visible of several redevelopment projects of the 1970s; at least there are good views from the top. Horror at its construction prompted a change in building regulations for central Paris; like Centre Point in London, it's an inescapable

landmark. At its foot are a shopping centre, the **Red Light** and **Amnesia** nightclubs (*see p329 and p331*), joined in winter by an outdoor **ice rink** (*see p338*). The old Montparnasse railway station witnessed two events of historic significance: in 1898 a runaway train burst through its façade (you've almost certainly seen the photo) and on 25 August 1944 the Germans surrendered Paris here. The train station was rebuilt in the 1970s, a grey affair that contains the surprising **Jardin de l'Atlantique** and the **Mémorial du Maréchal Leclerc/Musée Jean Moulin** (*see p174*) above its tracks.

Rue du Montparnasse, appropriately enough for a street near the station that sends travellers to Brittany, is clustered with crêperies. Nearby, strip joints have replaced most of the theatres on ever-saucy rue de la Gaîté, but boulevard Edgar-Quinet has pleasant cafés and a street market (Wed, Sat mornings), and the entrance to the **Cimetière du Montparnasse**. Nearby

Line up for the **Eiffel Tower**. *See p140.*

boulevard du Montparnasse still buzzes at night, thanks to its many cinemas and brasseries: giant art deco brasserie La Coupole (No.102, 14th, 01.43.20.14.20); opposite, classic café **Le Select** (see p237); Le Dôme (No.108, 14th, 01.43.35.25.81), now a top-notch fish restaurant and bar; and La Rotonde (No.105, 6th, 01.43.26.48.26). All were popularised by the heavyweight literary and arty set between the wars, all now use this heritage to their best advantage. Nearby, on boulevard Raspail, stands Rodin's statue of Balzac, whose rugged rather than flattering appearance caused such a scandal that it was only put in place in 1937.

For a whiff of Montparnasse's artistic past, wander down rue de la Grande-Chaumière. Bourdelle and Friesz taught at the venerable Académie de la Grande-Chaumière (No.14), frequented by Calder, Giacometti and Pompon among others (it still offers drawing lessons today); Modigliani died at No.8 in 1920, ruined by tuberculosis, drugs, alcohol and women; nearby **Musée Zadkine** (see p167) occupies the sculptor's old house and studio. Rues Vavin and Bréa, leading to the Jardin du Luxembourg, have become an enclave of children's shops. Make sure you look out for Henri Sauvage's sleek, white tiled apartment building at **6 rue Vavin**, constructed in 1911-12.

Further east on boulevard du Montparnasse, literary café La Closerie des Lilas (No.171, 6th, 01.40.51.34.50) was a favourite with everyone from Lenin and Trotsky to Picasso and Hemingway; brass plaques on the tables tell you who used to sit where. Next to it is the lovely Fontaine de l'Observatoire, with bronze turtles and thrashing sea horses by Frémiet and figures of the four continents by Carpeaux. From here the Jardins de l'Observatoire form part of the perspective running between the **Palais du Luxembourg** (see p136) and the **Observatoire de Paris** across the boulevard, the original royal observatory. A curiosity next door is the Maison des Fontainiers, built over a large (now dry-ish) underground reservoir commissioned by Marie de Médicis to supply water to fountains around the city. A recent addition is the glass-and-steel **Fondation Cartier** (see p168), designed by Jean Nouvel on boulevard Raspail, the jewellery company's HQ and an exhibition centre for contemporary art.

West of the train station the redevelopment of Montparnasse continues with the circular place de Catalogne, a piece of 1980s postmodern classicism by Mitterrand's favourite architect, Ricardo Bofill, and the housing estates of rue Vercingétorix. Traces of old arty Montparnasse remain here too: in impasse Lebouis, an avant-garde studio building has recently been converted into the **Fondation Henri Cartier-Bresson** (see p179 and p170 **Capturing defining moments**); at 21 avenue du Maine, an ivy-clad alleyway of old studios contains the **Musée du Montparnasse** (see p168), in the former academy and canteen of Russian painter Marie Vassilieff, and artist-run exhibition space Immanence; on rue Antoine-Bourdelle, the **Musée Bourdelle** (see p168) includes another old cluster of studios, where sculptor Bourdelle, Symbolist painter Eugène Carrière and, briefly, Marc Chagall also worked, while towards Invalides, on rue Mayet, craft and restoration workshops still hide in old courtyards.

Cimetière du Montparnasse

3 bd Edgar-Quinet, 14th (01.44.10.86.50). M° Edgar-Quinet or Raspail. **Open** *6 Nov-15 Mar* 8am-5.30pm Mon-Fri; 8.30am-5.30pm Sat; 9.30am-5.30pm Sun. *16 Mar-5 Nov* 8am-6pm Mon-Fri; 8.30am-6pm Sat; 9am-6pm Sun. **Admission** free. **Map** p407 G9.
This 1,800-acre cemetery was formed by commandeering three farms (there are the ruins of a rural windmill by rue Froidevaux) in 1824. As with much of the Left Bank, the Montparnasse cemetery scores high on lit cred: Samuel Beckett, Charles Baudelaire, Jean-Paul Sartre and Simone de Beauvoir, Guy de Maupassant, Tristan Tzara and Ionesco are all here; resident artists include Constantin Brancusi, Henri Laurens, Frédéric Bartholdi (sculptor of the Statue of Liberty) and Man Ray. The celeb roll-call features Serge Gainsbourg, André Citroën (of car fame), comic Coluche and actress Jean Seberg.

Jardin de l'Atlantique

Entry from Gare Montparnasse or pl des Cinq-Martyrs-du-Lycée-Buffon, 15th. M° Montparnasse Bienvenüe or Gaîté. **Open** dawn-dusk daily. **Map** p407 F9.
Perhaps the hardest of all Paris gardens to find, the Jardin de l'Atlantique was opened in 1995. It's an engineering feat: a small oasis of granite paths, trees and bamboo suspended 18m over the tracks of Montparnasse station. Small openings let you peer down on the trains below.

Observatoire de Paris

61 av de l'Observatoire, 14th (www.obspm.fr). M° St-Jacques/RER Port-Royal. **Open** *Tours* 1st Sat of mth by reservation in writing. **Map** p407 H10.
The Paris observatory was founded by Louis XIV's finance minister, Colbert, in 1667; it was designed by Claude Perrault, who worked on the Louvre, with labs and observation tower. The French meridian line mapped out by François Arago in 1806 (in use before the Greenwich meridian was adopted as an international standard) runs through the centre of the building, aligned on the compass points. The dome on the observation tower was added in the 1840s, but what with urban light pollution, now most gazing takes place in Meudon and Provence. A visit involves writing ahead, but check the website for openings linked to astronomical happenings. or visit on the Journées du Patrimoine (see p282).

Hidden Paris The great escape

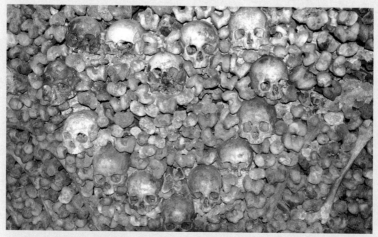

Unusual recent finds underneath Paris have alerted the authorities to what many have known all along – that the city's colossal network of passages, most of them closed to the public, have been regularly put to good use by pranksters and party-goers.

Two key discoveries made the news in the summer of 2004. First, a security alert was set off when tunnels were found heading towards the high-security Prison de la Santé. Originally believed to have been dug by either terrorists or criminals planning a prison escape, they turned out to be the work of the more extreme element of catacomb enthusiasts, or *cataphiles*. Another extreme faction ('Les Mexicains') was responsible for setting up an underground cinema – bar, seats, illegal electricity cables and all – far below the Trocadéro.

In 1944, the passages were used by the Resistance; in 1968, by students fleeing the police. Wishing to restrict public access to the short section of **catacombs** (*see p144*) below the official entrance at Denfert-Rochereau, the authorities have managed to seal up nearly a third of the 3,000-km tunnel network which extends under much of the city, particularly the 13th and 14th districts.

The passages originated as quarries, providing limestone for huge building projects such as Notre-Dame. By the late 18th century, when the city had extended this far south, many streets began to collapse. The

authorities set about building tunnels and supports to prop up the earth. At the same time, with public burial pits rising in the era of the Revolutionary Terror, the bones of six million people were transferred to the catacombes at Denfert-Rochereau. The bones of Marat, Robespierre and their cronies are tightly packed in with wall upon wall of their fellow citizens. It's an extraordinary sight, and one not for the claustrophic – although the sign 'Stop! This is the empire of death!' might be overdoing it a little. You descend an 85-step spiral staircase that takes you 20m below ground, to a mass of bones and carvings. Carry a torch – and don't try to take one of the bones as a souvenir: bags are checked at the end.

Meanwhile, the cataphiles continue to get their clandestine kicks. Armed with miners' lamps and overalls, graffiti artists and party people lead bemused visitors down the handful of concealed manholes dotted around the Left Bank (particularly around **Parc Montsouris**; *see p145*). Most of the tunnels are high enough to stand up in – workmen had to bring in the bones by wheelbarrow, remember – and most intersections are signposted with street names. While most manage to elude the police, they can do nothing about the passages sealed off by pumped-in concrete. Within 50 years or so only relatively small sections of the network will remain accessible.

Cimetière du Montparnasse.
See p142.

Tour Montparnasse

33 av du Maine, 15th (01.45.38.52.56/www.tour montparnasse.com). M° Montparnasse Bienvenüe.
Open *Winter* 9.30am-10.30pm daily. *Summer* 9.30am-11.30pm daily. **Admission** €8.20; €7 students, over-60s; €5.50 5s-14s; free under-5s.
Credit MC, V. **Map** p407 F9.

Built in 1974 on the site of the old station, this 209m steel-and-glass monster is shorter than the Eiffel Tower, but more central. A lift whisks you up to the 56th floor, where you'll find a display of aerial views of Paris. Classical concerts are held on the terrace.

Denfert-Rochereau & Montsouris

Just before the 1789 Revolution, the bones of six million Parisians were wheelbarrowed to the Catacombs at Denfert-Rochereau, taken from overcrowded city cemeteries to a network of tunnels that spreads under much of the 13th and 14th districts. The gloomy public entrance to one section is next to one of the toll gates of the Mur des Fermiers-Généraux built by Ledoux in the 1780s.

The bronze Lion de Belfort dominates the traffic-laden place Denfert-Rochereau, a favourite starting point for the city's countless political demonstrations. The regal beast was sculpted by Bartholdi, and is a scaled-down replica of the one in Belfort, commemorating Colonel Denfert-Rochereau's brave defence of the town in 1870. Nearby, the southern half of rue Daguerre is a sociable, pedestrianised market street (Tue-Sat, Sun morning) brimming with cafés and food shops.

One of the big draws here is the **Parc Montsouris**. Around the western edge of the park are small streets such as rue du Parc Montsouris and rue Georges-Braque that were built up in the 1920s and '30s with charming villas and artists' studios by avant-garde architects including Le Corbusier and André Lurçat. On the southern edge of the park is the **Cité Universitaire**, home to 6,000 students.

Les Catacombes

1 pl Denfert-Rochereau, 14th (01.43.22.47.63). M° Denfert Rochereau. **Open** 10am-6pm Tue-Sun; Closed public hols. **Admission** €5; €3.30 over-60s; €2.50 students, 14s-26s; free under-14s. **No credit cards.** **Map** 407 H10.

Official entrance for vast network of subterranean passages. *See p143* **The great escape.**

Cité Universitaire

Bd Jourdan, 14th (01.43.13.65.00/www.ciup.fr). RER Cité Universitaire.

The Cité Internationale Universitaire de Paris is an odd mix. Created between the wars in a mood of internationalism and inspired by the model of Oxbridge colleges, the 37 halls of residence spread across landscaped gardens were each designed in supposedly appropriate national style, some by appropriate national architects (take the De Stijl-style Collège Néerlandais by Willem Dudok); others in exotic pastiche like the Asie du Sud-Est building with its Khmer sculptures and bird-beak roof. The Brits get what looks like a minor public school; the Maison Internationale is based on Fontainebleau; the Swiss (1935) and Brazilians (1959) get Le Corbusier. You can visit the sculptural white

Pavillon Suisse (01.44.16.10.16, www.fondationsuisse.fr), which has a Le Corbusier mural on the ground floor. The Cité's spacious landscaped gardens are open to the public, and the newly renovated theatre puts on a spread of drama and contemporary dance.

Parc Montsouris

Bd Jourdan, 14th. RER Cité Universitaire. **Open** 8am-dusk Mon-Fri; 9am-dusk Sat, Sun.
The most colourful of the capital's parks was laid out for Baron Haussmann by Alphand. It boasts sweeping, gently sloping lawns, an artificial lake and artificial cascades. On its opening day in 1878 the lake inexplicably emptied and the engineer responsible committed suicide.

The 15th district

Centred on the shopping streets of rues du Commerce and Lecourbe, the expansive 15th has little to offer tourists, though as a largely residential district it has plenty of good restaurants and street markets. It's worth making a detour to visit **La Ruche** ('beehive'), designed by Eiffel as a wine pavilion for the 1900 Exposition Universelle and resituated here as artists' studios. Nearby is **Parc Georges Brassens**, opened in 1983, while at the Porte de Versailles, the sprawling **Paris-Expo** exhibition centre was created in 1923.

Parc Georges Brassens

Rue des Morillons, 15th. Mᵒ Porte de Vanves or Porte de Versailles. **Open** 8am-dusk Mon-Fri; 9am-dusk Sat, Sun. **Map** p406 D10.
Built on the site of the former Abattoirs de Vaugirard, Parc Georges Brassens prefigured the industrial regeneration of Parc André Citroën and La Villette. (*See p291* **From waste ground to playground**). The gateways crowned by bronze bulls have been kept, as have a series of iron meat-market pavilions, which house a second-hand book market at weekends. The Jardin des Senteurs is planted with aromatic species while, in one corner, a small vineyard produces 200 bottles of Clos des Morillons every year.

La Ruche

Passage de Dantzig, 15th. Mᵒ Convention or Porte de Versailles. **Map** p406 D10.
Take a peek through the grille or sneak behind an unsuspecting resident to see the iron-framed former wine pavilion built by Eiffel for the 1900 Exposition Universelle, and rebuilt by philanthropic sculptor Alfred Boucher to be let as studios for struggling artists. Chagall, Soutine, Brancusi, Modigliani, Lipchitz and Archipenko spent periods here, and the 140 studios are still sought after by artists today.

Paris-Expo

Porte de Versailles, 15th (01.43.95.37.00/www. parisexpo.fr). Mᵒ Porte de Versailles. **Map** p406 B10.

The vast exhibition centre, spread over different halls, hosts all kinds of trade and arts fairs. Many, such as the Foire de Paris (*see p279*) or art fair FIAC (*see p282*), are open to the public.

The 13th district

The contrasts don't get much greater than in the 13th, where villagey clusters of little houses alternate with '60s tower blocks and the new ZAC Rive Gauche. *See p146* **The lucky 13th**.

Les Gobelins & La Salpêtrière

Its image may be all tower blocks, but the 13th is also historic, especially where it borders the 5th. The **Manufacture Nationale des Gobelins**, home to the state weaving companies, continues a tradition founded in the 15th century, when tanneries, dyers and weaving workshops lined the river Bièvre (*see p136* **The lost river**). The waterway became notorious for its pollution, while the slums that grew up around it were later depicted in Hugo's *Les Misérables*. The area was tidied up in the 1930s when Square René-Le-Gall, a small park, was laid out on the allotments used by tapestry workers. The river was forced underground, but enthusiasts have reinstated a small stretch in the park. Nearby, through a gateway at 17 rue des Gobelins, you can spot the turret and first floor of a medieval house, recently renovated as apartments. The so-called Château de la Reine Blanche on rue Gustave-Geffroy is named after Queen Blanche of Provence who had a château here, but was probably rebuilt in the 1520s for the Gobelin family. Blanche was also associated with a nearby Franciscan monastery of which a fragmentary couple of arches survive on the corner of rue Pascal and rue de Julienne. On the western edge of the 15th, next to Gare d'Austerlitz, the station which serves most of central France, sprawls the huge Hôpital de la Pitié-Salpêtrière founded in 1656, with its striking **Chapelle St-Louis**.

The busy intersection of place d'Italie has seen more developments. Opposite the 19th-century town hall, Centre Commercial Italie 2, a bizarre high-tech confection designed by Kenzo Tange, houses a shopping centre and the **Gaumont Grand Ecran Italie** cinema (*see p297*). There's a food market on boulevard Auguste-Blanqui (Tue, Fri mornings).

Chapelle St-Louis-de-la-Salpêtrière

47 bd de l'Hôpital, 13th (01.42.16.04.24). Mᵒ Gare d'Austerlitz. **Open** 8.30am-6pm Mon-Fri, Sun; 11am-6pm Sat. **Map** p408 L9.
The austerely beautiful chapel was designed by Libéral Bruand in 1657-77 with an octagonal dome in the centre and eight naves in which to separate

Sightseeing

the sick from the insane, the destitute from the debauched. Around the chapel sprawls the vast Hôpital de la Pitié-Salpêtrière, founded on the site of a gunpowder factory (hence the name, derived from saltpetre) by Louis XIV to round up vagrant women, becoming a centre for research into insanity in the 1790s. That was when renowned doctor Philippe Pinel began to treat some of the inmates as sick rather than criminal – Charcot later pioneered neuro-psychology here, receiving a famous visit from Freud. Salpêtrière is now one of the city's main teaching hospitals, but the chapel is also used for contemporary art installations, notably for the Festival d'Automne (see p282), when its striking architecture proves a backdrop for such artists as Bill Viola, Anish Kapoor and Nan Goldin.

The lucky 13th

Seen from the glazed upper floor of the sleek MK2 arthouse cinema complex, the bridge where rue de Tolbiac and rue Nueve de Tolbiac meet at the new Bibliothèque François Mitterrand Métro station marks a frontier between new and old Paris. Below, the creation of the colossal new development zone of the ZAC Rive Gauche has been ten years in the making. transforming the forgotten 13th district.

Stretching along the Seine from the Gare d'Austerlitz to boulevard Masséna, after a decade of upheaval, the ZAC is set to be the most sought-after slice of real estate in Paris. Once the cranes and JCBs have gone, the area will accommodate four times as many people as it does today, which is to say 15,000 residents and 60,000 employees. By 2006, a footbridge will link the **Bibliothèque Nationale François Mitterrand** (see p147) with the **Parc de Bercy** (see p109), and an open-air swimming pool will float on the Seine by the Quai de la Gare. Moreover, the ZAC will be the centre of the new academic Latin Quarter, welcoming 25,000 students and 4,000 staff at four separate universities, including Paris VII and a French offshoot of the University of Chicago.

Everything began with the opening of the Bibliothèque in 1996. Around its four glass towers sprang up plush apartment blocks, elegant social housing, sleek company headquarters and, crucially, noteworthy places of culture and entertainment. All is now only ten minutes from the city centre, thanks to the high-tech driverless line 14 Métro and a new RER station at Bibliothèque. Along the boulevards des Maréchaux, the ring of earlier boulevards parallel to the Périphérique, the first stretches of a new tramway are being laid out, scheduled to start service in 2006.

It still takes a little imagination to picture what it's all going to be like, but after years when the library and scattered industrial remnants stuck up like islands in a sea of excavation, the area is starting to come alive. The arty Jean-Michel Wilmotte designed **MK2B** multiplex cinema (see p298), cafés and shops have opened to serve library users and residents of the new riverside housing. A main street, avenue de France, has now been constructed over the railway tracks. The project is combining offices, residential developments and the new university quarter in the Masséna area a little south of the Bibliothèque Mitterrand.

Unlike the 'stack-'em-up-and-hide-'em-away mentality of 1970s housing projects, the ZAC augurs 21st-century eclecticism. Big-name architects, among them Chemetov, Bofill, Foster, and Valode et Pistre have been commissioned. French wunderkind Christian de Portzamparc, who was responsible for designing the **Cité de la Musique** (see p315 and p323), has been entrusted with overseeing the new Latin Quarter.

Allied to the masterplan for the area is a district of research and innovation. East of the library, **Les Frigos** (quai Panhard et Levassor, 01.44.24.96.96, www.les-frigos.com), a hive of artists' and jazz studios in former refrigerated warehouses, is one of several existing industrial buildings to have been saved thanks to local pressure groups and artists' associations. The majestic Grands Moulins de Paris, partly burned down in 1996, are another, former flour mills which will be converted into a separate university administrative building by up-and-coming architect Rudi Ricciotti. The Compressed Air Building, next to the Périphérique, is set to become an architecture school.

In front of the library, the flotilla of music bars and clubs – the **Batofar** (see p328 and p323), the **Guinguette Pirate** (see p324) – moored on the Seine in front of the library are also providing signs of new life in the air; while the other side of the tracks, **rue Louise-Weiss** is the centre of a tight cluster of adventurous young art **galleries** (see p307), drawing crowds for their joint vernissages.

Manufacture Nationale des Gobelins

42 av des Gobelins, 13th (01.44.08.52.00). M° Les Gobelins. **Open** *Guided tours* (01.44.54.19.33) 2pm and 2.45pm Tue-Thur (90 mins). **Admission** €8; €6 7s-24s; free under-7s. **No credit cards. Map** p408 K10.

Named after Jean Gobelin, a dyer who owned the site, the royal tapestry factory was founded by Colbert in 1662, when he set up the Manufacture Royale des Meubles de la Couronne. It reached the summit of its renown during the *ancien régime*, when Gobelins tapestries were produced for royal residences under artists such as Le Brun and Oudry. Tapestries are still made here (mainly for French embassies) and visitors can watch weavers at work. The tour (in French) through the 1912 factory takes in the 18th-century chapel and the Beauvais workshops. Arrive 30 minutes before the tour.

Chinatown & La Butte-aux-Cailles

South of the rue de Tolbiac, the shop signs suddenly turn Chinese or Vietnamese, and even McDonald's is decked out *à la chinoise*. The city's main Chinatown is centred along avenue d'Ivry, avenue de Choisy and the 1960s tower blocks between; while many of the tower blocks in the Paris suburbs are bleak, here they have a distinctly Eastern vibe, with restaurants, Vietnamese *pho* noodle bars and Chinese pâtisseries, hairdressers and exotic groceries, as well as the large **Tang Frères** supermarket (*see p268*). There's even a Buddhist temple hidden in a car park beneath the tallest tower (avenue d'Ivry, opposite rue Frères d'Astier-de-la-Vigerie, 13th). Lion and dragon dances take to the streets at Chinese New Year (*see p282*).

In contrast to Chinatown, the villagey Butte-aux-Cailles, occupying the wedge between boulevard Auguste-Blanqui and rue Bobillot, is a neighbourhood of old houses, winding cobblestone streets, funky bars and restaurants. This workers' neighbourhood, home in the 19th century to many small factories, was one of the first to fight during the 1848 Revolution and the Paris Commune. The Butte has preserved its rebellious character: residents wear Fidel Castro T-shirts and resist the aggressive forces of city planning and construction companies. The cobbled rue de la Butte-aux-Cailles and the rue des Cinq-Diamants are the hub of the arty, *soixante-huitard* forces, where you'll find relaxed, inexpensive bistros like the eccentric Le Temps des Cérises (18 rue Butte-aux-Cailles, 13th, 01.45.89.69.48), run as a cooperative, Chez Gladines (30 rue des Cinq-Diamants, 13th, 01.45.80.70.10) and the more upmarket **Chez Paul** (*see p211*). The cottages built in 1912 in a mock-Alsatian style round a central green at 10 rue Daviel were one of the earliest public

housing schemes in Paris. Just across the rue Bobillot, the **Piscine de la Butte-aux-Cailles** (*see p340*) is a charming arts-and-craft style swimming pool, fed by artesian wells. Further south, explore passage Vandrezanne, the little houses and gardens of square des Peupliers, rue des Peupliers and rue Dieulafoy and the flower-named streets of the Cité Florale. By the Périphérique, the Stade Charléty (9 bd Kellermann, 13th, 01.44.16.60.60), designed by father and son Henri and Bruno Gaudin, is a fine piece of architecture with its swooping bird like floodlights. In 2002 the stadium saw the 100m world record fall to Tim Montgomery.

The developing east

The erection of the **Bibliothèque Nationale de France** breathed life into the desolate area between Gare d'Austerlitz and the Périphérique, formerly just lonesome railway yards and now known as the ZAC Rive Gauche. The project calls for the development of offices, residential developments and a new university quarter, an eastwards extension of the Latin Quarter. *See p146* **The lucky 13th**.

Further east, towards Porte d'Ivry, curious rue Watt is the lowest street in Paris (it runs below river level), while at 12 rue Cantagrel you can see Le Corbusier's Cité de Réfuge de l'Armée de Salut hostel, a long, reinforced concrete structure built from 1929 to 1933 to accommodate 1,500 homeless men, and a precursor of the architect's Unités d'Habitation.

Bibliothèque Nationale de France François Mitterrand

Quai François-Mauriac, 13th (01.53.79.59.59/www. bnf.fr). M° Bibliothèque François Mitterrand or Quai de la Gare. **Open** 2-7pm Mon; 9am-7pm Tue-Sat; noon-7pm Sun. **Admission** €3/day; €4.50/2 days; €30 or €15 concs/2 weeks; €46 or €23 concs/year. **Credit** MC, V. **Map** p409 M10.

Opened in 1996, the new national library was the last and most expensive of Mitterrand's Grands Projets. The architect, Dominique Perrault, was criticised for his curiously dated design, which hides readers underground and stores the books in four L-shaped glass towers. He also forgot to specify blinds to protect books from sunlight; they were added afterwards. In the central void is a garden (filled with 140 trees, uprooted from Fontainebleau at a cost of 40 million francs). The library houses over ten million volumes, and can accommodate 3,000 readers. The research section, just below the public reading rooms, opened in 1998; much of the library is open to the public. Books, newspapers and periodicals are accessible to anyone over 18, and an audivisual section lets you browse through photo, film and sound archives. There are classical music concerts and exhibitions. *See also p167*.

Sightseeing

Beyond the Périphérique

Ring in the changes.

Is it a bird? Is it a plane? Nope, just another skyscraper at **La Défense**. *See p151.*

Across the Périphérique ring road lies another world. It starts with the dense housing and industrial estates of the inner suburbs, built up since the 19th century as old villages and rural churches were absorbed into the urban sprawl, and stretches to the outer edge of new towns which colonised old farmland after the war.

For many Parisians, an expedition to the *banlieue* (especially the undesirable northern and eastern suburbs) takes on the aura of a journey to a foreign land, a land ventured into only for cheap supermarket petrol and DIY stores. For them, the banlieue (a term rarely used to include the sought-after districts such as Neuilly, St-Cloud or Boulogne, but with much the same unspoken meaning as 'inner-city' when applied to UK towns) is as much a mindset as a physical reality, with its image of housing estates, large immigrant populations, unemployment, car rodeos, drugs, urban gangs, its own accent, argot and style of dress. Part of the negative rep is true: there are dangerous, no-

go housing estates, the *quartiers sensibles* (for 'sensitive' read 'problem'), where even the architects and building workers trying to renovate them are attacked, and where attempts to reopen local shops are met by vandalism. But there are also swaths of very respectable residential districts, with their own self-contained provincial atmosphere quite different from the city itself.

There are signs of change. Rising property prices within Paris mean that many families are being forced out into the inner ring of suburbs. High business rents have seen companies, notably in the media and advertising sectors and, more recently, financial services, moving outwards. And if many Parisians wouldn't contemplate living anywhere other than Paris itself, the mistrust works in two ways – there are also *banlieusards*, proud of belonging to the *neuf-trois* (slang for the 93 *département* of Seine St-Denis) rather than the elitist *soixante-quinze* (75) of Paris. *See p323* **Banlieue blues.**

St-Denis & the north

North of Paris, the *département* of Seine St-Denis (and part of adjoining Val d'Oise) is the one that best fulfils the negative image of the *banlieue*. It's a victim of its own 19th-century industrial boom and the 20th-century housing shortage, when colossal estates went up in places like La Corneuve (where a tower block was recently dynamited), Aulnay-sous-Bois and Sarcelles, and includes some of the poorest *communes* in all of France. Yet the *département* also boasts a buzzing theatre scene, such as the MC93 in Bobigny, the Théâtre Gérard Philipe in St-Denis and Théâtre de la Commune in Aubervilliers, as well as prestigious jazz and classical music festivals. And amid all the sprawl stands one of the treasures of Gothic architecture: the **Basilique St-Denis**, the spot where most of France's monarchs were buried. St-Denis also contains the atmospheric Musée de l'Art et d'Histoire de St-Denis (22bis rue Gabriel Péri, 01.42.43.05.10), located in a scrupulously preserved Carmelite convent, and also a busy covered market. Its fine modern buildings include Niemeyer's head offices for Communist newspaper *L'Humanité* and Gaudin's extension to the town hall. Across the canal is the landmark **Stade de France** (*see p333*), built for the 1998 World Cup and which has provided a spur to the renewal of this long rundown area of small terraced houses, council flats, factories and wasteland. Indeed, it could be said that the area of La Plaine St-Denis is on the up.

The canal has been nicely landscaped with a footpath along the quay, the noisy motorway has been covered over by a series of garden squares and playgrounds, and smart canalside apartments, a multiplex cinema, shopping centre and a DIY superstore have gone up near the stadium, which is now attracting businesses into the area. Over in nearby Aubervilliers, acres of 19th-century brick warehouses buzz with import-export businesses and recently arrived audio-visual companies. Le Bourget, home to the city's first airport and still used for private business jets and an air fair, contains the **Musée de l'Air et de l'Espace** (*see p180*) in its original passenger terminals and hangars.

North-east of Paris, Pantin has new presence on the cultural scene with the opening in June 2004 of the **Centre National de la Danse** (*see p294* **Jailhouse rocks**) in a cleverly rehabilitated office block.

North-west of St-Denis, Ecouen, noted for its beautiful Renaissance château, now the **Musée National de la Renaissance** (*see p173*), allows glimpses of a more rural past.

Basilique St-Denis

6 rue de Strasbourg, 93200 St-Denis (01.48.09. 83.54). M°/Tram Basilique de St-Denis. **Open** *Oct-Mar* 10am-5.45pm Mon-Sat; noon-5.45pm Sun. *Apr-Sept* 10am-6.15pm Mon-Sat; noon-6.15pm Sun. *Tours* 11.15am Mon-Sat, 3pm daily. **Admission** €6.10; €4.10 18-25s; free under-18s. **Credit** AmEx, DC, MC, V.
Legend has it that when St Denis was beheaded, he picked up his noggin and walked with it to Vicus Catulliacus (now St-Denis) to be buried. The first church, parts of which can be seen in the crypt, was built over his tomb in around 475. The present edifice was begun in the 1130s by Abbot Suger, the powerful minister of Louis VI and Louis VII. It is considered the first example of Gothic architecture, by uniting the elements of pointed arches, ogival vaulting and flying buttresses. In the 13th century, master mason Pierre de Montreuil erected the spire and rebuilt the choir, nave and transept. This was the burial place for all but three French monarchs between 996 and the end of the *ancien régime*, so the ambulatory is a museum of French funerary sculpture, among them a fanciful Gothic tomb for Dagobert, the austere effigy of Charles V and richly sculpted Renaissance tomb of Louis XII and Anne de Bretagne. In 1792, all these tombs were desecrated and the royal remains thrown into a pit.

Vincennes & the east

The more upmarket residential districts in the east surround the Bois de Vincennes, such as Vincennes with its royal château, St-Mandé and Charenton-le-Pont. Joinville-le-Pont and Champigny-sur-Marne draw weekenders for the riverside *guinguette* dancehalls (*see p350* **Rock back in time**).

Château de Vincennes

Av de Paris, 94300 Vincennes (01.48.08.31.20). M° Château de Vincennes. **Open** *Oct-Mar* 10am-noon, 1.15-5pm daily; *Apr-Sept* 10am-noon, 1.15-6pm daily. **Admission** *Short visit* €4; €3.10 18-25s; free under 18s. *Long visit* €6.10; €4.10 18-25s; free under 18s. **No credit cards.**
An imposing curtain wall punctuated by towers encloses this medieval fortress, still home to an army garrison. The square keep was begun by Philippe VI and completed by Charles V, who added the curtain wall. Henry V died here in 1422; Louis XIII used the château for hunting expeditions and had the Pavillon du Roi and Pavillon de la Reine built by Louis Le Vau, though their decoration disappeared when they were turned into military barracks.

Pavillon Baltard

12 av Victor Hugo, 94130 Nogent-sur-Marne (01.43.24.76.76/www.pbpa.net). RER Nogent-sur-Marne. **Open** during salons/exhibitions only.
When Les Halles was demolished someone had the foresight to save one of its Baltard-designed iron and glass market pavilions (No.8, the egg and poultry shed) and resurrect it for the benefit of the suburbs.

Sightseeing

Boulogne & the west

The capital's most-desirable suburbs lie to the west, where expensive properties were built between the wars. La Défense, Neuilly-sur-Seine, Boulogne-Billancourt, Levallois-Perret and, across the river, Issy-les-Moulineaux have become work locations for Parisians, notably in the advertising, media and service industries. Neuilly-sur-Seine is home to many of France's finance brains and captains of industry, as well as the fief of politician Nicolas Sarkozy.

Boulogne-Billancourt is the main town in the region outside Paris, and a lively centre in its own right. In 1320 the Gothic Eglise Notre-Dame was begun in tribute to a miraculous statue of the Virgin washed up at Boulogne-sur-Mer. By the 18th century, Boulogne was known for its wines and laundries and, early in the 20th century, for its artist residents (Landowski, Lipchitz, Chagall, Gris), while Billancourt was known for car manufacture, aviation and its film studios. In the 1920s and '30s, Boulogne-Billancourt was proud of its modernity: Tony Garnier built the elegant new town hall on avenue André Morizet; a new post office, apartments and schools all went up in the Modern Style, and private houses were built by the leading avant-garde architects of the day including Le Corbusier, Perret, Lurçat, Mallet-Stevens, Pingusson and Fischer, notably on rue Denfert-Rochereau near the Bois de Boulogne and rue du Belvedère. The **Musée des Années 30** (*see p162*) focuses on artists and architects who lived or worked in the town at the time. The innovative glass-fronted apartment block by Le Corbusier including the flat where he lived from 1933 to 1965 can be visited each Wednesday morning at 24 rue Nungesser et Coli (reserve ahead with the Fondation Le Corbusier on 01.42.88.41.53).

The former Renault factory has been sitting in the Seine like a beached whale since it closed in 1992, but work has just begun on the Fondation Pinault contemporary art museum, due to open in 2006 in a building designed by Japanese architect Tadao Ando. The rest of the island is to be built up as offices and housing.

Across the Seine, villas in large gardens surround the Parc de St-Cloud, one of the loveliest bits of open space around Paris. South of St-Cloud is Sèvres, where the former royal porcelain manufacture is now the **Musée National de Céramique** (*see p173*).

In the 19th century, riverside towns like Chatou, Asnières and Argenteuil, accessible by train, became places of entertainment, for promenades, *guinguettes* and rowing on the Seine, depicted by the Impressionists. The Ile de la Grande Jatte, between Neuilly and Courbevoie,

was eternalised in Seurat's *La Grande Jatte*, and Renoir frequented the Ile de Chatou, where the old restaurant and dance hall, the Maison Fournaise, is now a small museum.

At Rueil-Malmaison, the romantic **Château de Malmaison** was loved by Napoleon and Josephine. Josephine had a second château, La Petite Malmaison (229bis av Napoléon Bonaparte, 01.47.49.45.15; by appointment only) built nearby. The empress is buried in the Eglise St-Pierre St-Paul in the old centre, as is her daughter Hortense de Beauharnais, Queen of Holland and mother of Napoleon III. At Port Marly, the fanciful Château de Monte Cristo (01.30.61.61.35) was built for Alexandre Dumas *fils* with a tiled Moorish room; in its leafy grounds is the Château d'If, a folly inscribed with the names of Dumas' numerous works.

Suresnes, across the Seine from the Bois de Boulogne, has been a wine-producing village since Roman times, and still celebrates the Fête des Vendanges grape harvest each autumn. The 162 metre-high hill of Mont Valérian here was a place of pilgrimage – one of the nearby streets is still named rue du Calvaire. In 1841, a huge fortress was built here to defend Paris. Occupied by the German army during World War II, thousands of French Resistants were brought here by night and shot. The fortress itself still belongs to the French army and is the centre of its eavesdropping network. On the surrounding hill is the American Cemetery (190 bd de Washington), which contains the graves of American soldiers from World Wars I and II.

St-Germain-en-Laye is a smart suburb with a historic centre and a château, rebuilt by François I on the foundations of the fortress of Charles V. Here Henri II lived in style with his wife Catherine de Médicis and his mistress Diane de Poitiers; here Mary Queen of Scots grew up, Louis XIV was born, and the deposed James II lived for 12 years. Napoleon III turned the château into the **Musée des Antiquités Nationales** (*see p171*).

Château de Malmaison

Av du Château, 92500 Rueil-Malmaison (01.41.29. 05.55). RER Rueil-Malmaison. **Open** Oct-Mar 10am-noon, 1.30-5.15pm Mon-Fri; 10am-noon, 1.30-5.45pm Sat, Sun. *Apr-Sept* 10am-5pm Mon-Fri; 10am-5.40pm Sat, Sun. **Admission** €4.50; €3 18-25s; free under-18s. **Credit** MC, V.

Napoleon and Josephine's love nest was bought by Josephine in 1799, and was the emperor's favourite retreat during the Consulate (1800-03). After their divorce, Napoleon gave the château to his ex, who died here in 1814. All that romance has not gone to waste: today the château is for sightseeing and for weddings. The couple redesigned the entrance as a military tent; inside you can see the emperor's office, the billiard room and Josephine's tented bedroom.

Mémorial du Mont-Valérien

Rue du Professeur-Léon-Bernard, 92150 Suresnes.
Train to Suresnes-Mont-Valérien. **Open** *Guided tour*
in French Oct-Mar 3pm Sun, public hols. *Apr-Sept*
3pm, 4.30pm Sun, public hols. **Admission** free.
Inaugurated in 1960 by Charles de Gaulle, set against
a massive cross of Lorraine in pink granite from the
Vosges, 16 bronze relief sculptures by 16 artists
represent France's struggle for liberation – giving a
Gaullist perspective. Behind an eternal flame, the
crypt contains 16 tombs of 16 heroes from 16 French
battles in World War II (with a 17th left empty for the
last liberation hero). Members of the Resistance were
brought at night from prisons in Paris. A staircase
from inside the crypt leads visitors inside the curtain
wall and takes them up around the wooded hill, into
the chapel where prisoners were locked before
execution, and down to the Clairière des Fusillés, the
clearing where the shootings took place. The chapel
walls were covered in last, desperate graffiti and
scratchings (of which only a small patch remains); it
also contains five of the wooden firing posts against
which the condemned were tied. Over a thousand men
were shot here (women were deported); no one is
known to have escaped. In 2003 a monument by artist
Pascal Convert was erected, which lists the names of
all the victims known to date, including figures such
as Communist politician Gabriel Péri.

St-Denis. See p149.

La Défense

La Défense's skyscrapers and walkways create
another world. It was named after a stand
against the Prussians in 1870. La Défense has
been a showcase for French business since the
mid 1950s, when the CNIT hall (01.46.92.11.11)
was built for trade shows, but it was the
Grande Arche that gave the district a true
monument. More than 100,000 people work here,
and another 35,000 live in the blocks of flats on
the southern edge, with the inevitable mall and
an IMAX cinema. Outside on the esplanade are
fountains and sculptures by Miró and Serra.
No particular skyscraper displays architectural
distinction, although together they make an
impressive sight. Recent development westward
includes a 40-storey tower and a church. A
kiosk in front of the CNIT has local maps.

La Grande Arche de La Défense

92400 Paris La Défense (01.49.07.27.57/www.
grandearche.com). M° La Défense. **Open** 10am-7pm
daily. **Admission** €7.50; €6 students, 6-18s; free
under-6s. **Credit** AmEx, MC, V.
Completed for the bicentenary of the Revolution in
1989, the Grande Arche, designed by Danish architect Johan Otto von Spreckelsen, lines up neatly on
the Grand Axe from the Louvre, up the Champs-
Elysées to the Arc de Triomphe – but then is skewed
to the side. A stomach-churning glass lift soars up
through the 'clouds' to the roof, from where there's
a fantastic view over Paris.

The Louvre

The world's biggest cultural attraction – now with its own cult following.

The most famous museum in the world is, in fact, many museums in one. A palace whose medieval origins were unearthed in the course of President Mitterrand's Grand Louvre project, it encompasses architecture from every era. Treasures from the Egyptians, Etruscans, Greeks and Romans each have their own extensive galleries, as do Middle Eastern and Islamic art. There are European decorative arts from the Middle Ages up to the 19th century, and in the Sully wing you can roam through rooms distinguished by lavish interior design. The main draw is the paintings and sculpture, most of which are contained in the vast Denon wing, with two glass-roofed sculpture courts, Italian and French painting, and Dutch masters. The minimalist new galleries of Primitive Arts in the Pavillon des Sessions foreshadow and promote the Quai Branly museum, scheduled to open in 2006.

So where did all the art come from? It's not all a testament to imperial greed, although this played a part. Much of the Royal collection was, after all, presented as offerings to the ruling monarchs and acted as diplomatic sweeteners. The talent of Leonardo Da Vinci was fought over as a commodity and prestige point during

the reign of Louis XII, who petitioned for a portrait in Lombardy while at the same time Milan was being sacked by his very own troops. It was François I who brought an entire Italian court to France, resulting in a rich collection of then contemporary art and antiquities. Some treasures were bequeathed to the state in lieu of death duty and others are acquired in an ongoing process by the Réunion des Musées Nationaux. The Louvre opened as a museum immediately after the French Revolution in 1793, a true expression of the art-for-all ethic still in force every first Sunday of the month when the museum is free to enter.

Mitterrand's Grand Louvre project expanded the museum two-fold by throwing out the Ministry of Finance and other government offices that once inhabited the Cour Napoléon. But its organisation and restoration is still a work-in-progress: check the website or lists in the Carrousel du Louvre to see which galleries are closed on certain days to avoid missing out on what you really want to see. It is unrealistic to expect to cover more than two sections in a day before museum fatigue sets in, so choose what you want to see before you go and follow the signs. What is wonderful about the Louvre, however, is the element of surprise – from the grandeur of the Winged Victory of Samothrace crowning the grand stairway to the two tiny dice that have survived a thousand years. Then there is the almost operatic setting provided by the building itself: what is more incongruous than finding Louis XIV's bedchamber in the Egyptian department? Nothing is quite like it, and you will wish you had more time to lose yourself in its 12 miles of corridors and 300,000 works of art. Fifty thousand do every day.

ADVANCE TICKETS AND ENTRANCE

IM Pei's glass pyramid is a wonderful piece of architecture but it has the effect of making you think this is the only entrance. Avoid it or you'll be standing in a queue waiting for your bag to go through the scanner. There are three other ways in. Buying a ticket in advance means you can go in directly via the passage Richelieu off rue de Rivoli, or via the Carrousel du Louvre shopping mall (steps down either side of the Arc de Triomphe du Carrousel, at 99 rue de Rivoli or from the Métro). Advance tickets are valid for any day, and are available from the Louvre website, or from branches of **Fnac**, **Virgin Megastore** (for both, *see p246*) or any of the major department stores or supermarkets (*see p240*). The Cour des Lions entrance in the south-west corner of the complex (closed Fridays) has its own ticket desk and gives directly on to the Arts premiers and entrance to the Italian collections – and the *Mona Lisa*.

The Louvre is also included in the museums accessible with an all-in **Carte Musées et Monuments** (www.intermusees.com; *see p161*), available in three formats.

OTHER TIPS

• Pick up a map at the information desk. The museum is divided into three wings: Denon (down the Seine side); Richelieu (down Rivoli); and Sully, which joins them up and runs around the Cour Carrée at the end. The eight collections are colour-coded on the map and signs show you to the way to the most popular exhibits. *Destination Louvre* (€7.50) from the Réunion des Musées Nationaux shop in the Carrousel du Louvre is a good English-language guide.
• Printed cards, available in a variety of languages in each room, give good background information. Audioguides (€5) are available at the main entrances in the Carrousel du Louvre.
• Take breathers – your ticket is valid all day and you can leave and re-enter as you wish.
• Evening visits are on Wednesdays and Fridays till 9.45pm. Late on Friday the museum is free for the under-26s, but if you are planning to make several visits the Carte Louvre Jeunes, at €15 for the year, is worth getting.

• Some rooms are closed on a weekly basis – check on 01.40.20.51.51 or www.louvre.fr.
• Save your shopping for the end. The RMN bookshop and separate souvenir shops are open an hour after closing, except when the museum stays open late (*see above*).
• Don't try to see everything on one visit. You're bound to get lost, so think of it as an excuse to discover the unexpected.

The Louvre

Rue de Rivoli, 1st (01.40.20.50.50/recorded information 01.40.20.51.51/www.louvre.fr). M° *Palais Royal Musée du Louvre or Louvre Rivoli.* **Open** 9am-6pm Mon, Thur, Sat, Sun; 9am-9.45pm Wed, Fri. Closed Tue. **Admission** *Permanent collections* €8.50 (includes entry to the Musée Delacroix but not exhibitions at the Salle Napoléon); €6 6-9.45pm Wed, Fri; free concs 6-9.45pm Fri, all day first Sun of mth; CM. *Exhibitions* €8.50. *Day pass* €13; €11 6-9.45pm Wed, Fri. **Credit** MC, V. **Map** p403 G5.
Wheelchair/disabled access 01.40.20.59.90/ handicap@louvre.fr.

EATING

Grab a bite at the **Cafés Richelieu**, **Denon** or **Mollien** on the Mollien staircase, which has a terrace. Under the pyramid there's a sandwich bar, café and the **Grand Louvre** restaurant serving French cuisine, and the **Restorama** in the Carrousel du Louvre has multiple self-service outlets. The terrace of chic **Café Marly** (93 rue de Rivoli, 1st, 01.49.26.06.60), with a view of the pyramid, serves pricy brasserie fare. Fast-food outlet **Aux Pains Perdus** (4 rue de l'Echelle, 1st, 01.49.26.96.96) has soups, salads, wraps and artisanal lemonades to take away or eat on their terrace; **Ragueneau** (202 rue St-Honoré, 1st, 01.42.60.29.20) has pastries, salads, soups and a full lunch menu.

The best Oddities

● The name 'Louvre' is thought to come from 'lupara' (it was built on the site of a wolfhound kennel) or the word for 'fortress' in Anglo-Saxon.
● In 1939 200 truckloads of art were evacuated to the Château of Chambord. On his fleeting visit to Paris in June 1940, Hitler didn't bother to look at the Louvre, much to Albert Speer's disappointment.
● The IM Pei pyramid has its own robot to clean the glass.
● In 1680 a bourgeois petitioned Louis XIV to put public water closets in the Louvre. The request was ignored.

The Collections

History of the Louvre

Sully: lower ground floor. Shown as dark brown on Louvre maps.

Here you can visit the medieval foundations of the Louvre which were uncovered in 1985. A scale model shows the fortress at the time of Charles V. You can walk round the moat of Philippe-Auguste's outer wall to see the pillars of two drawbridges, La Taillerie tower with heart symbols cut into the stone by masons, and the outside of the dungeon where treasure and prisoners were kept. A well and a portion of ground are left undug, showing artefacts just as they were found. An exhibition recounts the history of the Louvre – the Saint-Louis room, a guard room from the era of Philippe-Auguste which was discovered in 1882, exhibits rare archeological finds as well as an unfinished staircase and carved pillars.

Ancient Egypt

Denon: lower ground floor; Sully: lower ground, ground and 1st floors. Green on Louvre maps.

Announced by the Giant Sphinx in pink granite (1898-1866 BC), the Egyptian department divides into two routes. The Thematic Circuit on the ground floor presents Nile culture (fishing, agriculture, hunting, daily and cultural life, religion and death); one of the big draws is the Mastaba of Akhethetep, a decorated burial chamber from Sakkara dating to 2400 BC. Six small sphinxes, apes from Luxor and the lion-headed goddess Sekhmet recreate elements of temple complexes, while stone sarcophagi, mummies, amulets, jewellery and entrails form a vivid display on funeral rites. One of the best displays is on Egyptian furniture (room 8, ground floor); dating from 1550-1069 BC, it looks almost contemporary in design. On the first floor, the Pharoah Circuit is laid out chronologically, from the Seated Scribe and

Who built the Louvre?

From Philippe-Auguste to François Mitterrand, France's rulers have all added their *sou*'s worth to the Louvre. Here's who made it the bohemoth of today – and how:

Philippe-Auguste 1180-1223

Built a medieval castle on the site of a seventh-century Roman wolfhound kennel in 1190 to protect Paris from invasion. In the centre was a dungeon which also served as a treasure trove. The remains of Philippe-Auguste's Louvre were discovered under the Cour Carrée in 1985.

Louis IX (Saint-Louis) 1226-70

The Salle Saint-Louis, in one of the outer towers, is thought to date from the saintly king because of the carvings on the pillars.

Charles V (The Wise) 1364-80

Records show that Charles turned the Louvre into a sumptuous palace, with gardens, a zoo and a tennis court. There was little to show for it after the Hundred Years War.

François I (1515-47)

Having razed the Medieval tower, a year before his death François I had Pierre Lescot build a new wing fit for a Renaissance prince.

Henri II (1547-59)

Henri II added the Pavillon du Roi, the earliest example of a Mansart-style roof (now hidden by façades since erected by Napoleon). The

architecture is decorated with figures and royal monograms (F for François I, H for Henri II with C and D for his wife and favourite, Catherine de Médicis and Diane de Poitiers, K for Charles IX and HdB for Henri IV). Inside, the Salle des Caryatides and Escalier Henri II are from this era.

Charles IX (1560-74)

Charles carried on the work of Lescot. A façade with his motto 'Piety and Justice', dismantled by Napoleon, can be seen in the Rotonde Napoléon. At this time Catherine de Médicis had the Tuileries palace built. Thus began 'Le Grand Dessein', the plan to unite the two palaces finally achieved by Napoleon III 30 years before the Tuileries burnt down.

Henri III (1574-89); Henri IV (1589-1610)

The two Henris added to Charles IX's Petite Galerie the perpendicular Grande Galerie, a show of power and order alongside the Seine. Henri IV's second wife, Marie de Médicis, had nagged him that the palace was far too gloomy and medieval.

Louis XIII (1610-43)

Had Jacques Lemercier continue the Lescot wing on the western side of the Cour Carrée. Lemercier created a mirror image of Lescot's work, with the magnificent Sully Pavilion receiving pride of place in the middle.

other stone figures of the Ancient Empire, via the painted figures of the Middle Empire to the New Empire with its animal-headed statues of gods and goddesses, papyrus scrolls and hieroglyphic tablets. Look for the double statue of the God Aman protecting Tutankhamun, and the black diorite 'cube statues' of priests and attendants. The collection, one of the largest hoards of Egyptian antiquities in the world, has its origins in Napoleon's Egyptian campaign of 1798-99 and Egyptologist Champollion, who deciphered hieroglyphics in 1824. The Coptic gallery, on the lower ground floor, has a new display of textiles and manuscripts to replace those put away to protect them from the light.

Oriental antiquities

Richelieu: lower ground and ground floor; Sully: ground floor. Yellow on Louvre maps.

This section covers Mesopotamia, Persia and the Levant from the fifth millennium BC to the first century AD. The huge Mesopotamian rooms contain glistening diorite sculptures of the Akkad dynasty and Gudea from the third millennium BC, some with just their remarkable feet. Don't miss the serene alabaster sculpture of Ebih-II, the superintendent of Mari (room 1b), and the earliest found evidence of writing in the form of fourth-century BC Sumerian tablets (room 1a). The Hammurabi Code, an essential document of Babylonian civilisation in the form of a black basalt stele recording 282 laws beneath reliefs of the king and the sun god, is one of the most ancient collections of laws in the history of mankind (room 3). Then come two breathtaking palace reconstructions: the great court, c713 BC, from the palace of Sargon II at Khorsabad (in present-day Iraq) with its giant bearded and winged bulls and friezes of warriors and servants (room 4); and the palace of Darius I at Susa (now Iran), c510 BC, with its fine glazed-brick reliefs of rows of archers, lions and griffins (room 12). The double-bull-headed

Sightseeing

Louis XIV (1643-1715)

Superintendent Colbert had plans for the Louvre, but Louis XIV only spent a sixth of what he spent on Versailles on it. He added three sides to the Cour Carrée to complete the square. View it from the Pont des Arts on the south side or the east side from St-Germain l'Auxerrois, and you appreciate the work of Louis Le Vau and François d'Orblay. Place du Carrousel, now a traffic roundabout, is named after an equestrian event held on this site in 1662.

Napoleon (1799-1815)

Though Napoleon credited himself with 'the construction of the Louvre' in his memoirs, he did little except tamper – though he did build the rue de Rivoli and its galeries (now the **Musée des Arts Décoratifs**, *see p172*) and fill the museum with plunder from his campaigns. The Percier and Fontaine rooms in the Denon wing are all that is left of the grand staircase and entrance the Emperor ordered – this was where Napoleon married Marie-Louise of Austria in 1810. He also erected the handsome Arc de Triomphe du Carrousel, copied from the arch of Septimius Severus in Rome.

Napoleon III (1852-70)

With the exception of the Grande Galerie, Napoleon I's galeries on rue de Rivoli and the Pavillon de Rohan (built by Louis XVIII), the whole of the Cour Napoléon was built during the Second Empire by Louis Visconti and Hector Lefuel. Headed by Baron Haussmann, the whole project was completed in four years from 1852-1856. Though designed as a continuation, the stone decoration is more ornate than that of the 17th-century parts – note Denon's central *pavillon* with a statue of the Emperor in the centre.

François Mitterrand (1981-1995)

This French President will be remembered for his daring Grand Louvre project. Mitterrand threw out the Ministry of Finance and opened the Richelieu wing, doubling the exhibition space, but his most inspired decision was to commission IM Pei's glass pyramid as the new main entrance to the museum. Visitors now descend via a spiral staircase into the underground Carrousel du Louvre, which also incorporates shops and restaurants and an exhibition hall often used for fashion shows.

Jacques Chirac (1995-present)

There was little Chirac could do to top his Socialist predecessor, so he commissioned the **Musée du Quai Branly** (*see p161*) to house Primitive Arts from the Louvre and other collections. Jean-Michel Wilmotte's conversion of the Pavillon des Sessions in the Louvre in 2000 offers an hors-d'oeuvre. Chirac has also managed to renovate the Salle des Etats and the Cour d'Apollon.

column was one of a chequerboard of such gigantic columns. As you enter the Iranian section, 5,000-year-old statues from Suza are housed in circular room 8 which gives a great view of the Cour Napoléon. The Levantine section includes Cypriot animalistic vases and carved reliefs from Byblos.

Islamic arts

Richelieu: lower ground floor. Turquoise on Louvre maps.
The Islamic decorative arts displayed here include early glass, fine tenth- to 12th-century dishes decorated with birds and calligraphy, traditional Iranian blue-and-white wares, Iznik ceramics, intricate inlaid metalwork from Syria, tiles, screens, weapons and funerary stele. The highlight is three magnificent 16th-century kelims. The collection currently includes 30 masterworks on loan from the Museum of Modern Art in New York.

Greek, Roman & Etruscan antiquities

Denon: lower ground floor, ground floor; Sully: ground floor, 1st floor. Blue on Louvre maps.
The Winged Victory of Samothrace, a headless Greek statue dating from the second century BC, stands sentinel at the top of the grand staircase giving an idea of its original dramatic impact on a promontory overlooking the sea. This huge department is made up of pieces amassed by François I and Richelieu, plus the Borghese collection (acquired in 1808), and the Campana collection of thousands of painted Greek vases and small terracottas.

Endless dark rooms on the first floor harbour small bronze, silver and terracotta objects, but the really exciting stuff is on the ground floor. Grandiose vaulted marble rooms are a fitting location for knockout masterpieces including the 2.3m-high *Athena Peacemaker* and the *Venus de Milo* (room 12), and overflow with gods and goddesses, swords and monsters.

Also on the ground floor are examples of the culture of Etruscan civilisation of south-central Italy, spanning the seventh century BC until submission to the Romans in the first century AD. The highlight is the Sarcophagus of the Cenestien Couple (c530-510 BC) in painted terracotta, which illustrates a smiling couple reclining at a banquet. Key Roman antiquities include a vivid relief of sacrificial animals, intricately carved sarcophagi, mosaic floors and the Boscoreale Treasure, magnificent silverwork excavated at a villa near Pompeii. Glance through the railings into room 17, where you'll see statues packed in their boxes awaiting renovation. Pre-Classical Greek art on the lower ground floor includes a large Cycladic head and Mycenean triad.

French painting

Denon: 1st floor; Richelieu: 2nd floor; Sully: 2nd floor. Red on Louvre maps.

There are around 6,000 of the most famous paintings in the world on show here, the most impressive being the huge 18th- to 19th-century canvases hanging in the Grande Galerie in the Denon wing. Here art meets politics with Gros' suitably dashing *Napoléon visitant le champ de bataille d'Eylau*, David's enormous *Sacre de Napoléon* and Delacroix's flag-flying *La Liberté Guidant le Peuple*. Géricault's beautiful but disturbing *Le Radeau de la Méduse* shows his artistic vision of the true story of the abandoned men who resorted to cannibalism and murder after an 1816 shipwreck. Just as horrifying is

Girodet's *Le Déluge*, where a wild-eyed man tries to cling on to a woman being pulled down by her own children. Biblical and historical scenes rub shoulders with aristocracy and grand depictions of moments in mythology.

Here you can find the earliest known non-religious French portrait (c1350: an anonymous portrait of French king Jean Le Bon), the *Pietà de Villeneuve-les-Avignon* later attributed to Enguerrand Quarton, Jean Clouet's *Portrait of François I* (marking the influence of the Italian Renaissance on portraiture), and works from the Ecole de Fontainebleau, including the anonymous *Diana the Huntress*, an elegant nude who resembles Diane de Poitiers, the mistress of Henri II. Poussin's religious and

The cult of the Code

As if the *Mona Lisa* doesn't already receive more than her fair share of attention, the Louvre's Denon wing of Italian paintings is now almost impenetrable as tourists file past Leonardo Da Vinci's masterpieces with the awestruck admiration of pilgrims. These days most aren't here to admire the brushwork, and those aren't Bibles clutched tightly in their hands.

Ever since Dan Brown's novel *The Da Vinci Code* became a bestseller in 2003, and a cult by 2004, disciples have come to Paris to follow in the footsteps of fictional hero-sleuths, Robert Langdon and Sophie Neveu, who team up to solve the murder of the Louvre's curator. The scandalous plot is based on the thesis that the Holy Grail is not a cup at all, but Mary Magdalene, the bride of Jesus, whose secret offspring can be traced to the French monarchy. Add an albino monk-assassin, a Vatican cover-up, a secret society, and a high-speed car chase around Paris, and you've got coachloads of *Da Vinci* fans intent on visiting the places mentioned in the book. And since the post-Iraq schism twixt France and America, Paris has never accommodated so many Francophiles from across the Atlantic.

So what started out as a few tourists taking photographs of the Louvre's inverted glass pyramid (where the Grail is supposedly interred) has become a windfall for tour companies who quickly capitalised on the trend. Even the Louvre has begun to court potential American donors, hosting power breakfasts under the audacious banner: 'Your Business and the Louvre Museum'.

Sceptics might complain that some readers have failed to see where facts end and fiction takes over. At St-Sulpice, one of the key locations in Brown's book, the rector Paul Roumanet has posted up a sign (both in English and French) next to the Rose Line tersely explaining that, 'Contrary to fanciful allegations in a recent best-selling novel, this is not a vestige of a pagan temple', but part of a 17th-century scientific instrument to measure the earth's orbit. Neveu's threat to knee a hole in Da Vinci's fragile *Virgin of the Rocks* would have been difficult – it is painted on wood. Worse, parts of the book are simply crass. Are the Tuileries 'Paris' own version of Central Park'? Would any sporting Englishman ever refer to losing to France's 'football squad' on the 'soccer pitch'? A London librarian who serves instant Nescafé with *cream*?

But while many articles – three books, even – have been quick to point out the factual errors, the more spiritual challenges are open for debate. Because, as 'Louvre builder' Napoleon famously stated: 'What is history, but a fable agreed upon?'

mythological subjects epitomise 17th-century French classicism, full of erudite references for an audience of cognoscenti. Don't miss Charles Le Brun's wonderfully pompous *Chancellier Séguier* and his four grandiose battle scenes, in which Alexander the Great stands in for Louis XIV. The 18th century begins with Watteau's *Gilles* and the *Embarkation for Cythera*. Works by Chardin include sober still lifes, but also fine figure paintings. If you're used to the sugary images of Fragonard, don't miss the *Fantaisies*, which forgo sentimentality for fluent, broadly-painted fantasy portraits, intended to capture moods rather than likenesses. Also in the Sully wing are sublime neo-classical portraits by David, Ingres' *La Baigneuse* and *Le Bain Turc*, portraits and Orientalist scenes by Chassériau and landscapes by Corot.

French sculpture

Richelieu: lower ground floor, ground floor. Light brown on Louvre maps.

French sculpture is displayed in and around the two glazed sculpture courts created with the Grand Louvre scheme. A tour of the medieval regional schools takes in the *Virgins* from Alsace, 14th-century figures of Charles V and Jeanne de Bourbon that adorned the exterior of the Louvre, and the late 15th-century Tomb of Philippe Pot, an effigy of a Burgundian knight carried by eight black-clad mourners. Fine Renaissance memorials, fountains and portals include Jean Goujon's friezes from the Fontaine des Innocents. In the Cour Marly, pride of place goes to Coustou's *Chevaux de Marly*, rearing horses being restrained by their grooms, plus two earlier equestrian pieces by Coysevox. Hewn from single blocks of marble, they were sculpted for the royal château at Marly-le-Roi before being moved to the Tuileries gardens, where copies now stand. In Cour Puget are the four bronze captives by Martin Desjardins, Clodion's rococo frieze and Pierre Puget's twisting *Baroque Milo of Croton*. Amid the 18th-century heroes and allegorical subjects, look out for Pigalle's *Mercury and Voltaire*.

Italian and Spanish painting

Denon: 1st floor. Red on Louvre maps.

Big changes are going on in this department: by spring 2005, when restoration of the Salle des Etats (room 6) is complete, the museum's two most celebrated works, the *Mona Lisa* and Veronese's monumental, lavish *Wedding at Cana*, will be given pride of place under a new glass roof. They will be surrounded by other Italian Renaissance masterpieces such as Leonardo's *Virgin of the Rocks*, *Virgin, Child and Saint-Anne* and *Saint-Jean Baptiste*, Caravaggio's *Fortune Teller*, the celebrated *Fête Champêtre* attributed to Titian, and the fruit and leaf heads of Arcimboldo's *Four Seasons*, plus works by Tintoretto, Lotto and Bronzino. Queues for *la Joconde* are even more inevitable after the success of Dan Brown's bestselling phenomenon *The Da Vinci Code* (*see p157* **The cult of the Code**) – as if the bullet-proof glass wasn't off-putting already. Two rooms of fragile Renaissance frescoes by Botticelli, Fra Angelico and Luini open the Italian department. Cimabue's *Madonna of the Angels* (c1270) combines the composition of Byzantine icons with the modelling of form of the Renaissance: Fra Angelico's *Coronation of the Virgin* and Mantegna's *Calvary* for example. Highlights of the Sienese school are Simone Martini's *Christ Carrying the Cross* and Piero della Francesa's *Portrait of Sigismondo Malatesta*. High Renaissance treasures from Florence include Raphael's *Belle Jardinière Virgin and Child*, and two paintings of dragon slayers St George and St Michael. A small Spanish section takes in El Greco's *Christ on the Cross Adored by Two Donors* and Jusepe de Ribera's *Club Foot*.

Graphic arts

Denon, 1st floor; Sully 2nd floor. Pink on Louvre maps.

The Louvre's huge collection of drawings includes Raphael, Michelangelo, Dürer, Holbein and Rembrandt, but owing to their fragility, drawings are not shown as permanent exhibits. Four galleries (French and Northern schools on the 2nd floor; Italian and new acquisitions on the 1st) have changing exhibitions (*see below*). Other works can be viewed in the Salle de Consultation upon written application only (01.40.20.52.51, fax 01.40.20.53.51).

Italian, Spanish and Northern sculpture

Denon: lower ground floor, ground floor. Light brown on Louvre maps.

Michelangelo's *Dying Slave* and *Captive Slave* (sculptures planned for the tomb of Pope Julius II in Rome) are the real showstoppers here, but other Renaissance treasures include a painted marble relief by Donatello, Adrien de Vriesse's bronze *Mercury and Psyche*, Giambologna's *Mercury* and the ethereal *Psyche Revived by Cupid's Kiss* by Canova. Benvenuto Cellini's *Nymph of Fontainebleau* relief is on the Mollien staircase. Aptly positioned between ancient and modern worlds on the ground floor, Napoleon III's former stables were reopened in 2004 to house princely collections of statuary formed by Richelieu, Borghese and Albani families in the 17th and 18th centuries. The statues, either copies of classical works or heavily restored originals, demonstrate the links between antique and modern sculpture. The height of the room has also allowed oversized works such as *Jupiter* and *Albani Alexander* to be shown for the first time. Northern sculpture, on the lower ground floor, ranges from Erhart's *Gothic Mary Magdalene* to the Neo-Classical work of Thorvaldsen, while the pre-Renaissance Italians include Donatello's clay relief *Virgin and Child*.

Northern schools

Richelieu: 2nd floor; Sully: 1st floor. Red on Louvre maps.

The northern Renaissance includes Flemish altarpieces by Memling and Van der Weyden, Bosch's fantastical, proto-Surrealist *Ship of Fools*, Metsys' *The Moneylender and his Wife*, and the northern Mannerism of Cornelius van Haarlem. The Galerie Médicis houses Rubens' Médicis cycle. The 24 canvases commissioned in the 1620s for the Palais de Luxembourg by Marie de Médicis, widow of Henri IV, mix historic events and classical mythology for the glorification of the queen who was not afraid to put her best features on public display. Look for Rubens' more personal, glowing portrait of his second wife *Hélène Fourment and her Children*, along with Van Dyck's *Charles I and his Groom* and peasant-filled townscapes by Teniers.

Dutch paintings in this wing include early and late self-portraits by Rembrandt, his *Flayed Ox* and the warmly glowing nude *Bathsheba at her Bath*. There are Vermeer's *Astronomer* and *Lacemaker* amid interiors by De Hooch and Metsu, and the meticulously finished portraits and framing devices of Dou, plus works from the Haarlem school. German paintings in side galleries include portraits by Cranach, Dürer's *Self-Portrait* and Holbein's *Anne of Cleves*.

The rooms of Northern and Scandinavian paintings include Caspar David Friedrich's *Trees with Crows*, the sober, classical portraits of Christian Købke and pared-back views of Peder Balke. A fairly modest but high-quality British collection located on the 1st floor of Sully includes landscapes by Wright of Derby, Constable and Turner and portraits by the likes of Gainsborough, Reynolds and Lawrence.

Decorative arts

Richelieu: 1st floor; Sully: 1st floor. Magenta on Louvre maps.

The decorative arts collection runs from the Middle Ages to the mid 19th century, often with royal connections, and includes entire rooms decorated in the fashion of the day. Many of the finest medieval items came from the treasury of St-Denis amassed by the powerful Abbot Suger, counsellor to Louis VI and VII, among them Suger's *Eagle*, a serpentine plate surrounded by precious stones and the sacred sword of the kings of France, dubbed 'Charlemagne's sword' by the Capetian monarchs as they sought to legitimise their line.

The Renaissance galleries take in ornate carved chests, German silver tankards, and the *Hunts of Maximilien*, twelve 16th-century Brussels tapestries depicting months, the zodiac and hunting scenes. 17th- and 18th-century French decorative arts are displayed in superb panelled rooms, and include characteristic brass and tortoiseshell pieces by Boulle. Displays move on to French porcelain, silverware, watches and scientific instruments. Napoleon III's opulent apartments, used until the 1980s by the Ministry of Finance, have been preserved with chandeliers, upholstery and palms intact. Butting on to the Denon wing, the magnificent Galerie d'Apollon is newly reopened after four years of restoration work. A precursor to the Hall of Mirrors at Versailles, the gallery was built for Louis XIV and is a showcase of talents from this golden age: architecture by Louis Le Vau, painted ceilings by Charles Le Brun and sculpture by François Girardon, the Marsy brothers and Thomas Regnaudin. It was completed by Napoleon III, who had Delacroix paint the central medallion, *Apollo Vanquishing the Python*. It houses the crown jewels and Louis XIV vases. A Rotonde d'Apollon anteroom with Merry-Joseph Blondel's *Chute d'Icare* ceiling is impressive.

African, Asian, Oceanic and American arts

Denon: ground floor. White on Louvre maps.

A new approach to '*arts premiers*' is seen in these eight rooms in the Pavillon des Sessions, auguring what is to come in the future Musée du Quai Branly (*see p161*). The spare, modern design of Jean-Michel Wilmotte allows each of 100 key works to stand alone in something midway between an art gallery and a museum. The pure aesthetics of such objects as a svelte Zulu spoon with the breasts and buttocks of a woman, a sixth-century BC Sokoto terracotta head, a recycled iron sculpture of the god Gou that prefigures Picasso and a pot-bellied, terracotta Chupicaro from Mexico can be appreciated in their own right, while printed boards provide fascinating explanations of their uses. Computer terminals with mahogany benches provide multimedia resources.

Temporary exhibitions

Major exhibitions are to be found in the Salle Napoléon. 2005 features (4 Mar-6 June) Roman France 950-1150 and (1 July-26 Sept) Antique Faïences from Egypt, the Middle East and Greece. Drawing exhibitions, included in the Louvre ticket price, take in (17 Feb-16 May) *Comme le rêve, le dessin*, combining 16th- and 17th-century Italian drawing with works from the Centre Pompidou, and (12 May-16 Aug) *Florentine Drawings under the Last Medicis*.

Sightseeing

Museums

Stocked by imperial plunder and styled by the spirit of the avant-garde,
the museums of Paris are eclectic and exhaustive.

**L'Institut du
Monde Arabe.**
See p174.

The Louvre (*see chapter* **The Louvre**) is so
overwhelming that it tends to overshadow the
city's hundred-plus museums. The **Centre
Pompidou**, **Musée d'Orsay** and **Musée
Marmottan** are almost as famous, and you
shouldn't miss the world-class ethnic art on
show at **Musées Guimet** and **Dapper** and
the **Institut du Monde Arabe**; nor the many
science museums, from the **Musée des Arts
et Métiers** to the high-tech **Cité des Sciences
et de l'Industrie** at La Villette. For lovers of
the avant-garde, there are the **Palais de
Tokyo Site de Création Contemporain**
and the ARC wing of the **Musée d'Art
Moderne de la Ville de Paris**.

The reason for the rich trove is tied up with
French history. After the Revolution, the huge
royal collections became the property of the
state; then came the 19th-century zeal for *grand
tourisme* – although the ownership of foreign
plunder is a matter of current debate. Both the
French state and the city put large sums into
the upkeep and expansion of collections, while
tiny, unique private museums, like the **Musée
Edith Piaf** or **Musée de l'Eventail**, struggle.

The new museum of primitive and tribal art
on quai Branly has fallen behind schedule and
won't open until 2008. New things to see in
2005 include the stunning Galerie des Bijoux at
the **Musée des Arts Décoratifs**, the **Maison
Rouge** devoted to private art collections and –
if all goes to plan – the reopened **Musée
Cernuschi** and **Mémorial de la Shoah**.
The themes of big exhibitions in 2005 include
Dada at the Pompidou, 18th-century masters at
the **Galeries Nationales du Grand Palais**,
Neo-Impressionism at the Musée d'Orsay and
Matisse at the **Musée du Luxembourg**.

TICKETS AND PASSES

The most economical way to visit a large
number of museums is the **Carte Musées et
Monuments** (www.intermusees.com). Coming
in handy one-day (€18), three-day (€36) or five-
day (€54) formats, it lets its holder into 70
museums and monuments across Paris (though
you have to pay extra for special exhibitions)
and lets you jump queues. The card is sold at
museums, tourist offices, branches of **Fnac** (*see
p246*) and major Métro stations. In our listings
CM indicates venues where the card is accepted.

The Galeries Nationales du Grand Palais now have an annual pass, **Sésame** (www.rmn.fr), which grants queue-jumping rights, unlimited entry and other discounts (€74 couples; €39 solo; €22 concessions).

Museums often offer a reduced rate for students, children and the over-60s; bring ID to prove your status. In any case, all permanent collections at municipal-run museums are free, and a reduced rate is usually applicable on Sundays. All national museums are completely free on the first Sunday of the month, and most museums throw open their doors on one Sunday in April for **Printemps des Musées** (01.40.15.36.00, www.culture.gouv.fr; *see p278*).

OPENING HOURS

Most national museums close on Tuesdays; most municipal museums close on Mondays.

To avoid crowds, visit on weekdays, or take advantage of the late-night opening that most of the big museums offer. Pre-booking is essential before 1pm at the Grand Palais, and it's also possible to pre-book the Louvre, the Luxembourg and major exhibitions. Most ticket counters shut 30 to 45 minutes before closing.

Thousands turn out for the annual **Journées du Patrimoine** (*see p282*) in September to see behind the normally closed doors of some of the capital's oldest and most beautiful buildings.

Art

Centre Pompidou (Musée National d'Art Moderne)

Rue St-Martin, 4th (01.44.78.12.33/www.centre pompidou.fr). M° Hôtel de Ville or Rambuteau. **Open** 11am-9pm (last entry 8pm) Mon, Wed-Sun; until 11pm some exhibitions. **Admission** €7; €5 18s-25s; free under-18s, 1st Sun of mth, CM. *Exhibitions* €7-€9; €5-€7 13s-25s. *Day pass* (exhibitions, collection & Atelier Brancusi) €10, €8 18-25s. **Credit** MC, V. **Map** p408 K6.

The Centre Pompidou (or 'Beaubourg'), holds the largest collection of modern art in Europe, rivalled only in its breadth and quality by MOMA in New York. Sample the contents of its vaults (50,000 works of art by 5,000 artists) on the website, as only a fraction – about 600 works – can be seen for real at any one time. There is a partial rehang each year. For the main collection, buy tickets on the ground floor and take the escalators to level four for post-1960s art. Level five spans 1905 to 1960. There are four temporary exhibition spaces on each of these two levels (included in the ticket). Main temporary exhibitions are on the ground floor, in gallery two on level six, in the south gallery, level one and in the new Espace 315 devoted to the under-40s.

On level five, the historic section takes a chronological sweep through modern art history, via Primitivism, Fauvism, Cubism, dada and Surrealism

up to American Color-Field painting and Abstract Expressionism. Masterful ensembles let you see the span of Matisse's career on canvas and in bronze, the variety of Picasso's invention and the development of cubic orphism by Sonia and Robert Delaunay. Others on the hit list include Derain, Braque, Duchamp, Picabia, Mondrian, Malevich, Kandinsky, Dix, Ernst, Miró, Klee, Magritte, Rothko and Bacon. Don't miss the reconstruction of a wall of André Breton's studio, combining the tribal art, folk art, flea-market finds and drawings by fellow artists that the Surrealist artist and theorist had amassed. The photography collection also has an impressive roll call, including Brassaï, Kertész, Man Ray, Cartier-Bresson and Doisneau. Slotted in tinier vitrines between the main rooms are works on paper, photography and archive material; other galleries are devoted to design and architecture.

Level four, post-'60s art, is to be entirely rehung at the end of 2004. Thematic rooms concentrate on the career of one artist; others focus on movements such as Anti-form or arte povera. Recent acquisitions line the central corridor, while at the far end you can find architecture and design. Video and installations by the likes of Mathieu Mercier and Dominique Gonzalez-Foerster are in a frequently changing room devoted to *nouvelle création*.

Big shows for 2005 include Robert Mallet-Stevens (27 Apr-29 Aug), contemporary African art (25 May-15 Aug), acquisitions from Bibliothèque Kandinsky (8 June-26 Sept) and Dada (5 Oct-9 Jan 2005). The winner of the Prix Marcel Duchamp creates a new work for Espace 315 each winter.

Atelier Brancusi, a public library, cinemas, children's activities, trendy restaurant Georges the contemporary music and dance factory IRCAM form part of the Centre Pompidou. *See also chapters* **Architecture**, **Sightseeing: Right Bank**, **Children** and **Film**.

Auditorium. Café. Children's workshops. Cinema. Guided Visits. Restaurant. Shops. Wheelchair access.

Musée des Années 30

Espace Landowski, 28 av André-Morizet, 92100 Boulogne-Billancourt (01.55.18.46.45/www.annees 30.com). M° Marcel Sembat. **Open** 11am-6pm Tue-Sun. Closed Mon, 15-31 Aug, hols. **Admission** (includes Musée-Jardin Landowski, *see p166*, and temporary exhibitions) €4.20; €3.20 concessions; free under-16s. **Credit** MC, V.

The Musée des Années 30 shows how much second-rate art was produced in the 1930s, though there are decent Modernist sculptures by the Martel brothers, graphic designs and Juan Gris still lifes and drawings. The highlights are the designs by avant-garde architects like Perret, Le Corbusier and Fischer. *Guided visits: 2.30pm Sun. Shop. Wheelchair access.*

Musée d'Art Moderne de la Ville de Paris/ARC Couvent des Cordeliers

11 av du Président-Wilson, 16th (01.53.67.40.00/ www.paris.fr/musees/MAMVP). M° Iéna or Alma Marceau. **Open** reopens autumn 2005. *Couvent des*

Cordeliers, 15 rue de l'Ecole-de-Médecine, 6th.
M° Odéon. **Open** noon-8pm Tue-Sun. **Admission**
€4.50; €2.50 13s-25s; free under-13s. **No credit
cards. Map** p408 H7.
The monumental 1930s building that houses the
city's own modern art collection is due to reopen in
autumn 2005 with a Pierre Bonnard exhibition. Until
then, parts of its collection are being shown themat-
ically in town halls around Paris. Adventurous contemporary wing ARC has temporarily crossed the
river to the former Revolutionary cell of the Couvent
des Cordeliers. Meanwhile, Louise Bourgeois' huge
Spider lowers over the skeletons at the **Muséum
National d'Histoire Naturel** (*see p181*), Ange
Leccia's wave projection *La Mer* plays at the **Musée
de la Marine** (*see p177*), and Christian Boltanksi's
Theatre of Shadows is at the **Musée d'art et d'histoire du Judaïsme** (*see p176*) until mid-2005.

Musée Cognacq-Jay
*Hôtel Donon, 8 rue Elzévir, 3rd (01.40.27.07.21/
www.paris.fr/musees/cognacq_jay). M° St-Paul.*
Open 10am-6pm Tue-Sun. Closed some hols.
Admission free. **Map** p408 L6.
This cosy museum in a carefully restored *hôtel par-
ticulier* houses the collection put together in the early
1900s by La Samaritaine founder Ernest Cognacq
and his wife Marie-Louise Jay. They stuck mainly to
18th-century French, focusing on rococo artists like
Watteau, Fragonard, Boucher, Greuze and pastellist
Quentin de la Tour, though some English (Reynolds,
Romney, Lawrence), Dutch and Flemish (an early
Rembrandt, Ruysdael, Rubens) names, plus
Canalettos and Guardis, have slipped in. Pictures are
displayed in panelled rooms with furniture, porce-
lain, tapestries and sculpture of the same period.
Bookshop. Children's workshops.

Fondation Dubuffet. *See p165.*

Musée Départemental Maurice Denis, 'Le Prieuré'
*2bis rue Maurice-Denis, 78100 St-Germain-en-Laye
(01.39.73.77.87/www.musee-mauricedenis.fr). RER
St-Germain-en-Laye.* **Open** 10am-5.30pm Tue-Fri;
10am-6.30pm Sat, Sun. **Admission** €3.80; €2.20
12s-25s, students, over-60s; free under-12s; CM.
Exhibitions (museum included) €5.30; €3.80 12s-25s,
concessions; free under-12s. **No credit cards.**
This former royal convent and hospital was home
and studio to Nabi painter Maurice Denis, who in
1915 also decorated the chapel in the garden. This
remarkable suburban collection comprises paintings, prints and decorative objects by the Nabis –
the name means 'Prophets' – who included Sérusier,
Bonnard, Vuillard, Roussel and Valloton. Seeking a
renewed spirituality in painting, they took inspiration from Gauguin and Toulouse-Lautrec, who also
have some paintings on show here.
Bookshop. Children's workshops. Garden.

Musée Jacquemart-André
*158 bd Haussmann, 8th (01.45.62.11.59/www.
musee-jacquemart-andre.com). M° Miromesnil
or St-Philippe du-Roule.* **Open** 10am-6pm daily.
Admission €8.50; €6.50 7s-17s, students; free
under-7s. **Credit** AmEx, MC, V. **Map** p403 E3.
The collection built by Edouard André and his wife
Nélie Jacquemart – and the mansion they built to
house it – are magnificent, and worth visiting for
their illustration of life among the 19th-century
haute bourgeoisie alone. On the ground-floor are the
circular Grand Salon, rooms of tapestries and French
furniture, Boucher mythological fantasies, library
(with Dutch paintings including Rembrandts), the
smoking room hung with English portraits, and the
polychrome marble winter garden with double spiral staircase. On the stairway three Tiepolo frescoes
from the Villa Contarini depict the arrival of Henri
III in Venice. Upstairs, what was to have been Nélie's
studio became their 'Italian museum', a splendid
Early Renaissance collection that includes Uccello's
St George and the Dragon, Mantegna's Ecce Homo,
a superb Schiavone portrait, a Carpaccio panel and
Della Robbia terracottas. Even the tea room has a
Tiepolo ceiling. The free audio guide is useful.
*Audio guide in six languages. Bookshop. Café
(11.30am-6pm). Partial wheelchair access.*

Musée Marmottan – Claude Monet
*2 rue Louis-Boilly, 16th (01.42.24.07.02/www.
marmottan.com). M° La Muette.* **Open** 10am-6pm
Tue-Sun (last entry 5.30pm). **Admission** €6.50; €4
8s-25s; free under-8s. **Credit** MC, V.
Originally a museum of the Empire period left to the
state by collector Paul Marmottan, this old hunting
pavilion has become a famed holder of Impressionist
art thanks to two bequests: the first by the daughter of the doctor of Manet, Monet, Pissaro, Sisley and
Renoir; the second by Monet's son Michel. Its Monet
collection, the largest in the world, numbers 165 –
including the seminal *Impression Soleil Levant* –
plus sketchbooks, palette and photos. A special

circular room was created for the breathtaking series of late water lily canvases; upstairs are works by Renoir, Manet, Gauguin, Caillebotte and Berthe Morisot, 15th-century primitives, the Wildenstein collection of medieval manuscripts, a Sèvres clock and a collection of First Empire furniture.
Shop. Wheelchair access.

Musée de l'Orangerie

Jardin des Tuileries, 1st (01.40.20.67.71/www. rmn.fr). M° Concorde. **Open** 2006. **Map** p403 F5.
Discovery of chunks of the Louvre's original curtain wall in the basement means that renovation work on the Orangerie has been delayed. The museum, which houses Monet's eight huge, late *Nymphéas* (water lilies) paintings, left by the artist to the nation as a 'spiritual testimony', as well as the Jean Walter and Paul Guillaume collection of Impressionism and the Ecole de Paris, will not reopen until at least 2006.

Musée d'Orsay

1 rue de la Légion d'Honneur, 7th (01.40.49.48.14/ recorded information 01.45.49.11.11/www.musee-orsay.fr). M° Solférino/RER Musée d'Orsay. **Open** 10am-6pm Tue, Wed, Fri, Sat (from 9am June-Sept); 10am-9.45pm Thur; 9am-6pm Sun. **Admission** €7; €5 18s-25s, all on Sun; free under-18s; CM. *With exhibitions* €8.50; €6.50 18s-25s, all on Sun; free under-18s. **No credit cards. Map** p407 G6.
This Beaux-Arts station, built for the Exposition Universelle of 1900, was saved from demolition to become the Musée d'Orsay, devoted to the pivotal period between 1848 and 1914. Italian architect Gae Aulenti remodelled the interior, keeping the iron-framed, coffered roof and creating galleries either side of a light-filled canyon. The arrangement has its drawbacks: upstairs, the Impressionists and Post-Impressionists are knee-deep in tourists, while too much space is given downstairs to Couture's languid nudes or Meissonier's history paintings; but it somehow manages to maintain an open-plan feel.
The museum follows a chronological route, from the ground floor to the upper level and then to the mezzanine, showing links between Impressionist painters and their forerunners, and their revolutionary use of light and colour.
Running down the centre of the tracks, a central sculpture aisle takes in monuments and maidens by artists including Rude, Barrye and Carrier-Belleuse, but the outstanding pieces are by Carpeaux, including his controversial *La Danse* for the façade of the Palais Garnier. The Lille side, on the right of the central aisle, is dedicated to the Romantics and history painters: Ingres and Amaury-Duval contrast with the Romantic passion of Delacroix's North African period, Couture's vast *Les Romains de la Décadence* and the cupids of Cabanel's *Birth of Venus*. Further on are early Degas and works by Symbolists Moreau and Puvis de Chavannes; a gallery puts on selections from Orsay's vast holdings of early photography.
The first rooms to the Seine side of the main aisle are given over to the Barbizon landscape painters Corot, Daubigny and Millet. One room is dedicated

to Courbet, with *The Artist and his Studio*, his monumental *Burial at Ornans* and show-stopping *L'Origine du Monde*. This floor also covers pre-1870 works by Impressionists, including Manet's provocative Olympia, and their precursor Boudin.
Upstairs are the Impressionists, with masterworks by Pissarro, Renoir and Caillebotte, Manet's *Déjeuner sur l'Herbe*, several of Monet's paintings of Rouen cathedral, and works by Degas. Among the Van Goghs are *Church at Auvers* and last painting, *Crows*. This is where you'll find the primitivist jungle of the Douanier Rousseau, the gaudy lowlife of Toulouse-Lautrec, the colourful exoticism of Gauguin's Breton and Tahitian periods, Cézanne's still lifes, landscapes and *The Card Players*, Seurat, Signac and the mystical pastel drawings of Odilon Redon.
On the mezzanine are works by the Nabis painters – Vallotton, Denis, Roussel, Bonnard and Vuillard. Several rooms are given over to art nouveau decorative arts, including furniture by Majorelle, and Gallé and Lalique ceramics. Paintings by Klimt and Burne-Jones reside here, and there are sections on architectural drawings and early photography. The sculpture terraces include busts by Rodin, heads by Rosso and bronzes by Bourdelle and Maillol.
Exhibitions in 2005 include Néo-Impressionnisme (14 Mar-26 June) and Un Nouveau Théâtre (11 Apr-3 July), examining how the Nabis collaborated with dramatists Ibsen, Maeterlinck and Jarry.
Audioguide. Bookshop. Café-restaurant. Cinema. Guided tours. Library. Wheelchair access.

One-man shows

Atelier Brancusi

Piazza Beaubourg, 4th (01.44.78.12.33/www. centrepompidou.fr). M° Hôtel de Ville or Rambuteau. **Open** 2-6pm Mon, Wed-Sun. **Admission** (included with Centre Pompidou – Musée National d'Art Moderne) €7; €5 18s-26s; free under-18s, 1st Sun in mth. **Credit** AmEx, DC, MC, V. **Map** p408 K6.
When Constantin Brancusi died in 1957 he left his studio and its contents to the state. Rebuilt outside the Pompidou, the studio has been faithfully reconstructed. His fragile works in wood and plaster, including his endless columns and streamlined bird forms, show how Brancusi revolutionised sculpture.

Atelier-Musée Henri Bouchard

25 rue de l'Yvette, 16th (01.46.47.63.46/www.musee-bouchard.com). M° Jasmin. **Open** 2-7pm Wed, Sat. Closed last 2wks Mar, June, Sept & Dec. **Admission** €4; €2.50 students under-26; free under-6s. **No credit cards.**
Sculptor Henri Bouchard had this house and studio built in 1924. Tended by his son, its dusty workroom, crammed with sculptures, sketchbooks and tools, gives an idea of the official art of his day. He began with Realist-style peasants and maidens, but around 1907 adopted a pared-down, linear style, as seen in his reliefs for the Eglise St-Jean-de-Chaillot and the monumental Apollo at the Palais de Chaillot.
Partial wheelchair access.

Fondation Dubuffet

137 rue de Sèvres, 6th (01.47.34.12.63/www. dubuffetfondation.com). Mº Duroc. **Open** 2-6pm Mon-Fri. Closed Aug, public hols. **Admission** €4; free under-10s. **No credit cards**. **Map** p407 E8.

You have to walk up a winding garden path to get to this museum in an old three-storey mansion. Set up a decade before his death in 1985 by Jean Dubuffet, master of *art brut* and wine merchant, the foundation ensures that a fair body of his works is accessible to the public. There's a changing display of his lively drawings, paintings and sculptures, plus models of the architectural sculptures from the *Hourloupe* cycle. The foundation looks after the Closerie Falballa, 3-D masterpiece of the Hourloupe cycle, at Périgny-sur-Yerres east of Paris (by appointment only, €8).

Archives (by appointment). Bookshop.

Musée Bourdelle

16-18 rue Antoine-Bourdelle, 15th (01.49.54.73.73/ www.paris.fr/musees/bourdelle). Mº Montparnasse Bienvenüe or Falguière. **Open** 10am-6pm Tue-Sun. Closed public hols. **Admission** free. **No credit cards**. **Map** p407 F8.

Rodin's pupil, sculptor Antoine Bourdelle (1861-1929), produced monumental works including the Modernist relief friezes at the Théâtre des Champs-Elysées, inspired by Isadora Duncan and Nijinsky.

Set around a small garden, the museum includes the artist's apartment and studios used by Bourdelle, painter Eugène Carrière, Dalou and Chagall. A 1950s extension tracks the evolution of Bourdelle's equestrian monument to General Alvear in Buenos Aires, and his masterful *Hercules the Archer*. A new wing by Christian de Portzamparc houses bronzes like Bourdelle's studies of Beethoven in various guises. *Bookshop. Children's workshops. Garden. Reference library (by appointment). Wheelchair access.*

Musée National Delacroix

6 pl Furstenberg, 6th (01.44.41.86.50/www.musee-delacroix.fr). Mº St-Germain-des-Prés. **Open** 9.30am-5pm Mon, Wed-Sun. **Admission** €5; €2.60 18s-25s, all on Sun; free under-18s, 1st Sun of mth; CM. **Credit** MC, V. **Map** p407 H6.

Romantic painter Eugène Delacroix moved to this apartment and studio in 1857, in order to be near the Eglise St-Sulpice where he was painting murals. The Louvre and the Musée d'Orsay house his major canvas works, but this collection includes small oil paintings, among them an early self-portrait in the stance of a Walter Scott hero and *Madeleine au Désert*, free pastel studies of skies, sketches and lithographs, his palette and Moroccan memorabilia. Exhibits include correspondence between Baudelaire and George Sand.

Bookshop.

Sightseeing

Enter the artist's lair: **Musée Gustave Moreau**. *See p166.*

Musée National Hébert

Hôtel de Montmorency-Bours, 85 rue du Cherche Midi, 6th (01.42.22.23.82/www.rmn.fr). M° St-Placide. **Open** 12.30-5.30pm Mon, Wed-Fri; 2-5.30pm Sat, Sun, public hols. Closing for 4yrs in 2005. **Admission** €3; €2.30 18s-25s; free under-18s, 1st Sun of mth; CM. **No credit cards. Map** p407 F7.

Ernest Hébert (1817-1908) was a painter of Italian landscapes and figurative subjects, who started with portraits and sad depictions of shepherdesses before turning to colourful, Symbolist-influenced muses and Impressionist-tinged ladies. The watercolours and oils are unremarkable and soon begin to drag, but are a testament to 19th-century taste. The house, built in 1743, has a certain (run-down) appeal.

Musée-Jardin Paul Landowski

28 av André-Morizet, 92100 Boulogne-Billancourt (01.46.05.82.69/www.mairie-boulogne-billancourt.fr). M° Boulogne Jean Jaurès. **Open** 11am-6pm Tue-Sun. Closed 15-31 Aug, some hols. **Admission** €4.10 (€6.20 with garden); €3.10 students; free under-16s. **Credit** MC, V.

Sculptor Paul Landowski (1875-1961) won the Prix de Rome in 1900, and never lacked for state commissions, his work treating classical and modern themes on a monumental scale. One of his most intriguing creations is *Temple* – four sculpted walls depicting the history of humanity. Some 100 sculptures are on show in this garden and studio. *Garden. Wheelchair access.*

Musée Maillol

59-61 rue de Grenelle, 7th (01.42.22.59.58/www. museemaillol.com). M° Rue du Bac. **Open** 11am-7pm Mon, Wed-Sun (last admission 6.15pm). **Admission** €8; €6 students; free under-16s. **Credit** *Shop* AmEx, MC, V. **Map** p407 G7.

Dina Vierny was 15 when she met Aristide Maillol (1861-1944) and became his principal model for the next decade, idealised in such sculptures as *Spring*, *Air* and *Harmony*. In 1995 she opened this delightful museum over the renovated 18th-century Hôtel Bouchardon, with Maillol's drawings, engravings, pastels, tapestry panels, ceramics and his early Nabis-related paintings, as well as the sculptures and terracottas that epitomise his calm, modern classicism. The museum also has works by Picasso, Rodin, Gauguin, Degas and Cézanne, a whole room of Matisse drawings, rare Surrealist documents and works by naive artists. Vierny has also championed Kandinsky and Ilya Kabakov, whose *Communal Kitchen* installation recreates the atmosphere of Soviet domesticity. Monographic exhibitions are devoted to modern and contemporary artists, including Klimt: Papiers Erotiques (9 Mar-30 May 2005). *Bookshop. Café. Wheelchair access.*

Musée Gustave Moreau

14 rue de La Rochefoucauld, 9th (01.48.74.38.50/ www.musee-moreau.fr). M° Trinité. **Open** 10am-12.45pm, 2-5.15pm Mon, Wed-Sun. Closed Tue. **Admission** €4; €2.60 18s-25s, Sun; free under-18s; CM. **Credit** MC, V. **Map** p403 G3.

A wonderful private museum, this combines the small private apartment of Symbolist painter Gustave Moreau (1825-98) with the vast two-floor gallery he built to display his work – set out as a museum by the painter himself. Downstairs shows his obsessive collector's nature with family portraits, Grand Tour souvenirs and a boudoir devoted to the object of his unrequited love, Alexandrine Durem. Upstairs is his fantasy realm which plunders Greek mythology and biblical scenes for canvases filled with writhing maidens, trance-like visages, mystical beasts and strange plants. Printed on boards that you can carry around are Moreau's lengthy, rhetorical and mad commentaries. Don't miss the trippy masterpiece *Jupiter et Sémélé* on the second floor. *Bookshop.*

Musée National Picasso

Hôtel Salé, 5 rue de Thorigny, 3rd (01.42.71.25.21/ www.musee-picasso.fr). M° Chemin Vert or St-Paul. **Open** Oct-Mar 9.30am-5.30pm Mon, Wed-Sun. Apr-Sept 9.30am-6pm Mon, Wed-Sun. **Admission** €5.50; €4 18s-25s; free under-18s, 1st Sun of mth; CM. *With exhibitions* €6.70; €5.20 18s-25s, all on Sun; free under-18s. **Credit** *Shop* AmEx, MC, V. **Map** p408 L6.

This astonishing testament to one man's genius was acquired by the state in lieu of inheritance tax and is housed in a grand Marais mansion. The collection shows all phases of Picasso's long and varied career, revealing his continual inventiveness and sense of humour. Masterpieces include a gaunt, blue-period self-portrait, studies for the *Demoiselles d'Avignon*, *Paolo as Harlequin*, his Cubist and classical phases, the surreal *Nude in an Armchair*, beach pictures of the '20s, sand-covered *tableaux-reliefs*, portraits of models Marie-Thérèse and Dora Maar, and even the ribald artist-and-model paintings of later years. The unusual wallpaper collage, *Women at their Toilette*, gets its own small room, and there are prints and ceramics, Minotaur etchings and his collection of tribal art – juxtaposed with 'primitive' wood figures he carved himself. Finds include his bizarrely wonderful sculptures, from the vast plaster head on the staircase and the spiky *Project for Monument to Apollinaire* to *Girl on a Swing*. Look out, too, for the sculpture of an ape – its face is actually made out of a toy car. Exhibitions for 2005 include Francis Bacon drawings (until mid Apr) and Picasso's *Bathers* from the Museum of Stuttgart (Sept). *Audiovisual room. Bookshop. Café (outdoor, May-Oct). Wheelchair access.*

Musée National Rodin

Hôtel Biron, 77 rue de Varenne, 7th (01.44.18. 61.10/www.musee-rodin.fr). M° Varenne. **Open** Oct-Mar 9.30am-4.45pm (gardens 5pm) Tue-Sun. Apr-Sept 9.30am-5.45pm Tue-Sun (gardens 6.45pm). **Admission** €5; €3 18s-25s, all on Sun; free under-18s, all 1st Sun of mth; CM. Gardens €1. **Credit** MC, V. **Map** p407 F6.

The Rodin Museum occupies the *hôtel particulier* where the sculptor lived at the end of his life. *The Kiss, Cathedral, Walking Man,* portrait busts and

Musée Zadkine.

early terracottas are exhibited indoors, as are many of the individual figures or small groups that also appear on the *Gates of Hell*. Rodin's works are accompanied by several pieces by his mistress and pupil, Camille Claudel. The walls are hung with paintings by Van Gogh, Monet, Renoir, Carrière and Rodin himself. Most visitors have greatest affection for the gardens, spotted with trees and treasures: look out for the *Burghers of Calais*, the elaborate *Gates of Hell* (inspired by the *Inferno*), *The Thinker*, *Orpheus* under shade, and unfinished nymphs emerging from their marble matrix. Fans can also visit Villa des Brillants at Meudon (01.41.14.35.00; May-Oct, 1-6pm Fri-Sun, museum and gardens €2, gardens only €1), where Rodin worked from 1895. *Bookshop. Garden café. Partial wheelchair access. Visits for visually handicapped (by appointment).*

Musée Zadkine

100bis rue d'Assas, 6th (01.55.42.77.20/www.paris. fr/musees/Zadkine). M° Vavin/RER Port-Royal. **Open** 10am-6pm Tue-Sun. Closed Mon, public hols. **Admission** free. *Exhibitions* €4; €3 students, over-60s; €2 under-26s; free under-13s; CM. **No credit cards. Map** p407 G8.

Works by the Russian-born Cubist sculptor Ossip Zadkine are displayed around the tiny house and garden near the Jardin du Luxembourg, where he lived from 1928 until his death in 1967. Zadkine's works include musical, mythological and religious subjects and his style varies with the materials: bronzes tend to be geometrical, wood more sensuous. Sculptures are displayed at eye level, with drawings and poems by Zadkine and paintings by his wife, Valentine Prax. Changing exhibitions of contemporary artists are held in the former studio. *Partial wheelchair access.*

Temporary exhibition venues

The city's non-museum exhibition centres include the blockbusting Grand Palais and Palais du Luxembourg. Smaller foundations, libraries and buildings of architectural interest offer reasonable prices or free exhibitions. Most are open to the public only during exhibitions, so check listings in *Pariscope* before dropping by. Cultural centres include: **Centre Culturel Calouste Gulbenkian** (Portugal, 51 av d'Iéna, 16th, 01.53.23.93.93); **Centre Culturel Irlandais** (Ireland, 5 rue des Irlandais, 5th, 01.58.52.10.30); **Centre Culturel Suisse** (Switzerland, 32-38 rue des Francs-Bourgeois, 3rd, 01.42.71.38.38); **Centre Wallonie-Bruxelles** (Belgium, 127 rue St-Martin, 4th, 01.53.01.96.96); **Goethe Institut** (Germany, Galerie Condé, 31 rue de Condé, 6th, 01.40.46.69.60 & 17 av d'Iéna, 16th, 01.44.43.92.30); **Institut Finlandais** (Finland, 60 rue des Ecoles, 5th, 01.40.51.89.09); **Institut Néerlandais** (Holland, 121 rue de Lille, 7th, 01.53.59.12.40); **Maison de l'Amérique Latine** (Latin America, 217 bd St-Germain, 7th, 01.49.54.75.00).

Bibliothèque Forney

Hôtel de Sens, 1 rue du Figuier, 4th (01.42.78. 14.60). M° Pont Marie. **Open** 1.30-8pm Tue-Sat. Closed public hols. **Admission** €4; €2 students under 28, over-60s; free under-12s. **No credit cards. Map** p408 L7.

In the turrets of the oldest Marais mansion, the Forney library specialises in exhibitions of the applied and graphic arts.

Bibliothèque Nationale de France – Richelieu

58 rue de Richelieu, 2nd (01.53.79.81.26/www. bnf.fr). M° Bourse. **Open** 9am-6pm Mon-Sat. Closed Sun, 2wks Sept, public hols. **Admission** €5; €4 students, 13s-25s; free under-13s. *La Crypte* free. **Credit** AmEx, MC, V. **Map** p404 H4.

Within the old Bibliothèque Nationale, the Galeries Mansart and Mazarine take in works on paper from medieval manuscripts to photography. Gallery La Crypte shows modern and graphic art. *Wheelchair access.*

Bibliothèque Nationale de France – François Mitterrand

Quai François-Mauriac, 13th (01.53.79.59.59/ www.bnf.fr). M° Bibliothèque or Quai de la Gare. **Open** 10am-7pm Tue-Sat; noon-7pm Sun. Closed 2wks Sept, public hols. **Admission** €5; €4 students, 13s-25s; free under-13s. **Credit** MC, V. **Map** p409 M10.

The vast library offers an erudite programme of exhibitions, including photography, artists' books and an ongoing cycle on writing. The more populist topics covered include *chanson* and the sea. *Café. Wheelchair access.*

Sightseeing

Chapelle St-Louis de la Salpêtrière

47 bd de l'Hôpital, 13th (01.42.16.04.24). M° Gare d'Austerlitz. **Open** 8.30am-6.30pm daily. **Admission** free. **Map** p408 L9.

Libéral Bruand's austere 17th-century chapel provides a fine setting for contemporary art, such as installations by Kawamata, Kapoor and Nan Goldin. *Wheelchair access.*

Espace EDF Electra

6 rue Récamier, 7th (01.53.63.23.45/www.edf.fr). M° Sèvres-Babylone. **Open** noon-7pm Tues-Sun. Closed public hols. **Admission** free. **Map** p407 G7.

This old electricity substation, set up by Electricité de France for PR purposes, is used for varied, well-presented exhibitions, from garden designer Gilles Clément to pioneer filmmaker Georges Méliès.

Espace Paul Ricard

9 rue Royale, 8th (01.53.30.88.00/www.espacepaul ricard.com). M° Concorde. **Open** 10am-7pm Mon-Fri. Closed some hols. **Admission** free. **Map** p403 F4.

The pastis firm promotes modern art, notably with the Prix Paul Ricard – young French artists shortlisted by an indepedent curator for an annual prize – to coincide with FIAC (*see p282*) each autumn.

Fondation Cartier pour l'art contemporain

261 bd Raspail, 14th (01.42.18.56.72/recorded info 01.42.18.56.51/www.fondation.cartier.fr). M° Raspail. **Open** noon-8pm Tue-Sun. **Admission** €6.50; €4.50 concessions; free under-10s. **Credit** AmEx, MC, V. **Map** p407 G9.

Jean Nouvel's glass and steel building, an exhibition centre with Cartier's offices above, is as much a work of art as the installations inside. Shows by contemporary artists and photographers alternate with wide-ranging themes, such as Birds or Desert. Live events around the shows are entitled *Nuits Nomades*. *Bookshop. Wheelchair access.*

Fondation Mona Bismarck

34 av de New-York, 16th (01.47.23.38.88). M° Alma Marceau. **Open** 10.30am-6.30pm Tue-Sat. Closed Aug, public hols. **Admission** free. **Map** p402 C5.

The Fondation provides a chic setting for eclectic exhibitions from Etruscan antiquities to folk art.

Galeries Nationales du Grand Palais

3 av du Général-Eisenhower, 8th (01.44.13.17.17/ reservations 08.92.68.46.94/www.rmn.fr/galeries nationalesdugrandpalais). M° Champs-Elysées Clemenceau. **Open** 10am-8pm Mon, Thur-Sun; 10am-10pm Wed. Pre-booking compulsory before 1pm. **Admission** *Before 1pm with reservation* €11.10. *After 1pm without reservation* €10; €8 18s-26s; free under-13s. **Credit** MC, V. **Map** p403 E5.

The city's leading blockbuster venue is a striking leftover from the 1900 Exposition Universelle. The central hall is closed for works, but two other exhibition spaces remain. In 2005 it hosts Les Arts des Indiens du Brésil (23 Mar-27 June) and Poussin, Le Lorrain, Watteau, David and others (20 Apr-1 Aug). *Audioguides. Café. Cinema. Shop. Wheelchair access.*

Halle St-Pierre – Musée d'Art Naïf Max Fourny

2 rue Ronsard, 18th (01.42.58.72.89/www.hallesaint pierre.org). M° Anvers. **Open** 10am-6pm daily. Closed Aug. **Admission** €7; €5.50 students, 4s-26s; free under-4s. **Credit** (*shop*) MC, V. **Map** p404 J2.

The former covered market in the shadow of Sacré-Coeur specialises in *art brut* and *art naïf* from its own and other collections. *Bookshop. Café/restaurant. Children's workshops.*

Hôtel de Ville de Paris

Salon d'accueil, 29 rue de Rivoli, 4th (01.42.76. 43.43). M° Hôtel de Ville. **Open** 9.30am-7pm Mon-Sat; 2-7pm Sun. **Admission** free. **Map** p408 K6.

Exhibitions in the City Hall vary from nostalgia trips about Piaf to contemporary African art.

La Maison Rouge – Fondation Antoine de Galbert

10 bd de la Bastille, 12th (01.40.01.08.81/www. lamaisonrouge.org). M° Bastille or Quai de la Rapée. **Open** Wed, Fri-Sun 11am-7pm; Thur 11am-9pm. **Admission** €6.50; €4.50 students, 13s-25s; free under-13s. **Credit** MC, V. **Map** p408 M7.

This 2,000m^2 art space opened in 2004 occupies an old printworks, comprising three large exhibition rooms and basement. It presents two private collections and two thematic shows a year. *Café. Shop. Partial wheelchair access.*

Musée-Atelier Adzak

3 rue Jonquoy, 14th (01.45.43.06.98). M° Plaisance. **Open** hours vary, call in advance. **Admission** free.

The eccentric house, studio and garden built by the late Roy Adzak harbours traces of the conceptual artist's plaster body columns and dehydrations. Now a registered, British-run charity, it gives (generally foreign) artists a chance to exhibit in Paris. *Garden. Partial wheelchair access.*

Musée National du Luxembourg

19 rue de Vaugirard, 6th (01.42.34.25.95/www. museeduluxembourg.fr). M° Cluny La Sorbonne/RER Luxembourg. **Open** 10am-10.30pm Mon, Fri; 10am-7pm Tue-Thur, Sat, Sun. **Admission** €9; €6 students, 8s-25s; free under 8s. **Credit** MC, V. **Map** p408 H7.

When it opened in 1750, this small but imposing museum was the first public gallery in France, and later a forerunner of the Musée National d'Art Moderne. Its current stewardship by the national museums and the French Senate has brought a more imaginative touch and some impressive coups. 2005's highlight will be Matisse, une Seconde Vie (16 Mar-17 July), focused on the colours and abstraction of his last years. Book ahead to avoid queuing. *Café. Shop. Wheelchair access.*

Musée du Montparnasse

21 av du Maine, 15th (01.42.22.91.96/www.musee dumontparnasse.net). M° Montparnasse Bienvenüe. **Open** 12.30-7pm Tue-Sun. **Admission** €5; €4 students, 12s-16s; free under-12s. **No credit cards.** **Map** p405 F8.

Musée des Arts Décoratifs.
See p172.

Set in one of the last surviving alleys of studios, this was home to Marie Vassilieff, who opened her own academy and canteen where penniless artists – Picasso, Cocteau and Matisse – came for cheap food; Trotsky and Lenin were also guests. Shows focus on the area's creative past and present-day artists.

Palais de Tokyo: Site de Création Contemporaine

13 av du Président-Wilson, 16th (01.47.23.54.01/ www.palaisdetokyo.com). M° Iéna or Alma Marceau. **Open** noon-midnight Tue-Sun. **Admission** €6; free under-18s, art students. **Map** p402 B5.
Curators Nicolas Bourriaud and Jérôme Sans' fresh approach has secured the future of this contemporary art 'laboratory' for another three years. When it opened in 2002, many thought the stripped-back interior with visible air conditioning and lighting gubbins was a statement. In fact, it was a practical answer to tight finances, but the 1937 building has come into its own as an open-plan space with a skylit central hall, permitting the coexistence of exhibitions and installations, fashion shows and performances. The long opening hours and funky café have succeeded in drawing a younger audience, and the rollcall of artists is impressive (Pierre Joseph, Frank Scurti, Wang Du et al). Though the name dates from the 1937 Exposition Internationale, it links in with a new generation of artists from the Far East. *Bar. Restaurant. Shops. Wheelchair access.*

Passage de Retz

9 rue Charlot, 3rd (01.48.04.37.99). M° Filles du Calvaire. **Open** 10am-7pm Tue-Sun. **Admission** €6; €4 students under 26, over-60s; free under-12s. **Credit** (over €10) MC, V. **Map** p404 L5.
This gorgeous Marais mansion, once a toy factory, was resurrected as a gallery in the 1990s to host shows and installations by contemporary artists, architects, designers and photographers. Wooden floors, glass roof and walled garden give it a relaxing vibe. Cool designer café too.
Bookshop. Café. Partial wheelchair access.

Pavillon des Arts

Les Halles, 101 rue Rambuteau, 1st (01.42.33.82.50/ www.paris.fr/musees). M° Châtelet Les Halles. **Open** 11.30am-6.30pm Tue-Sun. Closed hols. **Admission** €5.50; €4 students; €2.50 14s-26s; free under-14s. **No credit cards. Map** p404 K5.
This municipal gallery in the Forum des Halles hosts exhibitions based around anything from photography to Paris history.
Wheelchair access.

La Pinacothèque de Paris

30bis rue de Paradis, 10th (01.43.25.71.41/ www.pinacotheque.com). M° Bonne Nouvelle or Poissonnière. **Open** from 2005 (call to check) 10am-10.30pm Mon, Fri; 10am-7pm Tue-Thur, Sat, Sun. **Admission** €12; €8 13s-25s, students; €6 8s-12s; free under-12s. **Credit** MC, V. **Map** p404 H5.

Capturing defining moments

2004 was the year the world lost Henri Cartier-Bresson. Known as 'the eye of the 20th century', his Leica – and his belief in the defining moment – captured crucial political events, key thinkers and doers, and seemed to be able to look right into the soul of his subjects. His 96 years gave him and his wife Martine Franck the chance to catalogue his photographs into a Master Collection of 385 images, held by the **Bibliothèque Nationale de France** (see p167) and three other museums around the world, as well as opening the **Fondation Henri Cartier-Bresson** (see p179) in 2003.

The tall, narrow atelier built in 1913 by Molinié has a two-floor gallery, a minutely catalogued archive open to researchers and a pleasant lounge on the fourth floor screening films on TV. In the spirit of Cartier-Bresson, who assisted on three Jean Renoir films, and drew and painted all his life (some drawings are on the fourth floor), the Fondation opens to other disciplines with three annual shows. The convivial feel of the Fondation, and its Le Corbusier armchairs, foster relaxed discussion with staff and other visitors.

2004 saw changes at the former Centre National de la Photographie, now the **Jeu de Paume** (see p179) after its new home in the Jardin des Tuileries. The light, airy building, once a court for real tennis, offers two large galleries, a hip café and basement video art and cinema suite. Programming includes ground-breaking films across the decades, while the video cycle, designed as an integral part of thematic exhibitions, might include modern experimental works. Forthcoming exhibitions include Jean-Luc Moulène and Tony Oursler, Charlie Chaplin and Burlesques Contemporains. The Jeu de Paume's second site, the old Patrimoine Photographique in the Hôtel de Sully (pictured), continues its visiting exhibitions with a political slant.

The **Maison Européenne de la Photographie** (see p179), housed in a Marais mansion with modern annexe, is devoted to contemporary works and stores a huge permanent collection. Up to six exhibitions run concurrently, from photojournalism to experimental art photography; the energetic MEP organises the biennial Mois de la Photo (next one in Nov 2006) and the Art Outsiders festival of new media web art in September.

The pivotal years 1848-1914 of the **Musée d'Orsay** (see p164) cover photography's birth and golden age. Photographers were perfecting the richness and detail of the image, its later commercialisation resulting in a backlash return to photography as art. The collection of 45,000 includes works by Nadar, Nègre and Atget, and writers who explored the medium such as Zola, Degas and Bonnard.

A hundred and eighty thousand visitors came to inaugural show Picasso Intime at this privately-funded venue in the former Musée Baccarat. This allowed for a renovation that will create 4,000m² of space for permanent and temporary exhibitions. Created by art historian Marc Restellini, responsible for major shows at the Musée du Luxembourg, its ambition is to bring over crowd-pulling shows, often as partnerships with exhibition centres in Japan and the USA. There's a café overseen by Ducasse. On the ground floor, a room will present changing displays of works on long-term loan from private collections. *Café.*

Le Plateau

Rue des Alouettes, 19th (01.53.19.84.10/www. fracidf-leplateau.com). M° Buttes Chaumont. **Open** 2-7pm Wed-Fri; 11am-7pm Sat-Sun. **Admission** free.

This modern art space has become the low-budget challenger to the Palais de Tokyo. Born out of a campaign for an arts centre in northeast Paris, the small exhibition space addresses the diversity of current art practice with installations, painting, photography, experimental cinema, music and dance.

Architecture

Cité de l'Architecture et du Patrimoine – Palais de la Porte Dorée

293 av Daumesnil, 12th (01.58.51.52.00/www. archi.fr/IFA-CHAILLOT). M° Porte Dorée. **Open** 10am-5pm Mon, Wed-Sun. **Admission** *Exhibitions* free. *Art Deco rooms & acquarium* €5.50; €4 under-25s. **No credit cards**.

Pending the inauguration of the Cité de l'Architecture in the Palais de Chaillot at the end of 2005, the combined Musée des Monuments Nationaux and Institut Français de l'Architecture has been given a temporary home in the old Musée des Arts Africains et Océaniques. Shows range from architects' projects to retrospectives on Auguste Perret. The fine building, designed for the 1931 Exposition Coloniale, has an art deco bas-relief glorying in France's colonial past – it will be the Cité Nationale de l'Histoire de l'Immigration in 2007. Meanwhile, the crocodiles brought in from Dakar in 1948 lurk in the basement. *See also chapter* **Children**.

It culminates with Man Ray's portrait of Proust on his deathbed. Other important collections are held at the **Centre Pompidou** (*see p162*) and the **Musée Carnavalet** (*see p176*); for contemporary photography try the

Fondation Cartier pour l'art contemporain (*see p179*), **Le Plateau** (*see p170*) and the **Passage de Retz** (*see p169*). Keep an eye out, too, for exhibitions run by the Mairie (www.paris.fr), usually on a local theme.

Pavillon de l'Arsenal

21 bd Morland, 4th (01.42.76.33.97/www.pavillon-arsenal.com). M° Sully Morland. **Open** 10.30am-6.30pm Tue-Sat; 11am-7pm Sun. **Admission** free. **Credit** *Shop* MC, V. **Map** p408 L7.
The Pavillon displays local building projects and acts as an archive. The fantastic 1880s gallery, with its iron frame and glass roof, has been refurbished; the ground floor houses a permanent exhibition on the history of Paris. Upstairs is a temporary displays, a library and *vidéothèque*. Entries for projects like the 2012 Olympic landmark are shown on the mezzanine. *Bookshop. Café.*

Decorative arts

For more on fashion museums, *see p175* **Wearing it well**.

Galerie-Musée Baccarat

11 pl des Etats-Unis, 16th (01.40.22.11.00/www. baccarat.fr). M° Iéna. **Open** 10am-7pm Mon, Wed-Sat. Closed hols. **Admission** €7; €3.50 students. **No credit cards. Map** p402 C4.

It didn't take long for this fantastical showcase to make the itinerary of every fashion victim in town. Philippe Starck has created a neo-rococo wonderland in the old Musée Baccarat, the former mansion of socialite, the Vicomtesse de Noailles. From the red carpet entrance with a chandelier in a fish tank to the Alchemy room decorated by Gérard Garouste, there's a play of light and movement that makes Baccarat's work, past and present, sing. See items by great designers like Georges Chevalier and Ettore Sottsass, services made for princes and maharajahs, and monumental show-off items made for the great exhibitions of the 1800s. Le Cristal Room (*see p198*) restaurant has a two-month waiting list. *Restaurant. Shop.*

Musée des Antiquités Nationales

Château, pl Charles de Gaulle, 78100 St-Germain-en-Laye (01.39.10.13.00/www.musee-antiquites nationales.fr). RER St-Germain-en-Laye. **Open** *Oct-Apr* 10am-5.15pm Mon, Wed-Sun. *May-Sept* 10am-5.15pm Sat, Sun, hols. **Admission** €4; €2.60 students 18s-25s; free under-18s, 1st Sun of mth; CM. **Credit** *Shop* V.

Thousands of years spin by from one cabinet to the next in this awe-inspiring museum tracing France's rich archaeological heritage: some of the Paleolithic animal sculptures existed long before the Ancient Egyptians. The redesigned Neolithic galleries feature statue-menhirs, female statues and an ornate tombstone from Cys-la-Commune. Exhibits are well presented and full of curiosities, like the huge antlers from a prehistoric Irish deer or the 18th-century cork models of ancient sites, though the gallery of artefacts from Roman Gaul is currently shut.
Guided visits. Shop. Wheelchair access.

Musée des Arts Décoratifs

107 rue de Rivoli, 1st (01.44.55.57.50/www.ucad.fr). M° Palais Royal Musée du Louvre. **Open** 11am-6pm Tue-Fri; 10am-6pm Sat, Sun. Closed some hols. **Admission** (with Musée de la Mode and Musée de la Publicité) €6; €4.50 18s-25s; free under-18s; CM. **Credit** MC, V. **Map** p404 H5.

This rich collection of decorative arts is currently undergoing a major facelift as part of the Grand Louvre project. Last year the much-fêted Galerie des Bijoux opened – two dramatic rooms linked by a glass bridge. Although 1,200 pieces are on show, you get an impression of quality rather than quantity – clever spotlighting on black lets you appreciate the exquisite treasures on offer, a history of France in jewellery from *châtelaines* made for medieval royalty to Maison Falize enamel. The second gallery includes modern works made from unlikely materials such as car inner tubes and celluloid. There are cases focused on the Japanese art of seduction through combs and Chinese head jewellery. The Renaissance and Middle Ages galleries are also open, with Flemish tapestries and 16th-century Venetian glass, two reconstructions of period rooms, religious art including a wonderful altarpiece of the life of John the Baptist by Luis Borassa, and a new hanging of medieval tapestries. Due to reopen in 2005 are the 17th- and 18th-century, art deco and art nouveau, modern and contemporary collections, plus galleries of glass, wallpaper, drawings and toys.
Library. Shop. Wheelchair access (105 rue de Rivoli).

Musée de la Chasse et de la Nature

Hôtel Guénégaud, 60 rue des Archives, 3rd (01.53. 01.92.40/www.chassenature.org). M° Rambuteau. **Open** 11am-6pm Tue-Sun. Closed most public hols. **Admission** €4.60; €2.30 16s-25s, students under 26; €0.75 5s-16s; free under-5s. **No credit cards.** **Map** p404 K5.

Housed on three floors of a fine, Mansart-designed 17th-century mansion is a store of objects with a hunting theme (including a stuffed polar bear and a pair of gorillas). Highlights are the ornate weapons: crossbows inlaid with ivory and mother-of-pearl, rifles decorated with hunting scenes, reminders that hunting's accoutrements were status symbols. There are bird and animal studies by the first great *animalier* in France, Alexandre-François Desportes, as well as his own portrait of Louis XIV's hunting dogs. The museum is linked to a nature reserve in the Ardennes woodland.
Bookshop. Wheelchair access.

Musée de l'Eventail

2 bd de Strasbourg, 10th (01.42.08.90.20/www.anne hoguet.com). M° Strasbourg St-Denis. **Open** 2-6pm Mon-Wed (Mon-Fri in school hols). *Children's activities* Wed afternoons. Closed Aug, public hols. **Admission** €6; €4 under-26s; €3 8s-12s; free under-8s. **No credit cards. Map** p404 K4.

Anne Hoguet keeps the tradition of her ancestors alive in this arcane museum in a 19th-century apartment, a fan-maker's *atelier* since 1805. One room houses the tools of the trade; beside, Hoguet's studio where she works on fans for fashion and the stage. The former *salle d'exposition*, lined in blue silk, is where the collection of almost 1,000 historic fans – from 18th-century fans painted alternately with sacred or profane themes to modern versions – are shown in glass cases and stored in cabinets.

Musée National des Arts et Traditions Populaires

6 av du Mahatma-Gandhi, Bois de Boulogne, 16th (01.44.17.60.00/www.musee-atp.fr). M° Les Sablons. **Open** 9.45am-5pm Mon, Wed-Sun. Closed some hols.

Musée de la Publicité.

Admission €4; €2.60 10s-25s, students; free under-10s, 1st Sun of mth; CM. *Museum & exhibition* €5; €3.80 10s-25s, concessions; free under-10s. **Credit** MC, V.
This collection spotlights the traditions and culture of rural France with tools, household objects and costumes. The liveliest sections are those devoted to customs and beliefs (a crystal ball, thunder stones and medicines) and leisure. Due to move in 2008.
Auditorium. Library/sound archive (by appointment). Shop. Wheelchair access.

Musée National de la Céramique

pl de la Manufacture, 92310 Sèvres (01.41.14.04.20). M° Pont de Sèvres. **Open** 10am-5pm Mon, Wed-Sun. Closed most public hols. **Admission** €4; €2.60 18s-25s; free under-18s, all on Sun; CM. **Credit** *Showroom* MC, V.
Founded in 1738 as a private concern, the famous porcelain factory moved to Sèvres from Vincennes in 1756 to be taken on by the state. Finely painted, delicately modelled pieces that epitomise French rococo style, together with later Sèvres, adorned with copies of Raphaels and Titians, demonstrate technical virtuosity. The collection also includes Delftware, Meissen and wonderful Ottoman plates.
Shop and showroom. Wheelchair access.

Musée National du Moyen Age – Thermes de Cluny

6 pl Paul-Painlevé, 5th (01.53.73.78.00/www.musee-moyenage.fr). M° Cluny La Sorbonne. **Open** 9.15am-5.45pm Mon, Wed-Sun. **Admission** €5.50; €4 18s-25s, all on Sun; free under-18s, 1st Sun of mth; CM. *With temporary exhibitions* €6.70; €5.20 18s-25s. **No credit cards. Map** p408 J7.
Occupying the Paris mansion of the medieval abbots of Cluny and the remains of a Roman bathing establishment, the museum of medieval art and artefacts retains a suitably domestic scale. New acquisitions include the 12th-century illuminated manuscript *L'Ascension du Christ* from the Abbey of Cluny and the 16th-century triptych *Assomption de la Vierge* by Adrien Isenbrant of Bruges. Most famous is the mesmerising Lady and the Unicorn tapestry cycle: six, late 15th-century Flemish mille-fleurs tapestries depicting convoluted allegories of the five senses, beautifully displayed in a special circular room. Other textiles include fragile Coptic embroidery and Edward III's emblazoned saddle cloth and a cycle of the life of St Stephen. One room features chivalric and everyday life at the end of the Middle Ages. The heads of the kings of Judah from Notre-Dame cathedral, mutilated in the Revolution and rediscovered (minus their noses) in 1979, are the highlight of the sculptures. Fronted by a themed garden.
Bookshop. Concerts. Guided tours in English 2pm Wed; 11.45am Sat.

Musée Nissim de Camondo

63 rue de Monceau, 8th (01.53.89.06.40/www.ucad.fr). M° Villiers or Monceau. **Open** 10am-5pm Wed-Sun. **Admission** €6; €4.50 18s-25s; free under-18s; CM. Closed some public hols. **Credit** AmEx, MC, V. **Map** p403 E3.
Put together by Count Moïse de Camondo, this collection is named after his son Nissim, killed in World War I. Moïse replaced the family's two houses near Parc Monceau with this palatial residence and lived here in a style in keeping with his love of the 18th century. Grand first-floor reception rooms are filled with furniture by leading craftsmen of the Louis XV and XVI eras, huge silver services and vast services of Sèvres and Meissen porcelain, Savonnerie carpets and Aubusson tapestries.
Bookshop.

Musées des Parfumeries-Fragonard

9 rue Scribe, 9th (01.47.42.04.56) & 39 bd des Capucines, 2nd (01.42.60.37.14). M° Opéra. **Open** 9am-6pm Mon-Sat (Apr-Oct rue Scribe open daily). **Admission** free. **Map** p403 G4.
Get on the scent at the two museums showcasing the collection of perfume house Fragonard. The five rooms at rue Scribe range from Ancient Egyptian ointment flasks to Meissen porcelain scent bottles, while the second museum has bottles by Lalique and Schiaparelli. Both have displays on scent manufacture and an early 20th-century 'perfume organ'.
Shop.

Musée de la Publicité

107 rue de Rivoli, 1st (01.44.55.57.50/www.ucad.fr). M° Palais Royal Musée du Louvre. **Open** 11am-6pm Tue-Fri; 10am-6pm Sat, Sun. Closed some public hols. **Admission** (with Musée des Arts Décoratifs and Musée de la Mode) €6; €4.50 18s-25s; free under-18s; CM. **Credit** MC, V. **Map** p404 H5.
Upstairs element of the triumvirate of museums, the advertising museum occupies an artfully distressed interior by Jean Nouvel. Only a fraction of the vast collection of posters, promo objects and packaging can be seen at one time; vintage posters can be accessed through the multimedia space.
Archives. Shop. Wheelchair access.

Musée National de la Renaissance

Château d'Ecouen, 95440 Ecouen (01.34.38.38.50/www.musee-renaissance.fr). Train from Gare du Nord to Ecouen-Ezanville, then bus 269. **Open** 9.45am-12.30pm, 2-5.15pm Mon, Wed-Sun. **Admission** €4; €2.60 18s-25s, Sun; free under-18s, 1st Sun of mth, CM. **Credit** MC, V.
The Renaissance château built 1538-55 for Royal Constable Anne de Montmorency and wife Margaret de Savoie is the setting for a wonderful collection of 16th-century decorative arts, arranged over three floors (some parts only open at certain times – phone ahead). Best are the original painted chimney pieces, decorated with biblical and mythological scenes.
Bookshop. Wheelchair access (call ahead).

Ethnic art

Musée Cernuschi

7 av Velasquez, 8th (01.45.63.50.75/www.paris.fr/musees). M° Villiers or Monceau. **Open** reopens June 2005. 10am-5.40pm Tue-Sun. Closed public hols. **Admission** free. **Map** p403 E2.

Since banker and Republican Henri Cernuschi built a *hôtel particulier* by the Parc Monceau for the treasures he found in the Far East in 1871, the collection has doubled in size. It now ranks as the fifth most important collection of Chinese art in Europe, so the museum is being expanded to twice its size. It reopens in June 2005 with a total exhibition area of 3,200m². The fabulous collection ranges from legions of Han and Wei dynasty funeral statues to refined Tang celadon wares and Sung porcelain.

Musée Dapper

35bis rue Paul-Valéry, 16th (01.45.00.01.50/ www.dapper.com). M° Victor Hugo. **Open** 11am-7pm Wed-Sun. Closed some public hols. **Admission** €5; €2.50 students, 16s-25s; free under-16s. **Credit** MC, V. **Map** p402 B4.

A specialist museum named after the 17th-century Dutch humanist Olfert Dapper, the Fondation Dapper began in 1983 as an organisation dedicated to preserving sub-Saharan art. Reopened in 2000, the new Alain Moatti-designed museum includes a performance space, bookshop and café. The exhibition space houses two themed exhibitions each year on Africa and the African diaspora; the performance space welcomes African musicians and story-tellers. *Bookshop. Café. Concerts. Wheelchair access.*

Musée de l'Institut du Monde Arabe

1 rue des Fossés-St-Bernard, 5th (01.40.51.38.38/ www.imarabe.org). M° Jussieu. **Open** 10am-6pm Tue-Sun. **Admission** €4; €3 12s-25s, students, over-60s; free under-12s; CM. **Credit** MC, V. **Map** p408 K7.

Opened as one of Mitterrand's Grands Projets, the institute of the Arab world brings together a library, cultural centre, exhibitions and the Museum of Arab Museums, displaying items on long-term loan from museums in Syria and Tunisia, alongside its own permanent collection. The objects cover a huge geographical and historical span from prehistory to the present. Of special interest are the collections of urns and masks from Carthage, early scientific tools, and 19th-century Tunisian costume and jewellery. *Bookshop. Cinema. Concerts. Lectures. Library. Restaurant. Tearoom. Wheelchair access.*

Musée National des Arts Asiatiques – Guimet

6 pl d'Iéna, 16th (01.56.52.53.00/www.musee guimet.fr). M° Iéna. **Open** 10am-6pm (last entry 5.30pm) Mon, Wed-Sun. **Admission** €7; €5 students, 18s-25s, Sun; free under-18s, 1st Sun of mth; CM. **Credit** *Shop* AmEx, MC, V. **Map** p402 C5.

Founded by Lyonnais industrialist Emile Guimet in 1889 to house his collection of Chinese and Japanese religious art, and later incorporating the Oriental collections from the Louvre, the expanded Musée Guimet has 45,000 objects from Neolithic times on, in a voyage to Asia that conveys the flow of religions and civilisations. Lower galleries focus on India and Southeast Asia, centred on the stunning collection of Hindu and Buddhist Khmer sculpture from Cambodia. You can't miss the massive Giant's Way, part of the entrance to a temple complex at Angkor

Wat. Upstairs, Chinese antiquities include mysterious jade discs and an elephant-shaped Shang dynasty bronze pot. Also Afghan and Pakistani glassware, Tibetan mandalas and Moghul jewellery. *Auditorium. Guided visits. Library. Restaurant. Shop. Wheelchair access.*

Fashion

Musée de la Mode et du Textile

107 rue de Rivoli, 1st (01.44.55.57.50/www.ucad.fr). M° Palais Royal. **Open** for exhibitions 11am-6pm Tue-Fri; 10am-6pm Sat, Sun. Closed Mon, some hols. **Admission** €6; €4.50 18-25s; free under-18s; CM. **Credit** MC, V. **Map** p404 H5.

Fashion icons in spectacular settings. *See p175* **Wearing it well.** *Wheelchair access.*

Musée Galliera

10 av Pierre-1er-de-Serbie, 16th (01.56.52.86.00). M° Iéna. **Open** for exhibitions 10am-6pm Tue-Sun. Closed Mon, public hols. **Admission** (includes audioguide) €7; €5.50 over-60s; €3.50 13-26s; free under-13s. **Credit** MC, V. **Map** p402 D5.

A comprehensive look at clothes through history. *See p175* **Wearing it well.**

Fondation Pierre Bergé Yves Saint Laurent

3 rue Léonce-Reynaud, 16th (01.44.31.64.00/www. fondation-pb-ysl.net). M° Alma Marceau. **Open** for exhibitions Wed-Sun 11am-6pm. **Closed** Aug. **Admission** €5; €2.50 students, 11s-16s; free under-11s. **Credit** MC, V. **Map** p402 D5.

The great Yves Saint Laurent's career and contemporaries. *See p175* **Wearing it well.**

History & religion

Mémorial du Maréchal Leclerc de Hauteclocque et de la Libération de Paris & Musée Jean Moulin

23 allée de la 2e DB, Jardin Atlantique (above Gare Montparnasse), 15th (01.40.64.39.44/www.paris.fr/ musees). M° Montparnasse Bienvenüe. **Open** 10am-6pm Tue-Sun. Closed public hols. **Admission** free. *Exhibitions* €4; €3 students, over-60s; €2 under-26s; free under-13s. **No credit cards.** **Map** p407 F9.

This rooftop double museum follows World War II and the Resistance through Free French commander General Leclerc and left-wing hero Jean Moulin. Documentary material and film archives complement an impressive 270° slide show, complete with sound effects retelling the Liberation of Paris. An exhibition marking the 60th anniversary of the Liberation, runs until 10 April 2005. *Bookshop. Lectures. Research centre. Wheelchair access (call ahead).*

Musée de l'Armée

Hôtel des Invalides, esplanade des Invalides, 7th (01.44.42.37.72/www.invalides.org). M° Varenne or Latour-Maubourg. **Open** *Oct-Mar* 10am-5pm daily.

Apr-Sept 10am-6pm daily. Closed 1st Mon of mth, 1 Nov. **Admission** €7; €5.50 students under 26; free under-18s, CM. **Credit** MC, V. **Map** p407 E6.

After seeing Napoleon's tomb at Les Invalides, few visitors bother with the army museum included in the price. For military history, the museum is a must, but even if sumptuous uniforms and hefty cannons are not your thing, the building is itself a splendour. Besides military memorabilia, the rooms are filled with fine portraiture, such as Ingres' *Emperor*

Napoleon on his Throne. The World War I rooms are moving, the conflict brought into vivid focus by documents and photos. The Général de Gaulle wing deals with World War II, taking in not only the Resistance but also the Battle of Britain and war in the Pacific, and alternating artefacts with film footage. A number of rooms in the west wing are closed as part of Athena II, a major renovation scheme, but key items are displayed in the east wing. *Café. Concerts. Films. Lectures. Shop.*

Wearing it well

As much a part of French national heritage as fine art or wine, fashion is documented in vast collections across Paris, only a fraction of which can be seen at any one time.

The municipal fashion collection that is the **Musée Galliera** (*see p174*) and the **Musée de la Mode et du Textile** (*see p174*), part of the Union des Arts Décoratifs in the Louvre, hold changing themed exhibitions. Fashion icon Marlene Dietrich, *chanson* star Sylvie Vartan (*pictured*), handbags and toile de Jouy have been recent subjects. Those at the Musée de la Mode tend to be more exciting: last year's show on Elsa Schiaparelli (the museum holds her entire archive, and borrowed works from

worldwide collections) was fab, and the millennium show on the subject of the play of light was memorable for its centrepiece, Jean-Paul Gaultier's Eiffel Tower dress. Dramatic black-walled rooms make a fine background to the clothes, while video screens and a small cinema space show you how they move, and display interviews with the creators.

Housed in an *hôtel particulier* built by Eiffel, the Galliera takes a more academic approach. Its historical costume collection is particularly strong: 1,300 garments from the 18th century alone. It has strong links with the industry, and its initiative with young designers shows examples of innovative work the moment it hits the shops. The programme for 2005 contrasts 18th-century Dutch costume and European fashion (Apr-Aug) with an exhibition on the runway show in the autumn.

When Yves Saint Laurent bowed out of designing in 2002 and reopened his fashion house as the **Fondation Pierre Bergé Yves Saint Laurent** (*see p174*), exhibiting Picasso and Warhol paintings with the dresses they closely inspired, haute couture's status as museum piece seemed to have been sealed. But this exacting designer had always known his work was history in the making. Every vital statistic from his very first client, every sketch and every *toile*, were catalogued and secreted away. Many of his friends and clients have presented the designer with the dresses he created for them, all stored in the upper floors of the building at precisely 18°C and a hygrometric level of 50 per cent.

For the opening show, mannequins were set on '60s-style curvy white staging; videos projected on to the furniture and walls showed full-size catwalk shows and a montage of Pop Art luminaries. Half the exhibitions to follow will be devoted to aspects of Saint Laurent's muse, such as Robert Wilson's *Fables of La Fontaine* to run until spring 2005. *See also* pp37-39 **Haute couture or high street?**

Welcome to the machines – the **Musée des Arts et Métiers**. *See p180.*

Musée d'Art et d'Histoire du Judaïsme

Hôtel de St-Aignan, 71 rue du Temple, 3rd (01.53.01.86.60/www.mahj.org). M° Rambuteau. **Open** 11am-6pm Mon-Fri; 10am-6pm Sun. Closed Jewish hols. **Admission** €6.80; €4.50 18s-26s; free under-18s. **Credit** MC, V. **Map** p408 K6.

Set in a Marais mansion, this museum sprung from the collection of a private association formed in 1948 to safeguard Jewish heritage after the Holocaust. Displays illustrate ceremonies, rites and learning, and show how styles were adapted across the globe through some fine examples of Jewish decorative arts: a silver Hannukah lamp made in Frankfurt, finely carved Italian synagogue furniture, embroidered Bar Mitzvah robes. There are also documents and paintings relating to the emancipation of French Jewry after the Revolution, and the Dreyfus case, from Zola's *J'Accuse!* to antisemitic cartoons. Paintings by the early 20th-century avant-garde and the Ecole de Paris includes El Lissitsky and Chagall. The Holocaust is marked by Christian Boltanski's work commemorating the Jews who were living in the building in 1939, 13 of whom died in the camps. The Shoah Memorial (*see p178*) is to open shortly. *Auditorium. Café. Library. Shop. Wheelchair access.*

Musée d'Art et d'Histoire de St-Denis

22bis rue Gabriel-Péri, 93200 St-Denis (01.42.43.05.10). M° St-Denis Porte de Paris. **Open** 10am-5.30pm Mon, Wed-Fri (until 8pm Thur); 2pm-6.30pm Sat, Sun. Closed some hols. **Admission** €4; €2 over-60s; free under-16s. **No credit cards**.

This museum in St-Denis is set around the cloister of a former Carmelite convent, which housed Louis XV's daughter Louise de France in the 1700s. Along with displays of archaeology, prints about the Paris Commune, Post-Impressionist drawings and documents relating to local poet Paul Eluard, the most vivid part is the first floor where items are displayed within the nuns' austere cells. *Partial wheelchair access.*

Musée du Cabinet des Médailles

58 rue de Richelieu, 2nd (01.53.79.81.26/www.bnf.fr). M° Bourse. **Open** 1-5.45pm Mon-Fri; 1-5pm Sat; noon-6pm Sun. Closed 2wks Sept, public hols. **Admission** *2-day pass for library* €4.50. **Credit** MC, V. **Map** p404 H4.

On the first floor of the old Bibliothèque Nationale is this collection of coins and medals (Greek, Roman and medieval), plus oddities like Merovingian king Dagobert's throne and Charlemagne's chess set. *Shop. Partial wheelchair access.*

Musée Carnavalet

23 rue de Sévigné, 3rd (01.44.59.58.58/www.paris.fr/musees). M° St-Paul. **Open** 10am-6pm Tue-Sun. Closed some public hols. **Admission** free. *Exhibitions* €5.50; €4 over-60s; €2.50 14s-26s; free under-14s; **Credit** *Shop* AmEx, MC, V. **Map** p408 L6.

This fine Marais building houses 140 rooms depicting the history of Paris, from pre-Roman Gaul to the 20th century. Built in 1548, transformed by Mansart in 1660, it became a museum when Haussmann persuaded the city in 1866 to buy the hôtel to preserve

its beautiful interiors. Displays are chronological. The original 16th-century rooms house the Renaissance collections with portraits by Clouet, and furniture and pictures relating to the Wars of Religion. The first floor covers the period up to 1789 with furniture, applied arts and paintings displayed in restored, period interiors. For 1789 onwards, move into neighbouring Hôtel Le Peletier de Saint-Fargeau. The Revolutionary items detail the convoluted politics and bloodshed of the period. There are portraits of all the major players, prints, objects and memorabilia including a chunk of the Bastille prison. There are items belonging to Napoleon, views of post-Haussmann Paris, a cradle given by the city to Napoleon III – and Proust's cork-lined bedroom.
Bookshop. Guided tours. Lectures. Reference section (by appointment). Wheelchair access.

Musée d'Histoire de France

Hôtel de Rohan, 87 rue Vieille-du-Temple, 3rd (01.40.27.60.96/www.archivesnationales.culture. gouv.fr/chan). M° Hôtel de Ville or Rambuteau. **Open** 10am-12.30pm, 2-5.30pm Mon, Wed-Fri; 2-5.30pm Sat, Sun. Closed public hols. **Admission** €3; €2.30 18s-25s; free under-18s. **Credit** MC, V. **Map** p408 K6.
Housed in one of the grandest Marais mansions, this museum is to be renovated in order to present a more pluralistic historical interpretation. In the meantime, a changing selection of documents and artefacts cover major political people and events – the Wars of Religion, the French Revolution, Napoleon – plus social issues and quirky aspects of daily life, from the founding of the Sorbonne to an ordinance about umbrellas. The adjoining Hôtel de Soubise boasts the finest rococo interiors decorated for the Prince and Princesse de Soubise in the 1730s and paintings by Boucher and Van Loo (visits on Sunday afternoons by reservation 01.40.27.62.18).
Concerts. Library. Shop. Workshops.

Musée des Lettres et Manuscrits

8 rue de Nesle, 6th (01.40.51.02.25). M° Odéon or Mabillon. **Open** 1-9pm Wed; 10am-6pm Thur-Sun. Closed Tue, public hols. **Admission** €8, €5.50 students, 12s-15s; free under-12s. **No credit cards**. **Map** p408 H7.
This intimate new space in the heart of the Latin Quarter presents modern history on paper. From Magritte to Mozart and Freud to François Mitterrand, more than 2,000 documents and letters give an insight into the lives of the great and the good. Einstein arrives at the theory of relativity on notes scattered in authentic disorder, Napoleon boards HMS *Northumberland* in its log-book, the day it took him to St Helena, and Baudelaire complains about his money problems in a letter to his mother.

Musée de la Marine

Palais de Chaillot, pl du Trocadéro, 16th (01.53. 65.69.69/www.musee-marine.fr). M° Trocadéro. **Open** 10am-6pm Mon, Wed-Sun. **Admission** €7; €5.40 under-25s, over-60s; €3.85 6s-18s; free under-6s, CM, under-18s to main collection. **Credit** *Shop* MC, V. **Map** p402 B5.

French naval history, outlined from detailed carved models of battleships and Vernet's imposing series of paintings of the ports of France (1754-65) to a model of a nuclear submarine. There's also the imperial barge, built when Napoleon's delusions of grandeur were reaching their zenith in 1810.
Shop.

Musée de la Monnaie de Paris

11 quai de Conti, 6th (01.40.46.55.35/ www.monnaiedeparis.fr). M° Odéon or Pont Neuf. **Open** 11am-5.30pm Tue-Fri; noon-5.30pm Sat, Sun. Closed public hols. **Admission** €8; free under-16s. **Credit** *Shop* MC, V. **Map** p408 H6.
Housed in the handsome Neo-Classical mint built in the 1770s, this high-tech museum tells the tale of local coinage from its pre-Roman origins using sophisticated displays and audiovisual presentations.
Shop. Visit to atelier (2.15pm Wed, Fri book ahead).

Musée de Montmartre

12 rue Cortot, 18th (01.46.06.61.11/www.museede montmartre.com). M° Lamarck Caulaincourt. **Open** 10am-12.30pm, 1.30-6pm Tue-Sun. **Admission** €5.50; €3.50 students, over-60s; free under-8s. **Credit** *Shop* MC, V. **Map** p404 H1.
At the back of a garden, this 17th-century manor illustrates the history of the historic hilltop, with rooms devoted to revolutionary Louise Michel, composer Gustave Charpentier, the porcelain factory at Clignancourt, and a tribute to the Lapin Agile cabaret, with original Toulouse-Lautrec posters. There are paintings by Suzanne Valadon, who occupied a studio above the entrance pavilion, as did Renoir, Raoul Dufy and Valadon's son Maurice Utrillo.
Shop.

Musée de la Poste

34 bd de Vaugirard, 15th (01.42.79.23.45/www. laposte.fr). M° Montparnasse Bienvenüe. **Open** 10am-6pm Mon-Sat. Closed public hols. **Admission** €5; €3.50 students under 26; free under-12s. **Credit** AmEx, MC, V. **Map** p407 E9.
Amid uniforms, pistols, carriages, official decrees and fumigation tongs emerge snippets of history: during the 1871 Siege of Paris, hot-air balloons and carrier pigeons were used to get post out of the city and *boules de Moulins*, balls containing hundreds of microfiche letters, were floated down the Seine in return, mostly never to arrive. The second section covers French and international philately.

Musée de la Préfecture de Police

4 rue de la Montagne-Ste-Geneviève, 5th (01.44. 41.52.50/www.prefecturepolice-paris.interieur. gouv.fr). M° Maubert Mutualité. **Open** 9am-5pm Mon-Fri; 10am-5pm Sat. Closed public hols. **Admission** free. **No credit cards**. **Map** p408 J7.
Housed in a hideous police station, this museum looks at criminal Paris history since the establishment of the Paris police force in the 16th century. Among eclectic treasures are prisoners' expenses from the Bastille (including those of dastardly jewel thief the Comtesse de la Motte), the crafty exploding

Sightseeing

flowerpot planted by Louis-Armand Matha in 1894, and the gory Epée de Justice, a 17th-century sword blunted by the sheer number of noble necks.

Musée de la Résistance Nationale

Parc Vercors, 88 av Marx Dormoy, 94500 Champigny-sur-Marne (01.48.81.00.80/www.musee-resistance.com). RER Champigny-St-Maur then bus 208. **Open** 9am-12.30pm, 2-5.30pm Tue-Fri; 2-6pm Sat, Sun. Closed weekends in Aug, Sept. **Admission** €4; €2 16s-25s; free under-16s. **No credit cards.**
Occupying five floors of a 19th-century villa, the Resistance museum starts at the top with the pre-war political background and works down, via defeat in 1940, through the Occupation and the rise of the Maquis, to victory. Hundreds of photographs aside, the material consists of newspaper files, three short archive films, a wall of machine guns and a railway saboteur's kit. Commendably, displays steer clear of Resistance hero tub-thumping.

Le Mémorial de la Shoah

17 rue Geoffroy-l'Asnier, 4th (01.42.77.44.72). M° St-Paul or Pont Marie. **Open** from early 2005. **Admission** ring for details. **Map** p408 K6.
The Mémorial du Martyr Juif Inconnu is due to reopen with a permanent collection and temporary exhibitions devoted to the Holocaust and the 76,000 Jews deported from France between 1942 and 1944.

Literary

Maison de Balzac

47 rue Raynouard, 16th (01.55.74.41.80/www.paris.fr/musees). M° Passy. **Open** 10am-6pm Tue-Sun. Closed public hols. **Admission** free. **No credit cards. Map** p406 B6.
Honoré de Balzac rented a flat at this address in 1840 to avoid his creditors and established a password to sift friends from bailiffs. The museum is spread over several floors, and although the displays are rather dry, the garden gives an idea of the villas that lined this street when Passy was a chic spa in the 19th century. Memorabilia includes first editions, letters, proofs, portraits of friends and the novelist's mistress Mme Hanska, with whom he corresponded for years before marrying her – plus a 'family tree' of Balzac's characters that covers several walls. You can see his desk and the monogrammed coffee pot that fuelled all-night work on his sprawling *Comédie Humaine*. *Children's trail. Library (by appointment).*

Maison de Chateaubriand

La Vallée aux Loups, 87 rue de Chateaubriand, 92290 Chatenay-Malabry (01.47.02.08.62). RER B Robinson then walk. **Open** (guided tours only) except Sun) *Oct-Mar* 2-5pm Tue-Sun. *Apr-Sept* 10am-noon, 2-6pm Tue-Sun. Closed Jan. **Admission** €4.50; €3 concessions; free under-12s. **No credit cards.**
In 1807, attracted by the quiet Vallée aux Loups, René, Vicomte de Chateaubriand (1768-1848) set about turning a simple 18th-century country house into his own Romantic idyll and planted the park with rare trees as a reminder of his travels. Most interesting

is the double wooden staircase, based on a maritime design, a reminder of the writer's noble St-Malo birth. Anyone familiar with David's *Portrait of Mme Récamier* in the Louvre will find the original chaise longue awaiting the sitter, one of Chateaubriand's many lovers. After publishing an inflammatory work, he was ruined and in 1818 was forced to sell up. *Concerts/readings (spring, autumn). Shop. Tearoom.*

Maison de Victor Hugo

Hôtel de Rohan-Guéménée, 6 pl des Vosges, 4th (01.42.72.10.16/www.paris.fr/musees). M° Bastille. **Open** 10am-6pm Tue-Sun. **Admission** €5.50; €4 12s-26s; free under-13s. **Credit** AmEx, MC, V. **Map** p408 L6.
Victor Hugo lived here 1832-1848, the house today a museum for France's favourite son. On show are his first editions, nearly 500 drawings, and, more bizarrely, the great man's home-made furniture. *Shop.*

Musée de la Vie Romantique

16 rue Chaptal, 9th (01.55.31.95.67/www.paris.fr/musees). M° Blanche or St-Georges. **Open** 10am-6pm Tue-Sun. Closed public hols. **Admission** free. *Exhibitions* €7; €5.50 18s-26s; €3.80 14s-18s; free under-14s. **Credit** AmEx, DC, MC, V. **Map** p403 G2.
When Dutch artist Ary Scheffer lived in this villa, this area south of Pigalle was home to so many composers, writers and artists, it was known as 'New Athens'. Aurore Dupin, Baronne Dudevant (George Sand) was a guest at Scheffer's soirées, and many other great names crossed the threshold, including Chopin, Delacroix and Liszt. The museum has a lovely rose garden and tearoom, but Sand fans will be disappointed: the watercolours, lockets and jewels she left behind reveal little of her ideas or affairs. *Archives. Bookshop. Children's workshops. Concerts. Tearoom.*

Musée Mémorial Ivan Tourguéniev

16 rue Ivan Tourguéniev, 78380 Bougival (01.45. 77.87.12). M° La Défense, then bus 258. **Open** 10am-6pm Sun; by appointment for groups during the week. **Admission** free. *Exhibitions* €5.50; €2.50 12s-26s; free under-12s. **Credit** MC, V.
The dacha where novelist Ivan Turgenev lived until his death in 1883 was a gathering spot for composers Saint-Saëns and Fauré, divas Pauline Viardot and Maria Malibran, and writers Henry James, Flaubert, Zola and Maupassant. Letters and editions (mainly Russian) are on the ground floor; above there's the music room where Viardot held court, and the writer's deathbed. The guided tour (in French) is worthwhile. *Bookshop. Concerts. Guided tours 5pm Sun.*

Music

Musée Edith Piaf

5 rue Crespin-du-Gast, 11th (01.43.55.52.72). M° Ménilmontant. **Open** by appointment 1-6pm Mon-Wed; 9am-noon Thur (call two days ahead). Closed June, Sept. **Admission** donation. **No credit cards. Map** p405 N5.

The association Les Amis d'Edith Piaf runs this tiny two-room museum in the heart of the singer's old stomping ground. The Little Sparrow's little black dress and tiny shoes are touching, and letters and photos provide a personal touch. There's a sculpture of her by Suzanne Blistène, wife of Marcel, who produced most of Piaf's films.
Library. Shop.

Musée de la Musique

Cité de la Musique, 221 av Jean-Jaurès, 19th (01.44. 84.44.84/www.cite-musique.fr). M° Porte de Pantin. **Open** noon-6pm Tue-Thur, Sat; noon-7.30pm Fri; 10am-6pm Sun. Closed public hols. **Admission** €6.10; €4.57 18s-25s; €2.29 6s-18s; free under-6s, over-60s; CM. **Credit** MC, V. **Map** p405 (inset).
Alongside the concert hall, the innovative music museum houses a gleamingly restored collection of instruments from the old Conservatoire, interactive computers and scale models of opera houses and concert halls. On arrival you are supplied with an audio guide in a choice of languages. The musical commentary is a joy, playing the appropriate instrument as you approach each exhibit. Alongside the trumpeting brass, curly woodwind instruments and precious strings are more unusual items, such as the Indonesian gamelan orchestra, whose sounds influenced the work of Debussy and Ravel. Some of the concerts in the museum's amphitheatre use historic instruments from the collection.
Audioguide. Library. Shop. Wheelchair access.

Musée de l'Opéra

Palais Garnier, 1 pl de l'Opéra, 9th (01.40.01.24.93). M° Opéra. **Open** 10am-6pm daily. **Admission** €6; €4 10s-25s, students, over-60s; free under-10s. **No credit cards**. **Map** p403 G4.
The Palais Garnier houses temporary exhibitions relating to current opera or ballet productions, and a permanent collection of paintings, scores and bijou opera sets housed in period cases. Entrance includes a visit to the auditorium, if rehearsals permit.
Guided tours in English.

Photography

Fondation Henri Cartier-Bresson

2 impasse Lebouis, 14th (01.56.80.27.00/www.henri cartierbresson.org). M° Gaité. **Open** 1-8.30pm Wed; 1-6.30pm Thur, Fri, Sun; 11am-6.45pm Sat. Closed 20 Dec-11 Jan. **Admission** €4; €3 students, 12s-26s; free under-12s, all 6.30-8.30pm Wed. **No credit cards**. **Map** p407 F10.
Two-floor gallery dedicated to the great photographer. *See p170* **Capturing defining moments**.

Jeu de Paume

Concorde *1 pl de la Concorde, 8th (01.47.03.12.50/ www.jeudepaume.org). M° Concorde.* **Open** noon-9.30pm Tue; noon-7pm Wed-Fri; 10am-7pm Sat, Sun (last admission 30min before closing). **Admission** €6; €3 concessions. **Credit** MC, V. **Map** p403 F5.
Sully *Hôtel de Sully, 62 rue St-Antoine, 4th (01.47.03.12.50). M° St-Paul or Bastille.* **Open** 10am-6.30pm Tue-Sun (last admission 30min before closing). **Admission** €5; €2.50 concessions. **Credit** MC, V. **Map** p408 L7.
New home of the National Centre for Photography. *See p170* **Capturing defining moments**.

Maison Européene de la Photographie

5-7 rue de Fourcy, 4th (01.44.78.75.00/www.mep-fr.org). M° St-Paul. **Open** 11am-8pm Wed-Sun (last admission 7.30pm). Closed public hols. **Admission** €5; €2.50 students, 8s-26s; free under-8s, all 5-8pm Wed. **Credit** MC, V. **Map** p408 L6.
Huge collection at this Marais mansion. *See p170* **Capturing defining moments**.

Science & technology

La Cité des Sciences et de l'Industrie

La Villette, 30 av Corentin-Cariou, 19th (01.40. 05.80.00/08.92.69.70.72/www.cite-sciences.fr). M° Porte de la Villette. **Open** 10am-6pm Tue-Sat; 10am-

The best Museum cafés

Centre Pompidou
By Georges! A rooftop resto. *See p162.*

Galerie-Musée Baccarat
Dining celebrities. *See p171.*

Institut du Monde Arabe
Great tagines with rooftop views. *See p174.*

Jeu de Paume
Hip café with fab cakes. *See above.*

Musée des Arts et Métiers
Brunch in the steam-themed café. *See p180.*

Musée Dapper
Trendy decor and African art. *See p174.*

Musée de la Musique
Costes brothers' terrace café. *See above.*

Musée du Fumeur
Organic food for healthy smokers. *See p183.*

Musée de la Vie Romantique
Chopin and confectionery. *See p178.*

Palais de Tokyo
Global lavs at Tokyo Eat canteen. *See p169.*

7pm Sun. Closed public holidays. **Admission** €7.50;
€5.50 7s-16s, students under 25, over-60s; free under-
7s, CM. **Credit** MC, V. **Map** p405 (inset).
The ultra-modern science museum at La Villette
pulls in five million visitors every year. Explora, the
permanent show, occupies the upper two floors,
whisking visitors through 30,000m² of space, life,
matter and communication, where scale models of
satellites including the Ariane space shuttle, planes
and robots make for an exciting journey. Experience
weightlessness in the section devoted to the con-
quest of space. In the Espace Images, try out the
delayed camera and other optical illusions, draw 3-D
images on computer or lend your voice to the Mona
Lisa. The hothouse garden investigates futuristic
developments in agriculture and bio-technology. On
the lower floors, temporary exhibitions include
Climax (until end June 2005), about climate change.
The Cité des Enfants runs workshops for children
(*see chapter* **Children**).
*Bookshop. Café. Cinema. Conference centre. Library
(multimedia). Wheelchair access & hire.*

Musée de l'Air et de l'Espace

*Aéroport de Paris-Le Bourget, 93352 Le Bourget
Cedex (01.49.92.71.99/recorded information
01.49.92.71.71/www.mae.org). M° Gare du Nord
then bus 350/RER Le Bourget then bus 152.* **Open**
Oct-Mar 10am-5pm Tue-Sun. *Apr-Sept* 10am-6pm.
Closed public hols. **Admission** €7; €5 students;
free under-18s. **Credit** MC, V.
The air and space museum is a reminder that France
is a technical and military as well as cultural power.
Set in the former passenger terminal at Le Bourget
airport, the collection begins with the pioneers,
including fragile-looking biplanes, the contraption
in which Romanian Vivia succeeded in flying 12
metres in 1906, and the command cabin of a Zeppelin
airship. On the runway are Mirage fighters, a US
Thunderchief with painted shark-tooth grimace and
Ariane launchers 1 and 5. A hangar houses the prototype Concorde 001 and wartime survivors. A section is devoted to ballooning, another to space travel.
Shop. Wheelchair access (except Space building).

Musée des Arts et Métiers

*60 rue Réaumur, 3rd (01.53.01.82.00/www.arts-et-
metiers.net). M° Arts et Métiers.* **Open** 10am-6pm
Tue, Wed, Fri-Sun; 10am-9.30pm Thur. Closed public
hols. **Admission** *With exhibition* €7.50; €5.50
students under-26s; free under-18s. *Exhibition only*
€3; €2 students, under-26s. **Credit** V. **Map** p404 K5.
After the monks of this 11th-century priory lost their
heads in the Revolution, Abbé Henri Grégoire kept
his by thinking up a brilliant new use for the building – as a repository of technological marvels that
could act as a 3-D encyclopedia for investors and
industrialists in the new republic. Three floors of the
neighbouring building contain glass cases of beautifully crafted scientific instruments from astrolabes
to steam engines including reconstructions of
famous inventors' workshops. Though it is a bit
short on moving-parts models, clever filmed dia-
grams explain the workings and there are themed

talks by staff at intervals throughout the day. The
best bit is the magnificently restored church – the
earliest example of Parisian Gothic – containing
Foucault's pendulum, Blériot's biplane and the history of the car on seven glass floors. The pleasant
terrace restaurant offers an all-in brunch and museum deal on Sundays (€19.50; €10 children).
*Lectures. Library. Restaurant. Wheelchair access.
Workshops.*

Musée de l'Assistance Publique

*Hôtel de Miramion, 47 quai de la Tournelle, 5th
(01.46.33.01.43). M° Maubert Mutualité.* **Open**
10am-6pm Tue-Sun. Closed Aug, public hols.
Admission €4; €2 students, over-60s; free under-
13s, CM. **No credit cards**. **Map** p408 K7.
The history of Paris hospitals, from the days when
they were receptacles for abandoned babies to the
start of modern medicine with anaesthesia, is shown
through paintings, prints, grisly medical devices and
a mock ward and pharmacy.

Musée d'Histoire de la Médecine

*Université René Descartes, 12 rue de l'Ecole-de-
Médecine, 6th (01.40.46.16.93). M° Odéon.* **Open**
Oct-mid July 2-5.30pm Mon-Wed, Fri, Sat. *Mid July-
Sept* 2-5.30pm Mon-Fri. Closed public hols.
Admission €3.50; €2.50 students; free under-8s.
No credit cards. **Map** p408 H7.
The medical faculty collection covers the history of
medicine from ancient Egyptian embalming tools
through to a 1960s electrocardiograph. There's a
gruesome array of saws used for amputations, the
instruments of Dr Antommarchi, who performed the
autopsy on Napoleon, and the scalpel of Dr Félix,
who operated on Louis XIV.

Muséum National d'Histoire Naturelle

*36 rue Geoffroy-St-Hilaire/2 rue Bouffon, pl
Valhubert/57 rue Cuvier, 5th (01.40.79.54.79/56.01/
www.mnhn.fr). M° Gare d'Austerlitz or Jussieu.*
Open *Grande Galerie* 10am-6pm Mon, Wed-Fri-Sun;
10am-8pm Sat. *Other galleries* 10am-5pm Mon, Wed-
Fri; 10am-6pm Sat, Sun. Closed Tue. **Admission**
Grande Galerie €7; €5 5s-16s, students, over-60s; free
under-5s (with exhibition €9 and €5. Other galeries
each €5; €3 5s-16s, students, over-60s; free under-5s.
No credit cards. **Map** p408 K9.
Within the Jardin des Plantes botanical garden, the
brilliantly renovated Grande Galerie de l'Evolution
has taken the city's natural history museum out of
the dinosaur age. Architect Paul Chemetov set modern lifts and the latest audiovisual techniques into
the 19th-century iron-framed structure. Upon entry,
you're confronted with the 13.7m skeleton of a
whale: the rest of the ground floor is dedicated to
other sea creatures. On the first floor are the mam-
mals, including Louis XVI's rhinoceros, stuffed on
a wooden chair frame. Videos and interactive computers give information on life in the wild. Glass-
sided lifts take you up through suspended birds to
the second floor, which deals with man's impact on
nature and considers demographic problems and

pollution. The third floor traces endangered and extinct species. The separate Galerie d'Anatomie comparée et de Paléontologie contains more than a million skeletons of virtually every creature you can imagine, and a fossil collection of world importance. *See also chapter* **Children**.

Auditorium. Bookshop. Café. Library. Wheelchair access (Grande Galerie).

Musée de l'Homme

Palais de Chaillot, 17 pl du Trocadéro, 16th (01.44. 05.72.72/www.mnhn.fr). M° Trocadéro. **Open** 9.45am-5.15pm Mon, Wed-Fri; 10am-6.30pm Sat, Sun. Closed Aug, most public hols. **Admission** €7; €5 concessions; €3 under-16s. **Credit** *Shop* MC, V. **Map** p402 B5.

The human department of the Muséum National d'Histoire Naturelle (*see above*) considers human evolution, genetic diversity and the reasons and consequences of the population explosion. The prehistoric section covers from 3.7 million years ago to the Bronze Age with artefacts including the skeleton of Lucy and the skull of the Man of Tautavel.

Café. Cinema. Lectures. Library. Photo Library. Wheelchair access (call ahead).

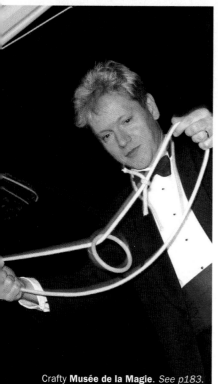

Crafty **Musée de la Magie**. *See p183.*

Musée Pasteur

Institut Pasteur, 25 rue du Dr-Roux, 15th (01.45. 68.82.83/www.pasteur.fr). M° Pasteur. **Open** 2-5.30pm Mon-Fri. Closed Aug. **Admission** €3; €1.50 students. **Credit** V. **Map** p407 E9.

The apartment where the famous chemist and his wife lived at the end of his life (1888-95) has hardly been touched since his death; you can still see their furniture and possessions, photos and instruments. The highlight is the extravagant mausoleum on the ground floor housing Pasteur's tomb, decorated with mosaics of his scientific achievements.

Musée de Radio France

Maison de Radio France, 116 av du Président-Kennedy, 16th (01.56.40.15.16/01.56.40.21.80/www.tourisme.fr/radio-france). M° Ranelagh or Passy/RER Kennedy Radio France. **Open** *Guided tours* 10.30-11am, 2.30pm, 4pm Mon-Fri. **Admission** €5; €3 concessions. **No credit cards. Map** p406 A7.

Audiovisual history is presented with an emphasis on French pioneers such as Edouard Branly and Charles Cros, including documentary evidence of the first radio message transmitted between the Eiffel Tower and the Pantheon. Note also the London broadcast of the Free French with its delightfully obscure coded messages.

Musée du Service de Santé des Armées

Val de Grace, pl Alphonse-Laveran, 5th (01.40.51. 51.94). RER Port Royal. **Open** *Groups* noon-6pm Tue, Wed. *Individuals* 1.30-5pm Sat, Sun. **Admission** €5; €2.50 6s-12s; free under-6s. **No credit cards. Map** p408 J9.

Housed in the royal convent designed by Mansart, next door to a military hospital, this museum traces the history of military medicine, via replicas of field hospitals and ambulance trains, and antique medical instruments. The chilling section on World War I demonstrates how speedily the conflict propelled progress in medical science.

Palais de la Découverte

av Franklin-D.-Roosevelt, 8th (01.56.43.20.21/www. palais-decouverte.fr). M° Champs-Elysées Clemenceau or Franklin D. Roosevelt. **Open** 9.30am-6pm Tue-Sat; 10am-7pm Sun (last entry 30min before). **Admission** €6.50; €4 5s-18s, over-60s, students under 26; free under-5s. *Planetarium* €3.50. **Credit** AmEx, MC, V. **Map** p403 E5.

The city's original science museum, housing designs from Leonardo da Vinci to the present day. Models, real apparatus and audiovisual material manage to bring displays to life, while permanent exhibits cover biology, astronomy, astophysics, chemistry, physics and earth sciences. The pertinent Planète Terre section highlights the latest developments in meteorology, while one room is dedicated to the sun. There are shows at the Planetarium too, and 'live' experiments (at weekends and during school holidays), ranging from the effect of pesticides to electrostatics. *See also pp287-292* **Children**.

Café. Experiments. Shop. Wheelchair access.

Sightseeing

Wonders & oddities

Musée des Arts Forains
53 av des Terroirs-de-France, 12th (01.43.40.16.15).
M° Cour Saint-Emilion. **Open** groups only, by
appointment. **Admission** €11.80; €3.85 concessions.
No credit cards. Map p409 P10.
Housed in a collection of Eiffel-era iron-framed wine
warehouses is a fantastic collection of 19th- and
early 20th-century fairground attractions, all working and imaginatively enhanced. The venue is hired
out for functions most evenings, and staff may well
be setting the tables when you visit. Of the three
halls the most wonderful is the Salon de la Musique,
where a musical sculpture by Jacques Rémus chimes
and flashes lights in time with the 1934 Mortier
organ and a modern-day digital grand piano playing *Murder on the Orient Express*. In the Salon de
Venise you will be twirled round on a gondola carrousel to 18th-century music, while in Salon des Arts
Forains you can play a ball-throwing game that sets
off a race of mustachioed waiters, and live out
Belleville Rendezvous fantasies on the Vélocipède, a
nightmarish carousel of penny-farthings. Open only
to groups of 15 or more, the venue can be visited as
an individual as part of a guided visit. Call ahead.

Musée de la Contrefaçon
*16 rue de la Faisanderie, 16th (01.56.26.14.00/
www.museedelacontrefacon.com). M° Porte-Dauphine.*
Open 2-5.30pm Tue-Sun. Closed most public hols.
Admission €2.50; free under-12s. **No credit cards.
Map** p402 A4.
This small museum was set up by the French anti-
counterfeiting association with the aim of deterring
forgers – but playing spot-the-fake with brands like
Reebok, Lacoste and Vuitton is fun. Fake Bic biros
too. Until 20 July 2005 Faussement vôtre! shows you
how to recognise fake car parts and electrical goods.

Musée de l'Erotisme
*72 bd de Clichy, 18th (01.42.58.28.73/www.erotic
museum.com). M° Blanche.* **Open** 10am-2am daily.
Admission €7, €5 students. **Credit** MC, V. **Map**
p403 H2.
Seven floors of erotic art and artefacts amassed by
collectors Alain Plumey and Joseph Khalif. The first
three run from 1st-century Peruvian phallic pottery
through Etruscan fertility symbols to Yoni sculptures from Nepal; the fourth gives a history of Paris
brothels; and the recently refurbished top floors host
exhibitions of modern erotic art. In the basement
you'll find titillations like a vaginal dinner plate.
Shop.

Musée du Fumeur.

Musée de la Franc-Maçonnerie

16 rue Cadet, 9th (01.45.23.20.92). M° Cadet. **Open**
2-6pm Tue-Sat. Closed public hols, 2wks July, Aug.
Admission €2; free under-12s. **No credit cards.**
Map p404 H3.
At the back of the Grand Orient de France (French
Masonic Great Lodge), the history of freemasonry is
traced from medieval stonemasons' guilds to the
prints of famous masons (General Lafayette and
1848 revolutionary leaders Blanc and Barbès).
Bookshop. Wheelchair access (call ahead).

Musée du Fumeur

7 rue Pache, 11th (01.46.59.05.51/www.museedu
fumeur.net). M° Voltaire. **Open** 11.30am-7.30pm
Tue-Sat; 12.30-7.30pm Sun. **Admission** free.
Map p409 N6.
If an organic café in a museum about smoking is
strange, the Musée du Fumeur relates to nature.
'Fumer moins et fumer mieux,' according to director
Monsieur Tigrane: smoking has lost touch with its
purpose as an aid to religious or philosophical contemplation. Here you'll find smoking contraptions
and their history and different tobacco strains in the
'plantarium'. Relax at the end of your tour with a
plant-based cocktail in the air-conditioned café.
Café. Shop.

Musée de la Magie

11 rue St-Paul, 4th (01.42.72.13.26/www.museedela
magie.com). M° St-Paul. **Open** 2-7pm Wed, Sat, Sun
(longer in hols). **Admission** €7, €5 3s-12s; free
under-3s. **No credit cards. Map** p408 L7.
This interactive museum of magic is run in the spirit of Robert-Houdin, the 19th-century French con-
jurer whose name was taken by Harry Houdini. The
sleight of hand starts outside in the queue and gets
craftier as you work your way through the exhibition. There's a broad array of conjuring tools, many
of which are put into practice before your very eyes.

Musée du Vin

Rue des Eaux, 16th (01.45.25.63.26/www.musee
duvinparis.com). M° Passy. **Open** 10am-6pm Tue-
Sun. **Admission** (with guide book and glass of wine)
€8; €7 over-60s; €5.70 students; free under-14s,
diners in the restaurant. **Credit** *Shop, restaurant*
AmEx, DC, MC, V. **Map** p406 B6.
Here the Confrères Bacchiques defend French wines
from imports and advertising laws. In the cellars of
an old wine-producing monastery are displays on
the history of viticulture with waxwork peasants,
old tools, bottles and corkscrews. Visits finish with
a wine tasting and, a paid extra, a meal.
Restaurant (noon-3pm). Shop. Wheelchair access.

Au Boeuf Couronné

In the legendary neighborhood of la Villette, once the site of Paris' main meat market, a mythical spot where connaisseurs enjoy the finest meats in the city. A generous gourmet heritage and flavours on a grand scale, in a superb Art Deco setting.

Open daily noon-3pm, 7pm-midnight
Valet parking lunchtime and evenings
188 avenue Jean Jaurès, 19th. Mº Porte de Pantin
Tel: 01.42.39.44.44 - Fax: 01.42.39.17.30

Montparnasse 1900

The registered-landmark Belle-Époque décor is a beautifully restored work of Art Nouveau. Discover the rich flavours, from traditional dishes to seafood and refined desserts... Le Montparnasse "1900" invites you into its historic past to sample cuisine marked by tradition and creativity.

Open daily noon-1am
Valet parking lunchtime and evenings
59 Bd du Montparnasse, 6th. Mº Montparnasse Bienvenue
Tel: 01.45.49.19.00 - Fax: 01.45.49.19.09

Eat, Drink, Shop

At the crossroads
of fashion,
entertainment
and business,
Maison Blanche
is where romance
meets design

maisonblanche
restaurantbar

15 avenue Montaigne, 8th.
M° Alma-Marceau

Open Mon-Fri , Sat & Sun
dinner only

Valet Parking - Reservations recommended
Tel: 01.47.23.55.99 - Fax: 01.47.23.51.09
www.maison-blanche.fr - info@maison-blanche.fr

Restaurants

The venerable capital of gastronomy gets hip.

Kong. *See p193.*

One of the first things that strikes you in the streets of Paris is that nobody is chewing. People don't eat on the run here – it remains a sacred activity, something to be undertaken with a certain amount of solemnity at the table. Things might be slowly changing, but you'd still be hard-pressed to find a bistro that would serve a three-course meal mid-afternoon. In Paris, there is a time and a place for food. This unbending attitude can be both charming and frustrating – there is nothing worse than emerging starving from a museum only to be turned away by a scornful waiter. When in

Paris, the wisest approach is to think like a Parisian and make food your top priority. As long as you remain focused on your next meal, you won't find yourself left in the lurch.

A restaurant (as opposed to a café) meal in Paris used to mean three courses. Now, perhaps as a result of the 35-hour work week most limit themselves to two courses at lunch and indulge in a full meal only at dinner. Euro inflation is a factor too, with many restaurants restricting their *prix fixe* lunch menus to two courses. Wine remains affordable at many restaurants, and thanks to a crackdown on drink-driving, most offer it by the glass.

The modern bistro has become firmly entrenched in the Paris food scene, setting a standard that even haute cuisine restaurants sometimes have trouble surpassing (*see p211* **A new breed of bistro**). The food at **L'Astrance**, **L'Atelier de Joël Robuchon** and **Flora** is likely to be as good as anything you might taste in Paris, if not the world. Add to that restaurants with spectacular settings, such as **Le Cristal Room** in the Maison Baccarat or **Kong** in La Samaritaine, and this city has plenty of surprises to offer even to those who know it well. Of course, one of the great pleasures of Paris is stumbling across a buzzing little neighbourhood bistro, and there are still plenty of these to be found.

Except for the very simplest restaurants, it is wise to book ahead. This can usually be done on the same day as your intended visit. More time should be allowed for really top-notch establishments, which require bookings weeks in advance and confirmation the day before. All bills include the service charge, so only tip if you're bowled over.

Restaurants in this chapter are presented by area, then by simple type: bistro & brasserie; French; haute cuisine and international. The average price given is for a standard main course à la carte. If no average price is listed, the option is the *prix fixe*. This indicates the price for the venue's set-price menu at lunch and dinner. If this is only offered at lunchtime, this is indicated as Lunch menu.

All listings have been checked at time of press, but are often liable to change. Many venues close for their annual break in August, some at Christmas. It pays to phone ahead. For more addresses, see *Time Out Paris Eating & Drinking*, on sale at www.timeout.com/shop.

Eat, Drink, Shop

Menu lexicon

Agneau lamb. **Aiguillettes** (*de canard*) thin slices (of duck breast). **Aïoli** garlic mayonnaise. **Aligot** mashed potatoes with melted cheese and garlic. **Aloyau** beef loin. **Anchoïade** spicy anchovy and olive paste. **Andouillette** sausage made from pig's offal. **Ananas** pineapple. **Anguille** eel. **Asperge** asparagus. **Aubergine** aubergine/eggplant.
 Ballotine stuffed, rolled up piece of meat or fish. **Bar** sea bass. **Bavarois** moulded cream dessert. **Bavette** beef flank steak. **Béarnaise** sauce of butter and egg yolk. **Beignet** fritter or doughnut. **Belon** smooth, flat oyster. **Biche** venison. **Bifteak** steak. **Bisque** shellfish soup. **Blanc** breast. **Blanquette** 'white' stew made with eggs and cream. **Boudin noir/blanc** black (blood)/white pudding. **Boeuf** beef; – **bourguignon** beef cooked Burgundy style, with red wine, onions and mushrooms; – **gros sel** boiled beef with vegetables. **Bouillabaisse** Mediterranean fish soup. **Bourride** a bouillabaisse-like soup, without shellfish. **Brochet** pike. **Bulot** whelk.
 Cabillaud fresh cod. **Caille** quail. **Canard** duck. **Cannelle** cinnamon. **Carbonnade** beef stew with onions and stout or beer. **Carré d'agneau** rack of lamb. **Carrelet** plaice. **Cassis** blackcurrants; blackcurrant liqueur. **Cassoulet** stew of white haricot beans, sausage and preserved duck. **Céleri** celery. **Céleri rave** celeriac. **Cèpe** cep mushroom. **Cervelle** brains. **Champignon** mushroom; – **de Paris** button mushroom. **Chateaubriand** thick fillet steak. **Chaud-froid** a sauce used to glaze cold dishes. **Chèvre** goat; goat's cheese. **Chevreuil** young roe deer. **Choucroute** sauerkraut, served garnie with cured ham and sausages. **Ciboulette** chive. **Citron** lemon. **Citron vert** lime. **Citronelle** lemongrass. **Civet** game stew. **Clafoutis** batter filled with fruit, usually cherries. **Cochon de lait** suckling pig. **Coco** large white bean. **Colin** hake. **Confit de canard** preserved duck. **Contre-filet** sirloin steak. **Coquelet** baby rooster. **Coquille** shell. **Coquilles St-Jacques** scallops. **Côte** chop; – **de boeuf** beef rib. **Crème brûlée** creamy custard dessert with caramel glaze. **Crème Chantilly** sweetened whipped cream. **Crème fraîche** thick, slightly soured cream. **Cresson** watercress. **Crevettes** prawns (UK), shrimp (US). **Croque-madame** sandwich of toasted cheese and ham topped with an egg; **croque-monsieur** sandwich of toasted cheese and

ham. **En croûte** in a pastry case. **Cru** raw. **Crudités** assorted raw vegetables. **Crustacé** shellfish.
 Daube meat braised in red wine. **Daurade** sea bream. **Désossé** boned. **Dinde** turkey. **Duxelles** chopped, sautéed mushrooms.
 Echalote shallot. **Eglefin** haddock. **Endive** chicory (UK), Belgian endive (US). **Entrecôte** beef rib steak. **Epices** spices. **Epinards** spinach. **Escabèche** sautéed and marinated fish, served cold. **Escargot** snail. **Espadon** swordfish. **Estouffade** meat that's been marinated, fried and braised.
 Faisan pheasant. **Farci** stuffed. **Faux-filet** sirloin steak. **Feuilleté** 'leaves' of (puff) pastry. **Filet mignon** tenderloin. **Fines de claire** crinkle-shelled oysters. **Flambé** flamed in alcohol. **Flétan** halibut. **Foie** liver; – **gras** fattened goose or duck liver. **Forestière** with mushrooms. **Au four** baked. **Fraise** strawberry. **Framboise** raspberry. **Fricassé** fried and simmered in stock, usually with creamy sauce. **Frisée** curly endive. **Frites** chips (UK); fries (US). **Fromage** cheese; – **blanc** smooth cream cheese. **Fruits de mer** shellfish. **Fumé** smoked.
 Galette round flat cake of flaky pastry, potato pancake or buckwheat savoury crêpe. **Garni** garnished. **Gelée** aspic. **Gésiers** gizzards. **Gibier** game. **Gigot d'agneau** leg of lamb. **Gingembre** ginger. **Girolle/chanterelle** small, trumpet-like mushroom. **Glace** ice-cream. **Glacé** frozen or iced. **Goujon** breaded, fried strip of fish; also a small catfish. **Gras** fat. **Gratin dauphinois** sliced potatoes baked with milk, cheese and garlic. **Gratiné** browned with breadcrumbs or cheese. **A la grècque** vegetables served cold in the cooking liquid with oil and lemon juice. **Cuisses de grenouille** frogs' legs. **Grillé** grilled. **Groseille** redcurrant. **Groseille à maquereau** gooseberry.
 Haché minced. **Hachis Parmentier** shepherd's pie. **Hareng** herring. **Haricot** bean; – **vert** green bean. **Homard** lobster. **Huître** oyster.
 Ile flottante whipped egg white floating in vanilla custard.
 Jambon ham; – **cru** cured raw ham. **Jarret** ham shin or knuckle. **Julienne** vegetables cut into matchsticks.
 Langoustine Dublin Bay prawns, scampi. **Lapin** rabbit. **Lamelle** very thin slice. **Langue** tongue. **Lard** bacon. **Lardon** small cube of

bacon. **Légume** vegetable. **Lièvre** hare. **Limande** lemon sole. **Lotte** monkfish.

Mâche lamb's lettuce. **Magret** duck breast. **Maison** of the house. **Maquereau** mackerel. **Marcassin** wild boar. **Mariné** marinated. **Marmite** small cooking pot. **Marquise** mousse-like cake. **Merguez** spicy lamb/beef sausage. **Merlan** whiting. **Merlu** hake. **Meunière** fish floured and sautéed in butter. **Miel** honey. **Mignon** small meat fillet. **Mirabelle** tiny yellow plum. **Moelle** bone marrow; **os à la** – marrow bone. **Morille** morel mushroom. **Moules** mussels; **– à la marinière** cooked with white wine and shallots. **Morue** dried, salted cod; **brandade de** – cod puréed with potato. **Mousseline hollandaise** sauce with whipped cream. **Myrtille** bilberry/blueberry.

Navarin lamb and vegetable stew. **Navet** turnip. **Noisette** hazelnut; small round portion of meat. **Noix** walnut. **Noix de coco** coconut. **Nouilles** noodles.

Oeuf egg; **– en cocotte** baked egg; **– en meurette** egg poached in red wine; **– à la neige** *see Ile flottante.* **Oie** goose. **Oignon** onion. **Onglet** cut of beef, similar to bavette. **Oseille** sorrel. **Oursin** sea urchin.

Palourde type of clam. **Pamplemousse** grapefruit. **Pané** breaded. **En papillote**

cooked in a packet. **Parfait** sweet or savoury mousse-like mixture. **Parmentier** with potato. **Paupiette** slice of meat or fish, stuffed and rolled. **Pavé** thick steak. **Perdrix** partridge. **Persil** parsley. **Petit salé** salt pork. **Pied** foot (trotter). **Pignon** pine kernel.

Pintade/pintadeau guinea fowl. **Pipérade Basque** dish of green peppers, onions, **Bayonne** ham and tomatoes, often served with scrambled egg. **Poivre** pepper. **Poivron** red or green (bell) pepper. **Pomme** apple. **Pomme de terre** potato. **Pommes lyonnaises** potatoes fried with onions. **Potage** soup. **Pot-au-feu** boiled beef with vegetables. **Potiron** pumpkin. **Poulet** chicken. **Poulpe** octopus. **Pressé** squeezed. **Prune** plum. **Pruneau** prune.

Quenelle light, poached fish (or poultry) dumpling. **Quetsche** damson. **Queue de boeuf** oxtail.

Ragoût meat stew. **Raie** skate. **Râpé** grated. **Rascasse** scorpion fish. **Réglisse** liquorice. **Rillettes** potted pork or tuna. **Ris de veau** veal sweetbreads. **Riz** rice. **Rognons** kidneys. **Rôti** roast. **Rouget** red mullet.

St Pierre John Dory. **Salé** salted. **Sandre** pike-perch. **Sanglier** wild boar. **Saucisse** sausage. **Saucisson sec** small dried sausage. **Saumon** salmon. **Seîche** squid. **Selle** (*d'agneau*) saddle (of lamb) **Suprême** fillets (of chicken) in a cream sauce. **Supion** small squid.

Tagine slow-cooked North African stew. **Tapenade Provençal** olive and caper paste. **Tartare** raw minced steak (also tuna or salmon). **Tarte aux pommes** apple tart. **Tarte Tatin** warm, caramelised apple tart cooked upside-down. **Timbale** dome-shaped mould, or food cooked in one. **Tisane** herbal tea. **Tournedos** small slices of beef fillet, sautéed or grilled. **Tourte** covered pie or tart, usually savoury. **Travers de porc** pork spare ribs. **Tripes** tripe. **Tripoux** dish of sheep's offal and sheep feet. **Truffes** truffles. **Truite** trout.

Vacherin cake of layered meringue, cream, fruit and ice cream; a soft, cow's milk cheese. **Veau** veal. **Velouté** stock-based white sauce; creamy soup. **Vichyssoise** cold leek and potato soup. **Volaille** poultry.

Cooking type ('La cuisson')

A point medium rare. **Bien cuit** well done. **Bleu** practically raw. **Cru** raw. **Rosé** pink (said of lamb, duck, liver, kidneys). **Saignant** rare.

Chez Georges.

shoulder of roebuck comes with celery, quince, chestnuts and prunes, along with a pretty Alsatian *faïence casserole*, generously filled with white beans stewed with garlic cloves, bay leaf and tomato, and topped with tender squid. The only complaint can be the pricey wine list with nothing less than €25.

Le Vieux Bistro
14 rue du Cloître-Notre-Dame, 4th (01.43.54.18.95). *M° Cité or St-Michel.* **Open** noon-2.15pm, 7.30-10.15pm daily. **Average** €30. **Lunch menu** €27. **Credit** MC, V. **Map** p408 J7.
Given its corny name and location opposite Notre-Dame, it is a great surprise to discover that the food here is often excellent, the dining room comfortable and well run, and prices, given the quality, reasonable. Choose a spot in the spacious front room, cosy back one or on the romantic terrace, and start with sliced pistachio-studded sausage and potatoes dressed in vinegar and oil or the sublime *pâté de tête*, chunks of head cheese in a dark amber-coloured beef aspic. Then sample the renowned *bourguignon*, a first-rate rib of beef for two, or even scallops sautéed in whisky. The house Bordeaux, a Château Layauga 1999, at €25, is superb and goes down a treat with cheese, or one of the homely desserts.

The Islands

Bistros & brasseries

Brasserie de l'Ile St-Louis
55 quai de Bourbon, 4th (01.43.54.02.59). M° Pont Marie. **Open** noon-midnight Mon, Tue, Fri-Sun; 6pm-midnight Thur. Closed Aug. **Average** €20. **Credit** MC, V. **Map** p408 K7.
Happily this old-fashioned brasserie soldiers on while exotic juice bars and fancy tea shops on the island come and go. The terrace has one of the best summer views in Paris, and is invariably packed – although the dining room exudes shabby chic. Stuffed game and nicotine-stained walls make for a convivial Parisian experience, as does the slightly gruff waiter. Nothing here is gastronomically exciting – a well dressed *frisée aux lardons*, a slab of fairly ordinary terrine, a greasy slice of foie de veau prepared *à l'anglaise* with a rasher of bacon, a more successful pan of warming tripes – and a dash more sophistication in the kitchen would transform this delightful place into something more exceptional.

Mon Vieil Ami
69 rue St-Louis-en-l'Ile, 4th (01.40.46.01.35). *M° Pont Marie.* **Open** 12.30am-2.30pm, 7.30-10.30pm daily. Closed 2wks Jan, 2wks Aug. **Average** €20. **Prix fixe** €38. **Lunch menu** €23.50. **Credit** MC, V. **Map** p408 K7.
You don't have to work too hard on the Ile St-Louis to pull a crowd, as the many candlelit places serving indifferent food prove, so it's a thrill that Antoine Westermann should be here. Chef of the acclaimed Buerehiesel in Strasbourg, Antoine is an investor at this bistro, and his touch is everywhere. His former second, chef Antony Clemot, deserves equal praise. The menu offers a short but tempting assortment. Outstanding starters include *pâté en croûte* – buttery pastry enclosing delicious terrine with a cap of beef aspic and a lobe of foie gras – and mixed root vegetables in bouillon with foie gras. A slow-braised

The Louvre, Palais-Royal & Les Halles

Bistros & brasseries

L'Ardoise
28 rue du Mont-Thabor, 1st (01.42.96.28.18). *M° Concorde or Tuileries.* **Open** noon-2.30pm, 6.30-11pm Tue-Sun. Closed Aug. **Average** €20. **Prix fixe** €30. **Credit** MC, V. **Map** p403 G5.
One of the flagship modern bistros in the capital, L'Ardoise has begun to open on Sundays. The rather anonymous room gets packed with gourmets eager to explore the €30 blackboard menu featuring Pierre Jay's reliably delicious cooking, while chewing on some sourdough bread accompanied by a herby dip. A wise choice might be six oysters with warm chipolatas and a pungent shallot dressing, an unusual combination from Bordeaux which works with unexpected force. A 'gamey' hare pie with an escalope of foie gras nestling in its centre or firm, shelled langoustines placed around a delicate mousseline of celery and coated in a luscious chervil sauce, are just as attractive. A lightly chilled, raspberry-scented Chinon provides a perfect complement, chosen from a wine list sensibly arranged by price.

Chez Georges
1 rue du Mail, 2nd (01.42.60.07.11). M° Bourse. **Open** noon-2pm, 7-9.30pm Mon-Sat. Closed Aug. **Average** €25. **Credit** AmEx, MC, V. **Map** p404 J4.
The solid food and conviviality at Chez Georges are confirmation that the Parisian bistro of old is alive and well. Every table in this classic, long, mirrored room is taken – every night. And people also come

Cosmopolitan trends at the **Café Moderne**. *See p195*.

for the atmosphere, as motherly waitresses glide about dishing out plates and advice. The starters are paragons of simplicity – a bowl of warm Puy lentils in a vinaigrette with grated onion; frisée tossed with warm bacon chunks and topped with a poached egg. Main courses are cooked with care; juicy, rose-coloured steak *de canard* with meaty ceps, textbook sole meunière. A small choice of wines on the stencilled menu are around €24, but if you've money to spend, peruse the longer, printed list.

Au Pied de Cochon

6 rue Coquillière, 1st (01.40.13.77.00/www. pieddecochon.com). M° Les Halles. **Open** 24 hours daily. **Average** €20. **Credit** AmEx, DC, MC, V. **Map** p404 J5.
Open round the clock, this brasserie is a piggy tourist favourite. *See p214* **One snack mind**.

French

Le Poquelin

17 rue Molière, 1st (01.42.96.22.19). M° Palais Royal Musée du Louvre. **Open** 7-10pm Mon, Sat; noon-2pm, 7-10pm Tue-Fri. Closed 3wks Aug. **Average** €25. **Prix fixe** *Dinner* €33. **Lunch menu** €25. **Credit** AmEx, DC, MC, V. **Map** p404 H5.
Next to the Comédie Française and bearing Molière's real name, this elegant little spot takes its classical inheritance seriously. The gilded portrait of the man himself, elaborately wigged, sets the tone but he is quickly forgotten amid the elegant stripes, grand mirrors and theatrical touches. Maggy and Michel Guillaumin, the hands-on co-owners, assure the evening runs smoothly – from the first bite of unctuous pork belly to the last lick of *crème anglaise*.

Most diners are sedate, monied and looking for a classic night out. The three-course *prix fixe* has plenty of choice, mixing refined standards (thin slices of rare duck breast paired with a chunk of rich duck confit) and more daring flavours: a pan-fried slice of dab (a cousin of sole) is enlivened with basil tapenade and set on a bed of ginger leeks and Puy lentils. St-Pourçain house wines (from the Massif Central, like the Guillaumins) are good value at €16 a bottle.

La Tour de Montlhéry (Chez Denise)

5 rue des Prouvaires, 1st (01.42.36.21.82). M° Les Halles/RER Châtelet Les Halles. **Open** noon-4pm daily; 7.30pm-6.30am Mon-Fri. Closed 14 July-15 Aug. **Average** €20. **Credit** MC, V. **Map** p404 J5.
At the strike of midnight, the place is packed, jovial and hungry. The red-checked dining room is intimate – you end up tasting a portion of your neighbour's roasted lamb or chatting by the barrels of wine stacked atop the bar. Savoury traditional dishes, washed down by litres of the house Brouilly, are the order of the day. Les Halles was the city's wholesale meat market and game, beef and offal still rule here. Diners devour towering rib steaks served with marrow (€52) and a heaping platter of fries, homemade and among the best in Paris. Adventurous souls can try *tripes au calvados*, grilled *andouillettes* or lamb's brain, or go for an interesting stewed venison, served with succulent celery root and homemade jam. There are a few fish dishes, too.

Willi's Wine Bar

13 rue des Petits-Champs, 1st (01.42.61.05.09/ www.williswinebar.com). M° Pyramides. **Open** noon-2.30pm, 7pm-10.30pm Mon-Sat. Closed 2wks Aug. **Average** €15. **Prix fixe** *Lunch* €25. *Dinner* €32. **Credit** MC, V. **Map** p404 H5.

If you haven't discovered Willi's, you're missing something. A narrow passage beside the long bar gives way to a small and elegant beamed room accented with crisp white linen. From certain tables you can watch through the hatch the daring-do of François Yon's tiny, perfect kitchen and whet your appetite on stray aromas. Courses are ambitious, but never gratuitously so; there's no such thing as a mistake. Starters – succulent quail breasts sizzled in a sophisticated version of barbecue sauce, and a creamy *cassolette* of cockles, Puy lentils and shredded leek – set the tone, but the mains, classic and innovative, are more than you'd hope for. Yon is a star meat chef who matches precision cooking and fine sauces with superb presentation. A thick fillet steak, crowned with a tiny shallot *tatin*, is tender and just-right rare; a flaky chunk of roast cod, set in a dark, earthy sauce of chanterelles and artichokes, robust. Willi's wine list is appropriately long (Côtes du Rhône loom large) and the bilingual staff offer informed, enthusiastic advice.

Haute cuisine

L'Espadon

Hôtel Ritz, 15 pl Vendôme, 1st (01.43.16.30.80/ www.ritzparis.com). M° Madeleine or Concorde. **Open** noon-2.30pm, 7.30-10.30pm daily. **Average** €70. **Prix fixe** *Dinner* €160. **Lunch menu** €68. **Credit** AmEx, DC, MC, V. **Map** p403 G4.

It's with high expectations that you tread the plush carpet towards the dining room of the Ritz. The gilded mirrors, silk and ceiling motif are, well, Ritzy, and you sink happily into velvet banquette and broad armchair, giving in to the temptation to have an aperitif. The €68 menu is reasonable, as it includes cheese and coffee. The meal begins in earnest with oysters marinated with orange, pineapple and fennel, a smooth combination of poached chicken and foie gras garnished with the *sot l'y laisse* (parson's nose) and silky green asparagus purée with spiced langoustines. Domes are whisked off in unison to reveal the mains, essentially bistro classics refined: meltingly tender duck breast with carved turnip and caramelised spring onions, sole in cockle-cream sauce with finecut broad beans, green beans and peas, and a thick slice of flaky cod with chunks of lobster, *grenaille* potatoes and a meaty jus. Choose either pricy wines by the glass, or more wisely one of the cheaper bottles at €40. A hefty cheese trolley then arrives, the waiter egging you on to try various *chèvres*, a delicious roquefort and nutty aged comté.

Le Grand Véfour

17 rue de Beaujolais, 1st (01.42.96.56.27/www.relais chateaux.com). M° Pyramides. **Open** 12.30-1.30pm Mon-Fri; 8-9.30pm Mon-Thur. Closed Aug, 2wks Dec. **Average** €110. **Prix fixe** *Dinner* €250. **Lunch menu** €75. **Credit** AmEx, DC, MC, V. **Map** p403 H5.

Here tables are randomly named after the famous people who once ate at this former political hotbed, overlooking the Palais-Royal. The decor, too, is a glamorous historical gem, even if the size of the room means that tables are slightly too close for absolute comfort. The lunch menu allows chef Guy Martin to show off his skills without the use of luxury ingredients. The starter of Jerusalem artichokes is stunning: creamy pallets of vegetable topped with fresh crab, an unctuous purée studded with crispy wafers, accompanied by seafood-and-artichoke bisque. A main course of *tête de veau* is prepared with a *sauce verte* and tarragon salad, reaching a level of sophistication which leaves other meaty mains standing. As Taittinger owns the place, champagne would seem apt, though you will be gently guided towards quality half-bottles of Pouilly Fuissé and a vintage Margaux. The staff embellish the fine experience. Perhaps Victor Hugo really did sit at your table.

Le Meurice

Hôtel Meurice, 228 rue de Rivoli, 1st (01.44.58.10.10). M° Tuileries. **Open** noon-2pm Mon-Fri; 7-10pm Mon-Sat. **Average** €70. **Prix fixe** *Dinner* €170. **Lunch menu** €68. **Credit** AmEx, DC, MC, V. **Map** p403 G5.

Soon after assuming these kitchens, chef Yannick Alléno, from Les Muses at the Hotel Scribe, has hit his stride and is doing some really stunning if understated contemporary French luxury cooking. There are few chefs who exercise such restraint when allowed really superb produce to star at table. Alléno has a magician's light touch, subtly teasing the flavour out of every leaf, *frond*, fin or filet that passes through his domain. It is a huge treat, for example, to begin with slowly roasted ormer gathered off the Channel Islands and slow roasted for 72 hours before being posed on a bed of white beans in a deeply reduced veal jus in the shell; this was one of Alléno's signature dishes at Les Muses, and it is good to see that it has made the journey here. Bresse chicken stuffed with foie gras and served with truffled *sardalaise* potatoes, cooked in the fat of the fowl, is equally superb. The complicity of the courtly waiters and sommeliers makes for a memorable meal.

International

Kong

1 rue du Pont-Neuf, 1st (01.40.39.09.00/www. kong.fr). M° Pont Neuf. **Open** 10.30am-2am daily. **Average** €20-€25. **Credit** AmEx, MC, V. **Map** p408 J6.

The pastel banquettes, clear plastic chairs and mesmerising video screens of Kong, on the glassed-in top floor of the Kenzo building, seem designed to soothe frayed nerves; so, too, the menu. The à la carte selection – conceived by Fumiko Kono, private chef at chic Paris dinner parties and a protégée of Alain Passard – takes a cautious approach to reinventing French classics. The beef 'tataki' with tea vinaigrette and the raw tuna rolls with avocado and lemon vinaigrette come with more lettuce than anything else, though the paper-thin slices of beef have an intriguing texture and taste. A small bowl of

Jerusalem artichoke soup spiked with black truffle proves earthy and satisfying, while sea bass with oyster mushroom risotto is competent, nothing more. Desserts by star pâtissier Pierre Hermé again take few risks for a place with so much style.

Takara
14 rue Molière, 1st (01.42.96.08.38). Mᵒ Palais Royal Musée du Louvre. **Open** 12.30-2.15pm Tue-Fri; 7-10.15pm Tue-Sun. Closed 3wks Aug; 2wks Dec. **Average** €20. **Prix fixe** €48-€60. **Lunch menu** €21-€25. **Credit** MC, V. **Map** p404 H5.
Some of the best Japanese food in Paris. Start the meal with four plump raw oysters, served out of the shell and in a light vinegar sauce topped with shredded green onions and a pinch of peppery, grated radish. Follow it with the monkfish liver sushi, an unusual and delightful *mélange* of cubed, creamy monkfish liver and rice wrapped in crispy nori. Move on to the fresh turbot sashimi: roll up each translucent sliver with a sprig of chives, a sprinkle of chopped green onion and a dab of grated radish. Dip it into the vinaigrette and chew slowly. The *maguro* tuna with blanched leeks in miso paste provides just the right kick. Then try the astonishing *agedashi* tofu: deep-fried cubes of the silkiest tofu coated in a light, subtly elastic batter, softened by a warm mirin-based broth. Ingenious. Takara also specialises in *sukiyaki* and *shabu shabu* – a kind of self-serve Japanese hotpot.

Opéra & Grands Boulevards

French

Café Moderne
40 rue Notre Dames des Victoires, 2nd (01.53.40.84.10). Mᵒ Bourse. **Open** noon-4.30pm, 7.30-10.30pm Mon-Thur; noon-4.30pm, 7.30-11pm Fri; 7.30-11pm Sat. **Prix fixe** €26, €30. **Credit** AmEx, DC, MC, V. **Map** p404 J4.
Just behind the old stock exchange, this sleek new restaurant is hip and cosy. The long, narrow butter-coloured dining room has stripped wood floors and a view on a pretty interior courtyard, creating an illusion of space. From a trendy and cosmopolitan menu, you can start with the delicious millefeuille of grilled vegetables and aubergine caviar or maybe the soup of the day, perhaps a ruddy mushroom *velouté* which comes with a goat-cheese filled samosa. Then try the chicken breast sautéed with lemongrass and served with mash, steak with tarragon butter, or lamb stuffed with *pecorino*, tapenade and tomatoes in a thyme-scented jus. Desserts are wonderful, such as a macaroon made with anise and figs and garnished with sautéed cherries.

J'Go
4 rue Drouot, 9th (01.40.22.09.09). Mᵒ Richelieu Drouot or Le Peletier. **Open** noon-2.30pm, 7.30pm-midnight Mon-Sat. **Average** €20. **Prix fixe** €28. **Lunch menu** €19. **Credit** AmEx, MC, V. **Map** p404 H3.

Paris offshoot of a successful Toulouse restaurant only specialising in farmer's lamb from Quercy. *See p214* **One snack mind**.

Aux Lyonnais
32 rue St-Marc, 2nd (01.42.96.65.04). Mᵒ Bourse or Richelieu Drouot. **Open** noon-2pm, 7.30-11pm Tue-Fri; 7.30-11pm Sat. Closed 1wk Aug, 1wk Dec. **Average** €25. **Prix fixe** €38. **Credit** AmEx, MC, V. **Map** p404 H4.
Still with its Majorelle interior and gorgeous Belle Epoque tiles, this place taken over by Alain Ducasse and Thierry de la Brosse of L'Ami Louis now has an antique zinc bar in the back dining room and rather more comfortable dark wood furniture. The menu of intelligently modernised Lyonnais, Bressane and Beaujolais classics is equally comforting. After pleasant glasses of Bugey sparkling wine, served with cheese and sausage nibbles, first courses of charcuterie from Sibilla (the best in Lyon), and luscious suckling pig meat confit with foie gras are excellent. Steak served with sautéed shallots and a side of cheesy, garlicky mash is similarly superb. A sublime *st-marcellin* and a Cointreau soufflé will have you coming back as soon as possible.

Le Mimosa
44 rue d'Argout, 2nd (01.40.28.15.75). Mᵒ Sentier. **Open** noon-4pm Mon-Fri. **Prix fixe** €12, €14. **Credit** MC, V. **Map** p404 J5.
Near Les Halles, the Mimosa has two- and three-course menus that change daily, proof of the durability of local lunch culture. *See p197* **No such thing as a cheap lunch?**

Champs-Elysées & western Paris

Bistros & brasseries

Le Bistrot d'à Côté Flaubert
10 rue Gustave-Flaubert, 17th (01.42.67.05.81/ www.michelrostang.com). Mᵒ Courcelles. **Open** 12.30-2.30pm, 7.30-10.45pm daily. **Average** €25. **Lunch menu** €19. **Credit** AmEx, MC, V. **Map** p402 D2.
Star chef Michel Rostang took over this old *épicerie*, kept the pretty period interior and began serving up what he felt genuine bistro food should be. Starters, though, have a degree of sophistication that reflect haute-cuisine roots. They include a wonderfully complex *pressé* of asparagus, sundried tomatoes and coppa ham accompanied by a raw artichoke and parmesan salad, and marinated *lisette* (small mackerel) with mushrooms, carrots and mesclun. Main courses are simpler but well prepared, with the emphasis on fine-quality meat (there's always a beef offering of the day), and a choice of accompaniments. Lamb from the Pyrenees comes in a crumble crust with garlic shortbread biscuit and a bowl of smooth purée and *dos de lieu* (pollack) with spicebread crust and jus, served with niçois vegetables. Just what a bistro should be, only better.

Restaurant L'Entredgeu

83 rue Laugier, 17th (01.40.54.97.24). M° Porte de Champerret. **Open** noon-2pm, 7-10.30pm Tue-Sat. Closed Aug, 1wk Dec. **Prix fixe** €28. **Lunch menu** €20. **Credit** MC, V. **Map** p402 C2.

This snug bistro has been packed since it opened thanks to excellent food at reasonable prices. Young chef Philippe Tredgeu mastered this sure-fire formula while heading the kitchen at Chez Casimir. You almost can't complain about the squeeze-'em-in seating, slow service or thick clouds of cigarette smoke – and let's hope for a jazzier wine list in the future. The blackboard menu changes daily – scallops cooked in their shells with salted butter and crumbled cauliflower, and a *croustillant* of pig's trotter with celeriac *rémoulade* are fine starters, followed by delicious main courses of chewy, flavourful roast pork with braised chicory and lamb stuffed with foie gras. Try to book ahead and be on time, as late arrivals get sent to the cramped back dining room.

Chez Rose

23 rue Guillaume-Tell, 17th (01.42.67.12.67). M° Porte de Champerret or Pereire. **Open** noon-2pm, 7.30-10pm Mon-Fri. Closed 3wks Aug, 2wks Dec. **Average** €20. **Prix fixe** *Dinner* €19.50, €23.10. **Lunch menu** €14.80. **Credit** MC, V. **Map** p402 C2.

The handsome marble interior of this popular bistro once housed a butcher's shop, which is why bits of old hardware are a feature. Now it's an insider's address for locals, which means it's full noon and night. Settle at a table here, you'll soon see why: very good food for very reasonable prices. Chose from the daily specials or dig into the carte for dishes such as lentil salad with foie gras or poached egg in sorrel sauce, and then follow with cod steak or a superb *onglet de veau* with *pommes dauphinoises* and green beans. Desserts change regularly, including the superb poached figs in salted-caramel sauce or an admirable crumble. The wine list is brief, but includes a fine Côtes de Bourg la Tuillière at €21.

Savy

23 rue Bayard, 8th (01.47.23.46.98). M° Franklin D. Roosevelt. **Open** noon-2.30pm, 7.30-11pm Mon-Fri. Closed Aug. **Average** €22. **Lunch menu** €19.50-€23.50. **Prix fixe** €26.50. **Credit** AmEx, MC, V. **Map** p403 E4.

It is comforting that his 1923 art deco bistro with its intimate rows of mirrored booths continues to produce simple regional food based on the fine products of the Aveyron. Starters include a generous plate of Cantal *charcuterie*, a creamy *oeuf en cocotte* with roquefort and the unusual *farçou aveyronnais*, fried herb and chard patties. Main courses feature some light and delicate *tripoux*, highly seasoned tripe-and-trotter parcels, a generous slice of *foie de veau*, and a meaty if rather solid Auvergne sausage served with a wholesome purée of split peas. A fine hunk of st-nectaire cheese and a timeless chocolate mousse finish a satisfactory meal, accompanied by well priced red Morgon. Service is old school, but challenged by any large parties.

Le Bistrot des Vignes

1 rue Jean-Bologne, 16th (01.45.27.76.64). M° Passy or La Muette. **Open** noon-2.30pm; 7-10.30pm daily. **Prix fixe** €19-€22, €25-€28. **Credit** AmEx, DC, MC, V. **Map** p406 A6.

Tucked away on a quiet corner in the 16th, this bistro pulls in a crowd of loyal locals. Some even have their own table constantly set aside, just in case they drop by. A relaxed, friendly vibe prevails with butter-yellow walls garnished with black and white photos of vineyards. Food follows the seasons, with starters from salads (spinach leaf and fresh parmesan, red peppers marinated in pesto), to feathery red mullet 'doughnuts' with a sweet chilli dipping sauce, to marinated salmon and broccoli tart. Mains of duck breast coated in honey, served sliced on triangles of toasted gingerbread, and John Dory fillets baked with spicy aubergine and peppers with a watercress sauce, show a chef adept at turning out likeable, nicely balanced fare.

French

L'Astrance

4 rue Beethoven, 16th (01.40.50.84.40). M° Passy. **Open** 12.30-1.30pm, 8-9.15pm Mon-Fri. Closed 1wk Feb, 3wks Aug, 1wk Dec. **Average** *Lunch* €50. **Prix fixe** *Dinner* €150. **Lunch menu** €45, €100. **Credit** AmEx, DC, MC, V. **Map** p406 B6.

L'Astrance is the quintessential modern French restaurant, thanks to the talent and gastronomic imagination of chef Pascal Barbot. Sample his magnificent millefeuille made with slices of button mushroom sprinkled with *verjus* (the juice of unripe grapes) and caramelised foie gras – a fine balance of flavours and textures. Next up, a fascinating dish of langoustines in a featherweight batter of egg and beer served with a colourful salad of mini cos, begonia and garlic flowers, pansy petals and a garnish of pleasantly astringent begonia juice surrounded by peppery nasturtium oil: sweet, sour and bitter. A pepper sorbet proceeds a dessert of *gariguette* strawberries on green tea mousse between two transparent rice *galettes*. The wine list and the service are superb. Reserve a month ahead.

Ballon & Coquillages

71 bd Gouvion-St-Cyr, 17th (01.45.74.17.98). M° Porte Maillot. **Open** noon-3pm, 7pm-midnight daily. Closed Aug. **Average** €25. **Credit** AmEx, MC, V. **Map** p402 B2.

Almost no larger than an oyster itself, this charming little bar is a great addition to the neighbourhood around the Porte Maillot and Palais des Congrès, its round mosaic-topped counter a haven of conviviality in corporate precincts. Take one of the red leather stools and design your own feast. The oysters (Gillardeau, *spéciales de Normandie*, Utah Beach, and *plates de Bretagne*) are sold by threes, and your first order should comprise a minimum of nine. Otherwise, garnish your tray with *bigorneaux* (sea snails), red prawns, grey shrimp, langoustines, clams, cockles

No such thing as a cheap lunch?

Euro inflation and the proliferation of sandwich shops have made the bargain lunch harder to come by around Paris. Tourist areas such as St-Michel, rue Mouffetard and Les Halles offer plenty of bargain set menus, but it's risky territory even for Parisians. A better idea is to trail the office workers, who are careful to make the most of their *tickets restaurant* (luncheon vouchers), worth about €7 each. This eliminates most well-known bistros, whose lunchtime *prix fixes* now average about €15 for two courses. Though sandwiches, soups and pastas to go are becoming popular options, traditionalists still insist on a sit-down meal.

White-collar workers and journalists in the offices near Bourse have their blow-out lunches at nearby brasseries, but the savviest among them frequent the Japanese noodle shops along rue Ste-Anne towards the Opéra, where a plate of gyoza and a giant bowl brimming with noodles, vegetables and meat goes for less than €10. Heading in the other direction, the streets off pedestrianised rue Montorgueil offer better-value restaurants than nearby Les Halles — one beloved address is **Le Mimosa** (*see p195*), which doesn't look like much but serves lovingly made food at democratic prices.

In the Latin Quarter, avoid St-Michel and head instead to Jussieu, where students munch on *sandwichs grecs* and pizza, while cost-conscious academics feast on bargain lunches at nearby restaurants. The **Foyer Vietnamien** (80 rue Monge, 5th, 01.45.35.32.54) attracts plenty of non-Vietnamese with its freshly made food and €8.40 lunch menu. St-Germain-des-Prés is hardly awash with bargain food, but head along rue Montparnasse for good crêperies. In the Marais, you can't do better than the lively felafel joints along rue des Rosiers, particularly **L'As du Fallafel** (34 rue des Rosiers, 4th, 01.48.87.63.60).

Around train stations, flee the tacky brasseries serving moules-frites and explore the back streets. Near Gare de Lyon, **L'Encrier** (*see p206*) has become a local favourite, while the slightly pricier **Chez Casimir** (6 rue de Belzunce, 10th, 01.48.78.28.80), the annex of Chez Michel two doors down, is a real find near Gare du Nord. Between Gare du Nord and Gare de l'Est are some authentic south Indian and Sri Lankan restaurants, including the **New Pondichery** (189 rue du Fbg-St-Denis, 10th, 01.40.34.30.70). Perhaps no one loves hearty French grub better than a civil servant, and the roads around ministries hide some old-fashioned bargains, such as the two cheapies in rue Nélaton, facing the Interior Ministry near the Eiffel Tower.

Eat, Drink, Shop

and mussels, or opt for one of their suggested platters, including a tempting four-oyster sampler. From a curious and rather dear wine list with almost twice as many reds as whites, a good pick is the Château Theullet Bergerac, a dry white suited to shellfish.

Le Cristal Room
11 pl des Etats-Unis, 16th (01.40.22.11.10). M° Iéna. **Open** 8.30-10.30am, noon-2.30pm, 8-10.30pm Mon-Sat. **Average** €50. **Credit** AmEx, DC, MC, V. **Map** p402 C4.
This sumptuous townhouse has become the glittering new HQ, boutique and showroom of Baccarat, the venerable French crystal company. There's also a restaurant, Le Cristal Room, with decor by Philippe Starck and a light luxury snack menu by chef Thierry Burlot – a roaring hit. The salon shows Starck's pastiche of grandeur, exposing the bricks to create a brilliant contrast to the ox-blood red marble mouldings and huge Baccarat chandeliers. The expensive menu was conceived to please puckish rich types, but you can still eat well here. Start with chestnut soup with white truffles or scallops with Petrossian caviar – then go with risotto with white truffles, spaghetti with cherry tomatoes, hare with quince or lobster spit-roasted with vanilla beans.

Flora
36 av George-V, 8th (01.40.70.10.49). M° George V. **Open** noon-2.30pm Mon-Fri; 7-11pm Mon-Sat. Closed 3wks Aug. **Average** €25. **Prix fixe** €34. **Lunch menu** €26. **Credit** AmEx, MC, V. **Map** p402 D4.
Engaging chef Flora Mikula, founder of Les Olivades and former second to Alain Passard at L'Arpège, runs this stylish restaurant. She has broadened her horizons to include an international version of Provence that visits Morocco, Turkey, India and Vietnam. The hospitality is southern too, as a meal begins with delicious amuse-bouches and generously concludes with *mignardises*, including chocolate caramels, Turkish delight and miniature *cannelés*. Starters such as a *croustillant de crabe* in tomato soup and lacquered prawns and aubergine are excellent, as is a main of lobster with broad beans and tiny girolles in a jus of its own coral. Desserts include a macaroon in rose syrup with lime sorbet, and the wine list is fair.

Pomze
109 bd Haussmann, 8th (01.42.65.65.83). M° Miromesnil. **Open** 8am-11pm Mon-Sat. **Average** €32. **Credit** AmEx, DC, MC, V. **Map** p403 E3.
Apple-themed restaurant with fine ciders and Calvados-scented food. *See p214* **One snack mind**.

La Soupière
154 av de Wagram, 17th (01.42.27.00.73). M° Wagram. **Open** 12.30-2pm, 8-10.30pm Mon-Fri; 8-10.30pm Sat. **Average** €25. **Prix fixe** €28, €55. **Credit** MC, V. **Map** p402 D2.
This quiet and well-mannered little spot specialises in mushrooms all year round. Autumn is, of course, the best season here, as ceps, girolles, morels and other fleshy fodder of the forest floor appear in local markets and on menus. They come in a variety of guises, including a sublime salad of finely sliced raw ceps sprinkled with olive oil and sea salt as a starter, along with a lusciously earthy mushroom soup, followed by main courses such as brill with a sauté of mixed mushrooms or a splendid sautée of girolles in wine sauce with cinammon. The wine list is a bit dull and service leisurely, especially at noon, but the cooking is impeccable.

La Table du Lancaster
Hôtel Lancaster, 7 rue de Berri, 8th (01.40.76. 40.18). M° George V. **Open** 12.30-2.30pm, 7-10pm Mon-Fri; 7-10pm Sat, Sun. **Average** €40-€50. **Credit** AmEx, DC, MC, V. **Map** p402 D4.
The intimate dining room of the Hôtel Lancaster is now open to anyone willing to dig up the €70-plus required for a meal here. Chef Michel Troisgros has created a fascinating, if not always perfect, menu divided into six subheads: tomatoes; citrus; condiments and spices; wine and vinegar; vegetables and herbs; and dairy produce. Each offer several starters and main courses. With good advice from the waiters, you'll eat very well indeed, as Troisgros is set on intelligent global inspiration and also knows what the fashionable folk here will want. Dishes such as a scallop tartare with sea urchin roe make for a successful starter. Mains are similarly racy and satisfying, including a brilliant dish of perfect cooked cod, smeared with Japanese mustard and set down on a bed of Japan's best rice before being doused with cod bouillon. Desserts are great fun, too. The wine list is front-loaded to Bordeaux, though there are lovely New World ones available.

The best Late eats

Alcazar
Eat and be seen at Terence Conran's Left Bank gastrodome. *See p213.*

Bofinger
Post-opera treats till 1am. *See p204.*

Ile de Gorée
African delights past midnight. *See p209.*

Juan et Juanita
Get fresh and flirty amid up-for-it diners. *See p206.*

Au Pied de Cochon
Twenty-four-hour piggery at Les Halles. *See p192.*

La Tour de Montlhéry (Chez Denise)
Jovially packed with midnight carnivores. *See p192.*

Haute cuisine

Alain Ducasse au Plaza Athénée

*Hôtel Plaza Athénée, 25 av Montaigne, 8th
(01.53.67.65.00/www.alain-ducasse.com). M° Alma
Marceau.* **Open** 5.45-10.15pm Mon-Wed; 12.45-
2.15pm, 5.45-10.15pm Thur, Fri. Closed mid July-
mid Aug, 2wks Dec. **Average** €300. **Credit**
AmEx, DC, MC, V. **Map** p402 D5.

Dinner at Alain Ducasse's lingers long in the mind:
the spectacular dishes, the engaging service. Chef
Jean-François Piège's art is almost undetectable,
enhancing the natural flavours of the best French
seasonal produce. *Amuse-bouches* of perfectly poached
langoustines are topped with caviar, spider crab is
served in its orange shell beneath a bubbly foam of
coral. First courses include French asparagus from
Pertuis in Provence, poached and served under fine
leaves of melted comté cheese with an exquisite sauce
of black truffles and *vin jaune* from the Jura; and
plump langoustines on a bed of first-of-season ceps
– both sautéed and raw – red onion and herbs.
Sautéed Breton lobster with asparagus tips and
morels in a light sauce of its own cooking juices is
exquisite. After superb cheeses from Bernard
Anthony, the Alsatian *fromager*, and Marie-Anne
Cantin, desserts conclude with strawberries from
Plougastel, cut into matchsticks and arranged on a
rectangle of puff pastry, topped with a caramelised
stalk of poached rhubarb. Brilliant.

Les Ambassadeurs

*Hôtel de Crillon, 10 pl de la Concorde, 8th
(01.44.71.16.17/www.crillon.com). M° Concorde.*
Open 12.30-2pm, 7.30-10pm daily. **Prix fixe** €250.
Lunch menu *Mon-Fri* €70. **Credit** AmEx, DC,
MC, V. **Map** p403 F5.

If you hanker for gilt and crystal, polished marble
and a velvet stool on which to perch your handbag,
then this is your place. Chef Dominique Bouchet has
a sure touch with produce and a flair for presentation: portly green-and-white asparagus crowned
with a perfectly poached, yolk-oozing egg, a sliver
of foie gras and truffle juice, or gem-coloured spring
vegetables drizzled with olive oil then sprinkled with
slices of cured ham and fresh coriander. The mains,
too, extol simple excellence: langoustine ravioli floating in a broth of shellfish and verbena, and delicately
sliced salmon arranged on tomato petals, dressed
with thyme flowers, olive oil, lemon and balsamic
vinegar. Cheese zealots will be sated by two heaving trolleys and chocophiles will swoon at the six-
chocolate *grand cru* desserts on one plate. You'll pay
(though the lunch menu is quite a bargain), but
flanks of doting waiters don't come cheap.

Lucas Carton

*9 pl de la Madeleine, 8th (01.42.65.22.90/www.
lucascarton.com). M° Madeleine.* **Open** 8-10.30pm
Mon, Sat; noon-2.30pm, 8-10.30pm Tue-Fri. Closed
3wks Aug, 1wk Dec. **Average** €60-€80. **Prix fixe**
€264; *with wine* €434. **Lunch menu** €76. **Credit**
AmEx, DC, MC, V. **Map** p403 F4.

Cosseted in a Merlot-coloured banquette, iris-
embossed silver cutlery at hand, you could opt for
the *déjeuner affaires*, good value next to à la carte
offerings of €95 lobster and a €65 glass of wine –
and still not feel that you're second-besting it.
Tender green asparagus comes surrounded by an
emerald asparagus 'cappuccino' with almond milk
and tiny chips of spicy pork sausage; plump little
just-cooked scallops studded with pink pickled ginger and bright green courgette float in a heady broth
of coconut milk, lemongrass and coriander. Alain
Senderens marries wine with food; each dish has a
suggested glass: Pouilly Fuissé Le Clos 1999 with
the asparagus, Condrieu Terrasses 2000 with the
scallops. The stand-out main is a featherweight tem-
pura of sole and peppery celery leaves, lightly
flavoured with Madras curry, and ringed with a
zingy cucumber emulsion. This marvellous layering
of flavours is ably washed down with Condrieu
Grandes Chaillées 2000 at €25 a glass.

Pierre Gagnaire

*6 rue Balzac, 8th (01.58.36.12.50/www.pierre-
gagnaire.com). M° George V.* **Open** noon-1.30pm,
7.30-9.30pm Mon-Fri; 7.30-9.30pm Sun. Closed 1wk
in Feb, 2wks July, 1wk Oct/Nov. **Average** €70.
Prix fixe €225. **Lunch menu** €90. **Credit** AmEx,
DC, MC, V. **Map** p402 D3.

Pierre Gagnaire is a creative genius, his dishes made
of several elements, served separately, telling the
story of one ingredient. *La langoustine* features a
pan-fried version with a lime tuile, a mousseline with
lemongrass, a tartare with apple and ginger, and
grilled, with thyme nougatine. Others illustrate surprising complementarities (veal and frogs, for example). The *prix fixe* offers an ideal introduction, with
nine separate courses, including a stunning turnip
soup with swede and black truffle, cuttlefish with
cinnamon and creamy polenta, a *pressé* of leeks with
crab and tuna loin, and pigeon with Malabar pepper
and foie gras. A few fine English ingredients –
Maldon salt and Stilton – make it on to the menu
(Gagnaire is consultant chef to Sketch). The grand
dessert is seven delights including fruit-based concoctions, chocolate creations, and a fab pistachio
cream with roasted hazelnuts. The split-level dining
room has something of an art deco, ocean-liner feel,
accentuated by choreographed staff in tailcoats.

Taillevent

*15 rue Lamennais, 8th (01.44.95.15.01/www.
taillevent.com). M° George V.* **Open** 12.30-2pm,
7.30-10pm Mon-Fri. Closed Aug. **Average** €60.
Prix fixe €130, €180. **Lunch menu** €70.
Credit AmEx, DC, MC, V. **Map** p402 D3.

The ascension of chef Alain Solivérès, formerly of
Les Elysées du Vernet, to the one of the best kitchens
in the world has been a success. He has a lusty style,
but always remains in control with his ability to concentrate flavour. His *amuse-bouche* of cauliflower
cream with a buttery, faintly poultry-nuanced jus is
brilliant. Tipping his toque at his own past – a native
of Montpellier, he reinvented the cooking of south-

This year's vintage

The Paris wine bar idiom is getting an edgy update, as drinkers warm to the idea of a glass or two of well-chosen wine served with light eating from creative, quality-conscious menus, and all in convivial settings.

What's most noticeable about the new vintage is that the standard-issue, folkloric *vieille France* decors of wine bars are being jettisoned in favour of streamlined new looks, often with a '50s or '60s retro slant. Foreign wines are getting a look in, and food served is healthier and more daring than in the past – high-protein Peruvian grain quinoa, for example, is in, while tripe sausages find fewer takers.

If any single event signalled a sea change in the genre, it was last year's renovation of **La Taverne Henri IV** (*pictured*; 13 pl du Pont-Neuf, 1st, 01.43.54.27.90), the doyen of Paris wine bars. Famous as a venue in the novels of Georges Simenon, this venerable spot has been stripped to the bones so its

fine 16th-century architectural pedigree is plainly visible, and the menu now includes a variety of imaginative *tartines*, or open-faced sandwiches.

Near Châtelet, **Les Dessous de la Robe** (4 rue Bertin-Poirée, 1st, 01.40.26.68.18) is the wine-bar annex of a popular *bistrot à vins*, and the menu and mood here make the point that wine bars are pre-eminently about having a good time – wine-critic types need not apply – and the chance to sip an unknown quaff or two.

The surest sign of the new bacchanalia in Paris, though, is the growing number of wine bars in the eastern 11th and 12th. **La Muse Vin** (101 rue de Charonne, 11th, 01.40.09.93.05), one of the most popular new wine bars, feels like a friendly, freewheeling party. Colourfully decorated with contemporary art and fluorescent colours, it's impressively professional when it comes to its wines, including really nice, offbeat and easy-drinking bottles from all over France. The young proprietors are justly proud of their food, too, and the cheese and cold meat plates, plus a couple of hot dishes, are excellent. In a similar vein, and even trendier, **Le Cercle Rouge** (7 rue St- Sabin, 11th, 01.40.21. 02.51) has a decor of exposed brick walls and contemporary art that recalls the NoLita quarter of Manhattan. It's a great place to meet before a show at the opera. Wines here are nicely selected and run to that realm of vintages often described as 'much improved' – Costières de Nîmes, Corbières, Minervois and the like. Aside from plates of excellent charcuterie and tartines, there are a number of hot main dishes, including a splendid *Parmentier de canard*.

Finally, **Le Zinc des Cavistes** (5 rue du Fbg-Montmartre, 9th, 01.47.70.88.64), by Métro Grands Boulevards, presages a self-service approach, where you select a bottle from open stock, and pay a corkage fee to drink it with a light meal in a souped-up high-design setting seated on stools at a *table d'hôte*.

ern France – he produces three plump scallops topped with a miniature dice of Lucca olives, chorizo and parmesan and garnished with tender leaves of dandelion and rocket: a superb starter. His mastery of the more traditional dishes is impressive, too, as seen in a creamy soup of *ratte* potatoes from Noirmoutier ladled over a dainty sauté of shelled crayfish. A seasonal suggestion is a long strip of tuna belly, immaculately cooked so that the firm texture of the fish plays off of its own almost buttery richness, served with an elegant tangle of Espelette peppers, lemon, capers and serrano ham.

International

Man Ray
34 rue Marbeuf, 8th (01.56.88.36.36/www.
manray.fr). M° Franklin D. Roosevelt. **Open** 7pm-midnight Tue-Sat. Closed Aug. **Average** €25. **Prix fixe** €27. **Credit** MC, V. **Map** p402 D4.
At Man Ray your conversation involves whispering: 'Don't look now, but at your four o'clock, Mick Jagger,' punctuated by lengthy gaping at the extravagant pan-Asian decor. The food is an afterthought, and comically bland, though you might have luck with the sashimi. Safe-bet fried spring rolls, labelled '*comme je les aime*', are greasy, and an insipid foie gras with chutney is like a butter and fig jam breakfast. Dry tuna steak is beached on spinach leaves drowned in tangy ginger sauce, turning blacker by the minute as you wait for your partner's course to arrive. Tiramisu comes in a sundae glass, with coffee jelly lurking beneath. Be warned. Better to taste the buzz from the mezzanine bar for the 'After Work' drink and free massage during the week.

Montmartre & Pigalle

Bistros & brasseries

Casa Olympe
48 rue St-Georges, 9th (01.42.85.26.01). M° St-Georges. **Open** noon-2pm, 8-11pm Mon-Fri. Closed 1wk May, 3wks Aug, 1wk Dec. **Prix fixe** €37. **Credit** AmEx, MC, V. **Map** p404 H3.
Once a star at her jet-setty Olympe restaurant in the 15th, chef Olympe Versini has made an admirable transition at her superb bistro off place St-Georges. The attractive mustard-coloured room with pretty chandeliers and sconces pulls a creative crowd, and well-paced, friendly service and a brief but very appealing wine list add to the experience. Entrées include a poached egg with spinach and salted butter on a chestnut-flour *galette*, and a casserole of autumn fruits and vegetables, including pears, celeriac, pumpkin, kale and cardoons, braised in an iron casserole in luscious veal stock. Main courses of guinea hen with wild mushroom ravioli, and pork fillet with home-made sauerkraut in a sublime sauce of vinegar, sugar, spices and veal stock, are rustic and satisfying. Desserts are exceptional, too, includ-

ing the Paris-Brest (choux pastry filled with hazelnut cream) and a *croustillant de pomme* (apple baked in pastry) in salted caramel sauce.

Georgette
29 rue St-Georges, 9th (01.42.80.39.13). M° St-Georges. **Open** noon-2.45pm, 7.30-11pm Tue-Fri. Closed 3wks Aug. **Average** €13. **Credit** AmEx, MC, V. **Map** p404 H3.
A mix of 1950s-vintage formica tables and ancient wooden beams provides external charm, but what has won Georgette a loyal following since this bistro opened three years ago is the lady chef's loving use of seasonal ingredients. Forget pallid supermarket tomatoes – here they are orange, yellow and green, layered in a salad or whizzed in a flavour-packed gazpacho. Hearty meat dishes satisfy the local business crowd, while lighter options might include slightly bony sea bream with Provençal vegetables, a charlotte of juicy lamb chunks and aubergine. There's an unsweetened prune-and-pear compote – though the creamy, cloudlike Fontainebleau with raspberry coulis takes some beating.

Le Petit Caboulot
6 pl Jacques-Froment, 18th (01.46.27.19.00). M° Guy Môquet. **Open** noon-2.30pm, 8-11pm Mon-Sat. **Average** €13. **Lunch menu** €10. **Credit** DC, MC, V.
This has all the trappings of a friendly neighbourhood bistro. *Brik de chèvre aux pommes*, a crisp pastry of apple and melting goat's cheese on a bed of salad, starts things off nicely. Foie gras *maison* is also well worth a try. The duck confit (ask for it *bien grillé*) is dark, succulent, with a skin that crunches like heaven and the haddock brandade features flakes of smoked fish blended with moist potato purée, oven-browned. Then the *tarte Tatin* arrives. Ubiquitous in bistros but so rarely right, this one, caramelised to the core, will have you booking your return. Mosaic pillars, a huge curved bar and a vast collection of old enamel adverts (look for the Arabic Kodak) evoke a bygone era.

A la Pomponette
42 rue Lepic, 18th (01.46.06.08.36). M° Abbesses or Blanche. **Open** noon-2.30pm, 7-11pm Mon-Thur; 7pm-midnight Fri, Sat. **Prix fixe** €18/€32. **Credit** AmEx, DC, MC, V. **Map** p403 H1.
Few other bistros evoke such unselfconscious charm as this almost century-old table founded by Arthur Delacroix, a retired soldier (hence the military paraphernalia), and run with great professionalism by his great-grandchildren. It remains a respected neighbourhood institution that doesn't go out of its way to pander to the tourist trade, but delights in teaching *les étrangers* about real bistro food. Starters such as snails sizzling in garlic butter, rabbit in aspic, country terrine or marrow bones, a real rarity, arrive at the table. Then come dishes such as braised veal with olives, *boeuf mode* (beef stewed with carrots, onions and bay leaf), chicken in cream with morels or skate *grenobloise*. The menu changes regularly, but remains a loveable battery of pre-war classics.

RESTAURANT

VESUVIO
Café

Italian Specialities
SUMMER TERRACE ON THE
CHAMPS-ELYSEES. NON-STOP SERVICE
144 av des Champs-Elysées, 8th. Tel: 01.43.59.68.69
M⁰ George V, Charles de Gaulle-Etoile

Branches:
25 rue Quentin Bauchart, 8th. Tel: 01.47.23.60.26
1 rue Gozlin, 6th. Tel: 01.43.54.94.78

Chez Toinette
20 rue Germain-Pilon, 18th (01.42.54.44.36).
M° Abbesses. **Open** 7.30-11pm Tue-Sat. Closed Aug.
Average €16. **Credit** MC, V. **Map** p403 H2.
This stalwart purveyor of bistro fare behind the
Théâtre de Montmartre has steadily upped its prices
in line with its burgeoning success. The blackboard
menu is still, however, good value in an area known
for rip-offs. As you squeeze into the seats, the ami-
able waiter describes each dish with pride, then presents an appetiser of olives, ripe cherry tomatoes and
crisp radishes. Of the starters, try the red-blooded
wild boar terrine, the pleasing *chèvre chaud* with a
glorious creamy st-marcellin on a bed of rocket and
lettuce, or the soufflé-like asparagus quiche.
Carnivorous mains include *mignon de porc*, spring
lamb and assorted steaks – the lamb seared in rosemary is a delicious lean morsel. If the desserts cover
standard ground, you can round off on a high note
with Armagnac-steeped prunes.

French

Chez Jean
8 rue St-Lazare, 9th (01.48.78.62.73). M° Notre-
Dame de-Lorette. **Open** noon-2.30pm, 8-10.30pm
Mon-Fri. Closed Aug. **Average** €28. **Prix fixe**
dinner €58. **Lunch menu** €34. **Credit** DC, MC, V.
Map p404 H3.
With a staff-to-diner ratio nearing levels of haute cuisine and a sumptuous high-ceilinged dining room
with pine panelling and comfy banquettes, it was
only a matter of time before prices rose at Chez Jean.
The great-value *prix fixe* has become a lunch-only
affair, and à la carte in the evening is a pretty expensive outing. Food is still well-prepared and creative,
while service combines politeness and efficiency.
Fine yellow Chinese-style ravioli stuffed with crab
burst with flavour, served with a light verbena
sauce, while a ramekin of plump snails with quar-
tered fresh artichokes are set off well by a tasty poultry gravy. Mains range from foie gras *mi-cuit*,
scattered with toasted almonds and served with a
bracing rhubarb sauce, to a delicious slow-cooked
farmhouse pork with a chutney of apricots, preserved lemons and sage. Pleasingly alcoholic eau-
de-vie marinated cherries scattered with pistachios
make for a fine dessert.

Pétrelle
34 rue Pétrelle, 9th (01.42.82 11.02). M° Anvers.
Open noon-1.30pm, 8-9.30pm Tue-Fri; 8-9.30pm Sat.
Closed 4wks July/Aug, 1wk Dec. **Average**
€25. **Prix fixe** €25. **Credit** MC, V. **Map** p404 J2.
Jean-Luc André is as inspired a decorator as he is a
cook, and the quirky charm of his dining room has
made it popular with fashion designers and film
stars. A faded series of early 20th-century tableaux
is his latest flea-market find, but behind this style is
some serious substance. André seeks out the very
best ingredients from local producers. The €25 no-
choice menu is huge value (on our last visit, mari-

nated sardines with tomato relish, rosemary-scent-
ed rabbit with roasted vegetables, deep purple
poached figs), or you can splash out with luxurious
à la carte dishes such as tournedos Rossini.

Beaubourg & the Marais

Bistros & brasseries

Le Hangar
12 impasse Berthaud, 3rd (01.42.74.55.44).
M° Rambuteau. **Open** noon-2.30pm, 7-11.30pm Tue-
Sat. Closed Aug. **Average** €14. **No credit cards**.
Map p404 K5.
It's worth making the effort to check out this bistro
by the Centre Pompidou, with its terrace and excellent cooking. The exposed stone walls and smartly
set tables are immediately welcoming, and the light,
long room fills with locals and slightly baffled
Americans. A bowl of tapenade and toast is set
down as you chose from the fairly comprehensive
carte. It yields, for starters, a tasty and grease-free
rillettes de lapereau (rabbit) alongside a perfectly balanced pumpkin-and-chestnut soup. Main courses
include a well-seasoned steak tartare, served with a
crisp salad and some *pommes dauphines*, and a
superb *ris de veau* on a bed of melting chicory. You
may also be tempted by the puddings, the chocolate
soufflé and warm white wine tart with cinnamon –
but if you're going to splurge, do remember that payment is by cash only.

Le Petit Marché
9 rue de Béarn, 3rd (01.42.72.06.67). M° Chemin
Vert. **Open** noon-3pm, 8pm-midnight daily.
Average €16. **Lunch menu** *Mon-Fri* €13.
Credit MC, V. **Map** 408 L6.
Just a step away from the place des Vosges, the Petit
Marché has become a hip Marais bistro, attracting
a fashion-conscious crowd. The woody interior is
warm and welcoming, while the heated terrace offers
a view of the gendarmerie. The menu is short and
modern with Asian touches. The raw tuna is flash-
fried in sesame seeds, and served with a Thai sauce,
making an original, refreshing starter, while crispy-
coated deep-fried king prawns have a similar oriental lightness. The main vegetarian risotto is rich in
basil, coriander, cream and al dente green beans,
contrasting winningly with the unctuous rice. Pan-
fried scallops with lime are accurately cooked to
avoid any hint of rubberiness, and accompanied by
a good purée and more beans. From the short wine
list the carafe of house red (€9) is unusually good.

French

L'Ambassade d'Auvergne
22 rue du Grenier-St-Lazare, 3rd (01.42.72.31.22/
www.ambassade-auvergne.com). M° Rambuteau.
Open noon-2pm, 7.30-10.30pm daily. Closed mid
July-mid Aug. **Average** €15. **Prix fixe** €27.
Credit MC, V. **Map** p404 K5.

This rustic auberge is a fitting embassy for the hearty, filling fare of central France. Go easy on the complimentary pâté and thick-sliced country bread while you look at the menu; it is impossible to feel hungry on leaving. The choice of cured ham comes as two hefty, plate-filling slices, as does the salad bowl chock full of green lentils cooked in goose fat, studded with bacon bits and shallots. The *rôti d'agneau* arrives as a pot of melting chunks of lamb in a rich meaty sauce with a helping of tender white beans. Dishes arrive with the flagship *aligot*, served with great pomp as the waiter lifts great strands of the creamy, elastic mash-and-cheese concoction into the air and lets it plop on to the plates with a dramatic flourish. Of the regional wines (Chanturgue, Boudes, Madargues), the quite fruity AOC Marcillac makes a worthy partner for a successful meal.

Le Dôme du Marais

53bis rue des Francs-Bourgeois, 4th (01.42.74.54.17). Mº Rambuteau. **Open** noon-2.30pm, 7.15-11pm Tue-Sat. Closed 2wks Jan, 3wks Aug. **Average** €18. **Prix fixe** €29. **Lunch menu** €17, €23. **Credit** AmEx, MC, V. **Map** p408 L6.

The building predates the Revolution; in the 1920s it was the auction room for the state pawnbrokers. The remarkable octagonal dining room is lavishly decorated with marble cherubs and gilt walls, crowned by a striking dome. Owner-chef Pierre Lecoutre's cooking is more confident than ever, with robust ingredients such as *tête de veau*, *andouille* and game (hare, pigeon and venison on one winter menu). Recent meals have included a delicate *blanquette de veau*, a top-notch sauté of free-range chicken with smoked garlic, saffron milk mushrooms and baby vegetables, and a thick fillet of sea bream with a spiced crust, served on a cauliflower purée. Crêpes are a feature – as a starter with pig's trotter and snails, or as a dessert with rhubarb compote and sorbet. Exceptional value for the quality.

Le Pamphlet

38 rue Debelleyme, 3rd (01.42.72.39.24). Mº Filles du Calvaire. **Open** 7.30-11pm Mon, Sat; noon-2.30pm, 7.30-11pm Tue-Fri. Closed 2wks Jan, 2wks Aug. **Prix fixe** €30, €45. **Credit** MC, V. **Map** p404 L5.

The beamed room with its elegantly dressed and spaciously placed tables, combined with cooking that is modern and sophisticated without being insubstantial or too elaborate, makes Le Pamphlet's €30 menu one of the best deals in town. Here you can chew on fragrant *saucisson sec* with your aperitif, before a ladle of creamy lentil soup arrives as a pre-starter. The first course keeps up the high standard of presentation, an outstanding combination of escargots and rabbit rillettes, while a mini-brandade is enlivened by the addition of tasty haddock. Mains include a well-prepared *Parmentier de canard*, a duck version of cottage pie, and glazed suckling pig, served French-style astride some roasted root vegetables. Charming service and a carefully chosen flinty Pouilly Fumé at €26 makes you feel as if you have eaten at a prestigious address for half the price.

International

Anahi

49 rue Volta, 3rd (01.48.87.88.24). Mº Arts et Métiers. **Open** 8pm-midnight daily. **Average** €20. **Credit** MC, V. **Map** p404 K5.

A rickety old building in a narrow and ill-lit street deep in the Marais houses this trendy Argentinian restaurant. Slabs of grilled beef fresh (well, vacuum-packed) from the pampas pull in the crowds, cheerily welcomed by Carmina and Pilat, the sisters who started up in this old charcuterie 20 years ago. The original white tiled walls are dotted with black and white photos of the pair – the art deco ceiling was painted by Albert Camus' brother. Tuck into *torta pascualina*, a sweetish spinach tart with onions, or try the standout *ceviche* made with sea bass. Mains of skewered chicken breast marinated in lemon and served with apple and pineapple salsa and sweet potato purée, and *cururù de camarào* (grilled gambas with peanuts and okra) are satisfying but the *bif angosto* – a juicy fillet served with a green salad – is the star. Wash it down with a choice Chilean red.

Bastille & eastern Paris

Bistros & brasseries

Bofinger

5-7 rue de la Bastille, 4th (01.42.72.87.82/www. bofingerparis.com). Mº Bastille. **Open** noon-3pm, 6.30pm-1am Mon-Fri; noon-1am Sat, Sun. **Average** €28. **Prix fixe** €31.90. **Lunch menu** Mon-Fri €21.50. **Credit** AmEx, DC, MC, V. **Map** p408 M7.

Opposite the Bastille opera house, Bofinger is a post-show haunt and draws big crowds at other times for its authentic art nouveau setting and brasserie atmosphere. Downstairs is the prettiest place to eat, upstairs is air-conditioned. As at many Flo-group restaurants, the food is always adequate but rarely aspires to great culinary heights. An à la carte choice might be plump, garlicky escargots, and a well-made langoustine terrine, followed by an intensely seasoned salmon tartare and a generous, if uneventful, cod steak. The calf's liver is accompanied by cooked melon. Alternatively, you could go for the foolproof brasserie meal of oysters and fillet steak, and expect a rabidly pungent plate of munster cheese and accompanying bowl of cumin, washed down by the fine raspberry-nosed Chinon at €35.50 a bottle.

Le Bistrot Paul Bert

18 rue Paul-Bert, 11th (01.43.72.24.01). Mº Charonne. **Open** noon-2pm, 7.30-11pm Tue-Sat. Closed Aug. **Average** €17. **Prix fixe** €28. **Lunch menu** €15. **Credit** MC, V. **Map** p409 N7.

This popular haunt of businessmen and artisans has a well-worn interior filled with a smell of garlic and red wine. The boss here chooses superb bottles, his list interesting with affordable treats. The is not of the sophisticated modern bistro type but good old-fashioned, no-nonsense cuisine. Egg mayo is raised from the mundane by a particularly good potato salad. Mains include a substantial and perfectly cooked piece of salmon with hollandaise sauce served with pasta, and a tender chuck steak with a couple of spoonfuls of flavoursome beef reduction accompanied by melting potato wedges. The cinnamon-rich apple crumble with crème fraîche sustains the high standards – the *prix fixe* menu features nobler products prepared with the same honest care.

French

Astier

44 rue Jean-Pierre-Timbaud, 11th (01.43.57.16.35). Mº Parmentier. **Open** noon-2pm, 8-10.15pm Mon-Fri. Closed 1wk Apr, Aug, 1wk Dec. **Prix fixe** €27. **Lunch menu** €22. **Credit** MC, V. **Map** p405 M4.
On entering Astier all your senses tell you that this is a serious bastion of traditional food: the unmistakeable smell of fine French cooking, the look of unbridled contentment on the crimson faces of businessmen, and the sound of frantic ordering across a crowded, unassumingly decorated room. The charming *patronne* squeezes you in to a corner table and gives you the handwritten menu. This is a place where homemade terrines lead the way, so go for the chicken liver and seafood versions, both highly flavoured. Firm yet tender lamb sweetbreads, served generously with tiny *mousseron* mushrooms, replace the controversial calf variety with aplomb, and the accompanying *gratin dauphinois* is sinfully good. Book ahead for the bargain lunch menu.

C'Amelot

50 rue Amelot, 11th (01.43.55.54.04). Mº Chemin Vert. **Open** noon-2pm, 7-10.30pm Tue-Fri; 7-10.30pm Sat. **Prix fixe** €16, €26, €32. **Credit** AmEx, MC, V. **Map** p408 M6.
Didier Varnier is a young bistro chef who relishes the contrast of serving inventive and often refined food in low-key settings. C'Amelot's long, narrow dining room in gloomy rue Amelot has a countrified, even dated, feel with its panelling and bare wood tables. There are two options for each course. You could start with a typically southwestern lentil soup with foie gras – earthy, with morsels of oozy goodness – or unusual cured salmon with braised chicory in a sweet vinegar sauce that contrasts nicely with its bitterness. Lamb chops in *poivrade* (white wine) sauce with porridgy polenta are remarkable for the quality of the rosy meat. Prunes in spiced wine provide a wintry end to a market-inspired meal.

Crêperie Bretonne Fleurie

67 rue de Charonne, 11th (01.43.55.62.29). Mº Ledru-Rollin or Charonne. **Open** noon-2.30pm, 7.30-11pm Mon-Fri; 7.30-11pm Sat. Closed Aug. **Average** €5. **Credit** MC, V. **Map** p409 M7.
Everything about this restaurant is authentic, including the crêpe chef's pointy chin thatch, wiggly pipe and striped sailor shirt. The menu is straightforward: to fill your savoury, freshly cooked buckwheat *galette*, choose a ham/cheese/egg combination (all three is a *complète*, presented in a perfect square, topped off with a gleaming egg yolk),

Interesting, affordable treats at **Le Bistro Paul Bert**. *See p204.*

andouille (tripe sausage) or the more inventive camembert with walnuts. Old-fashioned manners prevail: the sashaying waitress serve ladies first as gents politely contemplate the Celtic flags, Breton Tin-Tin book and puzzling tribal mask. Dessert crêpes feature pear-and-chocolate and banana-and-chocolate fillings. Dry cider would be the logical accompaniment, but a Breton Breizh cola in its nifty glass bottle is hard to resist.

L'Encrier

55 rue Traversière, 12th (01.44.68.08.16).
M° Ledru-Rollin or Gare de Lyon. **Open** noon-2.15pm, 7.30-11pm Mon-Fri; 7.30-11pm Sat. Closed Aug. **Average** €14. **Prix fixe** *Dinner* €17, €20.

Candlelit flirting at **Juan et Juanita**.

Lunch menu €12. **Credit** AmEx, DC, MC, V. **Map** p409 M8.
Tremendous value at this popular local. *See p197*
No such thing as a cheap lunch?

Juan et Juanita

82 rue Jean-Pierre-Timbaud, 11th (01.43.57.60.15).
M° Couronnes. **Open** 8pm-2am Tue-Sat. **Average** €15. **Credit** MC, V. **Map** p405 N4.
J 'n' J attract a fresh-faced clientele with its refined cuisine. Carine Francart's seven-year-old gem set off with a Californian menu but today is decidedly French and consistently good. With dripping candelabras on every table and one in the ladies, the look is polished and flirty – as are the staff. Starters include mesclun salads with toasted hazelnuts, one with a crispy st-marcellin brik. They are followed by the special of the night, perhaps a buttery rabbit with thyme, and a leg of lamb with mint, a house speciality so tender it needed no convincing off the bone. Desserts are too good to pass up, so indulge in a lime sorbet with vodka and vanilla ice-cream with a red fruit coulis. An ambitious wine list is strong on Graves and Gaillacs.

La Ravigote

41 rue de Montreuil, 11th (01.43.72.96.22).
M° Faidherbe Chaligny. **Open** noon-2.30pm, 7-10.30pm Mon-Fri; noon-2.30pm Sat. **Prix fixe** *Dinner* €18. **Lunch menu** €13. **Credit** MC, V. **Map** p409 P7.
Rue de Montreuil still has slight vestiges of its furniture-making past – artisans and assorted ebony specialists gather here. The narrow room has views of old Paris, the welcome is warm, and the oft-harassed chef potters around, chatting with typical Parisian truculence. The food is unremarkable, but reliable and generously served for €13 at lunch and €18 in the evening. A fine pâté can be followed with the restaurant's signature dish of *tête de veau*, *sauce Ravigote*, a gelatinous feast which always hits the spot. You might see a group devouring a steaming chicken tagine with obvious relish. The wine of the month, say a fruity Mâcon, nicely accompanies the meal through to the *gâteau de semoule*, served with a comfortingly large quantity of *crème anglaise*. This place is on borrowed time, so get here soon.

Le Square Trousseau

1 rue Antoine-Vollon, 12th (01.43.43.06.00). M°
Ledru-Rollin. **Open** noon-3pm, 8-11.30pm Tue-Sat. **Average** €20. **Lunch menu** €20. **Credit** AmEx, DC, MC, V. **Map** p409 N7.
This restaurant with its superb 1900s interior is a favourite with a fashion and media crowd; the friendly waiters, handsome in their long white aprons, appear as if on film. The food, though, is for real. Start with a silky-textured smoked salmon and candied lemon timbale; a tomato, cucumber and avocado millefeuille with mozzarella, refreshing red, green and white layers showered with chives; or poached eggs in a fine, nutmeg-scented cheese sauce with Japanese herbs. A main dish of plump farm

French classics in listed surroundings – all aboard **Le Train Bleu**.

chicken comes with a mini, creamy risotto; tender strips of duck with a delicious cherry sauce, and chicken is set in Moroccan-style pastry. The wine prices are a surprise, given the good-value food, but the selection does unearth the best from Touraine, Burgundy, Auvergne and the Vaucluse.

Le Train Bleu

Gare de Lyon, cour Louis-Armand, 12th (01.43.43.09.06/www.le-train-bleu.com). M° Gare de Lyon. **Open** 11.30am-3pm, 7-11pm daily. **Average** €26. **Prix fixe** €43. **Credit** AmEx, DC, MC, V. **Map** p409 M8.

This listed dining room with vintage frescoes of the alluring destinations served by the Paris-Lyon-Marseille railway and big oak benches with shiny brass coat racks exudes a pleasant air of expectation. Don't expect, though, cutting-edge cooking, but rather fine renderings of French classics and first-rate produce. Lobster served on walnut-oil-dressed salad leaves is a generous, beautifully prepared starter as is the pistachio-studded *saucisson de Lyon* with a warm salad of small *ratte* potatoes. Mains of veal chop topped with a cap of cheese and *sandre* (pike-perch) with a 'risotto' of *crozettes* are also pleasant, although given the size of the starters and the superb cheese tray, you could have a satisfying three-course meal here without a main. A few reasonably priced wines would be a welcome addition.

International

Chez Omar

47 rue de Bretagne, 3rd (01.42.72.36.26). M° Temple or Arts et Métiers. **Open** noon-2.30pm, 7-11.30pm Mon-Sat; 7-11.30pm Sun. **Average** €14. **No credit cards**. **Map** p404 L5.

The once-fashionable Omar doesn't take reservations and the queue can stretch the length of the zinc bar and out the door. Everyone is waiting for the same thing: couscous. Prices range from €11 (vegetarian) to €24 (*royale*); there are no tagines or other traditional Maghreb mains, only a handful of French classics (duck, fish, steak). Overstretched waiters slip through the crowds with mounds of semolina, steaming vats of vegetable-laden broth, and steel platters heaving with meat and more meat, including the stellar *merguez*. Even on packed nights an offer of seconds – gratis, of course – will encourage you to stay; big appetites might find room for the giant platter of Algerian pastries the waiter leaves at your table. Non-smokers beware: the proximity of your neighbours means that you'll share more than just their conversation.
Other locations: *Café Moderne, 19 rue Keller, 11th (01.47.00.53.62).*

Dong Huong

14 rue Louis-Bonnet, 11th (01.43.57.18.88). M° Belleville. **Open** noon-11pm Mon, Wed-Sun. Closed 3wks Aug. **Average** €7. **Credit** MC, V. **Map** p405 M4.

The excellent food attracts a buzzing crowd, but this is also, significantly, one of few Parisian restaurants that banishes smokers to a separate room, on the lower floor. Dishes arrived promptly and in generous portions. The delicious *bành cuôn*, steamed Vietnamese ravioli, are served piping hot, stuffed with minced meat, mushrooms, bean sprouts, spring onions and deep-fried onion. *Com ga lui*, chicken kebabs with tasty lemongrass, though not as delicate, are served on tasty rice. *Bò bùn chà giò* (noodles with beef and small *nem* topped with onion strips, spring onion and crushed peanuts) make a meal in itself. Be sure to try the dark, sickly sweet iced lotus flower tea with lotus seeds, lychees and seaweed jelly. For dessert, the mandarin, lychee and mango sorbets are tasty and authentic.

Ile de Gorée
70 rue Jean-Pierre Timbaud, 11th (01.43.38.97.69).
Mº Parmentier. **Open** 7pm-1am Mon-Sat. **Average**
€14. **Credit** MC, V. **Map** p405 M4.
The real Gorée Island is a 15-minute ferry ride off
the Senegal coast to Gorée Island. At its Paris namesake, mango-and-peach punch and live kora music
set the mood before simple but well-prepared *boudin
créole* (black pudding with cinnamon) and *aloco*
(sautéed plantains) with sweet tomato relish. The
mains are hearty and honest: a *dem farci* (stuffed
mullet) in brown sauce or *thiou poisson* (whole fish)
with tomatoes, bell peppers, carrots, potatoes and
basmati rice, richly marinated with a sauce tingling
with flavour. Muomuo the friendly house cat will lap
up the rest of your rum-raisin ice cream from the
bowl, sparing the exotic selection of coconut, mango
and pistachio sorbets. The cooks wave goodbye as
you plan your next trip to this enchanted isle.

Le Souk
*1 rue Keller, 11th (01.49.29.05.08). Mº Ledru-Rollin
or Bastille.* **Open** 7.30-10.30pm Tue-Fri; noon-
2.30pm, 7.30-10.30pm Sat, Sun. **Average** €15.
Prix fixe *for 8 or more* €31, €35. **Credit** MC, V.
Map p409 N7.
Potted olive trees mark the entrance where savvy
diners push past the battered kilim over the doorway into a lively den of Moroccan cuisine. Start with
b'stilla, a savoury pasty stuffed with duck, raisins
and nuts, flavoured with orange blossom water and
sprinkled with cinnamon and powdered sugar – or
a creamy eggplant dip scooped up with hunks of
fluffy Moroccan bread, baked on the premises. Don't
fill up though, as the enormous tagines and couscous are first rate. The favourite is *tagine canette*,
duckling stewed with honey, onions, apricots, figs
and cinnamon then showered with toasted almonds.
Couscous bidaoui arrives in handsome earthenware,
a hefty shank of lamb on the side. Cold beer goes
down well, but you might be happy with a bottle of
Algerian or Moroccan red, at €17. For dessert try
the excellent millefeuille with fresh figs, as sweet
mint tea is poured in a long stream by a djellaba-
clad waiter. Book ahead.

Zagros
*21 rue de la Folie-Méricourt, 11th (01.48.07.09.56).
Mº St-Ambroise.* **Open** noon-3pm, 7-11pm Mon-Sat.
Closed 2wks Dec. **Average** €13. **Prix fixe** €18,
€24. **Lunch menu** €11. **Credit** AmEx, MC, V.
Map p405 M5.
This relaxed off-Oberkampf address is frequented
by an arty Kurdish community: a stringed *bajlama*
is stashed behind the till in case musical inspiration
strikes. The menu roams over the area covered by
the Kurdish diaspora, with the usual dips, skewer-
grilled meats and a small selection of fish. The hot
oven-cooked aubergine with feta is melt-in-the-mouth
good, proving that the Kurdish village dishes are the
way to go. Ditto for the *hasti* – jarret of lamb boiled
then re-cooked in a tomato-flavoured sauce and
topped with a slice of grilled aubergine and pepper

– and chef's speciality *kavournas*, lamb preserved in
salt. You can finish with *fromage blanc*, one with
fresh diced fruit and the other with honey and walnuts. You leave the place to the sound of the bajlama and a bottle of Metaxa on the table.

North-east Paris

French

Chez Michel
*10 rue de Belzunce, 10th (01.44.53.06.20). Mº Gare
du Nord.* **Open** 7pm-midnight Mon; noon-2pm, 7pm-
midnight Tue-Fri. **Closed** 3wks Aug. **Prix fixe**
€30. **Credit** MC, V. **Map** p404 K2.
Thierry Breton is from Brittany (he's so proud of his
origins that he sports the Breton flag on his chef's
whites) and his menu is stacked with hearty offerings from said hearty region. Marinated salmon with
purple potatoes served in a preserving jar, pickled-
herring-style, is succulently tender. So too fresh
abalone, and the rabbit braised with rosemary and
Swiss chard might just be the best bunny in town.
Blackboard specials, which carry a €5-€15 supplement, follow the seasons. Game lovers are spoilt in
the cooler months with wood pigeon, wild boar and
venison, and there are usually some juicy fat, fresh
scallops on offer, too.

International

La Madonnina
*10 rue Marie-et-Louise, 10th (01.42.01.25.26).
Mº Goncourt.* **Open** noon-2.30pm, 8-11pm Mon-Sat.
Closed 3wks Aug. **Average** €12. **Lunch menu** €11.
Credit MC, V. **Map** p404 L4.

The best Vegetarian

L'Arpège
The best beetroot around. *See p217.*

L'Astrance
Quintessential modern French cuisine.
See p196.

Café Moderne
Hip, sleek and inventive. *See p195.*

Chez Omar
The finest vegetarian couscous in town.
See p207.

Le Petit Marché
Fashion-conscious Marais haunt. *See p203.*

La Soupière
Fun with all things fungi. *See p198.*

Eat, Drink, Shop

Host Gianna will pull up a chair to explain the entire (if small) menu and recommend a wine (like a ruby-red dry Rupicolo). Otherwise, no red-checked clichés here, surrounded by blinking lights and Virgin Mary shrines. They worship food, too: luscious salads and roasted veggies are displayed on an antipasti altar. Every dish features fresh ingredients – starters of tender marinated calamari amid potatoes and rocket and a scrumptious aubergine *parmiggiano*, also served with a generous heap of rocket; mains such as the exquisite pesto-truffle-mushroom ravioli or red pesto. A magician apppears for the Saturday special €8 children's menu.

Le Reminet has always been a favourite Left-Bank bistro, opening at weekends and serving a €13 lunch menu on three days during the week. The Sunday lunch might seem dear, but Hugues Gournay's cooking remains accurate and delicious. Start off with some crisp fried filo parcels of black pudding, or even ravioli – whole *gambas* in light pliable dough, bathing in coconut milk. Main courses feature a perfectly timed fillet of beef with a shallot purée, and some tender scallops on firm, well-sauced tagliatelle. A bottle of €29 red Gigondas bears up well – the wine of the month at over €50 could be a shock for the financially unwary.

The Latin Quarter & the 13th

Bistros & brasseries

L'Avant-Goût
26 rue Bobillot, 13th (01.53.80.24.00). M° Place d'Italie. **Open** noon-2pm, 7.30-11pm Tue-Fri. Closed 1wk Jan, 1wk May, 3wks Aug/Sept. **Prix fixe** €28; €36-€40. **Lunch menu** €12.50. **Credit** MC, V.
Owner-chef Christophe Beaufront has resisted the temptation to raise prices, lower quality and turn tables faster. The blackboard menu doesn't change much, but who cares when you eat so well at this price? During a recent meal, starters of tuna tartare with roasted vegetables, and a medley of spring vegetables in a light bouillon with a poached egg were all first rate. Beaufront's signature dish is a *pot-au-feu de cochon*, a big casserole brimming with pork cuts, fennel and sweet potato, served with gherkins, horseradish sauce and ginger chips. A delicious €21 Cairanne can be finished off with an intriguing terrine of roquefort, butter and preserved pear.

Le Bistrot Côté Mer
16 bd St-Germain, 5th (01.43.54.59.10/www. bistrocotemer.com). M° Maubert Mutualité. **Open** 12.15-2.15pm, 7.15-10.15pm Mon-Sat. Closed 3wks Aug. **Prix fixe** €23. **Lunch menu** €17, €22. **Credit** AmEx, MC, V. **Map** p408 K7.
Bistrot Côté Mer may be way inland, but its blue and yellow entrance reminds you of a beach cabin, its stone walls could be seaside St-Malo and even the plates are wave-shaped. A creamy mushroom *amuse-bouche* arrives with menus, written on a ceramic platter. Skipping standards such as oysters and tuna, opt for the succulent ravioli stuffed with scallops, tarama and a trace of ginger. The main courses feature sea bass, chard and artichokes in a tangy broth steamed inside an iron pot, and yellow pollock whose crispy skin is accompanied by a green pea sauce, sautéed mustard greens, and a winter vegetable mash. Pricy but tasty desserts.

Le Reminet
3 rue des Grands-Degrés, 5th (01.44.07.04.24). M° Maubert Mutualité or St-Michel. **Open** noon-2pm, 7.30-11pm Mon, Thur-Sun. Closed 3wks Aug. **Average** €15. **Lunch menu** *Mon, Thur, Fri* €13. **Credit** MC, V. **Map** p408 J7.

French

Atelier Maître Albert
1 rue Maître-Albert, 5th (01.56.81.30.01). M° St-Michel or Maubert Mutualité. **Open** noon-2.30pm, 6.30-11.30pm Mon-Wed; noon-2.30pm, 6.30pm-1am Thur, Fri; 6.30pm-1am Sat; noon-2.30pm Sun. **Average** €22. **Lunch menu** €22, €28. **Credit** AmEx, DC, MC, V. **Map** p408 J7.
With a slick new decor by Jean-Michel Wilmotte, who redesigned chef Guy Savoy's main table, this new Savoy annex in a sweet dog-leg street in the Latin Quarter looks like it could become a good restaurant even if the concept was launched by Jacques Cagna a decade ago. The indigo-painted and grey marble floored dining room with open kitchen and *rôtisseries* on view is attractive but noisy – book a table in the quieter bar area. The short menu lets you get at a Savoy classic or two to start, including oysters in sea-water gelee or more inventive dishes like the *ballotin* of chicken, foie gras and celery root in a chicken liver sauce. Next up, perhaps a rotisseried *faux-filet*, or a chunk of tuna, served with tiny iron casseroles of potatoes dauphinois and (much tastier) cauliflower in béchamel sauce. Once this place works out the noise and the ungarnished plates, it'll be ideal for a tasty feed with friends.

L'Ecurie
2 rue Laplace, 5th (01.46.33.68.49). M° Maubert Mutualité. **Open** noon-2.15pm, 7pm-11.30pm daily. **Average** €9. **Prix fixe** €15. **Lunch menu** €11.50. **No credit cards. Map** p408 J8.
The Stable draws hordes of carnivorous diners with a popular formula of grilled meat and chips washed down with copious amounts of drinkable wine. Minie, supposedly a descendant of the original 17th-century stable owner, runs a tight ship, cajoling waiters and hesitant customers while dispensing free drinks and teasing her favourite regulars. Follow her recommendation and opt for the €15 prix fixe. A selection of cold starters covers farmhouse pâté and a variety of salads, including '*salade au bleu*' lettuce scattered with an unidentifiable grated blue cheese. The main courses are all slabs of red meat, flame-grilled in the makeshift kitchen behind the bar and accompanied by thick chips. This is followed with one of the traditional desserts. The food

may be basic, the horse theme a little overdone and service occasionally rushed, but – aided by a complimentary aperitif and calvados digestif – one al most always emerges satisfied and replenished. A budget winner.

L'Ourcine

92 rue Broca, 13th (01.47.07.13.65). M° Les Gobelins. **Open** noon-2pm, 7-10.30pm Tue-Sat. **Closed** 2wks July/Aug. **Lunch menu** *Tue-Fri* €19. **Prix fixe** €28. **Credit** MC, V. **Map** p408 J10.

A great destination for Basque cuisine; booking a must. *See below* **A new breed of bistro**.

Chez Paul

22 rue Butte-aux-Cailles, 13th (01.45.89.22.11). *M° Place d'Italie.* **Open** noon-2.30pm, 7.30pm-12.30am daily. **Average** €14. **Credit** MC, V.

Chez Paul is a beacon to professional types who lurk in the 13th, its white-cloth-and-wood approach offering a chic alternative to other offbeat spots along the strip. Tradition takes pride of place – *pot-au-feu*, beef knuckle, bone marrow – and you can eat your way from one end of a beast to the other. Seafood makes an appearance on the blackboard menu with oysters, whelks, an excellent starter of pan-fried mullet

A new breed of bistro

While the classic Paris bistro is on the wane, a mini boom of new bistros has sprung up, mainly in the outlying 11th and 12th districts. Here a new generation of young restaurateurs is responding to growing demand by affluent young professionals newly arrived to these formerly sleepy neighbourhoods, who crave the homely fare they don't have the time or energy to make, along with child-friendly conviviality.

What distinguishes the new breed of bistro from the chequered-tablecloth spots of yore is the trend towards lighter and more cosmopolitan eating. Chefs grill, use jus instead of flour- or cream-thickened sauces, throw in formerly exotic herbs like fresh coriander and ginger alongside traditional ones like tarragon, and allow menus more space for fish and vegetables. The other noticeable feature is the relative rarity of the slow-simmered dishes like *blanquette de veau* that were once the stock in trade of the Paris bistro; France's 35-hour week has a had a withering effect on time-consuming cooking and many figure- and health-conscious Parisians have an aversion to dishes they perceive as rich and fatty.

Le Marsagny (73 av Parmentier, 11th, 01.47.00.94.25) is the perfect prototype of the new wave bistro: friendly, generous, fairly priced and reliably delicious. There's a lot of word of mouth operating when it comes to this address, and it's not unusual to see film, fashion and TV types having a low-key time. The crowd otherwise comprises a comfortable mix of liberal locals with arty aspirations (if not professions). The menu is a grand slam of traditional treats such as terrine or fricassee of rabbit with olives and more inventive dishes like a starter millefeuille of avocado and crayfish. **Le Sot l'y Laisse** (70 rue Alexandre-Dumas, 11th,

01.40.09.79.20) is not only a great place to relax at, but offers value for money. The yellow walls with miniature blackboards offering various wines make a homely setting, and the kitchen does some excellent cooking, such as a first-rate salad of artichoke hearts and country ham and a superb roast chicken.

In more traditional vein, chef Thierry Coué's **Le Vin de Zinc** (25 rue Oberkampf, 11th, 01.48.06.28.23) serves hearty classics like boudin with violette mustard – don't miss his odd but brilliant aubergine-filled crêpe for dessert. **Le Temps au Temps** (13 rue Paul Bert, 11th, 01.43.79.63.40) is another new sepia-toned place with stencilled profiles of famous French chefs on its walls and great Gallic grub like *boeuf aux carottes* or pan-roasted veal kidneys. With frosted glass globes and vanilla-coloured walls, **Le Vieux Chêne** (7 rue du Dahomey, 11th, 01.43.71.67.69) looks as though it's been around for at a century, but is actually a promising yearling, with a menu of bistro favourites that includes chicken cooked with shallots and vinegar, pigeon with cabbage, and fresh strawberries with rhubarb compote for dessert.

Though much of the innovative bistro action is to be found in eastern Paris, there are also some great new addresses on the Left Bank. **L'Ourcine** (*see above*) serves up an intriguing mixture of Basque and Béarnais dishes such as baby squid sautéed with garlic and Espelette pepper or cod-stuffed red peppers, along with modern recipes like roast cod with chorizo vinaigrette and white beans. And around the Latin Quarter, **Les Papilles** (30 rue Gay-Lussac, 5th, 01.43.25.20.79) is an epicerie-cum-bistro that offers a different, great value *prix fixe* menu every day of the week – maybe cauliflower soup with chorizo confetti, roast rack of lamb with ratatouille or goat's cheese with salad.

fillets with olive tapenade and a main of monkfish nuggets in a creamy garlic sauce with gleaming green spinach. Liquorice ice-cream and a carafe of chilled Brouilly also go down well. The joint is jumping, so if you want a bone to pick, book.

Chez René
14 bd St-Germain, 5th (01.43.54.30.23). M° Maubert Mutualité. **Open** 12.15-2.15pm, 7.45-10.30pm Tue-Sat. Closed Aug, 1wk Dec. **Average** €22. **Prix fixe** *dinner* €41. **Lunch menu** €30. **Credit** MC, V. **Map** p408 K7.
Every decade since René Cinquin opened this place in 1957, the staff have gathered for a photo that's framed and added to the others hanging by the door. As far as change is concerned, that's pretty much it. These days it's René's son Jean-Paul who chats with the diners, but there's still the same silver cutlery, starched linen and hard work in the kitchen. The coq au vin is the reason for coming here. The secret of the dark, succulent sauce is no stock, just a good 20 minutes constantly stirring flour and butter over the feeblest of flames before adding the wine – just as René's granny taught him. Similar skills go into the *boeuf bourguignon*. Cheese impressively comes in two courses: cow's milk and goat's milk.

St-Germain-des-Prés & Odéon

Bistros & brasseries

Allard
41 rue St-André-des-Arts, 6th (01.43.26.48.23). M° Odéon. **Open** noon-2.30pm, 7-11.30pm Mon-Sat. Closed 3wks Aug. **Average** €38. **Prix fixe** €32. **Lunch menu** €24, €32. **Credit** AmEx, DC, MC, V. **Map** p408 H7.
It's reassuring to come across this fine example of a traditional bistro. With its vanilla-coloured walls and a coat rack in the narrow hall connecting the two small dining rooms, Allard has a pre-war feel, a first impression confirmed by the kitchen itself, which sends out the glorious Gallic grub you come to Paris for. Winter here is perfect. Start with sliced Lyonnais sausage studded with pistachios and served with potato salad in delicious vinaigrette, or maybe a sauté of wild mushrooms, and then choose between roast shoulder of lamb, roast Bresse chicken with sautéed ceps or roast duck with olives. Finish up with the *tarte fine de pommes* and go with one of the good, if slightly pricey, Bordeaux.

Josephine 'Chez Dumonet'
117 rue du Cherche Midi, 6th (01.45.48.52.40). M° Duroc. **Open** 12.15-2.30pm, 7.15-10.30pm Mon-Fri. **Average** €22. **Credit** AmEx, MC, V. **Map** p407 F8.
This bastion of classic bistro cooking, where the use of luxury ingredients brings a splash of glamour, is guaranteed to please the well-heeled loyal clientele. The room looks comfortingly old-fashioned, while formal staff emphasise the impression of serious Parisian eating. All dishes are available as half portions, allowing you to explore some classy numbers

without breaking the bank. In truffle season, try the salad of lamb's lettuce, warm potatoes and truffle shavings in its €31 half-portion version. Delicious sautéed potatoes, rich in goose fat and a touch of garlic, accompany both the tournedos and an absolute top-quality *andouillette*. Sumptuous puddings, too.

French

Les Bouquinistes
53 quai des Grands-Augustins, 6th (01.43.25.45.94/ www.guysavoy.com). M° St-Michel. **Open** noon-2.30pm, 7-11.30pm Mon-Fri; 7-11.30pm Sat. **Average** €26. **Lunch menu** €26.50. **Credit** AmEx, DC, MC, V. **Map** p408 J6.
There are good and not-so-good things about this Guy Savoy offshoot. The food is smart and seasonally driven. The yellow walls with mirrors and multicoloured frames set a good mood. It's the service that jars; the wad of young waiters are a poor match for the food. Dishes include avocado and prawns in radicchio leaves with a curried herring sauce; tuna tartare with soy bean and sunflower sprouts; grilled saddle of rabbit with carrots and pearl-like steamed radish; and roast John Dory with capers, olives, yellow pepper and olive-oil-mashed potato. Desserts are crowd-pleasers – lime macaroon filled with regal mango sorbet and served with coconut cream, or a blood-red 'cappuccino' of sour cherries and strawberries. Wine comes by the glass (from €4.60), or by the bottle (chilled red Sancerre at €34). The word has spread far and wide; expect plenty of English speakers among the diners.

Lapérouse
51 quai des Grands-Augustins, 6th (01.43.26.68.04). M° St-Michel. **Open** noon-3pm, 7.30-10.30pm Mon-Thur; noon-3pm, 7.30-11pm Fri; 7.30-11pm Sat. Closed Aug. **Average** €28. **Prix fixe** €90. **Lunch menu** €30. **Credit** AmEx, DC, MC, V. **Map** p408 J6.
One of the most romantic spots in Paris, Lapérouse was formerly a clandestine rendezvous for French politicians and their mistresses: the tiny private dining rooms upstairs used to lock from the inside, though no longer. Chef Alain Hacquard does a modern take on classic French cooking: his beef fillet is smoked for a more complex flavour, a tender saddle of rabbit is cooked in a clay crust, flavoured with lavender and rosemary and served with ravioli of onions. The only snag is the price, especially of the wine (a half-bottle of Pouilly Fuissé is nearly €40). The lunch menu is limited – and frankly, the seductive Seine-side dining room has always been best savoured at night.

International

Alcazar
62 rue Mazarine, 6th (01.53.10.19.99/www. alcazar.fr). M° Odéon. **Open** noon-3pm, 7pm-12.30am daily. **Average** €30-€40. **Lunch menu** €27. **Credit** AmEx, DC, MC, V. **Map** p408 H7.

Eat, Drink, Shop

The success of Sir Terence Conran's Paris gastrodome might well have more to do with its see-and-be-seen cachet than with the food itself. The space is certainly impressive, but the open kitchen is more likely to have you knock on the window and complain about your chips than offer admiration of the deft preparation. The seafood remains a safe bet and their lunchtime 'menu minceur' is a nice alternative to the naked-salad-and-Marlboros favoured by Parisian calorie counters. As disappointing as dinner can be, the minions can rustle up a good

brunch. Perfect scrambled eggs, fluffy muffins and a diet-starts-on-Monday chocolate cake combine well with an upbeat crowd. *See also p236.*

Montparnasse & beyond

Bistros & brasseries

Restaurant Wadja
10 rue de la Grande-Chaumière, 6th (01.46.33.02.02). M° Vavin. **Open** 7.30-11pm Mon, Sat; noon-2.30pm,

One snack mind

The French have always been single-minded about cooking, and never more so than in Paris, where a new breed of restaurant is attracting an obsessive kind of diner. Reacting to food crises that led locals to bring in *traçabilité,* labelling the origins of meat ingredients, forward-thinking chefs are banishing the banal from their menus in favour of 'forgotten' vegetable varieties and pedigree chops. For those weary of tomatoes that have never seen the sun, **Rouge Tomate** (34 pl du Marché-St-Honoré, 1st, 01.42.61.16.09) shows how versatile this fruit can be with multicoloured salads (despite the name, its tomatoes need not be red) in summer and stewed dishes in winter. Rather than rely on imports, owner Valéry Sauzay persuaded local producers to grow unusual varieties, which his cooks turn into preserves. Inventive **Pomze** (*pictured; see p198*) is

equally creative with the humble apple, drawing on ancient varieties, putting to good use a selection of cider and Calvados that make wine seem positively pedestrian.

This singular approach also extends to meat. The recently opened **J'Go** (*see p195*) bases its menu on lamb from the Quercy region and exceptionally juicy Gascon pork (who decided pork had to be lean, anyway?),

while the neighbourhood bistro **Le Petit Canard** (19 rue Henry-Monnier, 9th, 01.49.70.07.95) proudly serves nearly every bit of the duck except the beak, all of it from the family farm. **Au Pied de Cochon** (*see p192*) was way ahead of its time: back in the distant days when Les Halles was the city's wholesale market, this institution was already serving pigs' trotters and its legendary onion soup all night long.

7.30-11pm Tue-Fri. **Average** €20. **Prix fixe**
€13.57. **Credit** MC, V. **Map** p407 G9.
Striking the right balance between simplicity and
sophistication, this creamy yellow bistro has
become a favourite destination for families, artists
from the next-door studios and foreign visitors. A
la carte you might find foie gras sautéed with
prunes, monkfish with bacon, seasonal game or a
classic *agneau de sept heures*, but you can opt for
the daily-changing *menu du jour*. With a choice of
two starters, two main courses (one meat, one fish)
and two desserts for only €13.57 (laudably not
rounded up), this surely has to be one of the best
bargains in town. This is also a place for some interesting wine discoveries – Madame will produce a
little-known white Burgundy, or an unfiltered
organic red Bergerac.

French

Apollo
3 pl Denfert-Rochereau, 14th (01.45.38.76.77).
M°/RER Denfert Rochereau. **Open** noon-3pm, 8-
midnight daily. **Prix fixe** €20. **Lunch menu** €18.
Credit AmEx, DC, MC, V. **Map** p407 H10.
From the same team that conceived Quai Ouest, this
high-design restaurant in the former RER station of
Denfert Rochereau brings a breath of novelty into a
staid part of town. The decor fits nicely with the
original design, but the menu is firmly 21st century.
Modern takes on comfort food include herring caviar
and potatoes, *blanquette de coquilles St-Jacques*, and
braised beef with carrots. The food is good and generously served, including desserts of pineapple and
bananas sautéed in vanilla-flavoured rum.

The 7th & the 15th

Bistros & brasseries

Le Troquet
21 rue François-Bonvin, 15th (01.45.66.89.00).
M° Sèvres-Lecourbe. **Open** noon-2.30pm, 7.30-11pm
Mon-Thur; noon-2.30pm, 7.30-11.30pm Fri, Sat.
Closed 1wk May, 3wks Aug, 1wk Dec. **Prix fixe**
Dinner €30, €37. **Lunch menu** €22, €26. **Credit**
MC, V. **Map** p406 D8.
After polishing his technique in Christian Constant's
kitchens, the burly Christian Etchebest took over
this bistro from his uncle. Decorated with 1930s light
fixtures and a proud Crillon certificate, the restaurant feels deceptively old-fashioned. If Etchebest's
Basque-inspired cooking has country touches, his
style is modern. From a brief but tempting lunch
menu, start with fresh goat's pastry,
sprinkled with Espelette pepper and served with
just-cooked red cabbage. Vegetable soup turns out
to be a creamy, cardamom-scented blend, which you
ladle yourself on to foie gras and a spoonful of *crème
fraîche*. Both mains are stunning: a thick tuna steak
wrapped in cured ham with a rich squash purée; a
plump farm chicken breast stuffed with tapenade

comes with cabbage cooked with juniper, pork and
olive oil. Desserts are less remarkable.

Le Voltaire
*27 quai Voltaire, 7th (01.42.61.17.49). M° Rue du
Bac.* **Open** 12.30-2.30pm, 7.30-10.30pm Tue-Sat.
Closed 1wk Feb, 1wk May, Aug. **Average** €30.
Credit MC, V. **Map** p407 G6.
With its perfect riverside setting, the Voltaire might
be just another tourist-led Parisian bistro, but past
the velvet curtains, after Antoine has escorted you
to one of the cosy tables, you realise that this is a
chic spot whose regulars treat it like a private club.
Ladies are greeted with a kiss on the hand, guests
are lovingly guided through the wide-ranging carte.
Opt for an exemplary bowl of lamb's lettuce and
beetroot salad, or a shining, golden *feuilleté* encas-
ing fresh and tangy goat's cheese. Lobster omelette
is just the sort of luxury (€41) that Le Voltaire does
so well; creamy and thick with firm morsels of shellfish. A tasty *sauté de lapin* is a real country treat,
too. An expensive but exquisite lunch is accompanied by raspberry-scented, chilled Chinon (€29.50).

French

L'Ami Jean
27 rue Malar, 7th (01.47.05.86.89). M° Invalides.
Open noon-2pm, 7pm-midnight Tue-Sat. Closed
Aug. **Average** €18. **Prix fixe** €28. **Credit** MC, V.
Map p407 D6.
This long-running Basque address has become a hit
since the arrival of La Régalade's former sous-chef,
Stéphane Jégo. Excellent bread from Poujauran, a
street away, is a perfect nibble when slathered with
a tangy, herby *fromage blanc* – as are starters of
sautéed baby squid on a bed of ratatouille, and little rolls of aubergine stuffed with perfectly seasoned
braised lamb. Tender veal shank comes de-boned
with a lovely side of baby onions and broad beans
with tiny cubes of ham, while house-salted cod is
soaked, sautéed and doused with an elegant vinaigrette. There is a great wine list, including a Cahors
at €15, and some lovely Brana eau de vie should you
linger – a party spirit sets in as the night grows long.

L'Atelier de Joël Robuchon
5 rue de Montalembert, 7th (01.42.22.56.56).
M° Rue du Bac. **Open** 11.30am-3.30pm, 6.30pm-
midnight daily. **Average** €30. **Prix fixe** €97.
Credit MC, V. **Map** p407 G6.
The star chef is back, with a Paris take on a New York
coffee shop-cum-sushi-and-tapas bar. The lacquer
interior and the two U-shaped bars – you sit on stools
at a wenge wood counter by Pierre-Yves Rochon –
has sassy Left Bank chic. The food is fine, with a bit
of inspiration from L'Astrance (*see p196*) and
Spain's El Bulli. The menu is set into three different
formulas – start with caviar, Spanish ham, a large
seasonal salad, or maybe an assortment of the little
tasting plates including veal sweetbreads skewered
with a bay leaf twig and served with Swiss chard in
cream. Then, go classic (a steak), fanciful (*vitello*

tonnato, veal in tuna and anchovy sauce) or lush (sublime cannelloni of Bresse chicken and foie gras). Desserts are less inspired, the passion fruit soufflé with pistachio ice-cream the star.

Au Bon Accueil

14 rue de Monttessuy, 7th (01.47.05.46.11). M° Alma Marceau. **Open** noon-2.30pm, 7.30-10.30pm Mon-Fri. **Average** €28. **Prix fixe** €31. **Lunch menu** €27. **Credit** MC, V. **Map** p406 D6.

Since Jacques Lacipière opened this bistro in 1990 it has been one of the best deals of the 7th. A pleasant dining room, with big windows and nice lighting provides the setting for excellent updating of French classics. Start with a tasty *chaud-froid* combination of raw marinated sardines sandwiched between tiny, new spring leeks and a frazzle of deep-fried onion and chervil. To follow, rosé veal kidneys are attractively presented pyramid-style on fresh spinach, while a richly braised beef cheek in deep red wine sauce, cleverly offset by the tart flavours of stewed rhubarb, shows how Lacipière injects tradition with a few surprising touches. A relaxed atmosphere and courteous, conscientious staff make this an address to cherish only a few metres from the Eiffel Tower.

Le Café Constant

139 rue St-Dominique, 7th (01.47.53.73.34). M° Ecole Militaire or RER Pont de l'Alma. **Open** noon-2.30pm, 7-10.30pm Tue-Sat. **Average** €12. **Credit** MC, V. **Map** p406 D6.

It's at this simple and brightly lit neighbourhood cafe that you again discover the brilliance of chef Christian Constant, who went from the Crillon to the Violon d'Ingres. Some have found Constant's Violon squeaky, while this café purrs with good times, good food and good value. The blackboard menu changes constantly – if you're hungry, start with the peppery *pâté de campagne* or maybe the salmon-wrapped poached eggs in gelatin with salad, and follow with the steak, grilled steak tartare or calf's liver, all of with generous side dishes. For a lighter feed, begin with the green bean salad, and follow with pasta *au pistou* or salmon tartare. All of the food served here is fresh and flavourful, portions are more than fair and the wine list is a true gift, with a lovely Cahors for €14. No booking.

D'Chez Eux

2 av de Lowendal, 7th (01.47.05.52.55/www.chezeux. com). M° Ecole Militaire. **Open** noon-2.30pm, 7.30-10.30pm Mon-Sat. Closed 3wks Aug, 1wk Dec. **Average** €35. **Prix fixe** €100. **Lunch menu** €32, €34. **Credit** AmEx, DC, MC, V. **Map** p407 E7.

A warm welcome from the owner and long-serving staff are a prelude to a complimentary kir and a hunk of excellent *saucisson*. The cosseting, interlinked rooms feel comfortably provincial and the menu is an essay in a certain type of traditional French cuisine. Begin with either the salad trolley, which includes plump fresh anchovies, delicious long-cooked pearl onions plus other delicacies, or the equally tempting range of charcuterie. Mains include a guinea fowl *grand-mère*, served in a copper pan and carved at the table on its comfortable bed of potatoes, bacon and mushrooms. If the bird itself is slightly dry, the intensely flavoured jus compensates. An enormous slab of calf's liver is coated in a melting mixture of shallots and sharp vinegar. Tuck into the dessert trolley for a winning chocolate mousse, creamy vanilla ice-cream and an impressive collection of stewed fruits.

Haute cuisine

L'Arpège

84 rue de Varenne, 7th (01.45.51.47.33/www.alain-passard.com). M° Varenne. **Open** noon-2.30pm, 8-10.30pm Mon-Fri. **Average** €100. **Prix fixe** €320. **Credit** AmEx, DC, MC, V. **Map** p407 F6.

Alain Passard's devotees are willing to overlook the surprisingly cramped conditions for his unique way with food. Outsiders feel they're paying more for his ideas than for the ingredients themselves. Take his famous €60 beetroot, baked in a pyramid of coarse grey Guérande sea salt. You'll never taste a beetroot this good – but the technique, as explained by a chatty waiter, is simple. You can opt for one all-vegetable and one fish meal à la carte – Passard no longer cooks with red meat. A starter of mussels in two froths – one made with nasturtiums, the other with herbs – is the kind of silky delight you expect from haute cuisine. The turbot is cooked over low heat for two hours yet shows no dryness, while vegetables from Passard's garden outside Paris retain their crunchiness and are served with a sprinkling of couscous in Moroccan argania oil. The sommelier selects intriguing white wines by the glass (€13-€20), but at an overall for €400-plus for two you might like to see more effort made on the extras.

International

Odori

18 rue Letellier, 15th (01.45.77.88.12). M° La Motte-Picquet Grenelle or Avenue Emile Zola. **Open** noon-3pm, 7pm-10.30pm Tue-Sun. Closed 2wks Dec. **Average** €17. **Credit** V, MC. **Map** p406 C8.

It's out of the way, hidden down an obscure street, yet it's perpetually packed with Korean diners. A sublime starter of steak tartare is worth the trek alone: ice-cold meat, scented with sesame oil and textured with slivers of Fuji apple, raw garlic and a raw egg, is fresh and cleanly prepared. Follow this with a comforting beef-and-leek soup, a Korean staple just hot and spicy enough. The classic Korean barbecue comes with the usual side dishes of kimchi and various root vegetables, marinated in vinegar or tossed in the same lively chilli paste. Korean beef arrives sizzling on a hot plate surrounded by a moat of sweet, but mild stock. Wear machine-washable clothes. Service is friendly, but harried, amid the pungent smoke from the sizzling, open grills.

Eat, Drink, Shop

Cafés & Bars

Paris refreshes the parts other cities cannot reach.

De la Ville Café.
See p221.

For all the 21st-century constraints of time, television and euro inflation, Paris is still a café society. Stroll into any of the capital's 10,000 establishments – at sunrise, say, or in the dead of night – and you are soon lulled into thinking that this is a city that never works, let alone sleeps. You can always get a drink.

Where and how to do so depend on taste and time of day. The term 'café', used in Paris since 1672, can cover a multitude of sins. There is the traditional corner bar, with its zinc counter and local clientele. At this grass-roots level, across-the-board rules are soon established: a draught beer, or *pression*, is served in 25cl measures as a *demi*, and costs €2-€3. It's cheaper to drink at the counter than be served at table, cheaper inside than on the terrace, and cheaper before 10pm when a *tarif de nuit* might be imposed. Wine in three colours is similarly ubiquitous, and coffee comes as a small, strong espresso unless otherwise stated. Even the most modest of the many trendy or expat establishments across town also offer happy hours.

Nearly every café serves at least a sandwich or three, most run to salads and meaty mains. For the more sturdy brasserie and noble bistro, food is as essential to trade as drink, and those just wishing to imbibe there will pay more for the social nicety of aproned-and-waistcoated service. Tipping is optional, usually a few coins left in the silver dish.

Such café customs would have been familiar to the pre-war arty set of Montparnasse, to the political intriguers of the late 18th century, to Picasso and Braque of the early 20th, and to the post-war Sartre circle of St-Germain. All met and mused over social and artistic change in the cafés of Paris. Since the early 1990s, the change has not been in art, literature or politics but in the bars themselves. A hip crowd converging on rue Oberkampf and Ménilmontant created a scene around the classic retro **Café Charbon** and its satellites, free of café cliché, infused with up-to-date DJ sounds and big on cocktails. Simultaneously, bunches of Brits and Irish began to set up bars in Paris. The Frog &

Eat, Drink, Shop

Rosbif (www.frogpubs.com) rugger-and-roast-dinner chain popularised Anglo pub custom; the Hip Bars crowd (www.hip-bars.com) and its various associates and offshoots established cool bars across town (**Stolly's**, **Zéro Zéro**), at which drinking and music were paramount. Bar crawling became a popular sport.

The slow crossover of Ménilmontant movers and booze-soaked, music-bothered Brits has seen scores of cool bars blossom over the 11th and in the Marais, around Pigalle, Abbesses, Belleville and obscure blobs of the 20th.

While the north and east thrive, the Left Bank still has its *intello* spots, the west sits swank and glitz. And everyone still has their favourite bar, whatever the corner, custom or constraints, somewhere to linger and ponder aloud. Anything otherwise would be antisocial.

The Louvre, Palais-Royal & Les Halles

Le Café des Initiés
3 pl des Deux-Ecus, 1st (01.42.33.78.29). M° Louvre Rivoli or Les Halles. **Open** 8am-1am Mon-Sat. **Credit** AmEx, MC, V. **Map** p404 H5.
Once a crumbling corner café, now a designer hangout, Le Café des Initiés is a top spot for a trendy tipple. The room is lined with ergonomic red banquettes, a long zinc bar provides character and sleek black articulated lamps peer down from the ceiling. Dotted around the windowsills are tall, slender vases filled with fresh, scented lilies. The friendly staff and central location have helped put this place firmly on the aperitif map.

Le Comptoir
37 rue Berger, 1st (01.40.26.26.66). M° Les Halles. **Open** noon-2am Mon-Thur, Sun; noon-3am Fri, Sat. **Credit** MC, V. **Map** p404 J5.
Amid the busy commerce of Les Halles, Le Comptoir is an oasis of calm overlooking the gardens behind St-Eustache church. The decor is Moroccan to the last detail: deep-red rugs, coloured-glass chandeliers, low-slung leather stools and banquettes piled high with cushions. A young, worldly crowd lounges around drinking *thé à la menthe* – served as it should be with pine nuts bobbing on top. Friendly service and a lethal selection of cocktails make a perfect spot for leisurely drinking. Attractive Franco-Moroccan menu, too.

Le Fumoir
6 rue de l'Amiral-de-Coligny, 1st (01.42.92.00.24). M° Louvre Rivoli. **Open** 11am-2am daily. Closed 2wks Aug. **Credit** AmEx, MC, V. **Map** p404 H6.
This elegant bar directly opposite the Louvre has now become a bit of a Parisian institution: inside neo-colonial fans whirr lazily, oil paintings adorn the walls and even the bar staff seem to have been included in the interior decorator's sketches. A sleek

crowd sipping Martinis or browsing the papers at the long mahogany bar (originally from a Chicago speakeasy) gives way to young professionals in the restaurant and pretty young things in the library. It can feel a little try-hard and well-behaved, but some expertly mixed cocktails and a little friendly flirting with the PRs on the prowl are guaranteed to take the edge off the evening.

Hemingway Bar at the Ritz
The Ritz, 15 pl Vendôme, 1st (01.33.43.16.30.30). M° Madeleine or Concorde. **Open** 6.30pm-2am Tue-Sat. Closed 3wks Aug. **Credit** AmEx, DC, MC, V. **Map** p403 F5.
This much lauded bar has become a cocktailers' cliché, but that's because it's simply one of the loveliest places in Paris to do drinkies. The dark wood, muffled laughter, black-and-white photos of Papa H and the old-school charm of Colin the head barman and lovely Ludo his second, make the bar a cocoon from the horrors of the outside world. Leather seating and five-star service (a glass of berry-scented water appears within 30 seconds of arrival) preface cocktails are as near to alcoholic nirvana as possible – not least the divine raspberry Martini. Pulling in its fair share of characters, honeymooners and expense-account nerds, it's also a wonderful place to see what the human race does in its spare time. Opened across the corridor is the Cambon Bar: original Ritz bar, done up as it was back in its '20s heyday. *See p222* **Hot hotel haunts**.

Kong
1 rue du Pont-Neuf, 1st (01.40.39.09.00). M° Pont Neuf. **Open** noon-2am Mon-Sat. **Credit** AmEx, MC, V. **Map** p408 J6.
Philippe Starck's latest addition to the Paris scene is, predictably, one of the city's hottest places to do cocktails, ideally located on the top two floors of the Kenzo building overlooking the Pont Neuf. The bright mishmash interior is manga-inspired with

The best Terraces

Le Café du Marché
Lounge around with the smart set in the 7th (*see p237*).

Le Dada
Art-inspired socialising (*see p223*).

Le Jemmapes
Canalside tables – dangle your feet in the water (*see p233*).

Le Trésor
No traffic, just trendies (*see p229*).

Tsé
Sun-trap roof terrace (*see p224*).

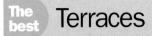

O'SULLIVANS
Irish Pubs Paris
everything you never expected ...
... WITHOUT THE USUAL BULL !

for a full on O'Sullivans experience visit :

 O'Sullivans café bar **1 Boulevard Montmartre 75002 Paris**
tel **01.40.26.73.41** metro line **8/9** stop **grands boulevards**
and

 O'Sullivans by the mill **92 Boulevard de Clichy 75018 Paris**
tel **01.42.52.24.94** metro line **2** stop **Blanche**

website : www.osullivans-pubs.com

lots of neon, Hello Kitty knick-knacks, comfy grey leather sofas and rocking chairs at the main dining tables, best avoided after a few too many *coupes*. The best bet is to perch at the long bar, flirt with the too-beautiful-to-bartend staff and order an excellent vodkatini or three. After dark you can make a music suggestion with each order – at weekends they somehow carve out a tiny dancing space for the trendy crowd to strut their stuff on. Wear lots of labels and try your best to look cool while half-cut.

Opéra & Grands Boulevards

Le Café Noir
*65 rue Montmartre, 2nd (01.40.39.07.36). M°
Sentier.* **Open** 8am-2am Mon-Sat. **Credit** AmEx, DC, MC, V. **Map** p404 J5.
Justifiably buzzing and enticingly kitsch corner bar, noir in name, scarlet in tone and brash in attitude. A framed Gainsbourg portrait and citation exhort 'Music Above All', although they're fighting for your attention with leopard-spotted bicycles, reindeer-antlered fishheads and dinky hanging baskets of papier-mâché lightshades, offset by a tiled bar counter – and all of it the size of a communal changing cubicle at the local baths. The clientele make the Noir nice and naughty, bright, bitchy and boho, forever picking up on the giggling conversation on the next banquette or prized pavement table. Modest lunchtime menu, too.

Le Coeur Fou
*55 rue Montmartre, 2nd (01.42.33.91.33). M°
Sentier.* **Open** 4pm-2am Mon-Sat. **No credit cards.**
Map p404 J4.
Be sure to arrive here early for a chance of some air-kissing space at the bar, as the hipsters, bohos and chancers who pack this place out start their soirées

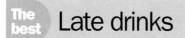

The best Late drinks

Le Bar
Quiet, dark, discreet and sexy (*see p236*).

Le Connétable
Oh-so-Paris place at which to get wrecked and fumble around at 1am (*see p227*).

Le Crocodile
More than 250 attitude-free cocktails on offer till late, late, late (*see p235*).

The Highlander
Quiet post-work pint turns into sunrise session – again and again (*see p236*).

La Taverne de Nesle
Something for everyone when you want to keep going all night (*see p237*).

while the rest of us are still staring into space at the office. It's ever-so-slightly self-consciously cool, but the squishy sofas, eye-grabbing canvases and masses of mingling make a night at Le Coeur Fou feel like a particularly fun gallery opening. Some of the lines overheard here can be works of art in themselves, and the stiff slush puppies and generous measures make everyone feel like the next big thing.

De la Ville Café
*34 bd Bonne-Nouvelle, 10th (01.48.24.48.09). M°
Bonne Nouvelle.* **Open** 11am-2am daily. **Credit** MC, V. **Map** p404 J4.
A former clip joint opened four years ago by the Charbon crew and other Ménilmontant movers (*see also p228* **Operation Oberkampf**), De la Ville has brought good news to Bonne Nouvelle. A recent expansion and refurb have upped the ante, so much so that the in-crowd is migrating north of the Marais to this otherwise ignored quarter. Note the recent arrival of a velvet rope guarding the large terrace. Inside, the distressed walls and hippy feel hang on, but the opulent new fittings and curvy club section at the back have become the hippest place at which to bag a table. A grand staircase leads to a first-floor lounge and exhibition space, and the interior is ambitious and arty with a fashion edge – Agnès b even designed the staff aprons. After elevating the 11th to bar legend, can the crew transform the 10th, and bring a café boom back to the boulevards?

Footsie
10-12 rue Daunou, 2nd (01.42.60.07.20). M° Opéra.
Open noon-2.30pm, 6pm-2am Mon-Thur; noon-2.30pm, 6pm-4am Fri, Sat. **Credit** AmEx, MC, V.
Map p403 G4.
The Footsie is based on an elementary play on words, and a principle so sound it should be floated on the stock market itself: bar prices modelled on shares which rise and fall every four minutes depending on how many people buy them. Popular brews and anything remotely stylish go up, cocktails you wouldn't touch with a rusty bargepole stay cheap. Footsie goads you into mixing your drinks and playing City whizz-kids till dawn. A whisky can fluctuate between €5.80 and €10.50 in seconds. A number of drinkers look up at the screens, scanning for bargains, most don't, waiting for the occasional crash and windfall booze-up.

Le Next
*17 rue Tiquetonne, 2nd (01.42.36.18.93). M°
Etienne Marcel.* **Open** 6pm-5am Mon-Sat. **Credit** MC, V. **Map** p404 J5.
Where once the simple old Baragouin billiard bar used to rock unpretentiously now swings the somewhat forced exotica of Le Next. Gaudy sheets billow from the ceiling, leopard-spot beermats brighten the dark bar counter, complemented by the occasional mounted giraffe. In the sunken chat-room through the dimly lit, narrow, intimate bar area a sign proclaims 'I Love My Wife', making you wish that everything was dimly lit instead of just dim, but it

doesn't distract a youngish, smart, non-discerning clientele freed from the onus of fidelity for the time being. Quasimodo could score here, no sweat. Happy hours help, as does a swift and discreet bar staff. Hippyish guff blows in from the DJ at the decks set up by the door.

Somo

168 rue Montmartre, 2nd (01.40.13.08.80/www.hip-bars.com). M° Sentier or Grands Boulevards. **Open** noon-2am Mon-Fri; 6pm-4am Sat. **Credit** AmEx, DC, MC, V. **Map** p404 J4.

The thoroughbred among the expat-owned Hip Bars stable, Somo is a sleeker, more grown-up offering than the Lizard Lounge (*see p229*), Stolly's (*see p229*) and The Bottle Shop (5 rue Trousseau, 11th, 01.43.14.28.04). Popular with suits from the nearby Bourse after work, it chills out later on in the evening and at weekends when bright young things arrive to party amid the fairy lights, aided and abetted by well-mixed €9 Absolut-based cocktails. Full menu, too, the €13.90 dinner a snip, the €9 bar snacks not so. Weekend DJ spots here have become new fixture on the Saturday-night circuit.

Hot hotel haunts

It's perhaps the possibility of slipping upstairs to a suite after a few too many that makes hotel bars such sexy places, or maybe it's the likelihood of spying an A-lister in the lavs. Whatever the reason, hotel bars are some of the city's best places to get messy.

The daddy of all hotel bars, the **Hemingway Bar at the Ritz** (*see p219*), is a wonderfully civilised place at which to get smashed. Bartenders Colin and Ludo dispense fabulous cocktails, compliments and flowers for the ladies in a gloriously suave manner. A little more lively, the refurbed **Bar Cambon** opposite (entrance at 38 rue Cambon, 1st, 01.43.16.30.90) is a good spot for posh partying and while the **Bar Vendôme** at the front of the hotel is still a little grim, the terrace is sublime in summer.

Stunning sundowners can also be found on the roof terrace of the **Hôtel Raphaël** (17 av Kléber, 16th, 01.53.64.32.00) and the interior bar, while not the prettiest in Paris, is the place at which to live out any Jane Birkin fantasies: Gainsbourg apparently wrote many of his songs propping up the bar here.

Equally sexy, the champagne bar **Le Dokhan's** (Hôtel Trocadéro Dokhan's, 117 rue Lauriston, 16th, 01.53.65.66.99) is the perfect choice for amorous encounters. Think high ceilings, ornate gilt, decorative panelling and service so discreet it's practically invisible. Perfect cocktails, too.

Those looking for something a little less subtle should head to the **V** (Hotel Four Seasons George V, 31 av George-V, 8th, 01.49.52.70.06) for a bling-bling beverage or three. It's sure swank at the Cinq. Higher on the see-and-be-seen scale is **Le Bar du Plaza** (Hôtel Plaza Athénée, 25 av Montaigne, 8th, 01.53.67.66.65), a cocktail bunny's most outré fantasy, with flattering lighting, high chairs offering maximum leg-crossing

exposure and ridiculous drinks. Avoid the savoury concoctions or the vodka jellies and go for an old-fashioned but expertly mixed standard or join the PR crowd in a Fashion Ice: alcoholic ice lollies that offer maximum flirting and slurping potential.

Traditionalist trendies still make a beeline for the **Costes** (239 rue St-Honoré, 1st, 01.42.44.50.00), for champers and air kisses, but the new hot hotel bar can be found at the **Murano Urban Resort** (13 bd du Temple, 3rd, 01.42.71.20.00). With an inventive interior, glamourous rather than glacial staff and great drinks (go for the Red Fruits and Love combo: vodka and summer fruits served in test tubes) this is the place at which to get rip-roaringly drunk, take a room and get any rock star fantasies out of your system. Until the next time.

Le Tambour

41 rue Montmartre, 2nd (01.42.33.06.90). M°
Sentier. **Open** 6pm-6.30am daily. **Credit** MC, V.
Map p404 J5.
Classic nighthawks' bar decked out with vintage
transport chic, its slatted wooden banquettes and
bus-stop-sign bar stools occupied by chatty regulars
who give the 24-hour clock its best shot. Neither
tatty nor threatening, Le Tambour comprises a
small counter area of friendly banter twixt staff and
souses, a busy conservatory and a long dining room
memorable for its retro Métro map from station
Stalingrad and iconic image of Neil Armstrong.
Pride of place is given to a philosophical quotation
about this being the perfect match of urban and
bucolic. Bang on, Tambour, bang on.

Le Truskel

10 rue Feydeau, 2nd (01.40.26.59.97). M° Bourse.
Open 8pm-2am Tue, Wed; 8pm-5.30am Thur-Sat.
Closed Aug. **Credit** AmEx, MC, V. **Map** p404 H4.
Oirish meets indie at this pub-cum-disco a stone's
throw from the stock exchange. The formula is quite
simple: an excellent selection of beers, fruity Belgian
and quality Czech included, attends to your throat
while a complete repertoire of Britpop assaults your
ears and, if you're sitting in the dark dog-leg bar
area, forces you to watch the videos, too. The back
area is for dancing, just like a school disco.
Malcontent expats love it, but not as much as French
boys who cannot hold their Murphy's, and for whom
a shoulder-hug and a communal wail of *Live Forever*
somehow allows access to a secret club. To add to
the pretence, a bar-bell rings for no reason whatso-
ever, causing first-time UK visitors to down their
drinks in one and dive for the bar.

Champs-Elysées & western Paris

Bindi

63 av Franklin-D.-Roosevelt, 8th (01.53.898.66.66).
M° St-Philippe du-Roule. **Open** 8-11pm Mon-Sat;
noon-3pm, 8pm-2am Tue-Fri. **Credit** AmEx, DC, MC,
V. **Map** p403 E4.
Rumour has it that Bindi's decor was modelled on
the nearby Buddha Bar, and you can see why. This
likeable underdog has all the trappings of its more
illustrious peer, though, thankfully, none of the gold-
chained punters to tarnish the furniture. It's essentially a classy Indian restaurant with a bar at the
back – a hybrid of Oriental bric-a-brac and neo-
kitsch – which plays host to relaxed trendsetters,
smitten couples and simpler folk who believe that
bars are basically about decent drinks and genuine
service. Perched above the lounge, DJs spin a blend
of ambient and down-tempo sounds.

Le Dada

12 av des Ternes, 17th (01.43.80.60.12). M° Ternes.
Open 6am-2am Mon-Sat; 6am-10pm Sun. **Credit**
AmEx, MC, V. **Map** p402 C3.

Nice and naughty **Le Café Noir**. *See p221.*

Perhaps the hippest café on this classy avenue in a
stuffy part of town, Le Dada is best known for its
well-placed, sunny terrace, but the kookily Dada-
influenced two-floor interior is ideal for a cheeky
afternoon tipple. The wood-block carved tables, and
the red walls provide a warm atmosphere for the
Parisian crowd which tends towards the well-heeled,
well-spoken and well, loaded. That said, the atmosphere is friendly and relaxed and if terracing is your
thing, you could happily spend a summer's day here.

Impala Lounge

2 rue de Berri, 8th (01.43.59.12.66). M° George V.
Open 9.30am-2am Tue-Sun. **Credit** AmEx, MC, V.
Map p402 D4.
Dubbed the 'African Bar' by regulars, this wannabe
hip spot hams up the colonial with zebra skins, tribal masks and a throne hewn from a tree trunk. Beer,
wine, tea and standard favourites can all be found
here, but best beverages are the cocktails, one of
which claims to boost a waning libido with its mystery mix of herbs and spices. It's not quite as cool as
it thinks it is, but at least it doesn't try too hard
either. DJs rock Sunday afternoon away. A snack-
and-mains menu includes ostrich.

Ladurée

75 av des Champs-Elysées, 8th (01.40.75.08.75/
www.laduree.fr). M° George V or Franklin D.
Roosevelt. **Open** 7.30am-midnight daily. **Credit**
AmEx, DC, MC, V. **Map** p402 D4.

Le Tambour. See p223.

Everything in this elegant tea room suggests decadence, from the 19th century-style interior to the service and the labyrinthine corridors that lead to the toilets. But what you came to this tea room for is not merely to wallow in bygone wealth: it's the teas, the pastries, and most of all, the hot chocolate. Thick, bitter, creamier than heaven, on first tasting it you will say to yourself: 'this is tar'. And so it is, but a rich, velvety tar that will leave you in the kind of stupor requisite for any afternoon of absolute lazing. Note that the original branch at 16 rue Royale (8th, 01.42.60.21.79) is more famed for its macaroons.

Nirvana

3 av Matignon, 8th (01.53.89.18.91). M° Franklin D. Roosevelt. **Open** 10am-4pm Mon-Thur, Sun; 10am-5am Fri, Sat. **Credit** AmEx, DC, MC, V. **Map** p403 E4.

Ever so hip and beautiful, the Nirvana is the type of place that will makes even the H&M-clad feel perfectly groomed and labelled-up – at least after a few brightly coloured cocktails. While the door folk can seem a little intimidating, the vibe inside is actually quite friendly, so it's worth brazening it out on the pavement to gain access to the inner sanctum, all acid brights, soft edges and sexy types shimmying on the dance floor to a hip soundtrack – they even have their own CD. An ex-Ritz chef runs the restaurant, so expect top-notch food at prices to match.

Petit Défi de Passy

18 av du Président-Kennedy, 16th (01.42.15.06.76/ www.defidepassy.com). M° Passy/RER Kennedy Radio France . **Open** 10am-2am Wed-Sat; 11am-midnight Sun. **Credit** AmEx, DC, MC, V. **Map** p406 B6.

In permanent rebellion against its posh postcode, this refreshingly no-fuss bar-restaurant challenges the local chi-chi rule, jollying along friendly students and English teachers through happy hour in a distinct whiff of late adolescence. It's positively bursting with toff totty (albeit rather on the young side) and the best bit is, it's exceedingly cheap. Guys can impress the fillies by buying a bottle of Absolut for €60 and keeping it behind the bar with their name on: not only might they gain entry into gilded youth, at the very least they can stake a claim in the 16th.

Tsé

78 rue d'Auteuil, 16th (01.40.71.11.90/www.groupe-bertrand.com). M° Porte d'Auteuil. **Open** 10am-2am Mon, Sun; 10am-3am Tue-Thur; 10am-4am Fri, Sat. **Credit** AmEx, MC, V.

The Asian fusion formula has even crept out as far as villagey Auteuil, a hot bed of snooty old people and thirtysomething hipsters in desperate need of a hotspot to call their own. Now they have it in the form of Tsé, a stylish sight squeezed into the old railway station. A Franco-Sino-Japanese bar-restaurant-club, it peddles kudos and alcoholic regeneration, at a price, to a vogueish clientele bearing sharp specs and media manners, talking into their dinky mobile phone ear-pieces rather than to their drinking partners. The enticing dark-red and gilt interior is rampant with Oriental lanterns, tassels and carved wood, while the drinks menu lapses into poncey Zen babble. To contemplate it, there's a handy Tibetan bed. Although a bit far up its own concept, this is a relaxing and opulent neighbourhood spot, with attentive pretty-boy staff, live jazz, funk DJs, sushi nibbles, simply fantastic Asian-styled cocktails and an utterly glorious sun-trap roof terrace.

Montmartre & Pigalle

Le Cyrano

3 rue Biot, 17th (01.45.22.53.34). M° Place de Clichy.
Open 9am-2am Mon-Fri; 5pm-2am Sat. **No credit cards. Map** p403 G2.

Once the finest football bar in France, the C has not lost its communal touch after a recent change of management. The missing scarves – hopefully dutifully mounted elsewhere – now give way to a series of bar scenes intricately created in papier-mâché, and allow the colourful tiling and tubas of the retro decor to shine through. A busy interior in which thesps from the nearby L'Européen theatre mingle with mechanics, students and layabouts reflects the multi-communal mix of the vicinity. A spot outside allows a view of the pedestrian flow along narrow rue Biot to and from its place de Clichy estuary.

La Divette de Montmartre

136 rue Marcadet, 18th (01.46.06.19.64). M° Lamarck Caulaincourt. **Open** 5pm-1am Mon, Fri-Sat; 3pm-1am Tue-Thur. **Credit** MC, V.

Serge, the barrel-bellied barman, runs this cavern of colourful nostalgia. Tucked away in Montmartre's hilly backstreets but worth the trek, this is Serge's *Recherche du temps perdu* in album cover, poster and table-football form. Beatles albums line up over the bar, Rolling Stones ones under it and an Elvis clock ticks in between – this decorative trinity is interrupted by *yé-yé* pop tack, the occasional green of St-Etienne football iconography and an old red telephone box. On tap, Wieckse Witte, Affligem and Pelforth, and bar-room gossip of the days when Manu Chao were regulars.

La Fourmi

74 rue des Martyrs, 18th (01.42.64.70.35). M° Pigalle. **Open** 8.30am-1.30am Mon-Thur; 8.30am-3.30am Fri, Sat; 10am-1.30am Sun. **Credit** AmEx, MC, V. **Map** p404 H2.

Flavour of the month in many quarters, and rightly so. Set on the cusp of the 9th and 18th, a short (steep) walk from lively Abbesses and busy boulevard stroll to place Pigalle, La Fourmi is retro-industrial at its best. An old bistro has been converted for today's tastes, i.e. picture windows giving natural light and visual bustle to the spacious, roughshod sand-coloured main interior, the prime seats on the podiums at the back. The classic zinc bar counter is crowned by industrial lights, the ornately carved backbar featuring the odd titular ant. An excellent music policy and hip clientele – although they'd have to go some to beat the bar staff – ensure a pile of flyers, and this is as good a place as any to pick up what's happening in town this week. Leffe, Hoegaarden and Guinness seal the recommendation.

Francis Labutte

122 rue Caulaincourt, 18th (01.42.23.58.26). M° Lamarck Caulaincourt. **Open** 8.30am-1.30pm daily. **Credit** MC, V. **Map** p404 H1.

In hitting distance of the Sacré-Coeur, yet tucked away from the main drag of tourist traps up the hill, stands this chilled-out drinkery. A tasteful faux-antique decor hinting at rustic pretensions is somewhat undermined by the constant traffic along the neighbouring main road, but that said, it's worth planting yourself in the cosy nook of the heated terrace. The wine selection may be small, but this can hardly be said for the platters of cheese and charcuterie, well-chosen and moreish.

Economy-class banter below decks at **Les Etages**. *See p227.*

Lush

16 rue des Dames, 17th (01.43.87.49.46/
www.lushbars.com). M° Place de Clichy. **Open** 4pm-
2am Mon-Fri; noon-2am Sat, Sun. **Credit** MC, V.
Map p403 G1.
At a prime address in Batignolles, Lush is a sleek
lair for chilled-out drinking with a loyal clientele of
laid-back trendies. Soft grape purples and comfy
banquettes provide a suitable setting for inexpensive pints, well-chosen New World wines and delicious cocktails. Premiership football and rugby on
big-screen TV, and half-decent live music, drag punters from across the city. A sister operation is due to
open on rue St-Sébastien in the 11th.

Le Sancerre

35 rue des Abbesses, 18th (01.42.58.08.20). M°
Abbesses. **Open** 7am-2am Mon-Thur; 7am-4am Fri,
Sat; 9am-2am Sun. **Credit** MC, V. **Map** p404 H1.
Of the many choices along rue des Abbesses, this is
probably the most popular, its terrace invariably
full, its large dark-wood interior an attractive mix
between cool and cosy. Impressive draughts of
Paulaner, Grimbergen and Record line up alongside
Belgian bottled beauties such as Kriek and Mort
Subite; the standard cocktails, all €5.50 on Mondays,
are made with the same care as the tastefully presented food, a couple of *plats du jour* and a good
range of mains and salads. So, where's the catch?
Well, the service is teeth-grindingly slow, shocking
considering the rapid turnover; this is particularly
galling on the evenings when a well-meaning duo
will be murdering your favourite Roy O number.
Loudly. That heinous crime apart, pull up a chair.

Beaubourg & the Marais

Andy Wahloo

69 rue des Gravilliers, 3rd (01.42.71.20.38). M° Arts
et Métiers. **Open** noon-2am Mon-Sat. **Credit** AmEx,
DC, MC, V. **Map** p404 K5.
Proving that size really doesn't matter (this place
brings new meaning to the word 'bijou') a formida-
bly fashionable set crowd in here and fight for a coveted place on an upturned paint can (who needs a
divan when you've got Dulux?). Andy Wahloo – created by the people behind its neighbour 404 and
London's Momo and Sketch – is Arabic for 'I have
nothing'. From head to toe, it's a beautifully
designed venue crammed with Moroccan artefacts,
and enough colours to fill a Picasso. Quiet early on,
there's a surge around nine and the atmosphere
heats up as the night gets longer.

Chez Richard

37 rue Vieille-du-Temple, 4th (01.42.74.31.65).
M° St-Paul. **Open** 6pm-2am daily. Closed Aug.
Credit AmEx, DC, MC, V. **Map** p408 K6.
This spacious if somewhat discombobulating cocktail bar is set back from the street bustle of narrow
rue Vieille-du-Temple. A mish-mash of brash decor
fails to hide the fact that Chez Richard is set in an
old courtyard, laid out on four levels, whose most
convivial spot is at the long, leather-coated counter.
Here you can call up excellent if expensive (€9)
Caribbean and classic cocktails, and take in a soundtrack of similarly Latin provenance. Grimbergen is
a welcome curiosity on draught, albeit at an unwelcome price tag of €4.50 for a 25cl glass. No one could

quite explain the bronze dragon mounted above (aren't they meant to be Welsh?), but concept schmoncept, it's a fair place to kick off the evening.

Le Connétable

55 rue des Archives, 3rd (01.42.77.41.40). M° Hôtel de Ville or Rambuteau. **Open** 7pm-2am Mon-Sat. Closed Aug. **Credit** AmEx, DC, MC, V. **Map** p408 K6.

Look no further for the ultra-Parisian Piaf-and-pastis bar that you always hoped you'll stumble on. Le Connétable is one of those wonderfully rare spots where you can find the much vaunted joie de vivre and bonhomie the French are supposed to be famous for and is normally in rather short supply. Expect old geezers getting hammered on rough red, faded divas holding court in the corner, young couples getting fruity on a stuffing-free sofa and up-for-it locals chatting to anything with a pulse and the ability to slur. Best enjoyed after midnight.

Les Etages

35 rue Vieille-du-Temple, 4th (01.42.78.72.00). M° St-Paul. **Open** 3.30pm-2am daily. **Credit** MC, V. **Map** p408 K6.

Take Les Etages at its word. Below decks, the street-level bar is so cramped economy-class syndrome is inevitable. Two lines of low chairs and metal stool tables link drinkers into a conspiracy of Chinese whispers – privacy is at a premium. Space, forget it. Backsides contort to shape the needs of someone's idea of fashionable furniture, hands grasp cocktails (€7-€8.50) presented in clunky Coke glasses, fingers pick from a bowl of stickly-sweet nuts. All it needs is for a net of red ants to drop from the ceiling and it would be perfect torture TV. In the relatively airy upstairs, though, these same seats serve as a sounding board for squatting intellectuals with more calf muscle than brain cell by the end of the evening. Pseudo as hell, so lapped up by locals.

Vintage venues

Every bar in Paris serves wine, but some serve it more seriously than others. Serious snobs should join the glitterati of the wine world at **Les Enfants Rouges** (9 rue de Beauce, 3rd, 01.48.87.80.61), where an extensive list full of heavy hitters and glam producers will challenge the most demanding of wine buffs. The staff will happily help those more used to grabbing anything for a fiver from the supermarket shelf. Rhône wines have a particularly strong showing. Bordeaux enthusiasts should head to the Madeleine branch of the **L'Ecluse** chain (15 pl de la Madeleine, 8th, 01.42.65.34.69). Here, the pretty old-school bar and charming cellar provide the perfect backdrop for an afternoon spent setting the world to rights over some seriously good red.

The trad but trendy **Clown Bar** (114 rue Amelot, 11th, 01.43.55.87.35) is a long-established favourite, stuffed with circus memorabilia, Oberkampf escapees and some wonderful wines, especially those from the Loire. Quintessentially French, **Le Baron Bouge** (1 rue Théophile Roussel, 12th, 01.43.43.14.32) offers a wide and frequently changing selection, including unusual choices from the Rhône and delicious charcuterie to accompany them.

If you're looking for a little clever chat with your Condrieu then **La Belle Hortense** (31 rue Vieille-du-Temple, 4th, 01.48.04.71.60) is the place for you. Bookshop and bottle shop combined, drink anything from Guigal, the cult producer favoured here.

When you're thinking of heading bravely into the New World then your first port of call should be **Juveniles** (47 rue de Richelieu, 1st, 01.42.97.46.49), an ebullient little bar run by an enthusiastic Scottish oenophile, whose staff will steer you towards some interesting, offbeat choices. More New World choices can be picked up at **Wine and Bubbles** (3 rue Française, 1st, 01.44.76.99.84), a handy shop-cum-bar. There's food here too, plus a nominal corkage fee.

L'Etoile Manquante

34 rue Vieille-du-Temple, 4th (01.42.72.48.34/ www.cafeine.com). M° Hôtel de Ville or St-Paul. **Open** 9am-2am daily. **Credit** MC, V. **Map** p408 K6.
L'Etoile Manquante forms part of a small coterie of venues on Vieille-du-Temple owned and designed by Xavier Denamur (*see also* La Belle Hortense, *p227* **Vintage venues**) – and this one is definitely the hippest of the bunch. The cocktails are punchy, the traditional tipples just as good, the salads and cold snacks reasonably priced and tasty – but it's the design and buzz that are the big draws here. The decor is both trendy and comfortable, embellished with wonderful lighting and interesting art works spread over the walls. As ever with Denamur's places, no visit is complete without a trip to the lavatory. There, an electric train shuttles between cubicles, starlight beams down on you from the ceiling and a hidden camera films you washing your hands. Don't worry, though, the images aren't bound straight for TF1 – just watch the small screen set up on the wall behind you.

Operation Oberkampf

For a decade or more, the epicentre of Paris alternative cool has been the bar scene centred on a cluster of streets at the Ménilmontant end of rue Oberkampf. The reason is simple: a cheap area, boho locals and the Charbon phenomenon. With its classic interior and studiously cool service, the **Café Charbon** (*pictured*; *see p231*) struck gold by serving funkified brasserie fare and well-priced booze (it's still €3.50 a pint in happy hour). And before you could say 'bandwagon', bars were popping up all over the place. One moment, three pissed Frenchmen; the next, a scene. And although the local in-crowd is notoriously fickle, Charbon customers have stayed loyal.

You can still get a sense of rue Oberkampf vibe with a quick bar crawl – one that involves a grand total of five minutes walking. Begin, then, at the Charbon itself, where the decor is still a wow, a booth seat a comfortable pleasure, and the DJing up to the mark.

Leaving this ostentatious hipness behind you, across the road you'll find **La Mercerie** (No.98, 01.43.38.81.30), where beer is cheap and plentiful, and you can chatter away in cosy little alcoves as DJs spin reggae in the background. The beauty of this place is sheer simplicity. Once you can heave yourself away, take a right and go up the hill. On your right you'll see a huddle outside **Cithéa** (No.112, 01.40.21.70.95), more of a music venue where admission is either free or nominal. It's open till 5.30am, so pass on and come back. Another 20 metres uphill brings you to the bizarre **Le Styx** (No.126, 01.48.05.92.88), with its mad mural and crazy toilets. Crossing back over the road you'll find **Gecko** (No.133, 01.43.57.81.44), a pick-up joint done out in luminous yellow. Another couple of swifties sunk in here should put you in fine fettle for the Cithéa (despite its drink prices); there they even lay on inviting sofas for you to pass out on.

Lucy gets legless again at **Le Fanfaran**. *See p230.*

Lizard Lounge

18 rue du Bourg-Tibourg, 4th (01.42.72.81.34/ www.hip-bars.com). M° Hôtel de Ville. **Open** noon-2am daily. **Credit** MC, V. **Map** p408 K6.
Anglophone/phile, hetro favourite deep in the Marais, this pick-up joint provides lager in pint glasses (€6), strong, well-mixed cocktails (€7) by the bucketload and a viewing platform from which the beer-goggled can ogle their prey from a predominantly loud and lively bar area. Bare brick and polished woodwork are offset by the occasional lizard, but the main backdrop is provided by a trip-hop and house soundtrack of consistent quality, as happy hours upstairs and in the sweaty cellar sweetly dovetail at 8pm. Mercifully, considering the five straight hours of bargain boozing from 5pm, the downstairs dancefloor is tiny, a spatial strait-jacket for those uncoordinated or incapacitated through drink. You can show off your catch at the popular weekend brunch.

Le Petit Fer à Cheval

30 rue Vieille-du-Temple, 4th (01.42.72.47.47). M° St-Paul. **Open** 9am-2am daily. **Credit** AmEx, DC, MC, V. **Map** p404 K6.
If Glasgow's Horseshoe boasts the UK's longest bar counter, its Parisian counterpart contains one of the smallest to be found across the Channel. Certainly by Parisian standards it's small, and far too charming by half, a marble ring surrounded by old film and promotional posters and headed by an old clock and an ornate mirror backdrop. Everything is done by mirrors, in fact, because behind the glassy façade hides a friendly dining room lined with old Métro

benches, offering space, but not the scenery of the handful of small tables out front looking out onto Vieille-du-Temple bustle. In business since 1903, the Little Horseshoe enjoyed a retro makeover by Xavier Denamur and his team in the 1990s.

Stolly's

16 rue Cloche-Perche, 4th (01.42.76.06.76/www.hip-bars.com). M° Hôtel de Ville or St-Paul. **Open** 4.30pm-2am daily. **Credit** MC, V. **Map** p408 K6.
This seen-it-all drinking den has been in action since 1991, serving a mainly expat crowd with expert vodka tonics and old Velvets tunes for nights immemorial. The staff make the place, really, helping you feel like part of what passes for furniture, and smoothing an easy passage from arriving sober to sinking them relentlessly until you're stotious. A summer terrace eases libation, as do long happy hours, but don't expect anyone to faff about with food. There's football on TV to compensate.

Le Trésor

5-7 rue du Trésor, 4th (01.42.71.35.17). M° St-Paul. **Open** 9am-2am daily. **Credit** AmEx, MC, V. **Map** p408 K6.
Still pulling in the punters after years as a top Marais tipple spot, Le Trésor has had a facelift. The luminous, eye-catching pinks, greens, whites and greys, and the concave fairground mirrors may be garish, but this hasn't deterred the mixed crowd of hotties. The food and wine (lunch, dinner and Sunday brunch) have a distinct Franco-Italian twist, and the lavatories are definitely worth a gander, with live goldfish swimming in the cisterns. Don't worry, you can't flush them away.

Le Caveau des
Oubliettes.
See p234.

Bastille & eastern Paris

China Club

*50 rue de Charenton, 12th (01.43.43.82.02/www.
chinaclub.cc). M° Bastille or Ledru-Rollin.* **Open** 7pm-
2am Mon-Thur, Sun; 7pm-3am Fri, Sat. Closed Aug.
Credit AmEx, MC, V. **Map** p409 M7.

With huge Chesterfields, low lighting and a sexy
long bar, it's impossible not to feel glamorous here.
In fact, if you've had a few, it's hard not to drop into
a gentle snooze. Yes, this is the domain of the
extremely relaxed gentlemen's club, all with a distinctly colonial Cohibas-and-cocktails feel. They
take their Martinis seriously but if you're more
Pussy Galore than James Bond you can't go wrong
with a well-made champagne cocktail. This is also
ideal seduction territory – although China Club is
equally suited to a civilised hands-off first date.
Those unconcerned by brewers' droop should plan
to schedule any rendezvous during the inhibition-
demolishing happy hour (7-9pm).

Le Fanfaron

*6 rue de la Main-d'Or, 11th (01.49.23.41.14). M°
Ledru-Rollin.* **Open** 6pm-2am Tue-Sat. Closed 2wks
Aug. **No credit cards**. **Map** p409 N7.

On a small backstreet, tucked away from Bastille,
Le Fanfaron (named after Dino Risi's cult 1962
movie) is the favoured haunt for musically inclined
retro dudes. Envious buffs come from far and wide
for owner Xavier's personal collection of rare film
soundtracks, while others pop in for the cheap
(€2.30) beer and bustle. The decor is an ode to kitsch-

cool with Stones and Iggy memorabilia, second-
hand furniture, 1960s film posters, wooden panelling
and Lucy the legless mannequin who props up one
side of the bar. At weekends Mr Raw spins LPs into
the wee hours and if too much cheap booze gets the
stomach acids rising, try the goat's cheese or an
entire *saucisson* for a measly hunger-quashing €4.

Le Lèche-Vin

13 rue Daval, 11th (01.43.55.98.91). M° Bastille.
Open 7pm-2am Mon-Sat; 7pm-midnight Sun. **Credit**
MC, V. **Map** p409 M7.

An old Bastille stand-by, best known for its kitsch
religious figures and pornographic pictures decking
out the toilet, tee hee. Yet the iconic imagery and
paper-mâché creations – e.g. the witch with archery
targets for nipples dangling over the bar – should
not distract from the fact that this is a damn good
bar even without the blasphemy. Quality Belgian
beers on tap and in bottles pass across the zinc
counter with regularity, to a bohemian clientele of
all ages and hairstyles, who prefer to avoid the sub-
urbanites and tourists strolling down bar-starred
but past-it rue de Lappe nearby. Generous happy
hours till 10pm usher in a €3.50 price tag on cocktails, and ensure lively banter till the early hours.

La Liberté

*196 rue du Fbg-St-Antoine, 12th (01.43.72.11.18).
M° Faidherbe Chaligny.* **Open** 9am-2am Mon-Fri;
11am-2am Sat, Sun. **Credit** MC, V. **Map** p409 N7.

By day La Lib is a relaxed spot to muse over a *plat
du jour*. The decor is a little primitive, to be sure,
and rubbing elbows is inevitable, but convivial is

Pop In

105 rue Amelot, 11th (01.48.05.56.11). M° St-Sébastien Froissart. **Open** 6.30pm-1.30am Tue-Sun. Closed Aug. **Credit** AmEx, MC, V. **Map** p408 L5.

The Pop In seems to be a contradiction in terms, or at the very least, an exercise in postmodern irony. A bar so uncool that it is in fact cutting-edge, a place that is so hip it seems tragic – Pop In is all things to all men. Since it hosted a Christian Dior after-show party and was subsequently colonised by fashion-hangers on, the Pop In has won a reputation as a place that doesn't care, doesn't try, but manages to be cool anyway. It's scruffy, cheap and the staff are genuinely nice. Add in a cellar bar that alternates between an open-mic night and a club for DJs and you have a recipe for a top night out.

North-eastern Paris

L'Atmosphère

49 rue Lucien-Sampaix, 10th (01.40.38.09.21). M° Gare de l'Est or Jacques Bonsergent. **Open** 5pm-midnight Mon; 10am-2am Tue-Fri; noon-2am Sat; noon-midnight Sun. **No credit cards. Map** p404 L3.

L'Atmosphère remains at the centre of the Canal St-Martin renaissance and sums up the spirit of the area. Parisians of all kinds chat, read and gaze from the waterside terrace while, within, the simple, tasteful interior, animated conversation and cheapish drinks provide entertainment enough. It's always packed, but brave the crowds on Sundays for the early-evening world and experimental music slots.

Café Charbon

109 rue Oberkampf, 11th (01.43.57.55.13/www.nouveaucasino.net). M° Parmentier or Ménilmontant. **Open** 9am-2am Mon-Thur, Sun; 9am-4am Fri, Sat. **Credit** MC, V. **Map** p405 N5.

This beautifully restored belle-époque building sparked the Oberkampf nightlife phenomenon, its booths, mirrors, chandeliers and adventurous music policy putting trendy locals at their ease, capturing the essence of café culture spanning each end of the 20th century. It was cool, it was grand. Fine dining, sound DJing, retro chic and high ceilings. After 15 years or more, the formula still works, inspiring scores of bar options nearby; *see p228* **Operation Oberkampf**. The management made a killing, opened the equally popular Nouveau Casino night-club next door (*see p329*) and plan to repeat the domino effect with the recently groovified De la Ville Café (*see p221*) in the 10th.

Café Chéri(e)

44 bd de la Villette, 19th (01.42.02.02.05). M° Belleville. **Open** 8am-2pm daily. **Credit** MC, V. **Map** p405 M3.

This splendid DJ bar (*see p327*) has expanded its brief and its opening hours to become an all-day café – without watering down any of the funky chic that keeps it well ahead of the pack after dark. Set in a rather gloomy corner of Belleville, the Chéri(e) sparkles with wit and invention. Large sealed jars

the word you're looking for. Good food too, a notch above the average bar grub and a notch cheaper. By night, though, it's ripped to the tits and still thirsty with it. If you're bored with twee bohemia elsewhere in Paris and are in need of a little edge, La Lib will provide. Attracting drunks of every stripe, La Lib comprises a small terrace and a narrow bar area dangling with knick-knacks and invariably packed. A back room is used for groups who might actually want to talk to each other. The rest are perfectly happy to guzzle (house punch or decent Belgian brews by the bottle), guffaw and cop off, and at some point everyone gets a turn to dance like a maniac on the bar counter. The music is always right. African beats, Burning Spear or Little Richard howling *Lucille*, it's just there. Reliably raucous.

Planète Mars

21 rue Keller, 11th (01.43.14.24.44). M° Ledru-Rollin. **Open** 6.30pm-2am Mon-Sat. Closed 2wks Aug. **Credit** MC, V. **Map** p409 M7.

From the dour grey of a Bastille backstreet, you enter a world of colour. Shimmery disco balls and bright red walls tell you straight off that, yes, you are in retro heaven. Kitsch objects line the walls, a space-age bar is buttressed by impatient queue jumpers, funky cocktails abound (including stellar Mojitos), and drink prices defy inflation so much you'd half suspect them to still be using old francs. Add to this DJs in a little corner spinning everything from funk to Northern Soul to 1980s disco and back again, and what have you got? A red planet full of fun, that's what. Set the controls for Planet Mars.

on en oublie d'aller ailleurs

café

42 rue vieille du temple 4th Paris • 01 42 72 16 94 •

amnesia-café.com

open every day from 11am to 2am

on the bar counter pack all kinds of punches, such as the €5 Chéri(e) of dark rum, and fruit vodkas are another speciality. DJ nights are conceived with equal craft, and the atmosphere around the red interior dotted with low-key artwork is one of suss and seduction. There's a branded front terrace if you need a little conversational respite from the BPM.

Café Parisien
2 pl de Rhin-et-Danube, 19th (01.42.06.02.75).
M° Danube. **Open** 7am-10pm Mon-Sat. Closed Aug.
No credit cards.
Emerge from Danube, an obscure stop on a one-way offshoot of line seven in the far 19th, and you'll find a pretty, open square lapped by this lovely oasis of nostalgic calm. At lunchtime, salads are served on the modest terrace bathed in sunlight – or around the small, tiled, quarter-circle counter and its half-dozen tables. After dusk, this cosy interior becomes a bar, an honest-to-goodness locals' bar, cigarette smoke wafted away by an enormous fan, showing the gaudy colours of the vintage film posters in their true glory. *Boulevard Crépuscule, Le Rock du Bagne* and *Autant En Emporte Le Vent,* the French titles bring a smile and, coupled with friendly service and near-provincial prices, should see you docking at the Danube again before too long.

Chez Prune
71 quai de Valmy, 10th (01.42.41.30.47).
M° République. **Open** 8am-2am daily. **Credit** MC, V.
Map p404 L4.
Bang in the heart of the Canal scene, Chez Prune is still a magnet for creative types, or local layabouts who like to think they're soaking up the atmosphere while waiting for the muse to strike. The black turtlenecks are many and the beards complicated; bindis, headscarves and Birkenstocks abound. Everyone seems to know everyone else, but it's far from cliquey: as long as you look suitably street and have a screenplay to talk about you'll fit right in.

Les Couleurs
117 rue St-Maur, 11th (01.43.57.95.61).
M° Parmentier. **Open** 4pm-2am daily. **No credit cards. Map** p405 M4.
Rue St-Maur at its squat-chic best. Plastic furniture, a tacky desert island mural, bare brick and naked lightbulbs compose the decor, 'Yes, what do you want, then?' the service, arty underground films the cultural programme and pool balls in primary colours the distinguishing signs on the beer taps – the tableau is set. And, *bien sûr,* locals flock here in droves (clock the mounted Kodak shots), ignoring the considerable claims of Le Marquis nearby. The soundtrack is as good as you'll find anywhere in these parts, the cocktails sharp, if presented with dutiful minimalism, and the vibe is vibrant and vital.

Favela Chic
18 rue du Fbg-du-Temple, 11th (01.40.21.38.14/ www.favelachic.com). M° République or Goncourt.
Open 7.30pm-2am Tue-Thur; 8pm-5am Fri, Sat.
Credit MC, V. **Map** p404 L4.

A hot and immensely popular Latin cocktail joint which makes the easy switch from eaterie to bar/club at some point before midnight. The dancefloor gets so crowded you can feel the air dripping sweat (this is a good thing, I assure you), and the cocktails err on the side of potent – with the Cuba Libre, you get the Coke's only there to add a bit of colouring. DJs occasionally veer from South America and don't be surprised if you end up in a drum 'n' bass night – or, for that matter, listening to anything from Britpop to Viennese waltzes.

Aux Folies Belleville
8 rue de Belleville, 20th (01.46.36.65.98).
M° Belleville. **Open** 6.30am-2am daily. **No credit cards. Map** p405 N4.
Zazou meets Zizou in this lively open-fronted café, its roots in the classic Hot Club days of waifs and wideboys, its current regulars and barstaff Kabyle expats originally from the mountains of Algeria. Touches of art deco, a little neon and old slices of vinyl on tabletops can be discerned during convivial daytime opening, but once the surrounding chairs and long zinc counter start filling, you'll see nothing but exaggerated hand gestures, elegant puffing of cigarette smoke and the occasional flash of a clean-shaven waiter in tie and apron. Four-euro Mojito punch is promised, as well as a boast of 75-year-old origins, but really this place is as timeless as it is unashamedly trendless.

Le Jemmapes
82 quai de Jemmapes, 10th (01.40.40.02.35).
M° Jacques Bonsergent or République. **Open** 11am-1am daily. **No credit cards. Map** p404 L4.
Destination canalside café and a sound reason to join the lazy throng along the St-Martin embankment. In fine weather, this leads to a bottleneck of content couples mini-picnicking on the waterfront, others brunching on the narrow bar terrace, where weekend tables are at a premium. Inside is small and arty, but not so much it puts you off, not with Chimay Bleue and Duval available anyway. Rare flavoured vodkas are another speciality – there's a slight Polish touch to the extensive lunchtime menu – but location is the deciding factor here. Visit during the week for a more boho crowd than the somewhat self-satisfied contingent of bric-a-brac browsers.

Lou Pascalou
14 rue des Panoyaux, 20th (01.46.36.78.10).
M° Ménilmontant. **Open** 9am-2am daily. **No credit cards. Map** p405 N4.
After a decade of loyal service, this Ménilmontant mainstay on a quiet square is still worth a visit. Here a bohemian crew of regulars and newcomers spills on to the pavement on clement evenings and crowds inside when things look a little grey and miserable in the outside world. Chess matches roll on for hours as locals settle scores over a *pression* or two (sets and a board are available from behind the bar). Guinness and Kilkenny are also available, and the selection of cocktails is remarkable.

Eat, Drink, Shop

La Patache

60 rue de Lancry, 10th (01.42.08.14.35). M° Jacques Bonsergent. **Open** 6pm-2am daily. **No credit cards. Map** p404 L4.

Abdel, the slavering old goat flirting and bickering with whichever barmaid happens to be on that week, presided over this dilapidated diamond long before the nearby Canal St-Martin became des res. The iconic *Hôtel du Nord* poster is no pose, but a reference to the real pre-war venue just over the bridge, now boasting a heritage sign, whose starring role in Marcel Carné's 1938 film classic would have been enjoyed by the bar regulars of the day. They're still here, in spirit, their present-day counterparts still arguing, cursing, smoking, drinking, falling in and out of love. Abdel provides scraps of paper at each table should they no longer be speaking to each other. Otis no longer wails from the long-dead jukebox, more's the pity, but it's a small price to pay for living history.

Le Piston Pélican

15 rue de Bagnolet, 20th (01.43.70.35.00). M° Alexandre Dumas. **Open** 8am-2am Mon-Fri; 10am-2am Sat, Sun. **Credit** MC, V. **Map** p409 Q6.

Since its change from a discarded old hostelry into a gleaming, semi-retro music bar-café, the PP has attracted younger regulars to this slightly obscure part of the 20th, the wrong side of Père-Lachaise from Ménilmontant. It comprises a large, raised dining area at the back, done out like a station waiting room (*Quai des Brumes* vintage), and a small, neat bar area out front. Attention is drawn to the long line of beer taps (Leffe, Pelforth, Guinness) before the eye discerns, amid the unwise maroon and mustard stucco of the decor, a shorter line of big old vats. House white, cider and... sweet mother of Abraham Lincoln, look at that, they've got snakebite on keg! DJs and live bands provide further entertainment.

La Soupière

12 rue Marie-et-Louise, 10th (01.42.08.10.41). M° Jacques Bonsergent. **Open** noon-2am Tue-Sun. **Credit** MC, V. **Map** p404 L4.

Part of the semi-underground scene in the burgeoning 10th of the mid-1990s, by the end of the decade La Soupière had breathed its last. Now blessed with dynamic new management, this boho classic down a narrow sidestreet near the St-Martin canal has reopened to provide a crowd-free, sunny alternative to the quayside snobbery nearby. Resolutely arty – poetry readings, the odd DJ at weekends – La Soup' features a jazzy interior of Chinese lanterns, vulgar oil paintings and cacti, and a scattering of streetside tables which catch the last of the afternoon's rays. The prices are friendly – Maes and rare draught Jenlain at under €2.50 a pop – and the clientele unpretentiously cool. Recommended.

Le Zéro Zéro

89 rue Amelot, 11th (01.49.23.51.00). M° St-Sébastien Froissart. **Open** 5pm-2am daily. **Credit** MC, V. **Map** p404 L5.

Revolutionary when it opened in 1999, the ZZ still has a chip on its shoulder. It's as wee as a wardrobe, it drinks like fish and its music kicks like a mule, so there. And many – menfolk, invariably – rally to the cause, they gather round the minuscule L-shaped bar and utter musings, so profound at the time, so pitiful when in chalked up in bare white-and-black over the counter. Attention should be drawn, though, to the cocktail blackboard, extensive and potent, incorporating a Zéro Zéro of dark rum, ginger and lime. And even the ZZ has had to succumb to happy hour discounts (6.30-8.30pm) despite a reasonable pricing structure. Oh, and the decorators don't seem to have touched it since the day it opened.

Le Zorba

137 rue du Fbg-du-Temple, 10th (01.42.39.68.68). M° Belleville. **Open** 5am-2am daily. **No credit cards. Map** p405 M4.

A simple Belleville café, its frontage open to the world, accommodates mainly Maghrebien gamblers by day and laid-back younger drinkers by night. It's cheap and working-class, with red strip lighting, squat toilets, tobacco-stained walls and a noisy terrace, but once the torn PMU slips are swept away, the Zorba can provide a swift *apéro* before an Asian meal or the perfect environment for a right old session. Full of character and characters, open for business laughably early and closing pleasingly late, the Zorba offers Leffe and Hoegaarden on draught, €5 cocktails and blue moods in spades.

The Latin Quarter & 13th

Le Caveau des Oubliettes

52 rue Galande, 5th (01.46.34.23.09). M° Maubert Mutualité. **Open** 5pm-2am Mon-Thur, Sun; 5pm-5am Fri, Sat. **Credit** MC, V. **Map** p408 J7.

Considered primarily as a music venue (*see p325*), this historically themed brick bar of Irish character attracts a good Franco-Euro mix of punters to its street-level pub before people venture down the stone staircase to the clammy cellar with its small stage and separate bar counter. Upstairs is best known for its tatty turf floor, scuffed by the soles of too many Doc Martens and spotted with too much Beamish, and its genuine guillotine from 1793. Not surprisingly, upstairs is called the Guillotine Bar. No barman has yet been executed for the odd burst of Guns 'N' Roses, nor banished to the similarly authentic medieval dungeon, now the music cellar. Atmosphere is provided by the sense of drinking in the heart of the Latin Quarter, in one of the oldest streets in all Paris. Sports TV, too.

Chez Lili et Marcel

1 quai de la Gare, 13th (01.45.85.00.08). M° Quai de la Gare. **Open** 6am-midnight Mon-Sat; 8am-8pm Sun. **Credit** AmEx, MC, V. **Map** p409 M9.

This large revamped bar-resto guards the entrance to the north-east corner of the equally revamped 13th, its yellow awnings pointing towards the river and Bercy opposite as you step down from Quai de la Gare Métro station high above. Done out like an old grocery, with packets of post-war Omo and the like on display, L&M's offers genuine *cuisine de famille* along with a patisserie. The sunlit terrace is as pleasant as you'll find along this stretch of the Seine, and all in all this is the nicest of the options before catching a movie at the MK2 a short walk around the corner.

Connolly's Corner

12 rue de Mirbel, 5th (01.43.31.94.22). M° Censier Daubenton. **Open** 4pm-2am daily. **No credit cards.** **Map** p408 K9.
Revellers from nearby rue Mouffetard join regulars to knock back stout and generous measures of Paddy whiskey or Breton beer Coreff at suitable whisky-barrel tables. Live music nights see a rush on seats, the regular darts matches are taken just as seriously, but everything else here is laid-back. The severed ties hanging around the bar are evidence that suits and the terminally straight will be taken down a peg or two.

Le Couvent

69 rue Broca, 13th (01.43.31.28.28). M° Les Gobelins. **Open** 9am-2am Mon-Fri; 6pm-2am Sat. **Credit** MC, V. **Map** p408 J10.
For an address located in the middle of nowhere, this heavily beamed bar creates a delightful hideaway. It first appeared in Pierre Gripari's two-part short-story collection *Contes de la rue Broca*, but it has come a long way since those dingy days. Nowadays it's the *chouchou* of students and thirtysomething couples, especially at concert time when live chords get feet tapping. Always busy, always smoky.

Le Crocodile

6 rue Royer-Collard, 5th (01.43.54.32.37). RER Luxembourg. **Open** 10.30pm-late Mon-Sat. Closed Aug. **Credit** MC, V. **Map** p408 J8.
Ignore the apparently boarded-up windows for a cocktail at Le Crocodile – if you're here late, it's open. Young, friendly regulars line the sides of this small, narrow bar and try to decide on a drink – somewhat difficult given the length and complexity of the cocktail list. It contains 267 choices, each one more potent than the other. Pen and paper are provided to note your decision; the pen comes in pretty handy for point-and-choose decisions when everything gets hazy. We think we can recommend an *accroche-coeur*, a supremely '70s mix of champagne and Goldschläger, served with extra gold leaf. But that was before we had to start pointing.

Le Pantalon

7 rue Royer-Collard, 5th (no phone). RER Luxembourg. **Open** 5.30pm-2am Mon-Sat. **No credit cards.** **Map** p408 J8.
Mad as a bag of frogs, Le Pantalon is a local café that seems familiar yet utterly surreal. It has the standard fixtures and fittings you find anywhere, including the old soaks at the bar – plus a strange vacuum-cleaner sculpture, disco-light toilets and the world's most prosaic proposal of marriage. Aside from the offbeat decor, the regulars and staff tip the balance firmly into eccentricity. Friendly and very funny French grown-ups and foreign students chat in a mish-mash of languages. Happy hours are generous, but drinks are always cheap enough to get tipsy without worrying about a cash hangover.

Those of you in the posh seats, rattle your jewellery – it's the **Alcazar**. *See p236.*

Le Piano Vache

8 rue Laplace, 5th (01.46.33.75.03/www.lepiano vache.com). M° Maubert Mutualité. **Open** noon-2am Mon-Fri; 9pm-2am Sat, Sun. **Credit** AmEx, MC, V. **Map** p408 J8.

A Left Bank drinking haunt for many a decade, this has all the hallmarks of what any beer-stained smoke hovel should be: dark, cramped, filled with a hardcore drinker/student clientele, the walls covered four times over with posters and indeterminate pub grime, and the greatest hits of alternative '80s synth-pop on repeat on the stereo. This is what the French mean by grunge, bless them. Note that weekday opening hours switch to evenings out of term time.

Rhubarb

18 rue Laplace, 5th (01.43.25.35.03). M° Maubert Mutualité. **Open** 5pm-2am daily. **Credit** MC, V. **Map** p408 J8.

A wonderful little spot near Mouffetard, Rhubarb is the latest offering from the crew that put the Fu Bar (*see below*) on the map. As Fu regulars would expect, the cocktails here are excellent and while Sean's famous apple Martini is still sublime, we think we might plump for his watermelon concoction or chocolate Martini in future. A relaxed vibe abounds and a mixed crowd mingle happily at the bar. The cellar is all crumbling pale stone and high ceilings, and while a quiet corner is ideal seduction territory, the space works equally well for gaggles of mates on a big night out.

St-Germain-des-Prés & Odéon

Alcazar

62 rue Mazarine, 6th (01.53.10.19.99/www. alcazar.fr). M° Odéon. **Open** 7.30pm-2am daily. **Credit** AmEx, DC, MC, V. **Map** p408 H7.

It would be fair to assume that the Alcazar would be over by now, hip bars tending to fade once their first flush of youth is gone. But the 'AZ bar' still somehow pulls it off. The sleek velvet banquettes, polished aluminium bar and the vantage point over the oh-so-trendy restaurant (*see p213*) and into the private dining room all help of course, but really this place is worth paying for because it's posh without being poncey – and the drinks are great. The Monday-night easy-listening sessions are *un must* in local hip circles and the weekend aperitif crowd still show no sign of defecting.

Le Bar

27 rue de Condé, 6th (01.43.29.06.61). M° Odéon. **Open** 8pm-late Mon-Sat. **No credit cards.** **Map** p408 H7.

Le Bar is one of those strange little places that you only ever visit when it's very very late and you're very very drunk. Surreal, but somehow familiar, it's almost completely pitch black, has a shrine-type affair at the back of the bar, gravel on the floor, everyone seems to talk in whispers and they serve very strong drinks. A few words of warning about this place: once you've been here, you'll find yourself strangely drawn back at inappropriate times when you really should go home to bed, and at least one member of the party falls asleep on the comfy black leather banquettes. Finally, there's a strange echo effect in the corridor down to the toilet, so if Le Bar is your last-ditch attempt to pull before the sun comes up, don't discuss your strategy too loudly.

Le Bar Dix

10 rue de l'Odéon, 6th (01.43.26.66.83). M° Odéon. **Open** 6pm-2am daily. **No credit cards.** **Map** p408 H7.

It's been here forever, this homely cavern of a bar, certainly longer than the brash Irish Horse's Tavern at one end of the street and even outlasting the neo-classical Odéon Theatre currently being modernised at the other. Generations of students have glugged back jugs of home-made sangria while squeezed into the cramped, twilit upper bar, tattily authentic with its Jacques Brel record sleeves, Yves Montand hand-bills and pre-war light fittings. The jukebox sadly no longer runs on vinyl, but the CDs weep suitably nostalgic pop nectar. Spelunkers and hopeless romantics negotiate the hazardous stone staircase for the cellar bar, its candlelight and century-old advertising murals. Someone slap a preservation plaque on this place, please.

Fu Bar

5 rue St-Sulpice, 6th (01.40.51.82.00). M° Odéon. **Open** 5pm-2am daily. **Credit** MC, V. **Map** p407 H7.

Things have changed at the Fu Bar since Sean and Gary sold up and moved to Rhubarb. It still looks the same, which is to say tiny, with a Tardis-like upstairs section you can cram into on busy nights and the drinks list is remarkably similar, but sadly the Fu Bar now feels a little less fun. It's still a welcome addition to the St-Germain pub crawl and we do still love the cosy atmosphere and mingling quota – the punters have retained their wont to table hop.

The Highlander

8 rue de Nevers, 6th (01.43.26.54.20/www.the-highlander.fr). M° Odéon. **Open** 5pm-5am Mon-Fri; noon-5am Sat, Sun. **Credit** MC, V. **Map** p408 H6.

The Highlander always feels a bit like a house party and if you don't already know everyone in there, you will by the end of your pint. A truly great local, this place has a fiercely loyal crowd of regulars, proba-bly because once you've spent a night getting ham-mered at the long wooden bar you'll definitely come back and do it again. It's quiet and cosy early evening with people nursing pints and setting the world to rights, and degenerates into a pissed-up pulling spot after 9pm. Barman Jimmy serves up generous measures and banter in equal parts, mak-ing this one of the best pubs in town. The cellar bar, used for anything from poetry readings to private do's, is open till 5am at weekends and resembles the type of school disco you know you really shouldn't want to go to anymore, but secretly still do.

Au Petit Suisse

16 rue de Vaugirard, 6th (01.43.26.03.81).
Mᵒ Odéon. **Open** 7am-midnight Mon-Sat; 7am-
10.30pm Sun. **Credit** DC, MC, V. **Map** p407 H7.
Named after Marie de Médicis' Swiss Guards, the
compact Au Petit Suisse has an enviable location
next to the Jardin du Luxembourg and so pulls in a
range of posh locals, au pairs escaping from their
charges and garret-banished Gauloise-puffing
Sorbonne students. The formal waiters excel in
French snottiness, but it makes this place all the
more authentic and tourist-free. Brave the haughty
stares for one of the handful of tables, order a kir
with a side of sneer and lap up a genuine 6th-district
café experience.

Le Rostand

6 pl Edmond-Rostand, 6th (01.43.54.61.58). RER
Luxembourg. **Open** 8am-2am daily. **Credit** MC, V.
Map p408 H6.
Le Rostand has a truly wonderful view of the Jardin
du Luxembourg from its classy interior, decked out
with Oriental paintings, a long mahogany bar and
wall-length mirrors. It's a terribly well-behaved
place and you should definitely consider arriving in
fur or designer sunglasses if you want to fit in with
the well-heeled regulars. The drinks list is lined with
whiskies and cocktails, pricy but not as steep as the
brasserie menu. Still, it's perfect for a civilised drink
after a spin round the gardens.

La Taverne de Nesle

32 rue Dauphine, 6th (01.43.26.38.36). Mᵒ Odéon.
Open 6pm-4am Mon-Thur, Sun; 6pm-6am Fri, Sat.
Credit AmEx, MC, V. **Map** p408 H6.
La Taverne, a late night staple for people who just
can't go home before daylight, has four distinct
drinking areas: a zinc bar at the front; a sort of
Napoleonic campaign tent in the middle; a trendily
lit ambient area at the back, and a dreadful 1980s
disco downstairs where girls in pearls do their best
to look sexy. The separate spaces correspond to
stages of drunkenness and encourage a gradual pro-
gression to the horizontal state. Among the hundred
or so brews you'll find the best of Belgium, but it's
the choice of French beers that really sets it apart.
Don't miss the house special L'Epi, brewed in three
different versions: Blond (100% barley); Blanc (oats)
and Noir (buckwheat) – or Corsican Pietra on tap.

Montparnasse

Le Select

99 bd de Montparnasse, 6th (01.42.22.65.27).
Mᵒ Vavin. **Open** 7am-2am Mon-Thur, Sun; 7am-
4.30am Fri, Sat. **Credit** MC, V. **Map** p407 G9.
For a decade between the wars, the junction of boulevards Raspail and Montparnasse was the centre of
the known universe. Man Ray, Cocteau and Lost
Generation Americans hung out at its vast glass-
fronted cafés (Le Dôme, La Coupule), socialising,
snubbing and snogging. Gregarious yet anonymous,
these bars allowed escape from a stifling box-room

flat. Hemingway first met F Scott Fitzgerald at the
notorious Dingo. Eighty years on, Le Select is the
best of these inevitable tourist traps. Sure, its pricy
menu is big on historical detail, but short on authenticity ('Cockney Brunch' of eggs, bacon and jam at
€15), but generally Le Select holds on to its Man Ray
heyday with dignity. *Intello* locals hang out at the
bar, spreading out the high-brow cultural section
while Mickey the house cat wanders over the
newsprint. Happy Hour from 7pm makes history
affordable, the cocktail and whisky list is extensive,
and pleasingly it's Mickey (not Ernie) who's honoured with a prominent framed portrait.

The 7th & the 15th

Le Bréguet

72 rue Falguière, 15th (01.42.79.97.00). Mᵒ Pasteur.
Open 5pm-1.30am Mon-Fri; 6pm-1.30am Sat. Closed
2wks Aug. **Credit** MC, V. **Map** p407 E9.
OK, so it's in the middle of nowhere and the decor is
nondescript, so why bother? Well, aside from the
fact that it's rare to find somewhere with this much
atmosphere in the fun-free 15th, it's worth the Métro
journey for the eclectic drinks list. As well as the
usual beers on tap, there are Strongbow cider, commendably smooth Guinness, vodkas and exotic
quaffs like Limoncello. Cheap cocktails, too. Work
your way down the list, you know you want to.

Le Café du Marché

38 rue Cler, 7th (01.47.05.51.27). Mᵒ Ecole Militaire.
Open 7am-midnight Mon-Sat; 7am-5pm Sun. **Credit**
MC, V. **Map** p407 D6.
This well-loved address is frequented by trendy
locals, shoppers hunting down a particular type of
cheese along this busy market street or tourists
who've managed to make it this far from the Eiffel
Tower before finding a truly charming place at
which to stop for drinks. Le Café du Marché really
is the hub of neighbourhood activity here. Their
pichets of decent house plonk go down a treat and
while it's fine just to drink here, mention must be
made of the food, such as the huge house salad with
lashes of foie gras and Parma ham.

Café Thoumieux

4 rue de la Comète, 7th (01.45.51.50.40/www.
thoumieux.com). Mᵒ La Tour-Maubourg. **Open**
noon-2am Mon-Fri; 5pm-2am Sat. Closed 2wks Aug.
Credit AmEx, MC, V. **Map** p407 E6.
The little brother to vintage bistro Thoumieux is a
laid-back destination for cocktails, tapas or big-
screen sport. Banquettes snake around the room and
spiky Aztec-pattern lamps send light flickering up
the walls and illuminate the faces of the pretty
young locals who have made this place their own.
The flavoured vodkas are delicious and include
vanilla, caramel and banana. Don't blame them for
any difficulties you might be suffering with the
extra-high bar stools (the banquettes are safest) or
for the sight of the monstrous, pebble-dashed sink
in the toilets – it's real.

Eat, Drink, Shop

Shops & Services

Whatever you want.

Antoine et Lili. *See p256.*

Eat, Drink, Shop

World capital of fashion, gastronomy and style, Paris is a discerning shopper's paradise. As the birthplace of couture (*see pp37-39* **Haute couture or high street?**), inventor of the bra and the stiletto, the French capital is home to showcase stores of all the world's top designers – but the luxury available on avenue Montaigne or rue du Faubourg-St-Honoré remains just a small slice of what's on offer at 30,000-plus emporia. Real Paris shopping reveals itself in specialist boutiques, family-run food shops, belle-époque department stores with rooftop views, and rustic markets that haven't changed in over a century (*see p267* **Market forces**).

Recent years have seen many family-run *fromageries, boulangeries, charcuteries* and quirky little treasure troves close. And although the chain concept is quickly catching on, the overall quality remains impressive, and almost everything, from a vintage bottle of Armagnac to a single praline chocolate, is lovingly served, wrapped and presented, whatever the store. Informative discussion is still very much part of the purchasing process. Beautiful old-style arcades – such as the galerie Vivienne (2nd) or passage Jouffroy (9th) – make shopping a sightseeing pleasure as well.

Different areas reveal different specialities. Classic clusters of shops include antiques in the 7th and second-hand and rare books in the 5th (a reminder of the days when there were publishing guilds there). Crystal and porcelain manufacturers still dot rue de Paradis in the 10th, furniture craftsmen on rue du Faubourg-St-Antoine, while the world's top jewellers can be found on place Vendôme. Street chic and lifestyle outlets live side by side in the Marais and around rue Etienne-Marcel, while quirky newcomers settle in Abbesses or near Canal St-Martin. Designer labels are scattered all over the 1st, 6th and 8th. Specialist enclaves include bikes and cameras on boulevard Beaumarchais.

Most shops open from 10am-7pm Monday to Saturday, specialist boutiques closing for an hour at lunch. Sunday shopping is no longer frowned upon, but is not as common as in the UK. Small corner grocery stores open late for essentials. Many family-run concerns close in August. *See p241* **Best after hours**.

Finally, no weekend shop would be complete without a visit to one of the city's extensive flea markets, the only place where haggling is still de rigueur and cash, not plastic, is the payment of choice. *See p273* **Hunt the heirloom**.

Sophisticated **La Samaritaine**.

One-stop shops

Department stores

The revamped *grands magasins* have brought in trendy designers and luxury spaces to lure shoppers away from independent boutiques.

Le Bon Marché

24 rue de Sèvres, 7th (01.44.39.80.00/www.bon marche.fr). M° Sèvres-Babylone. **Open** 9.30am-7pm Mon-Wed, Fri; 10am-9pm Sat. **Credit** AmEx, DC, MC, V. **Map** p407 G7.
Paris' oldest department store (1848) is also its most swish and user-friendly, thanks to an extensive redesign by LVMH. The prestigious Balthazar men's section offers a cluster of designer boutiques, while the Theatre of Beauty provides a comfort zone for women. Seven luxury boutiques, occupied by Dior and Chanel, among others, take pride of place on the ground floor; escalators designed by Andrée Putman take you up to the fashion floor, which includes the store's well-cut, own-label cotton shirts. The Grande Epicerie food hall (01.44.39.81.00, www. lagrandeepicerie.fr, 8.30am-9pm Mon-Sat) is next door, with an antiques gallery, bar and restaurant.

BHV (Bazar de l'Hôtel de Ville)

52-64 rue de Rivoli, 4th (01.42.74.90.00/www.bhv. fr); DIY hire annexe 40 rue de la Verrerie (01.42.74.97.23). M° Hôtel de Ville. **Open** 9.30am-7.30pm Mon, Tue, Thur, Fri; 9.30am-8pm Wed, Sat. **Credit** AmEx, MC, V. **Map** p408 J6.
DIY buffs spend hours in this hardware heaven, drooling over hinges, screws, nuts and bolts in the basement or dithering over paint colours upstairs;

there's even a Bricolage Café, with internet access. Upper floors of the store have a good range of men's outdoor wear, women's underwear, upmarket bed-linen, toys, household appliances – and an 800m² space devoted to every type of storage utility.

Galeries Lafayette

40 bd Haussmann, 9th (01.42.82.34.56/fashion shows 01.42.82.30.25/fashion advice 01.42.82. 35.50/www.galerieslafayette.com); cigar cellar 99 rue de Provence. M° Chaussée d'Antin La Fayette/RER Auber. **Open** 9.30am-7.30pm Mon-Wed, Fri, Sat; 9.30am-9pm Thur. **Credit** AmEx, DC, MC, V. **Map** p403 H3.
This department store has revamped its fashion, beauty and accessories sections, and, in hot compe-tition with Printemps (*see below*), opened a lingerie department, on the third floor. On the first, Le Labo and Trend have introduced progressive interna-tional creators, while 90 established designers are spread over the rest of the first and second floors. There are five fashion and beauty consultants to guide you through the sartorial maze, and the new men's fashion space on the third floor of Lafayette Homme is a must, with its natty designer corners and 'Club' space with net access. On the first floor, Lafayette Gourmet has exotic foods galore, and the second biggest wine cellar in Paris. The exquisite domed ceiling in the main shop is eminently photo-genic, and there's a rooftop café. On the other side of the boulevard, the old M&S building has become Lafayette Maison (www.lafayettemaison.com), 10,000m² of design for the home.

Printemps

64 bd Haussmann, 9th (01.42.82.50.00/www. printemps.com). M° Havre-Caumartin/RER Auber. **Open** 9.35am-7pm Mon-Wed, Fri, Sat; 9.30am-10pm Thur. **Credit** AmEx, DC, MC, V. **Map** p403 G3.
Printemps is the home of superlatives: the largest shoe department in Paris on the men's fifth floor, and – wait for it – the biggest beauty department in the world opened here in 2003, with some 200 brands. The lingerie department is the stuff of fantasy, too, stocked with luxury brands such as Erès and far-out frillies from Gaultier and Pucci. In all, there are six floors of fashion in both the men's and women's stores. On the second floor of Printemps de la Mode, French designers such as APC and Zadig et Voltaire sit side by side with the likes of Dolce e Gabbana and Moschino. Miss Code, on the fifth floor, targets the teen miss and offers a huge selection of jeans and sportswear. The Printemps de la Maison store, along with well-stocked home decoration and furnishings, has the more conceptual 'function floor', where saucepans and coffee machines are set out on steel shelving.The ninth-floor terrace restaurant sports an art nouveau cupola.

La Samaritaine

19 rue de la Monnaie, 1st (01.40.41.20.20/www. lasamaritaine.com). M° Pont Neuf. **Open** 9.30am-7pm Mon-Wed, Fri; 9.30am-9pm Thur; 9.30am-8pm Sat. **Credit** AmEx, DC, MC, V. **Map** p408 J6.

Now owned by LMVH, this venerable store was given an extensive facelift in 2003, with one part let out to high-street stalwarts such as Sephora (*see p243*) and the rest promoting beauty, leisure and designer fashion. It has a sophisticated selection of contemporary design and homewares, and the elaborate turquoise and gold wrought-ironwork and peacock mosaics around the glass roof still make it one of the best-preserved jewels of the belle epoque. Fabulous view from the top-floor restaurant.

Tati
4 bd de Rochechouart, 18th (01.55.29.52.50/ www.tati.fr). M° Barbès Rochechouart. **Open** 11am-7pm Mon; 10am-7pm Tue-Sat. **Credit** MC, V. **Map** p404 J2.

Financial difficulties threatened this shopping institution until an Italian buy-out in 2004. Expect to find anything from T-shirts to wedding dresses, as well as bargain children's clothes and household goods. Unbeatably cheap, but don't expect high quality. For other branches, see the website.

Shopping centres

Drugstore Publicis
133 av des Champs-Elysées, 8th (01.44.43.79.00/ www.publicisdrugstore.com). M° Charles de Gaulle Etoile. **Open** 8am-2am daily. **Credit** MC, V. **Map** p402 D4.

A 1960s legend for everyone from Jacques Dutronc to Fernand Raynaud, the reopening of the landmark Drugstore Publicis in 2004 drew throngs of nostalgic Parisians. A French take on US culture, this was a convenient rendezvous for gilded youth in the days when everything was closed on Sunday. Now after a long renovation, the 1970s building has been reclad with desultory fluo-lit spiral swirls by American architect Michele Saee, and a carbuncular glass and steel café oozes on to the pavement. But inside is what it's all about; on the ground floor are an international newsagent, a pharmacy and bookshop and a decadently upmarket deli full of quality olive oils and elegant biscuits; a screen running videos reminds you that Publicis is an advertising agency. The basement is a sort of macho take on Colette (*see p249*), keeping the selected design items (some exclusive) and lifestyle mags, but replacing high-fashion by fine wines (all New World) and a smart cigar cellar.

La Galerie du Carrousel du Louvre
99 rue de Rivoli, 1st (01.43.16.47.10/www. lecarrouseldulouvre.com). M° Palais Royal Musée du Louvre. **Open** 9am-8pm daily. **Credit** varies. **Map** p408 J6.

Paris doesn't have many malls, but this massive underground shopping centre – open every day of the year – surely qualifies as one. It's home to more than 35 shops: big-name chains such as Virgin, Esprit, Sephora, Nature et Découvertes, L'Occitane, Agatha, Bodum and Périgot, all vying for your attention and your cash. Great for last-minute gifts.

Beauty

Cosmetics

L'Artisan Parfumeur
24 bd Raspail, 7th (01.42.22.23.32). M° Rue du Bac. **Open** 10.30am-7pm Mon-Sat. **Credit** AmEx, DC, MC, V. **Map** p407 G7.

Among scented candles, potpourri and charms, you'll find the best vanilla perfume Paris can offer – Mûres et Musc, a bestseller for over 20 years.

By Terry
21 galerie Véro-Dodat, 1st (01.44.76.00.76). M° Palais Royal Musée du Louvre. **Open** 10.30am-7pm Mon-Sat. **Credit** AmEx, MC, V. **Map** p404 H5.

Terry de Gunzburg, once at Yves Saint Laurent, offers made-to-measure 'haute couleur' make-up, by chemists and colourists combining high-tech treatments and hand-made precision. Prêt-à-porter, too. **Other locations**: *1 rue Jacob, 6th (01.46.34.00.36); 10 av Victor-Hugo, 16th (01.55.73.00.73).*

The best After hours

Not quite the city that never sleeps, Paris nevertheless is home to a few places whose opening hours almost keep up with yours.

Black Block
This spot sells kooky Japanese gadgets and original art works until midnight, every day except Monday. *See p270.*

Drugstore Publicis
The Paris version of a mall sells stylish last-minute gifts until 2am every day. *See left.*

Librairie Flammarion
An outstanding selection of art books and children's titles until 10pm, every day except Tuesday. *See p245.*

Printemps
Most department stores stay open late on Thursday; here until 10pm you can delve into fantasy lingerie and the world's biggest beauty department. *See p240.*

Sephora
For emergency repairs, this prominent make-up and perfume emporium is open until midnight all week. *See p243.*

Virgin Megastore
Two mega branches of this CD and DVD bazaar are open until midnight, seven days a week. *See p246.*

Eat, Drink, Shop

Détaille 1905

*10 rue St-Lazare, 9th (01.48.78.68.50/www.detaille.
com). M° Notre-Dame de-Lorette.* **Open** 3-7pm Mon;
10am-1.30pm, 3-7pm Tue-Sat. **Credit** MC, V. **Map**
p403 H3.

Step back in time in this shop, opened, as the name
suggests, in 1905. Six fragrances, three for men and
three for women are made from original recipes.

Editions de Parfums Frédéric Malle

*37 rue de Grenelle, 1st (01.42.22.77.22). M° Rue du
Bac.* **Open** 11am-7pm Mon-Sat. **Credit** AmEx, MC,
V. **Map** p407 F6.

Olfactory minimalism: choose from eight perfumes
made by Frédéric Malle, former consultant for
Lacroix, Chaumet and Hermès.

Galérie Noémie

*17 rue du Cygne, 1st (01.44.76.06.26/www.galerie
noemie.com). M° Etienne Marcel.* **Open** 1-7.30pm
Tue-Sat. **Credit** DC, MC, V. **Map** p404 J5.

You can tell Noémie is a painter, not by the name of
the boutique but by the way all the make-up is set
out in palettes: artful indeed. Little pots of gloss (a
very reasonable €7.50) in myriad colours triple as
lip gloss, eyeshadow or blusher. For other locations,
see the website.

Guerlain

*68 av des Champs-Elysées, 8th (01.45.62.52.57/
www.guerlain.fr). M° Franklin D. Roosevelt.* **Open**
10.30am-8pm Mon-Sat; 3-7pm Sun. **Credit** AmEx,
MC, V. **Map** p403 E4.

This bijou boutique is one of the last vestiges of the
golden age of the Champs-Elysées. Although the
family sold the company to LVMH years ago, the
'maison' still produces outstanding creations and old
faves such as Samsara, Mitsouko and L'Heure Bleue.

Iunx

*48-50 rue de l'Université, 7th (01.45.44.50.14). M°
Rue du Bac.* **Open** 10.30am-7pm Mon-Sat. **Credit**
AmEx, MC, V. **Map** p407 G6.

Invisible from the street, this minimal, mysterious
space reinvents the way we choose and buy perfume. Iunx is Greek for 'seduction by scent', and this
futuristic temple to fragrance sells its own delicious
lines of perfumes, gels and candles. Try the Eau
Interdite, a curious, absinthe-scented eau de cologne.

Make Up For Ever Professional

*5 rue La Boétie, 8th (01.42.66.01.60). M°
Miromesnil.* **Open** 10am-7pm Mon-Sat. Closed Sat in
Aug. **Credit** AmEx, DC, MC, V. **Map** p403 E3.

With glitter, nail varnish, lipstick, fake eyelashes
and stick-on tattoos, prepare for a colour explosion
from this outfit beloved of catwalk make-up pros.
Other locations: *22 rue de Sèvres, 7th
(01.45.48.75.97).*

L'Occitane

*55 rue St-Louis-en-l'Ile, 4th (01.40.46.81.71/www.
loccitane.com). M° Pont Marie.* **Open** 10.30am-
7.30pm Mon-Sat. **Credit** AmEx, DC, MC, V.
Map p408 K7.

The many branches of this popular Provençal chain
proffer natural beauty products in neat packaging.
Soap rules, with also essential oils and perfumes.

Salons du Palais-Royal Shiseido

*Jardins du Palais-Royal, 142 galerie de Valois, 1st
(01.49.27.09.09/www.salons-shiseido.com). M° Palais
Royal Musée du Louvre.* **Open** 10am-7pm Mon-Sat.
Credit AmEx, DC, MC, V. **Map** p403 H5.

Under the arcades of the Palais-Royal is this luxury
perfume laboratory, where Shiseido's perfumer
Serge Lutens practises his aromatic arts. In this
wood-and-marble space, bottles of Lutens' concoctions – 'Tubéreuse Criminelle', 'Rahat Loukoum' or
'Ambre Sultan' – can be sampled. Many are exclusive to the Salons; prices start at around €100.

Sephora

*70 av des Champs-Elysées, 8th (01.53.93.22.50/
www.sephora.fr). M° Franklin D. Roosevelt.* **Open**
10am-midnight Mon-Sat; noon-midnight Sun. **Credit**
AmEx, MC, V. **Map** p403 E4.

The flagship of the cosmetic supermarket chain
houses 12,000 French and foreign brands of scent
and slap. Sephora Blanc (14 cour St-Emilion, 12th,
01.40.02.97.79) features beauty products in a blindingly minimalist interior. Sephoras are popping up
all over town; consult their website for a full list.

Salons & spas

Anne Sémonin

*Le Bristol, 108 rue du Fbg-St-Honoré, 8th (01.42.
66.24.22). M° Miromesnil or Champs-Elysées
Clemenceau.* **Open** 10.30am-7pm Mon-Sat. **Credit**
AmEx, DC, MC, V. **Map** p403 E3.

Facials are the thing here, delicious ones with basil,
lavender, lemon grass, ginger and plant essences.
Try the 'New Package' which includes an energis-
ing massage, a divine facial mask that smells and
feels so good you'll have to fight the urge to lick it,
a seaweed bath for your back, plus a reflexologist
studying your feet to see how every little thing is
holding up. Treatments cost from €60 to €135.

Les Bains du Marais

*31-33 rue des Blancs-Manteaux, 4th
(01.44.61.02.02/www.lesbainsdumarais.com). M° St-
Paul.* **Open** **Men** 11am-11pm Thur; 10am-8pm Fri;
10am-8pm Sat. **Women** 11am-8pm Mon; 11am-11pm
Tue; 10am-7pm Wed. **Mixed** 7-11pm Wed; 10am-8pm
Sat. Closed 3wks Aug. **Credit** AmEx, MC, V. **Map**
p408 K6.

This chic hammam and spa mixes modern and traditional (lounging beds and mint tea). Facials, waxing and essential oil massages are also available.
The hammam only costs €30; massage €30.

La Bulle Kenzo

*1 rue du Pont-Neuf, 1st (01.73.04.20.04/www.labulle
kenzo.com). M° Pont Neuf.* **Open** 10am-8pm Mon-
Sat. **Credit** AmEx, DC, MC, V. **Map** p408 J6.

Kenzo's flagship store, with the Starck-designed
restaurant Kong (*see p193*), houses a fourth-floor

Eat, Drink, Shop

Lashings of Left Bank literature at **Gibert Jeune**. *See p245.*

beauty salon of high chic and high concept. Their two massage rooms offer two different vibes – Pétillante has a disco ball, while the Japanese Zen cocoon provides calmer pleasures.

L'Esthétique de Demain

15 rue de la Grande-Truanderie, 1st (01.40.26.53.10). M° Châtelet or Etienne Marcel. **Open** 2-7pm Mon; 10am-7pm Tue-Sat. **Credit** MC, V. **Map** p404 J5.

If you're just looking to get the job done without a lot of hoopla, this low-key salon specialising in hair-removal is for you. It boasts some of the lowest prices in town, including waxing for men and women from €8, and facials from €30.

Hammam de la Grande Mosquée

1 pl du Puits-de-l'Ermite, 5th (01.43.31.18.14). M° Censier Daubenton. **Open** *Men* 2-9pm Tue; 10am-9pm Sun. *Women* 10am-9pm Mon, Wed, Sat; 2-9pm Fri. **Credit** MC, V. **Map** p408 K9.

To the sound of soft voices and Arabic music, clients are steamed, scrubbed and massaged in this 1920s mosque. Follow your session with a *gommage* (exfoliation with a rough mitt), then a massage. The hammam is €15, gommage €10 and massage €10.

Hammam Med Centre

43-45 rue Petit, 19th (01.42.02.31.05/www. hammammed.com). M° Ourcq. **Open** *Women* 11am-10pm Mon-Fri; 10am-8pm Sun. *Mixed* 10am-8pm Sat. **Credit** MC, V. **Map** p405 N5.

This hammam experience is hard to beat – spotless, mosaic-tiled surroundings; flowered sarongs and even a pool. But the main draw is masseuse Sonia Benothman, whose pioneering 'Rose de Nuit' treatment involves wrapping you in rose petals, using rare huile d'Argan from Morocco. Hammam and *gommage* cost €34, a 'Forfait florale' €119.

Institut Payot

10 rue de Castiglione, 1st (01.42.60.32.87). M° Concorde. **Open** 9.30am-6.30pm Mon, Wed, Fri, Sat; 9.30am-8.30pm Tue, Thur. **Credit** AmEx, DC, MC, V. **Map** p403 G5.

The former home of Countess Castiglione is as beautifully preserved as its clientele. Created by Dr Nadia Payot, one of the leading ladies in French skincare, it runs the gamut of luxurious face and body treatments. Prices range from €40 to €80.

Lancôme

29 rue du Fbg-St-Honoré, 8th (01.42.65.30.74). M° Madeleine. **Open** 10am-7pm Mon-Sat. **Credit** AmEx, DC, MC, V. **Map** p403 F4.

Massages are the name of the game here: try the 'Mineral Treatment', using smooth Arizona desert stones that have been warmed and rubbed in oil, or 'Flash Bronzer', with self-tanning creams. Facials cost €68 to €136, body treatments €74 to €149.

Toni & Guy

248 rue St-Honoré, 1st (01.40.20.98.20). M° Palais Royal Musée du Louvre or Pyramides. **Open** 10am-8pm Mon-Sat. **Credit** AmEx, DC, MC, V. **Map** p403 G5.

Strategically located in prime spots around Paris, these hairdressing salons have tariffs ranging from €45 to €92, depending on the 'artist' working on your new look. Drop by (or rather, book) for a cut on a Friday and Saturday afternoon and you can tax your hairdresser by nodding along to the resident DJ. Or you can let students experiment on you for free at Toni & Guy's training academy (122 rue du Fbg-St-Honoré, 8th, 01.40.20.15.93).

Other locations: 18 rue Tiquetonne, 2nd (01.40.41.11.00); 264 bd St-Germain, 7th (01.44.18.33.72); 6 rue de Charonne, 11th (01.43.14.01.43).

Books, CDs, DVDs

Books

Trawl around the 5th and 6th, and you'll find racks of €1 English-language paperbacks, heavyweight academic specialists and the quays lined with boxes of literary treasure. *See also p246* **Fnac** and **Virgin Megastore**; for cinema bookshops, *see p302*.

Artazart

83 quai de Valmy, 10th (01.40.40.24.00/www.
artazart.com) M° Jacques Bonsergent. **Open** 11am-8pm Mon-Fri; 2-7pm Sat, Sun. **Credit** MC, V. **Map** p404 L4.
A bright yellow beacon on trendy Canal St-Martin, this bookshop and gallery stocks cutting-edge publications on fashion, art, architecture and design.

Bouquinistes

Along the quais, especially quai de Montebello, quai St-Michel, 5th. M° St-Michel. **Open** times depend on stall, Tue-Sun. **No credit cards. Map** p408 J7.
The green boxes along the quais selling second-hand books are one of Paris' oldest institutions. Ignore the nasty postcards and rummage through the stacks of ancient paperbacks for something existential. Be sure to haggle – it would be rude not to.

Brentano's

37 av de l'Opéra, 2nd (01.42.61.52.50/www.
brentano.fr). M° Opéra. **Open** 10am-7.30pm Mon-Sat. **Credit** AmEx, MC, V. **Map** p403 G4.
Good for American classics, modern fiction and best-sellers, plus business titles. The children's section is in the basement, the French part towards the rear. Dinky gifts available next to the greetings cards.

La Flûte de Pan

49, 53, 59 rue de Rome, 8th (01.44.70.91.68). M° Europe. **Open** 10am-6.30pm Mon, Tue, Thur-Sat; 2.30-6.30pm Wed. **Credit** MC, V. **Map** p403 F3.
Three shops stocking books on classical music and – more importantly – scores for all kinds of instrument: strings, wind and orchestra, plus learning material at No.49; brass, sax and percussion at No.53, and piano, organ and vocal at No.59.

Galignani

224 rue de Rivoli, 1st (01.42.60.76.07). M° Tuileries. **Open** 10am-7pm Mon-Sat. **Credit** MC, V. **Map** p403 G5.
Opened in 1802, Galignani was reputedly the first English-language bookshop in Europe, and even published its own daily newspaper. Today it stocks fine and decorative arts books, and literature, in French and English, plus a range of magazines.

Gibert Jeune

10 pl St-Michel, 6th (01.56.81.22.52/www.gibert jeune.fr). M° St-Michel. **Open** 9.30am-7.30pm Mon-Sat. **Credit** AmEx, DC, MC, V. **Map** p408 J7.

This 'Langues et lettres' branch of the Left Bank chain claims to stock books published in 320 languages. For the full list of branches, see the website.

Gibert Joseph

26 bd St-Michel, 6th (01.44.41.88.88/www.gibert joseph.com). M° St-Michel. **Open** 10am-7.30pm Mon-Sat. **Credit** MC, V. **Map** p408 J7.
Best known as a bookshop for the Left Bank seats of learning, as well as a place at which to flog text books; Gibert Joseph (a separate company from Gibert Jeune, *see above* – both were formed by splitting parent company Gibert in 1929) also has stationery, CDs, DVDs and art supply emporia further up the street; for these details and other branches, see the website.

La Hune

170 bd St-Germain, 6th (01.45.48.35.85). M° St-Germain-des-Prés. **Open** 10am-11.45pm Mon-Sat; 11am-7.45pm Sun. **Credit** AmEx, MC, V. **Map** p407 G7.
A Left Bank institution, La Hune boasts a global selection of art and design books, and a magnificent collection of French literature and theory.

Librairie Flammarion

Centre Pompidou, 19 rue Beaubourg, 4th (01.44.78.43.22). M° Rambuteau. **Open** 10am-10pm Mon, Wed-Sun. **Credit** AmEx, MC, V. **Map** p404 K5.
This bookshop, on the ground floor of the Centre Pompidou, is one of the most pleasant places in Paris at which to browse through first-rate art, design, architecture, photography and cinema titles. It also stocks children's books, a huge selection of postcards (the post office next door is the quietest in town), arty magazines and other odds and ends.

The Red Wheelbarrow Bookstore

13 rue Charles-V, 4th (01.42.77.42.17). M° St-Paul. **Open** 10am-6.30pm Tue-Sun. **Credit** MC, V. **Map** p408 L7.
More literature than pulp fiction in this small but sincere English-language book-lined cranny, with a well-stocked children's corner. A larger branch can be found at 22 rue St-Paul (4th, 01.48.04.75.08, 10am-7pm Mon-Sat, 2-6pm Sun).

San Francisco Book Co

17 rue Monsieur-le-Prince, 6th (01.43.29.15.70). M° Odéon. **Open** 11am-9pm Mon-Sat; 2-7.30pm Sun. **Credit** MC. **Map** p408 H7.
Well-established second-hand bookstore with a wide range of English-language fiction, and more cheap paperbacks than you can shake a stick at.

Shakespeare & Co

37 rue de la Bûcherie, 5th (01.43.26.96.50). M° Maubert Mutualité/RER St-Michel Notre-Dame. **Open** noon-midnight daily. **No credit cards. Map** p408 J7.
George Whitman founded this institution in 1951, consisting of three floors crammed with books. It's staffed by struggling expat writers who calmly play chess while you browse in their bedrooms.

Eat, Drink, Shop

Village Voice

6 rue Princesse, 6th (01.46.33.36.47). M° Mabillon.
Open 2-8pm Mon; 10am-8pm Tue-Sat; 2-8pm Sun.
Credit AmEx, DC, MC, V. **Map** p407 H7.
An excellent selection of new fiction, non-fiction and literary magazines in English. It also holds literary events and poetry readings.

WH Smith

248 rue de Rivoli, 1st (01.44.77.88.99/www.
whsmith.fr). M° Concorde or Tuileries. **Open** 9am-
7.30pm Mon-Sat; 1-7.30pm Sun. **Credit** AmEx, MC,
V. **Map** p403 G5.
Some 70,000 English-language titles and a near impenetrable crush around the magazine section. Upstairs has English-language videos, DVDs and story tapes. Knowledgeable expat staff, too.

CDs & DVDs

Gibert Joseph (*see p245*) stocks CDs and DVDs; **WH Smith** (*see above*) stocks British DVDs; for specialist vinyl stores, *see p247* **That old black magic**.

Blue Moon Music

84 rue Quincampoix, 4th (01.40.29.45.60). M°
Rambuteau. **Open** 11am-7pm Mon-Sat. **Credit** V.
Map p408 J6.
Specialising in reggae and ragga, this is the place to come to for some authentic Jamaican sounds as it receives new imports on a weekly basis.

Crocodisc

40-42 rue des Ecoles, 5th (01.43.54.47.95).
M° Maubert Mutualité. **Open** 11am-7pm Tue-Sat.
Closed 2wks Aug. **Credit** MC, V. **Map** p408 J7.
An excellent, if expensive, range includes rock, funk, African, country and classical. For jazz and blues try Crocojazz (*see p247* **That old black magic**).

Fnac

74 av des Champs-Elysées, 8th (01.53.53.64.64/
www.fnac.com). M° George V. **Open** 10am-midnight
Mon-Sat; noon-midnight Sun. **Credit** AmEx, MC, V.
Map p402 D4.
Fnac's musical range is wide – the African section being particularly reliable. This is the only branch to open on Sunday; others also stock books, computers, music and photography equipment, and operate as a main concert box office.
Other locations: *Forum des Halles, 1st*
(01.40.41.40.00); 136 rue de Rennes, 6th
(01.49.54.30.00); music only 4 pl de la Bastille, 12th
(01.43.42.04.04).

Monster Melodies

9 rue des Déchargeurs, 1st (01.40.28.09.39). M° Les
Halles. **Open** 11am-7pm Mon-Sat. **Credit** MC, V.
Map p404 J5.
The owners of this store are prepared to help customers on their treasure hunt – and housing more than 10,000 second-hand, well-priced CDs of every variety, it's just as well.

Virgin Megastore

52-60 av des Champs-Elysées, 8th (01.49.53.50.00).
M° Franklin D. Roosevelt. **Open** 10am-midnight
Mon-Sat; noon-midnight Sun. **Credit** AmEx, DC,
MC, V. **Map** p403 E4.
The luxury of perusing the latest CDs till midnight makes this a choice spot, and the listening posts let you sample any CD by scanning its barcode. Sells concert tickets, too.
Other locations: *Carrousel du Louvre, 99 rue de*
Rivoli, 1st (01.44.50.03.10); 5 bd Montmartre, 2nd
(01 40 13 72 13); 15 bd Barbès, 18th
(01.56.55.53.70).

Children

Clothes & shoes

Stroll through St-Germain-des-Prés and you'll see toddlers decked out in designer gear that has never been anywhere near a sandpit. If you're looking for cheap 'n' cheerful, you'll find plenty of funky fashions at the chain **Du Pareil au Même**. Look for small boutiques with their own style, too, like **Gaspard de la Butte**. Children's shops are clustered on **rue Bréa** (6th), **rue Vavin** (6th) and **rue du Fbg-St-Antoine** (12th).

Bonton

82 rue de Grenelle, 7th (01.44.39.09.20/www.
bonton.fr). M° Rue du Bac. **Open** 10am-7pm Mon-
Sat. Closed 2wks Aug. **Credit** AmEx, DC, MC, V.
Map p407 F6.
At this concept store for kids and trendy parents, T-shirts, skirts and trousers come in rainbow colours, albeit at steep prices. There's also furniture, gadgets and accessories, plus a kids' hairdresser.

Du Pareil au Même

15-17 rue des Mathurins, 9th (01.42.66.93.80/www.
dpam.fr). M° Havre-Caumartin/RER Auber. **Open**
10am-7pm Mon-Sat. **Credit** MC, V. **Map** p403 G3.
Bright, cleverly designed basics for kids aged three months to 14 years, at low prices. Du Pareil Au Même Bébé, with fashionable accessories and clothing for kiddies up to two years, makes gifts that look more expensive than they are; check the musical cuddly chicken, a godsend at changing time. There's a homeware shop at No.23; for the other branches around town, see the website.

Gaspard de la Butte

10bis rue Yvonne-Le-Tac, 18th (01.42.55.99.40).
M° Abbesses. **Open** 10am-7pm Tue-Sun. Closed Aug.
Credit DC, MC, V. **Map** p404 H2.
Catherine Malaure creates the prototypes for the bright, graphic kids' wear (nought to six years) that she sells in this natty boutique. Malaure does a great line in sparky undersized accessories such as gloves and funky aviator hats.

Jacadi

76 rue d'Assas, 6th (01.45.44.60.44/www.jacadi.fr).
M° Vavin. **Open** 10am-7pm Mon-Sat. **Credit** MC, V.
Map p407 G8.

Jacadi's well-made clothes for babies and children;
pleated skirts, smocked dresses, dungarees and Fair
Isle knits are a hit with well-to-do parents. There's
funkier party stuff too. See website for branches.

Petit Bateau

26 rue Vavin, 6th (01.55.42.02.53/www.petit-bateau.
com). M° Vavin. **Open** 10am-7pm Mon-Sat. **Credit**
MC, V. **Map** p407 G8.

Renowned for comfortable, well-made cotton T-
shirts, vests and other separates in an extensive
range of colours and cuts, Petit Bateau carries an
equally coveted teen range. For the other branches
around town, check the website.

Six Pieds Trois Pouces

223 bd St-Germain, 7th (01.45.44.03.72). M°
Solférino. **Open** 10am-7pm Mon-Sat. Closed Mon
in Aug. **Credit** AmEx, V. **Map** p407 F6.

An excellent range of children's and teens' shoes
goes from classics by Startrite, Aster and Little
Mary to trendy Reeboks and Timberlands, as well
as shoes under the shop's less-expensive own label.
Other locations: *85 rue de Longchamp, 16th*
(01.45.53.64.21); 78 av de Wagram, 17th
(01.46.22.81.64).

That old black magic

Paris doesn't spring to mind as a prime spot
for feeding any vinyl addiction, but browsing
one of these specialist shops down an
obscure backstreet could lead to the kind of
find Camden just can't match.

The dance crowd are well catered for in
Paris. **DMC** (2 bd Richard-Lenoir, 11th,
01.43.38.00.00) has all the hip hop you can
shake a stick at, plus a quality house
selection thanks to Manchester Nick. **Urban
Music** (22 rue Pierre-Lescot, 1st,
01.40.13.99.28) specialises in the domestic
version. You'll find Jamaican 45s at **Black
Rain Musik** (55bis rue Jean-Pierre-Timbaud,
11th, 01.40.21.92.44).

For house and techno, the massive **12inch**
(18 rue Turbigo, 2nd, 01.40.13.90.00) has
a chill-out lounge as well as a good stock;
Vibe Station (57 rue du Fbg-St-Antoine, 11th,
01.44.74.64.18) specialises in garage and
the dark, sweaty cavern known as **Techno
Import** (16 rue des Taillandiers, 11th,
01.48.05.71.56), with techno and house
classified by label, has enough listening
posts you never have to queue. You'll find
house classics at **Club News** (37 rue St-
Honoré, 1st, 01.40.13.99.70) and a constant
flow of new electro at **Phat Beatz** (57 rue St-
Maur, 11th, 01.48.06.08.81). **Katapult** (2
rue de Franche-Comté, 3rd, 01.42.76.93.93)
is the place for German techno. For drum 'n'
bass, try **Black Label** (25 rue Keller, 11th,
01.40.21.92.44), while **Wave** (36 rue Keller,
11th, 01.40.21.86.98) is a nerds' paradise
of electronica. Exhaustive **Disco Puces** (102
bd Beaumarchais, 11th, 01.43.57.88.55)
stocks dance classics.

Paris is also a surprisingly fertile ground for
hardcore and underground sounds. Cool
Bimbo Tower (5 passage St-Antoine, 11th,

01.49.29.76.70) stocks all manner of
counter-culture music. **Hokus Pokus** (32 bd
Richard-Lenoir, 11th, 01.43.55.42.89) has
every hardcore genre under the BPM sun, and
you'll find more hardcore at **Sphénoïde** (30
rue St-Ambroise, 11th, 01.48.07.05.47).

Rare and vintage pressings of jazz, rock and
pop classics are thick on the ground. Tiny
Moby Disques (9 rue des Déchargeurs, 1st,
01.43.29.70.51) specialises in post-war jazz,
Crocojazz (64 rue de la Montagne-Ste-
Geneviève, 5th, 01.46.34.78.38) has some
8,000 jazz discs, while in nearby rue de
Navarre you'll find **Jazz Ensuite** (No.7,
01.43.37.61.80) and the **Paris Jazz Corner**
(No.5, 01.43.36.78.92). For pop, punk and
'60s beat, **Gibert Joseph Musique** (26 bd St-
Michel, 6th, 01.43.29.37 06) has bundles of
second-hand 45s, **Plus de Bruit** (35 rue La
Rochefoucauld, 9th, 01.49.70.08.70)
specialises in ska and chanson, while the
more sedate **Oldies But Goodies** (7 rue des
Filles du Calvaire, 3rd, 01.48.87.14.37) lives
up to the promise of its name. **Elvis Is
Happiness** (9 rue Notre-Dame-des-Victoires,
2nd, 01.49.27.08.43), home of the Paris
branch of the Elvis Fan Club, has discs,
clocks and models. Moving along, metal fans
can find that lost double-live gatefold at **Born
Bad** (17 rue Keller, 11th, 01.43.38.41.78).

In the classical stakes, there's **Papageno**
(1 rue de Marivaux, 2nd, 01.42.96.56.54,
www.papageno.fr), which specialises in rare
opera finds on vinyl, some dating back to the
early 20th century, as well as the usual large
selection of CDs.

Finally, what better place to browse through
vinyl recordings of moody French crooning than
Le Silence de la Rue (39 rue Faidherbe, 11th,
01.40.24.16.16)?

Colette. *See p249.*

Toys & books

Cosy traditional toyshops abound in Paris. **Department stores** (*see p240*) all provide animated windows and toy floors at Christmas. For children's books in English go to **WH Smith** (*see p246*) or **Brentano's** (*see p245*).

Arche de Noé

70 rue St-Louis-en-l'Ile, 4th (01.46.34.61.60). Mº Pont Marie. **Open** 11am-7pm daily. **Credit** AmEx, MC, V. **Map** p408 K7.
Far from the chaos of the *grands magasins*, Noah's Ark on the Ile St-Louis is just the place for Christmas shopping, with wooden toys from Eastern Europe, games and jigsaw puzzles, Babar paraphernalia and finger puppets.

Au Nain Bleu

406-410 rue St-Honoré, 8th (01.42.60.39.01/ www.au-nain-bleu.com). Mº Concorde. **Open** 9.45am-6.30pm Mon-Sat. **Credit** AmEx, MC, V. **Map** p403 G4.
Dating from 1836, France's most prestigious toy shop is stuffier and more old-fashioned than Hamley's. Its stock features toys from all around the world, from furry animals to electronic games.

Fnac Junior

19 rue Vavin, 6th (01.56.24.03.46/www.fnacjunior. com). Mº Vavin. **Open** 10am-7.30pm Mon-Sat. **Credit** AmEx, MC, V. **Map** p407 G8.
Fnac carries books, toys, videos, CDs and CD-Roms for the under-12s. Storytelling and activities (Wed, Sat) takes place for three-year-olds and up. For other branches around town, see the website.

La Grande Récré

7-11 bd Barbès, 18th (01.42.64.90.19/www.lagrande recre.com). Mº Barbès Rochechouart. **Open** 9am-7.30pm daily. **Credit** AmEx, MC, V. **Map** p404 J1.
France's answer to Toys 'R' Us, this massive toy chain stocks all manner of goodies. Check the website for other branch details.

Village Joué Club

3-5 bd des Italiens, 2nd (01.53.45.41.41/www.joue club.fr). Mº Richelieu Drouot. **Open** 10am-8pm Mon-Sat. **Credit** AmEx, MC, V. **Map** p404 H4.
The largest toy store in Paris is spread out on ground level in and around the passage des Princes.

Concept stores

Paris can't get enough of designerish one-stop shops, as instigated by the pioneering **Colette**, now with a branch in Tokyo. With their fusion of art, fashion and other creative pursuits, they result in a cool and popular alternative to the traditional high brow designer boutiques.

Castelbajac Concept Store

31 pl du Marché-St-Honoré, 1st (01.42.60.41.55). Mº Tuileries or Pyramides. **Open** 10.30am-7.30pm daily. **Credit** AmEx, DC, MC, V. **Map** p403 G5.
Aristo designer Jean-Charles de Castelbajac's humorous, colourful world of fashion – developed over 30 years either side of the Atlantic – is showcased in a 230m² gleaming white concept store. As well as his own eclectic fashion collections and accessories for men and women, Castelbajac contains funky furniture and any number of objects by invited artists and designers.

Colette

*213 rue St-Honoré, 1st (01.55.35.33.90/
www.colette.fr). M° Tuileries or Palais Royal Musée
du Louvre.* **Open** 10.30am-7.30pm Mon-Sat. **Credit**
AmEx, DC, MC, V. **Map** p403 G4.

Eight years on, the original concept/lifestyle store is
still the most cutting-edge and frighteningly minimalist. As well as exporting the one-stop concept
shop to Tokyo in 2004, Colette release CDs on their
own label and produce regular weighty style cata-
logues. 'Must Have' accessories are displayed away
from sticky fingers inside clinical glass cases, while
hipster books, media, Sony cameras, fancy Nokias
and the hair and beauty brands själ, Kiehl's, or uslu
airlines, are scattered amid the ultra-cool reviews,
magazines and photo albums on the ground floor
and mezzanine. Upstairs has a selection of 'in'
clothes (think Bless and Bernard Wilhelm), and
accessories such as the Chrome Hearts line. Lunch,
with a global selection of mineral water, can be nib-
bled at in the basement Water Bar.

Espace Lab 101

*44 rue de la Rochefoucauld, 9th (01.49.95.95.85).
M° Pigalle or St-Georges.* **Open** 12.30-7.30pm Tue-
Sat. **No credit cards. Map** p403 H2.

An off-shoot of creative clubbers Project 101, Espace
Lab has a changing collection of streetwear labels
(check out the customised military jackets by Super
Sapin), plus electronic music on independent labels
and DVDs. *See also p331* **Clubbing crossover**.

Spree

*16 rue de La Vieuville, 18th (01.42.23.41.40). M°
Abbesses.* **Open** 2-7.30pm Mon; 11am-7.30pm Tue-
Sat. Closed 2wks Aug, public hols. **Credit** MC, V.
Map p404 H1.

Run by artistic director Bruno Hadjadj and fashion
designer Roberta Oprandi, Spree mixes fashion,
design and contemporary art with a distinctly
Montmartre vibe. Here you'll find a '60s chair draped
in the latest fashions by designers such as Preen or
Isabel Marant.

Surface to Air

*46 rue de l'Arbre-Sec, 1st (01.49.27.04.54/
www.surface2air.com). M° Pont Neuf.* **Open** 11am-
7.30pm Mon-Sat. **Credit** MC, V. **Map** p408 J6.

A group of English and Americans created this inde-
finable, non-concept concept store; it also acts as a
gallery and graphic design agency. The cult clothing selection takes in cute T-shirt dresses, Sila and
Maria's trashy tank tops, Tatty Devine's hair accessories and men's themed sweatshirts. On its way to
rivalling Colette for tastemaking supremacy,
Surface to Air now runs biannual fashion salons, has
launched its own menswear label and has been
called upon by multinationals such as Motorola to
inject funkiness into their products.

Fashion

Fashion shopping in Paris is not always about
designer labels and selective boutiques. In
addition to pan-European brands such as H&M,
Zara and Mango, the French high street has its
fair share of Gallic cheapies: think **Etam**,
Jennyfer and Pimkie. The highest concentration
of these chains is in the Forum des Halles (1st),
and on nearby rue de Rivoli, between Métro
stations Châtelet and Louvre Rivoli. *See also
pp37-39* **Haute couture or high street?**

Designerwear

L'Eclaireur
3ter rue des Rosiers, 4th (01.48.87.10.22/
www.leclaireur.com). M° St-Paul. **Open** 11am-7pm
Mon-Sat. **Credit** AmEx, DC, MC, V. **Map** p408 L6.
Housed in a dandified warehouse, L'Eclaireur stocks
the most uncompromising of top labels' designs,
including Comme des Garçons, Martin Margiela,
Dries van Noten, Carpe Diem and Junya Watanabe.
See the website for details of other branches.

L'Eclaireur Homme
12 rue Malher, 4th (01.44.54.22.11/
www.leclaireur.com). M° St-Paul. **Open** 11am-7pm
Mon-Sat. **Credit** AmEx, DC, MC, V. **Map** p408 L6.

Amid the exposed ducts of this old printers you'll
find pieces by Prada, Comme des Garçons, Dries van
Noten and Martin Margiela. The star is Italian Stone
Island, whose radical technical clothing features
parkas with a steel shell to counteract pollution.

Kabuki Femme
25 rue Etienne-Marcel, 1st (01.42.33.55.65). M°
Etienne Marcel. **Open** 10.30am-7.30pm Mon-Sat.
Credit AmEx, DC, MC, V. **Map** p404 J5.
On the ground floor there's intrepid footwear and
bags by Costume National, Miu Miu and Prada,
along with Fendi's cult creations; Burberry belts and
Miu Miu sunglasses are also stocked here. Upstairs
is home to no-flies-on-me suits by Helmut Lang and
Véronique Leroy, Prada and Costume National.

Shopping by area

Châtelet & Les Halles
The **Forum des Halles** shopping centre is the
commercial and transport centre of Paris. In
the streets fanning out from this underground
hub are good vintage clothes and streetwear
shops. And along the **rue de Rivoli** between
the Métro stations Châtelet and Louvre-Rivoli
you'll find the pick of high-street fashion.
adidas (Fashion, *p259*); **Agnès b** (Fashion,
p256); **Boutique M Dia** (Fashion, *p259*);
La Bulle Kenzo (Beauty, *p243*); **By Terry**
(Beauty, *p241*); **Claudie Pierlot** (Fashion,
p256); **Clery Brice** (Fashion, *p259*); **E
Dehillerin** (Home, *p274*); **L'Esthétique de
Demain** (Beauty, *p244*); **Go Sport** (Sport &
games, *p275*); **Laguiole Galerie** (Home,
p275); **Legrand Filles et Fils** (Food & drink,
p265); **Monster Melodies** (Books, CDs,
DVDs, *p246*); **Papeterie Moderne** (Gifts,
p271); **Puma Store** (Fashion, *p259*); **Rag**
(Fashion, *p260*); **La Samaritaine** (One-stop
shops, *p240*); **Son et Image** (Fashion, *p260*);
Surface to Air (Concept stores, *p249*);
Le Vestibule (Fashion, *p259*).

Rue Etienne-Marcel & environs
When Rei Kawakubo set up **Comme des
Garçons'** first Paris boutique in this grungy
area just north of Les Halles in the 1980s,
she set in motion its transformation into the
rebellious but chic neighbour of fashionable
place des Victoires.
Barbara Bui (Fashion, *p256*); **Diesel** (Fashion,
p257); **Et Vous** (Fashion, *p257*); **Galérie
Noémie** (Beauty, *p243*); **Jean-Paul Gaultier**
(Fashion, *p255*); **Kabuki Femme** (Fashion,
p250); **Kanabeach** (Fashion, *p259*);
Kiliwatch (Fashion, *p259*); **Kokon To Zai**
(Fashion, *p251*); **Mandarina Duck** (Fashion,
p263); **Royal Cheese** (Fashion, *p259*);
Patrick Cox (Fashion, *p264*).

Rue St-Honoré & environs
The poshest part of the 1st, hugging the
Louvre, this area spreads out from rue St-
Honoré, and encompasses glamorous,
diamond-studded place Vendôme. The
success of concept store **Colette** has seen
a recent influx of new boutiques setting up
on and off rue St-Honoré.
Alice Cadolle (Fashion, *p260*); **Astier de
Villatte** (Home, *p272*); **Bali Barret** (Fashion,
p256); **Boucheron** (Fashion, *p262*); **Cabane
de Zucca** (Fashion, *p253*); **Colette** (Concept
stores, *p249*); **Castelbajac Concept Store**
(Concept stores, *p248*); **Chanel** (Fashion,
p254); **Chanel Joaillerie** (Fashion, *p262*);
Christian Louboutin (Fashion, *p263*); **Corinne
Cobson** (Fashion, *p257*); **Costume National**
(Fashion, *p254*); **Didier Ludot** (Fashion,
p259); **Dior Joaillerie** (Fashion, *p262*); **Erès**
(Fashion, *p260*); **Fauchon** (Food & drink,
p269); **Fifi Chachnil** (Fashion, *p260*; **La
Galerie du Carrousel du Louvre** (One-stop
shops, *p241*); **Galignani** (Books, CDs, DVDs,
p245); **Hédiard** (Food & drink, *p269*); **Maria
Luisa** (Fashion, *p251*); **Helmut Lang** (Fashion,
p254); **Institut Payot** (Beauty, *p244*);
Jacques Le Corre (Fashion, *p262*); **John
Galliano** (Fashion, *p255*); **Kioko** (Food &
drink, *p266*); **Louvre des Antiquaires** (Home,
p272); **Madelios** (Fashion, *p258*); **La Maison
de la Truffe** (Food & drink, *p269*); **La Maison
du Whisky** (Food & drink, *p270*); **Martin
Margiela** (Fashion, *p255*); **Au Nain Bleu**
(Children, *p248*); **Philippe Model** (Fashion,
p262); **Pierre Hardy** (Fashion, *p264*);

Eat, Drink, Shop

Kokon To Zai

48 rue Tiquetonne, 2nd (01.42.36.92.41). M°
Etienne Marcel. **Open** 11.30am-7.30pm Mon-Sat.
Credit AmEx, DC, MC, V. **Map** p404 J5.
Always a spot-on spotter of the latest creations, this
tiny, cutting-edge style emporium is sister to the
Kokon To Zai in Soho. The neon and club feel of the
mirrored space match the dark glamour of its
designs. Unique pieces straight off the catwalk share
space with creations by Alexandre et Matthieu,
Marjan Peijoski and new Norwegian designers.

Maria Luisa

2 rue Cambon, 1st (01.47.03.48.08). M° Concorde.
Open 10.30am-7pm Mon-Sat. **Credit** AmEx, DC,
MC, V. **Map** p403 G4.

Venezuelan Maria Luisa Poumaillou was one of
Paris' first stockists of Galliano, McQueen and the
Belgians, and has an eye for rising stars. Nearby
shops covers fashion (Olivier Theyskens, Diego
Dolcini, Ona Selfa, Rick Owens), accessories
(Manolos and Pierre Hardy shoes, Carel & Rubio's
gloves at 4 rue Cambon), streetwear (38 rue du Mont-
Thabor) and menswear (19bis rue du Mont-Thabor).

Onward

147 bd St-Germain, 6th (01.55.42.77.56). M° St-
Germain-des-Prés. **Open** 11am-7pm Mon, Sat;
10.30am-7pm Tue-Fri. **Credit** AmEx, DC, MC, V.
Map p407 G6.
Onward has a rapid turnover of young talents, who
seem to compete to see who can produce the most

Rodolphe Menudier (Fashion, *p264*); **Salons
du Palais-Royal Shiseido** (Beauty, *p243*); **Toni
+ Guy** (Beauty, *p244*); **Torréfacteur Verlet**
(Food & drink, *p269*); **Van Cleef & Arpels**
(Fashion, *p263*); **W H Smith** (Books, CDs,
DVDs, *p246*).

Rue du Fbg-St-Honoré & the Champs-Elysées

When St-Honoré crosses into the 8th and
becomes **rue du Faubourg-St-Honoré**, it takes
on an air of exclusivity. This neighbourhood
encompasses the gorgeous shops around
Madeleine, the famous A-grade fashion strip
the **avenue Montaigne**, as well as the brash
and buzzing **Champs-Elysées**.
Alléosse (Food & drink, *p265*); **Anne Sémonin**
(Beauty, *p243*); **Balenciaga** (Fashion, *p253*);
Black Block (Gifts, *p270*); **Les Caves
Taillevent** (Food & drink, *p270*); **CFOC**
(Home, *p272*); **Christian Dior** (Fashion,
p254); **Comme des Garçons** (Fashion, *p254*);
Décathlon (Sport & games, *p275*); **Drugstore
Publicis** (One-stop shops, *p241*); **Equistable**
(Sport & games, *p275*); **Etam** (Fashion,
p260); **La Flûte de Pan** (Books, CDs, DVDs,
p245); **Fnac** (Books, CDs, DVDs, *p246*);
Guerlain (Beauty, *p243*); **Hermès** (Fashion,
p254); **Izka** (Fashion, *p260*); **Jabugo Ibérico
& Co** (Food & drink, *p266*); **Lancôme** (Beauty,
p244); **Loft Design by** (Fashion, *p257*); **Louis
Vuitton** (Fashion, *p255*); **La Maison du
Chocolat** (Food & drink, *p266*); **Make Up For
Ever Professional** (Beauty, *p243*); **Marni**
(Fashion, *p255*); **Monceau Fleurs** (Gifts,
p270); **Petrossian** (Food & drink, *p268*);
Prada (Fashion, *p255*); **Roger Vivier** (Fashion,
p264); **Sephora** (Beauty, *p243*); **Virgin
Megastore** (Books, CDs, DVDs, *p246*).

Opéra & Grands Boulevards

The department stores provide the
commercial heartbeat to this busy *quartier.*
Brentano's (Books, CDs, DVDs, *p245*);
Cartier (Fashion, *p262*); **Les Caves Augé**
(Food & drink, *p270*); **Citadium** (Sport &
games, *p275*); **Du Pareil au Même** (Children,
p246); **Galeries Lafayette** (One-stop shops,
p240); **Jamin Puech** (Fashion, *p263*); **Lafont**
(Fashion, *p262*); **Pa Design** (Gifts, *p271*);
Printemps (One-stop shops, *p240*); **René
Pierre** (Sports & games, *p275*; **Sarl Velan
Stores** (Food & drink, *p268*); **Village Joué
Club** (Children, *p248*).

Montmartre

In the winding streets around Sacré-Coeur –
rue des Abbesses, **rue Houdon** and **rue des
Martyrs** – you'll find many funky, independent
designers. From the Métro station Barbès
Rochechouart, **bd de Rochechouart** is one
elongated strip of discount shops.
Arnaud Delmontel (Food & drink, *p265*);
Arnaud Lahrer (Food & drink, *p268*); **Detaille
1905** (Beauty, *p243*); **Espace Lab 101**
(Concept stores, *p249*); **Gaspard de la Butte**
(Children, *p246*); **La Grande Récré** (Children,
p248); **Spree** (Concept stores, *p249*); **Tati**
(One-stop shops, *p241*).

Canal St-Martin

This mini *quartier* provides the perfect canal-
side esplanade for relaxed browsing.
Antoine et Lili (Fashion, *p256*); **Artazart**
(Books, CDs, DVDs, *p245*); **Stocks and
Marques** (Fashion, *p260*). ▶

far-fetched and priciest design. It currently stocks over 20 established and up-and-coming designers, including Hussein Chalayan, The People of the Labyrinths and Martin Margiela. Accessories, too, are well chosen; try funky pieces by Tatty Devine, Pièce à Conviction and Yazbukey on for size.

Pressing Shop
13 rue du roi de Sicile, 4th (01.40.29.16.965). M° St-Paul. **Open** 1-8pm daily. **Credit** AmEx, DC, MC, V. **Map** p408 L6.

In this miniature, minimalist space run by David Naouri, this new and oh-so-chic Marais menswear store stocks a limited selection of pieces from London and Paris' most avant-garde labels, including Kim Jones, Bernhard Willhelm, Henrik Vibskov,

Stephan Schneider, Gaspard Yurkievich, Ziad Ghanem, Kostas Murkudis, Moritz Rogosky, Robert Cary Williams and Peter Jensen.

Shine
30 rue de Charonne, 11th (01.48.05.80.10). M° Bastille. **Open** 11am-7.30pm Mon-Sat. **Credit** AmEx, DC, MC, V. **Map** p409 M7.

If you're looking for a funkier, more youthful batch of cutting-edge clothes than Maria Luisa (*see p251*) can supply, Vinci d'Helia has just what you need: sexy T-shirts with unusual detailing, Luella's chunky knits and Earl Jeans trousers and jackets. A plethora of original if pricy accessories are here for the taking, and you could end up sharing shop space with Laetitia Casta and Emma de Caunes.

▶ ## Shopping by area (continued)

Bastille
Traditionally home to fine furniture craftsmen, **rue du Fbg-St-Antoine** and nearby **rue de Charonne** and **rue Keller** are peppered with new designer fashion and furniture shops.
Allicante (Food & drink, *p269*); **L'Autre Boulange** (Food & drink, *p265*); **Bières Spéciales** (Food & drink, *p270*); **Blue Moon Music** (Books, CDs, DVDs, *p246*); **Caravane Chambre 19** (Home, *p272*); **Come On Eileen** (Fashion, *p259*); **Les Domaines qui montent** (Food & drink, *p270*); **Galerie Patrick Seguin** (Home, *p274*); **Le Bihan** (Home, *p274*); **Isabel Marant** (Fashion, *p257*); **Ladies & Gentlemen** (Fashion, *p257*); **Moisan** (Food & drink, *p265*; **Résonances** (Gifts, *p271*); **Shine** (Fashion, *p252*).

The Marais
Particularly around **rue des Rosiers** and **rue des Francs-Bourgeois**, this trendy area is a treasure trove of designer boutiques, with a high concentration of design and interiors shops.
Anne et Valentin (Fashion, *p261*); **A-poc** (Fashion, *p253*); **Arche de Noé** (Children, *p248*); **L'Art du Buro** (Gifts, *p270*); **Les Bains du Marais** (Beauty, *p243*); **Bains Plus** (Home, *p274*); **Bô** (Home, *p272*); **BHV** (One-stop shops, *p240*); **Cappellini** (Home, *p272*); **Chône** (Home, *p274*); **Christophe Delcourt** (Home, *p274*); **CSAO** (Home, *p274*); **L'Eclaireur** (Fashion, *p250*); **L'Eclaireur Homme** (Fashion, *p250*); **L'Epicerie** (Food & drink, *p269*); **Espace Lumière** (Home, *p274*); **Finkelsztajn** (Food & drink, *p268*); **FR 66** (Home, *p274*); **Free 'P' Star** (Fashion, *p260*); **Goumanyat** (Food & drink, *p269*); **L'Habilleur**

(Fashion, *p260*); **Izraël** (Food & drink, *p266*); **Jack Henry** (Fashion, *p257*); **Jean-Paul Gardil** (Food & drink, *p269*); **Julien, Caviste** (Food & drink, *p270*); **Librairie Flammarion** (Books, CDs, DVDs, *p245*); **Mariage Frères** (Food & drink, *p269*); **Martin Grant** (Fashion, *p258*); **Nodus** (Fashion, *p258*); **Au Nom de la Rose** (Gifts, *p270*); **L'Occitane** (Beauty, *p243*); **Ozone** (Home, *p274*); **Paris-Musées** (Gifts, *p271*); **Pasta Linea** (Food & drink, *p268*); **Pressing Shop** (Fashion, *p252*); **The Red Wheelbarrow Bookstore** (Books, CDs, DVDs, *p245*); **Sentou Galerie** (Home, *p274*); **Tsumori Chisato** (Fashion, *p256*); **Le Village St-Paul** (Home, *p272*); **Zadig & Voltaire** (Fashion, *p258*).

St-Germain-des-Prés & Odéon
Chic shopping paradise of the Left Bank, with stores a-plenty on **bd St-Germain**, around **St-Sulpice church** and **rue de Buci**.
Alain Mikli (Fashion, *p261*); **APC** (Fashion, *p256*); **L'Artisan Parfumeur** (Beauty, *p241*); **Le Bon Marché** (One-stop shops, *p240*); **Bonton** (Children, *p246*); **Bruno Frisoni** (Fashion, *p263*); **Cacao et Chocolat** (Food & drink, *p266*); **Camper** (Fashion, *p263*); **Christian Constant** (Food & drink, *p266*); **Christian Liaigre** (Home, *p274*); **Christian Tortu** (Gifts, *p270*); **Corinne Sarrut** (Fashion, *p257*); **Da Rosa** (Food & drink, *p269*); **Debauve & Gallais** (Food & drink, *p266*); **Deyrolle** (Gifts, *p270*); **Editions de Parfums Frédéric Malle** (Beauty, *p243*); **Fnac Junior** (Children, *p248*); **Gérard Mulot** (Food & drink, *p268*); **Hervé Chapelier** (Fashion, *p263*); **Huilerie Artisanale Leblanc** (Food & drink, *p269*); **La Hune** (Books, CDs, DVDs, *p245*);

A-list

A-poc

47 rue des Francs-Bourgeois, 4th (01.44.54.07.05).
M° St-Paul. **Open** 11am-7pm Mon-Sat. Closed 3wks
Aug. **Credit** AmEx, DC, MC, V. **Map** p408 L6.
Acronymic for 'A Piece of Cloth', Issey Miyake's lab-
style boutique (designed by Erwan and Ronan
Bouroullec) takes a conceptual approach to clothes
manufacture. Alongside ready-to-wear cotton-Lycra
clothes are rolls of seamless tubular wool jersey
which is cut *sur mesure*; Miyake's assistants will
advise you on a unique ensemble. His original shop
(3 pl des Vosges, 01.48.87.01.86) houses the creations
of Naoki Takisawa, Miyake's latest design protégé.

Balenciaga

10 av George-V, 8th (01.47.20.21.11/www.
balenciaga.com). M° Alma Marceau or George V.
Open 10am-7pm Mon-Sat. **Credit** AmEx, DC, MC,
V. **Map** p402 D5.
With Nicolas Ghesquière at the Balenciaga helm, the
venerable Spanish fashion house has jumped ahead
of Japanese and Belgian designers in the hipper-
than-thou stakes. Floating fabrics contrast with dramatic cuts, producing a sophisticated urban style
that the fashion *haut monde* can't wait to slip into.

Cabane de Zucca

8 rue St-Roch, 1st (01.44.58.98.88). M° Tuileries.
Open 11am-7pm Mon-Sat. Closed Aug. **Credit**
AmEx, DC, MC, V. **Map** p403 G5.

Irié Wash (Fashion, *p257*); **Iris** (Fashion,
p263); **Iunx** (Beauty, *p243*); **Jacadi** (Children,
p247); **Jean-Paul Hévin** (Food & drink, *p266*);
Lagerfeld Gallery (Fashion, *p255*); **Marie
Mercié** (Fashion, *p262*); **Marithé et François
Girbaud** (Fashion, *p258*); **Martine Sitbon**
(Fashion, *p255*); **Miu Miu** (Fashion, *p255*);
Le Mouton à Cinq Pattes (Fashion, *p260*);
Onward (Fashion, *p251*); **Paul et Joe**
(Fashion, *p258*); **Paul Smith** (Fashion, *p258*);
Peggy Huyn Kinh (Fashion, *p264*); **Petit
Bateau** (Children, *p247*); **Pierre Hermé** (Food
& drink, *p268*); **Pierre Marcolini** (Food &
drink, *p266*); **Poilâne** (Food & drink, *p265*);
Princesse Tam Tam (Fashion, *p261*); **Richart**
(Food & drink, *p266*); **Robert Clergerie**
(Fashion, *p264*); **Ryst Dupeyron** (Food &
drink, *p270*); **Sabbia Rosa** (Fashion, *p261*);
Sadaharu Aoki (Food & drink, *p268*); **San
Francisco Book Co** (Books, CDs, DVDs,
p245); **Sennelier** (Gifts, *p271*); **Six Pieds
Trois Pouces** (Children, *p247*); **Sonia Rykiel**
(Fashion, *p255*); **Swarovski** (Fashion, *p262*);
Traction (Fashion, *p262*); **Vanessa Bruno**
(Fashion, *p258*); **Village Voice** (Books, CDs,
DVDs, *p246*); **Yohji Yamamoto** (Fashion,
p256); **Yves Saint Laurent** (Fashion, *p256*).

St-Michel & the 5th

St-Germain's bookish, intellectual cousin is
the hub of the Paris publishing world.
Le Boulanger de Monge (Food & drink,
p265); **Bouquinistes** (Books, CDs, DVDs,
p245); **Crocodisc** (Books, CDs, DVDs, *p246*);
Diptyque (Gifts, *p271*); **Gibert Jeune** (Books,
CDs, DVDs, *p245*); **Gibert Joseph** (Books,
CDs, DVDs, *p245*); **Hammam de la Grande
Mosquée** (Beauty, *p244*); **Kayser** (Food &

drink, *p265*); **La Maison des Trois Thés** (Food
& drink, *p269*); **Mexi & Co** (Food & drink,
p268); **Shakespeare & Co** (Books, CDs,
DVDs, *p245*); **Au Vieux Campeur** (Sport &
games, *p275*).

Trashy, cultish concepts at **Surface to Air**. *See p249.*

Belonging to the Issey Miyake group, this funky Japanese label produces expensive urban wear, distinguished by beautiful fabrics and detailing. Strong on accessories, it has a range of out-there watches.

Chanel

29 rue Cambon, 1st (01.42.86.28.00/www.chanel. com). M° Concorde or Madeleine. **Open** 10am-7pm Mon-Sat. **Credit** AmEx, DC, MC, V. **Map** p403 G4.
Practically synonymous with Paris, fashion legend Chanel is managing to stay relevant – thanks to Karl Lagerfeld. Coco opened her first boutique in this street, at No.21, in 1910, and the tradition continues in this elegant space. Lagerfeld has been designing for Chanel since 1983, and keeps on rehashing Chanel classics, like the little black dress and the Chanel suit with great success. For other branches, see the website.

Christian Dior

28 av Montaigne, 8th (01.40.73.54.44/www.dior. com). M° Franklin D. Roosevelt. **Open** 10am-7pm Mon-Sat. **Credit** AmEx, DC, MC, V. **Map** p402 D5.
To judge from the gaggles of girls who arrive en masse from the suburbs, life savings in hand, to choose a Dior bag, Nick Knight's sexy ad campaigns have been successful. Outrageous, gifted and acclaimed designer John Galliano is behind this label's upbeat, youthful and sexy image. For other branches, see the website.

Comme des Garçons

54 rue du Fbg-St-Honoré, 8th (01.53.30.27.27). M° Madeleine or Concorde. **Open** 11am-7pm Mon-Sat. **Credit** AmEx, DC, MC, V. **Map** p403 F4.
Rei Kawakubo's design ideas and revolutionary mix of materials have greatly influenced fashion of the past two decades, and are superbly showcased in this fire-engine red, fibreglass store. Exclusive perfume lines get a futuristic setting at Comme des Garçons Parfums (23 pl du Marché-St-Honoré, 1st, 01.47.03.15.03).

Costume National

5 rue Cambon, 1st (01.40.15.04.36/www. costumenational.com). M° Concorde. **Open** 11.30am-7pm Mon; 10.30am-7pm Tue-Sat. **Credit** AmEx, MC, V. **Map** p403 G4.
This Milan-based label produces young, sexy clothes for men and women. Its designer Ennio Capasa used to work for Yohji Yamamoto and is as keen on black as he is on giving women hourglass figures. A nice line in shoes and perfumes, too.

Helmut Lang

219 rue St-Honoré, 1st (01.58.62.53.20/www. helmutlang.com). M° Tuileries. **Open** 11am-7pm Mon-Sat. **Credit** AmEx, DC, MC, V. **Map** p403 G5.
Decorated with a work by Jenny Holzer – one of her LED pieces runs up the staircase – this minimal two-storey boutique houses the Austrian designer's chilly, monochrome designs for men and women. Ready-to-wear is downstairs and upstairs shoes and accessories lounge around on Lang's trademark black vinyl ottomans. Works by Louise Bourgeois, Lang's friend and frequent collaborator, are shown in a regularly rotating installation, and pieces by Jean Prouvé are also on show.

Hermès

24 rue du Fbg-St-Honoré, 8th (01.40.17.46.00/www. hermes.com). M° Concorde. **Open** 10.30am-6.30pm Mon-Sat. **Credit** AmEx, DC, MC, V. **Map** p403 F4.
Originally a prestigious saddler, this fashion and accessories house has managed to remain an independent, family-run business as well as a fashion star. For a long time its horse-themed scarves were associated with ladies who lunch, but after hiring avant-garde designer Martin Margiela as the womenswear head in 1997, Hermès brought its style right up-to-date. In 2004 Margiela handed the reins to Jean-Paul Gaultier. The fifth generation of the Hermès family continues to direct the company from this venerable building, inaugurated in the 1930s.

Jean-Paul Gaultier

*6 rue Vivienne, 2nd (01.42.86.05.05/www.gaultier.
fr). M° Bourse.* **Open** 10am-7pm Mon-Fri; 11am-7pm
Sat. **Credit** AmEx, DC, MC, V. **Map** p404 H4.
King of couture Gaultier has restyled his original
boutique as a boudoir with trapunto-quilted, peach
taffeta walls. Men's and women's ready-to-wear,
accessories and the cheaper JPG Jeans lines are sold
here, with haute-couture upstairs (by appointment,
01.42.97.48.12). For branches, see the website.

John Galliano

*384-386 rue St-Honoré, 1st (01.55.35.40.40/www.
johngalliano.com). M° Concorde.* **Open** 11am-7pm
Mon-Sat. **Credit** AmEx, DC, MC, V. **Map** p403 G4.
Designed by architect Jean-Michel Wilmotte (who
did stores for Cartier and Chaumet), this was the
most exciting store to open in Paris in 2003. Though
at Dior since 1996, Galliano still has his own range,
confirming his reputation as Britain's most original
designer. Passers-by can view the small but diverse
collection of well-cut delights through the showcase
window; once inside, Louis XVI-style leather chairs
complement the leather flooring in the changing
room, and the divine hand-embroidered wall panels
of Japanese cherry blossoms set in the candle-scent-
ed toilets. For outlets, see the website.

Lagerfeld Gallery

40 rue de Seine, 6th (01.55.42.75.51). M° Odéon.
Open 11am-7pm Tue-Sat. Closed Aug. **Credit**
AmEx, DC, MC, V. **Map** p408 H6.
Andrée Putman helped create this shrine to King
Karl's brand of stylish minimalism: Lagerfeld's fash-
ion creations and photography are both on display.
You could just sneak in to browse the latest output
of the fashion, beauty and art media, scattered over
a handsome round table at the front of the gallery.

Louis Vuitton

*38 av George-V, 8th (08.10.81.00.10/www.vuitton.
com). M° George V.* **Open** 10am-8pm Mon-Sat.
Credit AmEx, DC, MC, V. **Map** p402 D4.
Crossing this hallowed threshold has caused the odd
Tokyoite to faint from sheer shock and wonderment.
Since 1998 Marc Jacobs has been the artistic director of the luxury label, and was responsible for their
successful first ready-to-wear and shoe line in the
same year. Bringing the august label screamingly
up to date, Jacobs has made Vuitton's luggage and
accessories, as well as their fashion line, as much in
demand as water in the Sahara. In the meantime, you
and I might just be able to afford a monogrammed
pencil case. After slight renovations the flagship
Champs-Elysées store reopens some time in 2005;
till then, this temporary outlet keeps the flag flying.
See the website for other outlets.

Martine Sitbon

*13 rue de Grenelle, 7th (01.44.39.84.44). M° Rue du
Bac or Sèvres-Babylone.* **Open** 10.30am-7pm Mon-
Sat. **Credit** AmEx, MC, V. **Map** p407 G7.
Scents of orange and mimosa lure you into Sitbon's
vault-like store. Beneath its vast ceiling, few items

hang on the railings, but each appears to have a
secret history, born of the originality of the fabric
and cut and a singular harmony, often inspired by
modern art. The menswear will tickle you pink, and
there are cute accessories and candles for under €50.

Martin Margiela

*25bis rue de Montpensier, 1st (01.40.15.07.55). M°
Palais Royal Musée du Louvre.* **Open** 11am-7pm
Mon-Sat. **Credit** AmEx, DC, MC, V. **Map** p404 H5.
The first Paris boutique for the JD Salinger of the
fashion world (MM refuses to be photographed and
only gives interviews by fax) is an immaculate
white, unlabelled space. His clothes, bearing a blank
label but recognisable by external white stitching,
are famous worldwide among those in the know.
Here you can find the entire line 13, 0- and 0-10 accessories for men and women; line 6 (women's basics),
line 10 (menswear), plus magazines and shoes.

Marni

*57 av Montaigne, 8th (01.56.88.08.08). M° Franklin
D. Roosevelt.* **Open** 10am-7pm Mon-Sat. **Credit**
AmEx, DC, MC, V. **Map** p402 D5.
This neo-romantic Italian label was born in 1994
from a family fur company. Consuelo Castiglioni has
fun mixing leather, fur, silk, cashmere and prints,
creating an eccentric but cool mish-mash of textures
and colours. Also mens- and childrenswear lines.

Miu Miu

*16 rue de Grenelle, 7th (01.53.63.20.30). M° Sèvres-
Babylone.* **Open** 11am-7pm Mon; 10am-7pm Tue-Sat.
Credit AmEx, DC, MC, V. **Map** p407 G7.
A diminuitive of Miuccia, first name of Prada's
savvy director, Miu Miu is the principal label's
colourful younger (and cheaper) sister – notable for
its frivolous, reckless style and fabulous shoes. In
this simply decorated, massive two-storey boutique
you'll find both mens- and womenswear.

Prada

*10 av Montaigne, 8th (01.53.23.99.40/www.prada.
com). M° Alma Marceau.* **Open** 11am-7pm Mon;
10am-7pm Tue-Sat. **Credit** AmEx, DC, MC, V.
Map p402 D5.
Miuccia Prada dusted off her family's fine old leather
company in the 1980s, turning Prada's handbags
into the cognoscenti's accessory of choice. Ready-to-
wear was launched in 1989, and fashionistas haven't
been able to get enough of Prada's elegant designs
since. The Paris boutiques are recognisable for the
trademark cool, lime-green walls. See the website for
other outlets.

Sonia Rykiel

*175 bd St-Germain, 6th (01.49.54.60.60/www.sonia
rykiel.fr). M° St-Germain-des-Prés.* **Open** 10.30am-
7pm Tue-Sat. **Credit** AmEx, DC, MC, V. **Map** p407
G6.
Even if her fabrics aren't as super-soft as they once
were, the queen of stripes is still producing skinny
rib knitwear evoking the Left Bank babes of Sartre's
time. Menswear can be found across the street, while

two newer boutiques feature the younger, more affordable 'Sonia by Sonia Rykiel' collection (59 rue des Sts-Pères) and children's wear (6 rue de Grenelle, the site of her original 1966 shop). Just next door to this bastion of pre-pubescent fashion, her Sonia Rykiel Woman (4 rue de Grenelle, 6th, 01.49.54.66.21) store includes a range of designer sex toys – try the vibrating black rubber duck (€45). For other branches, see the website.

Tsumori Chisato

20 rue Barbette, 3rd (01.42.78.18.88). M° St-Paul or Hôtel de Ville. **Open** 11am-7pm Tue-Sat. Closed 3wks Aug. **Credit** AmEx, MC, V. **Map** p408 L6.
Known for her inventive use of colour and wispy fabrics, this Japanese designer has a cult following among fashion-conscious Parisiennes. Artistic director of Issey Sports in the 1980s, Chisato set up her own label in 1990 as part of Miyake's stable; her poetic, romantic designs are big on ingenious detail.

Yohji Yamamoto

3 rue de Grenelle, 7th (01.42.84.28.87). M° Sèvres-Babylone or St-Sulpice. **Open** 10.30am-7.30pm Mon-Sat. **Credit** AmEx, DC, MC, V. **Map** p407 G7.
One of the few true pioneers working in the fashion industry today, Yohji Yamamoto is a master of cut and finish, both strongly inspired by the kimono and traditional Tibetan costume. His dexterity with form makes for unique shapes and styles, largely in black, but when he does colour, it's a blast of brilliance.
Other locations: *47 rue Etienne-Marcel, 1st (01.45.08.82.45); Y's, 25 rue du Louvre, 1st (01.42.21.42.93); 69 rue des Sts-Pères, 6th (01.45.48.22.56).*

Yves Saint Laurent

6 pl St-Sulpice 6th (01.43.29.43.00/www.ysl.com). M° St-Sulpice. **Open** 11am-7pm Mon; 10.30am-7pm Tue-Sat. **Credit** AmEx, DC, MC, V. **Map** p408 H7.
Yves Saint Laurent retired in 2002 after an extraordinary 40-year career which began at Christian Dior, and continued with his fomenting an androgynous revolution in the 1960s under his own name, getting women into dinner and jump suits. It remains to be seen how the label will live on after Tom Ford's departure in 2004. For other branches around the city, see the website.

Boutiques

Agnès b

2, 3, 6, 10, 19 rue du Jour, 1st (women 01.45.08. 56.56/men 01.42.33.04.13/www.agnesb.fr). M° Les Halles or Etienne Marcel. **Open** 10am-7pm Mon-Wed, Fri, Sat; 10am-9pm Thur. **Credit** AmEx, MC, V. **Map** p404 J5.
Agnès b rarely wavers from her design vision: pure lines in fine quality cotton, merino wool and silk. Best buys are shirts, pullovers and cardigans that keep their shape for years. Her mini-empire of men's, women's and children's travel accessories and sportswear outlets is compact; see the site for details.

Antoine et Lili

95 quai de Valmy, 10th (01.40.37.41.55/www. altribu.com). M° Gare de l'Est. **Open** 11am-7pm Mon; 11am-8pm Tue-Fri; 10.30am-8pm Sat; 11.30am-7.30pm Sun. **Credit** AmEx, DC, MC, V. **Map** p404 L3.
Fuchsia-pink and apple-green shopfronts, reflected in the canal on a fine day, are a colour therapist's dream. Vibrant jumpers and neo-hippy skirts hang amid Mexican shrines, Hindu postcards and all sorts of miscellaneous kitsch. The three-shop Canal St-Martin 'Village' has an equally colourful home decoration outlet, florist and self-service café. For other branches, check out the barmy website.

APC

3, 4 rue de Fleurus, 6th (01.42.22.12.77/www.apc.fr). M° St-Placide. **Open** 10.30am-7pm Mon-Sat. **Credit** AmEx, MC, V. **Map** p407 G8.
APC is very very cool. Think of Muji crossed with a rough-cut Agnès b (*see above*) and you get an idea why Jean Touitou's gear is much sought after by the Japanese in-crowd. He recently collaborated with Jessica Ogden on an understated summer range, Madras. Men's clothes are at No.4, along with quirky accessories; cross the road to No.3 for the women's collection. All can be ordered and paid for online; see the website, too, for other branches.

Bali Barret

36 rue du Mont-Thabor, 1st (01.49.26.01.75/ www.balibarret.com). M° Concorde. **Open** 2.30-7.30pm Mon; 10.30am-7.30pm Tue-Sat. **Credit** AmEx, MC, V. **Map** p403 G5.
This French label opened its first boutique in 2002, stocking four different colours each season and offering an androgynous take on classic styles, with a sexy twist. The easy-to-wear collection for 2004 features bright primaries; look out for the funky belts and bags and the matching stripy knickers, stockings and cotton polo necks. Check out the mini-menswear collection for the soft, logoed sweatshirts.

Barbara Bui

23 rue Etienne-Marcel, 1st (01.40.26.43.65/www. barbarabui.fr). M° Etienne Marcel. **Open** 10.30am-7.30pm Mon-Sat. **Credit** AmEx, DC, MC, V. **Map** p404 J5.
Businesswomen who like to cut to the chase have a sartorial ally in Bui: lean, finely cut trousers, figure-hugging shirts and jackets and dagger heels. Bui has branched out into loungey CDs, and there's a café next door. For other branches, see the website.

Claudie Pierlot

1 rue Montmartre, 1st (01.42.21.38.38). M° Les Halles. **Open** 10.30am-7pm Mon-Sat. **Credit** AmEx, MC, V. **Map** p404 H4.
For true Paris chic, a black beret is essential – and Pierlot can always oblige, no matter what season. Wear it with her simple, elegant tank tops, cardigans and little black suits ideal for the office.
Other locations: *23 rue du Vieux-Colombier, 6th (01.45.48.11.96).*

Showcase **Comme des Garçons**. *See p254.*

Fashionable, mid upmarket womenswear in muted, neutral colours are the cornerstone of the Et Vous label. Its latest branch is ultra-minimal, with the collection displayed on pale, plywood units.
Other locations: (menswear) 271 rue St-Honoré, 1st (01.47.03.00.31); 6 rue des Francs-Bourgeois, 4th (01.42.71.75.11); 46 rue du Four, 6th (01.45.44.70.21); 69 rue de Rennes, 6th (01.40.49.01.64); 69 rue de Passy, 16th (01.45.20.47.15).

Irié Wash
8 rue du Pré-aux-Clercs, 7th (01.42.61.18.28). Mº Rue du Bac or St-Germain-des-Prés. **Open** 10.15am-7pm Mon-Sat. Closed 3wks Aug. **Credit** MC, V. **Map** p407 F7.
Elegant locals love this Japanese designer, whose search for new methods and materials includes laser cutting, hologram prints, and a mix of polyester and Elastane, such as ultra-supple suede (€190 a dress).

Isabel Marant
16 rue de Charonne, 11th (01.49.29.71.55). Mº Ledru-Rollin. **Open** noon-7pm Mon; 10.30am-7.30pm Tue-Sat. **Credit** AmEx, MC, V. **Map** p409 M7.
Marant's clothes are easily recognisable by their ethno-babe brocades, blanket-like coats and decorated sweaters in luxurious materials.
Other locations: 1 rue Jacob, 6th (01.43.26.04.12); 3 passage St-Sébastien, 11th (01.49.23.75.40).

Jack Henry
54 rue des Rosiers, 4th (01.44.59.89.44). Mº St-Paul. **Open** 2.30-8pm daily. **Credit** AmEx, DC, MC, V. **Map** p408 K6.
This New Yorker has been honing his sartorial skills here for over a decade. His spare, dark suits offer a fine, elongated silhouette, tastefully enhanced by chest-hugging knitwear. The look is inspired by US combat gear – meaning discipline in hidden details, rather than pockets in unlikely places.
Other locations: (women) 1 rue Montmartre, 1st (01.42.21.46.01).

Ladies & Gentlemen
4 passage Charles-Dallery, 11th (01.47.00.86.12). Mº Ledru-Rollin. **Open** noon-7pm Tue-Sat; 2-7pm Sun. Closed Aug. **Credit** MC, V. **Map** p409 N7.
Amid paintings and techno beats, red dummies are lovingly swathed in the classic yet slightly surreal creations of designers Isabelle Ballu (womenswear) and Moritz Rogorsky (menswear). Most clothes are hidden away in special alcoves – seek them out.

Loft Design by
12 rue du Fbg-St-Honoré, 8th (01.42.65.59.65). Mº Madeleine or Concorde. **Open** 10am-7pm Mon-Sat. **Credit** AmEx, DC, MC, V. **Map** p403 F4.
Patrick Frêche had the idea of making clothes to match the Paris skyline – heavy on the grey and black. A shrewd move, judging by Loft Design by's following with the Paris media and fashion crowd.
Other locations: 12 rue de Sévigné, 4th (01.48.87.13.07); 56 rue de Rennes, 6th (01.45.44.88.99).

Corinne Cobson
6 rue du Marché-St-Honoré, 1st (01.42.60.48.64). Mº Tuileries. **Open** noon-7.30pm Mon; 11am-7.30pm Tue-Sat. **Credit** AmEx, MC, V. **Map** p403 G4.
At this mirror-covered boutique Cobson favours simple lines combined with graphic prints; check out her anti-racism and pro-environment plunge-neck T-shirts and sumptuous chunky jumpers. Photos by her partner, Tanguy Loisance, provide the decor; droll designs by Samuel Lebaron in the window.

Corinne Sarrut
4 rue du Pré-aux-Clercs, 7th (01.42.61.71.60). Mº Rue du Bac or St-Germain-des-Prés. **Open** 10am-7pm Mon-Sat. **Credit** AmEx, MC, V. **Map** p407 F7.
Fans of *Amélie* will be charmed by the work of Corinne Sarrut, who dressed Audrey Tautou for the part. Anyone with a weakness for the 1940s silhouette will love her trapeze creations in silky viscose.
Other locations: 24 rue du Champ-de-Mars, 7th (01.45.56.00.65); 7 rue Gustave-Courbet, 16th (01.55.73.09.73); (wedding and evening) 42 rue des Sts-Pères, 7th (01.45.44.19.92).

Diesel
21 rue Montmartre, 1st (01.42.21.87.75/ www.diesel.com). Mº Etienne Marcel. **Open** 10.30am-7.30pm Mon-Sat. **Credit** AmEx, DC, MC, V. **Map** p404 K4.
After 20 years in the jeans business, Renzo Rossi is still tapping into teen dreams with brio.

Et Vous
42 rue Etienne-Marcel, 2nd (01.55.80.76.10). Mº Etienne Marcel. **Open** noon-7pm Mon; 10.30am-7pm Tue-Sat. **Credit** AmEx, MC, V. **Map** p404 J5.

Madelios

23 bd de la Madeleine, 1st (01.53.45.00.00/www. madelios.com). M° Madeleine. **Open** 10am-7pm Mon-Sat. **Credit** AmEx, DC, MC, V. **Map** p403 G4.

A one-stop-shop for men's fashion, with two floors and more than 100 labels. The decor is dull, but it's the stock that matters: suits by Paul Smith, Givenchy and Kenzo, plus shoes and accessories.

Marithé et François Girbaud

7 rue du Cherche Midi, 6th (01.53.40.74.20/www. girbaud.com). M° Sèvres-Babylone. **Open** noon-7pm Mon; 10am-7pm Tue-Sat. **Credit** AmEx, DC, MC, V. **Map** p407 J5.

This pioneering *soixante-huitard* pair came up with streetwear in high-tech fabrics using laser cutting and welding. Their flagship store has four floors and a garden of 250 plants. Check the web for branches.

Martin Grant

44 rue Vieille-du-Temple, 4th (01.42.71.39.49). M° St-Paul or Hôtel de Ville. **Open** 10am-6pm Mon-Fri. Closed 3wks Aug. **Credit** MC, V. **Map** p408 K6.

The chipped tiled floor and worn velvet chairs recall a retrofied Prada advert. This is couture, though, as interpreted by Australian designer Martin Grant. If you're a stickler for steady cutting and pure textiles devoid of fussy designs, pay this shop a visit.

Nodus

22 rue Vieille-du-Temple, 4th (01.42.77.07.96). M° St-Paul or Hôtel de Ville. **Open** 2pm-7.30pm Mon, Sun; 10.30am-7.30pm Tue-Sat. **Credit** MC, V. **Map** p408 K6.

Under the wooden beams of this cosy men's shirt specialist are neat rows of striped, checked and plain men's shirts, stylish silk ties with subtle, graphic designs and silver-plated crystal cufflinks.

Paul et Joe

62 rue des Sts-Pères, 7th (01.40.28.03.34). M° Rue du Bac or St-Germain-des-Prés. **Open** 11am-7.30pm Mon-Sat. **Credit** AmEx, DC, MC, V. **Map** p407 G6.

Fashion victims have taken a great shine to Sophie Albou's weathered '40s-style creations (named after her sons), so much so that she has opened a menswear branch and this flagship, with its out-to-be-noticed bubblegum pink gramophone.

Other locations: *46 rue Etienne-Marcel, 2nd (01.40.28.03.34); (men) 40 rue du Four, 6th (01.45.44.97.70).*

Paul Smith

22-24 bd Raspail, 7th (01.42.84.15.30/www.paul-smith.co.uk). M° Sèvres-Babylone. **Open** 11am-7pm Mon; 10am-7pm Tue-Sat. **Credit** AmEx, DC, MC, V. **Map** p407 G7.

Le style anglais in a wood-panelled interior. Smith's great suits and classic shoes are on the upper floor, while women and kids get a funkier space below.

Vanessa Bruno

25 rue St-Sulpice, 6th (01.43.54.41.04). M° Odéon. **Open** 10.30am-7pm Mon-Sat. **Credit** AmEx, DC, MC, V. **Map** p408 H7.

Bruno's feminine and very individual clothes have a cool and steady Zen-like quality that no doubt derives from her stay in Japan. She also makes great bags, seen hanging from the coolest wrists.

Other locations: *12 rue de Castiglione, 1st (01.42.61.44.60); 32 rue d'Argout, 2nd (01.40.26.70.65).*

Zadig & Voltaire

42 rue des Francs-Bourgeois, 3rd (01.44.54.00.60/ www.zadig-et-voltaire.com). M° St-Paul or Hôtel de Ville. **Open** 1.30-7.30pm Mon; 11am-8pm Tue-Sat; 2-8pm Sun. **Credit** AmEx, MC, V. **Map** p408 K6.

Louis Vuitton. *See p255.*

Z&V branches are popping up all over Paris; their relaxed, urban collection is clearly a winner. Popular separates include cotton tops, shirts and faded jeans; their winter range of cashmere jumpers is superb. For other branches, see the website.

Streetwear & clubwear

adidas
150 rue de Rivoli, 1st (01.58.62.51.60/www.adidas. com). M° Louvre Rivoli. **Open** 11.30am-7.30pm Mon-Sat. **Credit** AmEx, DC, MC, V. **Map** p404 H5.
Three techno floors of adidas products, whose shiny newness contrasts beautifully with this flagship store's raw surfaces. You'll be hard-pressed to find all these hard-to-find models on display anywhere else in the world; look out for re-editions of 1970s models (of course) nestle up with the entire Yohji Yamamoto-designed range.

Boutique M Dia
6-7 pl des Innocents, 1st (01.40.26.03.31). M° Châtelet/RER Châtelet Les Halles. **Open** 1-8pm Mon; 11am-8pm Tue-Sat. **Credit** AmEx, MC, V. **Map** p408 J6.
Mohammed Dia, the ultimate urban rebel from Paris' insalubrious Sarcelles suburb, went to America and came back with an idea to get him out of the ghetto: clothes design. €20 million later he has his own line of men and women's urban sports clothes and a shoe line called Tariq (worn by NBA's Dallas Mavericks). His first boutique is a shrine to his success, offering everything in the Dia range.

Clery Brice
11 rue Pierre-Lescot, 1st (01.45.08.58.70). M° Les Halles/RER Châtelet Les Halles. **Open** 11am-1pm, 2-7pm Mon-Sat. **Credit** MC, V. **Map** p404 J5.
Here you pay lofty prices to get limited editions of the coolest trainers six months before the rest of the world finds out they should be wearing them.

Kanabeach
78 rue Jean-Jacques-Rousseau, 1st (01.40.26.41.66). M° Etienne Marcel. **Open** 11am-7.30pm Mon-Sat. **Credit** MC, V. **Map** p404 J5.
With its mini waterfall, astroturf garden, mini caravan and changing rooms resembling beach cabins, this French youthwear store has a campsite vibe. The autumn/winter men's and women's collections include Jacquard check red and apricot coats, navy and cream trousers, and colourful separates.

Kiliwatch
64 rue Tiquetonne, 2nd (01.42.21.17.37/www. kiliwatch.tm.fr). M° Etienne Marcel. **Open** 2-7pm Mon; 11am-7pm Tue-Thur; 11am-8.30pm Fri; 11am-7.30pm Sat. **Credit** AmEx, MC, V. **Map** p404 J5.
The trailblazer of the rue Etienne-Marcel revival is filled to bursting with hoodies, casual shirts and washed-out jeans. Featured brands such as G-Star and Kulte accompany a selection of pricy but good-condition second-hand clothes (adidas tracksuit tops and mini-kilts especially) for that retro-chic look.

Puma Store
22 bd de Sébastopol, 4th (01.44.59.88.02/www.puma. com). M° Rambuteau/RER Châtelet-les-Halles. **Open** 10am-7.30pm Mon-Fri; 10.30am-7pm, Sat. **Credit** AmEx, MC, V. **Map** p404 J5.
Puma offers its particular brand of sport, lifestyle and fashion from this flashy two-floor flagship store. Speciality fixtures show off Christy Turlington's yoga clothes, and there are obscure versions of their popular Mostro trainer.

Royal Cheese
24 rue Tiquetonne, 2nd (01.40.28.06.56). M° Etienne Marcel. **Open** 11am-1pm, 2-8pm Mon-Sat. **Credit** AmEx, DC, MC, V. **Map** p404 J5.
Clubbers pop down to Royal Cheese to snaffle up hard-to-find imported items – Stussy, Evisu, Duffer, Gravy and Original Shopper for the boys, and Shariff, Bonds, Kitten and Evisu Donna for the girls – at fairly hefty prices (Japanese jeans €200).

Le Vestibule
3 pl Ste-Opportune, 1st (01.42.33.21.89). M° Châtelet. **Open** 10.30am-7pm Mon-Sat and one Sun in every month. **Credit** AmEx, DC, MC, V. **Map** p404 J5.
An eye-popping showcase for the wildest creations of the vintage streetwear and club gear genre, including exhibits by mainstream labels such as Dolce e Gabbana and Castelbajac. For effortless flash and panache, Cultura, Diesel StyleLab, Replay and its Coca-Cola Ware label are hard to beat.

Vintage & discount

The craze for vintage fashion has seen second-hand clothes shops flourish, though demand ensures that bargains are rare.

Come On Eileen
16-18 rue des Taillandiers, 11th (01.43.38.12.11). M° Ledru-Rollin. **Open** 11.30am-8.30pm Mon-Fri; 4-8pm Sun. **Credit** AmEx, DC, MC, V. **Map** p409 M7.
The owners of this three-floor vintage wonderland have an eye for what's funky, from cowboy gear to '60s debutantes frocks. With clients like Kylie Minogue, they can afford to charge high prices (Hermès scarves cost around €100), but the stock is well-sourced and in good condition.

Didier Ludot
19, 20 23, 24 galerie de Montpensier, 1st (01.42. 96.06.56/www.didierludot.com). Little black dress: 125 galerie de Valois, 1st (01.40.15.01.04). M° Palais Royal Musée du Louvre. **Open** 11am-7pm Mon-Sat. **Credit** AmEx, DC, V. **Map** p404 H5.
Didier Ludot's series of mini-temples to vintage-haute couture have been so successful that he now has concessions in Printemps, Harrods and Barneys New York, plus his own line of little black dresses, a perfume and a book. Ludot's prices are exorbitant, but then again he has stunning pieces – Molyneux, Balenciaga, Fath, Dior, Pucci, Féraud, Stern and of course Chanel, from the 1920s onwards.

Eat, Drink, Shop

Doursoux Michel
3 passage Alexandre, 15th (01.43.27.00.97). Mº Pasteur. **Open** 10am-7.30pm Tue-Sat. **Credit** MC, V. **Map** p407 E9.
This place is something of a classic in Paris' army surplus community. The stock is quite small, but includes good quality coats, boots and gloves.

Free 'P' Star
8 Ste-Croix-de-la-Bretonnerie, 4th (01.42.76.03.72). Mº St-Paul. **Open** noon-11pm Mon-Sat; 2-11pm Sun. **No credit cards. Map** p408 K6.
This Aladdin's cave of retro glitz, '60s, '70s and '80s glad rags and ex-army jackets is the best priced of the bargain basements.

L'Habilleur
44 rue de Poitou, 3rd (01.48.87.77.12). Mº St-Sébastien Froissart. **Open** 11am-8pm Mon-Sat. **Credit** MC, V. **Map** p404 L5.
Urbanites prowl this slick store for its severely cut men's and women's wear by Dries van Noten, Helmut Lang, John Richmond, Plein Sud, Martine Sitbon and Bikkembergs, and dagger-toed shoes by Patrick Cox. All the pieces, which are end of line or off the catwalk, are 50% to 70% off.

Le Mouton à Cinq Pattes
19 rue Grégoire-de-Tours, 6th (01.43.29.73.56). Mº Odéon. **Open** 10.30am-7.30pm Mon-Fri; 10.30am-8pm Sat. **Credit** AmEx, MC, V. **Map** p408 H7.
Designer vintage and last season's collection in mint condition: Vittadini, Buscat, Donn Adriana, Chanel and Lagerfeld. Turnover is fast, so this is no place for an indecision crisis. Labels are cut out, too, so make sure you know what you're buying.
Other locations: *15 rue Vieille-du-Temple, 4th (01.42.71.86.30); 138 bd St-Germain, 6th (01.43.26.49.25).*

Rag
83-85 rue St-Martin, 4th (01.48.87.34.64). Mº Rambuteau. **Open** 10am-8pm Mon-Sat; noon-8pm Sun. **No credit cards. Map** p404 K5.
While one half focuses on casual *fripes* – pilots' navy jumpers (€15), '70s shirts (€15), racks of colourful puffer jackets (€10), '70s heels (€30) and more – the other might yield a vintage Hermès scarf, '60s Paco Rabanne dresses or Gucci and Dior accessories.

Son et Image
87 rue St-Denis, 1st (01.40.41.90.61). Mº Châtelet. **Open** 10.30am-7.30pm Mon-Sat. **Credit** AmEx, MC,V. **Map** p404 J6.
This popular little second-hand clothes store is filled with vintage leather, fur coats and hip boots.

Stocks and Marques
65 rue de Lancry, 10th (01.42.00.00.46). Mº Jacques Bonsergent. **Open** noon-7.30pm Mon-Thur; noon-3.30pm Fri; 2-7pm Sun. **Credit** MC, V. **Map** p404 L3.
Closed on Saturday because its owner doesn't like crowds: the stock of top streetwear labels at 30% of their original price would certainly pull them in. Look out for Diesel jackets at €50.

Lingerie & swimwear

The third floor of **Galeries Lafayette** (*see p240*) devotes 2,600M² to underwear; for swimwear, *see also p275* **Sport & games**.

Alice Cadolle
14 rue Cambon, 1st (01.42.60.94.94/www.cadolle. com). Mº Concorde or Madeleine. **Open** 10am-1pm, 2-7pm Mon-Sat. Closed Aug. **Credit** AmEx, MC, V. **Map** p403 G4.
Five generations of lingerie here at this boutique, founded by Hermine Cadolle, the inventor of the brassière. Her great-great-granddaughter, Poupie Cadolle, continues the tradition on the belle epoque third floor. Her ready-to-wear speciality is bodices and corsets so *soigné* that Christian Lacroix and Thierry Mugler put them in their collections.

Erès
2 rue Tronchet, 8th (01.47.42.28.82/www.eres.fr). Mº Madeleine. **Open** 10am-7pm Mon-Sat. **Credit** AmEx, DC, MC, V. **Map** p403 G4.
Don't be misled by the demure interior: the label's beautifully cut, minimalist bikinis and swimsuits are hot and designed to make a splash. One advantage for the natural woman is that the top and bottom can be purchased in different sizes, or you can buy just one piece of a bikini should decide you don't want all your bases covered. See website for branches.

Etam
21 rue Tronchet, 8th (01.40.06.05.93/www.etam.fr). Mº Havre-Caumartin. **Open** 10am-7pm Mon-Sat. **Credit** AmEx, MC, V. **Map** p403 G3.
This high street shop has recently closed down many of its daywear branches in favour of its underwear shops (its original speciality). The result is all round underwear and swimsuits, catered to all tastes from sex kitten to cotton candies on a budget. See the website for other addresses.

Fifi Chachnil
26 rue Cambon, 1st (01.42.60.38.86/www. fifichachnil.com). Mº Madeleine. **Open** 11am-7pm Mon-Sat. **Credit** AmEx, MC, V. **Map** p403 G4.
Chachnil has a new take on frou-frou underwear in the pin-up tradition. Her chic mixes, such as deep red silk bras with boudoir pink bows and pale turquoise girdles with orange trim, will have you purring in delight. Transparent black babydoll negligées with an empire-line bust are also favoured.

Izka
140 rue du Fbg-St-Honoré, 8th (01.43.59.07.07). Mº St-Philippe du-Roule. **Open** 10am-7pm Mon-Sat. **Credit** AmEx, MC, V. **Map** p403 D3.
Gérard Petit's sporty, seamless lingerie has been snapped up by Warner's. The ten skimpy sets of bras and pants in microfibre (*so* tempting to buy the whole collection) have accompanying vests, and you can mix and match colours for gasps of admiration.
Other locations: *74 rue de Rennes, 6th (01.45.49.25.85).*

Princesse Tam Tam

*52 bd St-Michel, 6th (01.42.34.99.31). M° Cluny La
Sorbonne.* **Open** 1-7pm Mon; 10am-7pm Tue-Sat.
Credit AmEx, MC, V. **Map** p408 J7.
The commendable but inexpensive underwear and
swimwear brand favoured by Parisian trendy types
has launched out with provocative traffic-stopping
promotion. Bright colours, and sexily transparent
and sporty gear are most certainly in – though sadly
not for well-endowed girls.
Other locations: *9 rue Bréa, 6th (01.55.42.14.72).*

Sabbia Rosa

*73 rue des Sts-Pères, 6th (01.45.48.88.37). M° St-
Germain-des-Prés.* **Open** 10am-7pm Mon-Sat. **Credit**
AmEx, MC, V. **Map** p407 G7.
Settle yourself on the soft green leather sofa in this
lingerie heaven and let Moana Moatti slip on feather-
trimmed satin mules or spread before you satin, silk
and chiffon negligées in fine shades of tangerine,
lemon, mocha or pistachio. All the sizes here are
medium, others ones are made *sur mesure*; prices
are just the cheap side of extortionate for a slice of
absolutely exquisite luxury.

Accessories

Eyewear

Get an eye test at an *opthalmologiste*, then come
with your prescription for some cool French
specs to wow your friends back home.

Alain Mikli

*74 rue des Sts-Pères, 7th (01.53.63.87.40/www.
mikli.fr). M° Sèvres-Babylone.* **Open** 10am-7pm Mon-
Sat. **Credit** AmEx, DC, MC, V. **Map** p407 G7.
This cult French designer was among the first to
inject some vroom into prescription peepers. His signature material is cellulose acetate, a mix of wood
and cotton sliced from blocks. The Starck-designed
boutique has a glass counter where the frames are
laid out like designer sweeties, while upstairs 'travel
wear' is displayed in an 18th-century setting. See the
website for other branches.

Anne et Valentin

*4 rue Ste-Croix-de-la-Bretonnerie, 4th
(01.40.29.93.01/www.anneetvalentin.com). M° Hôtel*

Sales technique

The build-up to the Paris sales sees an edgy
but well-disguised hysteria among locals,
and even battalions of in-the-know fashion
guerrillas from neighbouring countries make
special expeditions to the French capital,
hoping to be the first to get their hands on,
say, a Comme des Garçons *chemise* for a
quarter of its original price.

Twice a year, Paris boutiques sell off what's
left of seasonal stock at hugely reduced
prices – up to 75 per cent – to make way for
incoming collections; winter stock is sold off
over four weeks in January, and over July
summer stock gets the boot. Not all shops
remain on sale for this entire period. The
exact national dates for the much-anticipated
sales, or *soldes*, are, not surprisingly for this
most bureaucratic of countries, imposed by
the government, more precisely by La
Direction départementale de la Concurrence,
de la Consommation et de la Répression des
Fraudes. (Dates for 2005 were not confirmed
at the time of writing; call 01.40.27.16.00.)

Because some prices drop progressively
over the sales period, this generates thorny
webs of desire, of risk and chance – are a
pair of size-40 Jean-Paul Gaultier-designed
Hermès boots going to last till the price drops
to half? Or will they be so in demand that a
fellow shopper (grrrr!) will happily snap them
up with only 25 per cent off the full price?

In other cases, however, it's definitely first
in, best dressed. Significant price cuts from
day one of the sales mean that being at the
door of the **Bon Marché** (*see p240*) when it
opens (often as early as 8am especially for
the start of the sales) means that you're in
with half a chance of getting your hot little
hands on bargain-priced must-haves. Some of
the smaller boutiques, Prada shoes (5 rue de
Grenelle, 6th, 01.45.48.53.14) for example,
put bouncers on the door to limit entry to ten
hysterical bargain-hunters at a time.

Other effective tactics for successful sales
shopping include going on a reconnaissance
patrol the week before the sales begin, in
order to identify your sartorial targets; once
the sales start you'll be able to zoom in on
them, aided by a little elbowing, speed and
precision. Your shopping uniform should be
comfortable and easy to get in and out of –
shoes with laces for example are a definite
no-no. And if queues for the changing room
are starting to resemble those for the toilets
at Munich's Oktoberfest, your foresight in
wearing a skirt will mean that you can save
time trying on, in a discreet corner of the
shop, other skirts or pants underneath it. And
finally, shopping at department stores means
you can cover the most ground without
running the risk of staining your new
Rodolphe Menudier (*see p264*) stilettos.

Eat, Drink, Shop

de Ville or St-Paul. **Open** 11am-8pm Tue-Sat. **Credit**
AmEx, DC, MC, V. **Map** p408 K6.
This modish French eyewear company occupies the
basement, ground and first floors of a cosy Marais
boutique. Anne et Valentin design very chic but
unpretentious unisex spectacle frames: lightweight
titanium models have names like Tagada, Tarzan,
Titus and Truman, and her coloured acetate frames
feature inventive details and colour combinations.

Lafont
*11 rue Vignon, 8th (01.47.42.25.93/www.lafont-
paris.com). M° Madeleine.* **Open** 10am-7pm Mon-Sat.
Credit AmEx, MC, V. **Map** p403 G4.
Philippe Lafont carries on the impeccable, finely
hand-finished work of his grandfather. The speciality of Philippe's designer wife Laurence is small oval
frames that tilt upwards like cat's eyes. For other
outlets, see the website.

Traction
*6 rue du Dragon, 6th (01.42.22.28.77). M° St-
Germain-des-Prés.* **Open** 2-7pm Mon; 10.30am-7pm
Tue-Sat. **Credit** AmEx, DC, MC, V. **Map** p407 H7.
This brand, owned by the Gros family, marries four
generations of know-how with a keen sense of
modernity. Try the heavy metal specs that are
super-light when worn, or the conversation-making
frames with quirky details on the shaft.

Hats

Jacques Le Corre
*193 rue St-Honoré, 1st (01.42.96.96.40). M°
Tuileries.* **Open** 10am-7pm Mon-Sat. **Credit** AmEx,
MC, V. **Map** p403 G4.
This flamboyant Breton experiments with textures
and pigments to create daywear hats and berets in
unusual fabrics. Some of his large lambskin bags
have bead patterns stamped on them like Braille;
others are dyed in fiery red or warm terracotta.

Marie Mercié
23 rue St-Sulpice, 6th (01.43.26.45.83). M° Odéon.
Open 11am-7pm Mon-Sat. **Credit** AmEx, DC, MC,
V. **Map** p408 H7.
Mercié's inspirations make you wish you lived in an
era when hat-wearing was de rigueur. What fun to
step out in a creation shaped like curved fingers
(complete with shocking-pink nail varnish and a
pink diamond ring), or a beret like a face with huge
turquoise eyes and red lips. Ready-to-wear starts at
around €300; *sur mesure* takes ten days.

Philippe Model
*33 pl du Marché-St-Honoré, 1st (01.42.96.89.02). M°
Pyramides.* **Open** 10am-7pm Mon-Sat. Closed Aug.
Credit AmEx, DC, MC, V. **Map** p403 H5.
With his exuberant colours and two-tone designs,
Model is your man if you're determined to stand out
in the wedding, racing or boating crowd. Prices from
around €50 for a beret to more than €3,000 for a
sumptuous, made-to-measure headdress.

Jewellery

Dotted in and around **place Vendôme**, Paris'
key *joailliers* define the city's luxurious spirit.

Boucheron
*26 pl Vendôme, 1st (01.42.61.58.16/www.boucheron.
com). M° Opéra.* **Open** 10am-7pm Mon-Sat.
Credit AmEx, DC, MC, V. **Map** p403 G4.
The grandest shop on place Vendôme, Boucheron
was the first to set up here, eager for celebrity custom from the nearby Ritz Hotel. Now owned by
Gucci, this venerable old jeweller still produces
voluptuous and sensual pieces. They reemploy traditional motifs with new accents: witness their innovative chocolate-coloured gold watch.

Cartier
*13 rue de la Paix, 2nd (01.42.18.53.70/www.cartier.
com). M° Opéra.* **Open** 10.30am-7pm Mon-Sat.
Credit AmEx, DC, MC, V. **Map** p403 G4.
This mythic French jeweller and watchmaker has
refocused on jewellery production after decades of
concentrating on fine leather goods and watches. Its
designs draw inspiration from its long, rich heritage:
panthers, pearls and the 'trinity' ring: interjoined
bands of white, yellow and rose gold. See the website for other branches.

Chanel Joaillerie
*18 pl Vendôme, 1st (01.55.35.50.05/www.chanel.
com). M° Concorde or Opéra.* **Open** 10.30am-6.30pm
Mon-Fri; 10.30am-1pm, 2-6.30pm Sat. **Credit** AmEx,
DC, MC, V. **Map** p403 G4.
You almost expect Coco to walk through the door of
this chic boutique, decorated in a style evocative of
'30s Paris. When Chanel launched their fine jewellery department in the early '90s, they reissued the
single jewellery collection – strong on platinum and
diamonds – that Coco had designed 60 years before.
The current collection reinterprets Coco's key motifs
– camellias, stars and comets – in a modern way.

Dior Joaillerie
*8 pl Vendôme, 1st (01.42.96.30.84/www.dior.com).
M° Concorde or Opéra.* **Open** 11am-7pm Mon, Sat;
10.30am-7pm Tue-Fri. **Credit** AmEx, DC, MC, V.
Map p403 G4.
Dior Jewellery is leading the pack, thanks to the
whimsical but unabashed bling of Victoire de
Castellane's designs. This former Chanel accessories
designer jumped ship to Dior in 1998, and is responsible for the fad of semi-precious, coloured stones
that has invaded place Vendôme.

Swarovski
*52 rue Bonaparte, 6th (01.56.24.15.60/www.
swarovski.com). M° St-Germain-des-Prés.* **Open**
10am-7pm Mon-Sat. **Credit** AmEx, MC, V. **Map**
p407 H6.
This lavish boutique houses the costume jewellery
of this century-old Austrian family company, who
produce glamorous pieces made from top quality
crystals that have seduced the celebrity set.

Royal Cheese. *See p259*

Van Cleef & Arpels

22 pl Vendôme, 1st (01.53.45.45.45/www.vancleef.
com). M° Concorde or Opéra. **Open** 10.30am-7pm
Mon-Fri; 11am-7pm Sat. **Credit** AmEx, DC, MC, V.
Map p403 G4.
Occupying this site since 1906, Van Cleef & Arpels
is a member of legendary 20th-century jewellers.
This French family dynasty grew out of the alliance
of two diamond merchant families and the girl's best
friend continues to take centre-stage in their elegant
designs. See the website for other addresses.

Shoes & bags

The luxury floor at **Printemps** (*see p240*) is a
good source of designer footwear labels and
rue du Dragon in the 6th is crammed with
boutiques offering young designers' creations.

Bruno Frisoni

24 rue de Grenelle, 7th (01.42.84.12.30). M° Rue du
Bac. **Open** 10.30am-7pm Tue-Sat. **Credit** AmEx,
DC, MC, V. **Map** p407 G7.
Innovative Frisoni used to work for Christian
Lacroix and Jean-Louis Scherrer. Inspired by the
1960s, he makes shoes with a cinematic, pop edge;
his modern theatrics are not for the conventional.

Camper

25 rue du Vieux-Colombier, 6th (01.45.48.22.00/
www.camper.es). M° St-Sulpice. **Open** 10am-7pm
Mon-Sat. **Credit** AmEx, DC, MC, V. **Map** p407 G7.
These chic Spanish cobblers were the first to bring
asymmetry into popular shoe design.

Christian Louboutin

19 rue Jean-Jacques-Rousseau, 1st (01.42.36.05.31).
M° Palais Royal Musée du Louvre. **Open** 10.30am-
7pm Mon-Sat. Closed Aug. **Credit** AmEx, DC, MC,
V. **Map** p404 J5.

Each of Louboutin's creations – with hallmark red
soles – is displayed in individual frames. His Trash
mules – incorporating old Métro tickets, glitter, torn
letters and postage stamps – are especially coveted.
Other locations: *38 rue de Grenelle, 7th*
(01.42.22.33.07).

Hervé Chapelier

1 rue du Vieux-Colombier, 6th (01.44.07.06.50). M°
St-Sulpice. **Open** 10.15am-7pm Mon-Fri; 10.15am-
7.15pm Sat. **Credit** AmEx, MC, V. **Map** 407 G7.
The top stop for the ultimate chic, hard-wearing, bi-
coloured totes. Often copied, never equalled, they're
available in pretty much every colour. Sizes and
prices range from a dinky little purse at €22 to a
stonking weekend bag at €130.

Iris

28 rue de Grenelle, 7th 01.42.22.89.81). M° Rue du
Bac. **Open** 10.30am-7pm Mon-Sat. **Credit** AmEx,
MC, V. **Map** p407 F7.
Iris is the Italian manufacturer of shoes by Marc
Jacobs, Ernesto Esposito, Alessandro Dell'Acqua
and Véronique Branquinho: its entire footwear
range is on display at this dazzling white boutique,
the pieces by Esposito being instantly recognisable
by their flower patterns.

Jamin Puech

61 rue de Hauteville, 10th (01.40.22.08.32). M°
Poissonnière. **Open** 10am-2pm, 3-7pm Mon-Sat.
Credit MC, V. **Map** p404 K3.
The full collection of Isabelle Puech and Benoît
Jamin's dazzling handbags, which use anything
from tapestry and raffia to sequins, are on show in
a boho setting complete with antler-horn chairs.

Mandarina Duck

36 rue Etienne-Marcel, 2nd (01.40.13.02.96/www.
mandarinaduck.com). M° Etienne Marcel. **Open**
11am-7pm Mon-Sat. **Credit** MC, V. **Map** p404 J5.

Beautifully cut, minimalist designs at **Erès**. *See p260.*

The yellow-and-white geometric Mandarina Duck features sleek, trendy, monotone handbags; the Italian brand's wallets, luggage, sunglasses and watches are also available.

Patrick Cox
62 rue Tiquetonne, 2nd (01.40.26.66.55). M°
Etienne Marcel. **Open** 10.30am-7.30pm Mon-Sat.
Credit AmEx, MC, V. **Map** p404 J5.
If the slipper fits, it'll be one of Cox's. Elegance off the catwalk is his forte, with ultra-feminine designs and mixes of fabric. His stiletto boots and kitten heels will have your feet feeling like a million euros.

Peggy Huyn Kinh
11 rue Coëtlogon, 6th (01.42.84.83.83). M° St-
Sulpice. **Open** 10am-7pm Mon-Sat. **Credit** AmEx,
MC, V. **Map** p407 G7.
This street may not scream fashion, but it doesn't deter Peggy Huyn Kinh, former creative director for Cartier and others, whose bags use boarskin and python. She does minimalist silver jewellery too.

Pierre Hardy
156 galerie de Valois, 1st (01.42.60.59.75/www.
pierrehardy.com). M° Palais Royal Musée du Louvre.
Open 11am-7pm Tue-Sat. **Credit** AmEx, DC, MC, V.
Map p404 H5.
This classy black-and-white shoebox is home to Hardy's range of superbly conceived footwear – with a price tag to match – for men and women. A shoe designer at Hermès, he has a feel for street-smart glamour that keeps him ahead of the pack.

Robert Clergerie
5 rue du Cherche Midi, 6th (01.45.48.75.47). M° St-
Sulpice. **Open** 10am-7pm Mon-Sat. **Credit** AmEx,
MC, V. **Map** p407 G7.

Robert Clergerie has thankfully settled back into designing exquisitely practical daywear; he has even managed to revive the two-tone loafer he originally created at the start of his career way back in 1981. His stylised 'boxing trainer' knocks the socks off other models.
Other locations: *46 rue Croix-des-Petits-Champs,*
1st (01.42.61.49.24); 18 av Victor-Hugo, 16th
(01.45.01.81.30).

Rodolphe Menudier
14 rue de Castiglione, 1st (01.42.60.86.27). M°
Concorde or Tuileries. **Open** 10.30am-7.30pm Mon-
Sat. **Credit** AmEx, MC, V. **Map** p403 G5.
This silver-and-black cylinder of a boutique is a perfect backdrop for Rodolphe Menudier's racy designs, which mingle moods and materials. Dozens of open, silver-handled drawers display his stilettos laid flat in profile. Top of the range are outrageous thigh-high boots with Plexiglass soles, but the more demure type of customer can opt for ballerina pumps or stock up on exclusive hosiery made by Gerbé and Chantal Thomass.

Roger Vivier
29 rue du Fbg-St-Honoré, 8th (01.53.43.00.00). M°
Madeleine or Concorde. **Open** 10.30am-7pm Mon-
Sat. **Credit** AmEx, DC, MC, V. **Map** p403 F4.
Before Blahnik there was Vivier. This extravagent shoe designer approached his craft like a sculptor, fashioning extraordinary forms for feet; Roger Vivier is widely credited with inventing the stiletto and made fans of celebrities as diverse as Queen Elizabeth II and The Beatles. The legend of this master shoemaker lives on in this exclusive boutique selling signature vintage models and new designs by Bruno Frisoni (*see p263*).

Food & drink

Though many *charcutiers* and quirky little places are increasingly rare, Paris still has plenty to offer the food-obsessed. It would be easy to spend an entire holiday (if not a lifetime) exploring the enormous variety of breads, pastries, cheeses and chocolate, and open-air markets continue to beckon with their displays of fresh, seasonal goods (*see p267* **Market forces**). The chain concept is catching on: there seems to be a **Paul** bakery on every corner and even renowned fromageries such as **Quatrehomme** have been popping up in different neighbourhoods. The good news is that overall quality remains impressive – and you need only look around to realise that cream-filled pastries won't make you fat.

Bakeries

Arnaud Delmontel

39 rue des Martyrs, 9th (01.48.78.29.33). M° St-Georges. **Open** 7am-8.30pm Mon, Wed-Sun. **No credit cards. Map** p404 H2.
With its crisp crust and chewy crumb scattered with irregular holes, Delmontel's Renaissance bread is easily one of the finest in Paris. He puts the same skill and perfectionism into his pastries.

L'Autre Boulange

43 rue de Montreuil, 11th (01.43.72.86.04). M° Nation or Faidherbe Chaligny. **Open** 7.30am-1.30pm, 4-7.30pm Mon-Fri; 7.30am-12.30pm Sat. Closed Aug. **No credit cards. Map** p409 P7.
Michel Cousin rustles up 23 kinds of organic loaves in his wood-fired oven, such as the *flutiot* (rye bread with raisins, walnuts and hazelnuts), the *sarment de Bourgogne* (sourdough and a little rye) and a spiced cornmeal bread ideal for foie gras. Great croissants and *chaussons* for superior snacking.

Le Boulanger de Monge

123 rue Monge, 5th (01.43.37.54.20). M° Censier Daubenton. **Open** 7am-8.30pm Tue-Sun. **Credit** MC, V. **Map** p408 K9.
Dominique Saibron uses spices in his starter to give inimitable flavour to his organic sourdough *boule*. About 2,000 bread-lovers a day visit his boutique, which also produces one of the city's best baguettes.

Kayser

8 & 14 rue Monge, 5th (01.44.07.01.42/ 01.44.07.17.81). M° Maubert Mutualité. **Open** 6.45am-8.30pm Mon-Fri; 6.30am-8.30pm Sat, Sun. **Credit** MC, V. **Map** p408 J7.
In a few years Eric Kayser has established himself as one of the city's star bakers, even if his baguette is a little on the salty side. The bakery at 14 rue Monge is devoted to organic loaves.
Other locations: *5 rue Basse des Carmes, 5th (01.44.07.31.61).*

Moisan

5 pl d'Aligre, 12th (01.43.45.46.60). M° Ledru-Rollin. **Open** 7am-1.30pm, 3-8pm Tue-Sat; 7am-2pm Sun. **No credit cards. Map** p409 N7.
Moisan's bakeries are spreading around Paris, but the quality of his organic bread, *viennoiseries* and rustic tarts remains outstanding. At this branch near place d'Aligre market the queue snakes out the door.
Other locations: *4 av du Général-Leclerc, 14th (01.43.22.34.13).*

Le Moulin de la Vierge

166 av de Suffren, 15th (01.47.83.45.55). M° Sèvres-Lecourbe. **Open** 7am-8pm Mon-Sat. **No credit cards. Map** p407 E8.
Basile Kamir learned breadmaking after falling in love with an old abandoned bakery. Each of his branches has an irresistible fragrance, matched by the quality of his sourdough breads.
Other locations: *82 rue Daguerre, 14th (01.43.22.50.55); 105 rue Vercingétorix, 14th (01.45.43.09.84).*

Poilâne

8 rue du Cherche Midi, 6th (01.45.48.42.59/ www.poilane.com). M° Sèvres-Babylone or St-Sulpice. **Open** 7.15am-8.15pm Mon-Sat. **No credit cards. Map** p407 G7.
Apollonia runs Poilâne after her father's demise in a helicopter crash. Nothing has changed in the tiny original shop, where locals queue for freshly baked country *miches*, flaky-crusted apple tarts and buttery shortbread biscuits. See website for branches.

Cheese

The sign *maître fromager affineur* denotes merchants who buy young cheeses from farms and age them on their premises; *fromage fermier* and *fromage au lait cru* signify farm-produced and raw milk cheeses respectively.

Alléosse

13 rue Poncelet, 17th (01.46.22.50.45). M° Ternes. **Open** 9am-1pm, 4-7pm Tue-Thur; 9am-7pm Fri, Sat; 9am-1pm Sun. **Credit** MC, V. **Map** p402 C2.
People cross town for these cheeses – wonderful farmhouse camemberts, delicate st-marcellins, a choice of *chèvres* and several rarities.

Fromagerie Dubois et Fils

80 rue de Tocqueville, 17th (01.42.27.11.38). M° Malesherbes or Villiers. **Open** 9am-1pm, 4-8pm Tue-Fri; 8.30am-8pm Sat; 9am-1pm Sun. Closed 3wks Aug. **Credit** MC, V. **Map** p403 E2.
Superchef darling Dubois stocks 80 types of goat's cheese plus prized, aged st-marcellin and st-félicien.
Other locations: *79 rue de Courcelles, 17th (01.43.80.36.42).*

Fromagerie Quatrehomme

62 rue de Sèvres, 7th (01.47.34.33.45). M° Vaneau. **Open** 8.45am-1pm, 2-7.45pm Tue-Sat. **Credit** MC, V. **Map** p407 F8.

The award-winning Marie Quatrehomme is behind this inviting *fromagerie*. Justly famous for classics such as comté fruité, beaufort and the squishy st-marcellin, it sells more unusual specialities such as goat's cheese with pesto and truffle-flavoured brie.

Marie-Anne Cantin

12 rue du Champ-de-Mars, 7th (01.45.50.43.94/ www.cantin.fr). M° Ecole Militaire. **Open** 8.30am-7.30pm Mon-Sat. **Credit** MC, V. **Map** p406 D6.
Cantin, a vigorous defender of unpasteurised cheese and supplier to many posh Paris restaurants, is justifiably proud of her dreamily creamy st-marcellins, aged *chèvres* and roquefort réserve.

Chocolate

Cacao et Chocolat

29 rue de Buci, 6th (01.46.33.77.63). M° Mabillon. **Open** 10.30am-7.30pm daily. **Credit** AmEx, DC, MC, V. **Map** p407 H7.
This shop decorated in burnt-orange and ochre recalls chocolate's ancient Aztec origins with spicy fillings (honey and chilli, nutmeg, clove and citrus), chocolate masks and pyramids.
Other locations: *63 rue St-Louis-en-l'Ile, 4th (01.46.33.33.33).*

Christian Constant

37 rue d'Assas, 6th (01.53.63.15.15). M° St-Placide. **Open** 8.30am-9pm Mon-Fri; 8.30am-8.30pm Sat; 8.30am-7pm Sun. **Credit** MC, V. **Map** p407 G8.
A true master chocolate maker and *traiteur*, Constant is revered by all. Trained in the arts of patisserie and chocolate, he scours the globe for new and delectable ideas. Ganaches are subtly flavoured with verbena, jasmine or cardamom.

Debauve & Gallais

30 rue des Saints-Pères, 7th (01.45.48.54.67/www. debauve-et-gallais.com). M° St-Germain-des-Prés. **Open** 9am-7pm Mon-Sat. **Credit** MC, V. **Map** p407 G7.
This former pharmacy, its façade dating from 1800, sold chocolate for medicinal purposes. Its intense tea, honey or praline-flavours still heal the soul.
Other locations: *33 rue Vivienne, 2nd (01.40.39.05.50).*

Jean-Paul Hévin

3 rue Vavin, 6th (01.43.54.09.85/www.jphevin.com). M° Vavin. **Open** 10am-7pm Mon-Sat. Closed Aug. **Credit** AmEx, MC, V. **Map** p407 G8.
Jean-Paul Hévin dares to fill his chocolates with potent cheeses, served with wine as an apéritif. Even more risqué are his aphrodisiac chocolates.
Other locations: *231 rue St-Honoré, 1st (01.55.35.35.96); 16 av de La Motte-Picquet, 7th (01.45.51.77.48).*

La Maison du Chocolat

89 av Raymond-Poincaré, 16th (01.40.67.77.83/ www.lamaisonduchocolat.com). M° Victor Hugo. **Open** 10am-7pm Mon-Sat. **Credit** AmEx, MC, V. **Map** p402 B4.

Robert Linxe opened his first Paris shop in 1977 and has been inventing new chocolates ever since, using Asian spices, fresh fruits and herbal infusions. See the website for other addresses.

Pierre Marcolini

89 rue de Seine, 6th (01.44.07.39.07/www.pierre marcolini.com). M° Mabillon. **Open** 10.30am-7pm Tue-Sat. **Credit** AmEx, MC, V. **Map** p407 H7.
This Belgian newcomer to Paris is known among chocoholics worldwide for his 44 ganache flavours, including ginger, jasmine and tea with lemon.

Richart

258 bd St-Germain, 7th (01.45.55.66.00/www. richart.com). M° Solférino. **Open** 10am-7pm Mon-Sat. **Credit** AmEx, MC, V. **Map** p407 F6.
Each chocolate ganache has an intricate design, packages look like jewel boxes and each purchase comes with a tract on how best to savour chocolate.

Global

Les Délices d'Orient

52 av Emile-Zola, 15th (01.45.79.10.00). M° Charles Michels. **Open** 7.30am-9pm Tue-Sun. **Credit** MC, V. **Map** p406 B8.
Shelves here brim with stuffed aubergines, halva, Lebanese bread, falafel, olives and all manner of Middle Eastern delicacies.
Other locations: *14 rue des Quatre-Frères-Peignot, 15th (01.45.77.82.93).*

Izraël

30 rue François-Miron, 4th (01.42.72.66.23). M° Hôtel de Ville. **Open** 9.30am-1pm, 2.30-7pm Tue-Fri; 9.30am-7pm Sat. Closed Aug. **Credit** MC, V. **Map** p408 K6.
A Marais fixture, this narrow shop stocks spices and other delights from Mexico, Turkey and India.

Jabugo Ibérico & Co

11 rue Clément-Marot, 8th (01.47.20.03.13). M° Alma Marceau or Franklin D. Roosevelt. **Open** 10am-8pm Mon-Sat. **Credit** MC, V. **Map** p402 D4.
This shop specialises in Spanish hams with the Bellota-Bellota label, meaning the pigs have feasted on acorns. Manager Philippe Poulachon compares the complexity of his cured hams (at €98 a kilo) to the delicacy of truffles.

Kioko

46 rue des Petits-Champs, 2nd (01.42.61.33.65). M° Pyramides. **Open** 10am-8pm Tue-Sat; 11am-7pm Sun. **Credit** MC, V. **Map** p403 H4.
From *koshi-hikari* rice to Kikkoman, this two-level supermarket has everything that fans of Japanese cooking might crave – including ready-made sushi.

Merry Monk

87 rue de la Convention, 15th (01.40.60.79.54). M° Boucicaut. **Open** 10am-7pm Mon-Sat. **Credit** MC, V. **Map** p406 B9.
Expat essentials such as ginger biscuits and loose tea, with a section dedicated to South Africa.

Market forces

Eat, Drink, Shop

When pressed, Parisians will shop at the *supermarché*, but they are far happier queuing (jostling, as often as not) at their local open-air market. Markets have eternal appeal, their products perceived as a more 'natural' alternative to supermarket fare. The city council has made them more accessible to working people by extending opening hours and creating late-afternoon markets in previously overlooked areas. Even if quality can be variable, there is no better place in Paris to soak up neighbourhood atmosphere while tracking down a farmer's pungent goat's cheese, a dozen fresh Cancale oysters, a bunch of ruby chard or a jar of sunflower-yellow honey.

The 66 roving markets in Paris have retained their atmosphere and variety, although street and covered markets can be a bit of a letdown, with clothing stores and chains replacing traditional food shops. Here is a selection of the best roving markets, open from 8am to 2pm unless otherwise specified:

Marché Monge (place Monge, 5th; Wed, Fri, Sun), though compact, is pretty, and set on a leafy square. It has an unusually high proportion of producers and is much less touristy than nearby rue Mouffetard, a long-established street market. Be prepared to queue for the best quality.

Saxe-Breteuil (av de Saxe, 7th; Thur, Sat) has an unrivalled setting facing the Eiffel Tower, as well as the city's most chic produce. Look for farmer's goat's cheese, rare apple varieties, Armenian specialities, abundant oysters and a handful of dedicated small producers.

Marché Square d'Anvers (9th; 3-8pm Fri) is a newly created afternoon market, adding to the village atmosphere of a peaceful *quartier* down the hill from Montmartre. Among its highlights are untreated vegetables, hams from the Auvergne, lovingly aged cheeses and award-winning honey.

Marché Bastille (bd Richard-Lenoir, 11th; Thur, Sun) is one of the biggest and most boisterous in Paris. A favourite of political campaigners, it's also a great source of local cheeses, farmer's chicken and excellent affordable fish.

Marché d'Aligre (rue d'Aligre, 12th; Tue-Sun), next a covered market, is proudly working class. Stallholders out-shout each other while price-conscious shoppers don't compromise on quality.

Marché Président-Wilson (av Président-Wilson, 16th; Wed, Sat) is a classy market attracting the city's top chefs, who snap up ancient vegetable varieties. Genuine Breton crêpes and buckwheat galettes available as you shop.

Marché Batignolles (bd de Batignolles, 17th; Sat) is more down-to-earth than the better-known **Raspail** organic market, with a quirky selection of stallholders, many of whom produce what they sell. Prices are higher than at ordinary markets, but worth it.

Prize-winning cheeses at **Fromagerie Quatrehomme**. See p265.

Mexi & Co

10 rue Dante, 5th (01.46.34.14.12). M° Cluny La Sorbonne. **Open** noon-midnight daily. **No credit cards. Map** p408 J7.
All you need for a fiesta: marinades for fajitas, dried chillies, Latin American beers, *cachaça* and tequilas.

Pasta Linea

9 rue de Turenne, 4th (01.42.77.62.54). M° St-Paul.
Open 11am-9pm Tue-Fri; noon-8pm Sat, Sun.
Credit AmEx, DC, MC, V. **Map** p408 L6.
Artichoke ravioli with truffle cream sauce or fresh linguine with tomato and rocket are among the heavenly hot pastas you might find here – or quality dried pastas and prepared sauces to eat at home.

Petrossian

18 bd de La-Tour-Maubourg, 7th (01.44.11.32.32/ www.petrossian.fr). M° Invalides. **Open** 9.20am-8pm Mon-Sat. **Credit** AmEx, DC, MC, V. **Map** p407 E6.
Russian-themed delicatessen downstairs from a trendy restaurant, offering silky smoked salmon, Iranian caviar and gift boxes with little drawers to impress even the most jaded of the jet set.

Sarl Velan Stores

87 passage Brady, 10th (01.42.46.06.06). M° Château d'Eau. **Open** 10am-8.30pm Mon-Sat. **Credit** AmEx, DC, MC, V. **Map** p404 K4.
In a crumbling arcade lined with Indian restaurants, this is a prime source of spices and Indian produce.

Tang Frères

48 av d'Ivry, 13th (01.45.70.80.00). M° Porte d'Ivry.
Open 9am-7.30pm Tue-Sun. **Credit** MC, V.
Leading supplier to local restaurants in Chinatown, this is the best one-stop shop for a Chinese or southeast Asian stir-fry.

Patisseries

Arnaud Lahrer

53 rue Caulaincourt, 18th (01.42.57.68.08). M° Lamarck Caulaincourt. **Open** 10am-7.30pm Tue-Sun.
Credit MC, V. **Map** p403 H1.
Look out for the strawberry-and-lychee flavoured *bonheur* and the chocolate-and-thyme *récif*.

Finkelsztajn

27 rue des Rosiers, 4th (01.42.72.78.91). M° St-Paul.
Open 11am-7pm Mon; 10am-7pm Wed-Sun. Closed 15 July-15 Aug. **No credit cards. Map** p408 L6.
This motherly shop stocks dense Jewish cakes filled with poppy seeds, apples or cream cheese.

Gérard Mulot

76 rue de Seine, 6th (01.43.26.85.77). M° Odéon.
Open 6.45am-8pm Mon, Tue, Thur-Sun. Closed Aug.
No credit cards. Map p408 H7.
Mulot rustles up stunning pastries. Typical is the *mabillon,* caramel mousse with apricot marmalade.

Pierre Hermé

72 rue Bonaparte, 6th (01.43.54.47.77). M° St-Sulpice. **Open** 10am-7pm Tue-Sun. **Credit** DC, MC, V. **Map** p407 G7.
Pastry superstar Hermé attracts the connoisseurs of St-Germain with his seasonal collections.
Other locations: *185 rue de Vaugirard, 15th (01.47.83.29.72).*

Sadaharu Aoki

35 rue de Vaugirard, 6th (01.45.44.48.90). M° St-Placide. **Open** 11am-7pm Mon-Sat. **Credit** AmEx, DC, MC, V. **Map** p407 G8.
This Japanese pastry chef combines French techniques to produce original (and pristine) pastries.

Treats & *traiteurs*

Allicante

26 bd Beaumarchais, 11th (01.43.55.13.02/
www.allicante.com). M° Bastille. **Open** 10am-7.30pm
Mon-Sat. **Credit** AmEx, DC, MC, V. **Map** p408 M6.
A trove of oily delights, including rare olive oils from
Liguria, Sicily and Greece, fragrant pine nut, pistachio and almond varieties, oils extracted from apricot, peach and avocado pits – even pricey argania
oil, pounded by hand by Berber women in Morocco.

Da Rosa

62 rue de Seine, 6th (01.40.51.00.09/www.darosa.fr).
M° Odéon. **Open** 10am-10pm daily. **Credit** AmEx,
MC, V. **Map** p408 H7.
José Da Rosa sought ingredients for top Paris restau-
rants before opening his own shop, designed by
Jacques Garcia: Spanish hams, spices from Breton
chef Olivier Roellinger, truffles from the Luberon.

L'Epicerie

51 rue St-Louis-en-l'Ile, 4th (01.43.25.20.14). M°
Pont Marie. **Open** 11am-8pm daily. **Credit** MC, V.
Map p408 K7.
This perfect gift shop is crammed with nice bottles
of blackcurrant vinegar, five-spice mustard, tiny
pots of jam, orange sauce, honey with figs and indulgent boxes of chocolate snails.

Fauchon

26-30 pl de la Madeleine, 8th (01.47.42.60.11/www.
fauchon.com). M° Madeleine. **Open** 9.30am-8pm
Mon-Sat. **Credit** AmEx, DC, MC, V. **Map** p403 F4.
It may be the city's most famous food shop, but
glitzy Fauchon seems to lack soul after a series of
revamps. It's still worth a pilgrimage, particularly
for the beautifully packaged gift items.

Goumanyat

3 rue Dupuis, 3rd (01.44.78.96.74/www.goumanyat.
com). M° Temple. **Open** 11am-7pm Tue-Fri. **Credit**
AmEx, DC, MC, V. **Map** p404 L5.
Jean-Marie Thiercelin's family has been in spice
since 1809, and his spacious, rather secretive shop
(buzzer entry) is a treasure trove of super-fresh
flavourings. Star chefs come here for Indonesian
cubeb pepper, gleaming fresh nutmeg, long pepper
(an Indian variety), and Spanish and Iranian saffron.

Hédiard

21 pl de la Madeleine, 8th (01.43.12.88.88/
www.hediard.fr). M° Madeleine. **Open** 8.30am-9pm
Mon-Sat. **Credit** AmEx, DC, MC, V. **Map** p403 F4.
The first establishment to introduce exotic foods to
Paris, Hédiard specialises in rare teas and coffees,
spices, jams and candied fruits. The original shop,
dating from 1880, has a posh tea room upstairs. See
the website for other addresses.

Huilerie Artisanale Leblanc

6 rue Jacob, 6th (01.46.34.61.55). M° St-Germain-
des-Prés. **Open** 2.30-7pm Mon; 11am-7pm Tue-Sat.
Closed 2wks Aug. **No credit cards**. **Map** p407 H6.

The Leblanc family started out making walnut oil
from its family tree in Burgundy before branching
out to press pure oils from hazelnuts, almonds, pine
nuts, grilled peanuts, pistachios and olives.

Jean-Paul Gardil

44 rue St-Louis en l'Ile, 4th (01.43.54.97.15). M°
Pont Marie. **Open** 9am-12.45pm, 4-7.45pm Tue-Sat;
8.30am-12.30pm Sun. **Credit** MC, V. **Map** p408 K7.
Rarely has meat looked so beautiful as in this fairy-
tale shop, where geese hang in the window and a
multitude of plaques confirm the butcher's skill in
selecting the finest meats, such as milk-fed veal and
lamb, coucou de Rennes chickens, Barbary free-
range ducklings, and Bresse poulard and geese.

La Maison des Trois Thés

1 rue St-Médard, 5th (01.43.36.93.84). M° Place
Monge. **Open** 11am-7.30pm Tue-Sun. **Credit** MC, V.
Map p408 K8.
Yu Hui Tseng, one of world's leading tea experts,
has moved to these larger premises. A hush reigns
as connoisseurs dip their lips into teas costing a
small fortune, though the cheapest is €10.

La Maison de la Truffe

19 pl de la Madeleine, 8th (01.42.65.53.22/
www.maison-de-la-truffe.com). M° Madeleine. **Open**
9.30am-9pm Mon-Sat. **Credit** AmEx, DC, MC, V.
Map p403 F4.
Come here in winter for truffles worth more than
gold, or for the more affordable (artificial) truffle oils,
sauces and vinegars.

Mariage Frères

30 rue du Bourg-Tibourg, 4th (01.42.72.28.11/www.
mariage-freres.com). M° Hôtel de Ville. **Open** *Shop*
10.30am-7pm daily. *Restaurant* noon-3pm daily.
Salon 3-7pm daily. **Credit** MC, V. **Map** p408 K6.
A wood-panelled, wonderfully aromatic, classically
old-fashioned tea emporium – one of the few places
in Paris where queuing is solemnly observed. Come
here to buy (or, in the salon, sample) teas of every
provenance, colour and strength, plus tea-related
accessories. For other outlets, see website.

Poissonnerie du Dôme

4 rue Delambre, 14th (01.43.35.23.95). M° Vavin.
Open 8am-1pm, 4-7pm Tue-Sat; 8am-1pm Sun.
Credit MC, V. **Map** p407 G9.
The fish here are individually selected, many com-
ing straight from small boats off the Breton coast.
Each one is bright of eye and sound of gill. Try the
drool-inducing (but bank-breaking) turbot, the giant
crabs or the scallops, when in season.

Torréfacteur Verlet

256 rue St-Honoré, 1st (01.42.60.67.39). M° Palais
Royal Musée du Louvre. **Open** *Shop* 9.30am-6.30pm
Mon-Sat. *Tea shop* 9.30am-6.30pm daily. **Credit** MC,
V. **Map** p403 G5.
The freshly roasted coffee here smells as heavenly
as the priciest perfume. Eric Duchaussoy roasts rare
beans to perfection – sip a *p'tit noir* at a wooden
table, or take home the city's finest coffee.

Wine, beer & spirits

Don't expect to see an international selection in Paris wine shops – seek out French wines at reasonable prices that rarely travel beyond the borders. The food hall of **Galeries Lafayette** (*see p240*) stocks spirits of impressive vintage.

Bières Spéciales

77 rue St-Maur, 11th (01.48.07.18.71). M° Rue St-Maur. **Open** 10.30am-1pm, 4-9pm Tue-Sat. **Credit** AmEx, DC, MC, V. **Map** p405 N5.
Belgian brews dominate but you'll also find Polish, Scottish, Corsican, Portuguese and Chinese types.

Les Caves Augé

116 bd Haussmann, 8th (01.45.22.16.97). M° St-Augustin. **Open** 1-7.30pm Mon; 9am-7.30pm Tue-Sat. Closed Mon in Aug. **Credit** AmEx, MC, V. **Map** p403 E3.
The oldest wine shop in Paris – Marcel Proust was a regular customer – is serious and professional.

Les Caves Taillevent

199 rue du Fbg-St-Honoré, 8th (01.45.61.14.09/ www.taillevent.com). M° Charles de Gaulle Etoile or Ternes. **Open** 2-7.30pm Mon; 9am-7.30pm Tue-Fri; 9am-7.30pm Sat. Closed 3wks Aug. **Credit** AmEx, DC, MC, V. **Map** p402 D3.
Half a million bottles make up the Taillevent cellar, supervised by three head sommeliers.

Les Domaines qui Montent

136 bd Voltaire, 11th (01.43.56.89.15). M° Voltaire. **Open** 10am-8pm Tue-Sat. **Credit** MC, V. **Map** p405 N6.
A shop and café, where wines cost the same as they would at the producer's. Saturday tastings, too.

Julien, Caviste

50 rue Charlot, 3rd (01.42.72.00.94). M° Filles du Calvaire. **Open** 9.30am-1.30pm, 3.30-8.30pm Tue-Fri; 9.30am-8.30pm Sat; 10am-1.30pm Sun. **Credit** MC, V. **Map** p404 L5.
The tireless Julien overflows with enthusiasm for the small producers he has discovered, and often holds free wine tastings on Saturdays.

Legrand Filles et Fils

1 rue de la Banque, 2nd (01.42.60.07.12). M° Bourse. **Open** 11am-7pm Mon-Fri; 10am-7pm Sat. **Credit** AmEx, DC, MC, V. **Map** p404 H4.
This old-fashioned shop offering fine wines and brandies, teas and bonbons has a showroom for its tasting glasses and gadgets, housed within galerie Vivienne. Wine tastings on Thursdays.

La Maison du Whisky

20 rue d'Anjou, 8th (01.42.65.03.16/www.whisky.fr). M° Madeleine. **Open** 9.30am-7pm Mon; 9.30am-8pm Tue-Fri; 9.30am-7.30pm Sat. **Credit** AmEx, MC, V. **Map** p403 F4.
Jean-Marc Bellier explains which whisky matches which food, waxes lyrical about flavours such as honey and tobacco, and hosts a whisky club.

Ryst Dupeyron

79 rue du Bac, 7th (01.45.48.80.93/www.ryst-dupeyron.com). M° Rue du Bac. **Open** 12.30-7.30pm Mon; 10.30am-7.30pm Tue-Sat. Closed 1wk Aug. **Credit** AmEx, DC, MC, V. **Map** p407 F7.
The Dupeyron family has sold Armagnac for four generations, and have bottles dating from 1868. Treasures include some 200 fine Bordeaux, vintage port and rare whiskies.

Gifts

Florists

Au Nom de la Rose

87 rue St-Antoine, 4th (01.42.71.34.24/www. aunomdelarose.fr). M° St-Paul. **Open** 9am-9pm Mon-Sat 9am-2pm Sun. **Credit** AmEx, MC, V. **Map** p408 L7.
Specialising in roses, Au Nom can supply a bouquet, plus rose-based beauty products and candles.
Other locations: *throughout the city.*

Christian Tortu

6 carrefour de l'Odéon, 6th (01.43.26.02.56). M° Odéon. **Open** 10am-8pm Mon-Sat. Closed 2wks Aug. **Credit** AmEx, DC, MC, V. **Map** p408 H7.
The city's most celebrated florist is famed for combining flowers, twigs, bark and moss into still lifes. Buy his vases at 17 rue des Quatre-Vents (6th).

Monceau Fleurs

60 av Paul-Doumer, 16th (01.40.72.79.27/ www.monceaufleurs.com). M° La Muette. **Open** 8.30am-9pm daily. **Credit** MC, V. **Map** p402 B6.
The city-wide branches sell an affordable range of fresh *fleurs*. Order and pay for bouquets online, too.
Other locations: *throughout the city.*

Souvenirs & eccentricities

L'Art du Buro

47 rue des Francs-Bourgeois, 4th (01.48.87.57.97). M° St-Paul. **Open** 10.30am-7.30pm Mon-Sat; 2-6.30pm Sun. **Credit** AmEx, DC, MC, V. **Map** p408 L6.
This Marais boutique sells sleek and modern desk accessories, including some sexy ones that bring a whole new meaning to the term 'stress balls'.

Black Block

Palais de Tokyo, 13 av du Président-Wilson, 16th (01.47.23.37.04/www.blackblock.org). M° Iéna. **Open** noon-midnight Tue-Sun. **Credit** AmEx, DC, MC, V. **Map** p402 C5.
Kooky Japanese items – toys, trainers, mayonnaise – in big fridges, with limited-edition artworks.

Deyrolle

46 rue du Bac, 7th (01.42.22.30.07). M° Rue du Bac. **Open** 10am-6.45pm Mon-Sat. **Credit** AmEx, MC, V. **Map** p407 G6.

Established in 1831, this dusty taxidermists' overflows with stuffed animals. Have your own pet stuffed (€500 for a cat) or hire a beast for a few days.

Diptyque
34 bd St-Germain, 5th (01.43.26.45.27). M° Maubert Mutualité. **Open** 10am-7pm Mon-Sat. **Credit** AmEx, MC, V. **Map** p407 G6.
Diptyque's divinely scented candles in 48 different varieties are probably the best you'll ever find.

Pa Design
2bis rue Fléchier, 9th (01.42.85.20.85/www.pa-design.com). M° Notre-Dame de-Lorette. **Open** 10am-2pm, 3-7pm Wed-Fri; 10am-1pm, 2-7pm Sat. **Credit** AmEx, MC, V. **Map** p404 H3.
This design company produces a range of ingenious, playful domestic products – tablecloths, vases, toys or photo frames with a twist. They also sell a hand-picked selection of other local designers' work.

Papeterie Moderne
12 rue de la Ferronnerie, 1st (01.42.36.21.72). M° Châtelet. **Open** 9am-12.30am, 1.30-6.30pm Mon-Sat. **No credit cards**. **Map** p408 J6.
The source of those enamel plaques that adorn Paris streets and forbidding gateways (*Attention! chien bizarre* and the like) for less than €10 a pop.

Paris Accordéon
80 rue Daguerre, 14th (01.43.22.13.48). M° Gaîté or M°/RER Denfert Rochereau. **Open** 9am-noon, 1-7pm Tue-Fri; 9am-noon, 1-6pm Sat. **Credit** AmEx, MC, V. **Map** p407 G10.
This joint brims with accordions, from simple squeeze-boxes to the most beautiful tortoise-shell models, both second-hand and new.

Paris-Musées
29bis rue des Francs-Bourgeois, 4th (01.42.74.13.02). M° St-Paul. **Open** 2-7pm Mon; 11am-7pm Tue-Sat; 11am-6.30pm Sun. **Credit** AmEx, DC, MC, V. **Map** p408 L6.
Run by Ville de Paris museums, this shop showcases funky lamps and ceramics by young designers, along with reproductions from the city's museums.

Résonances
9 cour St-Emilion, 12th (01.44.73.82.82). M° Cour St-Emilion. **Open** 11am-9pm daily. **Credit** AmEx, MC, V. **Map** p409 P10.
Stocks a well-chosen array of supplies and gadgets for the home. DIY enthusiasts will appreciate the tape measures, paints and brushes and interior design books; sybarites will dig the bath products.

Sennelier
3 quai Voltaire, 7th (01.42.60.72.15/www.sennelier. fr). M° St-Germain-des-Prés. **Open** 2-6.30pm Mon; 9.30am-12.30pm, 2-6.30pm Tue-Sat. **Credit** AmEx, DC, MC, V. **Map** p407 G6.
Old-fashioned colour merchant Sennelier has been supplying artists since 1887. The array of oil paints, watercolours and pastels includes rare pigments, and there are primered boards, varnishes and paper.

Fauchon. *See p269.*

Flower power at **Christian Tortu**. *See p270.*

Home

Antiques & flea markets

Knowing who specialises in what is essential for antique buying in Paris. Classy traditional antiques can be found in the **Louvre des Antiquaires** (1st), **Carré Rive Gauche** (6th), **Village Suisse** (15th) and **Fbg-St-Honoré** (1st). You'll find art deco in **St-Germain-des-Prés** (7th), retro by **rue de Charonne** (11th), old books in the galeries, in the *bouquinistes* by the Seine, or at parc Georges Brassens.

As well as flea markets (*see p273* **Hunt the heirloom**), don't forget auction house **Drouot** (recorded information on 01.48.00.20.17). There are also frequent *brocantes* and *braderies* – antiques' and collectors' markets.

Louvre des Antiquaires
2 pl du Palais-Royal, 1st (01.42.97.27.27/www. louvre-antiquaires.com). M° Palais Royal Musée du Louvre. **Open** 11am-7pm Tue-Sun. Closed Sun July-Aug. **Credit** varies. **Map** p408 H5.
This upmarket antiques centre behind the façade of an old *grand magasin* houses 250 antiques dealers: just the place for Louis XV furniture, tapestries, porcelain and jewellery, model ships and tin soldiers.

Le Village St-Paul
rue St-Paul, rue Charlemagne and quai des Célestins, 4th. M° St-Paul. **Open** 10am-7pm Mon-Sat. **No credit cards.** **Map** p408 L7.

This colony of antique sellers, spread across small courtyards linking rues St-Paul and Charlemagne, and quai des Célestins, is a source of 1930s and '50s furniture, kitchenware and wine gadgets.

Design & interiors

La **Samaritaine** (*see p240*) has a selection of current design and homewares, as does the vast **Lafayette Maison** (*see p240*).

Astier de Villatte
173 rue St-Honoré, 1st (01.42.60.74.13). M° Palais Royal Musée du Louvre. **Open** 11am-7.30pm Mon-Sat. Closed 3wks Aug. **Credit** AmEx, MC, V. **Map** p403 G4.
Once home to Napoleon's silversmith Biennet, this ancient warren of small rooms now houses white and platinum ceramics inspired by 17th- and 18th-century designs, handmade by the Astier de Villatte siblings in their Bastille workshop.
Other locations: *99 rue du Bac, 7th (01.42.22.81.59).*

Bô
8 rue St-Merri, 4th (01.42.72.84.64). M° Hôtel de Ville. **Open** 11am-8pm Mon-Sat; 2-8pm Sun. **Credit** AmEx, MC, V. **Map** p408 K6.
Pared-back contemporary style: candlesticks, vases, unusual lights, new-agey incense burners and elegant grey Limoges porcelain.

Cappellini
4 rue des Rosiers, 4th (01.42.78.39.39/www. cappellini.it). M° St-Paul. **Open** 10.30am-7pm Tue-Sat. **Credit** AmEx, DC, MC, V. **Map** p408 L6.
This major global design company knows talent when it sees it. In this former Marais hammam you'll find all the usual suspects – Jasper Morrison, Hella Jongerius, Tom Dixon, the Bourroullec brothers – and their first-rate contemporary pieces.

Caravane Chambre 19
19 rue St-Nicolas, 12th (01.53.02.96.96). M° Ledru-Rollin. **Open** 11am-7pm Mon-Sat. **Credit** AmEx, MC, V. **Map** p409 M7.
This offshoot of Françoise Dorget's original Marais shop has goodies such as exquisite hand-sewn quilts from West Bengal, crisp cotton and organdie tunics, Berber scarves and lounging sofas and daybeds. Also chic accessories such as silk-sheet sleeping bags and stripy neckrests with matching eyemasks.
Other locations: *6 rue Pavée, 4th (01.44.61.04.22).*

CFOC
170 bd Haussmann, 8th (01.53.53.40.80). M° St-Philippe du-Roule. **Open** 10am-7pm Mon-Sat. **Credit** AmEx, DC, MC, V. **Map** p403 E3.
La Compagnie Française de l'Orient et de la Chine is full of eastern promise, from Chinese teapots and celadon bowls, to Iranian blown glass.
Other locations: *163, 167 bd St-Germain, 6th (01.45.48.00.18); 65 av Victor-Hugo, 16th (01.45.00.55.46).*

Hunt the heirloom

Paris is the home of the flea market. Set up by scrap merchants outside the city gates in the 19th century, the vast Puces de St-Ouen now sprawls way beyond its original site. The ones at Vanves, Aligre and Montreuil still resemble an old-fashioned street market. Though your chances of stumbling on a priceless artefact are pretty slim, there are plenty of interesting buys to be found. Remember to carry cash, always bargain (dealers will generally come down by 10-15 per cent) and beware of pickpockets. Nearly all flea markets open Saturday to Monday, apart from Aligre (Tue-Sun) and Vanves (Sat, Sun). Further info can be found at www.les-puces.com and www.la-brocante.com.

The mother of all flea markets, the enormous **Puces de St-Ouen** (18th, Mº Porte de Clignancourt) is home to some 2,500 dealers at ten main markets, most of which are on or off spinal rue des Rosiers. Don't bother to get here early to nab bargains – most stalls won't open till 9am at the earliest. The most eclectic source of vintage bric-a-brac is at the **Marché Paul Bert** (104 rue des Rosiers, 01.40.11.54.14), with cast-iron fountains, fairground animals and hefty lunchtime salads. More upmarket **Marché Biron** (85 rue des Rosiers, 01.40.11.59.69) has gilt and chandeliers down allée 1, period furniture along allée 2. You'll find vintage posters here, too. The plushest venue is the **Marché Serpette** (110 rue des Rosiers, 01.40.11.54.14), with art deco and antique costume jewellery. For '50s furniture, try the **Marché Vallès-Lecuyer**, between the roads of the same name. Second-hand and vintage clothes can be found at the **Marché Malik** (53 rue Jules-Vallès/59 rue Jean-Henri Fabre), although discount leather-jacket merchants have ousted some of the more interesting retro stalls. The oldest, most authentic and best organised is the **Marché Vernaison** (99 rue des Rosiers), with all kinds of furniture and toys; of the newest ones, the **Marché Dauphine** (138-140 rue des Rosiers, 01.40.12.14.68) features 300 dealers of classic furniture across two floors, and the **Marché Malassis** (142 rue des Rosiers, 01.40.12.29.28) is best for children's toys and Tintin memorabilia.

The only central market is **Aligre**. Its origins pre-date the French Revolution, and Aligre stays true to its junk tradition, with a handful

of *brocanteurs* peddling books, phone cards, kitchenware and knick-knacks at what seem optimistic prices. It shares space with one of the city's cheapest fruit-and-veg markets. *See p267* **Market forces**.

Begun in the 1920s, **Vanves** (av Georges-Lafenestre/av Marc Sangnier, 14th, Mº Porte de Vanves) is the smallest and friendliest of the flea markets. Conviviality and civility reign, and a stroll round the colourful stands makes for a peaceful, gently stimulating Sunday morning outing. If you get there early enough, there are decent second-hand clothes, dolls, '50s costume jewellery and silverware.

The anarchic **Montreuil** (Montreuil-sur-Bois, Mº Porte de Montreuil) disgorges mountains of second-hand clothing, car parts and a jumble of rubbish. You'll find little pre-1900, but there are fun collectibles like Pastis jugs and old hats. Stallholders shout out their prices above the din; feisty women push their prams over your toes, but the souk-like soul of the place will win you over in the end.

Chône

60 rue Vieille-du-Temple, 3rd (01.44.78.90.00).
M° Rambuteau. **Open** 2-7pm Mon; 11am-7pm Tue-
Sat. Closed Aug. **Credit** AmEx, DC, MC, V. **Map**
p408 K6.
Camille Unglik designed shoes for Louis Vuitton
before opening this boutique dedicated to exclusive
and limited-edition tablewear. Big on Scandinavian
designers, it houses glasswear, cutlery or crockery
by Tapio Virkkala; other featured designers include
Karim Rashid, Ross Lovegrove and Philippe Starck.

Christian Liaigre

42 rue du Bac, 7th (01.53.63.33.66). M° Rue du Bac.
Open 10am-7pm Mon-Sat. Closed 2wks Aug.
Credit AmEx, DC, MC, V. **Map** p407 G6.
This famous French interior decorator fitted out
New York's Hotel Mercer, Marc Jacobs' boutique in
Soho and the Market restaurant here in Paris. At his
showroom, Liagre displays his furniture and light-
ing designs of sober elegance and comfort, in trade-
mark tones of cream and brown.

Christophe Delcourt

12 rue Volney, 2nd (01.42.78.44.97). M° Opéra.
Open 9am-noon, 1-6pm Mon-Fri. **Credit** AmEx, DC,
MC, V. **Map** p403 G4.
Delcourt's art deco-influenced geometrical lines are
given a contemporary edge by their combination of
stained wood with waxed black steel.

CSAO

1-3 rue Elzévir, 3rd (01.44.54.55.88/www.csao.fr).
M° St-Paul. **Open** 10am-7pm Mon-Sat; noon-7pm
Sun. **Credit** AmEx, DC, MC, V. **Map** p408 L6.
Africa in the heart of the Marais. Standing for
'Compagnie du Sénégal et de l'Afrique de l'Ouest'
this spacious, lively boutique sells traditional crafts
produced according to the principles of equitable
commerce. The artisans often make their objects out
of recycled materials, so you'll find funky furniture
made out of tins and colourful mats out of plastic.

Espace Lumière

17 rue des Lombards, 4th (01.42.77.47.71). M°
Châtelet. **Open** 10am-7pm Mon-Sat. **Credit** AmEx,
MC, V. **Map** p408 K6.
These sober showrooms parade the best European
and American lighting designers working today.
Nuzzling up to pieces by Starck, Wilmotte or
Artemide are re-editions of key industrial lighting.
Other locations: *48 rue Mazarine, 6th*
(01.43.54.06.28); 167 bd Haussmann, 8th
(01.42.89.01.15).

FR 66

25 rue de Renard, 4th (01.44.54.35.36). M° Hôtel de
Ville. **Open** 10am-7pm Mon-Sat. **Credit** MC, V. **Map**
p408 K6.
Somewhere between a gallery and a shop, this two-
level experimental space accommodates contemporary artists and designers who produce exciting and
original products for the home – not only furniture,
but electrical fittings and floor and wall coverings.

Galerie Patrick Seguin

5 rue des Taillandiers, 11th (01.47.00.32.35/www.
patrickseguin.com). M° Ledru-Rollin or Bastille.
Open 10am-7pm Mon-Sat. **Credit** AmEx, DC, MC,
V. **Map** p409 M7.
Seguin specialises in modern French design from the
'50s: original pieces by Charlotte Perriand or Jean
Prouvé, all on display in a gorgeous showroom.

Le Bihan

41 rue du Fbg-St-Antoine, 11th (01.43.43.06.75).
M° Bastille. **Open** 2-7pm Mon; 10am-7pm Tue-Sat.
Credit AmEx, MC, V. **Map** p409 M7.
In case you thought the Faubourg was now just
clothes shops or mock Louis XV, check out this
three-floor showcase for the best of modern design,
such as furniture and lighting from Perriand, Gray
and Mies van der Rohe to Pesce, Santachiara, Pillet,
Morrison, Arad and others.

Ozone

49 rue de Saintonge, 3rd (01.53.01.93.01/www.ozone
light.com). M° Filles du Calvaire. **Open** 11am-7pm
Mon-Sat. **Credit** AmEx, MC, V. **Map** p404 L5.
Ozone produces elegant, contemporary lighting
designs from this smart Marais showroom/work-
shop. Young duo Eric Jaehnke and Etienne Gounot
produce deceptively simple and original pieces like
the X lamp – a glowing X-shaped light-box which
can be hung from the ceiling or stacked on the floor.

Sentou Galerie

18 & 24 rue du Pont-Louis-Philippe, 4th
(01.42.71.00.01). M° Pont Marie. **Open** 11am-7pm
Tue-Sat. **Credit** AmEx, MC, V. **Map** p408 K7.
Favoured by *Marie Claire Maison*, this is a trendsetting shop for tableware and furniture. Among the
eye-catching colours, look out for painted Chinese
flasks, vases and a lime-green accordion bench.

Kitchen & bathroom

Bains Plus

51 rue des Francs-Bourgeois, 4th (01.48.87.83.07).
M° Hôtel de Ville. **Open** 11am-7.30pm Tue-Sat; 2.30-
7.30pm Sun. **Credit** AmEx, MC, V. **Map** p408 K6.
The ultimate gents' shaving shop: duck-shaped
loofahs, seductive dressing gowns, chrome mirrors,
bath oils and soaps.

E Dehillerin

18 rue Coquillière, 1st (01.42.36.53.13). M° Les
Halles. **Open** 9am-12.30pm, 2-6pm Mon; 9am-6pm
Tue-Sat. **Credit** MC, V. **Map** p404 J5.
Suppliers to great chefs since 1820, this no-nonsense
warehouse stocks just about every kitchen utensil
ever invented. A saucepan from Dehillerin is for life.

Kitchen Bazaar

11 av du Maine, 15th (01.42.22.91.17). M°
Montparnasse Bienvenüe. **Open** 10am-7pm Mon-Sat.
Credit AmEx, MC, V. **Map** p407 F8.
All chrome gadgetry and modish fixtures, Kitchen
Bazaar is perfect for luxury items. Sister shop Bath

Modern design at **Le Bihan**. *See p274.*

Bazaar Autrement (6 av du Maine, 01.45.48.89.00), across the street, sells bathroom goodies. **Other locations**: *23 bd de la Madeleine, 1st (01.42.60.50.32).*

Laguiole Galerie
1 pl Ste-Opportune, 1st (01.40.28.09.42). M° Châtelet. **Open** 10am-noon, 2-7pm Mon-Sat. **Credit** MC, V. **Map** p408 J6.
Philippe Starck designed this chic and sharp boutique, a showcase for France's classic knife, the Laguiole, plus limited-edition versions thereof.

Sport & games
For general sports equipment and clothes, the chains **Go Sport** and **Décathlon** are best. If you just want to look the part, *see p259* **Streetwear & clubwear**. For **Agnès b** sportswear, *see p256*. For **Paris St-Germain** football gear and match tickets, *see p334*.

Au Vieux Campeur
48 rue des Ecoles, 5th (01.53.10.48.48/www.au-vieux-campeur.com). M° Maubert Mutualité. **Open** 11am-7.30pm Mon-Tue, Thur-Fri; 11am-9pm Wed; 9.30am-7.30pm Sat. **Credit** MC, V. **Map** p408 J7.
This Paris institution runs several specialist shops between rue des Ecoles and the bd St-Germain. The group provides good advice and equipment for just about any kind of sporting activity except golf.

Citadium
50-55 rue de Caumartin, 9th (01.55.31.74.00). M° Havre-Caumartin. **Open** 10am-8pm Mon-Wed, Fri, Sat; 10am-9pm Thur. **Credit** AmEx, DC, MC, V. **Map** p403 G3.
One of France's biggest sports stockists, and a cult to boot. The latest surf 'n' skater vids blast out into the four themed circular floors, all manned by expert staff. Hip watches to cross-country skis.

Décathlon
26 av de Wagram, 8th (01.55.31.74.00/ www.decathlon.fr). M° Charles de Gaulle Etoile. **Open** 10am-8pm Mon-Fri; 9am-8pm Sat. **Credit** MC, V. **Map** p402 C3.
Sports megastore with a comprehensive catalogue and helpful staff to ensure you're decked out with the right equipment at a competitive price. The range is awesome; it's also a camper's heaven. See the website for other branches.

Equistable
177 bd Haussmann, 8th (01.45.61.02.57). M° St-Philippe du-Roule. **Open** 11am-7pm Mon-Fri; 10am-6pm Sat. **Credit** AmEx, DC, MC, V. **Map** p403 E4.
Well-stocked emporium selling quality equine gear, from Hermès saddles to horsey trinkets.

Go Sport
Forum des Halles, 1st (01.53.00.81.70/www.go-sport.com). M° Les Halles/RER Châtelet Les Halles. **Open** 10am-7.30pm Mon-Sat. **Credit** AmEx, MC, V. **Map** p408 J6.
An Olympian list of sports is covered by this well-priced chain: home exercise machine, saddle wax, wet suit, Nike, adidas and cheaper house clobber.

Nauti Store
40 av de la Grande-Armée, 17th (01.43.80.28.28). M° Argentine. **Open** 11am-7pm Mon; 10am-7pm Tue-Sat. **Credit** AmEx, MC, V. **Map** p402 C3.
This shop stocks a vast range of sailing clothes and shoes from labels such as Helly Hansen and Sebago.

René Pierre
35 rue de Maubeuge, 9th (01.44.91.91.21/www.rene-pierre.fr). M° Poissonnière. **Open** 10am-1pm, 2-6.30pm Mon-Fri. **Credit** V. **Map** p404 H3.
Paris showroom for France's finest table-football tables, crafted at the Chalon-sur-Saône factory of René Pierre, *Maître Billardier* since 1952. Spun, swivelled and slammed in cafés around the world, his classic models *Onze*, *Leader* et al can be admired and ordered here. For UK *baby-foot* aficionados, tables can be delivered free of charge as far as Calais. Jukeboxes and billiard tables also on sale.

Subchandlers – Plongespace
80 rue Balard, 15th (01.45.57.01.01/www. subchandlers.com). M° Balard. **Open** 2.30-7.30pm Mon; 10.30am-7.30pm Tue-Sat. **Credit** MC, V. **Map** p406 A9.
Diving experts provide all the basic apparatus, plus underwater cameras, DVDs, books, and monthly soirées on photography, film and all things aquatic.

Eat, Drink, Shop

Discover the Show of the Most Famous Cabaret in the World !

Dinner & Show at 7pm from €140 • Show at 9pm : €97, at 11pm : €87

Montmartre - 82, boulevard de Clichy - 75018 Paris
Reservations : 01 53 09 82 82 - www.moulin-rouge.com

Arts &
Entertainment

Features

Festivals & Events

The city of light sparkles all year round.

Nouvel An Chinois. *See p283*.

Paris thrives on *fêtes*. Along with a panoply of cultural events throughout the year, there are anniversaries and religious festivals aplenty. Paris has a propensity to turn every commemoration into a serious, state-funded, event: in 2004 it was the the Liberation of Paris; in 2005 it be will the centenary of Sartre's birth (*see p283* **Ol' four eyes is back**).

The pro-active reign of Mayor Delanoë (*see pp33-36* **Delanoë's Dream**) has done much to refresh the capital's diary. **Paris-Plage** (*see p280* **No Plage like home**), an urban beach set up by the Seine for the summer, and **Nuit Blanche**, an autumnal, all-night culture fest, have brought high-profile successes.

In terms of cultural seasons, Paris starts up in October, keeping busy until the beginning of summer, when companies heads south. Many summer events are free, such as Paris-Plage, the **Fête de la Musique** and **Bastille Day**.

PUBLIC HOLIDAYS

On *jours feriés*, banks, many museums, most shops and some restaurants close; public transport runs as on Sunday. New Year, May Day, Bastille Day and Christmas are the most piously observed holidays. The full list runs like this: New Year's Day (*Jour de l'An*); Easter Monday (*Pâques*); May Day (*Fête du Travail*); VE Day (*Victoire 1945*) 8 May; Ascension Day (*Jour de l'Ascension*); Whit Monday (*Lundi de Pentecôte*); Bastille Day (*Quatorze Juillet*) 14 July; Feast of the Assumption (*Fête de l'Assomption*) 15 Aug; All Saints' Day (*Toussaint*) 1 Nov; Remembrance Day (*L'Armistice 1918*) 11 Nov; Christmas Day (*Noël*).

Spring

Six Nations
Stade de France, 93210 St-Denis (08.92.70.09.00/ www.stadedefrance.fr). RER B La Plaine Stade de France or RER D Stade de France St-Denis. **Admission** varies. **Date** Feb-Mar.
Paris is invaded by Brits and Celts for three big rugby weekends in winter. Tickets are hard to come by – try www.6nations.co.uk months in advance.

Salon des Grands Vins
Le Carrousel du Louvre, 99 rue de Rivoli, 1st (www.salondesgrandsvins.com). M° Palais Royal Musée du Louvre. **Admission** €15. **Date** early Feb.

Tastings, workshops, world experts – and, of course, wine: the focus of this annual oenophile celebration.

Fashion Week
Various venues (www.modeaparis.com). **Date** Mar and Oct.
Paris presents its collections to invited guests only. The better hotels fill up, the trendier bistros too. *See also pp37-39* **Haute couture or high street?**

Le Printemps des Poètes
Various venues (www.printempsdespoetes.com). **Date** Mar.
'Passeurs de mémoire' ('Memory Smugglers') is the theme for the seventh, 2005 edition of this popular national poetry festival, set up by Jack Lang in 1999.

Les Festins d'Aden
Various venues (http://aden.lemonde.fr). **Date** Mar.
Le Monde arts supplement *Aden* assembles big names for a week of rock and indie music.

Printemps du Cinéma
Various venues (www.printempsducinema.com). **Date** Mar.
Film tickets all across the city drop to €3.50 for this popular three-day film event.

Banlieues Bleues
Seine St-Denis (01.49.22.10.10/www.banlieues bleues.org). **Admission** €11-€15. **Date** Mar-Apr.
Five weeks of quality French and international jazz, blues, R&B, soul, funk, flamenco and world music.

Le Chemin de la Croix
Square Willette, 18th (01.53.41.89.00). M° Anvers or Abbesses. **Date** Good Friday.
Mini-pilgrimage as crowds follow the Archbishop of Paris from the bottom of Montmartre up to Sacré-Coeur as he performs the Stations of the Cross.

Foire du Trône
Pelouse de Reuilly, 12th (01.46.27.52.29). M° Porte Dorée. **Admission** free; rides €1.50-€4. **Date** early Apr-end May.
France's biggest funfair: stomach-churning rides, bungee jumping and *barbe à papa* (candyfloss).

Marathon de Paris
Av des Champs-Elysées, 8th, to av Foch, 16th (01.41.33.15.68/www.parismarathon.com). **Date** Apr.
From the Champs-Elysées to the Bois de Vincennes and Boulogne, the marathon takes in the city's sights.

Festival du Film de Paris
Various venues (01.45.72.96.40/www.festivaldufilm deparis.com). **Admission** €6-€7. **Date** Apr.
Paris' own film festival. Public previews of international films, plus star-spotting opportunities.

Fête du Travail
Date 1 May.
May Day is strictly observed in France. Museums and sights (the Eiffel Tower aside) close; unions stage a march through eastern Paris via Bastille. Street sellers hawk lilies of the valley (*muguet*).

Printemps des Musées
Various venues (http://printempsdesmusees. culture.fr). **Date** May.
The Ministry of Culture's annual treat sees selected museums across France open their doors for free.

Foire de Paris
Paris-Expo, pl de la Porte de Versailles (01.49.09. 60.00/www.foiredeparis.fr). M° Porte de Versailles. **Admission** €9. **Date** May.
This enormous lifestyle salon includes world crafts and foods, plus the latest health and house gizmos.

Les Puces du design
Passage du Grand-Cerf, pl Goldoni, 2nd (01.53. 40.78.77/www.pucesdudesign.com). M° Etienne Marcel. **Admission** free. **Date** May.
Set in the cobbled pedestrian streets of the shabby-chic Montorgueil district, this popular bi-annual (also Oct), 20th-century design fleamarket draws some 20 specialist retailers from all over France.

Festival de St-Denis
St-Denis (01.48.13.06.07/www.festival-saint-denis.fr). M° St-Denis Basilique. **Admission** €9-€55. **Date** mid May-end June.
The Gothic St-Denis Basilica and other historic buildings host quality classical concerts.

Summer

French Tennis Open
Stade Roland Garros, 2 av Gordon-Bennett, 16th (01.47.43.48.00/www.frenchopen.org). M° Porte d'Auteuil. **Admission** €21-€53. **Date** May-June.
The glitzy Grand Slam tournament is always well attended by showbiz stars.

Quinzaine des Réalisateurs
Forum des Images, Porte St-Eustache, Forum des Halles, 1st (01.44.76.62.00/www.forumdesimages. net). M° Les Halles. **Admission** €5.50. **Date** May-June.
As soon as the dust has settled at Cannes, the Directors' Fortnight programme comes to Paris.

Le Printemps des rues
Information (01.47.97.36.06/www.leprintempsdes rues.com). **Admission** free. **Date** early June.
Despite financial worries, this annual street-theatre fest is all set to celebrate Poland in 2005.

Foire St-Germain
Pl St-Sulpice and venues in St-Germain-des-Prés, 6th (01.43.29.61.04/www.foiresaintgermain.org). M° St-Sulpice. **Admission** free. **Date** June-July.
St-Germain-des-Prés lets its hair down for a month-long event of concerts, theatre and workshops.

Paris Jazz Festival
Parc Floral de Paris, Bois de Vincennes (08.20.00.75.75/www.parcfloraldeparis.com). M° Château de Vincennes. **Admission** Park €3. **Date** June-July.
Free jazz weekends at the lovely Parc Floral.

Arts & Entertainment

Prix de Diane Hermès

Chantilly (03.44.62.41.00/www.france-galop.com).
Date June.
The French Derby draws high society in silly hats.

Festival Chopin à Paris

Orangerie de Bagatelle, parc de Bagatelle, Bois de Boulogne, 16th (01.45.00.22.19/www.frederic-chopin. com). M° Porte Maillot, then bus 244. **Admission** €16-€31. **Date** June-July.
Candlelit evening recitals in the Bagatelle gardens.

Fête de la Musique

All over France (01.40.03.94.70/www.fetedela musique.fr). **Admission** free. **Date** 21 June.
Summer solstice comes to France as concerts take place all over the city for this free music festival.

Gay Pride March

Information: Centre Gai et Lesbien (01.43.57.21.47/ www.fiertes-lgbt.org). **Date** late June.
Outrageous floats and costumes parade towards Bastille, followed by an official fête and club events.

No Plage like home

Now as essential to summer as rosé and ice cream, Paris-Plage is one of the genuine successes of Bertrand Delanoë's mayorship (*see p33-35* **Delanoë's Dream**). Each July, 2,000 tonnes of fine sand is spread around on the banks of the Seine and transforms a busy city centre into a traffic-free beach resort for a month – pretty beach huts and all.

Now in its fifth year, and taken up by 25 other French cities, Brussels, Berlin and beyond, Paris-Plage attracted four million visitors in 2004. With the recent addition of a 28m-long kids' paddling pool (doubling up as an aqua gym for adults), Paris-Plage comprises a two-mile thin stretch of riverbank of palm-tree fringed pleasure zone, from the Louvre to Pont de Sully.

Seen from the Pont Notre-Dame, the beach's blue banners make it look like the

beginning of a yachting regatta, brightened by festive sunshades, ice-cream booths and water sprinklers, and jazzed up with live music, rollerblading hip hop demonstrations, and Butlin's-style '*plagistes*' in matching T-shirts. Activities aren't limited to sunbathing on the 200 loungers, 40 hammocks, or bouncing on the four trampolines – there's tai-chi, painting, light gymnastics, beach volleyball, climbing, badminton and, recently, rollerskating. There's even a tropical garden of bamboo groves. Every lazy pursuit is catered for – swimsuits for sale, a five-language library of trashy novels, and professional sandcastle builders making crocodiles and human forms out of sand.

Each hour of the day brings its own attractions. Sporty types pitch up early for jogging; sunworshippers and picnickers find their spot in the hotter hours; and the evening brings a *passegiata* where licensed buskers – tango or Brazilian band sounds – get festive under the coloured lights. The Plage is open from 7am to midnight, after which an army of beach sweepers and a special Seine-cleaning boat move in to make everything pristine for the next day.

Ostensibly set up for locals who can't afford to go on holiday – you'll find picnicking families in from the *banlieue* – the Plage is a great tourist draw in a season when Paris largely shuts down. And although it costs ¤2 million for the Town Hall and sponsors, the city makes the most of its publicity value, organising state-visit-style hard-hat press-calls around the transport of sand from quarries by barge and the installation of the palm trees.

Still, it's the Seine that's the real star, neglected for so long before its Right Bank was slowly popularised pre-Plage by the gay fraternity. After Delanoë's smartest move to date, the river now commands attention and admiration, perfectly framing magnificent sunsets over Notre-Dame.

La Goutte d'Or en Fête

Square Léon, 18th (01.46.07.61.64/www.gouttedor enfete.org). M° Barbès Rochechouart. **Admission** free. **Date** late June-early July.

Established and local artists play raï, rap and reggae in this Arab and African neighbourhood.

Paris Cinéma

Various venues (www.pariscinema.org). **Admission** varies. **Date** early July.

Premieres, tributes and restored films make up the programme of Paris' summer film-going initiative.

Solidays

Longchamp Hippodrome (01.53.10.22.22/www. solidays.com). M° Porte d'Auteuil. **Admission** *Day* €20. *Weekend* €35. **Date** early July.

Three-day music bash with a mix of French, World and new talent, in the name of AIDS charities.

Le Cinéma en Plein Air

Parc de La Villette, 19th (01.40.03.75.75/www. villette.com). M° Porte de Pantin. **Admission** free. **Date** mid July-end Aug.

Settle back on the immaculate lawn at this annual summer fixture – a themed season of films screened under the stars on Europe's largest inflatable screen.

Le Quatorze Juillet (Bastille Day)

Date 14 July.

France's national holiday commemorates the events of 1789. On the eve, Parisians dance at place de la Bastille. At 10am on the 14th, crowds line up down the Champs-Elysées as the President reviews a full military parade. By night, the Champ de Mars fills for the firework display.

Miss Guinguette

38 quai Victor Hugo, Ile du Martin-Pêcheur, Champigny sur Marne (information 01.49.83.03.02). RER Champigny sur Marne. **Admission** €7.50. **Date** 14 July.

A quest to find the light-footed queen of the open-air dance hall scene at this river island venue.

Paris, Quartier d'été

Various venues (01.44.94.98.00/www.quartierdete. com). **Admission** free-€15. **Date** mid July-mid Aug.

A lively series of classical and jazz concerts, dance and theatre performances in outdoor venues.

Paris-Plage

Pont des Arts to Pont de Sully (08.20.00.75.75/www. paris.fr). M° Sully Morland, Louvre Rivoli, Châtelet, Hôtel de Ville, Pont Marie. **Admission** free. **Date** mid July-mid Aug.

Urban seaside (*see p280* **No Plage like home**).

Le Tour de France

Av des Champs-Elysées, 8th. **Information** (01.41.33. 15.00/www.letour.fr). **Date** July.

The ultimate endurance test comes to an end after 3,350km of calf-busting action. Blink and you'll miss the winner as the event concludes on the Champs-Elysées in a blur of pedals and yellow Lycra.

Lean streets: **Marathon de Paris**. *See p279.*

Fête de l'Assomption

Cathédrale Notre-Dame de Paris, pl du Parvis Notre-Dame, 4th (01.42.34.56.10). M° Cité/RER St Michel Notre-Dame. **Admission** free. **Date** 15 Aug.

A national holiday. Notre-Dame again becomes a place of religious pilgrimage for Assumption Day.

Rock en Seine

Domaine National de St-Cloud (08.92.68.08.92/ www.rockenseine.com). M° Porte de Sainte Cloud. **Admission** *Day* €39. *2 days* €65. **Date** end Aug.

Two days, two stages, one world-class rock line-up.

Autumn

Jazz à la Villette

Parc de la Villette, 211 av Jean-Jaurès, 19th (01.40.03.75.75/01.44.84.44.84/www.villette.com). M° Porte de Pantin. **Admission** €13-€16. **Date** early Sept.

One of Paris' best jazz fests, with a comprehensive cross-section of acts.

Techno Parade
Information: 01.42.47.84.76/www.technopol.net.
Date mid Sept.
This parade (usually finishing at Bastille) marks the start of the electronic music festival Rendez-vous Electroniques.

Journées du Patrimoine
All over France (www.jp.culture.fr). **Date** Sept.
Embassies, ministries, scientific establisments and corporate headquarters open their doors. The festive Soirée du Patrimoine takes place on the first Journée. Pick up a copy of *Le Monde* or *Le Parisien* for a full programme – and be prepared for huge queues.

Festival d'automne
Various venues. Information: 156 rue de Rivoli, 1st (01.53.45.17.00/www.festival-automne.com). **Admission** €9-€30. **Date** mid Sept-mid Dec.

Major annual festival of challenging contemporary theatre, dance and modern opera, intent on bringing non-Western culture into the French consciousness.

Nuit Blanche
Various venues (08.20.00.75.75/www.paris.fr).
Admission free. **Date** early Oct.
Culture by moonlight: galleries and museums host one-off installations, and swimming pools, bars and clubs stay open till very late.

Prix de l'Arc de Triomphe
Hippodrome de Longchamp, Bois de Boulogne, 16th (01.49.10.20.30/www.france-galop.com). M° Porte d'Auteuil, then free shuttle bus. **Admission** free-€8. **Date** early Oct.
France's richest flat race attracts the elite of horse racing amid much pomp and ceremony.

Fête des Vendanges à Montmartre
Rue des Saules, 18th (01.46.06.00.32/www.fetedes vendanges demontmartre.com). M° Lamarck Caulaincourt. **Date** early Oct.
Folk music, speeches, locals in costume and a parade celebrate the 800-bottle Montmartre grape harvest. Chansons accompany the village fête atmosphere, with produce stands in Montmartre all weekend.

FIAC
Paris-Expo, Porte de Versailles. 15th (01.41.90.47.80/www.fiac-online.com). M° Porte de Versailles.
Admission €15. **Date** end Oct.
This respected international art fair gives France a chance to strut its contemporary stuff.

Festival Inrockuptibles
Various venues (01.42.44.19.92/www.lesinrocks.com).
Admission varies. **Date** early Nov.
Once indie-centred, this festival curated by popular rock magazine *Les Inrockuptibles* now champions trance, techno and trip hop.

Armistice Day
Arc de Triomphe, 8th. M° Charles de Gaulle Etoile.
Date 11 Nov.
To commemorate French combattants who served in the World Wars, the President lays wreaths at the Tomb of the Unknown Soldier under the Arc de Triomphe. The *bleuet* (a cornflower) is worn.

Fête du Beaujolais Nouveau
Date mid Nov.
The third Thursday in November sees cafés and wine bars throng as patrons assess the new vintage.

Winter

Paris sur glace
Pl de l'Hôtel de Ville, 4th; M° Hôtel de Ville. Pl Raoul Dautry, 15th; M° Montparnasse Bienvenüe. Pl de la Bataille de Stalingrad, 19th; M° Stalingrad. Information: 08.20.00.75.75/www. paris.fr.
Admission free (skate hire €5). **Date** Dec-Mar.
Totter around the edges of these outdoor rinks while fearless five-year-olds zoom past.

Icy does it: **Paris sur glace**.

Africolor

Various venues in St-Denis (01.47.97.69.99/www. africolor.com). M° Basilique de St-Denis. **Admission** €13 approx. **Date** mid Dec.
African music festival with a spirited farewell party.

Noël (Christmas)

Date 24-25 Dec.
Christmas is a family affair in France, with a dinner on Christmas Eve (*le Réveillon*), normally after mass. Notre-Dame cathedral fills for the 11pm service.

New Year's Eve/New Year's Day

Date 31 Dec-1 Jan.
Thousands crowd the Champs-Elysées and let off bangers. Nightclubs and restaurants hold expensive soirées. On New Year's Day the Grande Parade de Paris brings floats, bands and dancers.

Fête des Rois (Epiphany)

Date 6 Jan.
Pâtisseries sell *galettes des rois*, cakes with frangipan filling in which a *fève*, or tiny charm, is hidden.

Mass for Louis XVI

Chapelle Expiatoire, 29 rue Pasquier, 8th (01.42. 65.35.80). M° St-Augustin. **Date** Jan.
On the Sunday closest to 21 Jan, anniversary of the beheading of Louis XVI in 1793, royalists and right-wing crackpots mourn the end of the monarchy.

Nouvel An Chinois

Around av d'Ivry and av de Choisy, 13th. M° Porte de Choisy or Porte d'Ivry, also av des Champs Elysées, 8th. **Date** Jan.
Lion and dragon dances, and lively martial arts demonstrations, celebrate the Chinese new year.

Ol' four eyes is back

He was the 20th century's Voltaire, foe of injustice and flabby thought. He was awarded (and turned down – 'a writer must refuse to let himself be transformed into an institution') the Nobel Prize for Literature. When he died in 1980, 50,000 people turned up for his funeral: that's a hell of a fan base.

Outside France, **Jean-Paul Sartre** (*pictured*) may be read far less often than he was, say, in the radical '60s and '70s, but at home he's always been held in the highest esteem. Writer, philosopher, political activist, friend of artists and the oppressed: from 1945 to his death, there were few corners of intellectual life he didn't reach. In 2005, France celebrates his towering influence and the centenary of his birth with, among other things, a wide-ranging exhibition (Mar-Aug) at the **Bibliothèque Nationale de France – François Mitterrand** (*see p167*), theatrical productions across town, publication of the plays in one volume by Gallimard's prestigious Pléiade imprint, and a slew of conferences and discussions. Daily paper *Libération* can be relied upon to write about him at length: in 1973, Sartre helped found it. And guess who's issuing the commemorative stamp? That's right, Monaco. For a detailed Sartre calendar see www.jpsartre.org.

You may be wondering: what can Sartre do for me? You may think he looked like a mad, bad-tempered cow, remembering shots of his glabrous mug, all weak mouth and contra-swivelling eyeballs. Perhaps you're put off by his reputation for nihilism (though when he said 'God is dead', he followed on

with 'don't take that to mean he doesn't exist; merely that he used to talk to us and now stays silent' – hardly the hardcore atheist of legend). Perhaps you've heard the rumblings about his beastly treatment of women; about his books being horribly difficult. *Being and Nothingness*?!?

As the man himself would have urged, think again. On the difficulty count, Sartre could, yes, be guilty as charged – but far from always, or even often. His novels, plays, autobiography *Les Mots* and hundreds of essays were often as entertaining as they were thought-provoking. To get his measure, read the play *Le Diable et le Bon Dieu*, a mordantly funny metaphysical siege drama, or dip into the essay collection *Situations*; both exist in English translation.

Arts & Entertainment

Cabaret, Circus & Comedy

Cancan, *cirque* and café-théâtre – plus *steak-frites* with your satire.

Cabaret in Paris is staunchly traditional – there are still more boobs and boas here than in any other city. Away from the razzle-dazzle, satire thrives in good old-fashioned café-théâtres, where songs and sketches come with a supper and a bottle of plonk. Venues often range from cellars to converted cinemas.

Two English-language houses ensure a stream of anglophone comedians. Veteran **Laughing Matters** has now been joined by **The Bowler** pub; both bring over comedians from across the Channel.

Paris has always been a circus capital. The **Parc de La Villette** boasts groundbreaking extravaganzas each year, and traditional circuses appear elsewhere every season.

Cabaret & café-théâtre

Glitzy cabaret

For the low-down on the tourist-friendly venues, *see p285* **Cancan and champers**.

La Belle Epoque

36 rue des Petits-Champs, 2nd (01.42.96.33.33). M° Opéra or Quatre Septembre. **Dinner** 9pm daily. **Shows** 10pm daily. **Admission** *champagne & show* €52; *dinner & show* €70-€100. **Credit** AmEx, DC, MC, V. **Map** p403 H4.

Crazy Horse Saloon

12 av George V, 8th (01.47.23.32.32/www. crazyhorse.fr). M° Alma Marceau or George V. **Shows** 8.30pm, 11pm Tue-Fri, Sun; 7.30pm, 9.45pm, 10.50pm Sat. **Admission** *two drinks & show* €69-€90. **Credit** AmEx, DC, MC, V. **Map** p402 D4.

Le Lido

116bis av des Champs-Elysées, 8th (01.40.76.56.10/ www.lido.fr). M° George V. **Dinner** 7.30pm. **Shows** 9.30pm, 11.30pm Mon-Thur, Sun; 9.30pm, midnight Sat. **Admission** *champagne & show* €80-€100; *dinner & show* €140-€200; €25 under-12s. **Credit** AmEx, DC, MC, V. **Map** p402 D4.

Moulin Rouge

82 bd de Clichy, 18th (01.53.09.82.82/www.moulin-rouge.fr). M° Blanche. **Dinner** 7pm. **Shows** 9pm, 11pm daily. **Admission** *champagne & show* €85-€95; *dinner & show* €135-€165. **Credit** AmEx, DC, MC, V. **Map** p403 G2.

Café-théâtre

L'Ane Rouge

3 rue Laugier, 17th (01.47.64.45.77). M° Ternes. **Shows** 8pm-2am daily. **Admission** *show & one drink* €30; *dinner & show* €50-€85. **Credit** MC, V. **Map** p402 C2.

The 'Red Donkey' is a glittery café-théâtre happy to combine comic cabaret with a great atmosphere. Dine on unusual regional dishes, then watch the comedians do their stuff.

Au Bec Fin

6 rue Thérèse, 1st (01.42.96.29.35). M° Pyramides. **Shows** 7pm, 8.15pm, 9.45pm Mon-Sat; *matinées for children* 2.30pm, 4.30pm Wed, Sat. Closed Aug. **Admission** €14; €9-€12 concs; *dinner & show* €30-€36. **Credit** AmEx, MC, V. **Map** p403 H5.

This tiny café-théâtre claims a 300-year-old pedigree and provides wholesome family entertainment. Dine downstairs on traditional cuisine, then head up the rickety staircase to see anything from Oscar Wilde in French to a modern-day *Cendrillon* for the kids.

Les Blancs Manteaux

15 rue des Blancs-Manteaux, 4th (01.48.87.15.84/ www.blancsmanteaux.fr). M° Hôtel de Ville. **Shows** daily from 7pm (ring for details). **Admission** €14; €11 concs; *double show* €22; *dinner & show* €25. **No credit cards**. **Map** p408 K6.

This Marais institution has kept the café-théâtre flame burning for over 30 years with its two theatres and multiple weekly performances. With a dinner-and-show ticket, punters can eat around the corner at the Epices et Délices, and there's new stand-up on the first Wednesday of the month.

Chez Michou

80 rue des Martyrs, 18th (01.46.06.16.04/www. michou.com). M° Pigalle or Abbesses. **Dinner** 9pm daily. **Shows** 11pm approx. **Admission** *Show and one drink* €35. *Dinner & show* €95. **Credit** MC, V. **Map** p404 H2.

Drag, sparkling costumes, good food and wine: come to Michou's if you're looking for larger-than-life impersonations of Brigitte Bardot and Tina Turner.

Au Lapin Agile

22 rue des Saules, 18th (01.46.06.85.87). M° Lamarck Caulaincourt. **Shows** 9pm-2am Tue-Sun. **Admission** *show & one drink* €24. **No credit cards**. **Map** p404 H1.

Arts & Entertainment

Cancan and champers

A century after cancan was born, busty babes are still slinking across the cabaret stages of Paris. The **Moulin Rouge** (*see p284*) created the concept in 1889 with skirt-raising called *Quadrille Réaliste* (later coined the cancan). Since then, the addition of two glitzy venues, **Le Lido** and the **Crazy Horse Saloon** (for both, *see p284*), institutionalised garter-pinging forever. The tacky, modern **Belle Epoque** (*see p284*) completes the quartet.

Today's cabaret, an all-evening, €100, smart-dress extravaganza, is served with a pre-show gourmet meal and champers. Male dancers, acrobats and magicians refreshingly complement the foxy foxtrots; the dancing is synchronised, the costumes beautiful, and the whole caboodle unreservedly respectable.

True to form, the Moulin Rouge is the most traditional glamour revue and the only place with cancan. Toulouse-Lautrec posters, glittery lampposts and fake trees bestow a tacky charm, while the 60 Doriss dancers cover every inch of the stage with faultless synchronisation. Costumes are flamboyant, the entr'acte acts funny and the sets solid: one daring number even takes place inside a giant tank of underwater boa constrictors. Sadly, elbow room is nil, with hundreds of tables packed in like sardines. But if you can bear intimacy with international businessmen, the Moulin Rouge, the cheapest of the food-serving cabarets, won't disappoint.

For space go to Le Lido. With 1,000 seats, this classy venue is the largest, priciest cabaret of the lot: the art nouveau hall and its high-tech touches (descending balcony and disappearing lamps) optimise visibility, and star chef Paul Bocuse has revolutionised the menu. The slightly tame show, with 60 Bluebell Girls, has boob-shaking, wacky costumes and numerous oddities: courtesan cats meeting Charlie Chaplin for example.

For a cheaper, more risqué show, see *Taboo* at the Crazy Horse. The Horse's *art du nu* was invented in 1951 by Alain Bernadin; since then, this ode to feminine beauty has entertained punters with 11 lookalike dancers whose names (Nooka Caramel and Misty Flashback) are as real as their wigs. Clad only in rainbow light and strategic sticky tape, the girls put on such tantalising numbers as their signature piece *Va Va Voom*. Not everyone's smiling, though. In 2004, the Sioux tribe descendants of the real Crazy Horse lodged a written complaint against the club's 'disrespectful' name and use of feathered headresses...

The prices have gone up, but that's all that seems to have changed since this quaint, pink bar first opened in 1860. Tourists now outnumber the locals, but the Lapin harbours an echo of old Montmartre.

Comedy & fringe theatre

Le Bout
6 rue Frochot, 9th (01.42.85.11.88/www.bout.com). M° Pigalle. **Shows** daily. **Admission** €14; €9 concs; *two shows* €18. **No credit cards. Map** p404 H2.
In the heart of Pigalle, this ex-café-théâtre school has been cramming them in to its 40-seater venue since 1999. The emphasis is on newcomers, but that does not mean amateurs. Annual comedy festival too.

Café de la Gare
41 rue du Temple, 4th (01.42.78.52.51/www.cafe-de-la-gare.fr.st). M° Hôtel de Ville or Rambuteau. **Shows** 7.30pm, 9pm Mon, Tue, Sun; 8pm, 10pm Wed-Sat. **Admission** €10-€20. **Credit** MC, V. **Map** p408 K6.
From a cobbled courtyard, customers are led to one of the 300 stage-hugging seats in this atmospheric venue. House specialities include French stand-up, and raucous, irreverent comedies.

Caveau de la République
1 bd St-Martin, 3rd (01.42.78.44.45/www.caveau.fr). M° République. **Shows** 8.30pm Tue-Thur; 4.30pm Sat; 3.30pm Sun. **Admission** €25 Tue-Thur; €32 Fri-Sun; €16 concs. Closed Aug. **Credit** MC, V. **Map** p404 L4.
Open since 1901, this is one of the last *chansonniers* on the block, where artists spurt out golden oldies before presenting their own sardonic compositions. The humour is of a political-satirical bent, so it helps if you're up on current affairs.

Le Point Virgule
7 rue Ste-Croix-de-la-Bretonnerie, 4th (01.42.78. 67.03/www.netkiri.fr). M° Hôtel de Ville. **Shows** 8pm, 9.15pm, 10.30pm daily. **Admission** €15, €12 concs. **No credit cards. Map** p408 K6.
This small Marais theatre is an ideal launch pad for up-and-coming comedians. The crowds tend to be animated, the acts well polished, the most popular appearing at its comedy festival in September.

Le Zèbre
63 bd de Belleville, 20th (01.43.55.55.55). M° Père Lachaise. **Shows** vary. **Admission** varies. **Credit** MC, V. **Map** p405 N4.
Impresario Francis Schoeller rescued the art deco Zèbre cinema in 2002. After forays in all kinds of directions, the Z has stuck to satirical cabaret and chirruping *chanson* in true vaudeville style.

Comedy in English

The Bowler Pub
13 rue d'Artois, 8th (01.45.61.16.60). M° St-Philippe du-Roule . **Shows** 9pm, days vary. **Admission** €10 including a pint of beer. **Credit** AmEx, MC, V. **Map** p403 E3.

Pints, chips and belly laughs are doled out in large portions in this British beer temple, where on-the-up comedians off the Eurostar test their new material.

Laughing Matters
Info (01.53.19.98.88/www.anythingmatters.com). **Shows** *Hôtel du Nord, 102 quai de Jemmapes, 10th. M° République or Jacques Bonsergent.* **Admission** €20; €17 concs. **No credit cards. Map** p408 L4.
The anglophone giggle gang no longer have a monopoly in Paris, but promoter Karel Beer seems to be the only guy UK and US joke jockeys will cross the seas for. In 2005, look out for Greg Proops, Ross Noble, Daniel Kitson and Lee Mack.

Circus

Circus – traditional big tops and avant-garde acts – is a year-round fixture. See *Cirque* in the children's section of *Pariscope* for listings info.

Cabaret Sauvage
Parc de La Villette, 19th (01.42.09.01.09/www.cabaret sauvage.com). M° Porte de la Villette. **Shows** vary. **Admission** €12-€20. **Credit** MC, V. **Map** p405 inset.
Housed in an old circus venue, a mixture of tent, saloon and hall of mirrors provides a platform for contemporary jugglers and acrobats.

Cirque d'Hiver Bouglione
110 rue Amelot, 11th (01.47.00.12.25/www.cirque dhiver.com). M° Filles du Calvaire. **Shows** vary. **Admission** €10-€35. **Credit** V. **Map** p404 L5.
In 2005, this fine circus built in 1852 celebrates 70 years in the same family with *Bravo*, a tribute to the bi-annual Bouglione classic circus tradition.

Cirque Pinder
37 rue de Coulagnes, 94370 Sucy-en-Brie (01.45. 90.21.25/www.cirquepinder.com). Pelouse de Reuilly, Bois de Vincennes, 12th. M° Porte Dorée or Porte de Charenton. **Shows** mid-Nov-early Jan, times vary. **Admission** €12-€35; free under-2s. **Credit** AmEx, DC, MC, V.
With horses, lions, elephants and monkeys, Pinder is the oldest and most traditional travelling circus in France. The final leg of its 20,000km tour is the Christmas show at the Pelouse de Reuilly.

Espace Chapiteaux
Parc de La Villette, 19th (01.42.09.01.09/www. villette.com). M° Porte de la Villette. **Shows** 7.30pm Wed-Sat; 4.30pm Sun. **Admission** €25; €13-€20 concs. **Credit** MC, V. **Map** p405 inset.
Cirque Plume are regulars at La Villette – 2005 sees the return of local aerial dancing act Les Arts Saut.

Grand Céleste Cirque
13 av de la Porte-des-Lilas, 19th (01.53.19.99.13/ www.grandceleste.com). M° Porte des Lilas. **Open** Oct-Apr. **Shows** *matinees* Wed, Fri, Sat, Sun (phone for details); 8.45pm Fri, Sun. **Admission** €10-€26. **No credit cards.**
Three blue tents comprise this circus of traditional acts. Also guinguette-style bar and circus courses.

Children

Bundles of attractions, indoor and out.

Jardin du Luxembourg. *See p289.*

For all its hassle and bustle, Paris is a remarkably child-friendly city, a place where kids are fêted and culturally sated. If you come here with youngsters, any idea that Parisians are stand-offish will soon disappear under a barrage of praise and advice. Most of the famous sights on every child's wish list are accessible, and a boat trip down the Seine makes for an ideal family outing. Kids are made welcome at most cafés and restaurants, and set mini-menus (€5-€8) of *poulet-frites* plus dessert and drink are the order of the day at many bistros.

Parks are an essential part of every Parisian childhood, doubling up as gardens for flat-dwelling nippers; generations of children have grown up amid the sandpits, swings, puppet shows, pony rides and the boating ponds of the **Luxembourg** and Tuileries gardens. Nearly all public parks offer a playground of some kind. The city has become much more cycle- and rollerblade-friendly (*see p337 and p338*), so family outings on both are feasible along newly-created bike lanes, by the Seine and Canal St-Martin. The Bois de Vincennes in the east and de Boulogne in the west offer woodland, picnic areas, boating lakes and cycle paths.

Gaps in the academic schedule – Wednesday afternoons, weekends and the holidays – are filled by all kinds of workshops, theatre productions and film seasons; long-term expat families will find much to keep their offspring occupied and switched on.

A perennial pleasure is the funfair, the best being La Fête à Neu-Neu (Bois de Boulogne, autumn) and the Foire du Trône (Bois de Vincennes, spring); La Fête des Tuileries in summer offers dizzying views from the big wheel. Other family-friendly events include the Chinese New Year parade down the Champs-Elysées in February, the impromptu outdoor gigs of Fête de la Musique (21 June), and Quartier d'Eté (www.quartierdete.com), when parks and boulevards form the backdrop for free concerts, theatre and circus shows all summer. Bastille Day (14 July) comes with a parade, flypast and firework display, Hallowe'en gets bigger every year, and Christmas brings free carousels and outdoor ice-rinks at Hôtel de Ville, Montparnasse and La Défense. *See also pp278-283* **Festivals & Events**.

Pariscope, *Télérama* and *L'Officiel des Spectacles* have children's sections in their listings publications. Leaflets are dispensed at town halls, such as the info-packed free annual *Guide de la Rentrée*; contact Paris Infos Mairie (08.20.00.75.75). Look out for the bi-monthly *Paris-Mômes* supplement in *Libération*.

Getting around

Don't even contemplate crossing the street unless you're at a zebra crossing, and watch out even then – some drivers try to jump red lights. Turning traffic should give priority to pedestrians, but often doesn't. Look out, too, for rollerbladers, scooter-riders and motorcyclists whizzing down narrow pavements.

Turnstiles, numerous stairs and crowded carriages make travelling by Métro tricky with a pushchair. Try to make your journey between

---

► *See pp356-357 for* **Disneyland Paris**, **Walt Disney Studios Park** and the **Parc Astérix**.

10.30am and 4pm, or use the easier, driverless line 14 (Gare St-Lazare to Bibliothèque François Mitterrand); kids love to sit at the front and watch the tunnel walls go by. The mostly overground line 6 (Nation to Charles de Gaulle Etoile) and line 2 (Nation to Porte Dauphine) offer attractive city views, and a number of RER stations have lifts.

Of bus routes (www.ratp.fr), 29 are accessible with a pushchair. Also look out for the four priority seats near the front of each bus, designed to be used if you're travelling with under-fours, who go free on public transport. Four- to ten-year-olds qualify for a half-price *carnet* (ten tickets) for all transport, including the Montmartrobus minibus, the funicular and the Balabus.

Taxi drivers will generally take a family of four, as under-tens count as half; they charge €2 for a folding pushchair. If you're stuck miles from nowhere, G7 taxis (01.41.27.66.99) have an English-speaking line for bookings.

The water-borne Batobus (01.44.11.33.99, www.batobus.com) links eight prime sights along the Seine, including the Eiffel Tower, Louvre and Notre-Dame, leaving from the quay on the Left Bank. *See p86* **Boat tours**.

Help & information

The American Church
65 quai d'Orsay, 7th (01.40.62.05.00/www. acparis.org). M° Invalides. **Open** 1-7pm, 8-10.30pm Mon-Sat; 8.30am-2pm, 3-6pm Sun. *Sunday worship* 9am and 11am. **Map** p407 E5.
The free noticeboard just inside the main entrance is a useful source of information on recommended English-speaking babysitters and au pairs.

Baby Sitting Services
01.46.21.33.16/www.babysittingservices.com. **Open** 24 hrs daily. *Babysitting for up to 2 children* €6.30/hr 8am-10pm + €10.90 tax Mon-Sat; €7/hr + €15.90 tax Mon-Sat 10pm-8am, Sun and hols. €1/hr supplement for each extra child. **Credit** MC, V.
Babysitting can be organised at short notice. Visits to museums and cinemas can also be arranged, plus tuition, activities and children's parties.

Inter-Service Parents
01.44.93.44.93. **Open** 9.30am-12.30pm, 1.30-5pm Mon-Fri.
Free state-funded advice service lists babysitting agencies as well as giving advice on schools, child psychologists and lawyers. For other main agencies, check out www.paris-touristoffice.com.

Message

www.messageparis.org.
This English-speaking support group dispenses all kinds of local advice for mothers and mothers-to-be, and publishes the handy *ABCs of Motherhood in Paris* (€18 to non-members, €12 members).

Babies & toddlers

If you're off out, make sure you pack a portable changing mat – facilities are not so common. It's almost worth crossing town to use the WC chalet at the **Jardin du Luxembourg**, where for 40¢ an attendant lays a white napkin on a padded changing table. **Galeries Lafayette** (*see p240*) and **Printemps** (*see p240*) department stores are handy, as is **La Samaritaine** (*see p240*), with clean, well-equipped change rooms and great views from the rooftop restaurant.

When it comes to breastfeeding, the French are quite fussy. This usually means feeding *en plein air*, or in a quiet corner of a museum or restaurant. Take a scarf if letting it all hang out at a café is too awful to contemplate.

A city break with tots in tow doesn't have to mean spending every waking hour at the park; nearly all the main attractions have child-friendly activities nearby. The **Carte Musées et Monuments** (*see p161*), valid for up to 70 museums for between one to five days, allows access via the members entrance, saving time and tempers. For the **Louvre** (*see pp152-160*), use the direct entrance from Métro station Palais Royal Musée du Louvre to avoid the queue forever snaking above ground. Nearby, the funfair at the Tuileries gardens runs from mid June to the end of August. Carousels are located throughout the city – opposite the **Eiffel Tower** (*see p140*), at the foot of the **Trocadéro** gardens (*see p112*) and most parks. If the queue at the Eiffel Tower is too much, there's always the view from the more pushchair-friendly **Tour Montparnasse** (*see p144*) – take the lift to the 56th floor, then walk up to the terrace on the 59th. The ninth-floor terrace at the **Musée de l'Institut du Monde Arabe** (*see p130*) has great views downstream plus sticky treats served on mosaic-topped tables. If you do tough it out for the Tour Eiffel, toddlers can be rewarded by the go-kart track, duck pond, play areas and pony rides at the Champ de Mars. Even the **Musée Rodin** (*see p166*) has sandboxes, shade and wide open spaces.

For stress-free leisure, you can sail down the Seine on a Batobus as far as **Notre-Dame** (*see p84*) – you can even schedule a sandpit stop in the play area alongside.

Parks & gardens

Public gardens offer playgrounds, sandpits and concrete ping-pong tables. There's a handy one by **Notre-Dame**, trampolines in the **Tuileries** and, at posh **place des Vosges**, wooden slides and rocking horses. Many parks have their own Guignol (Punch and Judy) puppet theatre, with shows at weekends and on most Wednesday afternoons. The language might be hard to follow, but the audience participation is contagious. For more modern attractions, *see p291* **From waste ground to playground**.

Jardin de l'Acclimatation

Bois de Boulogne, 16th (01.40.67.90.82/ www.jardindacclimatation.fr). Mº Les Sablons. **Open** *Oct-May* 10am-6pm daily; *June-Sept* 10am-7pm daily. **Admission** €2.50; free under-3s. **Credit** (minimum €15) MC, V.
A much-loved feature since the 19th century, this amusement park boasts bears, a Normandy farm and an aviary to complement the enchanted river boat rides, Chinese dragon rollercoaster and the romping fun of the Enchanted House for the two-to-fours. Older kids enjoy the interactive gadgetry of the Explor@dome and a mini racing circuit. Some attractions cost €2.50 (€30 for 15), others are free. A mini train (Wednesdays and weekends; €3.75-€5) runs from Porte Maillot through the Bois de Boulogne to the park entrance.

Jardin du Luxembourg

Pl Edmond-Rostand, pl Auguste-Comte, rue de Vaugirard, 6th (01.42.34.20.00/www.paris.fr). Mº Odéon or St-Sulpice/RER Luxembourg. **Open** *winter* 8am-one hour before sunset; *summer* 7.30am-one hour before sunset. **Map** p407 H8.
The biggest and best play area on the Left Bank, thanks to the swing boats, merry-go-round, pony rides, puppet shows and, in summer, a toy boating-pond and two paddling pools.

Parc des Buttes-Chaumont

19th (01.42.02.91.21). Mº Buttes Chaumont or Botzaris. **Open** *Oct-June* 7am-9pm daily; *15 June-15 Jul* 7am-10pm daily; *15 July-30 Sept* 7am-11pm daily. **Map** p405 N2.
Above ground the view is arguably better than from Sacré-Coeur, while below kids can play among the grottos and waterfalls. A playground, puppet shows and donkey rides come into play in the summer.

Parc Floral

Route de la Pyramide, 12th (01.49.57.24.84/www.parcfloraldeparis.com). Mº Château de Vincennes, then 10min walk or bus 112. **Open** *Winter* 9.30am-5pm daily. *Summer* 9am-8pm daily. **Admission** €1; €0.50 7s-25s; free under-7s. *Weekends* €3; €1.50 7s-25s. **No credit cards.**
The miniature train (€1.50) is just one outstanding feature of this verdant park, one of the city's best play areas for all ages. There's a nature resource centre and butterfly garden, plus a huge adventure

playground with any number of slides, swings and climbing frames. Older kids will enjoy the mini golf course laid out like Paris or the racetrack with its pedal-powered horses. Wednesday afternoons bring free theatre shows, suitable for the threes to tens.

Parc de la Villette

211 av Jean-Jaurès, 19th (01.40.03.75.03/www. *villette.com). M° Porte de Pantin or Porte de la* *Villette.* **Open** 6am-1am daily. **Map** p405 inset.
Part of the redeveloped Villette canal basin, this series of themed parks includes Le Jardin des Miroirs – a walk through a quite bizarre reflected landscape – and the even more weird Jardin des Frayeurs Enfantines ('Garden of Childish Fears'), with spooky music to recreate a fairy-tale forest.

Activity museums

Egyptian mummies at the **Louvre**, flying machines at the **Musée de l'Air et de l'Espace** (at Le Bourget), the Planetarium at the **Palais de la Découverte**... There's plenty for a child's imagination, and under-18s can usually get in free, or almost. Many places provide activity sheets (ask at the *Accueil*) and children's activities (in French) on Wednesdays, at weekends and in the holidays. The majority of museums close on Mondays or Tuesdays. *See also pp161-184* **Museums**.

At the Louvre, the programme for kids is led by artists, architects and filmmakers. Next door, the **Museé des Arts Décoratifs** (*see p172*) offers hands-on art workshops for ages four to 12. The Musée Rodin children's clay modelling workshops in August and the **Musée Picasso** (*see p166*) offers family visits on Sundays, with children's workshops on Wednesdays in term-time, exploring animal sculptures and pictures by Pablo himself.

Escape in France (01.44.71.35.30, www. escapeinfrance.com) offers treasure hunts around the city's monuments and museums, as well as Versailles; their Conservatoire des Arts et Métiers tour is suitable for the over-fives. **Paris walks** (01.48.09.21.40, www. paris-walks. com) also runs a series of child-friendly walks during school holidays.

Centre Pompidou – Galerie des Enfants

Rue St-Martin, 4th (01.44.78.49.13/www.centre *pompidou.fr). M° Hôtel de Ville/RER Châtelet Les* *Halles.* **Open** 11am-10pm Mon, Wed-Sun. *Workshops* most Wed & Sat afternoons. **Admission** *incl* *museum entry* €5-€7; free under-18s. W*orkshop* *& exhibition* €8. **Credit** MC, V. **Map** p404 K5.
Beautifully thought-out exhibitions by top artists and designers introduce children to modern art, design and architecture, with hands-on workshops for sixes to 12s, and family visits one Sunday a month (11.15am-12.30pm). Outside, look out for the

colourful Stravinsky fountain and animated clock in the Quartier de l'Horloge on the piazza's north side: every hour, its plucky, man-size bronze automaton *Le Défenseur du Temps* ('Defender of Time') fights off a crab, a dragon or a cockerel (and all three at midday and 5pm). *See also p162.*

Cité des Enfants

Niveau 1, Cité des Sciences et de l'Industrie, 30 av *Corentin-Cariou, 19th (01.40.05.80.00/www.cite-* *sciences.fr). M° Porte de la Villette.* **Open** *90min* *visits* 9.45am, 11.30am, 1.30pm, 3.30pm Tue, Thu, Fri; 10.30am, 12.30pm, 2.30, 4.30pm, Wed, Sat, Sun; times vary in hols. **Admission** €5 per session. **Credit** MC, V. **Map** p405 inset.
Two vast hands-on discovery zones cater for under-fives and five- to 12-year-olds. Highlights for the under-fives include the water cascades (switch the points and watch the wheels spin), and a building site with foam blocks, wheelbarrows, cranes and pulleys for aspiring *bricoleurs*. Under-12s can try the working TV studio or the walk-in ant-hill.

Musée Grévin

10 bd Montmartre, 9th (01.47.70.85.05/www.musee- *grevin.com). M° Grands Boulevards.* **Open** 10am-6.30pm (last admission 5.30pm) Mon-Fri; 10am-7pm (last admission 6pm) Sat, Sun & hols. **Admission** €16; €13.80 concessions; €9 6s-14s. **Credit** AmEx, DC, MC, V. **Map** p404 H4.
Zinédine Zidane or Lara Croft are the favourites, but this waxworks museum is educational too, with artists, writers and prominent historical figures.

Musée de la Magie

11 rue St-Paul, 4th (01.42.72.13.26/www.museeedela *magie.com). M° St-Paul or Sully Morland.* **Open** 2-7pm Wed, Sat, Sun & summer hols; 2-7pm daily in half-term, Christmas & Easter hols. **Admission** €7; €5 3s-12s; free under-3s. **No credit cards.** **Map** p408 L7.
Kids will enjoy even the queue for this wonderful museum of magic and illusions: a magician is on hand to pull scarves out of ears. There's conjuring, and a hands-on approach to optical illusions.

Muséum National d'Histoire Naturelle

36 rue Geoffrey-St-Hilaire, 2 rue Bouffon, 57 rue *Cuvier, 27, place Valhubert, 5th (01.40.79.30.00/www.* *mnhn.fr). M° Gare d'Austerlitz or Jussieu.* **Open** 10am-6pm (last admission 5.15pm) Mon, Wed-Sun. **Admission** €5-€7. **Credit** MC, V. **Map** p408 K9.
This eclectic museum stands within the Jardin des Plantes. The Grande Galerie de l'Evolution imaginatively displays its stuffed creatures and skeletons to create a Noah's Ark-like stream of animals (including Louis XV's pet rhino); the small Espace Découverte has microscopes and interactive games aplenty, there are hunks of meteorite and giant crystals in the Galerie de Minéralogie et de Géologie, and the Galeries de Paléontologie et d'Anatomie Comparée are a sure-fire hit with jars of such eerie pickled creatures as a 'cyclops' cat with one eye.

Aquaria, zoos & safari parks

Ferme du Piqueur

92210 St-Cloud (01.46.02.24.53). M° Boulogne-Pont de St-Cloud. **Open** *Sept-July* 10am-12.30pm, 1.30-5.30pm Sat, Sun & hols; *Aug* 10am-12.30pm, 1.30-5.30pm daily. *Children's workshops for 4s-12s* 10am, 2pm, 4pm Wed (advance bookings only). **Admission** €2. **No credit cards.**

Small children will enjoy the cows, chickens, pigs and rabbits at this Parc de St-Cloud farm.

La Ménagerie

57 rue Cuvier, 5th (01.40.79.30.00). M° Gare d'Austerlitz or Jussieu. **Open** *Winter* 9am-5pm daily. *Summer* 9am-6pm daily. **Admission** €6; €3.50 4s-18s, concessions; free under-4s. **Credit** MC, V (minimum €15). **Map** p408 K8.

This is one of the oldest zoos in the world and, although somewhat tatty, just the thing for younger children. Attractions here include vultures, monkeys and most of the big cats – plus the Microzoo, the world as seen through a microscope.

From waste ground to playground

Parks in Paris fall into two distinct groups, divided by 250 years of urban development. There are the traditional variety where smartly turned out *petits Parisiens* have enjoyed carousels, pony rides and puppet shows which haven't changed since Haussmann instigated his vision of fresh air and open spaces for all in the mid-1800s. Try the Tuileries, the Champ de Mars, parc Monceau and Jardin du Luxembourg for a taste of yesteryear playtime – then contrast them with the more recent additions to the Paris park scene, all industrial spaces since transformed into pleasure zones.

Futuristic **Parc André Citroën** (rue Balard, 15th, RER Javel; *see p141*) was built on the site of the former car factory and is one of the city's most hi-tech outdoor spaces, adorned with computer-controlled fountains which gush water in every direction (pack the kids' bathers), themed and coloured gardens, and a tethered helium balloon, billed as the world's largest. It rises to a height of 135m (443ft) for great views of the city.

Set over the Gare Montparnasse, the **Jardin de l'Atlantique** (*see p142*) is a feat of engineering and makes a fun play space, too. Enter (for free) from boulevard Pasteur or you'll have to climb a lot of stairs or use the temperamental lift from the station side. There are wooded walkways, sandpits surrounded by mosaic tiled walls, fountains gushing from concrete slabs and swishy bamboo bushes, creating a little haven surrounded by city architecture.

When the abattoir moved out of rue des Morillons in 1978, the space was turned into the **Parc Georges Brassens**, on the edges of the 15th (M° Convention or Porte de Vanves; *see p145*) – note the bronze bulls at the entrance, and the auction room bell tower. Now there are play areas for different ages as well as vines, beehives and herb gardens;

perfect for a nature walk. A climbing wall for children was created out of masses of earth and stones left over from the demolition.

1979 also saw the demolition of the Bercy warehouses in the 12th, putting an end to a century of wine trading. The park that now stands in their place hints at its industrial past. Railway tracks and cobbled roads wind past the cafés of **Bercy Village** (*pictured*; rue Paul Belmondo, 12th, www.bercyvillage.com; M° Cour St-Emilion; *see p109*). It makes an ideal pit stop after the play areas, ponds and gardens, tended by local schoolchildren.

Palais de la Porte Dorée

293 av Daumesnil, 12th (01.44.74.84.80/www.palais-portedoree.org). M° Porte Dorée. **Open** 10am-5.15pm Mon, Wed-Sun. **Admission** €5.50; €4 4s-25s, free under-4s. **Credit** *Shop* MC, V.

This art deco palace houses the city aquarium, and its colonial crocs brought from Dakar in 1948. It is also currently housing artefacts due to be displayed at the Cité de l'Architecture et du Patrimoine when it opens towards the end of 2005. *See p170.*

Parc de Thoiry

78770 Thoiry-en-Yvelines (01.34.87.53.76/www.thoiry.tm.fr). 45km west of Paris. By car A13, A12, then N12 direction Dreux until Pont Chartrain, then follow signs. **Open** *Winter* 11am-5pm daily. *Summer* 10am-6pm daily. **Admission** *Park* €20; €14-€18.50 concessions; €14 3s-12s. *Château* €6; €4 3-12s. **Credit** MC, V.

One of Europe's first and best safari parks, Thoiry lets zebras rub their noses all over your windscreen, while lions laze and bears amble down a forest track. The venue is only accessible by car.

Parc Zoologique de Paris

53 av de St-Maurice, 12th (01.44.75.20.00/www.mnhn.fr). M° Porte Dorée. **Open** 9am-6pm Mon-Sat; 9am-6.30pm Sun & hols. **Admission** €5; free under-4s. **Credit** AmEx, DC, MC, V.

Gibbons leap around the trees, baboons slide on the rocks and over-sevens climb the 65m Grand Rocher (by lift, not with crampons). Check the notice at the entrance for newborns and that day's feeding times, especially for seals. A mini train tours the zoo.

Sealife Paris

14 cours du Danube-Serris, 77711 Marne-La-Vallée (01.60.42.33.66/www.sealife.fr). RER Val d'Europe. By car A4, then exit 12. **Open** 10am-5.30pm daily. **Admission** €11; €8 3s-11s; free under-3s. **Credit** AmEx, MC, V.

Recreated maritime environments at Sealife Paris include the lost city of Atlantis, the Etretat cliffs and the Atlantic Ocean (complete with sharks swimming overhead; under-14s must be accompanied by an adult. It's part of La Vallée shopping village, with a big play area and bargain kids' clothes shops.

Sport & entertainment

Fables, fairy tales and folk stories from all over Francophone Africa are regular favourites at children's shows at theatres and café-théâtres in Paris on Wednesday afternoons, at weekends and in the school holidays. **Théâtre Dunois** (7 rue Louise-Weiss, 13th, 01.45.84.72.00; www.theatredunois.org) organises theatre, dance and musical creations.

Traditional **circuses** come to Paris every winter (*see p286*); for the other seasons there are funfairs for the other seasons at the Bois de Vincennes (spring), the Tuileries (summer) and the Bois de Boulogne (autumn).

Children's films are mostly dubbed into French, but you can see V.O. (original version) screenings of the latest Hollywood hits at dozens of cinemas across town. (*see p297*). Also keep a look out for children's showings and talks on Wednesdays at the Forum des Images (01.44.76.63.44/47, www.forumdesimages.net). French is not needed for the Théâtre du Châtelet's Pochette Surprise cinema club (01.42.56.90.10), which screens silent classics with live piano accompaniment. The IMAX cinema at the Géode at La Villette (01.39.17.00.00, www.lageode.fr) will keep kids goggle-eyed; for more of the same, plus some truly amazing 3-D computer animations-cum-rides, head for Futuroscope (www.futuroscope.com), a thrilling futuristic park near Poitiers, an 80-minute TGV ride from the Gare Montparnasse.

Paris is good for outdoor entertainment, too. For the over-fours, the Roller Squad Institut (01.56.61.99.61, www.rsi.asso.fr) runs beginners' roller tours from the Esplanade des Invalides (M° Invalides) on Sundays at 9.45am. As well as many open-air pools in town, indoor Aquaboulevard (4 rue Louis-Armand, 15th, 01.40.60.15.15, www.forest-hill.com) gives the over-threes the chance to splash down slides and ride the waves. **Paris-Plage** (*see p280* **No plage like home**) in summer sees a plunge pool installed along with 2,000 tonnes of sand – enough for the most ambitious sandcastle. Skating takes place at the **Palais Omnisports** (www.bercy.fr) from October to May; *see pp333-340* **Sport & Fitness**.

Une Journée au Cirque

Cirque de Paris, 115 bd Charles de Gaulle, 92390 Villeneuve la Garenne (01.47.99.40.40/www.journeeocirque.com). M° Porte de Clignancourt then bus 137/RER St-Denis then bus 261. **Open** *Oct-June* 10am-5pm Wed, Sun. *Performances* 3pm. **Admission** €36.50-€41; €29-€34.50 3s-11s. *Show* €11-€24; €7-€14.50 3s-11s. **Credit** AmEx, MC, V.

From 10am, children can try their hand at tightrope-walking, juggling, clowning and dressage (though not lion taming), followed by lunch with the stars, a tour of the menagerie and the fairground museum, then finally, at 3pm, the show itself.

La Mer de Sable

La Mer de Sable, 60950 Ermenonville (03.44.54.18.44/www.merdesable.fr). RER Roissy, then shuttle (01 48 62 38 33). 10-11.20am, return 5.25-6.45pm. By car A1, exit 7. **Open** *Apr-Sept* 10am-6.30pm Mon-Fri, 10.30am-7pm Sat, Sun. **Admission** €16.50; €13.50 3s-11s. **Credit** AmEx, MC, V.

A Wild West theme park in a geological curiosity, the 'sea of sand' in the Ermenonville forest. There are great shoot-outs and equestrian acrobatics, and rides include the Colorado Canyon roller coaster, Desert Train and Cheyenne river ride. Opening hours can be erratic, so always phone ahead.

Dance

With a National Dance Centre just opened, dance in Paris is making its best moves since the days of Nijinsky.

Centre National de la Danse. *See p294*.

Now that Paris has a prestigious **National Dance Centre**, it need no longer rest on its laurels. Twelve years in the making, the Centre National de la Danse (*see p294* **Jailhouse rocks**) was opened in June 2004 as the flagship of the nation's 600-plus dance companies and 500-plus dancers. Located just outside Paris city centre in Pantin – near the Cité de la Musique – the CND not only serves as major performance and rehearsal centre, but also as an archive of the city's stellar dance heritage.

Although Paris is revered for its sumptuous Opéra productions and groundbreaking avant-garde performances of a century ago, it boasts an impressive contemporary scene: locals are hungry for cutting-edge dance. Talent is constantly shuttling between Paris and Brussels – Anne Teresa de Keersmaeker and her company Rosas are among the commuters. Superstars Pina Bausch and William Forsythe also visit regularly, drawing healthy crowds.

For would-be performers, there are masses of dance classes, ballet and hip hop being the most popular – and there's no letting up of the Buena Vista-inspired Latin phenomenon.

INFORMATION AND RESOURCES

For listings, see *Pariscope* and *L'Officiel des Spectacles*, and the *Aden* supplement in *Le Monde*. For events coverage, look out for two monthlies: *La Terrasse* (distributed free at major dance venues) and the glossy *Danser*. The Centre National de la Danse publishes the bi-annual in-depth review *Kinem* (subscription only, 01.41.83.98.98). The centre also has, among its many information resources, an audition posting board. Another can be found at the **Centre de Danse du Marais**.

For shoes and equipment, **Repetto** (22 rue de la Paix, 2nd, 01.44.71.83.12) supplies the Opéra with pointes and slippers, and main department stores (*see p240*) also carry dance items.

Festivals

Every season sees some kind of contemporary dance festival in or near Paris. The year starts with **Faits d'Hiver** (www.faitsdhiver.com) in January; May/June welcomes the **Rencontres Chorégraphiques de Seine-St-Denis** (www.rencontreschoregraphiques.com); and the **IRCAM Agora festival** (www.ircam.fr). **Onze Bouge** (www.festivalonze.org) in June is followed by the street-dance **Rencontres** (www.villette.com) at La Villette in October. There are smaller festivals at the **Maison des Arts de Créteil** and **Ménagerie de Verre** in the 11th. *See also chapter* **Festivals & Events**.

Paris quartier d'été

01.44.94.98.00/www.quartierdete.com.
Dates *July-Aug.*
This festival features eclectic programmes and free outdoor performances. Public rehearsals and talks give the audience the chance to meet prestigious international choreographers.

Festival d'Automne

01.53.45.17.00/www.festival-automne.com.
Dates *Sept-Dec.*
For 30 years, the Festival d'Automne has shown the way forward in the performing arts. Performances are highbrow and experimental, with work by big-name choreographers as well as newcomers.

Centre National de la Danse

1 rue Victor-Hugo, 93507 Pantin (01.41.83.27.27/ www.cnd.fr). M° Hoche/RER Pantin. **Open** *Box office (01.41.83.98.98)* 10am-7pm Mon-Fri. **Admission** €5-€15. **Credit** AmEx, MC, V.
France's impressive newly established centre for dance. *See below* **Jailhouse rocks**.

Maison des Arts de Créteil

pl Salvador Allende, 94000 Créteil (01.45.13.19.19/ www.maccreteil.com). M° Créteil-Préfecture. **Open** *Box office* 1-7pm Tue-Sat. Closed July-Aug. **Admission** €8-€20. **Credit** MC, V.
This arts centre brings international acts to the Paris suburbs. In 2005, these include Bill T Jones and, in May, the Kubilai Khan Investigations. Don't miss, either, the EXIT festival in the spring.

Palais Garnier

Pl de l'Opéra, 9th (08.92.89.90.90/www.opera-de-paris.fr). M° Opéra. **Open** *Box office* 11am-6pm Mon-Sat. *Telephone bookings* 9am-6pm Mon-Sat. Closed 15 July-end Aug. **Admission** €7-€160. Concs 1hr before show. **Credit** AmEx, MC, V. **Map** p403 G4.

The Ballet de l'Opéra National de Paris manages to tread successfully between tutu classics and creations, between the Opéra Bastille (*see p318*) and lavish Palais Garnier, where the freshly renovated grand foyer is a must-see. Nureyev's *Romeo and Juliet* is revived in July 2005, there are new pieces by Trisha Brown in December and *Wuthering Heights* in March. There's also the black-tie event every New Year's Eve and a special performance on 14 July.

Théâtre National de Chaillot

1 pl du Trocadéro, 16th (01.53.65.30.00/www. theatre-chaillot.fr). M° Trocadéro. **Open** *Box office* 11am-7pm Mon-Fri. *Telephone bookings* 11am-7pm Mon-Sat. Closed July-Aug. **Admission** €19.50-€39; €10.50-€32 concs. **Credit** MC, V. **Map** p402 C5.
Chaillot features big names and home-grown talents. The 2004-2005 season is eclectic, with hip hop and flamenco evenings, plus *Mambo Místico*, a dance-musical by extravagant Argentinian director Alfredo Arias, starring iconic performer Marilù Marini.

Théâtre de la Ville – Abbesses

2 pl du Châtelet, 4th (01.42.74.22.77/www. theatredelaville-paris.com). M° Châtelet. **Open** *Box office* 11am-7pm Mon; 11am-8pm Tue-Sat. *Telephone*

Jailhouse rocks

Parisian cultural institutions and audiences abide by a long-standing principle: beyond the city ring road, there be dragons. With downtown real estate prices soaring and politicians determined to perk up the suburbs, the long-running saga of siting

France's prestigious National Dance Centre saw it eventually end up by the Canal de l'Ourcq at Pantin, on the city's northeastern edge. In the pipeline since 1991, too frequently sidelined for want of consistent political and artistic decision, the **Centre**

bookings 11am-7pm Mon-Sat. Closed July-Aug. **Admission** €11-€29. **Credit** MC, V. **Map** p406 J6. The leading contemporary dance venue has become a showcase for established choreographers; in 2005 Pina Bausch and Anne Teresa de Keersmaeker will visit, as will Sidi Larbi Cherkaoui. Book early: most shows sell out well before opening night. Sister venue Théâtre des Abbesses (31 rue des Abbesses, 18th, same number) showcases classical Indian performers.

Other dance venues

L'Etoile du Nord

16 rue Georgette-Agutte, 18th (01.42.26.47.47). M° Guy Môquet. **Open** *Box office* 1-6pm Mon-Fri. Closed July-Aug. **Admission** €19; €8-€13 concs. **Credit** MC, V.
Provides a needed platform for the contemporary multi-media dance scene.

Ménagerie de Verre

12-14 rue Léchevin, 11th (01.43.38.33.44/www. menagerie-de-verre.org). M° Parmentier. **Open** *Box office* 90mins before show. Closed end July-Aug. **Admission** €10-€13. **No credit cards. Map** p405 N5.

This multidisciplinary hothouse is rooted in the avant-garde, with contemporary dance and classes. Also hosts bi-annual festival Les Inaccoutumés.

Le Regard du Cygne

210 rue de Belleville, 20th (01.43.58.55.93/http:// redcygne.free.fr). M° Télégraphe. **Open** *Box office* 1hr before show. Closed Aug. **Admission** €5-€15. **No credit cards.** Map p405 Q3.
This picturesque studio is one of the few alternative spaces in Paris. Its Spectacles Sauvages allow unknowns to show a ten-minute piece to the public.

Théâtre de la Bastille

76 rue de la Roquette, 11th (01.43.57.42.14/www. theatre-bastille.com). M° Bastille or Voltaire. **Open** *Box office* 10am-6pm Mon-Fri; 2-6pm Sat. Closed July-Aug. **Admission** €12.50-€19. **Credit** MC, V. **Map** p409 M6.
Small theatre showcasing ribald dance and drama.

Théâtre du Châtelet

1 pl du Châtelet, 1st (01.40.28.28.00/www.chatelet- theatre.com). M° Châtelet. **Open** *Box office* 1hr before show. Closed July-Sept. **Admission** €9-€75. **Credit** AmEx, MC, V. **Map** p404 J5.

National de la Danse (*see p274*) was opened with grand ceremony in June 2004. Oddly enough, in a country with a prestigious ballet tradition and some 600 active companies, dance is not a cultural policy priority. The CND has had to make do with a 1972 concrete-and-glass building that hosted the local offices, jail and courtroom. Key architects Antoinette Robain and Claire Guieysse redesigned the dreary, grey edifice, transforming it into a hi-tech and spacious structure. The angular lines are softened by bold red panels, Michelangelo Pistoletto's pop furniture, and Hervé Audibert's colourful yet dramatic lights.

As a cultural resource, though, the CND is second to none. Intended to provide professionals with pedagogical, technical and financial support, it features 11 rehearsal studios, classrooms, an exhibition hall, film-viewing rooms, audition posting boards, and a multimedia-library stacked with books, videos, archives and periodicals. Several studios can accommodate an audience of up to 135, but there is no actual performance hall. As if to ▶

A classical music institution across the square from the Théâtre de la Ville (*see p344*), Châtelet indulges dance audiences every year when hosting Spanish dancer, choreographer and heartthrob Nacho Duato in the spring. French regional ballets also receive regular invites, including the Ballet National de Lyon – expect pieces by Mats Ek and Philippe Découflé in 2005.

Théâtre de la Cité Internationale

21 bd Jourdan, 14th (01.43.13.50.50/www.theatre delacite.ciup.fr). RER Cité Universitaire. **Open** *Box office* 2-7pm Mon-Fri. *Telephone bookings* 2-7pm Mon-Sat. Closed July-Aug. **Admission** €21; €7.50-€12.50 concs. **Credit** MC, V.

This well established contemporary dance venue at the Cité Universitaire hosts shows, workshops and other festive events.

Dance classes

As a dance-devoted, multicultural metropolis, Paris offers classes in virtually any dance you can name, no matter how exotic. Here is just a small selection of what's on offer:

Centre de Danse du Marais

41 rue du Temple, 4th (01.42.72.15.42/www.paris danse.com). M° Rambuteau. **Open** 9am-9pm Mon-Fri; 9am-8pm Sat; 9am-7pm Sun. **Map** 404 K5.

This Marais venue boasts big-name teachers such as *danse orientale* star Leila Haddad or ballet's Casati-Lazzarelli team, and offers a huge choice of classes at amateur and professional level. Look out for the five-class 'sampler' pass, at €65 a good deal.

Centre Momboye

25 rue Boyer, 20th (01.43.58.85.01/www.ladanse. com/centremomboye). M° Gambetta. **Open** 9am-10.30pm daily. **Map** p405 P4.

This is the only centre devoted entirely to African dance, taught to live drumming. Hip hop too.

Studio Harmonic

5 passage des Taillandiers, 11th (01.48.07.13.39/ www.studioharmonic.fr). M° Bastille. **Open** *Office* 10am-5pm Mon-Fri. *Classes* 9.30am-10pm Mon-Fri; 9am-7.30pm Sat. Closed 3wks Aug. **Map** p409 M7.

The rising star among Parisian dance schools, its claim to fame is teacher Laure Courtellemont and her trademark raggajam, a blend of hip hop and Afro-Caribbean dance.

► Jailhouse rocks (continued)

accentuate the venue's previous function, Robain and Guieysse have laid out the café-restaurant in the form of a prison canteen.

Most shows, lectures and seminars are open to all. With guests such as the extravagant Foofwa d'Imobilité or Congolese choreographer Faustin Linyekula, the 2005 season definitely sounds attractive enough for any dance or architecture aficionado to head for Pantin – only a single Métro stop away from the Cité de la Musique, the Conservatoire and the Parc de La Villette.

Film

Cinema paradiso.

Le Grand Rex: king-sized. *See p298.*

Paris belongs to the movies – or is it the other way around? Consider: 87 cinemas mustering 376 screens, 150 of them independently owned – and of those, 89 show nothing but arthouse. 700 crews, local and international, shooting in the city every year. More tickets per capita bought in Paris than anywhere else in Europe. And, in any given week, a choice of around 230 movies – not counting festivals and retrospectives (*see p302*). You like cinema? You'll love Paris.

Even if you're only in town for a couple of days, it would be a crying shame not to visit at least one of the city's many and varied picture palaces – nearly all now have a website. As well as festivals, retrospectives and cut-price promotions, there are any number of 'meet the director' events: if you're lucky, your trip may coincide with a visit from Scorsese or Kitano.

Local interest is large enough to sustain a small avalanche of monthly movie magazines (*see p380* **Media**) – there's even a whole book fair devoted to writing on film (*see p302*). French DVD labels produce some of the most expertly curated discs in the world, and by no means restrict their output to francophonia. Visit the film sections of **Fnac** or the **Virgin Megastore** (for both, *see p246*) and you're more than likely to find American and British titles unavailable in the US or UK.

INFORMATION AND TICKETS

New releases, sometimes 15 or more, hit the screens on Wednesdays. Hollywood is well represented, of course, but Paris audiences have a balanced diegetic diet and an insatiable appetite for international product and non-standard formats like shorts or documentaries; then there are the 150-plus annual releases funded or part-funded with French money (the French film industry is still the world's third largest after the US and India).

For venues, times and prices, consult one of the city's three main weekly listings mags: *L'Officiel des Spectacles*, *Pariscope* or *Zurban*. *Films nouveaux* are the week's new releases, *Exclusivités* are the also-showing titles and *Reprises* means rep. Take note, when picking a showing of a non-francophone flick, of the two letters printed somewhere near the title: VO (*version originale*) means a screening in the original language with French subtitles; VF (*version française*) means dubbed into French.

Tickets can be bought in the usual way at cinemas themselves (for new blockbusters, especially at multiplexes, it pays to buy tickets at least one screening in advance); by phone on **AlloCiné** (08.92.89.28.92, www.allocine.fr); or, in some cases, online – although this often entails a booking fee. Seats are often discounted by 20 to 30 per cent at Monday or Wednesday screenings, and the Mairie sponsors a number of cut-price promotions throughout the year. All the multiplex chains offer *cartes illimitées*, season tickets which allow unlimited access.

Cinemas

Giant screens & multiplexes

Gaumont Grand Ecran Italie

30 pl d'Italie, 13th (08.92.69.66.96/www. gaumont.fr). M° Place d'Italie. **Admission** *Big screen* €9.50. *Other screens* €8.20; €5.70 under-12s; €18 monthly pass. **Credit** MC, V. **Map** p408 J10.
This impressive three-screen complex, designed by Japanese architect Kenzo Tange, opened in 1992. Come here to see your favourite star emblazoned

across its vast 24m screen – the biggest in Paris. Gaumont's unlimited entry card is called Le Pass, and is also valid in MK2 and Pathé cinemas, plus selected independents like La Pagode (*see p301*). *Wheelchair access.*

La Géode

26 av Corentin-Cariou, 19th (08.92.68.45.40/www. lageode.fr). M° Porte de la Villette. **Admission** €9; €7 under-25s. **Credit** MC, V. **Map** inset p405.
The IMAX cinema at the Cité des Sciences (*see p179*) occupies a huge, shiny geodesic sphere. The 1,000m² hemispheric screen lets you experience 3-D plunges through natural scenery or animated adventures where the characters zoom out to grab you. *Wheelchair access (reserve ahead).*

Le Grand Rex

1 bd Poissonnière, 2nd (08.36.68.05.96/www. legrandrex.com). M° Bonne Nouvelle. **Admission** €9; €7 students, over-60s; €5.95 under-12s. *Les Etoiles du Rex tour* €7.50; €6.50 under-12s; €5.50 all 5-7pm. **Credit** MC, V. **Map** p404 J4.
With its wedding-cake exterior, fairy-tale interior, plush carpets and the largest auditorium in Europe (2,750 seats), Le Grand Rex is one of the few cinemas likely to upstage whatever it screens: no wonder it's a listed historic monument. Its blockbuster programming (usually in VF) is well suited to its vast, roll-down screen; it also hosts concerts and rowdy all-night compilation events. There are six smaller screens in the basement and an adjoining building. The Etoiles du Rex tour provides a 50-minute, SFX-laden taste of movie magic. *Wheelchair access.*

Max Linder Panorama

24 bd Poissonnière, 9th (08.92.68.00.31/www. maxlinder.com). M° Grands Boulevards. **Admission** €8.50; €6.50 Mon, Wed, Fri, students, under-12s. **Credit** MC, V. **Map** p404 J3.

The best **Screens**

La Cinémathèque Française

Last chance to see a film at its historic Trocadéro address. *See p299.*

Forum des Images

Something for everyone. *See p299.*

Le Grand Rex

An auditorium of heroic, even majestic proportions. *See above.*

MK2 Bibliothèque

What a multiplex *should* look like. *See above.*

La Pagode

Eastern promise – fulfilled. *See p301.*

This state-of-the-art cinema (THX sound and an 18m screen) is named after the dapper French silent comedian who owned it between 1914 and 1925. The walls and 700 seats are all black, to prevent even the tiniest twinkle of reflected light distracting the audience from what's happening on the screen. Look out for all-nighters and one-offs such as rare vintage films or piano-accompanied silents. *Wheelchair access.*

MK2 Bibliothèque

128-162 av de France, 13th (08.92.69.84.84/ www.mk2.com). M° Bibliothèque François Mitterrand or Quai de la Gare. **Admission** €8.80-€9.20; €6.50 students, 12s-18s (Mon-Fri before 6pm); €5.50 under-12s; €5.10 before noon; €18 monthly pass. **Credit** MC, V. **Map** p409 M10.
The latest addition to the MK2 chain offers an all-in-one night out, with 14 screens, three restaurants, a bar that stays open till 5am at weekends and two-person 'love seats'. MK2 is a paradigm of imaginative programming that aims to bring arthouse to the masses. For €18 per month their Le Pass card offers unlimited screenings at any MK2, Pathé or Gaumont venue, and at a few independents. *Wheelchair access.*

UGC Ciné Cité Bercy

2 cour St-Emilion, 12th (08.36.68.68.58/www.ugc.fr). M° Cour St-Emilion. **Admission** €9.20; €6.50 students, over-60s; €5.50 under-12s; €18 monthly pass. **Credit** MC, V. **Map** p409 N10.
This ambitious 18-screen development screens art movies and mainstream fodder, and hosts regular meet-the-director events. The 19-screen Les Halles original (7 pl de la Rotonde, Nouveau Forum des Halles, 1st, 08.92.70.00.00, M° Les Halles) serves the same mix. The UGC Illimitée card provides all-you-can-watch access for €18 per month; there's a non-refundable €30 handling fee for new applicants. *Internet café. Wheelchair access.*

Showcases

Auditorium du Louvre

Musée du Louvre, 99 rue de Rivoli, 1st (01.40.20.51.86/www.louvre.fr). M° Palais Royal Musée du Louvre. **Admission** €5; €3 under-26s. **Credit** MC, V. **Map** p404 H5.
This 420-seat auditorium was designed by IM Pei. Film screenings are often related to the exhibitions; silent movies with live music are regulars.

Centre Pompidou

Rue St-Martin, 4th (01.44.78.12.33/www.centre pompidou.fr). M° Hôtel de Ville or Rambuteau. **Admission** €5; €3 students. **Credit** MC, V. **Map** p408 K6.
The programme here features themed series, experimental and artists' films and a weekly documentary session. This is also the venue for the Cinéma du Réel festival in March which, for 25 years, has championed the cause of documentary film. *Wheelchair access.*

Arts & Entertainment

Movie-lovers' love-in:
MK2 Bibliothèque. *See p298.*

Le Cinéma des Cinéastes

7 av de Clichy, 17th (01.53.42.40.20). M° Place de Clichy. **Admission** €7.20; €5.70 Wed, students, under-12s, over-60s. **Credit** MC, V. **Map** p403 G2.
Done out to evoke the film studios of old, this three-screen showcase of world cinema holds meet-the-director sessions and festivals of classic, foreign, gay and documentary films. Also offers a monthly pass. *Bar-restaurant. Wheelchair access.*

La Cinémathèque Française

01.56.26.01.01/www.cinemathequefrancaise.com. **Admission** €5; €4 students; membership available. **No credit cards.**
Palais de Chaillot *7 av Albert-de-Mun, 16th. M° Trocadéro.* **Map** p402 C5.
Grands Boulevards *42 bd Bonne-Nouvelle, 10th (01.56.26.01.01). M° Bonne Nouvelle.* **Map** p404 J4.
The influence of the Cinémathèque Française is immense. Henri Langlois, patron saint of film archives, founded it in 1936 and turned it one of the finest cinema collections in the world; his sacking helped kick off the events of 1968 (the locked Chaillot entrance immortalised by Truffaut at the start of *Baisers Volés*); and its screenings have shaped scores of filmmakers. In 2003, mogul Claude Berri was elected president, forcing the long-mooted, oft-postponed plans to relocate to the former American Center on rue de Bercy – set for autumn 2005 (for updates check www.51ruedebercy.com).

Forum des Images

2 Grande Galerie, Porte St-Eustache, Forum des Halles, 1st (01.44.76.62.00/www.forumdesimages. net). M° Les Halles. **Open** 1-9pm Tue, Wed, Fri-Sun;
1-10pm Thur. Closed 2wks Aug. **Admission** €5.50 per day; €4.50 students, under-26s, membership available. **Credit** MC, V. **Map** p404 J5.
The hyperactive four-screen Forum des Images is both a film archive dedicated to Paris on celluloid and a thought-provoking, entertaining programmer of films grouped around themes such as Motherhood or Gangsters. It hosts the Rencontres Internationales du Cinéma, the trash treats of L'Etrange Festival (*see p302*) and films from the critics' selection at Cannes.

Arthouses

Accattone

20 rue Cujas, 5th (01.46.33.86.86). M° Cluny La Sorbonne/RER Luxembourg. **Admission** €6.50; €5.50 Wed, students, under-20s. **No credit cards.** **Map** p408 J8.
Named after Pasolini's first film, this tiny Latin Quarter cinema has a clear preference for old Italian arthouse. That said, there's plenty of room on the rolling weekly programme of around 30 films for the likes of Roeg, Oshima, Buñuel and Ken Russell. In the 1960s it was managed by François Truffaut.

Action

Action Christine *4 rue Christine, 6th (01.43.29. 11.30). M° Odéon or St-Michel.* **Admission** €7; €5.50 students, under-20s. **No credit cards.** **Map** p408 J7.
Action Ecoles *23 rue des Ecoles, 5th (01.43.29. 79.89). M° Maubert Mutualité.* **Admission** €7; €5.50 students, under-20s. **No credit cards.** **Map** p408 J8.

Arts & Entertainment

Le Balzac.

Grand Action *5 rue des Ecoles, 5th (01.43.29.44.40).*
M° Cardinal Lemoine. **Admission** €7; €5.50 students,
under-20s. **No credit cards. Map** p408 K8.
A Left Bank stalwart since the early 1980s, the
Action group is renowned for screening new prints
of old movies. Heaven for those nostalgic for 1940s
and '50s Tinseltown classics and US independents.

Le Balzac
1 rue Balzac, 8th (01.45.61.10.60/www.cinema
balzac.com). M° George V. **Admission** €8; €6 Mon,
Wed, students, under-18s, over-60s. **No credit
cards. Map** p402 D4.
Built in 1935 and boasting a mock ocean-liner foyer,
Le Balzac scores highly for design and programming. Genial manager Jean-Jacques Schpoliansky
often welcomes punters in person at the start of each
screening. It recently acquired a digital projector,
and awards prizes according to audience votes.

Le Cinéma du Panthéon
13 rue Victor-Cousin, 5th (01.40.46.01.21). RER
Luxembourg. **Admission** €7; €5.50 Mon, Wed,
students, 13-18s; €4 under-13s. **No credit cards.
Map** p408 J8.
Paris' oldest surviving movie house (founded in 1907
in the Sorbonne) is one of the few to have retained
its balcony. It still screens new, often quite obscure
international films; meet-the-director evenings and
discussions are regular events.

Le Champo
51 rue des Ecoles, 5th (01.43.54.51.60). M° Maubert
Mutualité. **Admission** €7; €5.50 under-20s, all Wed,
Sun last screening. **No credit cards. Map** p408 J7.
The two-screen Champo has been in operation since
1938; in 2000 it was awarded historic monument
status. In the 1960s it was a favourite haunt of
nouvelle vague directors such as Claude Chabrol.

Le Denfert
24 pl Denfert-Rochereau, 14th (01.43.21.41.01).
M° Denfert Rochereau. **Admission** €6.50; €5 Mon,
Wed, students, over-60s; €4.60 under-15s. **No credit
cards. Map** p407 H10.
This friendly little cinema offers an eclectic reper-
tory selection that ranges from François Ozon and
Hayao Miyazaki to shorts and new animation, as
well as new foreign films.
Wheelchair access.

L'Entrepôt
7-9 rue Francis-de-Pressensé, 14th (01.45.40.07.50/
www.lentrepot.fr). M° Pernéty. **Admission** €6.90;
€5.60 students, over-60s; €4 under-12s. **Credit** MC,
V. **Map** p407 F10.
Documentary, shorts, gay, Second and Third World
cinema are more common here than mainstream
stuff. A debate or a chance to meet the director often
accompany the film.
Café. Restaurant.

Images d'Ailleurs
21 rue de la Clef, 5th (01.45.87.18.09). M° Censier
Daubenton. **Admission** €5.80; €5.10 Mon. **No
credit cards. Map** 408 K9.
Opened in 1990, this cinema focuses on films from
Africa and other rare movie treats.

Le Latina
20 rue du Temple, 4th (01.42.78.47.86/www.
lelatina.com). M° Hôtel de Ville. **Admission** €7;
€5.50 students, under-20s, all Mon, Tue. **No credit
cards. Map** p408 K6.
Flag-bearer for Latin cultures whose programming
runs from Argentinian to Romanian films. Salsa or
tango with the €16 film-dinner-dancing deals on
Monday and Wednesday evenings.
Restaurant.

Le Mac Mahon
5 av Mac-Mahon, 17th (01.43.80.24.81). M° Charles de Gaulle Etoile. **Admission** €6.50; €4.50 students. **No credit cards. Map** p402 C3.
This single-screen, 1930s-era cinema has changed little since its 1960s heyday (tickets are, delightfully, of the tear-off type), when its all-American programming fostered the label '*mac-mahonisme*' among the gang of buffs who haunted the place. Americana of the '30s to '60s is still the bulk of what's shown.

La Pagode
57bis rue de Babylone, 7th (01.45.55.48.48). M° St-François-Xavier. **Admission** €7.30; €5.80 Mon, Wed, students, under-21s. **No credit cards. Map** p407 F7.
This glorious edifice is not, as legend might have it, a block-by-block import, but a 19th-century replica by a French architect (although authentic Japanese elements include carved beams). Renovated in the late 1990s, this historic venue is one of the world's loveliest cinemas.

Studio 28
10 rue Tholozé, 18th (01.46.06.36.07/www.cinema studio28.com). M° Abbesses. **Admission** €7; €5.80 students, under-12s. **No credit cards. Map** p403 H1.

Montmartre's historic Studio 28 was the venue for Buñuel's scandalous *L'Age d'Or*, and features in *Amélie*. It offers a decent repertory mix of classics and recent movies, complete with Dolby sound and the chance to have a drink before or after screenings.

Studio Galande
42 rue Galande, 5th (01.43.26.94.08). M° St-Michel or Cluny La Sorbonne. **Admission** €7; €5.50 students, all Wed. **No credit cards. Map** p408 J7.
Some 20 different films are screened at this cheerful Latin Quarter venue every week – international art-house with the occasional *Matrix*. Every Friday, fans of *The Rocky Horror Picture Show* turn up with drag, rice and water pistols.

Festivals & special events

Festival international de films de femmes
Maison des Arts, pl Salvador-Allende, 94040 Créteil (01.49.80.38.98/www.filmsdefemmes.com). M° Créteil-Préfecture. **Date** Mar.
A selection of retrospectives and new international films by women directors.

Short and sweet

Up to his death of TB at 29, Jean Vigo had made only four films, two of them shorts – yet today he is reckoned by every authority worth citing to be one of cinema's masters. Rated alongside Renoir, Carné and Buñuel, Vigo's entire output fits nicely on two DVDs. To coincide with the centenary of Vigo's birth, 2005 sees seasons of films about him or inspired by him, exhibitions, books and restored prints of his work.

The tragic Vigo, a filmmaker who never caught so much as a whiff of success in his lifetime, was one of cinema's few true poets. His first film, the 26-minute jaunty-savage *A Propos de Nice*, was shot on a second-hand camera he would never have been able to afford had his step-father not given him the money. Then came a second short and the featurette *Zéro de conduite*, which was banned in France until 1945; then his last and greatest film, 1934's *L'Atalante* (pictured).

L'Atalante is a love story set, largely, on a cat-infested canal barge. Its lovers marry, cast off together, argue, split and are joyfully reunited – and in telling their story Vigo produced some of the most enchanting, most ingenious and least sentimental sequences ever made. There's lyricism aplenty, as when the abandoned barge

skipper dives into the water and sees visions of his girl, happy in her bridal gown; but it's a perfectly realistic view of married life. Studio Gaumont thought otherwise, and hacked it about; although subsequently restored, it's still not a director's cut. Vigo died days after the film's first run.

If you've never seen a Vigo film, a centenary year is as good a time to do so as any. There aren't many great directors whose complete works you can see as part of a day trip.

Printemps du Cinéma

Various venues (www.printempsducinema.com).
Date Mar.
Three days of €3.50 films across Paris.

Festival du Film de Paris

*Gaumont Marignan, 27 av des Champs-Elysées,
8th (www.festivaldufilmdeparis.com). Mº Franklin
D. Roosevelt.* **Date** Mar-Apr. **Map** p403 E4.
Given the city's love of the cinema, it's odd that its
own film festival makes such a relatively minor
splash. Never mind: it's a chance to see some 80
French and foreign films and catch a few stars. 2005
brings the festival's 20th edition.

Côté Court

*Ciné 104, 104 av Jean-Lolive, 93500 Pantin (01.48.
46.95.08/www.cotecourt.org). Mº Eglise de Pantin.*
Date June.
A great selection of new and old short films at Ciné
104 and a handful of neighbouring venues.

Paris Cinéma

*Various locations (01.55.25.55.25/www.paris
cinema.org).* **Date** July.
The Mairie sponsors this celebration of the silver
screen. Its programme includes shorts, documentary, experimental and animated films along with a
slew of retrospectives and *avant-premières* and a
handful or two of stars.

Rencontres internationales de cinéma

Forum des Images (see p299). **Date** July. **Map** p406 J5.
A global choice of new independent features, documentary and short films, usually screened in the
presence of their directors.

Cinéma au clair du lune

*Various locations (01.44.76.62.18/www.forumdes
images.net).* **Date** Aug.
Films screened under the stars on giant open-air
screens set up in squares and public gardens around
town: party atmosphere guaranteed.

3 Jours/3 euros

*All cinemas across town (www.paris.fr/fr/culture/
missioncinema).* **Date** Aug.
This Mairie-sponsored promotion is timed to start
getting kids into cinemas before the schools go back.
For three days, every screening costs just €3.

L'Etrange Festival

*Forum des Images (see p299/www.etrangefestival.
com).* **Date** Sept. **Map** p406 J5.
Explicit sex, gore and weirdness in the screenings
and 'happenings' at this annual feast of all things
unconventional draw large crowds.

Paris Capitale du cinéma art et essai

Various venues. **Date** Oct.
Yet another Mairie-funded cinema initiative. For a
whole week, films at 60 arthouse screens across the
city cost just €4 a pop.

Salon du Livre de Cinéma et du DVD

*Espace des Blancs-Manteaux, 48 rue Vieille-du-
Temple, 4th (www.cinemathequefrançaise.com).
Mº Hôtel de Ville.* **Date** Oct.
Some 150 European publishers of cinema books sell
their wares. There are round-table discussions and
the chance to meet and question film-makers.

Bookshops

Unsurprisingly, Paris is generously supplied
with specialist film bookshops. **Virgin
Megastore** (*see p246*) also stocks a decent
range of English-language movie books.

Ciné Reflet

*14 rue Serpente, 6th (01.40.46.02.72). Mº Cluny La
Sorbonne.* **Open** 1-8pm Mon-Sat; 3-7pm Sun. **Credit**
MC, V. **Map** p408 J7.
An old projector stands in a corner of this sprawl-
ing shop, well stocked with old photos, posters, and
new and second-hand books. Subjects covered range
from Lithuanian formalism to Laurel and Hardy.
The strong English-language selection includes the
Time Out Film Guide and mags like *Sight & Sound*.
Current and back issues of *Les Cahiers du Cinéma*
and *Première* fill shelf after shelf, as do fanzines and
old press dossiers.

Cinédoc

*45-53 passage Jouffroy, 9th (01.48.24.71.36).
Mº Grands Boulevards.* **Open** 10am-7pm Mon-Sat.
Credit MC, V. **Map** p404 J4.
This long, narrow, tobacco-scented bookshop has so
much in its dusty old cabinets and drawers, it's hard
to find what you're looking for. Ask the helpful staff
or take pot luck among the old photos, older US film
mags and fanzines, disquisitions on the *nouvelle
vague* and books about special effects in *Star Wars*.

Contacts

*24 rue du Colisée, 8th (01.43.59.17.71/www.media
librairie.com). Mº St-Philippe du-Roule.* **Open** 10am-
7pm Mon-Fri; 2-7pm Sat. **Credit** DC, MC, V. **Map**
p403 E4.
Truffaut's favourite *librairie* has been selling books
on film for 40 years. The stock is well organised and
boasts a large and up-to-date selection of English-
language titles. You'll also find *Film Comment* and
American Cinematographer, plus a few videos. They
operate a mail-order service on their website.

Scaramouche

*161 rue St-Martin, 3rd (01.48.87.78.58).
Mº Rambuteau.* **Open** 11am-1pm, 2-8pm Mon-Sat.
Credit MC, V. **Map** p404 K5.
This large-ish shop covers cinema and *gestuelle*
(mime and puppetry). The film section stocks a wide
range of new and second-hand titles in English, plus
a huge collection of publicity photos and portraits
filed in manilla envelopes under film title and actor's
or director's name. Wim Wenders and Alain Renais
have been known to pop in.

Galleries

Art and design intertwine in a fresh gallery scene.

Galerie Loevenbruck. *See p306.*

No one would now pretend that France is the centre of the comtemporary art world, yet Paris began the 2004-2005 gallery season in relatively optimistic mood. New galleries continue to open, an adventurous new team at the head of international contemporary art fair **FIAC** (*see p282*) has raised hopes for a local revival, while the third **Nuit Blanche** (*see p282*) met with much success. This annual all-night opening of major and minor galleries at last married the concept of accessibility with quality, showing that an audience does exist even for cutting-edge pieces, not least for outdoor video selections. There's also a burgeoning design gallery scene, reflecting the strength of a young French generation such as **Patrick Jouin**, the **Bourrellec brothers** and **Matali Crasset**, occupying an ambiguous role between design as function and design as art.

The gallery sector lives in symbiosis with the city's public institutions, with the **Centre Pompidou** (where the Espace 315 focuses on the under-40s; *see p162*), the **Palais de Tokyo** (*see p169*), the **Plateau** (*see p170*) and **ARC** (the contemporary wing of the Musée d'Art Moderne de la Ville de Paris; *see p162*) at the forefront. Look out, too, for the growing field of art/music/DJ interactions both in public spaces and more alternative venues such as **Mains d'Oeuvres** (*see p331* **Clubbing crossover**). The Prix Duchamp, now in its fifth year, and the opening of **La Maison Rouge** (*see p168*) in 2004, has started to bring France's notoriously secretive collectors out of the woodwork. Indeed, contemporary art is acquiring a certain fashionability. As François Pinault's new foundation goes up on the Ile Seguin, his eternal rival Bernard Arnault, head of luxury goods company LVMH, has begun to commission sculptures and videos for his chic new avenue Montaigne headquarters (open to the public on Saturdays). Likewise, June's biennial fair **Parcours St-Germain** sees contemporary art works nestling amid the diamond watches and designer trainers of some of the district's most glamorous boutiques, giving welcome visibility – at the risk of becoming a fashion accessory.

For innovative work and global names, make for the northern Marais and the streets near the Centre Pompidou, where historic *hôtels*

Centre Pompidou.
See p303.

particuliers may well be the haven for video and installation art, or to 'Louise', the growing nucleus of young galleries in the **13th**. Both areas are refreshingly international, and the variety of media typically eclectic. Galleries in St-Germain-des-Prés, home of the post-war avant-garde, largely confine themselves to tamer, traditional sculpture and painting; those near the Champs-Elysées present big modern and contemporary names. October's FIAC (http://fiac.reed-oip.fr) gives a quick fix on the gallery scene, both French and global; **Art-Paris** (www.artparis.fr) has a more mainstream selection; **Paris-Photo** draws specialists in classic and contemporary photography.

To see what's on, pick up bi-monthly booklet *paris-art* (www.paris-art.com), or the *Galeries Mode d'Emploi* (www.artsiders.com) and *Association des Galeries* listings foldouts, or take the Art Bus (01.47.00.90.85/www.art-process.com) which tours new galleries once a month. Most galleries close on Sundays, Mondays, in summer and at Christmas. Admission is free.

Beaubourg & the Marais

Cosmic Galerie
76 rue de Turenne, 3rd (01.42.71.72.73). M° Filles du Calvaire. **Open** 11am-7pm Mon-Fri. **Map** p404 L5.
Matt Collishaw, Vanessa Beecroft and Pierre Bismuth lead the hip brigade at this spacious Italian-owned gallery, which aims to create a London-style scene with its fashionable, club-style openings.

Galerie Anne de Villepoix
43 rue de Montmorency, 3rd (01.42.78.32.24/ www.annedevillepoix.com). M° Rambuteau. **Open** 10am-7pm Tue-Sat. **Map** p404 K5.
Along with established names such as Chris Burden and Suzanne Lafont, you'll find virtuoso mono-chrome paintings by Ming, the varied conceptual work of Franck Scurti and videos by Sara Rossi.

Galerie Cent 8
108 rue Vieille-du-Temple, 3rd (01.42.74.53.57). M° Filles du Calvaire. **Open** 10.30am-1pm, 2.30-7pm Tue-Sat. **Map** p404 L5.
Stimulating, varied shows take in all media, from paintings by Rémy Zaugg and Jugnet & Clairet to photography by Esko Männikki.

Galerie Chantal Crousel
40 rue Quincampoix, 4th (01.42.77.38.87/www. crousel.com). M° Rambuteau. **Open** 11am-1pm, 2-7pm Tue-Sat. **Map** p408 J6.
One of the city's most cutting-edge galleries, Crousel features Rikrit Tiravanija, politically inspired Thomas Hirschhorn, video installation artist Graham Gussin and rising stars Anri Sala and Melik Ohanian. An on-going series entitled 'Géographies' explores notions of homelands and migrations.

Galerie Chez Valentin
9 rue St-Gilles, 3rd (01.48.87.42.55). M° Chemin Vert. **Open** 2-7pm Tue-Fri; 11am-1pm, 2-7pm Sat. **Map** p408 L6.
Urban angst pervades works here. Look for creeping detritus installations and videos by Véronique Boudier, photos by Nicolas Moulin and projects by 2003 Prix Duchamp winner Mathieu Mercier.

Arts & Entertainment

Galerie de France

54 rue de la Verrerie, 4th (01.42.74.38.00). M° Hôtel de Ville. **Open** 11am-7pm Tue-Sat. **Map** p408 K6.

This is one of the rare galleries that covers the whole 20th century and beyond, often featuring singular figures who don't fit into any movement – like painter Eugène Leroy – or exhibits such as Rebecca Horn's mechanical contraptions.

Galerie Frank

7 rue St-Claude, 3rd (01.48.87.50.04/www.galerie frank.net). M° St-Sébastien Froissart. **Open** 11am-7pm Tue-Sat. **Map** p408 L6.

Focusing mainly on young artists, shows here might feature painted Tergal colour scapes by Cécile Bart, 'wordworks' by Charles Sandison, and the output of a batch of Finnish artists. The 2005 season brings Ilkka Halzo and Sandrine Pelletier.

Galerie Jean Brolly

16 rue de Montmorency, 3rd (01.42.78.88.02/www. jeanbrolly.com). M° Rambuteau. **Open** 11am-7pm Tue-Sat. **Map** p404 K5.

Collector Jean Brolly shows mainly painting and drawings, such as nostalgic images by Adam Adach and conceptual, manipulated canvases by Claude Rutault and Stephen Parrino.

Galerie Karsten Greve

5 rue Debelleyme, 3rd (01.42.77.19.37). M° Filles du Calvaire. **Open** 11am-7pm Tue-Sat. **Map** p404 L5.

The Cologne gallery's smart Paris outpost is the venue for retrospective displays of top-ranking artists. Jannis Kounellis, Louise Bourgeois, Pierre Soulages and Jean Dubuffet have all featured.

Galerie Marian Goodman

79 rue du Temple, 3rd (01.48.04.70.52/www. mariangoodman.com). M° Rambuteau. **Open** 11am-7pm Tue-Sat. **Map** p408 K6.

The New York gallerist has an impressive Paris outpost in a beautiful 17th-century mansion. Alongside names like Jeff Wall and Lothar Baumgarten, she has snapped up Pierre Huyghe, Brit videomaker Steve McQueen and Finn Eija-Liisa Ahtila.

Galerie Michel Rein

42 rue de Turenne, 3rd (01.42.72.68.13/www.michel rein.com). M° Chemin Vert. **Open** 11am-7pm Tue-Sat. **Map** p408 L6.

Shows here are a bit hit or miss, but Rein presents some interesting, hard-to-classify individuals such as Didier Marcel and Jean-Pierre Bertrand, and young artists Delphine Coindet and Stefan Nikolaev.

Galerie Nathalie Obadia

3 rue du Cloître-St-Merri, 4th (01.42.74.67.68). M° Rambuteau. **Open** 11am-7pm Mon-Fri. **Map** p408 K6.

Nathalie Obadia recently moved to spacious new premises. You'll find all media (with a predilection for painting): Jean-Marc Bustamente, Manuel Ocampo and Pascal Pinaud are regulars, as are Fiona Rae, Carole Benzaken and Jessica Stockholder.

Galerie Nelson

59 rue Quincampoix, 4th (01.42.71.74.56/www. galerie-nelson.com). M° Châtelet or Rambuteau. **Open** 2-7pm Tue-Sat. **Map** p408 J6.

Nelson was the first gallery in France to show Thomas Ruff, Thomas Schutte and Rodney Graham. It also features rising French artists Guillaume Paris and Stéphane Calais, and represents the late Fluxus maverick Robert Filliou.

Galerie Templon

30 rue Beaubourg, 3rd (01.42.72.14.10/www. galerietemplon.com). M° Rambuteau. **Open** 10am-7pm Mon-Sat. **Map** p404 K5.

Now an institution, Daniel Templon opened his first gallery in the early 1970s. Galerie T is both a favourite with the French art establishment and – as it mainly shows painters – a place that presents work private collectors might envisage putting on their walls. David Salle, Jean-Marc Alberola, Claude Viallat, Vincent Corpet are regulars along with Raymond Hains and young German artists.

Galerie Thaddaeus Ropac

7 rue Debelleyme, 3rd (01.42.72.99.00/www.ropac. net). M° Filles du Calvaire. **Open** 10am-7pm Tue-Sat. **Map** p404 L5.

The Austrian-owned gallery is strong on American Pop, neo-Pop, Warhol, Tom Sachs and Alex Katz, but also features Ilya Kabakov, Gilbert & George and quirky theme shows with outside curators.

Galerie Yvon Lambert

108 rue Vieille-du-Temple, 3rd (01.42.71.09.33/ www.yvon-lambert.com). M° Filles du Calvaire. **Open** 10am-1pm, 2.30-7pm Tue-Fri; 10am-7pm Sat. **Map** p404 L5.

Probably France's most important gallery (with a New York offshoot), this place pulls out all the stops, whether for the latest production by names like Nan Goldin, Jenny Holzer or Christian Boltanski, for new installation by Claude Levêque or Carlos Amorales, or for the video generation. The side gallery is for experimental artists such as David Shrigley in 2005.

Galerie Zurcher

56 rue Chapon, 3rd (01.42.72.82.20/www. galeriezurcher.com). M° Arts et Métiers. **Open** 11am-7pm Tue-Sat; *Nov-Mar* 2-6pm Sun. **Map** p404 K5.

Amid the Chinese wholesalers north of Beaubourg, Zurcher shows young artists with a new take on painting and video: Camille Vivier, Gwen Ravillous, Marc Desgrandchamps and Elisa Sighicelli.

Gilles Peyroulet & Cie

80 rue Quincampoix, 3rd (01.42.78.85.11). M° Rambuteau or Etienne Marcel. **Open** 2-7pm Tue-Sat. **Map** p404 K5.

Peyroulet is strongest with photo-oriented artists such as Marin Kasimir and Nick Waplington, but he also bridges the gap between fine art and design, with retrospective shows of 20th-century pioneers such as Eileen Gray and Alvar Aalto.

Schleicher + Lange

12 rue de Picardie, 3rd (01.42.77.02.77/www.
schleicherlange.com). M° Filles du Calvaire.
Open 10am-7pm Tue-Sat. **Map** p404 L5.
The first shows at this new gallery (opened by a
young duo from Berlin by way of London) look
promising. They focus on artists yet to exhibit in
Paris and, in addition to London-based talents,
promise finds from the buzzing scene in Lithuania.

Bastille & eastern Paris

Galerie Alain Gutharc

47 rue de Lappe, 11th (01.47.00.32.10/www.alain
gutharc.com). M° Bastille. **Open** 2-7pm Tue-Fri;
11am-1pm, 2-7pm Sat. **Map** p409 M7.
Gutharc talent-spots young French artists. Check
out Delphine Kreuter's fetishistic, colour-saturated
slice-of-life photos, quirky text pieces by Antoinette
Ohanassian and videos by Joël Bartolomméo and
former fashion stylist François-Xavier Courrèges.

Galerie Jocelyn Wolff

65 rue Rébeval, 19th (01.42.03.05.65/www.galerie
wolff.com). M° Pyrénées. **Open** 2-7.30pm Thur-Sat.
Map p405 N3.
This gallery opened a year ago near Le Plateau and
is drawing attention with films by Clemens Von
Wedermeyer and installations by Guillaume Leblon.

Galerie Maisonneuve

24-32 rue des Amandiers, 20th (01.43.66.23.99/
www.saintmonday.net). M° Père Lachaise. **Open**
2-7pm Tue-Sat. **Map** p405 P5.
Its location on the fifth floor of a modern block gives
the unusual Galerie Maisonneuve something of an
out-of-the-ordinary atmosphere. It tends to feature
installations and happenings from artists such as
Claudia Triozzi and Jan Kopp.

Champs-Elysées & western Paris

Galerie Jérôme de Noirmont

38 av Matignon, 8th (01.42.89.89.00/www.denoir
mont.com). M° Miromesnil. **Open** 11am-7pm Mon-
Sat. **Map** p403 E4.
The location in the glitzy end of town could arouse
suspicions that Jérôme de Noirmont sells purely
business art. Not a bit of it – eye-catching exhibitions by AR Penck, Clemente, Jeff Koons, Pierre et
Gilles, Shirin Neshat and Bettina Rheims make this
gallery worth the trip.

Galerie Lelong

13 rue de Téhéran, 8th (01.45.63.13.19/www.galerie-
lelong.com). M° Miromesnil. **Open** 10.30am-6pm
Tue-Fri; 2-6.30pm Sat. **Map** p403 E3.
Lelong presents bankable, post-war international
names including Alechinsky, Bacon, Hockney,
Kounellis, Scully. There are other branches in New
York and Zurich.

St-Germain-des-Prés

Galerie 1900-2000

8 rue Bonaparte, 6th (01.43.25.84.20/www.galerie
1900-2000.com). M° St-Germain-des-Prés.
Open 2-7pm Mon; 10am-12.30pm, 2-7pm Tue-Sat.
Map p408 H7.
Marcel and David Fleiss show Surrealism, Dada,
Pop art and Fluxus, with works by anyone from
Breton, Picabia and De Chirico to Lichtenstein and
Rauschenberg, plus the odd photo show.

Galerie Denise René

196 bd St-Germain, 7th (01.42.22.77.57/www.
deniserene.com). M° St-Germain-des-Prés or Rue du
Bac. **Open** 10am-1pm, 2-7pm Tue-Sat. **Map** p408 H7.
Denise René is a Paris institution and has remained
committed to kinetic art, Op art and geometrical
abstraction by Soto, et al, ever since Tinguely first
presented his machines here in the 1950s.
Other locations: *22 rue Charlot, 3rd*
(01.48.87.73.94).

Galerie G-P et N Vallois

36 rue de Seine, 6th (01.46.34.61.07/www.galerie-
vallois.com). M° Mabillon or Odéon. **Open** 10.30am-
1pm, 2-7pm Mon-Sat. **Map** p408 H7.
Vallois is a rare, truly contemporary gallery in St-
Germain-des-Prés, worth the detour for *nouveau*
réaliste torn-poster veteran Jacques Villeglé, and a
clutch of young artists.

Galerie Jeanne Bucher

53 rue de Seine, 6th (01.44.41.69.65/www.
artnet.com). M° Mabillon or Odéon. **Open** 9am-
6.30pm Tue-Fri; 10am-12.30pm, 2.30-6pm Sat.
Map p408 H7.
A fixture on the Left Bank since 1925, Jeanne Bucher
specialises in post-war abstract (De Staël, Viera da
Silva, Rebeyrolle) and Cobra painters.

Galerie Lara Vincy

47 rue de Seine, 6th (01.43.26.72.51/www.lara-
vincy.com). M° Mabillon or St-Germain-des-Prés.
Open 2.30-7.30pm Mon; 11am-12.30pm, 2.30-7.30pm
Tue-Sat. **Map** p408 H7.
Lara Vincy is one of the few characters to retain
something of the old St-Germain spirit and sense of
1970s Fluxus-style 'happenings'. Interesting theme
and solo shows include master of the epigram Ben,
and artists' text, music, performance-related pieces.

Galerie Loevenbruck

40 rue de Seine, 6th (01.53.10.85.68/www.
loevenbruck.com). M° Mabillon. **Open** 2-7pm Tue-
Sat. **Map** p407 H6.
Funky Loevenbruck injected a dose of humour into
St-Germain with a bunch of young artists, such as
Virginie Barré, Bruno Peinado and Olivier Blankart,
who treat conceptual concerns with a light touch.

Galerie Maeght

42 rue du Bac, 7th (01.45.48.45.15/www.
maeght.com). M° Rue du Bac. **Open** 10am-6pm Mon;
9.30am-7pm Tue-Sat. **Map** p407 G6.

The gallery founded by Aimé Maeght in 1946 is now run by his grandchildren, but pales against a past that included Léger, Chagall, Giacometti and Miró. The shop sells prints, posters and limited editions.

13th district

&:
10 rue Duchefdelaville, 13th (www.gbagency.fr/ www.situ.com/www.daviet-thery.com). M° Chevaleret. **Open** 11am-7pm Tue-Sat. **Map** p409 M10.
This gallery is shared between the gb agency (works by young artists such as Elina Brotherus), Fabienne Leclerc's in SITU (Mark Dion, Gary Hill, Florence Paradeis and Patrick Corillon), and artists' book publisher Christophe Daviet-Thery.

Air de Paris
32 rue Louise-Weiss, 13th (01.44.23.02.77/www. airdeparis.com). M° Chevaleret. **Open** 2-7pm Tue-Sat. **Map** p409 M10.
This gallery, named after Duchamp's famous bottle of air, shows experimental, neo-conceptual, somewhat chaotic material. A young international stable includes Liam Gillick, Pierre Joseph, Carsten Höller, Bruno Serralongue, Sarah Morris, muralist Lily van der Stokker and fashionista Inez van Lamsweede.

Art:Concept
16 rue Duchefdelaville, 13th (01.53.60.90.30/www. galerieartconcept.com). M° Chevaleret. **Open** 11am-7pm Tue-Sat. **Map** p409 M10.
Installation-based artists include Michel Blazy, Martine Aballea, spectacular artist in glass Richard Faugeot, and painter Didier Schlier.

Galerie Almine Rech
127 rue du Chevaleret, 13th (01.45.83.71.90/www. galeriealminerech.com). M° Bibliothèque François Mitterrand or Chevaleret. **Open** 11am-7pm Tue-Sat. **Map** p409 M10.
A varied but classy agenda includes light maestro James Turrell, installations by Ugo Rondinone and films by Ange Leccia.

Galerie Emmanuel Perrotin
55 & 30 rue Louise-Weiss, 13th (01.42.16.79.79/ www.galerieperrotin.com). M° Chevaleret. **Open** 11am-7pm Tue-Sat. **Map** p409 M10.
Perrotin is the place to catch up on the provocative young Japanese generation: Noritoshi Hirakawa, manga maniac Takashi Murakami and glossy cyber-punkette Mariko Mori.

Galerie Kréo
22 rue Duchefdelaville, 13th (01.53.60.18.42/ www.kreo.com). M° Chevaleret. **Open** 2-7pm Tue-Fri; 11am-7pm Sat. **Map** p409 M10.
Occupying an ambiguous space between design as function and design as art, Kréo combines retrospectives with commissioning limited-edition pieces. Look for Ron Arad, Marc Newson and Jasper Conran, as well as native Radi Designers, Martin Szekely and the Bourrellec brothers.

Jousse Entreprise
24 & 34 rue Louise-Weiss, 13th (01.53.82.13.60/ www.jousse-entreprise.com). M° Chevaleret. **Open** 11am-1pm, 2-7pm Tue-Sat. **Map** p409 M10.
Philippe Jousse shows contemporary artists, such as Matthieu Laurette, Thomas Grünfeld and challenging young video artist Clarisse Hahn, with 1950s avant-garde furniture by Jean Prouvé, lighting by Serge Mouille and Georges Jouve ceramics.

Photography

Photoworks of all sorts can be found in many of the above galleries. The biennial **Mois de la Photo** (next in Nov 2006) covers historic and contemporary work, as does the **Paris Photo** (www.paris-photo.com) salon in November.

Galerie Françoise Paviot
57 rue Ste-Anne, 2nd (01.42.60.10.01/www. paviotfoto.com). M° Quatre Septembre. **Open** 2.30-7pm Tue-Sat. **Map** p404 H4.
Paviot presents contemporary and historic photographers with an emphasis on the great Surrealists.

Galerie Kamel Mennour
60-72 rue Mazarine, 6th (01.56.24.03.63/www. galeriemennour.com). M° Odéon. **Open** 11am-7.30pm Mon-Sat. **Map** p407 H7.
Oh-so fashionable, often provocative, guests include Nobuyoshi Araki, Guido Mocafico, Peter Beard, David LaChapelle and film-maker Larry Clark.

Galerie Michèle Chomette
24 rue Beaubourg, 3rd (01.42.78.05.62). M° Rambuteau. **Open** 2-7pm Tue-Sat. **Map** p404 K5.
Classic and experimental photography. Regulars Alain Fleischer, Eric Rondepierre, Lewis Baltz and Bernard Plossu are shown beside historic masters.

Alternative spaces

Chez Robert Electron Libre
59 rue de Rivoli, 1st (www.59rivoli.org). M° Châtelet. **Open** 1.30-7.30pm Tue-Sun. **Map** p408 J6.
This daisy-bedecked squat is a hive of paint-spattered activity. As well as giving visitors the chance to look in on the inhabitants' individual studios and living spaces, it has a gallery putting on temporary shows.

Immanence
21 av du Maine, 15th (01.42.22.05.68/www.art-immanence.org). M° Montparnasse Bienvenüe. **Open** 2-7pm Thur-Sat. **Map** p407 F8.
Set up by two artists in an alley of old studios, Immanence hosts installations and photo shows.

Public
4 impasse Beaubourg, 3rd (01.42.71.49.51/www. icono.org/public). M° Rambuteau. **Open** times vary. **Map** p404 K5.
Features an experimental programme of three-day features including sculptures, installations, short video projects and debates.

Arts & Entertainment

Gay & Lesbian

Gay marriage, Pink TV and tea dance revivals are all the rage.

Forget about your troubles at the **Amnesia Café**. *See p309.*

Something of a pink revolution took place in June 2004 with France's first gay marriage in the Bordeaux suburb of Bègles. The decision of local mayor Noël Mamère – a former TV personality and ex-presidential candidate – to marry Stéphane Chapin and Bertrand Charpentier led to his suspension, and a court later annulling the marriage. The issue has become a rallying point for the gay community, while the authorities threaten mayors who follow Mamère's lead with further suspensions, even fines. The event has divided the nation.

The debate follows the controversy of 1999, when cohabiting couples were given more rights under the so-called PACS (Pacte Civile de Solidarité). PACS let a slew of gay businesses open – estate agents, mobile phone companies, service industries – in the Marais, also the location for Paris' first gay beauty parlour.

Across the city, the last five years have seen gay Paris mayor Bertrand Delanoë easily remain the most popular Socialist politician (he is certainly still the most prominent; *see pp33-36* **Delanoë's dream**) – and the setting up of France's first gay TV channel. Launched

on cable and satellite in October 2004, Pink TV is subscription-only, with half the audience coming from the Paris region. 'A giant leap for television, a small step in high heels,' was how presenter Eric Gueho described the event at its grand unveiling.

Although the pink euro is still strong in the Marais, the axis is shifting northwest with the rebranding of the Scorp as Le Vogue (25 bd Poissonnière, 9th, 01.40.26.28.30), the high profile opening of the American-style sauna Westside (43 rue du Fbg-Montmartre, 9th, 01.47.70.57.89) and the return of legendary venue Scaramouche as the multi-purpose home of the arthouse **Twins** (*see p313* **Cool cuckoo**). **Le Dépôt**, behind the Marais sex club of the same name, have crashed Pigalle by taking over a multi-storey sauna and sex club.

On top of that is the return of a treasured Paris institution, the Sunday tea dance. The knees-up at **Amnesia** in Montparnasse has gays of a certain age bigging up the event as the return to the glory days of the Palace tea dances of the 1980s. Not to be left out, **Le Queen** (*see p332*) team is hosting a monthly tea dance at their swank straight venue, Cabaret, in the environs of the Palais-Royal.

Nearby in summer, trunk-wearing boys and old queens in corsets are out in force along the quai des Tuileries, renamed quai François Mitterrand – and referred to as Tata Beach by the strutting or sunbathing riverbank cruisers. At night, the Bois de Boulogne comes gaily alive, but do be warned: it can be dangerous, even to the most hardened cruiser.

The sapphic scene is increasingly lively, with good times guaranteed at **Pulp** and even on occasions Le Dépôt.

INFORMATION AND RESOURCES

The two must-have mags are freebie fortnightly *e.m@le*, which hits the streets every other Thursday, and the monthly *Tetu*, the glossy on sale at most outlets. Fréquence Gay, on the airwaves for over a decade, has shortened its name to Radio FG. Found on 98.2FM, it also has a nightlife resource at www.radiofg.com.

For information on Pink TV, *see p308*.

ARCL

Maison des Femmes, 163 rue de Charenton 12th (01.46.28.54.94/01.43.43.41.13/http://arcl.free.fr). M° Reuilly Diderot. **Open** 7-9.30pm Tue. Closed Aug. **Map** p409 N8.
Les Archives, Recherches, Culture Lesbiennes deal with audio-visual documentation and bulletins on lesbian and women's activities.

Centre Gai et Lesbien

3 rue Keller, 11th (01.43.57.21.47/www.cglparis.org). M° Ledru-Rollin. **Open** 4-8pm Mon-Sat. **Map** p409 M7.
A cherished community meeting space, information centre and gay press resource.

SNEG

59 rue Beaubourg, 3rd (01.44.59.81.01/www.sneg. org). M° Rambuteau. **Open** 1-7pm Mon-Fri. **Map** p404 K5.
The Syndicat National des Entreprises Gaies is a nationwide gay-and-lesbian business group, uniting over a thousand companies.

Bars & cafés

Amnesia Café

42 rue Vieille-du-Temple, 4th (01.42.72.16.94). M° Hôtel de Ville or St-Paul. **Open** 10am-2am daily. **Credit** MC, V. **Map** p408 K6.
This bar is the height of cosiness. Stools at the bar for a drink *tout seul*, mirrored walls, nice leather armchairs in secluded corners for relaxing with mates – comfort is a given. In the sweaty basement, camp French classics get the crowd roaring.

Banana Café

13 rue de la Ferronnerie, 1st (01.42.33.35.31/www. bananacafeparis.com). M° Châtelet. **Open** 5.30pm-7am daily. **Credit** AmEx, DC, MC, V. **Map** p404 J5.

One of Paris' only open-all-night gay bars – which guarantees a steady throng of cruisers craning to watch the go-go boys gyrating on the counter. The worse-for-wear head downstairs, to sing-a-long show tunes around the piano.

Le Central

33 rue Vieille-du-Temple, 4th (01.48.87.99.33). M° Hôtel de Ville or St-Paul. **Open** 4pm-2am Mon-Fri; 2pm-2am Sat, Sun. **Credit** MC, V. **Map** p408 K6.
One of the oldest gay bars in Paris, and feeling her age (30-plus), Le Central has seen the bright young things moved on to sprucer joints. Handy for a quick *pression* in the Marais – but on a slow night you'll rattle around in it, the silence only punctuated by the scrape of bar stools.

Le Coffee-Shop

3 rue Ste-Croix-de-la-Bretonnerie, 4th (01.42.74. 24.21). M° Hôtel de Ville or St-Paul. **Open** 10am-2am daily. **No credit cards**. **Map** p408 K6.
Mini-landmark snack bar that's been keeping the Marais boys in *café au lait* and gossip for more than two decades, morning, noon and night.

Le Cox

15 rue des Archives, 4th (01.42.72.08.00). M° Hôtel de Ville. **Open** 12.30pm-2am Mon-Thur; 1pm-2am Fri-Sun. **No credit cards**. **Map** p408 K6.
Despite the kitsch baroque style – what were they thinking with that animal mural? – this is one of the hottest outposts of the Marais, a gay zoo that sure packs them in. Afternoons are sedate, but after dark out come the nighthawks. In summer, they're spilling out on the street by 8pm.

Le Duplex

25 rue Michel-le-Comte, 3rd (01.42.72.80.86). M° Rambuteau. **Open** 8pm-2am daily. **Credit** MC, V. **Map** p404 K5.
Despite all the trappings of a philo-café – art on the walls (changed every month), an educated crowd of students, professors and saloon politicos, the near permanent smoky fug – this small split-level bar doubles up as a championship cruising ground. Pull up a stool and get, er, philosophical.

Okawa

40 rue Vieille-du-Temple, 4th (01.48.04.30.69). M° Hôtel de Ville or St-Paul. **Open** 10am-2am daily. **Credit** MC, V. **Map** p408 L6.
Impossible to miss this low-lit corner café-bar done out in lumberjack chic. It's an undressy, straight-friendly place with a fifty-fifty gay-lesbian split, and there are always a few high-backed stools and soft pouffes free, except during fortune-telling sessions.

Open Café

17 rue des Archives, 4th (01.42.72.26.18). M° Hôtel de Ville. **Open** 11am-2am Mon-Thur, Sun; 11am-4am Fri, Sat. **Credit** MC, V. **Map** p408 K6.
A magnetic corner bar where many gay boys meet up before a night out. The spectacular, gender-free WCs are a talking point. The same management runs

the Raidd (23 rue du Temple, 4th, 01.42.77.04.88), one of the ritziest, sexiest in the Marais, with bright lights, go-go dancers and plasma screens.

Quetzal

10 rue de la Verrerie, 4th (01.48.87.99.07/www.quetzalbar.com). M° Hôtel de Ville. **Open** 5pm-5am daily. **Credit** MC, V. **Map** p408 K6.
The cruisiest bar in the Marais, with a posey front bar popular with beur boys, and a dancier back area full of muscle men. It has just had a makeover and the terrace, at a strategic crossroads, is a vantage point for gay men of a certain age.

Le Thermik

7 rue de la Verrerie, 4th (01.44.78.08.18). M° Hôtel de Ville. **Open** 5pm-2am daily. **Credit** MC, V. **Map** p408 K6.
Technicolor signage belies the fact that this is a spit-and-sawdust kinda place. Downstairs at weekends it has a village-disco-meets-rugby-club feel, the DJ spinning CDs worthy of the finest wedding do.

Le Tropic Café

66 rue des Lombards, 1st (01.40.13.92.62). M° Châtelet. **Open** noon-5am daily. **Credit** AmEx, MC, V. **Map** p408 J6.
This bright, upbeat café-bar sees young clubbers fuel up around midnight on filling Frenchified tapas in between cocktails and shots: plates of goat's cheese in breadcrumbs and the like from €3.50, served up by a bare-legged staff. The noisy techno terrace is heated in winter. Ample happy hours, too.

Restaurants

Le Curieux

14 rue St Merri, 4th (01.42.72.75.97). M° Hôtel de Ville. **Open** 11.30am-midnight daily. **Credit** MC, V. **Map** p408 K6.
This brash new kid on the block is brightly lit by bar chandeliers which draw in crowds like moths. Wallpaper-and-pine-block decor decorate the long bar room around it. The menu is stripped down, a pasta with toppings, the atmosphere hot Latin.

Maison Rouge

13 rue des Archives, 4th (01.42.71.69.69). M° Hôtel de Ville. **Open** noon-3pm, 8pm-midnight daily. **Credit** MC, V. **Map** p408 K6.
This place has had a makeover of blue and a slight sobering down of the soft furnishing, after the designer edge failed to cut in the price-conscious Marais. Will it work? Who knows, but sitting in this goldfish bowl gives you plenty to look at.

Pig'z

5 rue Marie-Stuart, 2nd (01.42.33.05.89/www.pigz.fr) M° Etienne Marcel. **Open** 8pm-midnight Tue-Sun. **Credit** AmEx, DC, MC, V. **Map** p404 J5.
Where gay gourmets pig out on classic fusion food such as Scottish salmon with lemon vinaigrette, Oriental-influenced chicken, and ravioli stuffed with button mushrooms.

Au Tiborg

29 rue du Bourg-Tibourg, 4th (01.42.74.45.25). M° Hôtel de Ville. **Open** noon-2pm, 7pm-midnight Tue-Sun. **Credit** MC, V. **Map** p408 K6.
A beamed roof, glazed terracotta jugs and framed paintings – hallmarks of many a timewarped French restaurant. In this one, in a Marais side street facing a gay sauna, there are gay and lesbian couples at every table. Besides the meaty dishes of the day and à la carte options, there's a vegetarian menu for €15.

Le Trésor

5-7 rue du Trésor, 4th (01.42.71.35.17). M° Hôtel de Ville. **Open** noon-3pm, 7pm-midnight Mon-Fri; noon-2am Sat, Sun. **Credit** AmEx, MC, V. **Map** p408 K6.
Check Rocco de Rubiens' red-and-white wonderland in this VIP lounge-cum-Marais restaurant. And how about the tuna in sesame crust, or cold-cut brunch at weekends? Ace.

Aux Trois Petits Cochons

31 rue Tiquetonne, 2nd (01.42.33.39.69/www.auxtroispetitscochons.com). M° Etienne Marcel. **Open** 8pm-11.30m daily. Closed Aug. **Credit** AmEx, DC, MC, V. **Map** p404 J5.
Three Little Pigs eschews international boystown cuisine in favour of a tasty, daily-changing menu. High quality, so reservation only.

Gay clubs

Le Dépôt

10 rue aux Ours, 3rd (01.44.54.96.96/www.ledepot.com). M° Rambuteau. **Open** 2pm-7am daily. **Admission** *includes one drink* €6-€12. **Credit** AmEx, MC, V. **Map** p404 K5.
Your basic sex disco, cutely positioned next to a police station. The decor is jungle netting and exposed air ducts, the dancefloor surrounded by video screens for idle cruising. Most of the action goes on in the never-ending network of backrooms.

Full Metal

40 rue des Blancs-Manteaux, 4th (01.42.72.30.05/www.fullmetal.fr). M° Rambuteau. **Open** 5pm-4am Mon-Thur, Sun; 5pm-6am Fri, Sat. **Credit** MC, V. **Map** p408 K6.
At this basement drinking den, against a backdrop of brickwork decorated with netting and handcuffs, the cute staff wear black armbands and open-ended chaps. Grab your condoms at the bar and take your drinks to the cabins (each with a lube dispenser), and wait. Home to regular theme events, including Paris' only night for skins. Older, hardcore crowd.

QG

12 rue Simon-le-Franc, 4th (01.48.87.74.18/www.qgbar.com). M° Rambuteau. **Open** 4pm-8am daily. **Credit** MC, V. **Map** p408 K6.
There's no entrance fee but one of the strictest dress codes in town: only the hardest set (doormen favour military gear) get in. Those who make it past the chaps on the door earn a drink and can join the other lucky ones in the backroom, playing in the slings,

Arts & Entertainment

Le Curieux. *See p310.*

cabins and (gulp!) the bath. Get naked on Saturday nights and Sunday afternoons, wear only your underwear on Sunday nights.

Le Transfert

3 rue de La Sourdière, 1st (01.42.60.48.42/www. letransfert.com). Mº Tuileries or Pyramides. **Open** midnight-7am Mon-Fri; 4-10pm, midnight-7am Sat, Sun. Also 6-10pm 1st & 3rd Thur of mth. **Credit** AmEx, MC, V. **Map** p403 G5.

Small leather and S&M bar used by regulars, though trainers fetishists also get their kicks at a special Sunday nighter. At other times, it gets going late.

Gay saunas

IDM

4 rue du Fbg-Montmartre, 9th (01.45.23.10.03). Mº Grands Boulevards. **Open** midnight-1am, noon-1am Mon; noon-1am Tue-Thur; noon-2am Fri, Sat; 6am-midnight Sun. **No credit cards.** Map p404 J4.

The city's largest gay sauna is modern, split over four floors, with a small gym and plenty of cabins and corridors to prowl.

Key West

141 rue La Fayette, 10th (01.45.26.31.74). Mº Gare du Nord. **Open** noon-1am Mon-Thur, Sun; noon-2am Fri, Sat. **No credit cards.** Map p404 K2.

Key West is a clean, modern and cruisy four-floor sauna with a small pool, jacuzzi and – alongside the usual cabins – a number of cages for bad boys. It's used by off-scene Parisians and Eurostar passengers making the most of its proximity to Gare du Nord. Bring your sports kit and work out in the three-room multigym, too.

Univers Gym

20-22 rue des Bons-Enfants, 1st (01.42.61.24.83). Mº Palais Royal Musée du Louvre. **Open** noon-2am Mon-Sat; 6am-2am Sun. **Credit** AmEx, DC, MC, V. **Map** p404 H5.

More sauna than gym – despite the serious-minded buff guys working out – this is the busiest in Paris, attracting some of the best-looking Frenchmen you won't ever see in the clubs. Lubes on tap.

Gay shops & services

Agora Press

19 rue des Archives, 4th (01.41.74.47.24). Mº Hôtel de Ville. **Open** 8am-8.20pm Mon-Sat. **Credit** AmEx, DC, MC, V. **Map** p408 K6.

This browsable newsagent has just been renovated and is temptingly pitched opposite Open Café (*see p309*). It stocks plenty of international newspapers, with a permanent window display of the latest gay magazines. Browse and cruise in one spot.

Space Hair.

Boy'z Bazaar

*5 rue Ste-Croix-de-la-Bretonnerie, 4th (01.42.
71.94.00). M° Hôtel de Ville.* **Open** noon-8.30pm
Mon-Thur; noon-9pm Fri, Sat; 1-8pm Sun. **Credit**
AmEx, DC, MC, V. **Map** p408 K6.
A one-stop shop for your basic tight Ts, sportswear
and winsome classics, plus a wing devoted to
Vivienne Westwood, Bikkenberg and Evisu.

Eric Filliat

*24 rue Vieille-du-Temple, 4th (01.42.74.72.79).
M° Hôtel de Ville or St-Paul.* **Open** 11am-2pm,
2.30-7.30pm daily. **Credit** MC, V. **Map** p408 K6.
A tiny but terrific boutique with tight racks of chic
sportswear, tops and trousers for gay clubbing, and
a window full of funky pumps. Boys on a budget
will appreciate the fact that its prices are somewhat
cheaper than at other Marais boutiques.

IEM

*208 rue St-Maur, 10th (01.40.18.51.51/www.iem.fr).
M° Goncourt.* **Open** 10.30am-7.30pm Mon-Sat.
Credit AmEx, MC, V. **Map** p405 M4.
Sex hypermarket, with emphasis on the harder side
of gay life. Videos, clothes and gadgets, with leather
and rubber upstairs. Check website for branches.

Les Mots à la Bouche

*6 rue Ste-Croix-de-la-Bretonnerie, 4th (01.42.78.
88.30). M° Hôtel de Ville or St-Paul.* **Open** 11am-
11pm Mon-Sat; 2-8pm Sun. **Credit** AmEx, MC, V.
Map p408 K6.

Well into its third decade of serving the local gay
community, this shop carries gay-interest literature
from all over the world; there's even an excellent
English-language section.

Space Hair

*10 rue Rambuteau, 3rd (01.48.87.28.51).
M° Rambuteau.* **Open** noon-10pm Mon; 11am-11pm
Tue-Fri; 9am-10pm Sat. **Credit** MC, V. **Map** p404 K5.
This flamboyant barber, with its house music and
starry decor, is an institution on the gay scene. It is
split into two salons, Cosmic and Classic, where
energetic scissors make it destination hairdressing.
Staff are friendly and talkative.

Gay hotels

Hôtel Central Marais

*33 rue Vieille-du-Temple, 4th (01.48.87.56.08/
www.hotelcentralmarais.com). M° Hôtel de Ville
or St-Paul.* **Rates** double €87; breakfast €7.
Credit MC, V. **Map** p408 K6.
Paris' only strictly gay hotel (above Le Central; *see
p309*) has been in operation for over a quarter of a
century. It has seven rooms, with nothing by way of
a private bathroom to spoil the fun. English spoken.

Hôtel Saintonge

*6 rue de Saintonge, 3rd (01.42.77.91.13). M° Filles
du Calvaire.* **Rates** €105 single; €115 double.
Credit AmEx, MC, V. **Map** p404 L5.

Although this hotel is open to everyone, its owners cultivate a gay clientele. All rooms have a shower, hairdryer, minibar, safe and TV.

Lesbian Paris

With French female sexuality ever more upfront, lesbian Paris is more visible – risqué fashion ads and mainstream films are spicing the viewing diet with sapphic seasoning. **Pulp** is still the lesbian club of choice – on Wednesdays the girls take their turn at the glory holes in **Le Dépôt** (*see p310*).

Bliss Kfé

30 rue du Roi-de-Sicile, 4th (01.42.78.49.36).
M° St-Paul. **Open** 5pm-2am daily. **Credit** MC, V.
Map p408 K6.
Laidback lezza lounge offers (wo)Manhattan inside an old patisserie. For cocktails, *apéros* and weekend discothequing, too. Male friends of this lively crowd are also bar fixtures.

Le Boobsbourg

26 rue de Montmorency, 3rd (01.42.74.04.82).
M° Rambuteau or Arts et Métiers. **Open** 5.30pm-2am Tue-Sat. **Credit** V. **Map** p404 K5.
Named by expat ex-pop star Tanita Tikaram, who noticed how US tourists mispronouce Beaubourg, this scuffed, slightly off-scene and old-fashioned neighbourhood dyke bar has Marais prices – €3.80 a *vin rouge*. There's a kitchen serving *assiettes* of cheese and charcuterie – go on, treat your girlfriend – and an upstairs dancefloor used for monthly films.

La Champmeslé

4 rue Chabanais, 2nd (01.42.96.85.20). M° Bourse or Pyramides. **Open** 3pm-dawn Mon-Sat. **Credit** MC, V. **Map** p403 H4.
The oldest girl bar in town – it opened in 1979 – this pillar of the lesbian community is a welcoming, neighbourhoody retreat for sapphic out-of-towners. There are imported beers on draught, regular cabaret (the Fetish Fantasm night is a highlight) and art shows. It's also an unofficial part of the Lady Di tour – here her driver Henri Paul was allegedly drinking before he chauffeured her car.

Le Mixer

23 rue Ste-Croix-de-la-Bretonnerie, 4th (01.48.87.55.44). M° Hôtel de Ville or St-Paul. **Open** 5pm-2am daily. **Credit** MC, V. **Map** p408 K6.
In this clubbiest of the main Marais bars, music is taken most seriously. In this mixed crowd (as the name suggests), lesbians can hang easy. It's happy hour from 6pm to 8pm; open decks events pull in notable bedroom DJs.

Pulp

25 bd Poissonnière, 2nd (01.40.26.01.93/www.pulp-paris.com). M° Grands Boulevards. **Open** midnight-5am Wed-Sat. **Admission** free-€9. **Drinks** €5-€9. **Credit** MC, V. **Map** p404 J4.

The leading lesbian disco in Paris – and certainly the grooviest – Pulp has also opened its doors to a mixed midweek crowd (*see p330*). The gay girls come out on top with DJs such as UK-French Chloe. Check out the website for groovy animated flyers.

Unity Bar

176-178 rue St-Martin, 3rd (01.42.72.70.59).
M° Rambuteau. **Open** 4pm-2am daily. **No credit cards. Map** p404 K5.
This raucous pool bar near the Centre Pompidou (look for the subtle spray-painted graffiti sign and huge windows), attracts a cruisy female crowd, hard-drinking, militant but non-threatening. Chalk up a cue, or try cards and board games on Sundays.

Cool cuckoo

In keeping with capitals the world over, Paris has succumbed to the dominance of the generic gay bar – one size fits all. **Twins**, though, dances to a different beat.

It's already blessed with an impeccable choice of venue, setting up in the space of the long lamented Scaramouche. This former dark flipside to the nearby glitzy Palace, a one-time favourite of key designers Mugler and Montana, could claim to have inspired the ethos, even the uniforms, of French creations the Village People. After years of darkness, Scaramouche has reemerged as Twins.

Linked with hip design outlets **Colette** (*see p249*) and the **Palais de Tokyo** (*see p270*), this multi-media, multi-storey venue includes a dancefloor, lounge and a large video screen. On any given night you might seen a lesbian short in the early evening and end up dancing the night away at Bionic Boogie or Smile Honey, a post electro-trash night. The eclectic scheduling is the work of programmer Bruno, who puts a premium on the audiovisual work of gay and lesbian talents. One Twins stalwart is computer animation artist and filmmaker Tom of Peking. He has coined a funky cartoon animation style, where sexual politics are never far from the surface. Tom's animation for lesbian singalong 'Gode save the gouine' – loosely translated as 'Dildo, save the lezza' – is bawdy enough to put the Pistols to shame.

Twins

44 rue Vivienne, 2nd (01.40.41.05.55/www.twins.fr). M° Grands Boulevards. **Open** 9pm-2am Tue-Wed; 11pm-6am Thur-Sat. **Admission** €5-€10. **Credit** MC, V. **Map** p404 J4.

Music: Classical & Opera

A new broom at the Opéra but still no base for the city's top orchestras.

The reign of Gérard Mortier at the **Opéra National de Paris** has begun, and with it a welcome fanfare of change. (*See p317* **A new knight at the opera**.) There will no longer be one musical director of the house, but a collection of visiting top conductors including Pierre Boulez, who has been too long absent from the Opéra, Russian firebrand Gergiev and the great Finn Esa Pekka Salonen for Wagner's *Tristan and Isolde*. For all the long-awaited variety, it is bound to be a confusing period of transition for the Opera House orchestra.

For the **Orchestre de Paris** the question of a new concert hall has been resolved, but not wholly to everyone's satisfaction. Dynamic conductor Christoph Eschenbach, who had laid his directorship of the orchestra on the line in favour of a new hall, must be bitter at the turn of events. With their temporary home of the **Théâtre Mogador** still a playhouse, and the **Salle Pleyel** in private hands and out of action for renovation, the scene looked set for the state to approve a new concert space in the 20th.

Regrettably, budgetary constraints won the day and the Pleyel is to be put back into service, with improved acoustics and comfort. Eschenbach's dream of a new hall has been shelved. The two other city orchestras divide their time between the **Maison de la Radio** and the **Théâtre des Champs-Elysées**. Both musical directors are aiming high with the repertoire in 2005, Myung-Whun Chung taking on the complete Mahler symphonies with the **Orchestre Philharmonique de Radio France**, and the venerable Kurt Masur beginning a cycle dedicated to Bruckner with the **Orchestre National de France**.

The highlight of the recent contemporary music season was the world premiere of *Angels in America,* a new opera by Péter Eötvös performed as part of the **Châtelet**'s season, where Jean-Pierre Brossmann is completing his mandate culminating with a Wagner Ring cycle in 2005/2006. Eötvös has attracted a wide audience without compromising his musical language. Contemporary musical creation is a part of the city's musical make-up, in a tradition from Debussy to Messiaen, and climaxing in the tonal abstraction of composer/conductor Pierre Boulez, founder of the **Ensemble Inter-Contemporain** and brains behind **IRCAM** and the vibrant **Cité de la Musique**.

Paris is also strong on Early Music, led by William Christie's **Les Arts Florissants**, whose viol supremacy is unchallenged, with French conductor Emmanuelle Haïm joining gifted native experts such as Christophe Rousset and Jean-Claude Malgoire. Monteverdi fans have recently seen two interpretations of *L'Incoronazione di Poppea*: one was conducted by Ivor Bolton at the **Palais Garnier**, with a debut for French counter-tenor Christophe Dumaux in a production by controversial American David Alden; the other, part of the season at the Théâtre des Champs-Elysées staged by the imaginative Scot, David McVicar.

Lovers of church music in an authentic setting will be happy to discover the **Festival d'Art Sacré** (01.44.70.64.10) in the run-up to Christmas. **Les Grands Concerts Sacrés** (01.48.24.16.97) and **Musique et Patrimoine** (01.42.50.96.18) offer concerts at various churches, while music in Notre-Dame is taken care of by **Musique Sacrée à Notre-Dame** (01.44.41.49.99, tickets 01.42.34.56.10).

INFORMATION AND RESOURCES

For listings, see *Pariscope* and *L'Officiel des Spectacles*. Monthly magazines *Le Monde de la Musique* and *Diapason* also list classical concerts, while *Opéra International* provides good coverage. *Cadences* and *La Terrasse*, two free monthlies, are distributed outside concerts. Other info sources include www.arpeggione.fr and www.concertclassic.com.

Many venues and orchestras offer cut-rate tickets to students (under 26) an hour before curtain up. Be wary of smooth-talking ticket touts around the Opéra and at big-name concerts. For **La Fête de la Musique** on 21 June, events are free, as are some concerts at the Maison de Radio France, the **Conservatoire de Paris** and certain churches. The main music in summer is the **Paris Quartier d'Eté** festival (www.quartierdete.com), with concerts in gardens across the city. *See also pp278-283* **Festivals & Events**.

Orchestras & ensembles

Les Arts Florissants

(01.43.87.98.88/www.arts-florissants.com).
William Christie's 'Arts Flo' is France's highest regarded Early Music group, honoured by invitations from the Opéra National. The standards of the ensemble in Rameau and Lully have become bench-

marks in authentic European performance. For 2005, Christie has brought his frilly Handelian style to *Hercules* at the Opéra National.

Ensemble InterContemporain

(www.ensembleinter.com). Based at the Cité de la Musique, IRCAM, Centre Pompidou, Musée d'Orsay, Musée du Louvre and Goethe-Institut.
Jonathan Nott is now principal guest conductor of this groundbreaking contemporary music ensemble founded by Pierre Boulez. The standard of the 31 soloists is high, and 2005 sees cycles dedicated to Varèse, Bartók and Xenakis, plus an exploration of the work of Mauricio Kagel.

Ensemble Orchestral de Paris

(www.ensemble-orchestral-paris.com). Based at the Théâtre des Champs-Elysées.
After celebrating their 25th anniversary, the orchestra gets back to business under reliable American musical director John Nelson. The emphasis is on classical composers, with Haydn and Beethoven to the fore. Highlights to come include the complete Beethoven symphonies in June 2005.

Orchestre Colonne

(01.42.33.72.89/www.orchestrecolonne.fr). Based at the Théâtre Mogador and Salle Gaveau.
This venerable but underachieving orchestra now seems in better form with a new principal guest conductor, Paul Connelly, who has brought a dynamic edge to the programming. Forthcoming highlights include Mahler's *Resurrection* and an evening under the baton and bow of violinist Vladimir Spivakov.

Orchestre Lamoureux

(01.58.39.30.30/www.orchestrelamoureux.com). Based at the Théâtre des Champs-Elysées.
Revelling in a home base at the Champs-Elysées, and a decade of work with musical director Yutaka Sado, the Lamoureux is still under threat through lack of funding. Their demise would rob the city of an orchestra with a real educational mission.

Orchestre National de France

(01.40.28.28.40/www.radiofrance.fr). Based at the Maison de Radio France and Théâtre des Champs-Elysées.
The firm hands of Kurt Masur have changed the profile of this prestigious orchestra, and performances of the core symphonic repertoire now rank with the best in the world. For 2005, the musical director turns his attention to Bruckner. Invited conductors include Bernard Haitink, Riccardo Muti, Sir Colin Davis and a special 80th birthday celebration for French maestro Georges Prêtre.

Orchestre de Paris

(01.56.35.12.12/www.orchestredeparis.com). Based at the Théâtre Mogador.
Although Christoph Eschenbach and his orchestra go from strength to strength, they are still based at the outdated, unsatisfactory Théâtre Mogador and look set to stay there until renovation works at the

Arts & Entertainment

Salle Pleyel (*see p318*) are over. Upcoming programming features the complete Beethoven symphonies with guests conductors such as Janowski and Previn, a Brahms festival, and a survey of the chamber music of Mendelssohn.

Orchestre Philharmonique de Radio France

(www.radiofrance.fr). Based at the Maison de Radio France, Théâtre des Champs Elysées and Cité de la Musique.
In 2005 the highly respected musical director Myung-Whun Chung and his orchestra are to take on the complete Mahler symphonies, culminating in June 2005 with the eighth in the appropriately grand basilica of St-Denis, and the ninth in the Théâtre des Champs-Elysées.

Venues

Auditorium du Louvre

Entrance through Pyramid, Cour Napoléon, 1st (01.40.20.55.55/reservations 01.40.20.84.00/www.louvre.fr). M° Palais Royal Musée du Louvre. **Box office** 9am-7pm Mon, Wed-Fri. Closed July, Aug. **Admission** €20-€25. **Credit** MC, V. **Map** p403 H5.
A fine series is proposed at the Louvre with a full season of chamber music and lunchtime concerts. For 2005 there's an impressive line-up of international string quartets including the Takács and Ysaÿe.

Châtelet – Théâtre Musical de Paris

1 pl du Châtelet, 1st (01.40.28.28.40/www.chatelet-theatre.com). M° Châtelet. **Box office** 11am-7pm daily. *By phone* 10am-7pm Mon-Sat. Closed July, Aug. **Admission** €8-€106. **Credit** AmEx, MC, V. **Map** p408 J6.
Jean-Pierre Brossmann's reign moves towards his swansong, with Wagner's *Ring* cycle produced by Robert Wilson in 2005, after which Jean-Luc Choplin looks set to bring in more French repertoire. 2005 sees the premiere of the opera *Angels in America* by Péter Eötvös, and a crowd-pleasing appearance by Angela Gheorghiu in Puccini's *La Rondine* is scheduled for July 2005. The theatre also produces a series of chamber music and symphonic concerts.

Cité de la Musique

221 av Jean-Jaurès, 19th (recorded information 01.44.84.45.45/reservations 01.44.84.44.84/ www.cite-musique.fr). M° Porte de Pantin. **Box office** noon-6pm Tue-Sun. *By phone* 11am-7pm Mon-Sat; 11am-6pm Sun. **Admission** €4-€33. **Credit** MC, V. **Map** p405 inset.
The exciting, energetic programming here focuses on contemporary and Baroque – but also a vast non-classical repertoire, including excursions into ethnic music and jazz. 2005 is to see imaginative cycles ranging from music under the Third Reich to an exploration of Kurdish music. The museum has a smaller concert space; the adjacent Conservatoire (01.40.40.45.45) is host to world-class performers and professors, and features many free concerts.

IRCAM

1 pl Igor-Stravinsky, 4th (01.44.78.48.16/www.ircam.fr). M° Hôtel de Ville. **Box office** 9.30-7pm Mon-Fri. **Admission** €9-€12. **Credit** AmEx, DC, MC, V. **Map** p408 K6.
The bunker set up to create electronic microtonal music for the new century is looking rather less redundant nowadays, thanks largely to a full programme of conferences and courses, and the showcase festival Agora, now in its sixth year. Concerts are performed here and in the main hall of the adjoining Centre Pompidou.

Maison de Radio France

116 av du Président-Kennedy, 16th (01.56.40.15.16/ information 01.42.30.15.16/ www.radiofrance.fr). M° Passy/RER Kennedy Radio France. **Box office** 11am-6pm Mon-Sat. **Admission** free-€20. **Credit** MC, V. **Map** p406 A7.
State-owned radio station France Musique broadcasts an impressive range of classical concerts, operas and ethnic music from here. The main stage in the cylindrical building is the charmless Salle Olivier Messiaen, but the quality of music making – from the Orchestre National de France and the Orchestre Philharmonique de Radio France – compensates. Under-26s are entitled to buy a Passe Musique, which offers admission to four concerts for €18. There are free events on too.

Musée National du Moyen Age (Cluny)

6 pl Paul-Painlevé, 5th (01.53.73.78.16/www.musee-moyenage.fr). M° Cluny La Sorbonne. **Admission** €16. **Credit** MC,V. **Map** p408 J7.
The museum presents medieval concerts that are in keeping with the collection housed here, in a setting that inspires authenticity.

Musée d'Orsay

62 rue de Lille, 7th (01.40.49.47.57/www.musee-orsay.fr). M° Solférino/RER Musée d'Orsay. **Admission** €20-€25. **Credit** MC, V. **Map** p407 G6.
In 2005 the museum is running a full and stimulating series of concerts, including Ravel's complete piano works played by Alexandre Tharaud (June) and a cello cycle featuring the talents of Emmanuelle Bertrand, Mischa Maisky and Miklós Perényi. Popular lunchtime events too.

Opéra Comique/Salle Favart

Pl Boïeldieu, 2nd (01.42.44.45.40/reservations 01.42.44.45.46/www.opera-comique.com). M° Richelieu Drouot. **Box office** (*14 rue Favart, 2nd*) 9am-9pm Mon-Sat. *By phone* 11am-6pm Mon-Sat. **Admission** €7-€90. **Credit** AmEx, DC, MC, V. **Map** p404 H4.
Jérôme Savary has done a fine job at this bijou theatre. The reward is its promotion to national status for the 2005/2006 season. Works are in hand to bring the theatre up to date, but Savary is keeping on with performances of his own review-style shows, before launching new programming of Baroque works and revivals of *opéras comiques*.

A new knight at the opera

Known by his native Belgian press as the 'cultural pope', Gérard Mortier (*pictured*), new director of the Opéra National (*see p318*), is no stranger to controversy. After cutting his teeth in Germany, this baker's son from Ghent became director of Brussels' Théâtre de la Monnaie in 1981. This national opera house was virtually off the musical map when Mortier took control, but by renewing the repertoire and gaining subsidies for improving the theatre and casting, he managed to turn around its fortunes. Some still point to the heavy cost of this exercise. Mortier's next move was to the venerable Salzburg Festival, ill-prepared for the arrival of avant-garde producers and contemporary music. His controversial reign saw ticket sales rise.

His appointment as the new director of the Opéra National, succeeding Hugues Gall, was half expected, half dreaded. Gall had been a reliable administrator of the top job, dealing adroitly with the problems of managing two houses, where discontent runs hand in hand with creativity.

Whether Mortier will have the necessary flexibility to dodge the bullets remains to be seen. His philosophy of searching for new ways to deal with cultural heritage splits opinion down the middle. The function of a national opera house, while not that of a museum for routine revivals, includes an element of conservation. Post-Salzburg, Mortier is aware that the Paris Opéra is not the same as a global arts festival, and has even spoken of an exploration of 19th-century French opera, with talk of pieces by Dukas, Massenet and Saint-Saëns. In his first season, national music is represented by the more challenging *Pelléas et Mélisande* by Debussy and Messiaen's *Saint François d'Assise*. Neither piece makes for easy listening. The ticket take-up for the six-hour *Saint François* is likely to be the first challenge of the new season.

Mortier's aesthetic ideals are in many ways admirable, his dislike of Puccini permissible and his eagerness to explore the best of modern production values exciting – but introducing the audience to a repertoire and performing style that he alone finds worthy has a mildly dictatorial edge. His view on opera stars is equally challenging; they are welcome if part of a valid artistic project, which neatly sidelines visiting prima donnas in unchallenging productions of the Italian repertoire. This purist approach is fine for connoisseurs, but bad for anyone who wanted to see Pavarotti walk through *Tosca* just one more time – but these are just the people Mortier wants to help... Surely they'll realise that Janácek's *From the House of the Dead* is a better piece?

Opéra National de Paris Bastille

Pl de la Bastille, 12th (08.36.69.78.68/www.opera-de-paris.fr). M° Bastille. **Box office** (*120 rue de Lyon, 12th*) 11am-6pm Mon-Sat. **Admission** €5-€130. *Concerts* €5-€44. **Credit** AmEx, MC, V. **Map** p409 M7.

The modern building everybody loves to hate, from the disused main entrance to the unfinished *salle modulable*, also suffers from unflattering acoustics. Gérard Mortier takes on the highest-profile job in music and may yet convince the public that this is a cutting-edge institution. *See p317* **A new knight at the opera.** Controversial American producer Peter Sellars grapples with Wagner's *Tristan and Isolde* in April 2005; other upcoming treats are productions of Janácek's *From the House of the Dead* with José Van Dam and *Elektra* by Richard Strauss, with Christoph von Dohnányi conducting.

Opéra National de Paris Garnier

Pl de l'Opéra, 9th (08.36.69.78.68/www.opera-de-paris.fr). M° Opéra. **Box office** 11am-6pm Mon-Sat. *By phone* 9am-6pm Mon-Sat. **Admission** €7-€160. *Concerts* €7-€44. **Credit** MC, V. **Map** p403 G4.

The restored Palais Garnier is the jewel in the crown of Paris music making – yet the Opéra National favours the high-tech technology of the Bastille for most new productions. May 2005 sees Mozart's *Clemenza di Tito*, and Pina Bausch's all-singing, all-dancing version of Gluck's *Orfeo e Eurydice*.

Péniche Opéra

Facing 46 quai de la Loire, 19th (01.53.35.07.76/reservations 01.53.35.07.77/www.penicheopera.com). M° Jaurès or Laumière. **Box office** 10am-7pm Mon-Fri. **Admission** €11-€23. **Credit** MC, V. **Map** p405 M1.

Péniche Opéra is an enterprising boat-based company that produces a programme of chamber-scale shows; it's directed by the indefatigable Mireille Larroche. The highlight for 2005 is a celebration of French *mélodie*.

Salle Cortot

78 rue Cardinet, 17th (01.47.63.85.72). M° Wagram or Malesherbes. **No box office**. **Admission** phone for details. **Map** p403 E2.

This intimate concert hall in the Ecole Normale Supérieure de Musique has an excellent acoustic for occasional chamber music events.

Salle Gaveau

45 rue La Boëtie, 8th (01.49.53.05.07/www.salle gaveau.com). M° Miromesnil. **Box office** 11.30am-6.30pm Mon-Fri. **Admission** €21-€56. **Credit** AmEx, MC, V. **Map** p403 E3.

In addition to chamber music, the Salle Gaveau can accommodate full orchestras without losing its intimacy. 2005 sees French counter-tenor Philippe Jaroussky perform alongside the Baroque music Ensemble Artaserse, as well as piano recitals from Paul Badura-Skoda and Stephen Kovacevich. Elena Bashkirova concludes the season with two evenings of chamber music.

Salle Pleyel

252 rue du Fbg-St-Honoré, 8th (01.45.61.53.01/www.pleyel.com). M° Ternes. **Map** p402 D3.
Closed for renovation. Optimistic claims put the re-opening date as early as 2005.

Théâtre des Bouffes du Nord

37bis bd de la Chapelle, 10th (01.46.07.34.50/www.bouffesdunord.com). M° La Chapelle. **Box office** 11am-6pm Mon-Sat. **Admission** €8-€24.50. **Credit** AmEx, MC, V. **Map** p404 L2.

The eclectic programming here by Peter Brook and Stéphane Lissner is one of the city's musical highlights. 2005 sees the return of harpsichordist Gustav Leonhardt and a stylish range of chamber groups, culminating with a day dedicated to composer Karol Szymanowski devised by pianist Piotr Anderszewski.

Théâtre des Champs-Elysées

15 av Montaigne, 8th (01.49.52.50.50/www.theatre champselysees.fr). M° Alma Marceau. **Box office** 1pm-7pm Mon-Sat. *By phone* 10am-noon, 2-6pm Mon-Fri. **Admission** €5-€110. **Credit** AmEx, MC, V. **Map** p402 D5.

This beautiful theatre, with bas-reliefs by Bourdelle, witnessed the premiere of Stravinsky's *Le Sacre du Printemps* in 1913. Director Dominique Meyer is rightly proud of the theatre's unsubsidised status, and maintains its tradition of quality programming. The agenda for 2005 includes Luc Bondy's eagerly awaited production of Britten's *The Turn of the Screw*, and visits from the Vienna Philharmonic.

Théâtre Mogador

25 rue de Mogador, 9th (01.53.32.32.00/www.mogador.net). M° Trinité or St-Lazare. **Admission** phone for details. **Map** p403 G3.

With the closure of the Salle Pleyel for renovation, the Théâtre Mogador is filling in as a serious classical music venue. Built as a music hall, the Mogador staged large-scale musicals and operettas, even a week of dates by The Clash in 1981. Still, even with 'enhanced' acoustics, the theatre does not make an ideal concert hall, and strengthens the case for a major new music venue in the capital.

Théâtre du Tambour-Royal

94 rue du Fbg-du-Temple, 11th (01.48.06.72.34). M° Belleville or Goncourt. **Box office** 6.30-8pm Tue-Fri; 3-8pm Sat, Sun. *By phone* 10am-8pm Mon-Sat. **Admission** €12-€20. **Credit** MC, V. **Map** p405 M4.

Charming intimate venue where Maurice Chevalier began his career. Occasional concerts, operas and review style shows.

Théâtre de la Ville

2 pl du Châtelet, 4th (01.42.74.22.77/www.theatre delaville-paris.com). M° Châtelet. **Box office** 11am-7pm Mon-Sat. **Admission** €15. **Credit** MC, V. **Map** p408 J6.

Programming in this vertiginous concrete amphitheatre features hip chamber music outfits like the Kronos Quartet, Toyko Quartet and Fabio Biondi, and more conventional groups.

Music: Popular Music

While francophone rappers and garage bands go national, local acts are forced to learn their chops in a live scene regimented by authoritarian by-laws.

So maybe rock 'n' roll isn't the first thing you think of when you come to Paris. Indeed, this is a town where a curfew – yes, a real, police-imposed curfew, the kind of thing inflicted upon 16-year-olds in the provinces – ensures many gigs finish at 10.30pm. Moreover, a new noise clampdown – *la lutte contre la bruit* – dictates that any venue producing more than 75 decibels can be closed down by the police immediately.

But it's not all bad. The jazz scene is one of the healthiest in Europe, with a long tradition of legends (Miles Davis, Martial Solal) finding inspiration here. World music also finds a home in Paris, a global centre for Arabic and West-African sounds. And, of course, let's not forget *la chanson française*, France's contribution to musical culture. Rock bands may have to cut their amps but the *chansonnier* is sacrosanct.

Rock is trying its best. A new wave of exciting, homegrown bands, inspired by their UK and US counterparts, has broken through.

This class of 2004 (Les Prototypes, Luke and Déportivo) offer a Gallic take on three chords. French hip-hop acts, following the established lead of MC Solaar and Marseille collective IAM, have also broken into the mainstream and taken root. *See p323* **Banlieue blues**.

Paris is a stopping-off point for any major European tour, and a cluster of smaller venues (**Triptyque**, **Nouveau Casino**, **Batofar**) bring the best electronica and alternative rock to town. These venues are also getting together to persuade the Town Hall that kids should be able to have fun, and have it loud.

INFORMATION AND RESOURCES

To hear about gigs, check out radio stations **Nova** (101.5FM; predominantly electronica based), **TPS** (89.9FM; jazz), **Le Mouv'** and **OuiFM** (92.1FM & 102.3FM; rock). The best listing details are in the weekly *Zurban* and *Les Inrockuptibles*, whose site www.lesinrocks.com

El-easy does it: Femi Kuti gives it some welly at the **Elysée Montmartre**. *See p320*.

Arts & Entertainment

has a superb database with every concert in Paris on any given day. *Lylo*, a pocket-sized bi-monthly gig guide, is distributed free at **Fnac** (*see p246*) and bars such as **La Fourmi** (*see p225*). For advance tickets, try the **Virgin Megastore** (*see p246*) or Fnac. None of the venues listed below has a daytime box office unless otherwise stated. Get to the gig at the time stated on the ticket. Due to the stringent curfews, concerts aim to start on time, and not an hour after the doors open. For standard rock and chanson venues, entry fees are nominal.

Festivals

Paris

Rock en Seine
Parc de St-Cloud, 16th (www.rockenseine.com). M° Pont de St-Cloud. **Date** late Aug.
After the success of its first edition in 2003, the 2004 event starred the White Stripes, Muse, Sonic Youth plus home-grown talent.

Solidays
Hippodrome de Longchamp, 16th (01.53.10.22.22/ www.solidays.com). M° La Muette. **Date** mid July.
Anyone who's anyone in French rock does their bit for this festival, raising money for AIDS charities.

Further afield

Les Eurockéennes
(www.eurockeennes.com). Gare de Lyon or Gare de l'Est to Belfort (4hrs). **Date** early July.
As close as France gets to a rock festival experience, with tents, three stages and big names from the world of the alternative guitar.

La Route du Rock
(www.laroutedurock.com). Gare Montparnasse to St-Malo (3hr30mins). **Date** *mid Aug.*
The hip and the random (in 2004 The Kills were hip and Coco Rosie random) gather at this pretty port to rock out and scare families on caravan holidays.

Les Transmusicales
(02.99.31.12.10/www.transmusicales.com). Gare Montparnasse to Rennes (2hr30mins). **Date** early Dec.
A hive of musical activity at this Breton backwater, spread over every venue in town (tickets sold for each concert separately), showcasing veterans and unsigned sprogs yearning for a break. Great stuff.

Stadium venues

Palais Omnisports de Paris-Bercy
8 bd de Bercy, 12th (08.92.69.23.00/from abroad 01.46.91.57.57/www.bercy.fr). M° Bercy. **Box office** 11am-6pm Mon-Sat. **Admission** varies. **Credit** AmEx, MC, DC, V. **Map** p409 N9.

This sports arena hosts pop megaliths ranging from Radiohead to Phil Collins. Not really the place for the connoisseur, hidden amid 19,999 other punters.

Zénith
211 av Jean-Jaurès, 19th (01.42.08.60.00/www.le-zenith.com). M° Porte de Pantin. **Admission** varies. **No credit cards**. **Map** p405 inset.
Ignore the skate-rink atmosphere and the logistical headache of two thousand-plus all heading back to Paris via one Métro stop and a few taxis – here the amps go up to the max and the line-up (Franz Ferdinand, Black Eyed Peas) wows 365 days a year.

Rock venues

Le Bataclan
50 bd Voltaire, 11th (01.43.14.35.35). M° Oberkampf. **Box office** 11am-7pm Mon-Fri. **Credit** MC, V. **Map** p405 M5.
Stars of chanson and world music use this former theatre, which also hosts rock legends from Patti Smith to George Clinton. Salsa club at weekends.

Café de la Danse
5 passage Louis-Phillipe, 11th (information only 01.47.00.57.59/www.cafedeladanse.com). M° Bastille. **Open** 11am-6pm Mon-Fri. Closed July, Aug. **No credit cards**. **Map** p409 M7.
If it's folky, frail, expansive beauty you're after, this utterly lovely venue, with its high ceiling and cheery acoustics, is the place to find it. 2004 saw Mercury Rev and Granddaddy.

La Cigale/La Boule Noire
120 bd de Rochechouart, 18th (01.49.25.80.75/ www.lacigale.fr). M° Anvers or Barbès Rochechouart. **No credit cards**. **Map** p404 J2.
Upstairs (La Cig) hosts the likes of Supergrass or Peter Frampton (Peter Frampton!), while downstairs in La Boule lithe young things on the rise get their piece of the action in an old-fashioned rock cellar.

Le Divan du Monde
75 rue des Martyrs, 18th (01.42.52.02.46/www. divandumonde.com). M° Anvers or Pigalle. **Open** *Bar* 10pm-3am Tue-Sat. **Credit** MC, V. **Map** p404 H2.
It's been done up since Toulouse-Lautrec used to amble in for his absinthe, but the decadent spirit of this old Montmartre haunt is still in evidence. Indie, hip-hop and electro-dance gets showcased for labels (Rephlex, NinjaTune) to gawp at.

Elysée Montmartre
72 bd de Rochechouart, 18th (08.92.69.23.92/www. elyseemontmartre.com). M° Anvers. **Open** 11am-midnight daily. **Credit** MC, V. **Map** p404 J2.
One of the many Montmartre venues to start life as a showcase for girls in various states of undress, this is now a top city venue. Large yet intimate, it's run by Garance, France's biggest promoters in France. As well hosting the Rapture and Coldcut, it's used for a warm-up gig for the likes of the Beastie Boys.

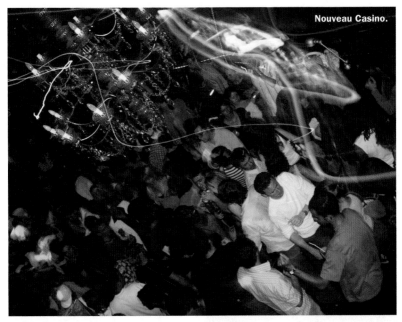

Nouveau Casino.

Mains d'Oeuvres

*1 rue Charles-Garnier, 93400 St-Ouen (01.40.
11.25.25/www.mainsdoeuvres.org). M° Porte de
Clignancourt.* Closed July, Aug. **No credit cards.**
This music hive offers rehearsal and recording space
to new acts, plus a 350-capacity venue in which to
headline or support an Aphex Twin or John Spencer
Blues Explosion. At occasional festivals, DJs spin in
the staff canteen. *See p331* **Clubbing crossover.**

La Maroquinerie

*23 rue Boyer, 20th (01.40.33.30.60/www.
lamaroquinerie.fr). M° Gambetta.* **Credit** AmEx, MC,
DC, V. **Map** p405 P4.
Previously a World Music venue, La Maroquinerie
now hosts alternative rock heroes such as Le Tigre
and the Beta Band. Adjoining literary café.

Nouveau Casino

*109 rue Oberkampf, 11th (01.43.57.57.40/www.
nouveaucasino.net). M° Parmentier or St Maur.*
Box office 30min before show. **Credit** DC, MC, V.
Map p405 N5.
A gem of a venue: great acoustics, a leftfield line-up
(post-rock, dub, garage) and fair drinks prices. Upstairs
chill-out area gives a great view of action onstage and
off. Run by the adjacent **Café Charbon** (*see p231*).

Olympia

*28 bd des Capucines, 9th (01.55.27.10.00/www.
olympiahall.com). M° Opéra.* **Box office** 10am-9pm
Mon-Sat; 10am-7pm Sun. **Credit** AmEx, MC, DC, V.
Map p403 G4.

Back in the day, this legendary venue was graced
by the Beatles, the Stones and top French names in
the Charles Aznavour line. Now it's Sting stopping
by on the nostalgia circuit.

La Scène Bastille

*2bis rue des Taillandiers, 11th (01.48.06.50.70).
M° Bastille.* **No credit cards. Map** p409 M7.
With chill-out alcoves overlooking the dancefloor,
the kids strut and smooch to hip hop, funk and jazz,
and there are club nights here, too.

Le Trabendo

*211 rue Jean-Jaurès, 19th (01.49.25.80.75/www.
trabendo.fr). M° Porte de Pantin.* **No credit cards.**
Map p405 inset.
Part minimo-futurist utopia, part wacky Ikea, this
spot in the Cité de la Musique complex cuts its niche
in all things alternative, from post-rock to drum 'n'
bass, avant-garde hip-hop to modern jazz.

Le Triptyque

*142 rue Montmartre, 2nd (01.40.28.08.03/www.
letriptyque.com). M° Bourse.* **Open** 8pm-2am
Mon-Wed; 9pm-6am Thur-Sat; 6pm-2am Sun.
Credit MC, V. **Map** p404 J4.
A welcome newcomer to the local nightlife scene, Le
Triptyque is one of the hippest places in town.
It boasts open, eclectic programming (The Zutons,
Luke Vibert) and the most sweat-drenched moshpit/
dancehall in Paris. You can freshen up on a sofa in
the chill-out area, away from all the action.

Rock in bars

The Cavern
21 rue Dauphine, 6th (01.43.54.53.82). M° Odéon.
Open 7pm-late daily. **Credit** MC V. **Map** p408 H6.
In the depths of St-Germain-des-Prés, this lively,
atmospheric cellar is the perfect place to check out
a couple of new acts.

Le Gambetta
*104 rue de Bagnolet, 20th (01.43.70.52.01/www.
gambetta-bar.com). M° Gambetta.* **Open** 10am-2am
daily. **Credit** AmEx, MC, DC, V. **Map** p409 Q6.
Here's the deal. You slump on the slummiest piece
of dilapidated sofa and are stirred rudely every now
and then by local lads power-chording away for all
they're worth. Deserves a gander, all said.

House of Live
*124 rue La Boétie, 8th (01.42.25.18.06/www.houseof
live.com). M° Franklin D. Roosevelt.* **Open** noon-5am
daily. **Credit** AmEx, MC, DC, V. **Map** p403 E4.
You sit down, cabaret-style, and watch indie sprogs
vying for that elusive break. Gospel music, too.

O'Sullivans by the Mill
92 bd de Clichy, 18th (01.42.52.24.94). M° Blanche.
Open noon-5am Mon-Thur, Sun; noon-6am Fri, Sat.
Credit MC, V. **Map** p403 G2.

The Cavern.

Downstairs is the home of new anglophone radio
station, Paris Live – bands provide the playlists in
the spacious back room of this sound drinking
emporium. Live acts play on Thursdays.

Le Réservoir
*16 rue de la Forge-Royal, 11th (01.43.56.39.60/www.
reservoirclub.com). M° Bastille.* **Open** 8pm-dawn Tue-
Sat; noon-5pm Sun. **Credit** MC, V. **Map** p409 N7.
As well as club nights and stand-up comedy, Le R
stages live chanson and indie acts, and jazzsters
musically accompanying the Sunday brunch.

Le Who's Bar
*13 rue du Petit Pont, 5th (01.43.54.80.71). M° St-
Michel.* **Open** 5pm-dawn daily. **Credit** MC, V.
Map p408 J7.
Candlelit and full of intimate nooks, Le Who's Bar
seems the perfect place for a lonesome troubadour
to unburden his soul in. And indeed it is.

Chanson

Roll up to one of these places and you could find
anything from Piaf covers to slam poetry, from
experimental theatre to a new *chansonnier*
clutching at the frail dream of stardom.

Chez Adel
*10 rue de la Grange-aux-Belles, 10th (01.42.08.
24.61). M° Jacques Bonsergent.* **Concerts** 5pm Tue-
Sun. **Credit** MC, V. **Map** p404 L3.
The repertoire spans chanson, World Music (often
Eastern European) and anything unclassifiable.
Atmosphere courtesy the house sangria, and patron
Adel himself, surely deserving of cult status.

Le Limonaire
*18 cité Bergère, 9th (01.45.23.33.33/http://limonaire.
free.fr). M° Grands Boulevards.* **Concerts** 10pm
Mon-Sat; 7pm Sun. **Credit** MC, V. **Map** p404 J4.
A *bistro à vins* where serious chanson takes the lime-
light. Performances vary from acoustic, piano-led
chansonniers to cabarets.

Le Magique
*42 rue de Gergovie, 14th (01.45.43.21.32/www.
aumagique.com). M° Pernéty.* **Concerts** 9.30pm
Wed, Thur; 10.30pm Fri, Sat. **No credit cards**.
Map p407 F10.
Artiste-in-residence Marc Havet serenades punters
with politically incorrect chanson, plus a monthly
diet of songs inspired by Baudelaire and Aragon.

Le Pataquès
*8 rue Jouye-Rouve, 20th (01.46.36.44.93/http://
pataques.bar.free.fr). M° Pyrénées.* **Concerts** 8pm
Fri, Sat. **No credit cards**. **Map** p405 N4.
Deep in Piaf country, Le Pataquès deals mainly in
chanson of the old school, with some jazz or debate.

Sentier des Halles
*50 rue d'Aboukir, 2nd (01.42.61.89.96/www.
sentierdeshalles.fr). M° Sentier.* **Concerts**
8-10pm Mon-Sat. **Credit** MC, V. **Map** p404 J4.

Banlieue blues

An ethnic minority, ghettoised in suburban blocks and alienated from cultural life and mainstream politics, finds its creative outlet spitting venom over sparse beats – welcome to *neuf-trois*, the fledging rap movement from the Seine-Saint-Denis département north of Paris, postcode 93. And before 9-3 came 9-2, and bad Booba, from the *banlieue* Boulogne, postcode 92. And while the current 9-3 mob of chancers gets their act together, Booba (*pictured*) has emerged from jail to produce a zillion-selling rap album.

Booba's influence on the French hip-hop scene has been huge. Having cut his teeth in the mid '90s on various local compilations, he first made real waves as one half of Lunatic, co-fronted by him and his mate Ali, known for their single 'Le crime paie' ('Crime Pays'). For Booba, this was not quite correct:

he was to spend a year in jail for assaulting a taxi driver. The release of Lunatic's debut *Mauvais Oeil*, shifting 90,000 copies in 1999, coincided nicely with Booba's. Despite much hype, Lunatic dissolved in the course of a particularly difficult second album and Booba went it alone.

This did pay, as 2002's debut *Temps Mort* became his second album to go gold, and brought him the accolade of becoming the first French artist to be nominated for best rapper in the American magazine *The Source Music Awards*. Once again there was a violence-induced hiatus, as Booba was connected with a brawl in which a young man was shot in the stomach outside a club (in the 9-3, natch). Undeterred, his second solo effort, *Panthéon*, sold 100,000 copies in a month, and became one of the biggest rap albums in France in 2004. In August he found himself supporting 50 Cent at Bercy stadium.

But far from merely being a French take on US hip-hop clichés, Booba's sound is unmistakeably French. Booba creates the landscape of the Paris *banlieue* through minimalist synthesised riffs and off-kilter drum machine sounds – a far cry from the R&B-based US equivalent, heavy on samples and verse-chorus-verse songs. And then there's his delivery. All gruff monotones, in fact recalling 50 Cent, but whereas the American's take on the gangsta bling is one of laid-back complacency, Booba's voice cracks with underlying rage. Naming an album *Panthéon* – last resting place of the greats of the French (white) intellectual hierarchy – can be seen as an attack on the hegemony that defines Frenchness. There's much more to his sound than basic rapper egoism – it is indelibly political. And providing he stays out of trouble, Booba might just be the most imaginative and enduring artist to come out of any grass-roots music scene this side of the Channel.

A concert venue rather than a bar with music, Le Sentier des Halles is where celebrated and new artists entertain a seated, sentient crowd.

Le Vieux Belleville
12 rue des Envierges, 20th (01.44.62.92.66/www.le-vieux-belleville.com). M° Pyrénées. **Concerts** 9pm Tue-Thur. **Credit** MC, V. **Map** p405 N4.
From the terrace you'll get a superb view of Paris; inside, you get accordions, 20-a-day voices and the feeling you've just walked into an old movie.

Floating venues

Batofar
11 quai François-Mauriac, 13th (01.56.29.10.33/www.batofar.net). M° Bibliothèque François Mitterand or Quai de la Gare. **Open** 9pm-late Wed-Sat. **Admission** €5-€20. **Credit** V. **Map** p409 N10.
As good as it gets, with live acts from hip hoppers to underground noise merchants all enjoyed by an up-for-it crowd. Terrace open from 7pm in summer.

Guinguette Pirate

11 quai François-Mauriac, 13th (01.43.49.68.68/
www.guinguettepirate.com). M° Bibliothèque François
Mitterrand or Quai de la Gare. **Open** 8pm-late Wed-
Sat. **Admission** €8-€12. **Credit** V. **Map** p409 N10.
Not the sturdiest vessel to have braved the seas, and
as the speakers have a propensity to cut out, so rock
gigs can be sober affairs. Stick to *chanson* nights.

World & traditional music

On any given night you can see anyone from
Youssou N'Dour (a regular) to musicians from
tiny Afghan villages. If ethnic music is your
drop, you've come to the right place.

Cité de la Musique

221 av Jean-Jaurès, 19th (01.44.84.44.84/www.cite-
musique.fr). M° Porte de Pantin. **Concerts** Tue-Sat,
times vary. **Admission** €16-€35. **Credit** MC, V.
Map p405 inset.
This Villette venue welcomes the best from all four
corners of world. It also does a fine line in contemporary classical, avant-jazz and electronica.

Institut du Monde Arabe

1 rue des Fossés-St-Bernard, 5th (01.40.51.38.38/
www.imarabe.org). M° Jussieu. **Concerts** 8.30pm Fri,
Sat. **Admission** varies. **Credit** AmEx, MC, V. **Map**
p408 K7.
This huge, plush auditorium attracts the leading
performers from the Arab world.

Kibélé

12 rue de l'Echiquier, 10th (01.48.24.57.74).
M° Bonne Nouvelle. **Concerts** 9.30pm Wed-Sat.
Admission €5-€10. **Credit** MC, V. **Map** p404 K4.
Music from across the Mediterranean and beyond.
Turkish restaurant in the same building.

Satellit' Café

44 rue de la Folie-Méricourt, 11th (01.47.00.48.87/
www.satellit-cafe.com). M° Oberkampf. **Concerts**
8.30pm Tue-Thur. **Admission** €10. **Credit** MC, V.
Map p405 M5.
This spacious bar lends its sound system to all
things global, though the focus is on traditional
African music. Great late-night bar, too.

Théâtre de la Ville

2 pl du Châtelet, 4th & 31 rue des Abbesses, 18th
(01.42.74.22.77/www.theatredelaville-paris.com).
M° Châtelet or Abbesses. **Box office** 11am-7pm
Mon-Sat. **Concerts** 8.30pm Mon-Fri; 5pm, 8.30pm
Sat. **Admission** €11.50-€30. **Credit** MC, V.
Map p408 J6.
Bringing in musicians and dancers of the highest
calibre to both its sites, the venue is homing in on
East Africa and Central Asia for 2005.

La Vieille Grille

1 rue du Puits-de-l'Hermite, 5th (01.47.07.22.11).
M° Place Monge. **Concerts** 9pm Tue-Sat; 5pm, 8pm
Sun. **Admission** varies. **No credit cards**. **Map**
p408 K8.
From Kurt Weill to tango, Offenbach to klezmer,
plus theatre, book-readings and children's shows,
this artist-run venue in the heart of the Mouffetard
area offers fun for all the family.

Jazz & blues

Jazz and Paris go way back. The city is dotted
with medieval cellars where you can get your
fill of quality live jazz and blues. The big names
from around the world stop off as often as they
can – and not just for old time's sake. Younger
French musicians, bringing in electronic and

Le Bilboquet. *See p325.*

ethnic influences (Magic Malik Orchestra or Truffaz) make sure the Paris jazz scene isn't a 'heritage' feature, but a living culture.

Baiser Salé
*58 rue des Lombards, 1st (01.42.33.37.71). M°
Châtelet.* **Concerts** *chanson* 7pm daily; *jazz* 10pm daily. **Tickets** €8-€20. **Credit** AmEx, DC, MC, V.
Map p408 J6.
The 'salty kiss' provides a platform for passing *chansonniers* and jazzmen of every stripe.

Le Bilboquet
*13 rue St-Benoît, 6th (01.45.48.81.84). M° St-
Germain-des-Prés.* **Concerts** 9.30pm-2am Tue-Sat.
Tickets €18 inc one drink. **Credit** AmEx, MC, V.
Map p407 H6.
This was the joint where Miles changed modern music forever. Now it's a sumptuous restaurant with dinner jazz and occasional star names.

Caveau de la Huchette
*5 rue de la Huchette, 5th (01.43.26.65.05). M° St-
Michel.* **Concerts** 9.30pm daily. **Admission** €10.50-
€13. **Credit** MC, V. **Map** p408 J7.
Tourists boogie away in this medieval cellar, a mainstay of the Left Bank scene. Quality acts.

Caveau des Oubliettes
52 rue Galande, 5th (01.46.34.23.09). M° St-Michel.
Concerts 10pm Fri, Sat. **Admission** €4.20. **Credit**
MC, V. **Map** p408 J7.
A foot-tapping frenzy thrives in this medieval dungeon, replete with instruments of torture. Jam sessions in the week. Upstairs bar too (*see p234*).

Au Duc des Lombards
*42 rue des Lombards, 1st (01.42.33.22.88).
M° Châtelet.* **Concerts** 9.30pm Mon-Sat. **Admission**
€19-€23. **Credit** MC, V. **Map** p408 J6.
One of a number of venues along this street, this one intimate (to say the least) and with a varied agenda.

Jawad K-Fé
*114 rue de Bagnolet, 20th (01.43.67.73.35). M°
Gambetta or Alexandre Dumas.* **Concerts** 9.30pm
Wed-Sun. **Admission** varies. **Credit** V MC.
Map p409 Q6.
Miles from the haunts of the Left Bank, this place serves up jazzy beats for a nominal fee.

Lionel Hampton Jazz Club
*Hôtel Méridien Etoile, 81 bd Gouvion-St-Cyr, 17th
(01.40.68.30.42/www.jazzclub-paris.com). M° Porte
Maillot.* **Concerts** 10.30pm, 12.30am Mon-Sat; 10pm
Sun. **Admission** €23 inc one drink. **Credit** AmEx,
DC, MC, V. **Map** p402 B2.
This classy hotel venue invites top American names to perform blues, jazz and gospel.

New Morning
*7-9 rue des Petites-Ecuries, 10th (01.45.23.51.41/
www.newmorning.com). M° Château d'Eau or Le
Peletier.* **Box office** 3-7pm Mon-Fri. **Concerts**
9.30pm daily. **Admission** €15-€25. **Credit** MC, V.
Map p404 K3.

While featuring some of the best electronic jazz – 2004 brought both Roy Ayers and John McLaughlin – blues and hip hop get a look-in at this prestigious and consistently exciting venue.

Parc Floral de Paris
*Route de la Pyramide, Bois de Vincennes, 12th
(08.20.00.75.75). M° Château de Vincennes.*
Concerts *May-July* 4.30pm Sat, Sun. **Admission**
€1.50-€3. **No credit cards**.
Well-known names serenade a chilled-out crowd at this open-air venue every summer.

Petit Journal Montparnasse
*13 rue du Commandant-René-Mouchotte, 14th
(01.43.21.56.70/www.petitjournal-montparnasse.
com). M° Gaité.* **Concerts** 10pm daily. **Admission**
€20 inc one drink. **Credit** MC, V. **Map** p407 F9.
A two-level jazz brasserie with Latin sounds, R&B and soul-gospel. Dinner (€50) starts at 8pm.

Quai du Blues
*17 bd Vital-Bouhot, Ile de la Jatte, 92200 Neuilly-
sur-Seine (01.46.24.22.00). M° Pont de Levallois.*
Concerts 10.30pm Fri, Sat. **Admission** €20;
dinner & show €39. **Credit** MC, V.
Ike Turner has been just one of the big-name stars to grace this exclusively African-American stage.

Les 7 Lézards
*10 rue des Rosiers, 4th (01.48.87.08.97/www.
7lezards.com). M° St-Paul.* **Concerts** 10pm daily.
Admission €11-€16. **No credit cards**. **Map** p408 L6.
From fusion to bop, *chanson* to improv, and one of the best jam sessions around (Sundays), this cellar hosts the hottest sounds. No pre-booking.

Le Slow Club
130 rue de Rivoli, 1st (01.42.33.84.30). M° Châtelet.
Concerts 10pm Fri, Sat. **Tickets** €9-€13. **Credit**
MC, V. **Map** p408 J6.
The medieval cellar may be tiny, but it thinks big: boogie-woogie big bands and dance-friendly R&B. One of the most famous jazz hovels in Europe.

Le Sunset/Le Sunside
*60 rue des Lombards, 1st (01.40.26.21.25/www.
sunset-sunside.com). M° Châtelet.* **Concerts** 9-10pm
daily. **Admission** €12-€22. **Credit** MC, V.
Map p408 J6.
Sunset dabbling in the electric, Sunside the acoustic, and a reputation that pulls big names from both sides of the Atlantic: this duo of venues is one of the main ports of call on any Paris jazz pilgrimage. Its small, smoky rooms lend authenticity as well.

Théâtre du Châtelet
*1 pl du Châtelet (information 01.40.28.28.00/booking
01.40.28.28.41/www.chatelet-theatre.com).
M° Châtelet.* **Concerts** vary. **Admission** €10-€65.
Credit AmEx, DC, MC, V. **Map** p408 J6.
When this theatre and classical music hall dabbles in jazz, it does it properly. Its yearly Bleu sur Scène Festival is the place where biggies like Herbie Hancock and Ornette Coleman come out to play.

Nightlife

Morning-after parties might prove more exciting than the night before.

The French are not clubbing folk, preferring a friendly house party or *resto-ciné* evening to bouncing BPMs, sweaty strangers and strobes. Those who prefer to dance with someone rather than face a DJ booth can choose between salsa and sing-along-a-rock-classic, at nights such as Gala des Ringards at **Le Glaz'art** and Le Bal at **Elysée Montmartre**. There are a plenty of standard discos, too: Friday nights at Le Globo (8 bd de Strasbourg, 10th, 01.42.41.55.70), all week at Le Saint (7 rue St-Séverin, 5th, 01.43.25.50.04), swing, be-bop and rock 'n' roll after the club's jazz concerts at the Slow-Club (130 rue de Rivoli, 1st, 01.42.33.84.30).

Purist clubbers should not despair, though. There are promoters and venues that have been battling the authorities and convincing a poorly informed public to keep Paris pulsing at night. The annual Rendez-Vous Electroniques, run by Technopol preceding the main annual Techno Parade of mid September, help spread the word. *See pp278-283* **Festivals & Events**.

Name clubs (**Club 287**, **Queen**, **Amnesia**, Elysée Montmartre) rarely venture beyond house music played to mixed and mainstream crowds. Most of the smaller venues have opted for a combination of house, techno and electro with many adding a live music element to make for a more complete night (**Pulp**, **Nouveau Casino**, Le Glaz'art, **Batofar**, **Triptyque**). Hip-hop and R&B fans will be surprised at how under-represented the scene is in comparison to the high record sales and radio play. Pure hip-hop nights are held in the week at Triptyque and Batofar; R&B is featured at Wednesday's Break'n at Queen, and on Thursdays at **La Scène**. Drum 'n' bass is close to the hardcore party scene although there are mainstream nights such as Meet at Glaz'art and Santa Cruz at Nouveau Casino. Hardcore is kept to squat parties and outdoor events organised by local collectives Mas I Mas and Heretik Sound System – **Le Gibus** run events on Tuesday and Thursday nights. Péniche Alternat (quai de

Batofar. *See p328.*

Bercy, 12th, info@alternat.org) specialises in both drum 'n' bass and hardcore events.

ADVICE AND INFORMATION

Paris clubs don't really get going until 2am as people often hit a DJ bar beforehand. Many visit several clubs in one night and finish their evening at an after-party on Sunday morning (*see p328* **Morning glory**). This can be costly, but free passes can be found on various flyers. Flyer info is available at www.flyersweb.com. Other useful sites are www.novaplanet.com, www.radiofg.com and www.lemonsound.com, for house and techno events. Radio FG 96.2FM and Radio Nova 101.5FM give regular listings. You can also find quality DJing at free nights in certain clubs during the week.

Do go out in proper shoes and don't wear a baseball cap or tracksuit bottoms. Bouncers are notorious for denying entrance on the slightest pretext. Similarly, groups of men might be unwelcome. If you're coming back another time, say goodbye to the door attendant – even learn their first name – as you leave. Recognition is all. If you're in a posey place, it might make sense to order a bottle of spirits at the door. This can mean free entrance, VIP treatment and your own table. Though the price will be astronomical, it works out the same as a couple of rounds of drinks if you've come as a group.

Note that the last Métro leaves at around 12.45am, and the first gets rolling at 5.45am; in between those times you'll have to get home by night bus or taxi.

Club bars

Café Chéri(e)

44 bd de la Villette, 19th (01.42.02.02.05). *M° Belleville.* **Open** 11am-2am daily. **Admission** free. **Drinks** €3-€7. **Credit** MC, V. **Map** p405 M3.
A popular DJ bar, not least thanks to its terrace. Mondays are devoted to female DJs; during the rest of the week, the soundwaves flit between electro and house. Used as a daytime bar too. *See also p231.*

La Fabrique

53 rue du Fbg-St-Antoine, 11th (01.43.07.67.07/ *www.fabrique.fr). M° Bastille.* **Open** 11am-5am Mon-Sat. **Admission** *Mon-Thur* free. *Fri, Sat* €10. **Drinks** €2-€8. **Credit** AmEx, DC, MC, V. **Map** p409 M7.
A buzzy DJ bar/club/restaurant that has just opened a branch in Japan. Local house DJs spin the wheels of steel to the appreciation of a trendy Bastille crowd. Formidable bouncers, though.

L'Ile Enchantée

65 bd de la Villette, 10th (01.42.01.67.99). *M° Colonel Fabien.* **Open** noon-2am Mon-Fri; 5pm-2am Sat, Sun. **Admission** free. **Drinks** €2.50-€6.50. **Credit** MC, V. **Map** p405 M3.

Morning glory

There are almost as many Sunday morning after-hours parties in Paris as Saturday nights. As any adept local clubber will tell you, this is the time when the city comes alive, when the clubbing utopian dream comes true, when stars share their champagne with telephone salesmen, models have philosophical conversations with schoolteachers, a dealer will buy you a drink and no one cares if your dancing skills need serious attention. Why are 'afters' so popular in Paris? Simply because it takes that long for everyone to relax and finally have fun.

French Kiss at **Red Light** (see p330), held Saturday night into Sunday morning, has a very strong gay following with a hard house sound emphasised by extra-powerful lasers. **Club 287** (*see below*) attracts over 2,000 party goers to their Kit Kat Forever held every Sunday morning with resident DJ W.A.R.R.I.O. mixing percussive house to a very wide-eyed public and **Folies Pigalle** (*see p329*) attracts the clubbing workforce to its Luxe on Saturday and Sunday mornings. Be Friends at the central **Panam** (28 bd Bonne Nouvelle, 10th, www.le-panam.com), a hop away from the **Rex** (*see p330*), has a deeper house policy whereas **Queen** (*see p332*) punters end up at **La Médina** (52 rue des Petites-Ecuries, 10th, www.illegalparty.com/Be_Friends_La_Medina_Paris_3103.html). Those who really don't want the party to the end usually find themselves dragged along to Follow Me (**Charlie's Pub**, 24 rue Keller, 12th, no phone), which ends at 6pm on Sunday night only to start again on Monday morning. The **Batofar** (*see below*) has been a popular 'after' venue since it opened and now holds the monthly Miniboum, one of the rare 'after' events interested in the music featured, with global live acts and DJs invited to play minimal house and techno. The resident British DJ, Princess Lea, weaves breakbeats into progressive house and techno, which keeps punters on their toes until closing-time eventually arrives. They have a chill-out area with somewhat more experimental sounds for intimate conversation.

This popular bar has invested in a mini club area upstairs where the city's new electro generation hand out flyers and exchange gossip.

Le Man Ray

34 rue Marbeuf, 8th (01.56.88.36.36). M° Franklin D. Roosevelt. **Open** 7pm-2am Mon-Thur; 6pm-5am Fri-Sun. **Admission** *Mon-Thur, Sun* free; *after 12.30am Fri, Sat* €20. **Drinks** €10-€15. **Credit** MC, V. **Map** p402 D4.

This be-seen bar-restaurant attracts glitzy folk who willingly slide on the dancefloor. DJs spin house at weekends. *See also p201.*

La Mezzanine de l'Alcazar

62 rue Mazarine, 6th (01.53.10.19.99/www.alcazar.fr). M° Odéon. **Open** 7pm-2am daily. **Admission** free. **Drinks** €9-€12. **Credit** AmEx, DC, MC, V. **Map** p408 H7.

The impressive DJ line-up at the stylish, Conran-owned mezzanine bar draws local yuppies; the music gets pumping past midnight. *See p213 and p236.*

Le Troisième Lieu

62 rue Quincampoix, 4th (01.48.04.85.64). M° Rambuteau. **Open** 6pm-2am Mon-Sat. **Admission** free. **Drinks** €2.50-€5. **Credit** MC,V. **Map** p404 J5.

This vast new venue is a new concept by les Ginettes Armées, famous for their Sunday afternoon lesbian and mixed events. The ground floor features DJs mixing eclectic sounds for chatting and relaxing to, while the clubbier basement is strictly dancefloor.

Cool

Bateau Concorde Atlantique

By 25 quai Anatole-France, 7th (01.47.05.71.03). M° Assemblée Nationale. **Open** 11pm-5am Mon-Fri; 5pm-5am Sat; 6pm-5am Sun. **Admission** free-€15. **Drinks** €5-€8. **Credit** MC, V. **Map** p403 F5.

This two-level boat has become the clubbers' spot during the summer with its terrace and voluminous dancefloor. From July until September the Respect team hold a popular weekly Wednesday night bash with free admission before 10pm.

Batofar

By 11 quai François-Mauriac, 13th (01.56.29.10.00/www.batofar.org). M° Quai de la Gare. **Open** 11pm-6am Mon-Sat; 6am-noon 1st Sun mth. **Admission** €8-€12. **Drinks** €3.50-€8. **Credit** MC, V. **Map** p409 N10.

Some clubbers jumped ship after a new management crew boarded this popular lighthouse boat. The change means more eclectic, less experimental programming, straight club nights at weekends and a loyal following for the miniboum after-party once a month. In summer clubbers chill on the quayside while DJs play on deck. A rock venue too. *See p323.*

Club 287

33 av de la Porte d'Aubervilliers, 18th (01.48.34.00.00). M° Porte de la Chapelle. **Open** 11pm-5am Tue-Sat; 6am-noon Sat, Sun. **Admission** €10-€16. **Drinks** €8-€16. **Credit** AmEx, MC, V.

When it opened the 287 was the place to be – its trendy followers have since moved on and the club is populated by a non-Parisian crowd who have just discovered house music. Under new management, so phone ahead. A fair distance from any Métro stop.

Elysée Montmartre

72 bd de Rochechouart, 18th (01.44.92.45.38/ www.elyseemontmartre.com). M° Anvers. **Open** midnight-6am Fri, Sat. **Admission** €10-€15. **Drinks** €4-€9. **Credit** MC, V. **Map** p404 J2.
Although more of a concert venue than a club (*see p320*), promoters hire it for big nights such as the monthly Open House and Panic nights, which attract a thousand clubbers at weekends.

Folies Pigalle

11 pl Pigalle, 9th (01.48.78.25.26/www.folies-pigalle.com). M° Pigalle. **Open** midnight-dawn Mon-Thur; midnight-noon Fri, Sat; 6pm-midnight Sun. **Admission** €5-€20. **Drinks** €10-€12. **Credit** MC, V. **Map** p404 G2.
Pigalle types, *banlieue* bad boys and tourists squelch to pumping and percussive house by resident DJs.

Le Gibus

18 rue du Fbg-du-Temple, 11th (01.47.00.78.88/ www.gibus.fr). M° République. **Open** midnight-dawn Tue-Sat. **Admission** free-€20. **Drinks** €9-€11. **Credit** AmEx, DC, MC, V. **Map** p404 L4.

This '80s punk hot spot has gone through plenty of different styles, settling on house and disco at the weekends, R&B on Thursdays and trance every Wednesday and Friday. The crowd is essentially non-Parisian and remarkably mellow.

Le Glaz'art

7-15 av de la Porte-de-la-Villette, 19th (01.40.36. 55.65). M° Porte de la Villette. **Open** 8.30pm-2am Thur (sometimes Weds); 10pm-5am Fri, Sat. **Admission** €10-€12. **Drinks** €4-€9. **Credit** AmEx, MC, V. **Map** p405 inset.
The converted Eurolines station is a wee bit far-flung, but its strong live programming and theme nights attract a loyal crowd. Watch out for regular dub, techno and drum 'n' bass nights.

Minuit Maroquinerie

23 rue Boyer, 20th (01.40.33.30.60). M° Gambetta. **Open** midnight-5am Fri, Sat. **Admission** €10-€14. **Drinks** €4-€8. **No credit cards. Map** p405 P4.
This eclectic theatre and concert hall has become a pumping club at weekends with minimal house, hip hop, funk and nu school breaks.

Nouveau Casino

109 rue Oberkampf, 11th (01.43.57.57.40). M° Parmentier. **Open** midnight-5am Wed-Sat. **Admission** €5-€10. **Drinks** €5.50-€9. **Credit** *Bar only* MC, V. **Map** p405 M5.

Birds and blokes love a midnight flit at the **Café Cheri(e)**. *See p327.*

Arts & Entertainment

The annexe of the Café Charbon (see p231) is a prime rock concert venue (see p321) and hosts club nights from Wednesday to Saturday. Local collectives and international names play dub, techno and much more.

Pulp

25 bd Poissonnière, 2nd (01.40.26.01.93). M° Grands Boulevards. **Open** midnight-5am Wed-Sat. **Admission** free-€9. **Drinks** €5-€9. **Credit** MC, V. **Map** p404 J4.

Essentially a lesbian club (see p313), Pulp has opened its doors to a mixed crowd on Wednesdays and Thursdays, when free entrance creates an atmosphere midway between a late-hours bar and a club. Watch out for top international DJs dropping in and a regular spot from local Ivan Smagghe.

Red Light

34 rue du Départ, 15th (no phone). M° Edgar Quinet or Montparnasse Bienvenüe. **Open** 11pm-2am Fri, Sat. **Admission** €20. **Drinks** from €10. **Credit** AmEx, MC, V. **Map** p407 F9.

House mecca with local and global DJs spinning harder house music. Fridays centre on monthly nights BPM and Strictly House; Saturdays attract a very preened gay clientele for events such as King$ with resident DJ David Guetta.

Rex

5 bd Poissonnière, 2nd (01.42.36.10.96). M° Bonne Nouvelle. **Open** 11.30pm-dawn Wed-Sat. **Admission** free-€13. **Drinks** €5-€12. **Credit** MC, V. **Map** p404 J4.

The Rex has held its reputation as a prime venue for electronic music for a decade or more. It's Laurent Garnier's home-from-home, where he often gives spectacular 12-hour sets. Friday favours techno, Wednesdays and Thursdays are frequently free. Saturdays feature house with residencies by DJs such as Dan Ghenacia and Ivan Smagghe.

La Scène

2bis rue des Taillandiers, 11th (01.48.06.50.70/ www.la-scene.com). M° Bastille. **Open** midnight-6am Wed-Sat. **Admission** €5-€12. **Drinks** €5-€9. **Credit** MC, V. **Map** p409 M7.

This Bastille restaurant/bar/club complex holds regular concerts as well as club events from Thursday to Saturday. There's an alternative gay emphasis on Fridays; when popular nights such as Eyes Need Sugar attract a very fashionable crowd.

Le Triptyque

142 rue Montmartre, 2nd (01.40.28.05.45/www. letriptyque.com). M° Grands Boulevards. **Open** 8.30pm-2am Tue-Sun. **Admission** €5-€15. **Drinks** €3-€8. **Credit** AmEx, MC, V. **Map** p404 J4.

Eclectic programming allowed this prime club and concert venue to attract a very stylish local and international crowd. Good live agenda. *See p321.*

Twins

44 rue Vivienne, 2nd (01.40.41.05.55). M° Bourse or Grands Boulevards. **Open** midnight-5am Thur-Sat. **Admission** free-€8. **Credit** MC, V. **Map** p404 H4.

This new two-storey gay and mixed club offers a venue for a gay crowd bored of being ghettoised and confined to tacky house and disco. The enthusiastic followers sweat it out to chunky electro, R&B and booty bass. *See p313* **Cool cuckoo.**

Cut a rug to a commercial soundtrack at **La Scala**. *See p332.*

Arts & Entertainment

Clubbing crossover

In an effort to provide something other than the basic three-DJ menu, more and more venues are starting to combine clubbing with mixed media. Artists, film-makers, VJs, poets, designers and dancers are invited to perform and interact with audiences, creating a sort of digital age cabaret and attracting a crowd that's as much art school as clubber. Such events are held at venues like **Batofar** (see p328), **Nouveau Casino** (see p329), **Le Glaz'art** (see p329) and **Le Tryptique** (see p330) in the week, although they tend to launch into traditional clubbing after 1am for fear of scaring away their regulars. What's more, as DJ culture, art and fashion cross paths, galleries bring DJs and live acts to their openings. The **Centre Pompidou** (see p162), **Fondation Cartier pour l'art contemporain** (see p168) and **Palais de Tokyo** (see p169) regularly include electronic music concerts in their programme and no fashion event is complete without a DJ, live act or multi-media artist to entertain the crowds. Crossover venues include:

Ars Longa

94 rue Jean-Pierre-Timbaud, 11th (01.43.55.47.71/www.arslonga.org). Mº Couronnes, Parmentier or Ménilmontant.

This former modest internet café now features happenings in an old metalworks, La Maison des Métallos, whose seasonal Métalosmix has film, live acts, fashion shows and DJ mixes. Their monthly short-film night Court-z'y has become a spot for amateur directors.

Mains d'Oeuvres

1 rue Charles-Garnier, 93400 Saint-Ouen (01.40.11.25.25/www.mainsdoeuvres.org). Mº Porte de Clignancourt.

This vast disused factory turned semi-legal squat at Porte de Clignancourt has studios for producers, artists and dancers by day; by night, it hosts concerts and club nights, with a surprising number of international DJs, live acts and performers (plus regular nights by local label Tricatel and promoters Ping-Pong. The team behind it are soon to open a space called Point Ephemère on the Canal St-Martin.

Project 101

44 rue de La Rochefoucauld, 9th (01.49.95.95.85/www.project-101.com). Mº Pigalle or Saint-Georges.

Cosy shop Espace Lab 101 is the venue for Friday night's Basement Lounge. DJs and VJs interact against a wall of visuals and sound, intimate concerts are held as well as screenings of experimental films and shorts.

Wagg

62 rue Mazarine, 6th (01.55.42.22.00). Mº Odéon. **Open** 11.30pm-6am Fri, Sat. **Admission** €12. **Drinks** €8-€18. **Credit** AmEx, DC, MC, V. **Map** p408 H7.

This old Jim Morrison hangout attracts a Left Bank crowd with house and disco at weekends.

Glitzy

Amnesia

24 rue de l'Arrivée, 15th (01.56.80.37.37/www.amnesia.fr). Mº Montparnasse Bienvenüe. **Open** 11.30pm-6am Tue-Sat; 6pm-2am Sun. **Admission** €10-€20 (ladies free Thur). **Drinks** €10. **Credit** MC, V. **Map** p407 F9.

Music is strictly house – the most popular event is the gay tea dance on Sundays. *See also p309.*

Les Bains

7 rue du Bourg-l'Abbé, 3rd (01.48.87.01.80). Mº Etienne Marcel. **Open** 11pm-6am Mon-Sat. **Admission** €10-€20. **Drinks** €10. **Credit** AmEx, MC, V. **Map** p404 J5.

This club, having lost its kudos with the in-crowd, is now used by tourists and out-of-towners.

Le Cab

2 pl du Palais-Royal, 1st (01.58.62.56.25/www.cabaret.fr). Mº Palais Royal Musée du Louvre. **Open** 11.30pm-5am Wed-Sat. **Admission** Mon-Thur free. *Fri, Sat* €20. **Drinks** €13. **Credit** AmEx, MC, V. **Map** p404 H5.

The Cabaret, now 'Cab', has had an interior facelift by Franco-Japanese designer Ora Ito – but the music is dated: revival nights, R&B and commercial house.

L'Etoile

12 rue de Presbourg, 16th (01.45.00.78.70). Mº Charles de Gaulle Etoile. **Open** 11pm-5am Mon-Sat. **Admission** *girls, Mon-Tue* free; *Wed-Sat* €20. **Drinks** €16-€20. **Credit** AmEx, DC, MC, V. **Map** p402 C3.

Don't bother if you're not wearing Armani, as the door policy is strict. Have a model in tow.

Le Hammam

94 rue d'Amsterdam, 9th (01.55.07.80.00). Mº Place de Clichy. **Open** 11.30pm-5am Wed-Sun. **Admission** €16-€20. **Drinks** €8-€13. **Credit** MC, V. **Map** p403 G2.

The music volleys between R&B and raï, attracting gilded North African youths, film stars, designers and TV personalities. Lavish cuisine, too.

Arts & Entertainment

Nirvana

3 av Matignon, 8th (01.53.89.18 91). M° Franklin D. Roosevelt. **Open** 8am-4am daily. **Admission** free. **Drinks** €12. **Credit** AmEx, MC, V. **Map** p403 E4.
Opened by Buddha Bar disc compiler Claude Challe, Nirvana has a vague eastern theme with the music varying from lounge to Ibiza house. *See also p224.*

La Suite

40 av George-V, 8th (01 53 57 49 49). M° George V. **Open** 8pm-4.30am Wed-Sat (often closed for private parties). **Admission** free. **Drinks** €20. **Credit** AmEx, MC, V. **Map** p402 D4.
Cathy and David Guetta, who made their name at Les Bains, have launched this venture with a lounge area attracting models and their walking wallets.

Le VIP

76-78 av des Champs-Elysées, 8th (01.56.69.16.66/ www.viproom.fr). M° George V. **Open** midnight-5am Tue-Sun. **Admission** free. **Drinks** €20. **Credit** AmEx, DC, MC, V. **Map** p402 D4.
Run by celebrity Jean Roch, this club has become the place for launch parties and celebrity birthdays.

Mainstream

Bus Palladium

6 rue Fontaine, 9th (01 53 21 07 33/www. buspalladium.fr). M° Blanche. **Open** 11pm-5am Tue-Sun. **Admission** €20. **Drinks** €13. **Credit** AmEx, MC, V. **Map** p403 H2.
'Le Bus' has been around for ever (Serge Gainsbourg mentions it in one of his early songs). After several revamps, its still a prime chat-up spot for suits and well-to-do young things got up in their mums' clothes, especially on Tuesdays when women get in – and drink – for free.

Club Med World

39 cour St-Emilion, 12th (08.10.81.04.10). M° Cour St-Emilion. **Open** 7pm-2am Tue-Thur; 7pm-6am Fri, Sat. **Admission** €15-€20. **Drinks** €10. **Credit** AmEx, MC, V. **Map** p409 N10.
This huge venue in the Bercy Village hosts popular disco and '80s nights at weekends for people who don't really like nightclubs but like to dance.

La Loco

90 bd de Clichy, 18th (01.53.41.88.88/ www.laloco.com). M° Place de Clichy. **Open** 11pm-5am Tue-Sun. **Admission** €6-€20. **Drinks** €5. **Credit** AmEx, MC, V. **Map** p403 G2.
After trying to pull in trendy and gay clubbers, La Loco has returned to the mainstream, and has a big teenage and *banlieue* following. The three dance-floors offer house, dance and chart hits on weekends and metal and gothic concerts during the week.

Queen

102 av des Champs-Elysées, 8th (08.92.70.73.30/ www.queen.fr). M° George V. **Open** midnight-dawn daily. **Admission** €10-€20. **Drinks** €10. **Credit** AmEx, MC, V. **Map** p402 D4.

Queen was once a top-notch gay club, but in recent years the place has become rather commercial and unimaginative (apart from evenings when an international DJ is invited to play). The crowd is a mix of unhip tourists, gym queens and business-school students except on Wednesdays when a hipper bunch grind to maximum R&B.

La Scala

188bis rue de Rivoli, 1st (01.42.60.45.64/www. lascalaparis.fr). M° Palais Royal Musée du Louvre. **Open** 10.30pm-6am Tue-Sun. **Admission** €12-€15. **Drinks** €9. **Credit** MC, V. **Map** p403 H5.
This huge central club has plenty of potential, but a chart-oriented, commercial soundtrack attracts a wet-behind-the-ears clientele.

World, Latino & rock 'n' roll

Le Cabaret Sauvage

59 bd Macdonald, 19th (01.42.09.03.09/www. cabaretsauvage.com). M° Porte de la Villette. **Open** 8pm-dawn, days vary. **Admission** €10-€20. **Drinks** €4-€8. **Credit** AmEx, MC, V. **Map** p405 inset.
This circus venue (*see p286*) is hired out for all sorts of nights, the best dedicated to North African music.

Caveau de la Huchette

5 rue de la Huchette, 5th (01.43.26.65.05). M° St-Michel. **Open** 9.30pm-2.30am Mon-Thur; 9.30pm-3.30am Fri, Sat. **Admission** €10-€13. **Drinks** *from* €4.50. **Credit** MC, V. **Map** p408 J7.
A popular haunt for fun-seeking divorcees and veterans not ready to settle down quite yet. Music varies from funky jazz to rock 'n' roll classics.

La Chapelle des Lombards

19 rue de Lappe, 11th (01.43.57.24.24/www. chapelledeslombards.com). M° Bastille. **Open** 11pm-dawn Tue-Sun. **Admission** *Tue, Wed, Sun* free; *Thur-Sat* €15-€19. **Drinks** €6-€12. **Credit** MC, V. **Map** p409 M7.
Latinos and Africans sweat it out in this friendly venue specialising in world music with zouk, salsa, soukous and raï. Occasional concerts, too.

Les Etoiles

61 rue du Château d'Eau, 10th (01.47.70.60.56). M° Château d'Eau. **Open** 9pm-4am Thur-Sat. **Admission** €10. **Drinks** €4-€6. **Credit** MC, V. **Map** p404 K3.
A quality live salsa band electrifies the dancefloor every weekend. Anyone looking a little uncertain will be swept into a frenzy of footwork with free advice dished out to the less adept.

La Java

105 rue du Fbg-du-Temple, 10th (01.42.02.20.52). M° Belleville. **Open** 10pm-6am Thur-Sat; 2-7pm Sun. **Admission** €10-€16. **Drinks** €8-€12. **Credit** MC, V. **Map** p405 M4.
Hidden away in a disused Belleville market, La Java is a mecca for the salsa-loving community with live bands featured at weekends.

Arts & Entertainment

Sport & Fitness

Steeped in sport history, the prime candidate city to host the Olympic Games of 2012 can provide venues for every occasion.

The candidate best placed to host the Olympic Games in 2012 – the decision due in July 2005 – Paris has been instrumental in setting up the world's major sports bodies and events. The modern Games, football's FIFA, World Cup and European cups were planned and developed in the boardrooms of the French capital.

Much is owed to a dynamic, outward-looking sports press, particularly the daily *L'Equipe* and bi-weekly *France Football*. Their fin-de-siècle forebear, *L'Auto*, under Henri Desgrange, introduced the world's biggest annual sporting event into the calendar: the **Tour de France**. Beset by doping scandals, the three-week summer Tour (www.letour.fr) is still a national festival. In cycling circles, many believe France to be a 'cleaner' ground for the sport thanks to stricter local drug controls – yet locals despair of a home rider emulating Bernard Hinault's 1985 triumph. Millions still flock to the Champs-Elysées every July to welcome in the winner.

For details of other major sports events, *see chapter* **Festivals & Events**.

Cycling is one of many participation sports in Paris, details in *Parisports: Guide du Sport à Paris* issued by the Mairie (www.sport.paris.fr). Many venues ask for proof of health insurance, ID and passport-sized photos for membership.

Spectator sports

The national stadium is the **Stade de France** (93210 St-Denis, 08.92.70.09.00, www.stadedefrance.fr, RER B La Plaine-Stade de France or RER D Stade de France-St-Denis). Indoor events take place at **Palais Omnisports de Paris-Bercy** (8 bd de Bercy, 12th, 08.92.69.23.00, www.popb.fr, M° Bercy). **Stade Roland Garros** (Porte des Mousquetaires, 2 av Gordon-Bennett, 16th, 01.47.43.48.00, www.fft.fr/rolandgarros, M° Porte d'Auteuil) stages the French tennis open; the **Parc des Princes**, home of flagship football club Paris St-Germain (*see p334*), also hosts other sports events.

Tickets are sold at branches of **Fnac** and the **Virgin Megastore** (*see p246*).

Piscine Pontoise Quartier Latin. *See p340*.

Basketball

Paris Basket Racing

Stade Coubertin, 82 av Georges-Lafont, 16th (01.46.10.93.60/www.parisbasket.com). M° Porte de St-Cloud. **Admission** *from* €8. **Credit** MC, V.
After leading the San Antonio Spurs to the top of the NBA, Bruges-born Tony Parker has bought Pro A division Paris Basket Racing, where he began his career. Could it be a glorious homecoming?

Football

Paris St-Germain

Parc des Princes, av du Parc-des-Princes, 16th (01.47.43.71.71/www.psg.fr). M° Porte de St-Cloud. **Admission** *from* €14 (08.92.68.36.22; *mobile* 32.75). **Credit** MC, V. **Shop** *53 av des Champs-Elysées, 8th (01.56.69.22.22). M° Franklin D. Roosevelt.* **Open** 10am-9.45pm Mon-Sat; noon-9.45pm Sun. **Credit** AmEx, MC, V. **Map** *shop* p403 E4.

If PSG didn't exist, it would have been necessary to invent them – which is precisely what happened. Starved of top-class soccer in the capital since the demise of the famous Racing (now in the French third division), a group of donors set up PSG by amalgamating local clubs 30 years ago. Backed by TV channel Canal+, PSG bought top stars to win silverware in the '80s and '90s, much to the chagrin of poorer, traditional clubs from the provinces like Olympique Marseille. PSG's raucous following from the suburbs hardly endears them, either. Much to OM's glee, PSG have since lost form, so much so that Canal+ are selling back their shares. A dismal start to 2004-05 does not bode well...

Horse racing

There are seven courses in and around Paris. The full schedule, the *Calendrier des Courses*, is published by France Galop (08.21.21.32.13, www.france-galop.com). For information on trotting, consult www.cheval-francais.com.

A day at the races

With seven tracks in and around Paris, a day at the races is an ideal way to experience French sport at its most elegant and grass-roots level. For course information, *see p335*.

The most fashionable social event is the champagne-drenched **Prix de l'Arc de Triomphe Lucien Barrière** at **Longchamp** in October, the richest flat-race of the season, with total prize money of €1.6 million. Some 15,000 British and Irish racing fans head over to Paris for the 16-race programme, with the big race taking place on the Sunday. The fauna on the *pelouse* is just as colourful as that in the paddock, and women in wild hats get in for free.

The same fashion parade turns out for the **Prix de Diane Hermès** at **Chantilly** (*pictured*) in June, a major international event at which Hooray Henris mingle with Kazakhs in full costume. Picnics are set up among the yurts and races are interspersed by displays of bravado bare-back riding. The full length of the course at Chantilly, with its adrenalin-raising climb at the end, is used for the **Prix du Jockey Club** the weekend before.

For steeplechasing, head for **Auteuil** in the Bois de Boulogne on any weekend in season, accessible by Métro. This is the place where Hemingway used to bet. The free *pelouse* is basic, with a concrete bunker for betting, and no toilets. For more comfort, pay for a *tribune* (grandstand) seat. The biggest event is the **Gras Savoye Grand Steeplechase de Paris** on the last Sunday in May.

The third type of racing is *le trot*, or trotting, and takes place at the **Hippodrome de Vincennes**. Though shunned by the purists,

Tickets are €1.50-€8 (free for under-18s), with free babysitting and pony rides for under-tens. See *p334* **A day at the races**.

Hippodrome d'Auteuil
Route des Lacs, 16th (01.40.71.47.47). Mº Porte d'Auteuil.
Steeplechasing in the Bois de Boulogne.

Hippodrome de Chantilly
16 av du Général-Leclerc, 90209 Chantilly (03.44.62.41.00). Train from Gare du Nord.
Flat racing 40km from Paris.

Hippodrome d'Enghien
pl André-Foulon, 95230 Soissy-sous-Montmorency. (01.34.17.87.00). Train from Gare du Nord.
Steeplechasing and trotting 18km from Paris.

Hippodrome de Longchamp
route des Tribunes, 16th (01.44.30.75.00). Mº Porte d'Auteuil then free bus.
Flat racing in the Bois de Boulogne.

Hippodrome de Maisons-Laffitte
1 av de la Pelouse, 78602 Maisons-Laffitte (01.39.12.81.70). RER Maisons-Laffitte then bus.
Flat racing.

Hippodrome de Paris-Vincennes
2 route de la Ferme, 12th (01.49.77.17.17). Mº Château de Vincennes/RER Joinville le-Pont then free bus.
Trotting in the Bois de Vincennes.

Hippodrome de St-Cloud
1 rue du Camp Canadien, 92210 St-Cloud (01.47.71.69.26). RER Rueil-Malmaison.
Flat racing.

Rugby

Stade Français Paris
Stade Jean-Bouin, 26 av du Général-Sarrail, 16th (08.92.69.21.92/www.stade.fr). Mº Porte d'Auteuil. **Admission** €8-€40. **Credit** AmEx, MC, V.

two-wheeled chariots make for an exciting race and attract a colourful, high-spending crowd. Floodlights on winter evenings add to the atmosphere.

A day at the races is considered a family occasion, and all courses except **Maisons-Laffitte** have an *espace enfants* with games, face-painting and pony rides to keep the children entertained while the grown-ups happily blow the housekeeping.

Auteuil, Longchamp and Chantilly have a free *pelouse*, and grandstand seats cost €3 or €4, rising to €8 for a big race. The major difference between betting in France and elsewhere is that there are no bookmakers, only the state-owned PMU, which operates rather like the Tote. All the money goes into a kitty and winnings depend on the odds at the starting gun. Form and tips can be found at www.pmu.fr, www.paris-turf.com, in the day's *L'Equipe* or Equidia (www.equidia.fr) on satellite TV.

Most courses will have English-language information on how to bet, on a noticeboard or on the back of the betting slip. A *pari simple* is a bet on one horse, for one race, either a win (*gagnant*) or a place (*placé*). A *jumelé* is two horses in the correct order, a *jumelé placé* two horses placed in the first three past the post. A *trio* is the same for three horses. The *quinté* of five horses in correct order is offered once a meeting. Finally, *la cote* is the odds.

Le Stade Français Paris (the name of the team, not the stadium) were French rugby champions in 2003 and 2004. Already on a roll for 2005, the team will probably pose for another *Dieux du Stade* calendar – naked except for strategically placed rugby balls.

Activities & team sports

All-round sports clubs

The **Standard Athletic Club** (route Forestière du Pavé de Meudon, 92360 Meudon-la-Forêt, 01.46.26.16.09, www.standac.com) is a private sports and social club aimed at local English speakers. Full membership is €675 per year, plus a joining fee. As well as football, cricket and hockey teams, there are tennis and squash courts, a heated outdoor pool, billiards table, and a work-out room with fitness classes.

Local top-level multi-sports clubs include **Racing Club de France** (01.45.67.55.86, www.racingclubdefrance.org), **ASPTT de Paris** (01.45.69.01.01, www.asptparis.com), **Paris Université Club** (01.44.16.62.62, www.puc.asso.fr) and **Le Stade Français** (01.40.71.33.33, www.stadefrancais.com).

American football

There are about 15 teams in the suburbs with teams for all ages. There are also 'no-tackle' Flag Football teams open to both men and women – and even cheerleader squads. Contact the Fédération Française de Football Américain (01.43.11.14.70, www.fffa.org) for details.

Athletics & running

Paris has many municipal tracks (including eight indoor ones) of a good standard, open to individual runners outside scheduled events for a monthly subscription of about €4. Details will be in the *Guide du Sport* (*see p333*). Joggers use the banks of the Seine and the parks (Jardin du Luxembourg, Tuileries, and Parc de la Villette). Note that the Bois de Boulogne and Bois de Vincennes are also cruising spots. The Paris Marathon takes place in April (*see chapter* **Festivals & Events**).

The **Hash House Harriers** organise weekly runs through their four clubs in the Paris region. Contact http://parishhh.free.fr or the Sans Clue HHH at http://schhh.free.fr.

Baseball, softball & cricket

Most Paris teams practise in the Bois de Vincennes. Contact the Fédération Française de Baseball, Softball et Cricket (01.44.68.89.30, www.ffbsc.org). An English expat runs the

Château de Thoiry Cricket Club (78770 Thoiry, 01.34.87.55.70, www.thoirycricket.com) 40km from Paris. The **Paris University Club** (01.44.16.62.62, www.pucbaseball.com) has baseball teams for all ages.

Basketball

Almost every municipal sports centre has a court and club. The Fédération Française de Basketball (01.53.94.25.00, www.basketfrance.com) has details. Public spots include courts under the Métro tracks near M° Glacière in the 13th and the Jardin du Luxembourg in the 6th.

Boules, pool & bowling

For boules or *pétanque*, try square des Arènes de Lutèce (5th) or the *boulodrome* at the Jardin du Luxembourg (6th). The Fédération Française de Pétanque (www.petanque.fr) has details.

Some pool venues require your ID or passport. Paris has 25 ten-pin bowling centres; those listed below rent shoes and open late:

Academy Billard Beaugrenelle

32 rue Linois, 15th (01.45.79.67.23/www.aka-billard.com). M° Charles Michels. **Open** noon-2am Mon-Fri; noon-4am Sat, Sun. **Admission** €10.50-€13.50/hour. **No credit cards. Map** p406 B8.
The largest pool hall has 22 US, five French and four UK tables, accompanied by live DJ tunes.

Bowling-Mouffetard

73 rue Mouffetard, 5th (01.43.31.09.35/www.bowling-mouffetard.fr). M° Place Monge. **Open** 3pm-2am Mon-Fri; 10am-2am Sat, Sun. **Admission** *from* €2.30-€5.50/set. **No credit cards. Map** p408 J9.
Centrally located venue with eight bowling lanes.

Cercle Clichy Montmartre

84 rue de Clichy, 9th (01.48.78.32.85/www.academie-billard.com). M° Place de Clichy. **Open** 10am-6am daily. **Admission** *pool from* €4.80/hour; *billiards from* €11.70/hour. **No credit cards. Map** p403 G2.
Historic venue decorated in frescos with a huge bar and pool tables a-plenty. No under-18s.

Climbing

To use any municipal climbing wall, you need to obtain a personal ID card. Take a photo, your passport, proof of valid insurance and €4 per month to the centre you want to use. Those who prefer the real thing can find superb boulder formations at the Forêt de Fontainebleau, 45 minutes south of Paris. **Grimporama** (www.grimporama.com) has full details; the **Club Alpin Français de Fontainebleau** (01.53.72.87.00, http://caf77.free.fr) organises group climbs and weekend excursions.

Centre Sportif Poissonnier

2 rue Jean-Cocteau, 18th (01.42.51.24.68). M° Porte de Clignancourt. **Open** *Winter* noon-2pm Mon-Fri; noon-4pm Sat, Sun. *Summer* noon-2pm, 6-10pm Mon-Fri; noon-4pm Sat, Sun. **Admission** *from* €3. **No credit cards**.

The largest of the six municipal walls in Paris.

Mur Mur

55 rue Cartier-Bresson, 93500 Pantin (01.48.46. 11.00/www.mur.mur.online.fr). M° Aubervilliers-Pantin Quatre Chemins. **Open** noon-11pm Mon-Fri; 9.30am-6.30pm Sat, Sun. **Admission** €7-€14; €4-€7 under-12s. **No credit cards**.

Considered the best climbing wall in Europe, with 1,500sq m of wall, 10,000 holds and ice-climbing. The joining fee is €24, €12 for under-12s. Hire kit and tuition available.

Cycling

Cycling has improved dramatically with Mayor Delanoë's expansion of bike lanes throughout the city. Ideal spots include the embankment, and the Canal St-Martin on Sundays and holidays, when local roads are closed to traffic. The Bois de Vincennes can be reached via the Promenade Plantée, along the Viaduc des Arts.

The Fédération Française de Cyclisme (01.44.16.88.88, www.ffc.fr) has details of the many local cycle clubs. The **Stade Vélodrome Jacques-Anquetil** (Bois de Vincennes, 12th, 01.43.68.01.27) is regularly open to cyclists, and the track at **Longchamp** (*see p335*) is open to speed cyclists when there are no horse races.

The non-profit **Mieux se Déplacer à Bicyclette** (01.43.20.26.02, www.mdb-idf.org) organises free rides for members, €30/year.

Gepetto & Vélos

59 rue du Cardinal-Lemoine, 5th (01.43.54.19.95/ www.gepetto-et-velos.com). M° Cardinal Lemoine. **Open** 9am-7pm Tue-Sat; 9.30am-7pm Sun. **Credit** MC, V. **Map** p408 K8.

Rents, sells and repairs all types of bicycles.

Vélo Bastille

37 bd Bourdon, 4th (01.48.87.60.01/www.parisvelo sympa.com). M° Bastille. **Open** 9.30am-1pm, 2-6pm Mon, Tue, Thur, Fri; 9am-1pm, 2-7pm Sat, Sun. **No credit cards**. **Map** p408 L7.

Repairs, rental and guided cycling tours of the city.

Diving

Courses for the French licence are offered at the **Club de Plongée du 5ème** (01.43.36.07.67), which uses the Piscine Jean-Taris (*see p340*) and runs trips to the Med. **Surplouf** (06.14.10. 26.11/01.42.21.18.14) offers courses in English. **Bleu Passion** (94 bd Poniatowski, 12th, 01.43.45.26.12, www.bleu-passion.fr) organises a diving school and sells all kinds of equipment.

Fencing

For a list of clubs, consult www.escrime-ffe.fr. The fencing section at the **Racing Club de France** (5 rue Eblé, 7th, 01.45.67.55.86, www.racingclubdefrance.org) is suitable for leisure or competition, with 12 fencing masters and 18 pistes. All levels and ages are welcome.

Fitness clubs

The **Club Med** gyms (www.clubmedgym.fr) dominate the health-club scene, with 22 branches in Paris and the western suburbs, including five Waou Clubs with spa facilities. The gyms have state-of-the-art machines, pools, dance classes, plus roller outings, a solarium and even a piano room (at Montparnasse). One visit costs €25, annual memberships from €726.

The non-profit **La Gym Suédoise** (01.45.00.18.22, www.gymsuedoise.com) is an association which holds one-hour gym sessions in ten locations across Paris. Their method mixes stretching, cardio exercises and running to music. Membership is €75-€100 per term, or €10 per session. Unlike most gyms, there are free trials at specified locations.

There are free weekly 'Sport Nature' session of outdoor stretching, aerobics and running, set up by the Mairie at 13 locations around town. Check the annual *Guide du Sport* (*see p333*) or visit www.sport.paris.fr.

Club Quartier Latin

18 rue de Pontoise, 5th (01.55.42.77.88/www.club quartierlatin.com). M° Maubert Mutualité. **Open** 9am-midnight Mon-Fri; 9.30am-7pm Sat, Sun. **Admission** €16. **No credit cards**. **Map** p408 K7.

Home to the Pointoise pool (*see p340*), this venerable centre just off the boulevard St-Germain houses no-frills fitness facilities, a room for step, aerobics, stretching and yoga classes. There's a sauna as well.

Espace Vit'Halles

48 rue Rambuteau, 3rd (01.42.77.21.71/www.vit halles.com). M° Rambuteau. **Open** 8am-10pm Mon-Fri; 9am-7pm Sat, Sun. **Admission** *non-members* €25/day. **Credit** AmEx, V. **Map** p408 K5.

This sunken-level health club behind the Centre Pompidou has some of the best classes in Paris, step and spinning especially; payment is extra for each. There are Technogym fitness machines and a sauna.

Football

For information on the local amateur leagues, contact the Ligue Ile de France de Football (01.42.44.12.12, http://paris-idf.fff.fr). To take part in a kickabout, try the Bois de Boulogne near Bagatelle, the Bois de Vincennes, or the Champ de Mars at weekends.

Golf

The suburbs are full of top-rated courses for all levels and all budgets. Contact the Fédération Francaise de Golf (68 rue Anatole-France, 92309 Levallois-Perret, 01.41.49.77.00, www.ffg.org).

Golf du Bois de Boulogne

Hippodrome d'Auteuil, 16th (01.44.30.70.00/ www.golfduboisdeboulogne.fr). M° Porte d'Auteuil. **Open** 8am-8pm daily. **Admission** €4-€5. **No credit cards.**
The municipal green has one main course, putting greens and crazy golf. It's closed on horse-racing days, so check before you head out.

Golf National

78280 Guyancourt (01.30.43.36.00/www.golf-national.com). RER St Quentin en Yvelines, then taxi. **Open** 8am-7pm Mon-Fri; 8am-8pm Sat, Sun. **Admission** €28-€89. **Credit** AmEx, MC, V.
Home of the French Open, this has two 18-hole courses and one nine-hole course.

Horse riding

To enjoy the lovely horse-riding trails in the Bois de Boulogne or the Bois de Vincennes, you have to join a riding club such as **La Société d'Equitation de Paris** (Centre Hippique du Bois de Boulogne, 16th, 01.45.01.20.06, www.equitation-paris.com), the **Centre Hippique du Touring** (Bois de Boulogne, 16th, 01.45.01.20. 88) or the **Cercle Hippique du Bois de Vincennes** (94130 Nogent-sur-Marne, 8 rue de Fontenay, 01.48.73.01.28). Beginners have the chance to learn at the **Club Bayard Equitation** at Vincennes (Centre Bayard, UCPA Vincennes, 12th, 01.43.65.46.87, www.clubbayard.com). Membership runs for three months (€230), or you can take a five-day course in July or August for €265. Out near Versailles, the **Haras de Jardy** (92430 Marnes-la-Coquette, bd de Jardy, 01.47.01.35.30, www.haras-de-jardy.com) offers lessons by the hour for all ages, with no membership fee.

Leisurely rides at all levels in the forests of Fontainebleau are run by **La Belle Aventure** (01.60.55.02.64, http://la.belle.aventure.free.fr), as well as **La Bleausière** (06.82.01.21.18, http://la.bleausiere.free.fr).

Ice skating

The most popular open-air skating rink is the free one in front of the **Hôtel de Ville** which runs from December to February, skate rental €5. There is another rink set up at the Tour de Montparnasse. If it's cold enough, people will be skating on the **Lac Supérieur** in the Bois de Boulogne. *See chapter* **Festivals & Events**.

Patinoire de Boulogne

1 rue Victor-Griffuelhes, 92100 Boulogne-Billancourt (01.46.08.09.09). M° Marcel Sembat. **Open** 4-7pm Mon; 3-6pm Wed; 3.45-5pm Fri; 10.30am-1pm, 3-6pm, 9pm-midnight Sat; 10am-1pm, 3-6pm Sun. **Admission** €5. **No credit cards.**
Year-round indoor rink with free skate rental.

Patinoire Sonja Henie

Palais Omnisports de Paris-Bercy (01.40.02.60.60/ www.bercy.fr). M° Bercy. **Open** Sept-mid June 3-6pm Wed; 9.30pm-12.30am Fri; 3-6pm, 9.30pm-12.30am Sat; 10am-noon, 3-6pm Sun. **Admission** €3-€6. **No credit cards. Map** p409 N9.
Protection, helmets and skates for hire (€3).

Rowing & watersports

Paris residents can row, canoe and kayak for free on Saturdays at the **Base Nautique de la Villette** (41bis quai de la Loire, 19th, 01.42.40.29.90). Reserve a week in advance and bring along proof of residence and two photos. Waterskiing and wakeboarding can be enjoyed at the **Club Nautique du 19ème** (Bassin de Vitesse de Saint Cloud, 92100 Boulogne-Billancourt, 01.42.03.25.24) and the **Ski Nautique Club de Paris** (01.47.71.76.01) between the Pont de Saint-Cloud and pont de Suresnes in the 16th. Serious rowers can join the annual **Traversée de Paris**, part of the Randon'Aviron EDF outings open to the public. Contact the Ligue Ile-de-France d'Aviron (94736 Nogent-sur-Marne, 01.48.75.79.17, http://aviron-iledefrance.org). For a leisurely paddle, hire a boat at the **Lac Daumesnil** and **Lac des Minimes** in the Bois de Vincennes or on **Lac Supérieur** in the Bois de Boulogne.

Rugby

For a good club standard, try the **Athletic Club de Boulogne** (Stade du Saut du Loup, av de la Butte-Mortemart, 16th, 01.46.51.11.91), which fields two teams. The **British Rugby Club of Paris** (58-60 av de la Grande Armée, 17th, 01.40.55.15.15, www.brfcparis.com) fields two teams in the corporate league.

Skateboarding

You'll see skateboarders around the fountain at **place des Innocents** (by the Forum des Halles, 1st) and on the esplanade at **Trocadéro** (16th), where ramps are available. The **Palais Omnisports Paris-Bercy** (*see p333*) is also popular. Official centres include:

Centre Sportif Suzanne Lenglen

2 rue Louis-Armand, 15th (01.44.26.26.50). M° Balard. **Open** 7am-10pm Mon-Fri; 7am-7pm Sat, Sun. **Admission** from €3. **No credit cards.**

Friday night fever

As brightness falls on a Friday night, the neon-lit square between Montparnasse station and the Tower fills with skaters. Most are in their 20s and look like they were born on skates, easily navigating between the pedestrians. Some are wearing the latest, four-wheeled, in-line skates that sparkle; others, the bulky five-wheelers; and some purists don '70s-style roller-skates with the toe-brake. This is where communal sport and fashion combine – Friday Night Fever, a high-speed, three-hour nocturnal tour of Paris on skates organised by **Pari-Roller** (01.43.36. 89.81, www.pari-roller.com). By 10pm, there are thousands of them, plus roller-mounted cops and ambulances waiting for the bright Pari-Roller staff to give the word. Then they're off, like a swarm of bees taking over the streets. Cars have no choice but to wait until the pack – numbering anywhere from a thousand to a record 40,000 – passes by.

The phenomenon started with a handful of skaters in 1993. By 1995 there were 500, so city officials decided to provide police escorts to prevent traffic chaos. Today it's the biggest weekly sporting fixture in Paris.

Friday Night Fever is free and open to anyone who can keep up. Skaters must move with a fast-moving crowd of thousands for three hours of cobblestone streets, steep climbs and even steeper descents. Those who aren't quite up to speed yet can join the more sedate 'family' skate run by **Roller et Coquillage** (www.rollers-coquillages.org) on Sundays at 2.30pm by Nomades skate shop off place de la Bastille (37 bd Bourdon, 4th, 01.44.54.94.42); the shop rents out skates. **Roller Squad Institute** (www.rsi.asso.fr, 01.42.74.70.00) organises lessons for all ages. For real rollerblading and skateboarding acrobatics, head for the vast **Rollerparc Avenue** (see p340) in Vitry-sur-Seine.

Arts & Entertainment

This huge venue has two outdoor ramps for skaters, skateboarders and mountain-bikers.

Rollerparc Avenue

100 rue Léon-Geffroy, Z.I. Les Ardoines, 94400 Vitry-sur-Seine (01.47.18.19.19/www.rollerparc.com). RER Les Ardoines. **Open** 2pm-midnight Wed; 4pm-midnight Fri; 10am-8pm Sat, Sun. **Admission** €10; €8 concs. **No credit cards.**
This is the best skate park around, with an extensive network of indoor and outdoor tracks for roller-skaters or skateboarders; equipment rental, too. *See p339* **Friday night fever**.

Squash

No membership is necessary to play at squash at the **Club Quartier Latin** (*see p337*), with rates from €20 per game and racket rental from €2.50. The **Standard Athletic Club** (*see p336*) has squash courts for members or on payment of a €185 seasonal fee.

Squash Montmartre

14 rue Achille-Martinet, 18th (01.42.55.38.30/ www.squash-montmartre.com). M° Lamarck Caulaincourt. **Open** 10am-11pm Mon-Fri; 10am-7pm Sat, Sun. **Admission** *from* €10. **No credit cards.**
Period memberships available, plus equipment hire.

Swimming

Pools are plentiful and cheap, some with fine views or historical architecture. Most require a swimming hat (available on-site) and ban Bermudas. Many open late – and swimming to music is integral to Nuit Blanche night in October. *See chapter* **Festivals & Events.**

Aquaboulevard

4 rue Louis-Armand, 15th (01.40.60.15.15/www. aquaboulevard.com). M° Balard/RER Bd Victor. **Open** 9am-11pm daily. **Admission** *six hours* €20; €10 concs. **No credit cards. Map** p406 A10.
With year-round summer temperatures, this tropical water park under a giant atrium is great fun for kids. An extra charge gets you a steam bath and three saunas of varying intensity.

Piscine Butte-aux-Cailles

5 pl Paul-Verlaine, 13th (01.45.89.60.05). M° Place d'Italie. **Open** 7-8am, 11.30am-1pm, 4.30-6.30pm Tue; 7am-6.30pm Wed; 7-8am, 11.30am-6pm Thur, Fri; 7-8am, 10am-6pm Sat; 8am-5.30pm Sun. **Admission** €2.40; €1.35 concs. **No credit cards.**
This listed complex built in the 1920s has one main indoor pool and two outdoor pools. The water is a warm 28°C thanks to the natural sulphurous spring.

Piscine Georges-Vallery

148 av Gambetta, 20th (01.40.31.15.20). M° Porte des Lilas. **Open** 10am-5pm Mon, Fri; 10am-10pm Tue, Thur; 10am-5pm Weds; 9am-5pm Sat, Sun. **Admission** €3.95, €3.20 concs. **No credit cards.**

Built for the 1924 Olympics, this complex features a retractable Plexiglas roof, a 50-m pool and one for kids. Due to reopen in April 2005 after renovation.

Piscine Jean-Taris

16 rue Thouin, 5th (01.55.42.81.90). M° Cardinal Lemoine. **Open** 7-8am, 11.30am-1pm Tue, Thur; 7-8am, 11.30am-5.30pm Wed; 7-8am, 11.30am-1pm, 5-8pm Fri; 7am-5.30pm Sat; 8am-5.30pm Sun. **Admission** €2.40; €1.35 concs. **No credit cards. Map** p408 J8.
This 25m pool has huge bay windows overlooking a sloping garden, and with the Panthéon visible just above the trees. Mixed showers and locker area.

Piscine Pontoise Quartier Latin

18 rue de Pontoise, 5th (01.55.42.77.88/www.club quartierlatin.com). M° Maubert Mutualité. **Open** 7-8.30am, 12.15-1.30pm, 4.30-11.45pm Mon, Tue; 7-8.30am, 12.15-11.45pm Wed; 7-8.30am, 12.15-1.30pm, 4.30-7.15pm, 9-11.45pm Thur; 7-8.45am, noon-1.30pm, 4.30-8pm, 9-11.45pm Fri; 10am-7pm Sat; 8am-7pm Sun. **Admission** €3.80; €3.35 concs; €9 9-11.45pm. **No credit cards. Map** p408 K7.
This beautiful art deco pool has two mezzanine levels with private locker rooms, plus night swimming to underwater music. Small fee for lockers.

Piscine Suzanne-Berlioux

Forum des Halles, 10 pl de la Rotonde, 1st (01.42. 36.98.44). M° Les Halles. **Open** 11.30am-10pm Mon, Tue, Thur, Fri; 10am-10pm Wed; 9am-7pm Sat, Sun. **Admission** €3.80; €3 under-16s. **No credit cards. Map** p404 J5.
This 50m pool with its own tropical greenhouse is good for lap swimming – but there are no lockers (check your belongings in to the attendants).

Tennis & table tennis

It used to be impossible to reserve a council court unless you had a special card. But thanks to the new Paris Tennis system, you can register a password and reserve a court online (www.tennis.paris.fr) or on 01.71.71.70.70. Fees are €5.75 per hour, €11.40 indoor. Among the 44 municipal courts, the six at the **Jardin du Luxembourg** (01.43.25. 79.18) are good, but there's a better selection at the **Centre Sportif La Falguère** (route de la Pyramide, 01.43. 74.40.93) at the Bois de Vincennes, with 22 courts, of which eight are acrylic. There are even two covered clay courts at the **Centre Sportif Suzanne-Lenglen** (*see p338*).
To find public table-tennis tables in parks around town, consult the *Guide du Sport* (*see p333*). Club information is at www.paristt.com.

Club Forest Hill

4 rue Louis-Armand, 15th (01.40.60.10.00/www. aquaboulevard.com). M° Balard/RER Bd Victor. **Open** 9am-11pm daily. **Admission** varies. **No credit cards. Map** p406 A10.
Twelve branches in and around Paris.

Theatre

Grand, absurd or politically challenging, there's no shortage of drama here – just fewer anglophone troupes to practise it.

Paris is rich in dramatic history. From moody medieval plays to revolutionary street theatre in 1968, French drama has always mirrored, shaped and commented on French society. Paris has led the pack in the development of new acting styles, popular dramatic movements and landmark theatre buildings.

Two stalwarts of theatrical tradition, the **Comédie Française** on the Right Bank and the **Théâtre de la Huchette** on the Left, have repertoires which have defined French drama, from the neoclassicists to the Theatre of the Absurd. Beyond these, nearly native Peter Brook still reigns as an influential director at **Les Bouffes du Nord**, featuring smart programming with global flair. To the east in the Bois de Vincennes, the **Cartoucherie** is a factory turned theatre commune with five resident companies, accessible by a theatre bus; *see p342* **Five go down to the woods**.

Just south of Bastille is the petite **Théâtre de l'Opprimé**, a pocket-sized theatre with lofty productions. There are often more actors on stage than spectators, but the company tackles important issues, and demonstrates directorial and comedic prowess. For more

experimental theatres, such as the legendary **Café de la Gare**, *see pp284-286* **Cabaret, Circus & Comedy**.

Outside the centre, the **Théâtre Gérard-Philipe** (93207 St Denis, 55 bd Jules Guesde, 01.48.13.70.00, www.theatregerardphilipe. com), housed in a century-old building, offers quality fare for the 2005 spring season, including the Festival Jeune Public for youngsters. In the north-east, the **MC93 Bobigny** (93000 Bobigny, 1 bd Lénine, 01.41.60.72.72, www.mc93.com) is a slick institution dedicated to promoting global cross-cultural exchange.

Productions in English, German and Spanish come to the **Odéon**, Bouffes du Nord, **Théâtre de la Cité Internationale**, and the stage at the **Centre Georges Pompidou** (www.cnac-gp.com). Numbers of local English-language troupes, though, have dwindled. Led by Kim Broderick, **One World Actors Productions** (www.oneworldactors.com) is the principal source of anglophone theatre. Shakespeare is performed in June at the Bois de Boulogne's pleasant **Théâtre de Verdure du Jardin Shakespeare** (08.20.00.75.75) by London's Tower Theatre Company (www.towertheatre.org.uk).

TICKETS AND INFORMATION

For details of scheduling and programming, look in the Theatre section of the weekly *L'Officiel des Spectacles*. Further information can be found at www.parisvoice.com. Tickets can be bought at the theatres directly, at **Fnac** or the **Virgin Megastore** (for both, *see p246*) and at www.theatreonline.com. Check www.theatresprives.com for half-price tickets to performances at many of the private theatres during the first week of a new show. Two agencies which sell same-day tickets at half price are **Kiosque de la Madeleine** (15 pl de la Madeleine, 8th, closed Mon); and Kiosque Montparnasse (parvis de la Gare Montparnasse, 15th, closed Mon). These agency tickets, however, tend to be for commercial offerings. Queues can be long, and there's no way to contact the kiosks by phone or internet. For students, special subscriptions are available at many theatres, and almost all offer same-day rates with significant reductions.

La Comédie Française. *See p342.*

Five go down to the woods

Théâtre du Soleil.

Past the Château and the Parc Floral, buried deep in the Bois de Vincennes, is a drama-lover's paradise, an idyllic complex of five theatres which features relentlessly new, exciting spectacles: the Cartoucherie. This ex-army munitions warehouses (note the stone guard's hut as you enter the grounds) could not be better located – in bucolic meadows, with a rope swing and stables.

The best known of the quintet is the **Théâtre du Soleil** (01.43.74.87.63, www.theatre-du-soleil.fr), a troupe born in the political strife of the mid-1960s. Since then, the group has been producing unabashedly political, technically decadent spectacles at the rate of one every three or four years. The rehearsal process is long and thorough, including extensive international research done by the whole team. The Soleil runs as a collective (everyone is included in all aspects of production, from set-building to music-making), but the productions are largely shaped by de facto leader Ariane Mnouchkine; not only does she serve as director, she even dishes up food during the intermission.

The Théâtre du Soleil's work is Brechtian in nature, a true example of epic theatre – using puppets, masks and onstage musicians to distance the spectators, the troupe creates an arena of reflection. The stories they tell focus on ancient Chinese myths, contemporary refugee crises and more. When the company is in Paris (and not on tour) they are a must-see.

Right Bank

Les Bouffes du Nord
37bis bd de la Chapelle, 10th (01.46.07.34.50/ www.bouffesdunord.com). M° La Chapelle. **Box office** 11am-6pm Mon-Sat. **Admission** €8-€24.50. **Credit** MC, V. **Map** p404 K2.
Theatre worshippers cannot come to Paris without paying tribute to director Peter Brook, whose experimental company CICT is based at this unrenovated venue. Stéphane Lissner's co-direction has added classical music and opera.

Cartoucherie de Vincennes
Route du Champ de Manoeuvre, bois de Vincennes, 12th. M° Château de Vincennes, then shuttle bus or bus 112.
Five independent theatres housed in old munitions warehouses. *See above* **Five go down to the woods**.

Comédie Française
www.comedie-francaise.fr.
Salle Richelieu *1 pl Colette, 1st (08.25.10.16.80). M° Palais Royal Musée du Louvre.* **Box Office** 11am-6pm daily. **Admission** €11-€30; €10 under-27s (1hr before play). **Credit** AmEx, MC, V. **Map** p403 H5.

The four other residents are as inspiring. The **Théâtre de l'Aquarium** (01.43.74.99.61, www.theatredelaquarium.com) was started in 1963 by students at the Ecole Normale Supérieure. From that upper-crust background they delved into the realm of radical street theatre. 2005 includes productions of *Timon of Athens*, and a reprise of artistic director Julie Bohen's successful 2004 staging of *Uncle Vanya*. The **Théâtre de la Tempête** (01.43.28.36.36, www.la-tempete.fr) derives its name from Aimé Césaire's adaptation of Shakespeare's last play. Founded in 1970, today it is led by director/playwright Philippe Adrien. In their two performance spaces, the Tempête produce new plays from around the globe as well as contemporary French works. The **Théâtre de l'Epée de Bois** (01.48.08.39.74) and the **Théâtre du Chaudron** (01.43.28.97.04) complete the Cartoucherie quintet. June 2005 sees the *Rencontres à la Cartoucherie*, a gathering of more than 150 actors, writers and directors meeting to discuss the state of performance and theatre's role in society.

Théâtre de l'Aquarium.

Performing in sheds, old warehouses and factories on the outskirts of town, these troupes have revised not only the purpose of theatre but the definition of theatre spaces. For spectators, this means a free bus through the woods to a beautiful forest setting, home-made soup and bread in the lobby, a starlit backdrop – and challenging, politically committed theatre.

Studio Theatre *galerie du Carrousel du Louvre, 99 rue de Rivoli, 1st (01.44.58.98.54). M Palais Royal Musée du Louvre*. **Box office** 5.30pm on day. **Admission** €13; €7.50 under-27s. **Credit** MC, V. **Map** p403 H5.
Théâtre du Vieux Colombier *21 rue du Vieux Colombier, 6th (01.44.39.87.00). Mᵒ St Sulpice*. **Box office** 1-6pm Mon, Sun; 11am-7pm Tue-Sat. **Admission** €26; €19 over-60s; €13 under-27s. **Credit** MC, V. **Map** p407 G7.
The gilded mother of all French theatres, the Comédie Française turns out season after season of classics, as well as lofty new productions. The red velvet and

gold-flecked Salle Richelieu is located right by the Palais-Royal; under the same umbrella are the the Studio, a black box inside the Carrousel du Louvre, and the Théâtre du Vieux Colombier. Spring 2005's line-up includes *Tartuffe* and *Le Malade Imaginaire*; their author Molière suffered a fatal coughing fit while performing the latter here 330 years ago.

Théâtre de l'Athénée-Louis Jouvet

7 rue Boudreau, square de l'Opéra Louis Jouvet, 9th (01.53.05.19.19/www.athenee-theatre.com). Mᵒ Opéra. **Box office** 1-7pm Mon-Sat. **Admission** €6-€28. **Credit** MC, V. **Map** p403 G4.

Arts & Entertainment

This theatre is among the most beautiful in France, its Italianate decor like the interior of a jewellery box. The Athénée's mission stages new spins on classic works; the 2005 season boasts Kleist's *Prince of Homburg* and Genet's *Le Balcon*.

Théâtre de la Bastille
76 rue de la Roquette, 11th (01.43.57.42.14/ www.theatre-bastille.com). M° Voltaire. **Box office** 10am-6pm Mon-Fri; 2-6pm Sat. **Admission** €12.50-€19. **Credit** MC, V. **Map** p409 N6.
Effervescent, exotic productions are emblematic of the kind of spirit found here; the Bastille is a little smaller, a little edgier, and a bit funkier than many of the more grand Parisian theatres.

Théâtre National de Chaillot
1 pl du Trocadéro, 16th (01.53.65.30.00/www. theatre-chaillot.fr). M° Trocadéro. **Box office** 11am-7pm Mon-Sat; 1-5pm Sun. **Admission** €9-€39. **Credit** MC, V. **Map** p402 B4.
Get here early and grab a cocktail; the lobby has a huge window with an Eiffel Tower view. Highlights for 2005 include virtuoso director Deborah Warner's newest project (in English) in May and June; Robert LePage brings his pensive solo piece *La Face Cachée de la Lune* in early summer. Three auditoria range from an intimate, experimental space to a 2,800-seater.

Théâtre de l'Opprimé
78 rue du Charolais, 12th (01.43.40.44.44/ www.theatredelopprime.net). M° Dugommier. **Box office** 1hr before show. **Admission** €10-€15. **No credit cards**. **Map** p409 P9.
This small theatre with great vision borrows its name – and vision – from Brazil's Augusto Boal, who believed that theatre can change the world. The repertory is largely contemporary, their methods inspired by Boal, and the troupe offers workshops in his technique and teachings.

Théâtre de la Ville
2 pl du Châtelet, 4th (01.42.74.22.77/www.theatre delaville-paris.com). M° Châtelet. **Box office** 11am-7pm Mon; 11am-8pm Tue-Sat. **Admission** €11.50-€30. **Credit** MC, V. **Map** p408 J6.
The 'city theatre' turns out the most consistently innovative and stimulating programming in Paris. Instead of running a standard rep company, the house imports music, dance and theatre productions from the classics to the avant-garde.

Left Bank

Odéon, Théâtre de L'Europe
Until late 2005: Ateliers Berthier, 36 bd Berthier, 17th (01.44.85.40.00/www.theatre-odeon.fr). M° Porte de Clichy. **Box office** *By phone* 11am-6.30pm Mon-Sat. *On site* 2hrs before show. **Admission** €13-€26. **Credit** MC, V.
In May 1968 the Odéon was occupied by striking students and workers, a black anarchist flag was flown from the roof and a banner declaring 'L'Odéon est ouvert' was draped over its sculpted façade. The

Odéon is again sheathed, closed for renovation until the end of 2005. The company lives on, producing consistently smart, well-executed productions at the Ateliers Berthier, the space where the Paris Opéra rehearse. The agenda for 2005 sees productions of Ibsen's *Hedda Gabler* and *Peer Gynt* and an eclectic international programme.

Théâtre de la Cité Internationale
21 bd Jourdan, 14th (01.43.13.50.50/www.theatrede lacite.com). RER Cité Universitaire. **Box office** 1hr before show. **Admission** €9.50-€19. **Credit** MC, V.
A polished professional theatre on the campus of the Cité Universitaire, the Théâtre de la Cité displays an international flair worthy of its setting. The 2005 season includes Lorca's *The House of Bernarda Alba* and de Ghelderode's *L'Ecole des Bouffons*. In addition to the main theatre and dance season, the prestigious Ecole du Théâtre National de Strasbourg occupies the stage for a short stint each summer.

Théâtre de la Huchette
23 rue de la Huchette, 5th (01.43.26.38.99). M° St-Michel. **Box office** 5-9pm Mon-Sat. **Admission** €18; €13 concessions. **Credit** MC, V. **Map** p408 J7.
Eugene Ionesco's absurdist classic *La Cantatrice Chauve* ('The Bald Soprano') premiered in Paris in 1950; Nicolas Bataille first staged the play at this tiny theatre in 1957. While the actors have changed, the same production plays, on a double bill (€28/€20) with another of Ionesco's plays, *La Leçon*. Each runs just short of an hour. A reasonable level of French should get you through the evening.

Bald is best: **Théâtre de la Huchette**.

Trips Out of Town

Trips Out of Town

Visit soaring Gothic spires, swinging riverside dances, the sumptuous palace of the Sun King – or the tiny attic of a tortured artist.

The Loire Valley splendour of the **Château de Villandry**. *See p362*.

Day Trips

Auvers-sur-Oise

This charming rural retreat was where Van Gogh spent his last weeks, painting frantically. Many of his most well-known works, of crows over wheatfields or the local church, were completed here and are now displayed on illustrated panels around the village, allowing you to compare them to their locations today.

The tiny attic room at the **Auberge Ravoux** that Vincent rented in May 1890 for 3.50 francs is open to the public and gives an evocative sense of the artist's stay. Previous Auvers residents had included Camille Pissarro, Paul Cézanne and Charles Daubigny, whose widow was still living in the village when Van Gogh arrived – he painted their garden. Today you can visit Daubigny's museum (Manoir des Colombières, 01.30.36.80.20) and studio (61 rue Daubigny, 01.34.48.03.03), still decorated with his murals.

A further attraction here, linked with the artistic community of the day, is the Absinthe Museum (44 rue Callé, 01.30.36.83.26), a modest collection of art and artefacts related to the favoured drink of the late 19th century. Since banned in France, the lethal green concoction is not available at the replica café-bar upstairs.

Local artistic legacy has not been overlooked by Auvers' main historical attraction either. The 17th-century Château d'Auvers (01.34.48.48.50) features a walk-through tour (for which visitors must wear a special helmet) themed around the Impressionists and their surroundings.

Auberge Ravoux

52 rue du Général-de-Gaulle, 95430 Auvers-sur-Oise (01.30.36.60.60). **Open** 10am-6pm Tue-Sun. **Admission** €5. **No credit cards**.

Where to eat & stay

You can always do as Vincent might have done, and dined at the **Auberge Ravoux** itself (*see above*) – these days they serve two traditional courses for €23, three for €30. **La Guinguette** (rue de Léry, 01.34.48.43.29) can rustle up lunch for €15. The **Hostellerie du Nord** (6 rue Général-de-Gaulle, 01.30.36.70.74; closed Sat lunch, Sun eve, Mon) have master chef Joël Boilleaut running the kitchen – there's a menu for €45. Upstairs are eight comfy rooms (www.hostelleriedunord.fr) for €92-€122 each.

Getting there

By car
35km north from Paris by the A15, exit 7, then N184 exit Méry-sur-Oise for Auvers.

By train
From Gare du Nord, changing at St Ouen L'Aumone (whole journey takes about 1hr).

Chantilly

From the 14th century until 1897, the town of Chantilly was the domain of the Princes of Condé, the cousins of the French kings. As well

as its impressive **château**, Chantilly has a rich equestrian history, with its hunting forests and prestigious horse-racing centres.

The cream-coloured château stands as a fine example of the French Renaissance, its domes and turrets set high above the surrounding lake. In reality, much of the original palace was destroyed during the Revolution, leaving the main wing to be reconstructed in the 19th century by Henri d'Orléans, Duc d'Aumale, to house his collection of paintings and rare books.

When the duke died in 1897, he bequeathed the Domaine de Chantilly to the Institute de France – including the Grand Stables, the Hippodrome (*see p334* **A day at the races**) and the 15,000-acre forest – on the condition that the château be opened to the public as the Musée Condé, and that none of the artworks would be moved or loaned to other museums. His remarkable collection is complemented by the surrounding **park**, beautifully landscaped by Le Nôtre of Versailles fame.

Thanks to the duke's foresight, the unique character of Chantilly and its forest have been

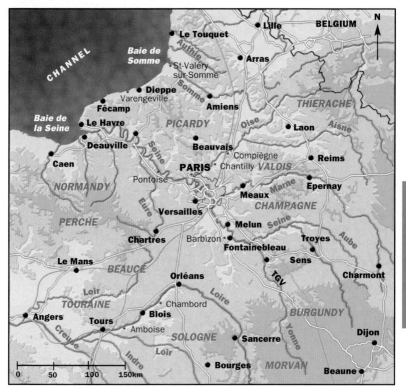

preserved. It's still an important equestrian centre, known for the prestigious Prix de Diane Hermès at the Hippodrome in June.

The Great Stables at the château were commissioned in 1719 by Prince Louis-Henri de Bourbon (who believed that he would be reincarnated as a horse), and once housed 240 horses, 500 hunting dogs and a hundred palfreys and hunting birds. It was only lightly battered during the Revolution, and then became one of Napoleon's equestrian training grounds. In 1982 the great horseman Yves Bienaimé restored the stables and turned them into the **Musée Vivant du Cheval**. The Bienaimé family has also restored and reopened the **Potager des Princes**, the princes' old vegetable garden.

The Forêt de Chantilly is full of hiking and cycling trails. A pleasant walk of around 7km circles the four small lakes, the Etangs de Commelles, and passes the Château de la Reine Blanche, a mill converted in the 1820s into a pseudo-medieval hunting lodge. Steer clear of the sand alleys which criss-cross the forest by the hippodrome; they're used each morning to train the racehorses. For details of forest trails, ask at the Office National des Forêts (1 av de Sylvie, 03.44.57.03.88, www.onf.fr).

Senlis, 9km east of Chantilly, is known as the birthplace of the French monarchy – although little else has happened since the tenth century. Its historic centre has half-timbered houses, fine mansions, a Gothic cathedral and the remains of Gallo-Roman city walls and amphitheatre. For more details, contact the Senlis tourist office (03.44.53.06.40, www.ville-senlis.fr).

Château de Chantilly

Musée Condé, 60500 Chantilly (03.44.62.62.62/ www.chateaudechantilly.com). **Open** *Nov-Feb* 10.30am-12.45pm, 2-5pm Mon, Wed-Fri; 10.30am-5pm. Sat, Sun. *Mar-Oct* 10am-6pm Mon, Wed-Sun. **Admission** €7; €6 12-17s; €2.80 4-12s. **Credit** MC, V.

Set in beautiful surroundings, the château's main attraction is the remarkable collection of paintings and drawings at the Musée Condé. It includes three paintings by Raphael, Filippo Lippi's *Esther and Assuarus* and the *Très Riches Heures du Duc de Berry*, a medieval Book of Hours. Usually it'll be a facsimile on show.

Château Park

Open *Nov-Feb* 10.30am-5pm Mon, Wed-Sun. *Mar-Oct* 10am-7pm daily. **Admission** *Park only* €3.50; €2 4-11s; free under-4s. *Combined tickets* (boat tour, carriage ride, mini-train rides) *from* €8.50. **Credit** MC, V.

The main section of the château's sprawling park, designed by royal landscape architect Le Nôtre, features traditional French formal parterres and an extensive canal system, where visitors can see the

park from the electric-powered boats. Get off the beaten path to explore the English Garden, the Temple of Venus, the Island of Love, the kangaroo zoo and the hamlet which inspired Marie-Antoinette to build her own version at Versailles. Horse-drawn carriages and mini-trains also run.

Musée Vivant du Cheval

Les Grandes Ecuries, Chantilly (03.44.57.13.13/ www.musee-vivant-du-cheval.fr). **Open** *Nov-Feb* 10.30am-5pm Mon, Wed-Sun. *Apr, July-Oct* 10.30am-6.30pm Mon, Wed-Fri; 10.30am-7pm Sat, Sun. *May, June* 10.30am-6.30pm Mon, Wed-Fri; 10.30am-5.30pm Tue; 10.30am-7pm Sat, Sun. **Admission** €8; €7.50 students; €6.50 13-17s; €5.50 4-12s; free under-4s. **Credit** MC, V.

More than 40 breeds live at these historic stables, a real treat for horse-mad youngsters. As opposed to the formal showmanship displayed at Versailles, this museum is an interactive affair where kids can pet the ponies and everyone gets to learn how the horses are trained to perform in the ring. There are demonstrations every day at 11.30am, 3.30pm and, in summer, also at 5.15pm.

Potager des Princes

Parc de la Faisanderie (17 rue de la Faisanderie/ 03.44.57.40.40/www.potagerdesprinces.com). **Open** *Mar-Oct* 2-5pm Mon, Wed-Fri; 11am-12.30pm, 2-5.30pm Sat, Sun. **Admission** €7; €5.50 4-12s; free under-4s. **Credit** MC, V.

The restored princes' kitchen garden is now a 19th-century English garden with vegetable plots, trained fruit trees, a small farmyard, and open-air theatre next to the lake. Musical performances all summer.

Trips Out of Town

Château de Fontainebleau. *See p352.*

Where to eat & stay

Try the home-style cooking at **Le Goutillon** (61 rue du Connétable, 03.44.58.01.00), a cosy wine bistro on the high street. Lunch menus from €18. **La Capitainerie** (03.44.67.40.00) offers good French food in the old château kitchens, a three-course deal available for €21. To sample Chantilly whipped cream, invented by one of the princes in the late 1700s, stop by for afternoon tea at **Aux Goûters Champêtres** (03.44.57.46.21; closed mid Nov-mid Mar) in the hameau at the château.

One of the only hotels in the town centre is the **Hotel du Parc Best Western** (36 av du Maréchal Joffre, 03.44.58.20.00, www.hotel-parc-chantilly.com), lacking in charm but equipped with the essentials for a good night's rest. Doubles here are around €90.

Further information is available at the local **tourist office** (60 av Maréchal Joffre, 03.44.67.37.37, www.chantilly-tourisme.com; closed Sun Oct-Apr), in a white house near the station.

Getting there

By car
40km from Paris by A1, exit Chantilly or N16 direct.

By train
SNCF Chantilly-Gouvieux from Gare du Nord (30 mins), then 5min walk to town, 20mins to château. Some trains stop at Creil, then loop back to Chantilly.

Chartres

Seen from afar, the mismatched spires and brilliant silhouette of **Chartres cathedral** burst up out of the Beauce cornfields and dominate the skyline of this otherwise modest town some 90km south-west of Paris.

One of the finest examples of Gothic architecture impresses millions of tourists today – what would it have been like to have walked here as a fervent believer and seen it 800 years ago?

Chartres was a pilgrimage site long before the cathedral was built, ever since the Sacra Camisia (said to be the Virgin Mary's birthing garment) was donated in 876 by the king. The sublime stained glass of the cathedral, and its doorways bristling with sculpture, embody a complete medieval world view, with earthly society and civic life reflecting the divine order.

Modelled on **St-Denis** (*see p149*), the west front, or 'Royal Portal' has three richly sculpted doorways. Inside, another era of sculpture is represented in the lively 16th-century scenes of the life of Christ that surround the choir. Note the circular labyrinth of black and white stones in the floor – such mazes used to exist in many cathedrals, but most have been destroyed.

The cathedral is, above all, famed for its stained-glass windows depicting Biblical scenes, saints and medieval trades in brilliant 'Chartres blue', punctuated by rich reds. Climb the tower for a fantastic view of it all. English-language tours, some still given by one of the world's most knowledgeable and entertaining experts on Chartres cathedral, Malcolm Miller.

Chartres town is an attractive tangle of narrow, medieval streets on the banks of the Eure which makes for a pleasant post-cathedral walk. Two sights merit mentioning: the Musée des Beaux-Arts (29 Cloître Notre-Dame, 02.37. 36.41.39) in the former bishop's palace, housing a collection of 18th-century French paintings by Watteau and others; and the Memorial to Jean Moulin, the legendary figure of the Resistance, a war-time prefect of Chartres until dismissed by the Vichy government through his refusal to cooperate with the Nazi authorities. He became Gaulle's right-hand man on the ground, and died under torture in Lyon in 1943. Moulin's memorial stands a ten-minute walk west of the cathedral, at the corner of rue Collin d'Arleville and boulevard de la Résistance.

Rock back in time

If you're looking for a true out-of-town French experience an easy journey away from Paris, look no further than a canal boat ride along the sleepy River Marne to the *guinguette* capital of the east, Joinville-le-Pont.

Before rock 'n' roll, there were guinguettes. These suburban dance halls grew up in the 19th century in old riverside wine-producing communities just outside Paris and got their name from *guinget*, the cheap local wine that was even cheaper when sold outside Paris. The early versions were fanciful constructions built along the Seine at Sceaux and Robinson or the Maison Fornaise on the Ile de Chatou, then along the Marne after a suburban rail service was put in. Guinguettes were a chance for a day out in the country, offering boat trips and rowing races, as well as lively drinking and dancing. This tradition has endured along the more working-class Marne, reaching its peak in the interwar years and the 1950s, depicted in vintage films and in the popular song, *Joinville-le-Pont*.

The canal cruise to guinguette heaven is no less nostalgic – and more suited to relaxation than ticking the boxes on a nysightseeing itinerary. Starting at the Port de l'Arsenal in Bastille (get there by 8.45am to ensure a good seat), the good barge Alliance trudges through the Bastille Lock onto the Seine, and past Bercy, the Ministry of Finance, new apartment blocks and old factories. Look out for the haunting 19th-century compressed air factory SUDAC, soon be turned into a school of architecture, before heading on past Ivry and Charenton.

As soon as the Seine joins the Marne at Alfortville (dominated by the Chinese hotel and restaurant complex Chinagora), the city and its pressures feel far behind you. This is the point when the guide will begin to wax lyrical about the passing faded mansions and the famous dance hall, L'Ile du Moulin Brulé, rebuilt from the days when Johnny Halliday made young hearts flutter. Break out the picnic breakfasts and set sail for Joinville.

Cathédrale Notre-Dame

Pl Cathédrale (02.37.21.59.08). **Open** *Jan-Apr, Nov, Dec* 8am-7pm daily. *May-Oct* 8am-8pm. *Tower Sept-Apr* 9am-12.30pm, 2-4.30pm Mon-Sat; 2-4.30pm Sun. *May-Aug* 9am-12.30pm, 2-5.30pm Mon-Sat; 2-5.30pm Sun. **Admission** free. *Tower* €4. **No credit cards.**
English lecturer Malcolm Miller has given English-language tours here for 40 years or more. They run Mondays to Saturdays, at noon and 2.45pm, from April to November, and cost €10.

Where to eat & stay

Tourists flock to the **Café Serpent** (2 Cloître Notre-Dame, 02.37.21.68.81) near the cathedral – if full, there are plenty of other easy options nearby. For restaurant cuisine with a riverside view, **L'Estocade** (1 rue de la Porte Guillaume, 02.37.34.27.17) does the job. Two chain hotels fringe the town centre on the ring road: **Grand Monarque** (22 rue Epars, 02.37.18.15.15,

Once you arrive, you have the choice of a swiftish lunch and the 2pm slow barge back to Paris – or the chance to party like it's 1959 then a night-time stagger to the nearest RER station 20 minutes away.

Back on the quays at Joinville-le-Pont, **Chez Gégène** is your dyed-in-the-wool classic dance hall. Still run by descendents of the original Gégène, it has changed little since it was photographed by Doisneau, with garlands of lights at the entrance, bistro at the front and dance hall at the rear, with tables around the slippery wooden dance floor, where you can get up and dance between courses. On Saturday nights and Sunday afternoons, the live band draws multi-generational families celebrating birthday parties, suburban couples and groups of young Parisians. But don't wear jeans or trainers here, please. This is the sort of place where elderly gallants will come over and ask unaccompanied young (and not so young) ladies to dance. Beware – the standard is frighteningly high, as you'll see when the regulars start to foxtrot, waltz and tango around the floor. A few simpler rock 'n' roll and *yé-yé* numbers are slipped in for the beginners.

So attractive has the retro culture celebrated at guinguettes become, that the most popular venue was only opened in 1991. Set on its own romantic tree-shaded island a short stretch down the Marne from Joinville near a bend in the river by Champigny, **Guinguette de la Martin-Pêcheur** is accessible by a little raft. Every 14 July, this is the setting for the highly competitive **Miss Guinguette** competition (*see p281*), based not only on dancing ability but also on dress and knowledge of guinguette culture. But generally things aren't taken too seriously here: you're in for a nostalgic afternoon out of town, with moules-frites and strawberries, accompanied by a little dancing *à deux* to the sound of the accordion.

Canauxrama

Port de l'Arsenal, opposite 50 bd de la Bastille, 12th. (01.42.39.15.00). Mº Bastille. **Departures** *Apr-Oct* 9am, 2.30pm Thur, Sat, Sun. **Admission** €14; €11 students, over-60s; €8 6-12s; free under 6s. No concs for 2.30pm departures Sat, Sun and public hols. **Credit**, MC, V. **Map** p408 L7.

Chez Gégène

162 quai de Polangis, 94340 Joinville-le-Pont (01.48.83.29.43). RER A Joinville-le-Pont. **Open** *Apr-Oct* from noon Tue-Sun. **No credit cards**.

Guinguette de la Martin-Pêcheur

41 quai Victor-Hugo, 94500 Champigny-sur-Marne (01.49.83.03.02). RER Champigny. **Open** *May-Sept* from noon daily. *Apr, Oct* from noon Sat, Sun. **No credit cards.**

Giverny. See p353.

www.bw-grand-monaque.com, €105-€125) and the more basic **Ibis Centre** (pl Drouaise, 02.37.36.06.36, €62-€68), with regular weekend rates of €45. The **tourist office** (pl Cathédrale, 02.37.18.26.26) can also book accommodation.

Getting there

By car
90km from Paris by the A10, then A11.

By train
Direct from Gare Montparnasse (1hr).

Fontainebleau

Home to 14 French kings since François I, Fontainebleau ('Fon-ten-blow') was once a sort of an aristocratic club where gentlemen of the day came to hunt and learn the art of chivalry. The town grew up around the **château** in the 19th century, and today is a pleasant and lively place to visit, dominated by three major elements: the sumptuous royal palace which dominates the town centre; the hunting forest and its rock formations, and the INSEAD business school (the 'European Harvard') on the forest edge, which adds a cosmopolitan touch.

The château is bite-sized compared to the sprawling grandeur of Versailles, but has been completely furnished since its restoration. The style adopted by the Italian artists brought in by François I is still visible, as are the additions

put in by later rulers – Napoleon redecorated much in Empire style before leaving for exile on Elba from the front courtyard, the Cour des Adieux. The château gardens, park and grand canal, all free to enter, are also worth exploring.

The 42,000-acre Forêt de Fontainebleau is part of the Gâtinas Regional Nature Park, with its bizarre geological formations and diverse wildlife. Its ravines, rocky outcrops and mix of forest and sandy heath where François I liked to hunt is the wildest slice of nature near Paris and popular with weekenders for walking, cycling, riding and rock climbing. There are a number of well-marked trails such as the GR1 from Bois-le-Roi train station, but more serious yompers would be better off with an official map such as the TOP25 IGN series 2417-OT covering all the forest, highlighting climbing sites, campsites and picnic areas. Maps are on sale at the **Fontainebleau Area Tourist Office** (4 rue Royale, 01.60.74.99.99, www.fontainebleau-tourisme.com), which rents out bicycles (€19/day) and has details on the nearby villages of Barbizon and Moret-sur-Loing. Bikes can also be rented from La Petite Reine (32 rue Sablons, 01.60.74.57.57, www.la-petite-reine.fr; closed Mon), plus baby seats, at around €15 per day – passport or €300 deposit required.

La Bleausière riding school (06.82.01.21.18, http://la.bleausiere.free.fr), on the edge of the Fontainebleau forest in Barbizon, offers year-round short and long guided tours for adults and children of all levels.

Château de Fontainebleau

77300 Fontainebleau (01.60.71.50.60/www.musee-château-fontainebleau.fr). **Open** *Château Oct-May* 9.30am-5pm Mon, Wed-Sun. *June-Sept* 9.30am-6pm Mon, Wed-Sun. *Park & Gardens Winter* 9am-5pm daily. *Summer* 9am-7pm. **Admission** *Château* €5.50; €4 18-25s; free under-18s & holders of the Carte Musées et Monuments. *Park & Gardens* free. **Credit** MC, V.

This former hunting lodge is fascinating for its mish-mash of styles after centuries of additions and changes. In 1528, François I brought in Italian artists and craftsmen to help architect Gilles le Breton transform a neglected lodge into the finest Italian Mannerist palace in France. This style, noted for its grotesqueries, contorted figures and crazy fireplaces, is still visible in the Ballroom and Long Gallery. Henri IV then added a tennis court, Louis XIII built a double-horseshoe entrance staircase, Louis XIV and XV added classical trimmings. Napoleon and Louis-Philippe also spent a fortune on redecoration.

The château gardens include Le Nôtre's formal Grand Parterre, the Jardin de Diane and a carp pond in the Jardin Anglais. There is also an informal château park just outside, with green lawns and a canal where locals fish and visitors picnic. Other activities include dinghy rental on the lake and horse-drawn carriage rides.

Where to eat & stay

Rue Grande is lined with restaurants, such as the inventive, stylish **Au Délice Impérial** (No.1, 01.64.22.20.70) and **Au Bureau** (No.12, 01.60.39.00.01) with Tex-Mex specialities and global beers in a pub setting. DJs and live bands comprise the evening agenda here. At No.92, picnickers can find excellent local cheese at **Fromagerie Barthélémy** (01.64.22.21.64).

For a blow-out meal, head for **Le Caveau des Ducs** (24 rue Ferrare, 01.64.22.05.05), with traditional French cuisine in a 17th-century interior of heavy oak tables and tapestries. Lunch menus range from €19 to €30.

The charming **Hôtel de Londres** (1 pl Général-de-Gaulle, 01.64.22.20.21, www.hotelde londres.com; €90-€150) is centrally located and has free, private parking. Some of the dozen rooms have balconies overlooking the château. Set in a 19th-century post house, the elegant **Hôtel Napoléon** (9 rue Grande, 01.60.39.50.50, www.hotelnapoleon-fontainebleau.com; €122-€190) overlooks an interior garden, and boasts decent restaurant, La Table des Maréchaux.

Getting there

By car

60km from Paris by A6, then N7 (about 75 minutes). Beware of traffic jams back to Paris on Sundays.

By train

Gare de Lyon to Fontainebleau-Avon (35mins), then bus AB (marked Château). Ask for a Forfait Château de Fontainebleau (€20; €16 10-17s; €8 4-9s) at the Gare de Lyon, covering train fare, bus connection, château entrance and audio guide.

Giverny

In 1883 Claude Monet moved his mistress and eight children into his quaint pink-brick house in bucolic Giverny, and concentrated as much time on cultivating a beautiful garden here as painting the water lilies in it.

Monet was fascinated by light. The leader of the Impressionist movement – his *Impression: Sunrise* gave rise to the group's name in 1874 – thrived on outdoor scenes, whether along the Seine near Argenteuil or by the Thames. Having seen the tiny village of Giverny from the window of a train, he was smitten. By 1890 he had bought his dream home and soon had a pond dug, bridges built and a tableau of greenery weaved together. As Monet's eyesight began to fail, he produced endless impressions of his man-made paradise, each trying to capture how the leaves and water refracted light. He died here in 1926.

Of the hundreds of tourists who visit here on any given day, not all are art-lovers – there are no original Monets in the large studio and two-storey house, though no few Japanese prints. Most are simply here for the lilies, and to have their picture taken beside them. In fact, Giverny is overrun with visitors snapping each other.

The garden, it must be said, is a masterpiece, its famous water-lily pond, weeping willows and Japanese bridge remarkably intact; and the charming house, the **Fondation Claude Monet**, is dotted with touching momentos. But once you're back in the village, be prepared for heated arguments over finding a table at one of the scarce eating places and long queues of impatient tourists almost everywhere you turn. Get here early, or alternatively in time for evening dinner (around €15) at the famous **Hôtel Baudy** museum-restaurant (81 rue Claude Monet, 02.32.21.10.03; book ahead) where Monet's American disciples (such as Willard Metcalf and Dawson-Watson) set up their easels for several decadent years, expanding the old hotel into an art-atelier extraordinaire with a ballroom, rose garden and tennis courts – Cézanne even stayed in one of the attic rooms for a month. After dinner, stay overnight in Giverny (always reserve; *see p354*) and get to the Monet museum first thing in the morning. Up the road, the **Musée Americain de Giverny** (02.32.51.94.65) has a collection of works by the American Impressionist colony.

Fondation Claude Monet

Giverny 27620 (02.32.51.28.21). **Open** *Apr-Oct*
9.30am-6pm Tue-Sun. **Admission** *House & garden*
€5.50; €4 students; €3 7-13s; free under-7s.
Credit AmEx, MC, V.

Where to stay

Les Rouge Gorges B&B run by Eric and
Christelle Carrière (6 rue aux Juifs, 02.32.51.
02.96) has pretty country lodgings available at
€50-€70. **Le Coin des Artistes** (65 rue
Claude Monet, 02.32.21.36.77; €50-€80) is a
comfortable B&B that doubles as an art gallery.
For more suggestions, http://giverny.org links
to hotels and B&Bs in the area.

Getting there

By car
80km west of Paris by A13 to Bonnières and D201.

By train
Gare St-Lazare to Vernon (45mins); then 5km taxi
ride or bus from the station.

Versailles

Centuries of makeovers have made Versailles
the best known and most sumptuously clad
châteaux in the world – a veritable bouquet of
over-the-top brilliance, and an absolute must-
see. Architect Louis Le Vau first embellished
the original building – a hunting lodge built in
the centre of marshlands during Louis XIII's
reign – after Louis XIV saw Vaux-le-Vicomte,
the impressive residence of his finance minister,
Nicolas Fouquet. The Sun King had the unlucky
minister jailed and stole away not only his
architect, but also his painter Charles Le Brun
and the landscaper André Le Nôtre, who turned
the boggy marshland into terraces, parterres
fountains and lush groves.

After Le Vau's death in 1670, Jules Hardouin-
Mansart took over as principle architect,
transforming Versailles into the **château** we
know today, dedicating the last 30 years of his
life to adding the two main wings, the Cour des
Ministres and the Chapelle Royale. In 1682
Louis moved he and his court in – thereafter he
rarely set foot in Paris. In the 1770s, Louis XV
had Jacques-Ange Gabriel add the sumptuous
Opéra Royal, used for concerts by the Centre de
Musique Baroque (01.39.20.78.10). It still has the
original spy holes Louis' bodyguards used to
keep an eye on him. The expense of building
and running Versailles cost France dear. With
the fall of the monarchy in 1792, most of the
furniture was lost but the château was saved
from demolition after 1830 by Louis-Philippe.

Versailles has hosted the official signings of
many historic treaties – European recognition
of the United States, the unification of Germany
in 1871, the division of Europe after 1918 – and
is still used by the French government for
major summits. In the **Gardens**, **Grand
Trianon** accommodates the Heads of State.

The Gardens are works of art in themselves,
their ponds and statues now embellished by a
fully working fountain system. On summer
weekends, the spectacular jets of water are set
to music, a prelude to the occasional firework
displays of the Fêtes de Nuit.

Beyond the Gardens is the park and Grand
Canal where visitors can laze around in small
boats, wooded parkland and sheep-filled
pastures. This is where the Grand Trianon, the
Petit Trianon – and Marie Antoinette's
replica village Hameau are hidden. Outside the
château gates are the recently restored Potager
du Roi, the Sun King's vegetable garden, and
his stables, now housing the **Académie du
Spectacle Equestre**.

Versailles is currently undergoing a complete
overhaul, notably in its entrance and ticketing
area. The first phase won't be ready until 2010,
so expect a little chaos for the next few years.

In the town of Versailles, grab a *Historical Places*
brochure free from the tourist office (*see below*) and
explore. Quartier Saint-Louis opposite the Potager
was developed by Louis XV around the Cathédrale
St-Louis. Just off rue d'Anjou are the Carrés Saint-
Louis, four market squares surrounded by 18th-

Versailles.

century boutiques housing galleries and antique shops. North-east of the château is the Quartier Notre-Dame, part of the 'new town' designed by the Sun King himself. Eglise Notre-Dame is where members of the royal family were baptised and married. Around the corner is the market square of the same name, surrounded by restaurants and cafés dating back to 1671 and restored in 1841. The covered market is closed on Mondays.

Bicycles can be rented from outside RER Versailles-Chantiers (place Raymond Poincaré, 01.39.20.16.60) for €5 and hour or €12 a day.

Château de Versailles

78000 Versailles (01.30.83.76.20/advance tickets 08.92.68.46.94/www.chateauversailles.fr). **Open** *Nov-Mar* 9am-5pm Tue-Sun. *Apr-Oct* 9am-6pm Tue-Sun. **Admission** €7.50; *after 3.30pm* €5.30; free under-18s; CM. **Passeport Versailles** *Nov-Mar* €14.50; €4 10-17s; free under-10s. *Apr-Oct* €20; €6 10-17s; free under-10s. **Credit** AmEx, DC, MC, V.
Versailles is a masterpiece. Allow yourself a whole day to appreciate the sumptuous State apartments, and the Hall of Mirrors, the highlights of any visit – and mainly accessible with just a day ticket. The Grand Appartement, where Louis XIV held court, consists of six gilded salons (Venus, Mercury, Apollo and so on), all opulent examples of baroque craftsmanship. No less luxurious, the Queen's Apartment includes the Queen's Bedroom, where royal births took place in full view of the court. Hardouin-Mansart's 75m-long showpiece, the Hall of Mirrors, where a united Germany was proclaimed in 1871 and the Treaty of Versailles signed in 1919,

floods with natural light from its 17 spacious windows. Designed to catch the last of the day's rays, it was here that the Sun King would hold extravagant receptions. A host of other private apartments can only be seen as part of a guided tour.

The easiest, but not the cheapest way, to see Versailles is with the Passeport. It allows quick access via Porte C to the main section of the château, the audio-guided tour of the Chambre du Roi, Grand and Petit Trianon, the Gardens and their displays. Buy the Passeport in advance from Fnac stores (*see p246*), tourist offices or any RER station (price of journey added to the ticket); or go directly to Porte C2 or D before 2pm. Those who hold a Carte Musées et Monuments (*see p161*) can enter via Porte B-2. Those just wanting a day ticket must queue with the masses at Porte A. Any number of guided tours are available from Porte D; it's essential to book early that morning, and then meet by Porte F.

Grand Trianon/Petit Trianon

Open *Nov-Mar* noon-5pm daily. *Apr-Oct* noon-6pm daily. **Admission** €5; €3 after 3.30pm; free under-18s, holders of a Passeport Versailles or Carte Musées et Monuments. **Credit** AmEx, DC, MC, V.
After so many extensions to the château, in 1687 Louis XIV had Hardouin-Mansart build the pink marble Grand Trianon in the north of the park away from the protocol of the court. Here Louis and his chidren's governess, and his secret second wife, Madame de Maintenon, could admire the intimate gardens from the lovely colonnaded portico. It still retains the Empire decor of Napoleon, who stayed here with his second Empress, Marie-Louise.

The Mouse and the Gaul

Mickey and Astérix are slugging it out for your euros. The figureheads of two huge theme parks outside Paris – **Disneyland Paris** 32km south-east and **Parc Astérix** 36km north – attract millions of families here every year. Astérix is cheaper, but Disneyland Paris also boasts the Walt Disney Studios Park and white-knuckle rides of Adventureland and Frontierland. Parc Astérix has hit back with Goudurix and Le Grand Splach. Astérix scores higher for its educational benefits, Disneyland Paris turns out thousands of satisfied customers every week, all the year round – Parc Astérix closes for the winter. And it is Disneyland Paris which attracts families over from the UK by the bucketload – Astérix scores heavily with the domestic and European market.

Split into neat historical sections (Ancient Greece, the Roman Empire, the Middle Ages and 19th Century Paris), Parc Astérix is packed with varietyand easy to get around. Thrill seekers can defy gravity on Goudurix, Europe's largest roller coaster with seven stomach-churning loop-the-loops, while younger kiddies will squirm to get wet on Le Grand Splach log-flume. Astérix, Obélix and their fellow Roman bashers hang out in the spanking new Gaul Village (an exact replica of the one in Albert Uderzo's original comic book) that adjoins the Druid's Forest adventure playground and nearby magic school (Ecole des Druides), where evil Romans have been turned into real pigmy goats. A jamboree of live acts also pump up the pace, with quality shows from dancing dolphins in the Théâtre de Poséidon to awe inspiring acrobatics and synchronised swimming inside the Roman Circus. The food in the park is reassuringly French with an attractive huge choice of eateries including the Rélais Gaullois canteen, where three courses run at €11.

Despite rumours, Disneyland Paris was not built in the shape of Mickey's ears – but that doesn't detract from the frivolous fun on offer in this huge resort (one-fifth the size of Paris) with its main Disneyland park and adjacent film studio complex. Enter the Walt Disney Studios via the Front Lot and head into Animation courtyard for a lesson in cartoon production at Animagique, a 'black light' show based on cult moments from Disney classics. From there, the special effects Studio Tram Tour in Production Courtyard takes you onto an imitation film set with real fireballs and cascading torrents of water. Daredevils should try the Rock 'n' Roller Coaster in the Back Lot which rips off at mega speed before hurtling round hairpin turns and loops to the sounds of Aerosmith. In the main park, little ones can enjoy Fantasyland with Sleeping Beauty's pink fairy-tale castle, while white-knuckle seekers will prefer Adventureland and Frontierland with bone-shaking rides like Indiana Jones et le Temple du Péril which tears around backwards. If you've not much time, get to the park early for a free Fastpass so you can jump the queues on most big rides. Disneyland Paris comes into its own at Hallowe'en and Christmas when there are parades and performances. A golf course and seven Disney-themed hotels make up the resort. For both Disneyland Paris and Parc Astérix certain rides have height restrictions.

Disneyland Paris/Walt Disney Studios Park

Marne-la-Vallée (01.60.30.60.30/UK 0870 503 0303/www.disneylandparis.com). RER A or TGV Marne-la-Vallée-Chessy. By car A4 Metz-Nancy exit 14. **Open** *Sept-Mar* 10am-8pm Mon-Fri; 9am-8pm Sat-Sun. *Apr-Jun* 9am-8pm daily. *July-Aug* 9am-11pm daily. **Studios Park** *Winter* 10am-6pm Mon-Fri; 9am-6pm Sat, Sun. *Summer* 9am-6pm daily. All times may vary for public hols. **Admission** *Disneyland Park or Walt Disney Studio Park* €40; €30 3-11s. Free under-3s. *One-day Hopper for both parks* €49; €39 3-11s. Free under-3s. *Three-day Hopper* €107; €80 3-11s. Free under-3s. **Credit** AmEx, MC, V. One-day tickets are valid for the main Park *or* the Studio Park; and for both only after 6pm in summer and 5pm in winter. They are also sold at UK Disney stores, and in Paris at Fnac, Virgin Megastore (*see p246*) and at tourist offices. All-in one-day RER-Disneyland Paris tickets are sold at major stations. Hoppers for both parks are sold at the venue.

Parc Astérix

60128 Plailly (08.26.30.10.40/www. parcasterix.fr). RER B Roissy-Charles de Gaulle 1, then shuttle bus (9.30am-1.30pm, 4.30pm-closing time). By car A1 exit Parc Astérix. **Open** *Apr-Jun* 10am-6pm daily. *July-Aug* 9.30am-7pm daily. *Sep-Oct* 10am-6pm Wed, Sat-Sun. Closed Nov-Mar. Call ahead for extra closure dates. **Admission** €32; €23 3-11s; under-3s free. **Credit** MC, V.

Greetings from the Norman Riviera: **Deauville**. *See p360.*

The Petit Trianon, built for Louis XV's mistress Mme de Pompadour, is a wonderful example of neo-classicism. Marie-Antoinette took this as her main residence, and had the gardens completely changed to include an open-air theatre and her fairy-tale farm and dairy known as the Hameau de la Reine. Built for her by Mique in 1783, here the queen escaped from the discontent of her subjects and the Revolutionary fervour of Paris by pretending to be a humble milkmaid.

Gardens

Open *Nov-Mar* 8am-dusk daily. *Apr-Oct* 7am-dusk daily. **Admission** *Winter* free (statues covered over). *Summer* €3; €1.50 for 10-17s; free under-10s. **Grandes Eaux** (01.30.83.78.88). **Open** *Apr-Oct* Sun. *July-Sept* Sat, Sun. **Admission** €5; €3.50 10-17s; free under-10s, holders of a Passeport Versailles. **Credit** AmEx, DC, MC, V. **Park Open** dawn-dusk daily. **Admission** free. **Potager du Roi** (10 rue Maréchal Joffre/01.39. 24.62.62/www.potager-du-roi.fr). **Open** *Apr-Oct* 10am-6pm Mon-Fri. *Guided tours only* Sat, Sun. **Admission** Mon-Fri €4.50; €3 concs; free under-6s. Sat, Sun €6.50; €3 for students; free under-6s. **Credit** AmEx, DC, MC, V.

Stretching over 815 hectares, these meticulously planned Gardens consist of formal parterres, ponds, elaborate statues – many commissioned by Colbert in 1674 – and a spectacular series of fountains served by an ingenious hydraulic system only recently restored to working order. On weekend afternoons from spring to autumn, these great fountains are set in action to music for the 'Grandes Eaux Musicales' – and also serve as a backdrop,

seven times a year, for the extravagant Fêtes de Nuit, capturing the ancient finery of the Sun King's celebrations with fireworks, music and theatre.

Potager du Roi, the restored vegetable garden, features 16 small squares surrounded by 5,000 fruit trees espalier-grown into fabulous shapes.

Académie du Spectacle Equestre

Grandes Ecuries, Château de Versailles (01.39.02. 07.14/www.acadequestre.fr). **Les Matinales des écuyers** *(practice & visit)* **Open** *Mar-Dec* 9am-noon Tue-Fri; 11am-2pm Sat, Sun. Closed Jan, Feb. **Admission** €7; €3 5-18s, students. **Credit** MC, V. **Reprise Musicale** *(performance & visit)* **Open** *Mar-Dec* 2-3.30pm Sat, Sun. Closed Jan, Feb. **Admission** €15; €7 under-18s, students. **Credit** MC, V.

Across from the château entrance is the Sun King's magnificent stables, restored in 2003. It houses the Académie du Spectacle Equestre, which performs elaborate shows of tightly choreographed theatrics on horseback run by the famous horse trainer and former circus showman Bartabas. Visitors can catch a show on the weekends, or attend training sessions to see how the white horses and their young riders learn their tricks.

Where to eat & stay

Set in a building dating back to the construction of the château, **Le Chapeau Gris** (7 rue Hoche, 01.39.50.10.81, www.auchapeaugris.com) is the oldest restaurant in Versailles, offering French country cuisine served under wooden beams. Look out for the set lunch at €17 and menus at €26, with a lunch formule for €17. It's closed on Tuesday night and all day Wednesday. **Boeuf à la Mode** (4 rue au Pain, Marché Notre-Dame, 01.39.50.31.99) is an authentic 1930s brasserie serving steak and seafood specialities. For a proper splurge, Michelin-starred haute-cuisine **Les Trois Marches** (Hôtel Trianon Palace, 1 bd Reine, 01.39.50.13.21; closed Mon, Sun) has menus at €160 or set lunches from €58.

You'll find plenty of bars which open late around the Marché Notre-Dame. The centre of town also boasts several reasonably-priced hotels for under €100. One of them is the **Hôtel du Cheval Rouge** (18 rue André Chenier, 01.39.50.03.03, www.chevalrouge.fr.st), built in Louis XIV's former livery, overlooking the Marché Notre-Dame. Located in an 18th-century townhouse across from the château, the **Hôtel de France** (5 rue Colbert, 01.30.83.92.23, www.hotelfrance-versailles.com) is a classic hotel with period furnishings. Doubles run from €145, triples and suites also available.

For details, contact the **Versailles Tourist Office** (Sofitel building, 2bis av de Paris, 01.39.24.88.88, www.versailles-tourisme.com).

Getting there

By car
20km from Paris by the A13 or D10.

By RER
RER C5 (VICK or VERO trains) run from the Left Bank to Versailles-Rive Gauche, nearest the château.

By SNCF
Transilien from Gare St-Lazare run to Versailles-Rive Droit (10mins on foot to the château).

Further Afield

The Champagne region

Named after the region in which it's produced, champagne – nearly all 300 million bottles a year of it – comes from the towns of **Reims** (nasally pronounced 'Rrance') and **Epernay**, some 25km apart. At less than two hours by train from Paris, both are ideal destinations for a day trip or a weekend break, with historical sites and champagne houses to visit. Most champagne cellars give detailed explanations of how champagne is produced – from the Pinot Noir, Chardonnay and Pinot Meunier grape varieties, to strict name and quality controls – and tours finish with a sample. Don't forget your woollies as the cellars are chilly and damp.

Epernay developed in the 19th century as expanding champagne houses moved out from Reims to acquire more space. Today, the aptly named avenue de Champagne is home to most major brands – but the best tours are at **Moët & Chandon** and **Champagne Mercier**.

In Reims, nearly all the major champagne houses are open by appointment only: Krug (03.26.84.44.20); Lanson (03.26.78.50.50); Louis Roederer (by appointment *and* recommendation only 03.26.40.42.11) and Veuve Clicquot (03.56.89.54.41). **Champagne Pommery** is set in an intriguing Elizabethan building.

Home of the coronation church of most French monarchs dating back to Clovis in 496, Reims was an important city since Roman times. The present **Cathédrale Notre-Dame** (03.26.47.55.34, www.catedrale-reims.com; open 7.30am-7.30pm daily), begun in 1211, has rich Gothic decoration that includes thousands of well-preserved figures on the portals. Look out too for Chagall's designs, visible through the stained glass at the back of the cathedral. The statues damaged during heavy shelling in World War I can be seen next door in the former archbishop's palace, the Palais de Tau (2 place du Cardinal-Luçon, 03.26.47.81.79).

L'Ancien Collège des Jésuites (1 pl Museux, 03.26.85.51.50; closed Tue, Sat morn, Sun morn) is a classic example of 17th-century baroque architecture, housing a panelled library decorated with religious carving and paintings by Jean Hélart. The college has also given over a considerable space to modern art.

Moët et Chandon
20 av de Champagne, Epernay 51200 (03.26.51. 20.00/www.moet.com). **Open** *mid Nov-mid Mar* 9.30-11.30am, 2-4.30pm Mon-Fri. *Mid mar-mid Nov* 9.30-11.30am, 2-4.30pm daily. **Admission** *includes one glass* €7.50; 12-16s €4.50; free under-12s. **Credit** AmEx, DC, MC, V.

Moët & Chandon started life in 1743 as champagne supplier to Madame de Pompadour, Napoleon and Alexander I of Russia. Since then, they have kept pole position with the largest domain (543 hectares) and more than 250 global suppliers. In the hour-long tour, visitors are led through a huge section of chalk tunnels, 28km in length, under the grand house.

Mercier
68 av de Champagne, Epernay 51200 (03.26.51. 22.22/www.champagne-mercier.fr). **Open** *mid Nov-mid Mar* 9.30-11.30am, 2-4.30pm Mon, Thur-Sun. *Mid mar-mid Nov* 9.30-11.30am, 2-4.30pm daily. **Admission** *includes 1 glass* €6.50; 12-15s €3; free under-12s. **Credit** MC, V.

Some 7,000 tonnes of chalk were extracted to create the 18km of cellars at Mercier, opened in 1858. Note the 20-tonne champagne barrel at the entrance: it took 24 bulls and 18 horses to drag it all the way from Epernay to Paris for the 1889 Universal

Exposition. The 45-minute subterranean tour takes place on a little train and covers a stretch of tunnel used for mini-car races in the 1950s.

Champagne Pommery

5 pl du Général Gouraud, Reims 51100 (03.26.61. 62.63/www.pommery.com). **Open** *appointment only Mid Nov-mid Apr* 10am-6pm daily. *Mid Apr-mid Nov* 9.30am-7pm daily. **Admission** *includes one glass* €7.50; *includes two glasses* €10. **Credit** MC, V.
Built in 1868, this unusual château was modelled on Elizabethan architecture so that it would stand out from surrounding competitors. The visit takes place 30m underground, in 18km long tunnels, which link 120 chalk mines from the Gallo-Roman period.

Where to eat & stay

In Reims, countless cafés and brasseries line lively **place Drouet d'Erlon**, as well as many hotels. Contact the **tourist office** next to the cathedral for details (03.26.77.45.00, www. reims-tourisme.com). If you fancy staying at a working champagne domain, contact **Ariston Fils Champagne**. They offer three double rooms at €45-€48 and pamper their guests (4-8 Grande Rue, Brouillet, 03.26.97.43.46).

In Epernay, **La Cave à Champagne** (16 rue Gambetta, 03.26.55.50.70) does good traditional French food. The chain **Hôtel de Champagne** (30 rue Eugène Mercier, 03.26.53.10.60) provides comfortable rooms from €75-€115 and the **Hôtel Kyriad** (rue Lorraine, 03.26.51.88.78) has basic, clean rooms from €54.

Getting there

By car
Porte de Bercy then 150km by A4 (direction Marne-la- Vallée and Metz). For Epernay exit at Château Thierry and take the N3.

By train
From Gare de l'Est trains take about 90mins for Reims and Epernay.

Deauville-Trouville

Fabulous, glamorous Deauville – just a two-hour train journey from Paris – knows how to look after its guests. Whether you come here to inhale sea air, spot celebrities or up the star rating of your all-over tan, you'll find a town that is primed and equipped to rejuvenate, satiate and titillate – it can't help it, it was designed that way.

Deauville was born in the mid-19th century when the Duc de Morny, Napoleon III's half-brother, recognised an opportunity to tap a spawning tourist trade and built a racecourse on an empty patch of the Côte Fleurie, just across a narrow stretch of water from Trouville. Later he added grandiose hotels and a casino, and by the 1910s the town was established as the prime holiday destination for Parisian jet-setters and British aristocracy. This early growth period has indelibly left its mark on the town's personality: the bright bathing huts and famous beach-side boardwalk, designed to protect ladies' flowing dresses, hark back to more genteel days, while the local spa centres, horse-riding and gourmet food market (place du Marché, Tues, Fri and Sat mornings) honour the tenets of 'bien-vivre'.

Like the French Riviera, Deauville caters to old-style leisure and wealth: there are two marinas, three golf courses, including the only floodlit course in Europe (02.31.14.42.00) and a yacht school (01.31.88.38.19). The occasions to drop coin are endless: serious designer boutiques, top-dollar restaurants and Parisian-style cafés (with prices to match) line the streets. Then there's the casino, just behind the seafront. This massive belle-époque edifice stands like a bastion of decadence and cannot be missed. *Faites vos jeux* at the roulette tables graced by Coco Chanel – but unless you are Coco herself, ID will be required and, for some rooms, formal attire.

Deauville is no museum piece. Its population swells from 4,500 to around 75,000 in season when the sweeping expanse of beach fills with a multicoloured festival of parasols; watersports and sand-surfing keeping the restless occupied. An energetic calendar also brings in the crowds, with international polo and racing events all year and the American Film Festival in September (www.festival-deauville.com), when Harrison Ford usually turns up to crease a grin.

Just a dice tumble away, the 17th-century port town of Trouville, shares the same railway station. Family-owned shops, narrow back streets and a daily fish market lend Trouville an authenticity which its flashier sister lacks. Check out the beach, casino (with one room decorated as a Louisiana paddle steamer) and Napoleon's summer residence, Villa Montebello (64 rue du Maréchal-Leclerc, 02.31.88.16.26), which regularly hosts exhibitions of art.

Casino Barrière de Deauville

Rue Edmond-Blanc, Deauville (02.31.14.31.14). **Open** 11am-2am Mon-Thur; 11am-3am Fri; 10am-4am Sat, 10am-3am Sun. **Admission** Over-18s only, formal dress €12. **Credit** AmEx, MC, V.

Where to eat & stay

Tuck in to oysters at **Le Ciro's** (2 rue-Edmond Blanc, 02.31.14.31.31) on the seafront or tackle a roast lobster and rich Normandy treats at **Le Spinmaker** (52 rue Mirabeau, 02.31.88.24.40;

menus €27, €42). The twin peaks of Deauville's hotel selection are the palatial **Royal Barrière** (bd Cornuché, 02.31.98.66.33, from €280) and the half-timbered **Normandy Barrière** (38 rue Jean Mermoz, 02.31.98.66.22, from €260), with an underground tunnel to the casino.

Those visiting here on a budget should look in from the seafront – or find somewhere in Trouville. A comfortable and quite cheap option overlooking the sea is the **Flaubert Hôtel** (rue G-Flaubert, 02.31.88.37.23, www.flaubert.fr), where €85 gets you a double room, and €115 one with a sea view.

For more information, contact the **Office de Tourisme de Deauville** (pl de la Bastille, 02.32.14.40.60, www.deauville.org); the one in **Trouville** is found at 32 bd Fernand-Moureaux (02.31.14.60.70, www.trouvillesurmer.org).

Getting there

By car
195km west from Paris by the A13.

By train
From Gare Saint-Lazare to Deauville-Trouville (2hrs).

Faites vos jeux

Paris has a 100-km safety net thrown around it. Not real, of course, but legislative: within this area, no casinos are allowed to operate. Such was the rule laid down by a 1920 gambling law, designed to protect the poor from the alluring clack of the roulette wheel. But only 15km from Paris, there is a legal loophole: Enghien-les-Bains. A sleepy, suburban town of 10,000, Enghien made an appropriate cameo in hit film *Amélie* as the retirement place of the heroine's docile father. But it also has a special quality, which came to the attention of gaming entrepreneurs a decade after the town's 19th-century casino, opened by Hippolyte de Villemessant, founder of *Le Figaro*, fell foul of the legislation. Healing sulphurous waters make Enghien a spa town, and spa towns are exempt from the gambling law. Bingo! Or rather, casino. In 1931, the casino reopened and picked up its reputation as a gaming pioneer – Villemessant had been the first to introduce the private casino game of *petit cheval* to the public.

In the 21st century, the casino is a place of mildly crumpled glamour: not Las Vegas, certainly not James Bond, but hardly run-of-the-mill. It sits next to a gleaming, moonlit lake; its gaming halls are wood-panelled and hung with Klimt mosaics. Ritzy jazz singers barely dent the overall atmosphere of infatuated concentration, while tuxed day-trippers scope the room in vain for showings of sequins and thighs. This is a locals' joint as much as anything, something that perturbed the town population when the casino announced it was introducing 130 fruit machines. Blackjack, stud poker, chemin de fer and punto banco meant big money and big players; fruit machines meant coins and ruffians. The proximity of edgy suburbs such

as Epinay, Villetaneuse and St-Denis made the prospect gloomy, but the decline has not materialised. In fact, now you need smart dress for the slots as well as the casino. The owners now plans to open a deluxe spa here, with all the treatments, in 2005.

Casino d'Enghien
3 av de Ceinture, 95880 Enghien-les-Bains (01.39.34.13.00/www.ot-enghienlesbains.fr). Train from Gare du Nord to Enghien-les-Bains (10 mins). **Open** *Slots* 10am-4am daily. *Casino* 4pm-4pm daily. **Admission** €10-€25. **No credit cards.**

The Loire Valley

Renowned for its sumptuous Renaissance châteaux, the relics of the Valois kings who preferred ruling from Amboise and Blois than overcrowded Paris, the stunning Loire valley is full of historical splendour and intrigue. Like the UNESCO protected Loire River, untamed and picturesque, this huge region is an ode to all that is good in France: awe-inspiring architecture, lavish countryside, excellent food and some of the best wines in the world.

The selection of visits featured below, set between Amboise and Saumur, should provide an architecturally diverse range of châteaux, from medieval to 19th-century, and plenty of opportunity to taste some fine wines en route.

A railway line serves the valley, with Tours as the hub – most of the château towns are less than an hour's journey away. Buses also run, but less frequently. The TGV between Paris and Tours takes one hour. There are also a couple of car-hire offices at Tours station (Avis 02.47.20.53.27 or Budget 02.47.46.22.21), plus desks at Tours airport, served by Ryanair from London Stansted. The Loire Valley is also perfect cycling country – there are cycle hire offices at and near Tours station.

The lively town of **Amboise** grew up at a strategic crossing point on the Loire. The **Château Royal d'Amboise** (02.47.57.00.98), built within the walls of a medieval stronghold, was the first royal Renaissance residence in the Val de Loire. Although only a small part of

Charles VIII and Louis XIIs' complex remains today, the château's interior spans several styles from vaulted Gothic to Empire. The exquisite Gothic St-Hubert chapel holds the tomb of Leonardo Da Vinci who died at Amboise in 1519. It's a short walk up the hill, past several cave dwellings, to reach Clos Lucé (02.47.57.62.88), the Renaissance manor where Leonardo lived at the invitation of François I for the three years before his death. Beneath the château on place Michel Debré, the Caveau des Vignerons (02.47.57.23.69) has plenty of local wine to sample, including the region's speciality – Cremant de Loire – a light sparkling wine made from Pineau and Chardonnay grapes.

The last Renaissance château to be built on the Loire was **Villandry** (02.47.50.02.09), famed for its spectacular Renaissance knot gardens by Jacques Androuet du Cerceau. The castle's interior was refitted in the 18th century and shelters a collection of Spanish paintings and a Hispanic-Moresque ceiling. However, the true attraction has to be its three-tiered gardens, most unusual of which is the colourful and appetisingly aromatic *jardin potager*, where patterns have been created with ornamental artichokes, cabbages and pumpkins.

Rising from an island in the river Indre west of Tours, **Azay-le-Rideau** (02.47.45.42.04) is the quintessential fairy-tale castle, especially when viewed during the nocturnal garden visits in summer. Built in 1518-27 by François I's treasurer Gilles Berthelot (although he died in hiding before it was finished), it combines

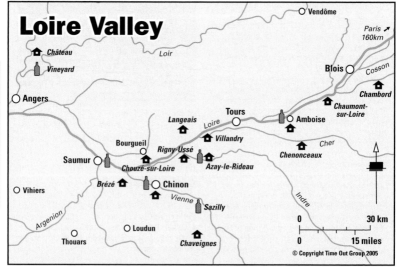

Loire Valley

period features (high roofs, narrow pepper-pot turrets) with the imposing symmetry of new Italian Renaissance style. The château's interior is mostly Gothic and Renaissance with intricate tapestries, paintings and 16th-century furniture.

At the end of Louis-Philippe's Pont de Langeais (built in 1849), the **Château de Langeais** (02.47.96.72.60), where Charles VIII married Anne de Bretagne in 1491, stands as a stern, archetypal medieval fortress. Although Louis XI transformed it into the comfortable lodgings we see today, the present castle, dating from 1465, still has a moat, wooden drawbridge and the vestiges of the oldest medieval stone *donjon* in France. Amid the lovely furnishings, don't miss the 16th-century Flanders tapestries.

The genuine Sleeping Beauty castle is **Rigny-Ussé** (02.47.95.54.05), Charles Perrault's inspiration before writing the classic fairy story. The pivotal spinning-wheel scene is even reconstituted at the top of one of the turrets. Initially built in the 15th and 16th centuries on the site of a medieval bastion, the north wing was knocked down by the Marquis de Valentinay in the 17th century to provide a view onto his beautiful terraces, designed by Le Nôtre. The interior dates mostly from this period, with striking Flanders tapestries.

High on a cliff, looming over the picturesque town of **Chinon** (famous for its wine), are the ghostly ruins of the **Château de Chinon** (02.47.93.13.45). You can admire the scale of this huge medieval fortress is from the south bank of the Vienne. Split into three distinct forts, separated by deep moats, the castle was the property of the counts of Blois in the tenth century, before the Plantagenets took it for the English crown in the 1200s. The Fort Saint-Georges cannot be visited, but the Château du Milieu (the entrance to the castle) and the 13th century Tour de l'Horloge with its museum on Jeanne d'Arc (who met with Charles VII here in 1429) provide attractive compensation. Down in the medieval town, Au Vieux Marché by the river (2 route de Tours, 02.47.93.04.10) offers daily wine-tasting with a tour around the wine cellar on request. Chinon wine is recognisable by its ruby colour and violet aroma.

Brézé (02.41.51.60.15) is a château unlike any other. Still inhabited by descendants of the original owners (from 1060), the Renaissance- and Empire-style main buildings could easily be misconstrued as intentional trompe-l'oeil additions to what is hiding in the moat: a subterranean medieval city, which can still be visited, including a bakery (last used by the Germans World War II) and the magnificent Cathédrale d'images, where strange lights are projected onto the cave walls to produce eerie art. After your unusual upstairs-downstairs

visit, you can taste the estate's own Saumur wine (classed as one of the best vintages in the Anjou region) in the Espace Dégustation.

Chocolate-box **Saumur** – as known for its wine as for its striking **Château de Saumur** (02.41.40.24.40) – was a stronghold for the Anjou dynasty. In the 16th century governor Philippe Dupleiss-Mornay decided to fortify the castle, then turn it into a jail. The Marquis de Sade was imprisoned here in 1768. The château is an example of 14th-century architecture, with a collection of decorative pieces and a horse-riding museum. Behind the castle, 12m underground, the Caves Louis de Grenelle (20 rue Marceau, 02.41.50.17.63) gives a tasting tour through their stone cellars, including sparkling varieties from Château de Brézé.

If you're driving back to Paris, the **Château de Chambord** (02.54.50.40.00), **Château de Chaumont** (02.54.51.26.26) and **Château de Chenonceaux** (08.20.20.90.90) are Renaissance castles near Amboise well worth a detour.

Where to stay

Amboise is a pleasant, centrally-located stop-off point. In town, try the **Manoir de la Maison Blanche** (18 rue de l'Epinetterie, 02.47.23.16.14, double €70) near the centre. In Azay-le-Rideau, **Le Biencourt** (7 rue Balzac, 02.47.45.20.75, www.hotelbiencourt.com) offers basic rooms for two to four people (€47-€70).

For a taste of the high life at low prices, the **Château de la Vrillaye** (02.47.58.24.40, www. chateaudelavrillaye.com) in **Chaveignes** (18km from Chinon, 23 km from Azay-le Rideau) offers stunning rooms, wine-tasting, tennis courts and a swimming pool for €75-€90 a double. The **Château des Réaux** (02.47.95.14.40) at Chouzé-sur-Loire has doubles for €80-€230.

Among the number of hotels in Saumur, the **St-Pierre** (8 rue Haute-St-Pierre, 02.41.50. 33.00, www.saintpierresaumur.com) is set between the church of the same name and the château. Room prices range from €72 in low season to €126. **Saumur tourist office** (pl de la Bilange, 02.41.40.20.60, www.saumur-tourisme.com) will have many other options.

Getting there

By car

Take the A10 to Blois (174km), then follow the Loire along the N152 to Saumur via Amboise and Tours. Sights should be signposted along this road.

By train

TGV from Gare de Montparnasse takes 2hrs 30mins to Saumur (change at Angers), to Langeais (change at St-Pierre-des-Corps) and to Chinon (change at Tours). From Gare d'Austerlitz to Amboise takes 2hrs.

TimeOut Film

timeout.com/film

'the best films, the hottest news
and the sharpest writers'

All the best new releases, all the listings,
and 15,500 films and DVDs reviewed –
all in one place

Directory

Features

Directory

Getting Around

By air

Roissy-Charles-de-Gaulle airport

Most international flights arrive at Roissy-Charles-de-Gaulle airport, 30km north-east of Paris. Its two main terminals are some way apart, so check which one you need for your return flight; for information in English, call 01.48.62.22.80 or see www.adp.fr (under 'flight schedules'). The **RER B** is the quickest and most reliable way to central Paris (about 40min to Gare du Nord; 45min to RER Châtelet-Les Halles; €7.75 single). A new station gives direct access from Terminal 2 (including Air France flights); from Terminal 1 you take the free shuttle bus. RER trains run every 15min, 5.24am-11.56pm daily. SNCF information: 08.91.36.20.20. **Air France buses** (€10 single, €17 return) leave every 30min, 6am-10.30pm Mon-Fri, 7am-10.30pm Sat, Sun, from both terminals, and stop at Porte Maillot and pl Charles-de-Gaulle (35-50 min trip). Air France buses run to Gare Montparnasse and Gare de Lyon (€11.50 single, €19.55 return) every 30min (45-60min trip), 7am-9.30pm daily. There's also a bus between Roissy and Orly (€15.50) every 20-30min, 6am-11pm daily. Information on 08.92.35.08.20, www.cars.airfrance.fr. The RATP **Roissybus** (€8.30) runs every 15min, 6.30am-11pm daily, between the airport and the corner of rue Scribe/rue Auber (at least 45min); buy tickets on the bus.

Information: 08.92.68.77.14. **Paris Airports Service** is a door-to-door minibus service between airports and hotels, 24/7. It works on the 'more passengers the less you pay' system. Roissy prices go from €24 for one person to €12.40 each for eight people, 6am-8pm (minimum €34, 5-6am, 8-10pm); Orly from €22 for one to €9 each for eight; book on 08.21.80.08.01, www.paris airportservice.com. **Airport Connection** (01.44.18.36.02, www.airport-connection.com; reservations 7am-8pm) runs a similar service, 5am-8pm, at €25 per person, €37 for two, then €15 per extra person. A **taxi** to central Paris can take 30-60 mins depending on traffic and your point of arrival. Expect to pay €30-€50, plus €1 per piece of luggage.

Orly airport

French domestic and several international flights use Orly airport, 18km south of the city. It has two terminals: Orly-Sud (mainly international flights) and Orly-Ouest (mainly domestic flights). English-speaking information service on 01.49.75.15.15, 6am-midnight daily. **Air France buses** (08.92.35.08.20, www.cars. airfrance.fr; €7.50 single, €12.75 return) leave both terminals every 15min, 6am-11.30pm daily, and stop at Invalides and Montparnasse (30-45min). The RATP **Orlybus** at Denfert-Rochereau leaves every 15min, 5.35am-11.05pm daily (30-minute trip); tickets (€5.80) are available on the bus. Information: 08.92.68.77.14. The high-speed **Orlyval** shuttle train runs every 7min (6am-11pm daily)

to RER B station Antony (Orlyval and RER together cost €8.85); getting to central Paris takes about 35min. You could also catch the **Orlyrail** (€5.50) to Pont de Rungis, where you can take the RER C into central Paris. Trains run every 15min, 6am-11pm daily; 50min trip. A **taxi** into town takes 20-40min and costs €16-€26, plus €1 per piece of luggage. The minibus services listed above also run to and from Orly.

Paris Beauvais airport

Beauvais, 70km from Paris, is served by UK budget airlines, such as **Ryanair** (03.44.11.41.41, www.ryanair.com), which flies from Dublin, Shannon and Glasgow. A bus service (€10) between the airport and Porte Maillot leaves 20min after each arrival and 3hr 15min before each departure. Tickets can be bought at the arrival lounge or from the Beauvais shop at 1 bd Pershing, 17th. Information: 08.92.68.20.64, www.aeroportbeauvais.com.

Airline contacts

Aer Lingus 01.70.20.00.72, www.aerlingus.com
Air France 08.20.82.08.20, www.airfrance.fr
American Airlines 08.10.87.28.72, www.aa.com, www.americanairlines.com
bmibaby +44 (0)890 710 081, www.bmibaby.com
British Airways 08.25.82.54.00, www.britishairways.fr
British Midland 01.41.91.87.04, www.flybmi.com
Continental 01.42.99.09.09, www.continental.com
Easyjet 08.25.08.25.08, www.easyjet.com
KLM & NorthWest 08.90.71.07.10, www.klm.com
United 08.10.72.72.72, www.united.com

By car

For travel between France and the UK by car, options include tunnel **Le Shuttle** (Folkstone-Calais 35mins) (08.10.63.03.04, www.eurotunnel.com); fast service **Hoverspeed** (Dover-Calais, Newhaven-Dieppe) (03.21.46.14.00, www.hover speed.com); ferries **Brittany Ferries** (08.25.82.88.28, www. brittanyferries.com), **P&O Stena Line** (01.55.69.82.28, www.posl.com) and **SeaFrance** (08.25.04.40.45, www.seafrance.com).

Shared journeys

Allô-Stop *1 rue Condorcet, 9th (01.53.20.42.42/08.25.80.36.66, www.allostop.net; M° Poissonière).* **Open** 10am-1pm, 2-6.30pm Mon-Fri; 10am-1pm, 2-5pm Sat. **Credit** MC, V. Call several days ahead to be put in touch with drivers. There's a fee (€4.50 under 200km; up to €10 over 500km), plus €0.50 per km to the driver. Routes most travelled: Cologne, Lyon, Marseille, Nantes, Rennes, Toulouse.

By coach

International coach services arrive at the Gare Routière Internationale Paris-Galliéni at Porte de Bagnolet, 20th. For reservations (in English) call **Eurolines** on 08.92.69.52.52 (€0.34 min), or in the UK 01582 404511, www.eurolines.fr.

By rail

The new, speedier **Eurostar** service between London and Paris now takes 2hrs 25min direct; allow slightly longer for trains stopping in Ashford and Lille. You must check in at least 30min before the train is due to leave. Passports must be carried on the Eurostar. Eurostar trains from London Waterloo (01233 617575, www.eurostar.com) arrive at Gare du Nord (08.92.35.35.39, www.sncf.fr) with easy access to public transport and taxi ranks (the huge queues do move fairly quickly). **Bicycles**

can be transported as hand luggage if they are dismantled and carried in a bike bag. You can also check them in at the Eurodispatch depot at Waterloo (Esprit Parcel Service, 08705 850850) or Sernam depot at Gare du Nord (08.25.84.58.45). Check-in must be done 48hr in advance, a Eurostar ticket must be shown and the service costs £20 or €49.

Travel agencies

Nouvelles Frontières *13 av de l'Opéra, 1st (08.25.00.08.25/www. nouvelles-frontieres.fr). M° Pyramides.* **Open** 9am-7pm Mon-Sat. **Credit** MC, V. Agent with 16 branches in Paris.

Thomas Cook *26 av de l'Opéra, 1st (01.53.29.40.00/www.thomascook.fr). M° Opéra.* **Open** 10am-7pm Mon-Sat. **Credit** AmEx, DC, MC, V. General travel agent with more than 33 branches in Paris.

USIT *6 rue de Vaugirard, 6th (01.42.34.56.90/08.92.88.88.88/ www.usitconnections.fr). M° Odéon.* **Open** 10am-7pm Mon-Fri; 10am-6pm Sat. Credit MC, V. Provides coach, air and train tickets.

Maps

Free maps of the Métro, bus and RER systems are available at airports and Métro stations. Other brochures from Métro stations are *Paris Visite – Le Guide*, with details of transport tickets and a small map, and *Plan de Paris*, a fold-out map that shows *Noctambus* night bus lines. Maps sponsored by Galeries Lafayette and Printemps can be picked up at most hotels. A Paris street map (called *Plan de Paris*) can be bought from newsagents or stationers (*papeteries*). The blue-covered *Paris Pratique* is nicely clear and compact.

Public transport

The public transport system (**RATP**) consists of bus routes, the Métro (underground), the **RER** suburban express railway (which connects with the Métro inside Paris) and

All change!

The Carte Orange will soon no longer be orange, and staffed kiosks are to disappear from some stations. Yes, it's all change on the Paris Métro, with the introduction of the new electronic **Navigo** card. Simply swiping this chip-carrying smart card over a scanner opens the turnstile. The system has been in place since 2001 for annual subscribers, but now monthly and weekly Carte Orange holders can also choose to go electronic – and purple (the colour of Navigo). Carrying encrypted information about the holder – digital photo and personal details – the Navigo card can be charged with credit on the Internet or at portals in Métro stations. While its

main use is for regular travel in Paris, the card can also be charged for one-off journeys to anywhere on the RER network (such as Versailles). In the future, Navigo could theoretically allow users to connect with other forms of transport, and there are plans to give it a extra, new role: that of electronic purse for low-value purchases in *boulangeries*, newsagents, and *tabacs*. Technophobes needn't panic, though: the traditional magnetic-strip cards are still around – as Paris Visite, carnets, and single tickets. But in the years to come, these too will be phased out and replaced by disposable, contactless tickets. For more details, see www.ratp.fr.

two suburban tramways. Paris and its suburbs are divided into eight travel zones; zones 1 and 2 cover the city centre. Information: 08.92.68.77.14, in English 08.92.68.41.14, www.ratp.fr. State rail system **SNCF** serves the French regions and abroad (*Grandes Lignes*) and the suburbs (*Banlieue*). Information: 08.92.35.35.35, www.sncf.com.

Fares & tickets

RATP **tickets** and passes are valid on the Métro, bus and RER. Tickets and *carnets* can be bought at Métro stations, tourist offices and *tabacs* (tobacconists); tickets can be bought on buses. Keep your ticket to exit from RER stations and in case of spot checks. A ticket costs €1.40; it's more economical to buy a *carnet* of ten tickets for €10.50. *Carte Orange* passes (passport photo needed) offer unlimited travel in the relevant zones for a week or month. A *coupon mensuel* (valid from the first day of the month) for zones 1-2 costs €50.40; a weekly *coupon hebdomadaire* (valid Mon-Sun inclusive) for zones 1-2 costs €15.40 and is better value than *Paris Visite* passes; three-day pass for zones 1-3 is €18.25; a five-day pass is €26.65, with discounts on some tourist attractions. A one-day *Mobilis* pass goes from €5.40 for zones 1-2 to €18.40 for zones 1-8 (not including airports).

Métro & RER

The Paris **Métro** is at most times the fastest and cheapest means of getting around. Trains run daily 5.30am-12.40am.

Individual lines are numbered, with each direction named after the last stop. Follow the orange *Correspondance* signs to change lines. Some interchanges, such as Châtelet, Montparnasse-Bienvenüe and République, involve long walks. The exit (*Sortie*) is indicated in blue. The driverless line 14, also known as the Météor, runs from Gare St-Lazare to the new Bibliothèque Nationale. Pickpockets and bag-snatchers are rife on the Métro – pay special attention as the doors are closing. The five **RER** lines (A, B, C, D and E) run 5.30am-1am daily across Paris and into commuterland. Within Paris, the RER is useful for making faster journeys – for example, Châtelet-Les Halles to Charles de Gaulle-Etoile in only two stops on the RER compared with eight on Métro line 1. Métro tickets are valid for RER journeys within zones 1-2.

Buses

Buses run 6.30am-8.30pm, with some routes continuing until 12.30am, Mon-Sat; more limited services operate on selected lines Sun and public holidays. You can use a Métro ticket, a ticket bought from the driver (€1.40) or a travel pass. Tickets should be punched in the machine next to the driver; passes should be shown to the driver. When you want to get off, press the red request button, and the *arrêt demandé* (stop requested) sign lights up.

Night buses

After the Métro and normal buses stop, the only public transport – apart from taxis – are the 18 **Noctambus** lines, between place du Châtelet and the suburbs (hourly 1.30am-5.35am Mon-Thur; half-hourly 1am-5.35am Fri, Sat); look out for the owl logo on bus stops. Routes A to H, P, T and V serve the Right Bank and northern suburbs; I to M, R

Technology to go

Thanks to all things wireless, travellers can now keep up to speed with everything from delayed departures to breaking business news. Worried you'll miss your plane boarding time or can't find the gate number? The new AéroSMS service lets jetsetters at Paris's two main airports keep tabs on their flights. The service sends text messages to mobile phones, with details of estimated arrival or departure times, departure gates, baggage hall location, and any delays or cancellations to their flights. Not to be outdone, the SNCF has equipped the country's 50 biggest railway stations (including all those in Paris) with WiFi hotspots, allowing passengers with appropriately-equipped laptops to surf while they wait for their train.

Going underground, malodorous Métros could soon be a thing of the past. Using micro-encapsulation technology, the RATP has come up with a new perfume that is sprinkled inside carriages on its driverless line 14. The more crowded the train, the more the perfume crushed and the more fragrance released. The future could also see every motorist's fantasy realised: traffic lights that turn green just as you roll up. Not satisfied with the city's multiple bus lanes, the RATP is looking into exploiting the existing GPS equipment aboard its buses to assure a red light-free journey for bus passengers. For the time being, though, the project is awaiting the green light.

and S serve the Left Bank and southern suburbs. A ticket costs €2.70 and allows one change; travel passes are valid.

River transport

Batobus (www.batobus.com). River buses stop every 15-25 mins at: Eiffel Tower, Musée d'Orsay, St Germain-des-Prés (Quai Malaquais), Notre-Dame, Jardin des Plantes, Hôtel de Ville, Louvre, Champs-Elysées (Pont Alexandre III). They run June-Sept 10am-9pm; Apr-Oct 10am-7pm. A short-trip ticket (four stops max) costs €7.50 (€3.50 children, €7 students, €6 Carte Orange holders); one-day pass €11 (€5, €9, €7.50); two-day pass €13 (€7, €11, €9); one-month pass €22 (€12 children); season-ticket €50 (€30 children). Tickets can be bought at Batobus stops, RATP ticket offices and the Office de Tourisme.

Trams

Two modern tramlines operate in the suburbs, running from La Défense to Issy-Val de Seine and from Bobigny Pablo Picasso to St-Denis. They connect with the Métro and RER; fares are the same as for buses.

Rail services

Several suburban attractions, Versailles and Disneyland Paris in particular, are served by the RER. Most locations farther from the city are served by the SNCF railway; there are few long-distance bus services. The TGV high-speed train has revolutionised journey times and is slowly being extended to all the main regions.

Tickets can be bought at any SNCF station (not just the one from which you'll travel), SNCF shops and travel agents. If you reserve online or by phone, you can pay and pick up your tickets from the station or have them sent to your home. SNCF automatic machines (billeterie automatique) only work with French credit/debit cards. Regular trains have full-rate White (peak times) and cheaper Blue periods. You can save on TGV fares by buying

special cards. Carte 12/25 gives under-26s a 25%-50% reduction; without it, under-26s are entitled to 25% off. Buy tickets in advance to secure the cheaper fare. Pensioners over 60 benefit from similar terms with a Carte Senior. Before you board any train, stamp your ticket in the orange composteur machines located on the platforms, or you might have to pay a hefty fine.

SNCF reservations & tickets
SNCF national reservations and information: 08.92.35.35.35 (€0.34 per min) www.sncf.com. **Open** 7am-10pm daily. Line can also be reached by dialling 3635 and saying 'billet' at the prompt.

SNCF information (no reservations) in Ile-de-France: 08.91.36.20.20. **Open** 7am-10pm daily.

Paris mainline stations

Gare d'Austerlitz: Central and SW France and Spain.

Gare de l'Est: Alsace, Champagne and southern Germany.

Gare de Lyon: Burgundy, the Alps, Provence, Italy.

Gare Montparnasse: West France, Brittany, Bordeaux, the Southwest.

Gare du Nord: Northeast France, Channel ports, Eurostar, Belgium and the Netherlands.

Gare St-Lazare: Normandy.

Taxis

Paris taxi drivers are not known for their charm, nor for their knowledge of the Paris street plan; if you have a preferred route, say so. Taxis can also be hard to find, especially at rush hour or early in the morning. Your best bet is to find a taxi rank (station de taxis, marked with a blue sign) on major roads, crossroads and at stations. A white light on a taxi's roof indicates the car is free; an orange light means the cab is busy. Taxi charges are based on zone and time of day: **A** (7am-7pm Mon-Sat, €0.62 per km); **B** (7pm-7am Mon-Sat, all day Sun; 7am-7pm Mon-Sat suburbs and airports, €1.06 per km); **C** (7pm-7am daily suburbs and airports, €1.24 per km). Most journeys in

central Paris average €6-€12; there's a minimum charge of €5.10, plus €0.90 for each piece of luggage over 5kg or bulky objects, and a €0.70 surcharge from mainline stations. Most drivers will not take more than three people, although they should take a couple and two children. Don't feel obliged to tip, although rounding up by €0.30-€0.70 is polite. Taxis are not allowed to refuse rides because they are too short and can only refuse to take you in a particular direction during their last half-hour of service – though both rules are blatantly ignored. If you want a receipt, ask for un reçu or la note. Complaints should be made in writing to the **Bureau de la réglementation publique de Paris**, 36 rue des Morillons, 75732 Paris Cedex 15.

Phone cabs

The following accept phone bookings around the clock; you also pay for the time it takes your radioed taxi to get to where you are (assuming it does actually turn up). If you wish to pay by credit card (€15 minimum), mention this when you order. **Airportaxis** (to and from Paris airports) 01.48.40.17.17/www.airportaxis. com; **Alpha** 01.45.85.85.85; **Artaxi** 01.42.06.67.10/www. artaxi.fr; **G7** 01.47.39.47.39/ 01.41.27.66.99 (in English); **Taxis Bleus** 01.49.36.10.10/ www.taxis-bleus.com.

Driving

If you bring your car to France, you must bring its registration and insurance documents – an insurance green card, available from insurance companies and the AA and RAC in the UK, is not compulsory but is useful. As you come into Paris you will meet the Périphérique, the giant ring road that carries traffic in, out and around the city. Intersections, which lead

Directory

onto other main roads, are called *portes* (gates). Driving on the Périphérique is not as hair-raising as it might look, though it's often congested, especially at rush hour and peak holiday times. If you've come to Paris by car, it may be a good idea to park at the edge of the city and use public transport. Some hotels have parking spaces which can be paid for by the hour, day or by various types of season tickets. In peak holiday periods, the organisation Bison Futé hands out brochures at motorway *péages* (toll gates), suggesting less-crowded routes. French roads are categorised as *Autoroutes* (motorways, with an 'A' in front of the number), *Routes Nationales* (national 'N' roads), *Routes Départementales* (local, 'D' roads) and rural *Routes Communales* ('C' roads). *Autoroutes* are toll roads, though some sections, including most of the area immediately around Paris, are free. *Autoroutes* have a speed limit of 130km/h (80mph); this is not adhered to with any degree of zeal by French motorists. The limit on most *Routes Nationales* is 90km/h (56mph); within urban areas the limit is 50km/h (30mph), and 30km/h (20mph) in selected residential zones. **Traffic information for Ile-de-France**: 08.26.02.20.22/www.bison-fute.equipement.gouv.fr.

Breakdown services

The AA or RAC do not have reciprocal arrangements with an equivalent organisation in France, so it's advisable to take out additional breakdown insurance cover, for example with **Europ Assistance** (01.41.85.85.41/www.europ assistance.co.uk). If you don't have insurance, you can use its service (01.41.85.85.85), but it will charge you the full cost. Other 24-hour breakdown services in Paris include:

Action Auto Assistance (01.45.58.49.58); **Dan Dépann Auto** (01.42.66.67.58).

Driving tips

● At junctions where no signposts indicate right of way, the car coming from the right has priority. Many roundabouts now give priority to those on the roundabout. If this is not indicated (by road markings or a sign with the message *Vous n'avez pas la priorité*), priority is for those coming from the right.
● Drivers and all passengers must wear seat belts.
● Children under ten are not allowed to travel in the front of a car, except in baby seats facing backwards.
● You should not stop on an open road; pull off to the side.
● When drivers flash their lights at you, this means they will not slow down and are warning you to move out of their path or keep out of the way. But friendly drivers also flash their lights to warn you when there are *gendarmes* lurking in the vicinity.
● Try to carry plenty of change, as it's quicker – and less stressful – to make for the exact-money line on *péages*. If you are caught short, cashiers do give change and *péages* accept credit cards.

Parking

There are still a few free on-street parking areas left in Paris, but they are, unsurprisingly, often full. If you park illegally, you risk getting your car clamped or towed away (*see below*). It is forbidden to park in zones marked for deliveries (*livraisons*) or taxis. Parking meters have now been replaced by *horodateurs*, pay-and-display machines, which take a special card, *carte de stationnement* (€15 or €30 available from *tabacs*). Parking

is often free at weekends, after 7pm and in August. There are numerous underground car parks in central Paris. Most cost €2.50 per hour; €19 for 24 hours; some offer lower rates after 6pm, and many offer various types of season ticket – a week, for instance, at €80, and a month at around €150. More information at www.parkingsdeparis.com.

Clamps & car pounds

If you've had your car clamped, contact the local police station. There are eight car pounds (*préfourrières*) in Paris. You'll have to pay a €136 removal fee plus €10 storage charge per day, and a parking fine of €35 for parking in a no-parking zone. Bring your driving licence and insurance papers. But before you can pay, you need to find that treasured vehicle – not a small task given the labyrinth that represents the world of impounded cars in Paris and the affability of those who run it. Here goes. Once clamped, your car will first be sent to the *préfourrière* closest to where it was snatched. The six *préfourrières* roughly correspond to the following districts: **Les Halles** 1st, 2nd, 3rd, 4th (01.40.39.12.20); **Bercy** 5th, 12th, 13th, 14th (01.53.46.69.20); **Pantin** 10th, 11th, 19th, 20th (01.44.52.52.10); **Balard** 6th, 7th, 14th, 15th, 16th (01.45.58.70.30); **Foch** 8th, 16th, (01.53.64.11.80); **Pouchet** 9th, 17th, 18th (01.53.06.67.68). After a 72hr spell in the *préfourrière*, if no-one has claimed it, a car will be sent to one of the following two *fourrières* (pounds): **Paris Nord Macdonald** 1st-4th, 8th-10th, 16th-19th (01.40.37.79.20); **Paris Sud Bonneuil** 5th-7th, 11th-15th, 20th (01.45.13.61.40). But if your car is deemed not necessarily worth retrieving, it will be sent to one of the following *fourrières*:

Prefecture de Police Paris Nord 1st-4th, 8th-10th, 16th-19th (01.48.38.14.81); **Fourrière Clichy** 5th-7th, 11th-15th, 20th (01.47.31.22.15). Information: www.prefecture-police-paris.interieur.gouv.fr.

Car hire

To hire a car you must be 25 or over and have held a licence for at least a year. Some agencies accept drivers aged 21-24, but a supplement of €20-€22 per day is usual. Take your licence and passport with you. There are often good weekend offers (Fri evening to Mon morning). Week-long deals are better at the bigger companies: with Avis or Budget, for example, it's around €270 a week for a small car with insurance and 1,750km included. Costlier hire companies allow the return of a car in other French cities and abroad. Bargain companies may have an extremely high charge for damage: read the small print before signing.

Hire companies

Ada *01.45.54.63.63/08.25.16.91.69/ www.ada-location.fr.*
Avis *08.20.05.05.05/www.avis.com.*
Budget *08.25.00.35.64/www.budget rentacar.com.*
Calandres *04.93.76.03.50.* Has a *flotte prestige* of luxury cars (for those who've held a licence for at least five years).
EasyRentacar *www.easycar.com.*
Europcar *01.30.43.82.82.*
Hertz *01.39.38.38.38/www.hertz.com.*
Rent-a-Car *08.92.69.46.95/ www.rentacar.fr.*
Valem *01.43.14.79.79/www.axeco.fr.*

Chauffeur-driven cars

Carey *(01.41.40.84.84/www.carey-first.com).* **Open** 24hr daily. **Prices** from €145 airport transfer; €240 for 4 hours. **Credit** AmEx, DC, MC, V.

Cycling

Since 1996, the Mairie de Paris has been promoting cycling in the city. There are now 353km of bike lanes and there are even plans for a bicycle 'Périphérique' circling Paris. Mayor Delanoë has continued with predecessor Jean Tiberi's enthusiasm, though his decision to close 3km of the Right Bank beside Paris-Plage for cyclists, rollerbladers and pedestrians was clearly aimed at leisure cyclists rather than commuters. The Itinéraires Paris-Piétons-Vélos-Rollers – scenic strips of the city that are closed to cars on Sundays and holidays – have been consistently multiplied; the city website (www.paris.fr) can provide an up-to-date list of routes and a downloadable map of cycle lanes. A free *Paris à Vélo* map can also be picked up at any Mairie or from bike shops. Cycle lanes (*pistes cyclables*) run mostly N-S and E-W. N-S routes include rue de Rennes, av d'Italie, bd Sébastopol and av Marceau. E-W routes take in the rue de Rivoli, bd St-Germain, bd St-Jacques and av Daumesnil. You could be fined (€22) if you don't use them, which is a bit rich considering the lanes are often blocked by delivery vans and the €135 fine for obstructing a cycle lane is barely enforced. Cyclists are also entitled to use certain bus lanes (especially the new ones, which are set off by a strip of kerb stones): look out for traffic signs with a bike symbol. The Bois de Boulogne and Bois de Vincennes offer paths away from traffic although they are still criss-crossed by roads bearing menacing motor vehicles.

Don't let the Parisians' blasé attitude to helmets and lights convince you it's not worth using them. Be confident, make your intentions clear and keep moving – and beware of scooter-mounted bag-snatchers. If the thought of pedaling around alone in a city known for the verve of its drivers fazes you, consider joining a guided bike tour (*see p77,* **Guided Tours**).

Cycles & scooters for hire

Note that bike insurance may not cover theft: be sure to check before you sign on the dotted line.

Atelier de la Compagnie *57 bd de Grenelle, 15th (01.45.79.77.24). M° Dupleix.* **Open** 9.30am-7pm Mon-Fri. Closed one week in Aug. **Credit** MC, V. A scooter for €30 per day or €130 per week. Deposit of €1,200, plus passport, required.

Freescoot *63 quai de la Tournelle, 5th (01.44.07.06.72/www.freescoot. com). M° St Michel.* **Open** 9am-7pm daily. **Credit** MC, V. Scooter for €30 per day or €145 per week. Deposit of €1,300, plus passport, required.

Maison Roue Libre *1 passage Mondétour, 1st (08.10.44.15.34). M° Châtelet.* Plus (Mar-Oct) four RATP cyclobuses at Stalingrad, pl du Châtelet, porte d'Auteuil and parc Floral in the Bois de Vincennes (01.48.15.28.88/www.rouelibre.com). **Open** 9am-7pm daily. **Credit** MC, V (for weekend hire only). Bike hire costs €3 an hour; €12 a day. Helmets come free. Passport and €150 deposit required.

Paris-Vélo *2 rue du Fer-à-Moulin, 5th (01.43.37.59.22/www.paris-velo-rent-a-bike.fr). M° Censier-Daubenton.* Also (15 Apr to 15 Oct) in the Bois de Boulogne (rond-pont du Jardin d'Acclimatation) and the Bois de Vincennes (av Daumesnil, by Lac Daumesnil). **Open** 10am-7pm daily. **Credit** MC, V. Good selection of mountain bikes (VTT) and 21-speed models for hire. Five hours costs €12, a weekend €30, a month €116. Passport and €300 deposit required.

Walking

Walking is the best way to explore Paris; just remember that to anything on wheels (cyclists and rollerskaters included), pedestrians are the lowest form of life. Crossing Paris streets can be perillous, as the 3,000 or so pedestrians who end up in hospital – or worse – each year can tell you. Brits must realise that traffic will be coming from the 'wrong' direction and that zebra crossings mean little. By law, drivers are only obliged to stop at a red traffic light – and even then, many will take a calculated risk.

Directory

Resources A-Z

Addresses

Paris arrondissements are reflected in the last two digits of the postal code: 75005 denotes the 5th, 75012 the 12th. The 16th arrondissement is divided into two sectors, 75016 and 75116. Some business addresses have a more detailed postcode, followed by a Cedex number which indicates the arrondissement; *bis* or *ter* is the equivalent of 'b' or 'c' after a building number.

Age restrictions

You must be 18 or over to drive, and 18 in order to consume alcohol in a public place. There is no age limit for buying cigarettes. The age of consent for heterosexuals and homosexuals is 15.

Attitude & etiquette

Parisians take manners seriously and are generally more courteous than their reputation may lead you to believe. If someone brushes you accidentally they will more often than not say *'pardon'*; you can do likewise, or say *'c'est pas grave'* (don't worry). In shops it is normal to greet the assistant with a *'bonjour madame'* or *'bonjour monsieur'* when you enter and say *'au revoir'* when you leave. The business of *'tu'* and *'vous'* can be tricky for English speakers. Strangers, people significantly older than you and professional contacts should be addressed with the respectful *'vous'*; friends, relatives, children and pets as *'tu'*. Among themselves young people often launch straight in with *'tu'*.

Business

The best first stop in Paris for initiating business is the CCIP (*see below* **Useful Organisations**). Banks can refer you to lawyers, accountants and tax consultants. Other US and British banks provide expatriate services.

Conventions & conferences

The world's leading centre for trade fairs, Paris hosts over 500 exhibitions a year.

CNIT *2 pl de la Défense, BP 321, 92053 Paris La Défense (01.43.95.37.00/www.parisexpo.fr).* M°/RER Grande Arche de La Défense. Mainly computer fairs.

Palais des Congrès *2 pl de la Porte-Maillot, 17th (01.40.68.22.22/www.palaisdescongres-paris.com). M° Porte-Maillot.*

Paris-Expo *Porte de Versailles 15th (01.43.95.37.00/www.parisexpo.fr). M° Porte de Versailles.* Paris' biggest expo centre, from fashion to pharmaceuticals.

Parc des Expositions de Paris-Nord Villepinte *SEPENV 60004, 95970 Roissy-Charles de Gaulle (01.48.63.30.30/www.expoparisnord.com). RER Parc des Expositions.* Trade fair centre near Roissy airport.

Courier services

ATV *(01.41.72.13.63/www.atoutevitesse.com).* **Open** 24-hr daily. **No credit cards**. 24-hr bike or van messengers. Higher rates after 8pm and at weekends.

Chronopost *(Customer service: 08.25.80.18.01/www.chronopost.com).* **Open** 9am-8pm Mon-Fri; 9am-1pm Sat. **Credit** MC, V. This overnight delivery offshoot of the state-run post office is the most widely used service for parcels of up to 30kg.

UPS *(0800.877.877/www.ups.com).* **Open** 8am-7pm Mon-Fri; 8am-1pm Sat. **Credit** AmEx, MC, V. International courier services.

Secretarial services

ADECCO International *14 pl de la Défense, 92974 Paris La Défense (01.49.01.45.06/www.adecco.fr). M° Grande Arche de La Défense.* **Open** 8.30am-12.30pm, 2-6.30pm Mon-Fri. Large international employment agency specialising in bilingual secretaries and office staff – permanent or temporary.

Translators & interpreters

Certain documents, from birth certificates to loan applications, must be translated by certified legal translators, listed at the CCIP (*see below*) or embassies. For business translations there are dozens of reliable independents.

Travel advice

For up-to-date information on travel to a specific country – including the latest news on safety and security, health issues, local laws and customs – contact your home country government's department of foreign affairs. Most have websites packed with useful advice for would-be travellers.

Australia
www.smartraveller.gov.au

Canada
www.voyage.gc.ca

New Zealand
www.mft.govt.nz/travel

Republic of Ireland
http://foreignaffairs.gov.ie

UK
www.fco.gov.uk/travel

USA
http://www.state.gov/travel

Association des Anciens Elèves de L'Esit *(01.44.05.41.46)*. **Open** by phone only, 8am-8pm Mon-Fri; 8am-6pm Sat. A translation and interpreting co-operative whose 1,000 members are graduates of the Ecole Supérieure d'Interprètes et de Traducteurs.

International Corporate Communication *3 rue des Batignolles, 17th (01.43.87.29.29).* *M° Place de Clichy.* **Open** 9am-1pm, 2-6pm Mon-Fri. Translators of financial and corporate documents plus simultaneous translation.

Useful organisations

American Chamber of Commerce *262 rue de Fbg-St-Honoré, 8th (01.53.89.11.00/www. faccparisfrance.com). M° Ternes.* (Closed to the public, calls only.)

British Embassy Commercial Library *35 rue du Fbg-St-Honoré, 8th (01.44.51.34.56/www.amb-grandebretagne.fr). M° Concorde.* **Open** by appointment. Stocks trade directories, and assists British companies that wish to develop or set up in France.

CCIP (Chambre de Commerce et d'Industrie de Paris) *27 av de Friedland, 8th (01.55.65.55.65/ www.ccip.fr). M° Charles de Gaulle.* **Open** 9am-6pm Mon-Fri. This huge organisation provides a variety of services for people doing business in France and is very useful for small businesses. Pick up free booklet *Discovering the Chamber of Commerce* from its head office (above). There's also a legal advice line: 08.92.70.51.00 (9am-4.30pm Mon-Thur; 9am-1pm Fri). **Other locations**: *Bourse du Commerce, 2 rue de Viarmes, 1st (01.53.40.46.00). M° Louvre-Rivoli or Chatelet.* **Open** 9am-1pm, 2-5pm Mon, Tue, Thur, Fri; 9am-noon Wed. Has a free library and bookshop. *2 rue Adolf Jullien, 1st (01.55.65.40.16). M° Louvre-Rivoli or Châtelet.* **Open** 8.30am-12.30pm, 1.30-4.35pm. Support for businesses wishing to export goods and services to France.

Chambre de Commerce et d'Industrie Franco-Britannique *31 rue Boissy d'Anglas, 8th (01.53.30.81.30/fax 01.53.30.81.35/ www.francobritishchamber.com). M° Madeleine.* **Open** 2-5pm Mon-Fri. This organisation promotes contacts through conferences and social/cultural events. It publishes its own trade directory, as well as *Cross-Channel*, a trade magazine.

INSEE (Institut National de la Statistique et des Etudes Economiques) *Salle de consultation: 195 rue de Bercy, Tour Gamma A, 12th (01.41.17.50.50/ 08.25.88.94.52/www.insee.fr).*

M° Bercy. **Open** 9.30am-12:30pm, 2-5pm Mon-Thu, 9.30-12.30pm, 2-4pm Fri. Source of seemingly every statistic to do with French economy and society. Visit the reading room or search the website for free stats.

US Commercial Service *US Embassy, 2 av Gabriel, 8th (01.43.12.28.14/fax 01.43.12.21.72/ www.buyusa.gov/france). M° Concorde.* **Open** by appointment 9am-6pm Mon-Fri. Helps US companies looking to export to France. Advice by fax and e-mail.

Consumer

The customer is always right? If only. Shop staff surliness is an everyday occurrence, but in the event of a more serious misdemeanour, try one of the following.

Direction Régionale de la Concurrence, de la Consommation et de la Répression des Fraudes *8 rue Froissart, 3rd (01.40.27.16.00). M° St-Sébastien Froissart.* 9am-noon, 1.15-5.30pm Mon-Fri. Come here to file a consumer complaint concerning Paris-based businesses.

Institut National de la Consommation *80 rue Lecourbe, 15th (08.92.70.75.92). M° Sèvres Lecourbe.* **Open** *by phone* 9am-5pm Mon-Fri; recorded information at other times. Queries on consumer, regulatory, housing and administrative matters

Customs

There are no customs on goods for personal use between EU countries, provided tax has been paid in the country of origin. Quantities accepted as being for personal use are:

● 800 cigarettes or 400 small cigars or 200 cigars or 1kg loose tobacco.

● 10 litres of spirits (over 22% alcohol), 90 litres of wine (under 22% alcohol) or 110 litres of beer.

For goods from outside the EU:

● 200 cigarettes or 100 small cigars or 50 cigars or 250g loose tobacco.

● 1 litre of spirits (over 22% alcohol) or 2 litres of wine and beer

● 50g perfume

● 500g coffee

Tax refunds

Non-EU residents can claim a refund or *détaxe* (around 12%) on VAT if they spend over €175 in any one day and if they live outside the EU for more than six months in the year. At the shop ask for a *bordereau de vente à l'exportation*, and when you leave France have it stamped by customs. Then send the stamped form back to the shop. *Détaxe* does not cover food, drink, antiques, services or works of art.

Disabled travellers

Time Out guides include wheelchair access in listings, but it's always wise to check beforehand.

Association des paralysés de France *13 pl de Rungis, 13th (01.53.80.92.97). M° Place d'Italie.* **Open** 9am-12.30pm, 1.30-6pm Mon-Fri (closes 5pm Fri). Publishes *Guide 98 Musées, Cinémas* (€3.81) listing cinemas and museums accessible to those with limited mobility, and a guide to restaurants and sights.

Fédération APAJH (Association pour Adultes et Jeunes Handicapés) *185 Bureaux de la Colline, 92213 St-Cloud Cedex (01.55.39.56.00/www.apajh.org). M° Chemin Vert.* Advice for disabled people living in France.

Platforme d'accueil et d'information des personnes handicapées de la Marie de Paris *(08.00.03.37.48)*. Advice in French to disabled persons living in or visiting Paris. The Office de Tourisme website www.paris bienvenue.com also gives useful information for disabled visitors.

Getting around

Neither the Métro nor buses are wheelchair-accessible, with the exception of Métro line 14 (Méteor), bus lines 20, PC (Petite Ceinture) and some 91s. Forward seats on buses are intended for people with poor mobility. RER lines A and B and some SNCF trains are wheelchair-accessible in parts. All Paris taxis are obliged by law to take passengers in wheelchairs.

Directory

Aihrop *(01.41.29.01.29).* Open
9.30am-12.30pm, 1.30-5.30pm Mon-
Fri. Closed Aug. Transport for the
disabled, anywhere in Paris and Ile-
de-France; book 48 hours in advance.

Drugs

French police have the power
to stop and search anyone. It's
wise to keep prescription drugs
in their original containers and,
if possible, to carry copies of
the original prescriptions. If
you're caught in possession of
illegal drugs you can expect a
prison sentence and/or a fine.
An excellent source of advice
for young people with drug
problems is **Centre DIDRO**
(01.45.42.75.00/www.didro.net).
See also **Health**, **Helplines**.

Electricity & gas

Electricity in France runs on
220V. Visitors with British
240V appliances can change
the plug or use an adapter
(*adaptateur*). For US 110V
appliances, you'll need to use a
transformer (*transformateur*)
available at BHV or branches
of Fnac and Darty. Gas and
electricity are supplied by
state-owned Electricité de
France-Gaz de France. Contact
EDF-GDF (01.45.44.64.64/
www.edf.fr/www.gazdefrance.
com) about supply, bills,
power failures or gas leaks.

Embassies & consulates

For a full list of embassies and
consulates, see the Pages
Jaunes (www.pagesjaunes.fr)
under 'Ambassades et
Consulats'. Consular services
are for citizens of that country
(passports, etc) only.

Australian Embassy *4 rue
Jean-Rey, 15th (01.40.59.33.00/
www.austgov.fr). M° Bir-Hakeim.*
Open *Consular services* 9.15am-
noon, 2-4.30pm Mon-Fri; *Visas*
10am-12am Mon-Fri.

British Embassy *35 rue du Fbg-
St-Honoré, 8th (01.44.51.31.00/
www.amb- grandebretagne.fr). M°
Concorde. Consular services 18bis*

rue d'Anjou, 8th. Open 9.30am-
12.30pm, 2.30-5pm Mon, Wed-Fri;
9.30am-4.30pm Tue. *Visas 16 rue
d'Anjou, 8th (01.44.51.33.01/03/
recorded info 01.44.51.33.02/
emergency consular services
01.44.51.31.00).* Open 9am-noon
Mon-Fri; by phone 2.30-5pm Mon-Fri.
British citizens wanting consular
services (new passports etc) should
ignore the long queue along rue
d'Anjou for the visa department,
and walk straight in at No 18bis.

Canadian Embassy *35 av
Montaigne, 8th (01.44.43.29.00/
www.amb-canada.fr). M° Franklin
D. Roosevelt. Consular services
(01.44.43.29.02).* Open 9am-noon,
2-4.30pm Mon-Fri. *Visas 37 av
Montaigne (01.44.43.29.16).*
Open 8.30-11am Mon-Fri.

Irish Embassy *12 av Foch, 16th.
Consulate 4 rue Rude, 16th
(01.44.17.67.00). M° Charles de
Gaulle Etoile.* Open (consular/visas)
9.30am-noon Mon-Fri; by phone
9.30am-1pm, 2.30-5.30pm Mon-Fri.

New Zealand Embassy
*7ter rue Léonard-de-Vinci, 16th
(01.45.01.43.43/www.nzembassy.
com/france). M° Victor Hugo.* Open
9am-1pm, 2pm-5.30pm Mon-Fri
(closes 4pm Fri). July, Aug 9am-1pm,
2-4.30pm Mon-Thur; 9am-2pm Fri.
Visas 9am-12.30pm Mon-Fri. Visas
for travel to New Zealand can be
applied for using the website
www.immigration.govt.nz.

South African Embassy *59 quai
d'Orsay, 7th (01.53.59.23.23/www.
afriquesud.net). M° Invalides.* Open
by appointment; by phone 8.30am-
5.15pm Mon-Fri. Consulate and visas
9am-noon.

US Embassy *2 av Gabriel, 8th
(01.43.12.22.22/www.amb-usa.fr).
M° Concorde. Consulate and visas
2 rue St-Florentin, 1st
(01.43.12.22.22). M° Concorde.*
Open (consular services) 9am-
12.30pm, 1-3pm Mon-Fri. For visas,
phone 08.99.70.37.00 or check
website for non-immigration visas.

Emergencies

Most of the following services
operate 24 hours a day. In a
medical emergency, such as a
road accident, call the Sapeurs-
Pompiers, who have trained
paramedics. *See also* **Health:
Accident & Emergency,
Doctors; Helplines**.

Ambulance (SAMU)	**15**
Police	**17**
Fire (Sapeurs-Pompiers)	**18**
Emergency (from a mobile phone)	**112**

GDF (gas leaks)
08.10.43.32.75
EDF (electricity)
08.10.33.39 + number of
arrondissement (01-20)
Centre anti-poison
01.40.05.48.48

Gay & lesbian

For information on HIV and
AIDS, see **Health**. See also
Gay & Lesbian, *pp308-313.*

Health

Nationals of non-EU countries
should take out insurance
before leaving home. EU
nationals staying in France are
entitled to use of the French
Social Security system, which
refunds up to 70% of medical
expenses. British nationals
should obtain form E111 from
a post office before leaving the
UK (or E112 for those already
in treatment). If you're staying
for longer than three months,
or working in France but still
paying NI contributions in
Britain, you'll need form E128
filled in by your employer and
stamped by the NI contributions
office in order to get a French
medical number. Consultations
and prescriptions have to be
paid for in full on the spot, and
are reimbursed on receipt of a
completed *fiche.* If you undergo
treatment the doctor will give
you a prescription and a *feuille
de soins* (bill of treatment).
Stick the small stickers from
the medication boxes on to the
feuille de soins. Send this, the
prescription and form E111 to
the local **Caisse Primaire
d'Assurance Maladie** for a
refund. For those resident in
France, more and more doctors
(especially in Paris) now accept
the **Carte Vitale**, which lets
them produce a virtual *feuille
de soins* and you to pay only
the non-reimbursable part of
the bill. Information on the
health system can be found
at www.ameli.fr. You can
track refunds with Allosecu
(08.20.90.09.00).

Accident & emergency

Note that many hospitals specialise in one type of medical emergency or illness. Consult the Assistance Publique's web site (www.ap-hop-paris.fr) for details. In a medical emergency, call the Sapeurs-Pompiers or SAMU (*see p374* **Emergencies**). Following (in order of arrondissement) are Paris hospitals with 24-hr accident and emergency services:

Adults

Hôpital Hôtel Dieu *1 place du Parvis Notre-Dame, 4th (01.42.34.82.34).*

Hôpital St-Louis *1 av Claude Vellefaux, 10th (01.42.49.49.49).*

Hôpital St-Antoine *184 rue du Fbg-St-Antoine, 12th (01.49.28.20.00).*

Hôpital de la Pitié-Salpêtrière *47-83 bd de l'Hôpital, 13th (01.42.16.00.00).*

Hôpital Cochin *27 rue du Fbg-St-Jacques, 14th (01.58.41.41.41).*

Hôpital Européen Georges Pompidou *20 rue Leblanc, 15th (01.56.09.20.00).*

Hôpital Bichat-Claude Bernard *46 rue Henri Huchard, 18th (01.40.25.80.80).*

Hôpital Tenon *4 rue de la Chine, 20th (01.56.01.70.00).*

Children

Hôpital Armand Trousseau *26 av du Dr Arnold Netter, 12th (01.44.73.74.75).*

Hôpital St Vincent de Paul *82 av Denfert Rochereau, 14th (01.40.48.81.11).*

Hôpital Necker *149 rue de Sèvres, 15th (01.44.49.40.00).*

Hôpital Robert Debré *48 bd Sérurier, 19th (01.40.03.20.00).*

Private Hospitals

American Hospital in Paris } *63 bd Victor-Hugo, 92200 Neuilly (01.46.41.25.25/www.american-hospital.org). M° Porte Maillot, then bus 82.* **Open** 24hrs daily. English-speaking hospital. French Social Security refunds only a small percentage of treatment costs.

Hertford British Hospital (Hôpital Franco-Britannique) *3 rue Barbès, 92300 Levallois-Perret (01.46.39.22.22). M° Anatole-France.* **Open** 24hrs daily. Most of the medical staff speak English.

Complementary medicine

Académie d'homéopathie et des médecines douces *2 rue d'Isly, 8th (01.43.87.60.33). M° St-Lazare.* **Open** 11am-8pm Mon-Fri. Health services include acupuncture, aromatherapy and homeopathy.

Contraception & abortion

To get the pill (*la pilule*) or coil (*stérilet*), you need a prescription, available on appointment from the first two places below, from a *médecin généraliste* (GP) or from a gynaecologist. The morning-after pill (*la pilule du lendemain*) is can be from pharmacies without prescription but is not reimbursed. Condoms (*préservatifs*) and spermicides and are sold in pharmacies and supermarkets, and there are condom machines in most Métro stations, club lavatories and on some street corners. If you're considering an abortion (IVG – *interruption volontaire de grossesse*) but want to discuss options in detail, you may get better information and counselling from the *orthogénie* (family planning) department of a hospital than from the two organisations below (see www.ap-hop-paris.fr for IVG services). While abortion rights are strongly grounded in France, some doctors remain opposed. Ultrasound examinations to ascertain the exact stage of pregnancy are obligatory.

Centre de planification et d'éducation familiales *27 rue Curnonsky, 17th (01.48.88.07.28). M° Porte de Champerret.* **Open** 9am-5pm Mon-Fri. Free consultations on family planning and abortion. Abortion counselling on demand; otherwise phone for an appointment.

MFPF (Mouvement français pour le planning familial) *10 rue Vivienne, 2nd (free info: 08.00.80.38.03 or 01.42.60.93.20). M° Bourse.* **Open** 9.30am-5.30pm Mon, Tue, Thur, Fri; 9.30am-7.30am Wed. Phone for an appointment for prescriptions and contraception advice. For abortion advice, turn up

at the centre at one of the designated time slots. The approach here, however, is brusque.
Other locations: 94 bd Masséna, 13th (01.45.84.28.25; open 10am-3.30pm Wed; 11am-4pm Fri).

Dentists

Dentists are found in the *Pages Jaunes* under *Dentistes*. For emergencies contact:

Urgences Dentaires de Paris *(01.42.61.12.00).* **Open** 8am-10pm Sun, holidays.

SOS Dentaire *87 bd Port-Royal, 13th (01.43.37.51.00). M° Les Gobelins/RER Port-Royal.* **Open** *phone* 9am-midnight. Phone service for emergency dental care.

Hôpital de la Pitié-Salpêtrière *(see above,* **Accident & Emergency***)* also offers 24hr emergency dental care.

Doctors

A complete list of GPs is in the Pages Jaunes under *Médecins: Médecine générale*. To get a Social Security refund, choose a doctor or dentist who is *conventionné* (state registered). Consultations cost €20 or more, of which a proportion can be reimbursed. Seeing a specialist costs still more.

Centre Médical Europe *44 rue d'Amsterdam, 9th (01.42.81.93.33/ dentists 01.42.81.80.00). M° St-Lazare.* **Open** 8am-7pm Mon-Fri; 8am-6pm Sat. Practitioners in all fields, charging minimal consultation fees.

House calls

SOS Infirmiers (Nurses) *(01.47.07.00.73).* House calls 6am-midnight; daytime Sat-Sun. Costs vary, and are higher after 8pm.

SOS Médecins *(01.43.37.77.77 or 08.20.33.24.24).* House calls at least €60 if you don't have French social security; €30 if you do, before 7pm; from €50 after.

Urgences Médicales de Paris *(01.53.94.94.94).* Doctors make house calls around the clock for €35 and more per visit. Some speak English.

Opticians

Branches of **Alain Afflelou** (www.alainefflelou.com) and **Lissac** (www.lissac.com) stock hundreds of frames and can make prescription glasses within the hour. For an eye test you'll need to go to an *ophtalmologiste* – ask the optician for a list. Contact lenses can be bought over the counter if you have your prescription details.

Hôpital des Quinze-Vingts
28 rue de Charenton, 12th (01.40.02.15.20). Specialist eye hospital offers on-the-spot consultations for eye problems.

SOS Optique *(01.48.07.22.00/ www.sosoptique.com)*. 24hr repair service for glasses.

Pharmacies

Pharmacies sport a green neon cross. Paris has a rota system of *pharmacies de garde* at night and on Sunday. If closed, a pharmacy will have a sign indicating the nearest one open. Staff can provide basic medical services like disinfecting and bandaging wounds (for a small fee) and will indicate the nearest doctor on duty. *Parapharmacies* sell almost everything pharmacies do but cannot dispense prescription medication. Toiletries, sanitary products and cosmetics are often cheaper in supermarkets.

Night pharmacies

Pharma Presto *(01.42.42.42.50/ www.pharma-presto.com)*. **Open** 24hrs daily. Delivery charge €39 8am-6pm; €54 6pm-8am. Delivers prescription medication (may make non-prescription exceptions). Will also chauffeur your ailing pet to the vet.

Pharmacie des Halles *10 bd de Sébastopol, 4th (01.42.72.03.23)*. *M° Châtelet*. Open 9am-midnight Mon-Sat; 9am-10pm Sun.

Dérhy/Pharmacie des Champs *84 av des Champs-Elysées, 8th (01.45.62.02.41)*. *M° George V*. Open 24hrs daily.

Matignon *2 rue Jean-Mermoz, 8th (01.43.59.86.55)*. *M° Franklin D Roosevelt*. **Open** 8.30am-2am daily.

Pharmacie Européenne de la Place de Clichy *6 pl de Clichy, 9th (01.48.74.65.18)*. *M° Place de Clichy*. Open 24hrs daily.

Pharmacie de la Place de la Nation *13 pl de la Nation, 11th (01.43.73.24.03)*. *M° Nation*. Open 8am-11pm daily.

Pharmacie d'Italie *61 av d'Italie, 13th (01.44.24.19.72)*. *M° Tolbiac*. Open 8am-2am daily.

STDs, HIV & AIDS

Centre Medico-Sociale (Mairie de Paris) *2 rue Figuier, 4th (01.49.96.62.70)*. *M° Pont-Marie*. Open 9am-5.30pm Mon, Tue, Thur; 1.30-5.30pm Wed, Fri; 9.30am Sat. Free, anonymous tests (*dépistages*) for HIV, Hepatitis B and C and syphillis (wait one week for results). Excellent counselling.

Le Kiosque Infos Sida-Toxicomanie *36 rue Geoffroy l'Asnier, 4th (01.44.78.00.00)*. *M° St-Paul*. **Open** 10am-7pm Mon-Fri; 2-7pm Sat. Youth association offering information on AIDS and sexuality, as well as drug addiction and abuse. Face-to-face counselling service.

FACTS *(01.44.93.16.69/www.facts-line.com)*. **Open** 7-9pm Mon, Wed. English-speaking crisis line gives info and support for those touched by HIV/AIDS and runs groups for friends and relatives.

SIDA Info Service *(08.00.84.08.00)*. **Open** 24hrs daily. Confidential AIDS information in French. English-speaking counsellors 2-7pm Mon, Wed, Fri.

Helplines

Alcoholics Anonymous in English *(01.46.34.59.65/www.aaparis.org)*. 24-hr recorded message gives details of AA meetings at the American Church or Cathedral *(see p383)*.

Allô Service Public *(39.39/www.service-public.fr)*. **Open** 8am-7pm Mon-Fri; 9am-2pm Sat. Efficient source of information and contacts for all aspects of officialdom, tax, work and administrative matters. They even claim to be able to help if you have problems with neighbours. The catch: you can only dial from inside France, and operators speak only French.

The Counseling Center *(01.47.23.61.13)*. English-language counselling service, based at the American Cathedral.

Drogues Alcool Tabac Info Service *(08.00.23.13.13/www.drogues.gouv.fr)*. Phone service, in French, for help with drug, alcohol and tobacco problems.

Narcotics Anonymous *(01.43.72.12.72/www.nafrance.org)*. Meetings in English three times a week.

SOS Dépression *(01.40.47.95.95)*. Open 24hrs daily. People listen and/or give advice. Can send a counsellor or psychiatrist to your home in case of a crisis.

SOS Help *(01.46.21.46.46)*. **Open** 3-11pm daily. English-language helpline.

ID

French law demands that some form of identification is carried at all times. Be ready to produce a passport or *carte de séjour* in response to that old police refrain, 'Papiers, s'il vous plaît'.

Insurance

See p374 **Health**.

Internet

ISPs

America Online *(08.26.02.60.00/www.aol.fr)*.

Club-Internet *(08.26.02.70.28/www.club-internet.fr)*.

CompuServe *(03.21.13.49.49/www.compuserve.fr)*.

Free *(08.92.13.51.51/www.free.fr)*.

Microsoft Network *(08.25.82.78.29/www.fr.msn.com)*.

Noosnet *(08.25.34.54.74/08.00.114.114/ www.noos.com)*.

Wanadoo (France Télécom) *(08.10.63.34.34/www.wanadoo.fr)*.

Internet access

Many hotels offer Internet access, some from your own room. For websites *see p391*.

Access Academy *60-62 rue St-André des Arts, 6th (www.access academy.com)*. *M° Odéon*. **Open** 8am-2am daily.

Clickside *14 rue Domat, 5th (01.56.81.03.00)*. *M° Maubert-Mutualité*. **Open** 10am-midnight Mon-Fri; 1pm-11pm Sat-Sun.

Cyber Cube *12 rue Daval, 11th (01.49.29.67.67/www.cybercube.fr)*. *M° Bastille*. **Open** 10am-10pm daily.

Language

See p389 **Essential vocabulary**; for food terms, *see p188* **Menu lexicon**.

Left luggage

Gare du Nord

There are self-locking luggage lockers (6.15am-11.15pm daily) on Level -1 under the main station concourse: small (€3.50), medium (€7) and large (€9.50) for 48 hours. SNCF luggage service on 01.55.31.54.54 can give basic details.

Roissy-Charles-de-Gaulle airport

Bagages du Monde
(01.48.16.84.90/www.bagagesdumonde.com). **Terminal 1** *Niveau Arrivée, Porte 14 (01.48.16.34.90).* **Open** 8am-8pm daily. **Terminal 2** *Porte 3 (01.48.16.20.61).* **Open** 8am-8pm daily. **Terminal 2F** *Niveau Arrivée, Porte 4 (01.48.16.20.64).* **Open** 7am-7pm daily. Company with counters in CDG terminals and an office in Paris (102 rue de Chemin-Vert, 11th, 01.43.57.30.90) that can ship excess baggage anywhere in the world, or store luggage.

Legal help

Mairies can answer some legal enquiries; phone for timetables of their free *consultations juridiques.*

Direction départementale de la concurrence, de la consommation, et de la répression des fraudes *8 rue Froissart, 3rd (01.40.27.16.00). Mº St-Sébastien-Froissart.* **Open** 9-11.30am, 2-5pm Mon-Fri. Part of the Ministry of Finance; deals with consumer complaints.

Palais de Justice Galerie de Harlay *Escalier S, 4 bd du Palais, 4th (01.44.32.48.48). Mº Cité.* **Open** 9.30am-noon Mon-Fri. Free legal consultation. Arrive early.

SOS Avocats (08.25.39.33.00). **Open** 7-11.30pm Mon-Fri. Closed July, Aug. Free legal advice by phone.

Libraries

All arrondissements have free public libraries. For a library card, you need ID and evidence of a fixed address in Paris.

American Library *10 rue du Général-Camou, 7th (01.53.59.12.60/www.americanlibraryinparis.org). Mº Ecole-Militaire/RER Pont de l'Alma.* **Open** 10am-7pm Tue-Sat (shorter hours in Aug). **Admission** day pass €11; annual €96. The largest English-language lending library in continental Europe. Receives 400 periodicals, as well as popular magazines and newspapers (mainly American).

Bibliothèque Historique de la Ville de Paris *Hôtel Lamoignon, 24 rue Pavée, 4th (01.44.59.29.40). Mº St-Paul.* **Open** 9.30am-6pm Mon-Sat. Closed first two weeks in Aug. Admission free (bring passport photo and ID). Books and documents on Paris history in a Marais mansion.

Bibliothèque Marguerite Durand *79 rue Nationale, 13th (01.45.70.80.30). Mº Tolbiac or Place d'Italie.* **Open** 2-6pm Tue-Sat. Closed 3 weeks in Sept. **Admission** free. 40,000 books and 120 periodicals on women's history and feminism. Collection includes letters of Colette and Louise Michel.

Bibliothèque Nationale de France François Mitterrand *quai François-Mauriac, 13th (01.53.79.59.59/www.bnf.fr). Mº Bibliothèque.* **Open** 10am-8pm Tue-Sat; noon-7pm Sun. Closed 2wks in Sept. **Admission** day pass €3; annual €30. Books, papers and periodicals, plus titles in English. An audio-visual room lets you browse photo, film and sound archives. Wheelchair access.

Bibliothèque Publique d'Information (BPI) *Centre Pompidou, 4th (01.44.78.12.71/www.bpi.fr). Mº Hôtel de Ville/RER Châtelet Les Halles.* **Open** 12am-10pm Mon, Wed-Fri; 11am-10pm Sat, Sun. **Admission** free. Now on three levels, the Centre Pompidou's vast library has a huge international press section, reference books and language-learning facilities. Wheelchair access.

BIFI (Bibliothèque du Film) *100 rue du Fbg-St-Antoine, 12th (01.53.02.22.30/www.bifi.fr). Mº Ledru-Rollin.* **Open** 10am-7pm Mon-Fri. Closed 2 weeks in Aug. **Admission** €3.50 day pass; €34 annual; €15 students annual. Film buffs' library offers books, magazines film stills and posters, as well as films on video and DVD.

Documentation Française *29-31 quai Voltaire, 7th (01.40.15.72.72/www.ladocumentationfrancaise.fr). Mº Rue du Bac.* **Open** 10am-6pm Mon-Wed, Fri; 10am-1pm Thur. Closed Aug and first week Sept. The official government archive and central reference library has information on French politics and economy since 1945.

Locksmiths

Numerous round-the-clock repair services handle locks, plumbing and, sometimes, car repairs. Most charge a minimum €18-€20 call-out *(déplacement)* and €30 per hour, plus parts. Charges are higher on Sunday and at night.

Allô Assistance Dépannage *(08.00.00.00.18).* No car repairs.

Numéro Un Dépannage *(01.40.71.55.55).* No car repairs.

SOS Dépannage (01.47.07.99.99). Double the price of most, but claims to be twice as reliable.

Lost property

Bureau des Objets Trouvés *36 rue des Morillons, 15th (08.21.00.25.25/www.prefecture-police-paris.interieur.gouv.fr). Mº Convention.* **Open** 8.30am-5pm Mon-Thur; 8.30am-4.30pm Fri. Visit in person to fill in a form specifying details of the loss. This may have been the first lost property office in the world, but it is far from the most efficient. Huge delays in processing claims mean that if your trip to Paris is short you may need to nominate a proxy to collect found objects after you leave, although small items can be posted. If your passport was among the items lost you'll need to go to your consulate to get a single-entry temporary passport in order to leave the country.

SNCF lost property Some mainline SNCF stations have their own lost property offices.

Media

See also **Websites** *p391.*

Magazines

Arts & listings

Three smallish publications compete for basic Wed-to-Tue listings information: **Pariscope** (€0.40); **L'Officiel des Spectacles** (€0.35); and **Zurban** (€0.80). Linked to Radio Nova, monthly **Nova** gives multi-ethnic information on where to drink, dance and hang out. **Technikart** tries to mix clubbing with the arts. Highbrow TV guide **Télérama** has superb arts coverage and a Paris listings insert. **Les Inrockuptibles** (fondly known as **Les Inrocks**) is strong on contemporary music scenes at home and abroad; strong coverage of film and books, too. Specialist arts magazines meet every interest. The choice of film-related titles is especially wide, and includes long-established intellectual heavyweights **Les Cahiers du Cinéma**, **Positif** and

Directory

Trafic, fluffy **Studio** and celebrity-heavy **Première**.

Business

Capital, its sister magazine **Management** and weightier **L'Expansion** are notable monthlies. **Défis** has tips for the entrepreneur; **Initiatives** is for the self-employed.

English

The springtime **Time Out Paris Free Guide** is widely distributed in visitor venues and the **Time Out Paris Visitors' Guide** is on sale in newsagents across the city. **FUSAC** (France-USA Contacts) is a small-ads magazine that lists flat rentals, job ads and appliances for sale.

Gossip

The French love gossip. **Public** gives weekly celebrity updates; **Oh Là!** (sister of Spain's *Hola!* and UK's *Hello!*) showcases celebs. **Voici** is the juiciest scandal sheet; **Gala** tells the same stories without the sleaze. **Paris Match** is a French institution founded in 1948, packed with society gossip, celeb interviews and regular photo scoops. **Point de Vue** specialises in royalty (no showbiz fluff). Monthly **Entrevue** aims to titillate and tends toward features on nonconformist sex.

News

Weekly news magazines are an important sector in France, offering news, cultural sections as well as in-depth reports; they range from serious **L'Express**, **Le Point** and **Le Nouvel Observateur** and sardonic, chaotically arranged **Marianne**. Weekly **Courrier International** publishes a fascinating selection of articles, translated into French, from newspapers all over the world.

Women, men & fashion

Elle was a pioneer among women's mags and has editions across the globe. In France it's a weekly, and spot-on for interviews and fashion. Monthly **Marie-Claire** takes a more feminist, campaigning line. Both have design spin-offs (**Elle Décoration**, **Marie-Claire Maison**) and *Elle* has spawned foodie **Elle à Table**. **DS** has lots to read and coverage of social issues. **Vogue**, bought for its fashion coverage and big-name guests, is rivalled during fashion week by **L'Officiel de la Mode**. The underground buys more radical publications **Purple** (six-monthly art, literature and fashion tome), **Crash**, and the new wave of fashion/lifestyle mags: **WAD** (stands for We Are Different), **Citizen K**, **Jalouse** and **Numéro**. Men's mags include the naughty-bizarre **Echo des Savanes**

Listen up!

A new commercial radio station in Paris has become the first to broadcast entirely in English. Launched in May 2004, **Paris Live Radio** mixes Paris-centric content with the best of back home, making it a complete aural accompaniment for the capital's estimated 200,000 anglophone residents. But there's one catch: for the moment you can only tune in via cable, satellite, the internet, and DAB Digital Radio. Technology barrier notwithstanding, the station still reckons to attract some 30,000 listeners daily – and technophobes shouldn't have to wait long; plans are under way to apply for an AM and eventually an FM licence, perhaps in 2005.

Targeted at anglophiles as well as anglophones, Paris Live Radio has assembled a fittingly cosmopolitan broadcasting team – meaning you're as likely to tune in to an American accent as an Aussie, Welsh, English, or even Swedish one. The formula is classic enough: news, music and 'what's on' articles, but the blend of French and Anglo is what sets the station apart.

If you've not yet acquired a taste for French music, you may prefer to retune your digital dial, as French law obliges DJs to play at least 40 per cent home-grown artists. On the whole, though, the music is likely to appeal to the twenty- to thirtysomething crowd (which also happens to be the biggest demographic group among the capital's anglo ex-pats). During the daytime, think Coldplay, Red Hot Chilli Peppers, Air and the occasional classic from Pink Floyd or Bowie; weekend and evening sessions are given over to more eclectic tastes, such as jazz, hip-hop or classical. The station's niche, though, is its focus on Paris. Local news is delivered on the hour, and there are regular previews and reviews of the latest concerts, plays, shows, and art exhibitions in town. Self-proclaimed ex-pat cultural guerrilla David Applefield also hosts a weekly chat show for the more intellectually-inclined.

You can sample the full anglo aural experience at **www.parislive.fm**.

Paris Live Radio
01.53.09.26.20/www.paris liveradio.fm.

and French versions of lad bibles **FHM**, **Maximal** and **Men's Health**.

Newspapers

National dailies have relatively high prices and low print runs. Only 20% of France reads a *national* paper; regional dailies dominate outside Paris. Serious, centre-left **Le Monde** is must-read material for business types, politicians and intellectuals. Despite its lofty reputation, subject matter is surprisingly eclectic; its Wednesday issue comes with **Aden**, an excellent Paris listings supplement. Founded in the aftershocks of 1968 by a group that included Sartre and de Beauvoir, snappier **Libération**, fondly known as *Libé*, is now centre-left but still the read of the *gauche caviar*, worth buying for wide news and arts coverage. Conservative upper and middle classes go for daily broadsheet **Le Figaro**, which has a devotion to politics, shopping, food and sport. Its sales are boosted by lots of property and job ads and Wednesday's **Figaroscope** Paris listings. The Saturday edition has three magazines. For business and financial news, the French dailies **La Tribune**, **Les Echos** and the weekly **Investir** are the tried and trusted sources. The easy-read tabloid **Le Parisien** is strong on consumer affairs, social issues, local news, events and vox pops. Downmarket **France Soir** has gone tabloid. **La Croix** is a Catholic, right-wing daily. The Communist Party **L'Humanité** (shortened to *L'Huma*) struggles on. Sunday broadsheet **Le Journal du Dimanche** comes with **Fémina** mag and a Paris section. **L'Equipe** is the doyen of European sports dailies, its sister bi-weekly magazine **France Football** the bible of world soccer. Each was instrumental in setting up the game's top competitions

during the golden age of French sports journalism after the war. **Paris-Turf** is for horse fans.

English papers & magazines

Paris-based **International Herald Tribune** is on sale throughout the city; British dailies, Sundays and **USA Today** are widely available on the day of issue at larger kiosks in the centre, though often without their supplements. Most popular (and many esoteric) English and US magazines can be had in central bookshops (*see p245*).

Satirical papers

Wednesday institution **Le Canard Enchaîné** is the Gallic *Private Eye* – in fact it was the inspiration for the *Eye*. It's a broadly left-wing satirical weekly broadsheet that's full of in-jokes and breaks political scandals. **Charlie Hebdo** is mainly bought for its cartoons.

Radio

For a complete list of all Paris radio frequencies, go to www.bric-a-brac.org/radio/ville/paris; for up-to-date info on TV and radio see www.csa.fr. Many of the following can be heard on-line at their respective websites. A mandatory state-defined minimum of 40% French music has led to overplay of Gallic pop oldies and to the creation of dubious hybrids by local groups that mix words in French with a refrain in English. Trashy phone-in shows also proliferate. Wavelengths are in MHz.

87.8 France Inter Highbrow, state-run; jazz, international news and discussion slots aplenty. Good cultural coverage.

90.4 Nostalgie As you'd expect.

90.9 Chante France 100% French chanson.

91.3 Chérie FM Lots of oldies.

91.7 France Musiques State classical music channel: highbrow concerts and top jazz.

92.1 Le Mouv' New public station aimed at luring the young with pop and rock music.

93.1 Aligre From local Paris news to literary chat.

93.5/93.9 France Culture Talky state culture station.

94.8 RCJ/Radio J/Judaïque FM/Radio Shalom Shared wavelength for Jewish stations.

95.2 Ici et Maintenant/Neo New stations hoping to stir local public debate about current events.

96.0 Skyrock Pop station with loudmouth presenters. Lots of rap.

96.4 BFM Business and economics.

96.9 Voltage FM Dance music.

97.4 Rire et Chansons A non-stop diet of jokes and pop oldies.

97.8 Ado Music for adolescents.

98.2 Radio FG Beloved of clubbers for its on-the-pulse tips, this station ditched its all-gay remit in 1999.

99.0 Radio Latina Great Latin and salsa music.

100.3 NRJ 'Energy' – geddit? National leader with the under-30s.

101.1 Radio Classique Top-notch, state-run classical music station.

101.5 Radio Nova Hip hop, trip hop, world, jazz.

101.9 Fun Radio Now embracing techno alongside Anglo pop hits.

102.3 Ouï FM Ouï will rock you.

103.9 RFM Easy listening.

104.3 RTL The most popular French station nationwide mixes music and talk programmes.

104.7 Europe 1 News, press reviews, sports, business, entertainment. Much the best weekday breakfast news broadcast, with politicians interviewed live.

105.1 FIP Traffic and weather info, what's on in Paris and a mix of jazz, classical, world and pop. 'Fipettes', female continuity announcers employed for their come-to-bed voices, are a much-loved feature.

105.5 France Info 24-hr news, weather, economic updates and sports bulletins. Reports get repeated every 15 minutes: good if you're learning French.

106.7 Beur FM North African music and discussion.

English

You can receive the **BBC World Service** (648 KHz AM), with its English-language international news, current events, pop and drama; also on 198KHz LW, from midnight to 5.30am daily. At other times 198KHz LW carries **BBC Radio 4**, with British news,

Directory

talk and *The Archers*. **RFI** (738 KHz AM; www.rfi.fr) has an English-language programme of news and music from 7-8am, 2-3pm and 4.30-5pm daily. There's also the French capital's first all-English radio station, **Paris Live** (*see p378* **Listen up!**).

Television

TF1 *(www.tf1.fr)*. The country's biggest channel, first to be privatised (in 1987). Reality shows, dubbed soaps and football are staples.

France 2 *(www.france2.fr)*. State-owned station mixes game shows, chat, documentaries, and the usual cop series and films.

France 3 *(www.france3.fr)*. The more heavyweight of the two state channels offers wildlife and sports coverage, debates, *Cinéma de Minuit* – classic films in V.O. (*version originale*, or original language) – and endearing cookery show *Bon Appétit Bien Sûr*, fronted by superchef Joël Robuchon.

Canal+ *(www.canalplus.fr)*. Subscription channel shows recent films, exclusive sport and late-night porn. A week's worth of the satirical puppets show *Les Guignols* is broadcast unscrambled on Sunday at 1.40pm.

Arte/France 5 *(www.arte-tv.fr)*. Intellectual Franco-German hybrid Arte shares its wavelength with educational channel France 5 (3am-7pm).

M6 *(www.m6.fr)*. Dubbed US sci-fi series and made for TV movies, plus investigative reportage, popular science and kids' shows.

Cable TV & satellite

France offers a decent range of cable and satellite channels but content in English remains limited. CNN and BBC World offer round-the-clock news coverage. BBC Prime keeps you up to date on *Eastenders* (omnibus Sun 2pm), while Teva features comedy such as *Sex and the City*.

Noostv *(08.00.114.114/www.noos.fr)*. First cable provider to offer an interactive video service via Internet.

Money

Visitors can carry a maximum of €7,600 in currency (www.finances.gouv.fr).

The euro

Non-French debit and credit cards can automatically be used to withdraw and pay in euros, and currency withdrawn in France can be used all over the euro zone. Daylight robbery occurs, however, if you try to deposit a euro cheque from any country other than France in a French bank: they are currently charging around €15 for this service, and the European parliament has backed down on its original decision that cross-border payments should be in line with domestic ones across the euro zone. Good news for Brits though – if you transfer money from the UK to France in euros you'll pay the same charges as if Britain were within the euro zone (watch the exchange rate carefully though). For useful euro information online, *see p391*.

ATMs

Withdrawals in euros can be made from bank and post office automatic cash machines. The specific cards accepted are marked on each machine, and most can give instructions in English. Credit card companies charge a fee for cash advances, but their rates are often better than bank rates.

Banks

French banks usually open 9am-5pm Mon-Fri (some close at lunch); some banks also open on Sat. All are closed on public holidays, and from noon on the previous day. Note that not all banks have foreign exchange counters. Commission rates vary between banks; the state-owned Banque de France usually offers good rates. Most banks accept travellers' cheques, but may be reluctant to accept personal cheques even with the Eurocheque guarantee card, which is not widely used in France.

Bank accounts

To open an account (*ouvrir un compte*), French banks require proof of identity, address and your income (if any). You'll probably be required to show your passport, *carte de séjour*, an electricity/gas or phone bill in your name and a payslip/letter from your employer. Students need a student card and may need a letter from their parents. Of the major banks (BNP, Crédit Lyonnais, Société Générale, Banque Populaire, Crédit Agricole), Société Générale tends to be most foreigner-friendly. Most banks don't hand out a Carte Bleue/Visa until several weeks after you've opened an account. A chequebook (*chéquier*) is usually issued in about a week. Payments made with a Carte Bleue are debited directly from your current account, but you can choose for purchases to be debited at the end of every month. French banks are tough on overdrafts, so try to anticipate any cash crisis in advance and work out a deal for an authorised overdraft (*découvert autorisé*) or you risk being blacklisted as 'interdit bancaire' – forbidden from having a current account – for up to ten years. Depositing foreign currency cheques is slow, so use wire transfer or a bank draft in euros to receive funds from abroad.

Bureaux de change

If you arrive in Paris early or late, you can change money at the **American Express** bureaux de change in terminals 1 (01.48.16.13.70), 2A, 2B, 2C and 2D (01.48.16.48.40) and 2F (01.48.16.63.81) at Roissy, and at Orly Sud (01.49.75.77.37); all are open 6.30am-11pm daily. **Travelex** has bureaux de change at main train stations. Opening hours can vary.

Gare d'Austerlitz *01.53.61.92.40.*
Open 10am-6pm daily.
Gare de l'Est *01.42.09.51.97.* **Open** Mon-Sat 7am-10pm, 7am-7pm Sun.
Gare Montparnasse
01.42.79.03.88. **Open** 8.30am-7.20pm daily.
Gare du Nord *01.42.80.11.50.*
Open 7am-11.25pm daily.
Gare St-Lazare *01.43.87.72.51.*
Open 8.30am-7pm Mon-Sat;
11am-6pm Sun.

Credit cards

Major international credit cards are widely used in France; Visa (*Carte Bleue* in French) is the most readily accepted. French-issued credit cards have a security microchip (*puce*) in each card. The card is slotted into a reader, and the holder keys in a PIN to authorise the transaction. Non-French cards also work, but generate a credit slip to sign. In case of credit card loss or theft, call one of the following 24hr services that have English-speaking staff: **American Express** 01.47.77.72.00;
Diners Club 08.10.31.41.59;
MasterCard/Visa 08.92.70.57.05.

Foreign affairs

American Express *11 rue Scribe, 9th (01.47.77.70.00/www.american express.com/France). M° Opéra.*
Open 9am-6.30pm Mon-Sat.
Travel agency, bureau de change, poste restante (you can also leave messages here for other card holders Euro-travelling), card replacement, travellers' cheque refund service, international money transfers and a cash machine for AmEx cardholders.
Barclays *6 rond point des Champs-Elysées, 8th (01.44.95.13.80/www. barclays.fr). M° Franklin D Roosevelt.*
Open 9.15am-4.30pm Mon-Fri.
Barclays' international Expat Service handles direct debits, international transfer of funds, etc.
Citibank *125 av des Champs-Elysées, 8th (01.53.23.33.60/www. citibank.fr). M° Charles de Gaulle-Etoile.* **Open** 10am-5.30pm Mon-Fri.
Existing clients get good rates for international money transfers, preferential exchange rates and no commission on travellers cheques.

Global Change *150 av des Champs-Elysées, 8th (01.45.61.05.62)*
M° Charles de Gaulle-Etoile. **Open** 24hrs daily. Other branches have variable hours. No commission.
Travelex *52 av des Champs-Elysées, 8th (01.42.89.80.32/www. travelex.fr). M° Franklin D. Roosevelt.*
Open 9am-9.30pm daily. Hours of other branches (over 20 in Paris) vary. Issues travellers' cheques and insurance; deals with bank transfers.
Western Union Money Transfer
(08.25.00.98.98). 48 post offices provide Western Union services. Money transfers from abroad should arrive within 15 minutes; charges are paid by the sender. The following branch of the CCF bank (and four other branches located in tourist neighbourhoods) also act as an agent for Western Union, offering the same:
CCF Change, *4 rue du Cloître-Notre-Dame, 4th (01.43.54.46.12/ www. intl.westernunion.com).*
M° Cité. **Open** 9am-5.10pm daily (till 6pm in summer).

Tax

French VAT (*taxe sur la valeur ajoutée* or TVA) is arranged in three bands: 2.1%, for items of medication and newspapers; 5.5%, for food, books, CDs and DVDs; and 19.6% for all other types of goods and services.

Natural hazards

Paris has no natural hazards as such, though in recent years the town hall has produced evacuation plans to cover flooding. The deadly heatwave of 2003 led to *anti-canicule* measures for 2004, though these were widely ridiculed in the press. *See also* **Walking**.

Opening hours

Standard opening hours for shops are 9am/10am-7pm/8pm Mon-Sat. Some shops close on Mon. Shops and businesses often close at lunch, usually 12.30-2pm; many shops close in August. While Paris doesn't have the 24-hr consumer culture beloved of some capitals, some branches of Monoprix stay open until 10pm. Also most areas have a local grocer that stays open

until around 10pm and will often open on Sundays and public holidays, too – although you do pay for the convenience.
24-hr florist Elyfleur *82 av de Wagram, 17th (01.47.66.87.19).*
M° Wagram.
24-hr newsagents include:
33 av des Champs-Elysées, 8th, M° Franklin D Roosevelt. 2 bd Montmartre, 9th, M° Grands Boulevards.
24-hr garage Select Shell *6 bd Raspail, 7th (01.45.48.43.12). M° Rue du Bac.* This round-the-clock garage has a large if pricey array of supermarket standards from the Casino chain. No alcohol sold 10pm-6am.
Late-night *tabacs* Le Brazza *86 bd du Montparnasse, 14th (01.43.35.42.65). M° Montparnasse-Bienvenüe.* **Open** 24-hr daily.
La Favorite *3 bd St-Michel, 5th (01.43.54.08.02). M° St-Michel.*
Open 7am-2am daily.

Photo labs

Photo developing can often be more expensive than in the UK or USA (though developing slide films can often be cheaper). **Fnac Service**, **Photo Station** (www.photostation.fr) and **Photo Service** (www.photoservice.com) have numerous branches.

Police stations

The French equivalent of 999/911 is **17** and **112** from a mobile, but don't expect a speedy response. That said, the Préfecture de Police has no fewer than 94 outposts in the city. If you're assaulted or robbed, report the incident as soon as possible. You'll need to make a statement (*procès verbal*) at the *point d'accueil* closest to the site of the crime. To find the nearest, call the Préfecture Centrale (08.91.01.22.22) day or night, or go to www.prefecture-police.paris.interieur.gouv.fr.
Stolen goods are unlikely to be recovered, but you'll need a police statement for insurance purposes.

Directory

Postal services

Post offices (*bureaux de poste*) are open 8am-7pm Mon-Fri; 8am-noon Sat. All are listed in the phone book: under Administration des PTT in the *Pages Jaunes*; under Poste in the *Pages Blanches*. Most post offices have automatic machines (in French and English) that weigh your letter, print out a stamp and give change, saving you from wasting time in an enormous queue. You can usually buy stamps and often envelopes at a tobacconist (*tabac*). For info see www.laposte.fr.

Main Post Office *52 rue du Louvre, 1st (01.40.28.76.00). M° Les Halles or Louvre Rivoli.* **Open** 24hrs daily for Poste Restante, telephones, stamps, fax, photocopying and some banking operations. This is the best place to get your mail sent to if you haven't got a fixed address in Paris. Mail should be addressed to you in block capitals, followed by Poste Restante, then the post office's address. There's a charge of €0.50 for each letter received.

Recycling & rubbish

The city has a recently-established system of colour-coded domestic recycling bins. A yellow-lidded bin can take paper, cardboard cartons, tins and small electrical items; a white-lidded bin takes glass. All other rubbish goes in the green-lidded bins except for used batteries (all shops that sell batteries should accept them), medication (take it back to a pharmacy), toxic products (call 08.20.00.75.75 to have them picked up) or car batteries (take them to an official tip or return to garages exhibiting the 'relais verts auto' sign). Green hive-shaped bottle banks can be found on street corners.

Allô Propreté
(08.20.00.75.75/www.paris.fr). **Open** 9-5pm Mon-Fri. Recycling information and collection of cumbersome objects.

Religion

Churches and religious centres are listed in the *Pages Jaunes* under 'Eglises' and 'Cultes'. Paris has several English-speaking churches. The *International Herald Tribune*'s Saturday edition lists Sunday church services in English.

American Cathedral *23 av George V, 8th (01.53.23.84.00/www.us.net/ amcathedral-paris). M° George V.*

American Church in Paris *65 quai d'Orsay, 7th (01.40.62.05.00/ www.americanchurchparis.org). M° Invalides.*

Emmanuel Baptist Church of Paris *56 rue des Bons Raisins, 92500 Rueil-Malmaison (01.47.51.29.63/www.ebcparis.org). RER Reuil-Malmaison, then bus 244.*

Kehilat Gesher *10 rue de Pologne, 78100 St Germain-en-Laye (01.39.21.97.19). RER St-Germain-en-Laye.* The Liberal English-speaking Jewish community has rotating services in Paris and the western suburbs.

La Mosquée de Paris *2 pl du Puits de l'Ermite, 5th (01.45.35.97.33). M° Place Monge.*

St George's Anglican Church *7 rue Auguste-Vacquerie, 16th (01.47.20.22.51/www.stgeorgesparis. com). M° Charles de Gaulle-Etoile.*

St Joseph's Roman Catholic Church *50 av Hoche, 8th (01.42.27.28.56/www.stjoeparis.org). M° Charles de Gaulle-Etoile.*

St Michael's Church of England *5 rue d'Aguesseau, 8th (01.47.42.70.88/www.saintmichaels paris.org). M° Madeleine.*

Renting a flat

Flats are generally cheapest in northern, eastern and southeastern Paris. Expect to pay roughly €20 per month/m² (so, say, €700 per month for a 35m² flat). Studios and one-bedroom flats fetch the highest prices proportionally; lifts and cellars will also boost the rent. *See also p383* **Vive la colocation!**

Flat hunting

Given the scarcity of housing in Paris, it's a landlord's world; you'll need to search actively, or even frenetically, in order to find an apartment. The site www.logement.com is a reassuring place to start. In addition to giving reliable information about most aspects of the real estate world, it provides links to at least 20 other sites that list rental ads. See also www.explorimmo.fr, which lists rental ads from *Le Figaro* and specialist real estate magazines. Thursday morning's *De Particulier à Particulier* (www.pap.fr) is a must for those who want to rent directly from the owner, but be warned – most flats go within hours. Fortnightly *Se Loger* (www.seloger.com) is also worth getting, though most of its ads are placed by agencies. Landlords keen to let to foreigners advertise in the *International Herald Tribune* and English-language *FUSAC* (www.fusac.fr); rents tend to be higher than in the French press. There are also assorted free ad brochures that can be picked up from agencies. Private landlords often set a visiting time; prepare to meet hordes of other flat-seekers and have your documents and cheque book to hand. There's also the option of flat-sharing (*see p383* **Vive la colocation!**).

Rental laws

The minimum lease (*bail de location*) on an unfurnished flat is three years (though the tenant can give notice and leave before this period is up); furnished flats are generally let on one-year leases. During this period the landlord can only raise the rent by the official construction inflation index. At the end of the lease, the rent can be adjusted, but tenants can object before a rent board. Tenants can be evicted for non-payment, or if the landlord wishes to sell the property or use it as his own residence. It is illegal to throw people out in winter. Landlords will probably insist you present a dossier with pay slips (*fiches de paie/bulletins de salaire*) showing income equivalent to three to four times the monthly rent, and, for foreigners in particular, to provide a financial guarantor (someone who will sign a document promising to pay the rent if you abscond). When taking out a lease, payments usually include the first month's rent, a deposit (*une caution*) equal to two month's rent, and an agency fee, if applicable. It's customary for an inspection of the premises (*état des lieux*) at the start and end of the rental, the cost of which (around €150) is shared by landlord and tenant. Landlords may try to rent their flats *non-declaré* – without a written lease – and get rent in cash. This can make it hard for tenants to establish their rights – one reason why landlords do it.

Centre d'information et de défense des locataires *9 rue Severo, 14th (01.45.41.47.76). M° Pernety.* **Open** *by appointment* 10am-12.30pm, 2.30-3.30pm Mon-Fri. Helps sort out problems with landlords, rent hikes, etc.

Safety & security

Beware pickpockets, especially in crowded tourist hotspots. See also **Métro & RER**.

Shipping services

Hedley's Humpers *6 bd de la Libération, 93284 St-Denis (01.48.13.01.02/www.hedleyshumper s.com). M° Carrefour Pleyel.* **Open** 9am-1pm, 2-6pm Mon-Fri. Closed 2 weeks in Aug. **Other locations**: *102 rue des Rosiers, 93400 St-Ouen (01.40.10.94.00). M° Porte de Clignancourt.* **Open** 9am-5pm Mon, Fri-Sun. Specialist in transport of furniture and antiques. **In UK**: 3 St Leonards Rd, London NW10 6SX, UK (0208 965 8733). **In USA**: 21-41 45th Road, Long Island City, New York NY 11101, USA (1.718.433.4005).

Smoking

Although smoking seems to be an essential part of French life (and death), the French state and public health groups have recently waged war against the cigarette on several fronts. Smoking is now banned in most public spaces, such as theatres, cinemas and public

---

Vive la colocation!

Traditionally, young Parisians would rather live in a tiny *chambre de bonne* than give up their privacy, and the last population census found over half of Paris households were inhabited by people living alone. Change, however, is afoot. Over the last couple of years, the trend towards *la colocation*, or flat-sharing, has been occupying column inches. From conservative daily *Le Figaro* to trendy youth magazine *Nova*, the topic has been a must.

Why? For one, rents are going up. It's harder being aloof when flats get pricey. Then, there's the increasing influence of role models – *Friends* and reality TV shows like *Loft Story* (a Gallic version of *Big Brother*). The result is that the anglophone idea of flat-sharing is catching on.

This will come as a relief to any ex-pat who remembers the frustrations of finding a first flat in Paris. Answer an ad placed in heavyweight accommodation weekly *De Particulier à Particulier*, and you're likely to face 20-odd candidates outside the flat's door, brandishing all the relevant documents, pay slips and guarantees demanded by the landlord. If you're foreign, you probably won't have all that paperwork for a good year after your arrival in France.

So where to look for the ideal French housemate? There should be scope for the right match on **www.colocation.fr**, as the site claims to display some 3,000 new offers per week. Flat-hunters can track down their ideal *colocation* by selecting the age and sex of potential flatmates, as well as deciding whether to accept someone who smokes or has children. And candidates aren't just students and penniless young people; some 30 per cent of users are between 35 and 49. You can even check out potential flatmates in the flesh at **Le Jeudi de la Colocation**, a monthly soirée organised by the website.

Of course, once you've met your perfect roomie, you still need to convince him or her of *your* own qualities.

Beyond the web, the most useful sources of potential partners are of anglophone origin. *FUSAC*, the free fortnightly French-American listings magazine (distributed in anglo pubs, shops and other hangouts), includes a 'sharing' section in its accommodation pages – although rents are often exorbitant. The American Church (*see p382*) also posts flat-sharing ads from private individuals on its busy notice board. As with all ads, the earlier birds tend to nab the juiciest worms: in other words, decent flats disappear fast.

Further resources

www.appartager.fr
www.easycoloc.fr and
www.kel-koloc.fr are run by the same people behind www.colocation.fr; all three provide details of Jeudi de a Colocation events.

Directory

transport, and there are increasingly strident anti-smoking campaigns. Health warnings on cigarette packets are now unignorable, and prices have soared. Restaurants are obliged to have a non-smoking area (*espace non-fumeurs*) – though it will often be the worst corner in the house, and there's no guarantee other people seated in the section won't light up anyway. For information about stopping smoking, contact the Tabac Info Service (08.25.30.93.10/ www.tabac-info.net). If you're a dedicated smoker, you'll soon learn that most *tabacs* close at 8pm (for a few that don't, *see p381* **Opening hours**). Some bars sell cigarettes behind the counter, generally only to people who stay for a drink.

Study

Language

Most large multinational language schools, such as **Berlitz** (www.berlitz.com) have at least one branch in Paris. **Konversando** (01.47.70.21.64/ www. konversando.fr) specialises in exchanges and talk.

Alliance Française *101 bd Raspail, 6th (01.42.84.90.00/ ww.alliancefr.org). M° St-Placide*. Non-profit French-language school. Beginner and specialist courses start every month. Film club and lectures.

British Institute *11 rue Constantine, 7th (01.44.11.73.83/ www.bip.lon.ac.uk). M° Invalides*. Linked to the University of London, the 4,000-student Institute offers English courses for Parisians, and French courses (not beginner). Also offers a degree course and MAs.

Ecole Eiffel *3 rue Crocé-Spinelli, 14th (01.43.20.37.41/www.ecole-eiffel.fr). M° Pernéty*. Intensive classes, business French, and phonetics.

Eurocentres *13 passage Dauphine, 6th (01.40.46.72.00/www.eurocentres. com). M° Odéon*. Intensive classes with emphasis on communication. Also has a *médiathèque*.

Institut Catholique de Paris *12 rue Cassette, 6th (01.44.39.52.68/ www.icp.fr). M° St-Sulpice*. Traditional courses in French language and

culture. You must hold a *baccalauréat*-level qualification and be 18 or over (but don't have to be Catholic).

Institut Parisien *87 bd de Grenelle, 15th (01.40.56.09.53). M° La Motte Picquet-Grenelle*. Dynamic private school offers courses in language and French civilisation, business French.

La Sorbonne – Cours de Langue et Civilisation *47 rue des Ecoles, 5th (01.40.46.22.11/www.fle.fr/ sorbonne). M° Cluny-La Sorbonne/ RER Luxembourg*. Classes for foreigners ride on the name of this eminent institution. Teaching is grammar-based. Courses are open to anyone over 18 and fill up quickly.

Specialised

Many of the prestigious Ecoles Nationales Supérieures (including film schools La Fémis and ENS Louis Lumière) offer summer courses in addition to their full-time degree courses – ask for formation continue.

Adult education courses
Information: www.paris.fr or from your local mairie. A huge range of inexpensive adult education classes is run by the City of Paris, including French as a foreign language, computer skills and applied arts.

American University of Paris
31 av Bosquet, 7th (01.40.62.07.20/ www.aup.edu). RER Pont de l'Alma. An international college awarding four-year American liberal arts degrees (BA/BSc).

Christie's Education Paris
Hôtel Salomon de Rothschild, 11 rue Berryer, 8th (01.42.25.10.90/ www.christies.com/education). M° George V. The international auction house offers a one-year diploma, ten-week intensive courses and specialisations.

Cordon Bleu
8 rue Léon-Delhomme, 15th (01.53.68.22.50). M° Vaugirard. Courses range from three-hour sessions on classical and regional cuisine to a nine-month diploma for those starting a culinary career.

Ritz-Escoffier Ecole de Gastronomie Française *38 rue Cambon, 1st (01.43.16.30.50/www. ritzparis.com). M° Madeleine*. Everything from afternoon demos in the Ritz kitchens to diplomas, but at a price. Courses are in French with English translation.

Ecole du Louvre *Porte Jaugard, Aile de Flore, Palais du Louvre. quai du Louvre, 1st (01.55.35.17.35/ www.ecoledulouvre.fr). M° Palais*

Royal-Musée du Louvre. Art history and archaeology courses. Foreign students not wanting to take a degree can attend lectures.

INSEAD *bd de Constance, 77305 Fontainebleau (01.60.72.40.00/ www.insead.edu)*. Highly regarded international business school offers a ten-month MBA in English, and PhDs in business subjects.

Parsons School of Design
14 rue Letellier, 15th (01.45.77.39.66/ www.parsons-paris.pair.com). M° La Motte-Picquet-Grenelle. Subsidiary of New York art college offers BFA programmes in fine art, photography, fashion, marketing and interior design.

Spéos – Paris Photographic Institute *7 rue Jules-Vallès, 11th (01.40.09.18.58/ www.speos.fr). M° Charonne*. Full-, part-time and summer programmes. Exchange programmes with four art schools, including the Rhode Island School of Design.

Student life

Cartes de séjour and housing benefit

Take a deep breath before you read the following. Foreign students wishing to qualify for housing benefit or to work legally during their course in Paris must get a *carte de séjour* (*see p387*). You may then (note the 'may') be eligible for the ALS (*allocation de logement à caractère social*), which is handled by four CAFs (*caisses d'allocations familiales*). The '*calculez votre aide au logement*' feature of their website (www.caf.fr) lets you see how much you'll receive. www.droitsdesjeunes.gouv.fr gives information on your rights.

CAFs *19 rue Pot de Fer, 5th (08.20.25.75.10), M° Place Monge; 101 rue Nationale, 13th, M° Nationale; 18 rue Viala, 15th, M° Dupleix; 47 rue de la Chapelle, 18th, M° Marx Dormoy; 67 av Jean-Jaurès, 19th, M° Laumière*. **Open** 8.30am-4pm Mon-Fri.

Accommodation

The simplest budget accommodation for medium-to-long stays can be found at the **Cité Universitaire** or *foyers* (student hostels). Another option is a *chambre contre travail* – free board in exchange for childcare, housework or English lessons. Look out for ads at language schools and the American Church. For cheap hotels and youth hostels, *see chapter* **Where to Stay**. As students often cannot provide proof of income, a *porte-garant* (guarantor) is required who will guarantee payment of rent and bills.

Cité Universitaire *19 bd Jourdan, 14th (01.44.16.64.46/48/www.ciup.fr). RER Cité Universitaire.* **Open** *Offices* 8.30am-7pm Mon-Fri. Foreign students enrolled on a university course, or interns who are also studying, can apply for a place at this campus of halls of residence (but be forewarned: only about 10% of the students that apply get in). Rooms can be booked for a week or for an entire academic year. Rents are around €300-€400/month single, €200-€300 per person double. UK citizens must apply to the Collège Franco-Britannique, and Americans to the Fondation des Etats-Unis.

CROUS (Centre régional des oeuvres universitaires et scolaires) *39 av Georges-Bernanos, 5th (01.40.51.36.00/www.crous-paris.fr). Service du Logement: (01.40.51.55.55). RER Port-Royal.* **Open** 9am-5pm Mon-Fri. Manages all University of Paris student residences, posts ads for rooms and has a list of hostels. Requests for rooms must be made by 1 April for the next academic year. CROUS also runs cheap canteens (listed on website) and is the clearing house for all *bourses* (grants) issued to foreign students. Call the Service des Bourses on 01.40.51.37.35.

UCRIF (Union des centres de rencontres internationales de France) *27 rue de Turbigo, 2nd (01.40.26.57.64/www.ucrif.asso.fr). M° Etienne Marcel.* **Open** 9am-6pm Mon-Fri. Operates cheap, short-stay hostels from four help centres: 5th (01.43.29.34.80); 12th (01.44.75.60.06); 13th (01.43.36.00.63); 14th (01.43.13.17.00); 20th (01.40.313.45.45).

Student & youth discounts

To claim a *tarif étudiant* (around €1.50 off cinema seats, up to 50% off museums and standby theatre tickets), you must have a French student card or International Student Identity Card (ISIC), available from CROUS, student travel agents and the Cité

Universitaire. ISIC cards are only valid in France if you are under 26. Under-26s can get up to 50% off rail travel on some trains with the SNCF's Carte 12/25 and the same reduction on the RATP network with the 'Imagine R' card.

Working

Foreign students can legally work up to 20hrs per week. Non-EU members studying in Paris must apply for an *autorisation provisoire de travail* from the DDTEFT. CROUS's job service (01.40.51.37.52 through 57) finds part-time jobs for students. For pointers to vacancies, consult www.crous-paris.fr/emploi.

DDTEFT (Direction Départementale du Travail, d'Emploi et du Formation Professionelle) *109 rue Montmartre, 2nd (01.44.76.69.30/www.travail. gouv.fr). M° Bourse.*

Useful organisations

CIDJ (Centre d'information et de documentation jeunesse) *101 quai Branly, 15th (01.44.49.12.00/www.cidj.com). M° Bir-Hakeim/RER Champ de Mars.* **Open** 10am-6pm Mon-Fri; 9.30am-1pm Sat. Library gives students advice on courses and careers; youth bureau of ANPE (Agence Nationale Pour l'Emploi/www.anpe.fr) helps with job applications.

Edu France *173 bd St-Germain, 6th (01.53.63.35.00/www.edufrance.com). M° St Germain des Prés.* **Open** 9am-6pm Mon-Fri (call as hours vary). Fees €200-€500. Government-run organisation promotes the French university system abroad and assists foreign students in France. The website has some useful free information.

Maison des Initiatives Etudiantes (MIE) *50 rue des Tournelles, 3rd (01.49.96.65.30/www.paris.fr).* Provides student associations with logistical assistance and Paris-based resources like meeting rooms, grants and on-line computers. From September 2004, Radio Campus Paris, a radio station for students, will be broadcast.

Socrates-Erasmus Programme *Britain: UK Socrates-Erasmus Council, R&D Building, The University, Canterbury, Kent CT2 7PD (01227-762712).* **France:**

Agence Socrates-Leonardo Da Vinci, 25 quai des Chartrons, 33080 Bordeaux Cedex (05.56.00.94.00/ www.socrates-leonardo.fr). The Socrates-Erasmus scheme lets EU students with reasonable written and spoken French spend a year of their degree in the French university system. Applications must be made via the Erasmus co-ordinator at your home university. Non-EU students should find out from their university whether it has an agreement with the French university system. US students can find out more from **MICEFA** (*26 rue du Fbg-St-Jacques, 14th, 01.40.51.76.96/www.micefa.org*). **Relais d'accueil** (Foreign students helpdesk) *Cité Universitaire, 19 bd Jourdan, 14th. RER Cité Universitaire. CROUS de Paris, 39 av Georges-Bernanos, 5th. RER Port Royal. Information (01.43.13.66.46/ www.eduparis.net).* **Open** Sept-Nov. By-appointment advice on housing, getting a bank account, a Carte de Séjour, social security and university registration is available to foreign students at the two addresses above.

Telephones

Mobile phones

A subscription (*abonnement*) will normally get you a free phone if you sign up for at least one year. Two hours' calling time a month costs about €35/month. International calls are normally charged extra – a lot extra. The three companies that rule the cell phone market in France are:

Bouygues Telecom *(08.10.63.01.00/www.bouygues telecom.fr).*

France Telecom/Orange *(08.25.00.57.00/www.orange.fr).*

SFR *(08.05.80.08.05/www.sfr.fr).*

Dialing & codes

All French phone numbers have ten digits. Paris and Ile de France numbers begin with 01; the rest of France is divided into four zones (02-05). Mobile phone numbers start with 06; 08 indicates a special rate (*see below*). If you are calling France from abroad leave off the 0 at the start of the ten-digit number. The country code is 33. To call abroad from France dial 00, then country code, then the number. Since 1998 other phone companies have been allowed to enter the market, but France Télécom still has the monopoly on basic service. It has a useful website with information on rates, contracts and the like: http://www.agence.france telecom.com.

France Telecom English-Speaking Customer Service *(08.00.36.47.75)*. **Open** 9am-5.30pm Mon-Fri. Freephone information line in English on phone services, bills, payment, Internet.

Public phones

Most public phones in Paris (of which almost all are maintained by France Télécom) use *télécartes* (phonecards). Sold at post offices, *tabacs*, airports and train and Métro stations, they cost €7.50 for 50 units and €15 for 120 units. For cheap international calls you can also buy a *télécarte à puce* (card with a microchip) or a *télécarte pré-payée* that features a numerical code that you dial before making a call; these can be used on domestic phones, too. Travelex's International Telephone Card can be used in more than 80 countries (from Travelex agencies, *see p381*). Cafés have coin phones, while post offices usually have card phones. In a phone box, the display screen should read 'Décrochez'. Pick up the phone. When 'Introduisez votre carte' appears, put your card into the slot; the screen should then read 'Patientez SVP'. 'Numérotez' is your signal to dial. 'Crédit épuisé' means you have no more units left. Finally, hang up ('Raccrochez'), and don't forget your card. Some public phones take credit cards. If you're using a credit card, insert the card, key in your PIN number and 'Patientez SVP' should appear.

Operator services

Operator assistance, French directory enquiries *(renseignements)* 12. To make a reverse-charge call within France, ask to make a call *en PCV*.

International directory enquiries 32.12, then country code. €3 per call.

Telephone engineer 10.13.

International news (France Inter recorded message, in French), 08.92.68.10.33 (€0.34 per min).

Telegram *all languages, international* 08.00.33.44.11; *within France* 36.55.

Time 36.99.

Traffic news 08.26.02.20.22.

Weather 08.99.70.12.34 (€1.39 then €0.34 per min) for enquiries on weather in France and abroad, in French or English; dial 08.92.68.02.75 (€0.34 per min) for a recorded weather announcement for Paris and region.

Airparif (01.44.59.47.64). Mon-Fri 2-5.30pm. Information about pollution levels and air quality in Paris and Ile-de-France: invaluable for asthmatics.

Telephone directories

Phone books are found in all post offices and most cafés. The *Pages Blanches* (White Pages) list people and businesses alphabetically; *Pages Jaunes* (Yellow Pages) list businesses and services by category. Online versions can be had at www.pagesjaunes.fr.

Telephone charges

Local calls in Paris and Ile-de-France beginning with 01 cost €0.11 for three minutes, standard rate, €0.04/min thereafter and only apply to calls towards other land phones. Calls beyond a 100km radius (*province*) are charged at €0.11 for the first 39 seconds, then €0.24/min. International destinations are divided into 16 zones. Reduced-rate periods for calls within France and Europe: 7pm-8am during the week; all day Sat, Sun. Reduced-rate periods for the US and Canada: 7pm through to 1pm Mon-Fri; all day Sat, Sun.

Cheap providers

Getting wise to market demand, smaller telephone providers are becoming increasingly prolific and popular, as rates from giant France Télécom are not exactly

bargain-basement. The following can offer alternative rates for calls (you'll still need to rent your telephone line from France Télécom):

AT&T Direct (local access) *08.00.99.00.11*.

Fast Télécom *08.11.02.60.61*.

Free *www.free.fr*. With the Freebox (Free's modem for ASDL connection) €29.99 per month gets you ten hours of free calls to land lines (additional calls: €0.01 per minute), €0.19 per minute to mobiles and €0.03 per minute for most international calls.

IC Télécom *08.05.10.25.05/www.ictelecom.fr*.

9 Télécom *08.00.95.99.59/www.neuf.fr*.

Onetel *www.onetel.fr*.

Télé 2 *08.05.04.44.44*.

3U Télécom *08.05.10.16.45*.

Special-rate numbers

0800 Numéro Vert Freephone.

0810 Numéro Azur €0.11 under three min, then €0.04/min.

0820 Numéro Indigo I €0.118/min.

0825 Numéro Indigo II €0.15/min.

0836.64/0890.64/0890.70 €0.112/min.

0890.71 €0.15/min.

0891.67/0891.70 €0.225/min.

0836/0892 €0.337/min. This rate is for the likes of ticket agencies, cinema and transport information lines.

10.14 France Télécom information; free (except from mobile phones).

Minitel

France Telecom's Minitel, launched in the 1980s, is a videotext service available to any telephone subscriber, though the Internet has made it virtually redundant. If you come across one of these beige plastic boxes, type in 3611 for Minitel directory in English, wait for the beep, press 'Connexion', type MGS, then hit 'Envoi'. Then type 'Minitel en anglais' for the English service.

Ticket agencies

The easiest way to reserve and buy tickets for concerts, plays and matches is from a **Fnac** store. You can also reserve on www.fnac.com or by phone

(08.92.68.36.22; 9am-8pm Mon-Sat) and pick them up at one of their *points de vente* (see site for complete list) or pay with your credit card and have them sent to your home. **Virgin** has teamed up with **Ticketnet** to create an online ticket office (www.virginmega.fr). Tickets can also be purchased by phone (08.25.02.30.24) and sent to your home for a €5.35 fee.

Fnac Forum
1 rue Pierre Lescot, Forum des Halles, 1st
(01.40.41.40.00/www.fnac.com). Mº Les Halles/RER Châtelet-Les Halles. **Open** 9am-7.30pm Mon-Sat. **Credit** AmEx, MC, V.

Virgin Megastore
52-60 av des Champs-Elysées, 8th (01.49.53.50.00). Mº Franklin D Roosevelt. **Open** 10am-midnight Mon-Sat; noon-midnight Sun. **Credit** AmEx, DC, MC, V.

Time & seasons

France is one hour ahead of Greenwich Mean Time (GMT). France uses the 24-hr system (eg. 20h for 8pm).

Tipping

A service charge of ten to 15% is legally included in your bill at all restaurants, cafés and bars. However, it's polite to either round up the final amount for drinks, and to leave a cash tip of €1-€2 or more for a meal, depending on the restaurant and, of course, on the quality of the service.

Toilets

Automatic street toilets are not as terrifying as they look. You place your coin in the slot, and – open sesame – you're in a disinfected wonderland (each loo is completely washed down and disinfected after use, so don't try to avoid paying by sneaking in as someone is leaving: you'll get covered in bleach). Once inside, you have 15 minutes. If a space-age-style lavatory experience doesn't appeal, you can always nip in

to the loos of a café; although theoretically reserved for customers' use, a polite request and a smile should win sympathy with the waiter – and you may find you have to put a 20¢ coin into a slot in the door-handle mechanism, customer or not. Fast food chain toilets often have a code on their toilet doors which is made known to paying customers only.

Tourist information

Espace du Tourisme d'Île de France *Carrousel du Louvre, 99 rue de Rivoli, 1st (08.26.16.66.66/www.paris-ile-de-france.com). Mº Palais Royal Musée du Louvre.* **Open** 10am-7pm daily. Information showcase for Paris and the Ile-de-France.

Maison de la France *20 av de l'Opéra, 1st (01.42.96.70.00/www.franceguide.com). Mº Opéra.* **Open** 10am-6pm Mon-Fri; 10am-5pm Sat. The state organisation for tourism in France: information galore.

Office de Tourisme et des Congrès de Paris *Carrousel du Louvre, 99 rue de Rivoli, 1st (08.92.68.30.00 recorded information in English & French/www.paris-touristoffice.com). Mº Palais Royal Musée du Louvre.* **Open** 10am-6pm daily. Information on Paris and the suburbs, shop, bureau de change, hotel reservations, phonecards, museum cards, travel passes and tickets. Multilingal staff. Branches can also be found at the following addresses: 11 rue Scribe, 9th. Mº Opéra. Open 9am-6.30pm Mon-Sat. Closed Sun, 1 Jan, 1 May, 25 Dec. Gare de Lyon, 20 bd Diderot, 12th, Mº Gare de Lyon. Open 8am-6pm, Mon-Sat. Closed Sundays and public holidays. Gare du Nord, 18 rue de Dunkerque, 10th, Mº Gare du Nord Open 12.30pm-8pm daily, closed 25 Dec, 1 May.

Visas

European Union nationals do not need a visa to enter France, nor do US, Canadian, Australian or New Zealand citizens for stays of up to three months. Nationals of other countries should enquire at the nearest French Consulate before leaving home. If they are travelling to France from

one of the countries included in the Schengen agreement (most of the EU, but not Britain, Ireland, Italy or Greece), the visa from that country should be sufficient.

Cartes de séjour

Officially, all foreigners – EU citizens and non-Europeans – who stay in France for more than three months must apply at the Préfecture de Police for a *carte de séjour*, valid for one year. Those who have had a *carte de séjour* for at least three years, have been paying French income tax, can show proof of income and/or are married to a French national can apply for a *carte de résident*, valid for ten years. Students arriving from England wishing to make a first application for a student's carte de séjour should go directly (no appointments) to 13 rue Miollis, 15th, Mº Ségur or Cambronne, 8.35am-4.30pm Mon-Thur, 8.35am-4.15pm Fri. Applicants must bring ID, three recent photos, plus proof of studies, of an address in Paris and of sufficient funds.

CIRA (Centre interministeriel de renseignements administratifs) *(0821.08.09.10 0.12€/min/www.service-public.fr).* **Open** 8am-7pm Mon-Fri; 8am-noon Sat. Advice on French admin procedures.

Préfecture de Police de Paris Service Étrangers *7-9 bd du Palais, 4th (01.53.71.51.68/www.prefecture-police-paris.interieur.gouv.fr). Mº Cité.* **Open** 9am-4pm Mon-Fri. Information on residency and work permits for foreigners.

Weights & measures

France uses only the metric system; remember that all speed limits are in kilometres per hour. One kilometre is equivalent to 0.62 mile (1 mile = 1.6km). Petrol, like other liquids, is measured in litres; one UK gallon = 4.54 litres; 1 US gallon = 3.79 litres).

Directory

What to take

Binoculars or opera-glasses for studying high-altitude details of monuments, a pocket knife with corkscrew (the better to improvise picnics with food bought in markets) and – vital – comfortable shoes.

When to go

In July and August, when there are good deals on hotels and a good range of fun summer events: the city seems empty but is more relaxed than usual. Avoid October, with its glut of fashion weeks and trade shows.

Women in Paris

Though Paris is not especially threatening for women, the precautions you would take in any major city apply: be careful at night in areas like Pigalle, the rue St-Denis, Stalingrad, La Chapelle, Château Rouge, Gare de l'Est, Gare du Nord, the Bois de Boulogne and Bois de Vincennes. If you receive unwanted attention a politely scathing *N'insistez pas!* (Don't push it!) makes your feelings clear. If things get too heavy, go into the nearest shop or café and ask for help.

CIDFF (Centre d'Information et de Documentation des Femmes et des Familles) *7 rue du Jura,*

13th (01.42.17.12.34). Mº Gobelins. **Open** 1.30-5.30pm Tue-Thur (Mon by phone 9.30am-noon).The CIDFF offers health, legal and professional advice for women.

Violence conjugale: Femmes Info Service *(01.40.33.80.60).* **Open** 7.30am-11.30pm Mon-Sat. Telephone hotline for battered women, directing them towards medical aid or shelters.

Viols Femmes Informations *(08.00.05.95.95).* **Open** 10am-7pm Mon-Fri. Freephone service. Help and advice, in French, to rape victims.

Working in Paris

All EU nationals can work legally in France, but should apply for a French social security number and *carte de séjour*. Some job ads can be found at branches of the French national employment bureau, the **Agence nationale pour l'emploi** (ANPE), or on its website, www.anpe.fr. Branches are also where to go to sign up as a *demandeur d'emploi*, to be placed on file as available for work and possibly to qualify for French unemployment benefits. Britons can only claim French unemployment benefit if they were already signed on before leaving the UK. Non-EU nationals need a work permit and cannot use the ANPE network without valid work papers.

CIEE (Council on International Educational Exchange) *112ter rue Cardinet, 17th (01.58.57.20.50/www.council exchanges-fr.org). Mº Malesherbes.* **Open** 9am-6pm Mon-Fri. The CIEE provides three-month work permits for US citizens at or recently graduated from university (the 'Work in France' programme), has a job centre, mostly for sales and catering, and a housing placement service for those participating in the programme.

Espace emploi international (OMI et ANPE) *48 bd de la Bastille, 12th (01.53.02.25.50/www.emploi-international.org). Mº Bastille.* **Open** 9am-5pm Mon, Wed-Fri; Tue 9am-noon. Provides work permits of up to 18 months for Americans aged 18-35 and has a job placement service.

The Language Network *(01.44.64.82.23).* Helps to orient native English speakers who wish to teach.

Job ads

Help wanted ads sometimes appear in the *International Herald Tribune*, in *FUSAC* and on noticeboards at language schools and the American Church. Bilingual secretarial/ PA work is available for those with good written French. If you're looking for professional work, have your CV translated, including French equivalents for any qualifications. Most job applications require a photo and a handwritten letter (employers often use graphological analysis).

Average monthly climate

Month	High temp (C°/F°)	Low temp (C°/F°)	Rainfall
Jan	7/45	2/36	53cm
Feb	10/50	2/36	43cm
Mar	13/55	4/39	49cm
Apr	17/63	6/43	53cm
May	20/68	9/48	65cm
June	23/73	12/54	54cm
July	25/77	15/59	62cm
Aug	26/79	16/29	42cm
Sept	23/73	12/54	54cm
Oct	20/68	8/46	60cm
Nov	14/57	4/39	51cm
Dec	7/44	3/37	59cm

Essential Vocabulary

In French the second person singular (you) has two forms. Phrases here are given in the more polite *vous* form. The *tu* form is used with family, friends, children and pets; you should be careful not to use it with people you do not know sufficiently well. Courtesies such as *monsieur, madame* and *mademoiselle* are used more than their English equivalents.

General expressions

good morning/afternoon, hello bonjour; **good evening** bonsoir; **goodbye** au revoir; **hi** (familiar) salut; **OK** d'accord; **yes** oui; **no** non; **how are you?** comment allez vous?/vous allez bien?; **how's it going?** comment ça va?/ça va? (familiar); **sir/Mr** monsieur (Mr); **madam/Mrs** madame (Mme); **miss** mademoiselle (Mlle); **please** s'il vous plaît; **thank you** merci; **thank you very much** merci beaucoup; **sorry** pardon; **excuse me** excusez-moi; **do you speak English?** parlez-vous anglais?; **I don't speak French** je ne parle pas français; **I don't understand** je ne comprends pas; **speak more slowly, please** parlez plus lentement, s'il vous plaît; **I am going** je vais; **I am going to pay** je vais payer; **it is** c'est; **it isn't** ce n'est pas; **good** bon/bonne; **bad** mauvais/mauvaise; **small** petit/petite; **big** grand/grande; **beautiful** beau/belle; **well** bien; **badly** mal; **a bit** un peu; **a lot** beaucoup; **very** très; **with** avec; **without** sans; **and** et; **or** ou; **because** parce que **who?** qui?; **when?** quand?; **what?** quoi?; **which?** quel?; **where?** où?; **why?** pourquoi?; **how?** comment?; **at what time/when?** à quelle heure?; **forbidden** interdit/défendu; **out of order** hors service (HS)/en panne; **daily** tous les jours (tlj)

On the phone

hello allô; **who's calling?** c'est de la part de qui?/qui est à l'appareil?; **this is... speaking** c'est... à l'appareil; **I'd like to speak to...** j'aurais voulu parler avec...; **hold the line** ne quittez pas; **please call back later** rappellez plus tard s'il vous plaît; **you must have the wrong number** vous avez du composer un mauvais numéro

Getting around

where is the (nearest) Métro? où est le Métro (le plus proche)?; **when is the next train for... ?** c'est quand le prochain train pour... ?; **ticket** un billet; **station** la gare; **platform** le quai; **entrance** entrée; **exit** sortie; **left** gauche; **right** droite; **straight on** tout droit; **far** loin; **near** pas loin/près d'ici; **street map** le plan; **road map** la carte; **bank** la banque; **is there a bank near here?** est-ce qu'il y a une banque près d'ici?

Sightseeing

museum un musée; **church** une église; **exhibition** une exposition; **ticket** (*for museum*) un billet; (*for theatre, concert*) une place; **open** ouvert; **closed** fermé; **free** gratuit; **reduced price** un tarif réduit

Accommodation

do you have a room (for this evening/for two people)? avez-vous une chambre (pour ce soir/pour deux personnes)?; **full** complet; **room** une chambre; **bed** un lit; **double bed** un grand lit; **(a room with) twin beds** (une chambre à) deux lits; **with bath(room)/shower** avec (salle de) bain/douche; **breakfast** le petit déjeuner; **included** compris

At the café or restaurant

I'd like to book a table (for three/at 8pm) je voudrais réserver une table (pour trois personnes/à vingt heures); **lunch** déjeuner; **dinner** le dîner; **coffee** (espresso) un café; **white coffee** un café au lait/café crème; **tea** le thé; **wine** le vin; **beer** la bière; **mineral water** eau minérale; **fizzy** gazeuse; **still** plate; **tap water** eau du robinet/une carafe d'eau; **the bill, please** l'addition, s'il vous plaît

Shopping

cheap pas cher; **expensive** cher; **how much?/how many?** combien?; **have you got change?** avez-vous de la monnaie? **I would like...** je voudrais...; **may I try this on?** est-ce que je pourrais essayer cet article?; **do you have a smaller/larger size?** auriez-vous la taille en-dessous/au dessus?; **I'm a size 38** je fais du 38; **I'll**

take it je le prends; **could you gift wrap it for me?** pourriez-vous me faire un paquet cadeau?

Behind the wheel

no parking stationnement interdit/gênant; **toll** péage; **speed limit 40** rappel 40; **petrol** essence; **speed** vitesse; **traffic moving freely** traffic fluide

The come-on

do you have a light? avez-vous du feu?; **what's your name?** comment vous vous appelez?; **would you like a drink?** vous voulez boire un verre?; **you have lovely eyes, you know** tu as de beaux yeux, tu sais?; **your place or mine?** chez toi ou chez moi?

The brush-off

leave me alone laissez-moi tranquille; **get lost, you cretin** casse-toi, imbécile

Staying alive

be cool restez calme; **I don't want any trouble** je ne veux pas d'ennuis; **I only do safe sex** je ne pratique que le safe sex

Numbers

0 zéro; **1** un, une; **2** deux; **3** trois; **4** quatre; **5** cinq; **6** six; **7** sept; **8** huit; **9** neuf; **10** dix; **11** onze; **12** douze; **13** treize; **14** quatorze; **15** quinze; **16** seize; **17** dix-sept; **18** dix-huit; **19** dix-neuf; **20** vingt; **21** vingt-et-un; **22** vingt-deux; **30** trente; **40** quarante; **50** cinquante; **60** soixante; **70** soixante-dix; **80** quatre-vingts; **90** quatre-vingt-dix; **100** cent; **1000** mille; **10,000** dix mille; **1,000,000** un million

Days, months & seasons

Monday lundi; **Tuesday** mardi; **Wednesday** mercredi; **Thursday** jeudi; **Friday** vendredi; **Saturday** samedi; **Sunday** dimanche; **January** janvier; **February** février; **March** mars; **April** avril; **May** mai; **June** juin; **July** juillet; **August** août; **September** septembre; **October** octobre; **November** novembre; **December** décembre; **spring** le printemps; **summer** l'été; **autumn** l'automne; **winter** l'hiver

Directory

Further Reference

Books

Non-fiction

Petrus Abaelardus & Heloïse *Letters* The full details of Paris' first great romantic drama.

Robert Baldick *The Siege of Paris* The bloodshed, the hunger, the rats for supper: a gripping account of the Paris Commune of 1871.

Antony Beevor & Artemis Cooper *Paris after the Liberation* Rationing, freedom and Existentialism.

NT Binh *Paris au cinéma* Gorgeous coffee-table round-up of Paris sights on film.

Henri Cartier-Bresson *A propos de Paris* Classic black and white shots by a giant among snappers.

Danielle Chadych, Dominique Leborgne *Atlas de Paris* Lavishly appointed survey of Paris bricks and blocks and their movements through the centuries.

Rupert Christiansen *Tales of the New Babylon* Blood and sleaze in Napoléon III's Paris.

Vincent Cronin *Napoleon* A fine biography of France's most famous megalomaniac.

Christian Dupavillon *Paris Côté Seine* Nicely illustrated history of riverside Paris.

Julien Green *Paris* Short, sweet, personal account of Green's favourite city.

Alastair Horne *The Fall of Paris* Detailed chronicle of the Siege and Commune 1870-71.

J-K Huysmans *Croquis Parisiens* The world that Toulouse-Lautrec painted.

Douglas Johnson & Madeleine Johnson *Age of Illusion: Art & Politics in France 1918-1940* French culture in a Paris at the forefront of modernity.

Marc Lemonier, Jacques Lebar *Fascinating Paris* All the photos – in colour – you wish you could take yourself.

Ian Littlewood *Paris: Architecture, History, Art* Paris' history and its treasures.

Colin MacCabe *Godard* Ostensibly a biography of one man, but also an accessible introduction to intellectual life in late 20th-century France.

Patrick Marnham *Crime & the Académie Française* Scandals in Mitterrand-era Paris.

François Maspero *Roissy Express: Journey Through the Paris Suburbs* Take the train: Maspero examines day-to-day life mid-1990s Paris with photographer in tow.

Nancy Mitford *The Sun King; Madame de Pompadour* Great gossipy accounts of the courts of the *ancien régime*.

Noel Riley Fitch *Literary Cafés of Paris* Who drank what, where and when.

Virginia Rounding *Les Grandes Horizantales* Racy, entertaining lives of four 19th-century courtesans.

Renzo Salvadori *Architect's Guide to Paris* Plans, maps and a guide to Paris' growth.

Simon Schama *Citizens* Epic, wonderfully readable account of the Revolution.

William Shirer *The Collapse of the Third Republic*. Forensic account of the reasons for France's humiliating 1940 defeat.

Fiction & poetry

Louis Aragon *Le Paysan de Paris* A great Surrealist view of the city.

Honoré de Balzac *Illusions perdues*; *La Peau de chagrin*; *Le Père Goriot*; *Splendeurs et misères des courtisanes* Many of the best-known novels in the 'Comédie Humaine' cycle are set in Paris.

Charles Baudelaire *Le Spleen de Paris* Prose poems with Paris settings.

Simone de Beauvoir *Les Mandarins* Paris intellectuals and idealists just after the Liberation.

Louis-Ferdinand Céline *Mort à crédit* Vivid, splenetic account of an impoverished Paris childhood.

Victor Hugo *Notre Dame de Paris* Romantic vision of medieval Paris. Quasimodo! Esmerelda! The bells!

Guy de Maupassant *Bel-Ami* Gambling and dissipation.

Patrick Modiano *Honeymoon* Evocative story of two lives that cross in Paris.

Gérard de Nerval *Les Nuits d'octobre* Late-night Les Halles and environs, mid 19th-century.

Georges Perec *La Vie, mode d'emploi* Cheek-by-jowl life in a Haussmannian apartment building.

Raymond Queneau *Zazie dans le Métro* Paris in the 1950s: bright and very *nouvelle vague*.

Nicolas Restif de la Bretonne *Les Nuits de Paris* The sexual underworld of Louis XV's Paris, by one of France's most famous defrocked priests.

Jean-Paul Sartre *Les Carnets de la drôle de guerre* Existential angst as the German army takes over Paris.

Georges Simenon The Maigret books. Many of Simenon's novels featuring his laconic detective provide vivid pictures of Paris and its underworld. See also *L'Homme qui regardait passer les trains*.

Emile Zola *L'Assommoir*; *Nana*; *Le Ventre de Paris* Vivid accounts of the underside of the Second Empire from the master Realist.

The ex-pat angle

Adam Gopnik *From Paris to the Moon* A 'New Yorker' raises a family in this alien city.

Ernest Hemingway *A Moveable Feast* Big Ern chronicles 1920s Paris.

Henry Miller *Tropic of Cancer* Love, lust, lice and low-life: bawdy, yes. Funny, too.

Anaïs Nin *Henry & June* More lust in Montparnasse with Henry Miller and his wife.

George Orwell *Down and Out in Paris and London* Work in a Paris restaurant (it's hardly changed), hunger in a Paris hovel, suffering in a Paris hospital.

Edmund White *The Flaneur: a Stroll through the Paradoxes of Paris* US ex-pat maps out some of the hidden nooks of the city's history.

Film

Olivier Assayas *Irma Vep* Jean-Pierre Léaud and Maggie Cheung endeavour to remake Feuillade's vampire classic in 1990s Paris. And fail.

Luc Besson *Subway* Christophe Lambert goes underground. Hokum, but easy on the eye.

Marcel Carné *Hôtel du Nord* Atmosphère! Arletty's finest hour.

Jean-Luc Godard *A Bout de Souffle* Belmondo, Seberg, Godard, the Champs-Elysées, the attitude, the famous ending. Essential.

Jean-Luc Godard *Une Femme est une femme* Belmondo, Karina, Godard, the Grands Boulevards, the attitude, the riffing on musical tropes.

Edouard Molinaro *Un Témoin dans la ville* Lino Ventura on the run in 1950s nocturnal Paris. Superb *noir*.

Bertrand Tavernier *L.627* The drugs war in the 1990s, as seen from the cops' side. Gritty and polemic-making.

François Truffaut *Les 400 Coups* The first of the Antoine Doinel cycle.

Agnès Varda *Cléo de 5 à 7* The *nouvelle vague* heroine spends an anxious afternoon drifting around Paris.

Claude Zidi *Les Ripoux (Le Cop)* Cops Philippe Noiret and Thierry Lhermitte scam the whole of the Goutte d'Or.

Music

Air *Moon Safari* Relaxing, ambient beeps and sonics from that rara avis, a credible French pop group.

Serge Gainsbourg *Le Poinçonneur des Lilas* Classic early Gainsbourg: jazzy, elegant, mordant.

Thelonius Monk *The Paris Concert* A blend of the experimental and the romantically gentle.

Pink Martini *Sympathique* 'Je ne veux pas travailler' and other dinner-party starters by some French singing Americans.

Websites

paris.webcity.fr Compendious cultural calendar, plus small ads and information on shops, hotels, restaurants, traffic conditions and more.

www.culture.fr Current and forthcoming cultural events of all kinds, in Paris and other big French cities.

www.edible-paris.com Customised gastronomic itineraries in Paris – you send your requirements before you arrive – by the editor of Time Out's *Eating & Drinking in Paris* guide.

www.eduparis.net Lots of practical advice for anyone thinking of studying in Paris.

www.euro.gouv.fr Official euro website: information, updates and online currency converter.

www.fnac.com Browse and buy the multidisciplinary Fnac's books, CDs, DVDs and electronics – and reserve tickets for all sorts of events.

www.fusac.org Online version of the free fortnightly small ads mag: jobs, removals, personals, classes and more.

www.leparisien.com Selection of articles from the Paris daily newspaper.

www.mappy.fr Maps of Paris and France.

www.meteo.fr Weather forecasts and stats from the state meteorology office.

www.pagesjaunes.fr The Paris yellow pages, with maps and multi-angle photos of every address in the city. Also has a link to the Pages Blanches phone directory.

www.paris-anglo.com An abundance of nuts-and-bolts information, in English, on living in Paris.

www.paris-art.com Contemporary art exhibitions and galleries.

www.parisdigest.com Paris listings, shopping tips and general information in English.

www.parissi.com Films, concerts and a strong calendar of clubbing events.

www.paris-touristoffice.com Official site of the Office de Tourisme et des Congrès de Paris.

www.pidf.com Official site of the Paris regional tourist board: a goldmine of info on museums, events, transport, shopping et al.

www.quidonc.fr The phone book in reverse: type in a number, it tells you the owner. Can only be used in France.

www.ratp.com Everything you'll need to know about using the buses, Métro, RER and trams.

www.timeout.com/paris A pick of current events and good hotels, eateries and shops.

Directory

Note: page numbers in **bold** indicate section(s) giving key information on topic; *italics* indicate illustrations.

Restaurants

Maps

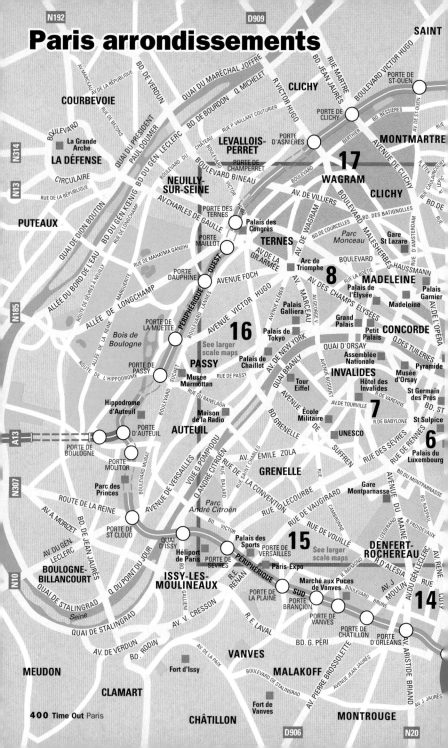

Paris arrondissements

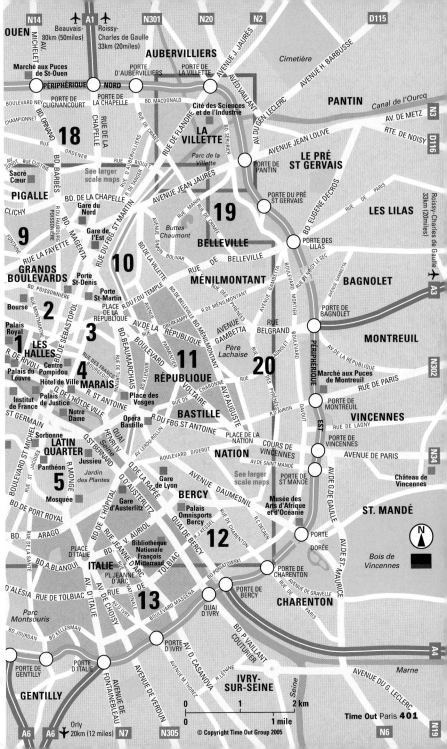

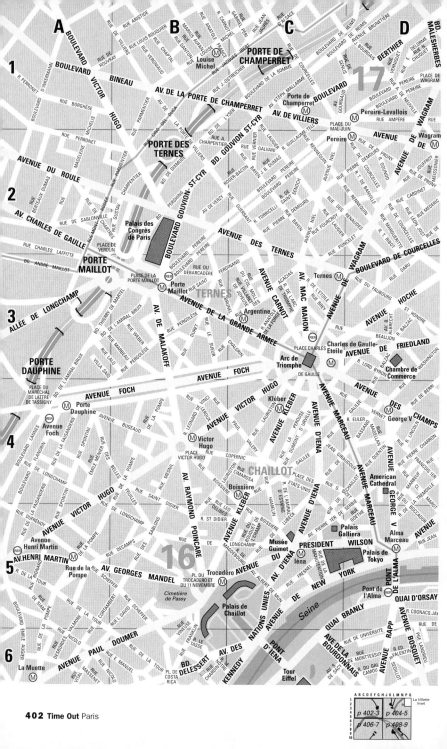

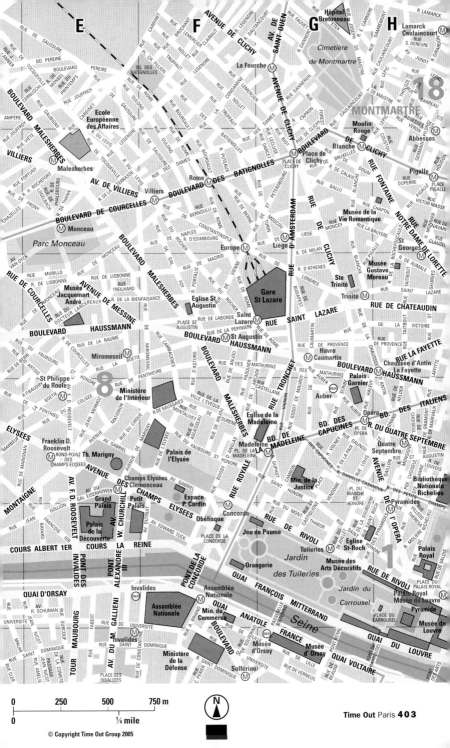

© Copyright Time Out Group 2005

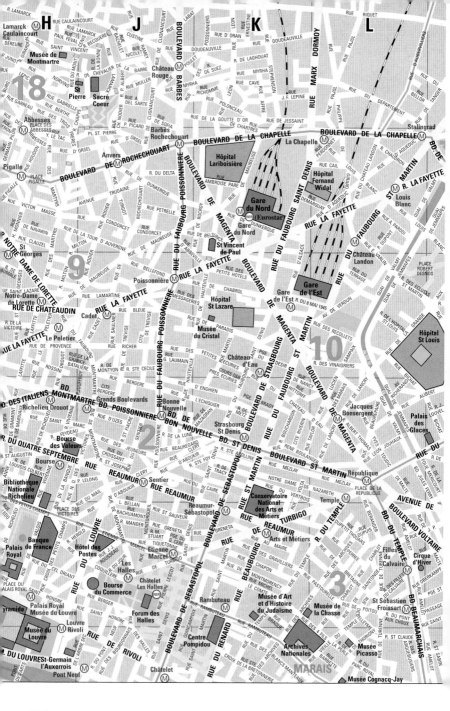

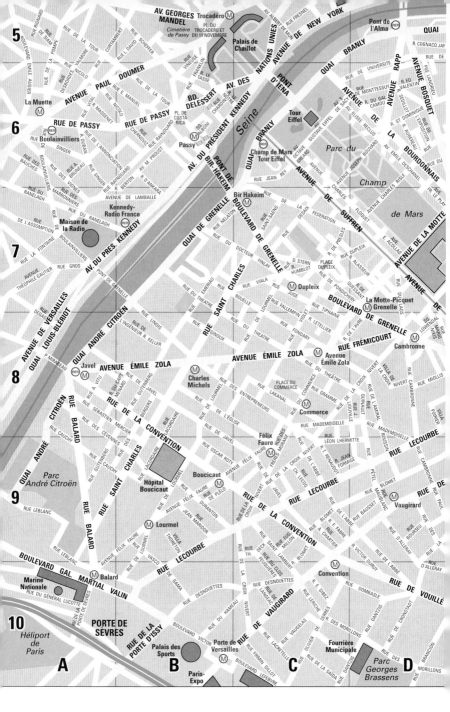

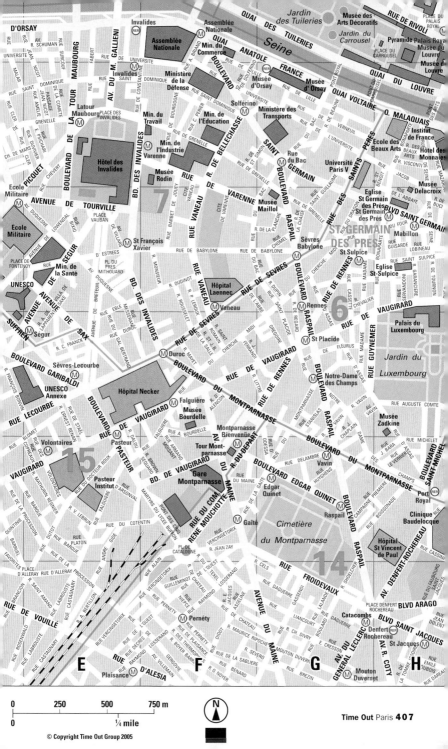

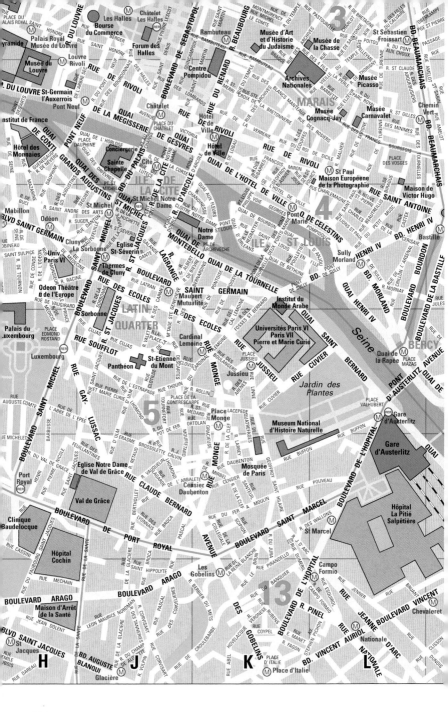

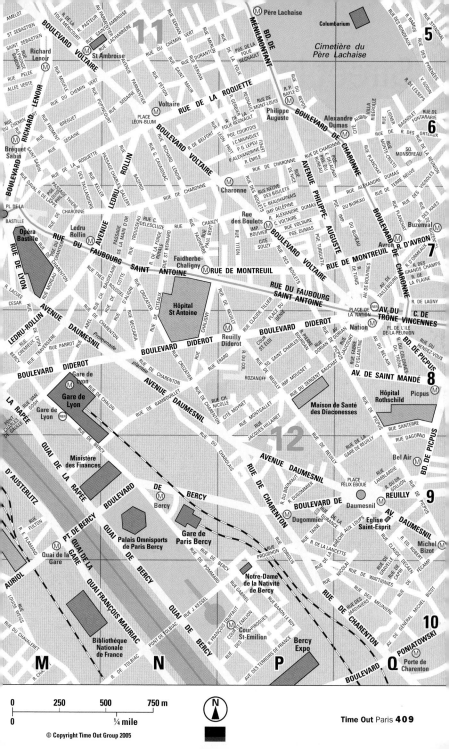

© Copyright Time Out Group 2005

Street Index

Paris RER

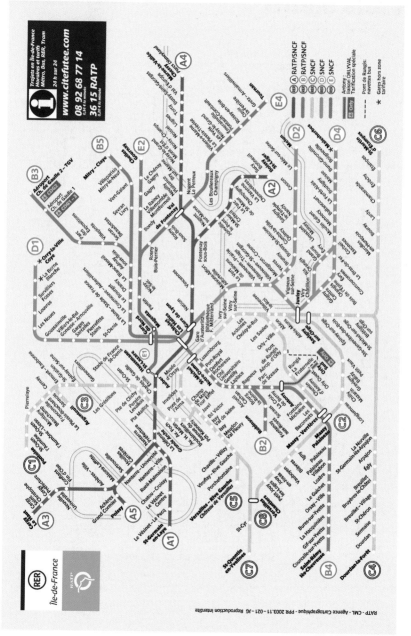

Paris Métro

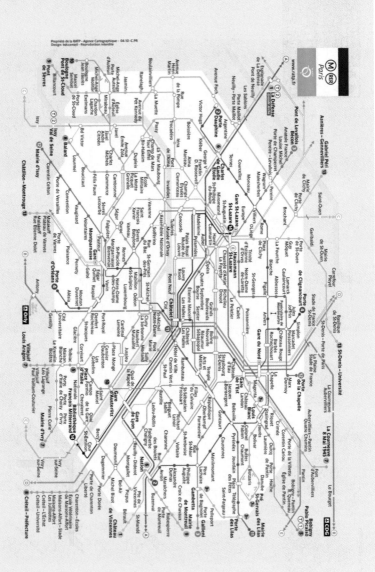